JAPAN
GOVERNMENT AND POLITICS

Contents

Preface

Japan, which consists of the four large islands of Honshu, Kyushu, Shikoku and Hokkaido and about 1000 small islands with an area of 377,727 sq. km., is one of the four countries in the world whose history as a sovereign nation goes back to the pre-Christian era. Militarists and bureaucrats almost continuously controlled Japanese politics since the days of the Meiji era, which marked the collapse of the Tokugawa feudalist regime. Constitutional government was introduced in Japan as a result of political reforms which followed the overthrow of the Tokugawa Shogunate and the restoration of Imperial rule on the 3rd of January, 1868. The Imperial Rescript of 1881 was another landmark in the constitutional development by which the Parliament was established in 1890. Later the Emperor promulgated the Meiji Constitution on 11th of February, 1889 which came into force from 1890. This constitution was the fundamental law of the Japanese State until 1947 when another constitution was enforced.

The present volume is divided into three parts. Part I consists of articles on Tradition and Modernity change of Leadership; Reforms in the Government; Local Government in Japan; and Rearmament; Part II deals with Japan as an economic power; Part III throws light on the foreign policy of Japan.

This book is a systematic piecing together of articles contributed by scholars and specialists to various journals of national and international repute. I am greatly indebted to the *Indian Political Science Review, India Quarterly, Foreign Affairs Reports, World Focus, Link, Indonesian Quarterly, China Report, BIISS Journal* (Bangladesh) and *The Statesman's Yearbook*, from which I have drawn freely. I express my deep sense of appreciation to all contributors for their scholarly papers and to various librarians and eminent scholars in the field who extended their cooperation to me.

New Dehli

VERINDER GROVER

Japan: An Introduction

(NIHON or NIPPON)

(Land of the Rising Sun)

CAPITAL: TOKYO

TERRITORY AND POPULATION

Japan consists of 4 major Islands, Honshu, Hokkaido, Kyushu and Shikoku, and many small islands, with an area of 377,819 sq. km. Census population (1 Oct. 1995) 125,568,504 (males 61,575,570, females 63,992,934). Estimate (1996) 125.86 m. Population estimate 1997, 126.17 m; density 337 per sq. km. Foreigners registered 31 Dec. 1997 were 1,482,707 of whom 645,373 were Koreans, 252,164 Chinese, 233,254 Brazilians, 93,265 Filipinos, 43,690 Americans, 40,394 Peruvians, 20,669 Thais, 14,438 British, 11,897 Vietnamese, 7,946 Iranians, 8,841 Canadians, 11,936 Indonesians, 6,940 Australians, 7,478 Indians, and 2,194 stateless persons. Estimated population for 2000 is 126.43 m.

RELIGION

The ancient religions of Shintoism and Buddhism are practised by a large number of Japanese. In 1968 Shinto was designated as the national religion, and all Shinto shrines acquired the privileged status of a national institution. In 1947, complete freedom of religion was given and state support to Shinto religion was completely stopped. All religious teachings have been stopped in public schools. In Dec. 1996 Shintoism claimed 102.0 m. adherents, Buddhism 91.58 m.; these figures obviously overlap. Christians numbered 3.17 m.

CLIMATE

The islands of Japan lie in the temperate zone, north-east of the main monsoon region of South-East Asia. The climate is temperate with warm, humid, summers and relatively mild winters except in the island of Hokkaido and northern parts of Honshu facing the Japan Sea. There is a month's rainy season in June-July, but the best seasons are spring and autumn, though Sept. may bring typhoons. There is a summer rainfall, maximum being: Tokyo: Jan. 5.2°C, July 25.2°C. Annual rainfall 1,405 mm.; Hiroshima: Jan. 4°C, July 25.7°C, Annual rainfall 1.555 mm.; Nagasaki: Jan. 6.4°C, July 26.6°C. Annual rainfall 1,945 mm.; Osaka: Jan. 5.5°C, July 27°C. Annual rainfall 1.318 mm.; Sapporo: Jan. 4.6°C, July 20.2°C. Annual rainfall 1,130 mm.

National Flag: White, with a red disc.

National Anthem: 'Kimi ga yo wa' ('May your Peaceful reign long last'); words 9th century, tune by Hiromori Hayashi.

SYSTEM OF GOVERNMENT

The Constitution of Japan which was promulgated on 3 November 1946 and came into force on 3 May 1947 provides for the structure and system of Government of Japan. Under this Constitution, the Emperor is the Head of State but has no governing power. Legislative power is vested in the bicameral Diet, consisting of the House of Representatives whose members are elected for a four-year term, and the House of Councillors or upper house, members of which are elected for six years, one-half being elected every three years. The election of members to both houses is a novel mixture of single-seat constituencies and proportional representation. Out of a total membership of 500 in the House of Representatives, there are 300 single-seat constituencies and 200 proportional representation seats. Similarly in the upper house, 50 national seats are determined according to the number of votes for each party, out of a total membership of 252 seats. The right to vote is given to every one at the age of 20 and above. Executive power is vested in the Cabinet. The Prime Minister is appointed by the Emperor on the designation by the Diet and he himself appoints the other Ministers. The Cabinet, like all other parliamentary system of governments, is responsible to the Diet (The Parliament of Japan).

JUSTICE

The Constitution of Japan lays down the basic principles of the legal system. Accordingly, the Supreme Court is the highest legal authority in the land, and consists of a Chief Justice and 14 associate judges. The Supreme Court has original as well as appellate jurisdiction. It bears appeals from the lower courts and is the final court to decide the constitutionality of a law, ordinance, regulation, or disposition. Below the Supreme Court are 8 regional higher courts, district courts in each prefecture and the local courts. In addition, there are Family Courts and Summary Courts.

PERSONNEL OF GOVERNMENT

Head of State

His Imperial Majesty Akihito, Emperor of Japan (succeeded to the throne 7 January 1989).

CABINET

(As on March 1999)

Prime Minister: Keizo Obuchi
Minister of Justice: Shozaburo Nakamura
Minister of Foreign Affairs: Masahiko Komura
Minister of Finance: Kiichi Miyasawa
Minister of Education: Akito Arima
Minister of Health and Welfare: Sohei Miyashita
Minister of Agriculture, Forestry and Fisheries: Soichi Nakagawa
Minister of International Trade and Industry: Karu Yosano
Minister of Transport: Jiro Kawasaki

Minister of Posts and Telecommunications: Seiko Noda

Minister of Labour: Akira Amari

Minister of Construction: Katsutsugu Sekiya

Minister of Home Affairs: Takeshi Noda

Chief Cabinet Secretary: Hiromu Nonaka

Director General, National Land Agency: Hakuo Yanagisawa

Director General, Defence Agency: Fukushiro Nukaga

Director General, Economic Planning Agency: Taichi Sakaiya

Director General, Environment Agency: Kenji Manabe

Director General, Science and Technology Agency: Yutaka Takeyama

Director General, Hokkaido and Okinawa Development Agency: Kichio Inoue

MAJOR POLITICAL PARTIES

Japan Communist Party, founded in 1922.

Komei, founded in 1964.

Liberal Democratic Party, founded in 1955.

New Frontier Party, founded in 1994.

New Party Sakigake, founded in 1993.

Ni-In Club, Kakushin Kyoto, founded in 1946.

Social Democratic Party of Japan, founded in 1945.

Sports Peace Party, founded in 1945.

MAJOR NEWSPAPERS

Asahi Shimbun (Japanese language: Daily) founded in 1879.

Asahi Evening News (English: Daily) founded in 1954.

Daily Sports (Japanese: Daily) founded in 1948.

Dempa Shimbun (Japanese: Daily) founded in 1950.

Hochi Shimbun (English: Daily) founded in 1897.

The Japan Times (English: Daily) founded in 1897.

Mainichi Shimbun (Japanese: Daily) founded in 1882.

Mainichi Daily News (English: Daily) founded in 1922.

Nihon Keizai Shimbun (Japanese: Daily) founded in 1876.

Naigai Times (Japanese: Daily) founded in 1949.

Nihon Kaiji Shimbun (Japanese: Daily) founded in 1942.
Nihon Kogyo Shimbun (Japanese: Daily) founded in 1933.
Nihon Nogyo Shimbun (Japanese: Daily) founded in 1928.
Nihon Sen-i Shimbun (Japanese: Daily) founded in 1943.
Nikkan Kogye Shimbun (Japanese: Daily) founded in 1917.
Nikkan Sports (Japanese: Daily) founded in 1946.
Sankei Shimbun (Japanese: Daily) founded in 1933.
Sankei Sports (Japanese: Daily) founded in 1963.
Shipping and Trade News (English: Daily) founded in 1949.
Sports Nippon (Japanese: Daily) founded in 1949.
Suisan Kezai Shimbun (Japanese: Daily) founded in 1949.
Tokyo Chunichi Sports (Japanese: Daily) founded in 1956.
Tokyo Shimbun (Japanese: Daily) founded in 1942.
Tokyo Sports (Japanese: Daily) founded in 1959.
Yukan Fuji (Japanese: Daily) founded in 1969.

MAJOR BANKS

ABN AMRO Bank Nv., Tokyo.
Asahi Bank Ltd., Tokyo.
Ashikaga Bank Ltd., Tochigi.
Bangkok Bank Public Co. Ltd., Tokyo.
Bank of Tokyo Ltd., Tokyo.
Bank of America NT & SA, Tokyo.
Bank of Yokohama Ltd., Yokohama.
Bank of India, Tokyo.
China Bank Ltd., China.
Chase Manhattan Bank, Tokyo.
Chao Trust and Banking Co. Ltd., Tokyo.
City Bank NA, Tokyo.
Dai-Ichi Kangyo Bank Ltd., Tokyo.
Deutsche Bank AG, Tokyo.
Daiwa Bank Ltd., Osaka.
Dresdner Bank AG, Tokyo.
Fuji Bank Ltd., Tokyo.
First National Bank of Chicago.

Hokkaido Takushoku Bank Ltd., Sapporo.
The Hongkong and Shanghai Banking Corpn. Ltd., Tokyo.
Hokuriku Bank Ltd., Toyama.
International Commercial Bank of China, Tokyo.
Joyo Bank Ltd., Ibaraki.
Korea Exchange Bank, Tokyo.
The Long-Term Credit Bank of Japan Ltd., Tokyo.
Lloyds Bank PLC, Tokyo.
Midland Bank PLC, Tokyo.
Mitsubishi Bank Ltd., Tokyo.
Mitsubishi Trust and Banking Corporation, Tokyo.
Mitsui Trust and Banking Co. Ltd., Tokyo.
The Nippon Credit Bank Ltd., Tokyo.
Sakura Bank Ltd., Tokyo.
Sanwa Bank Ltd., Osaka.
Shizuoka Bank Ltd., Shizuoka.
Standard Chartered Bank, Tokyo.
Sumitomo Bank Ltd., Osaka.
State Bank of India, Tokyo.
Sumitomo Trust and Banking Co. Ltd., Osaka.
Swiss Bank Corpn., Tokyo.
Toyo Trust and Banking Co. Ltd., Tokyo.
Tokai Bank Ltd., Nagoya.
Yasuda Trust and Banking Co. Ltd., Tokyo.
Zenshinren Bank, Tokyo.

WEIGHTS AND MEASURES

The Metric System is in force.

CURRENCY

100 Sen = 1 Yen

EDUCATION

In Japan, education is compulsory upto the age of 15. The elementary schools (*Shogakko*) admit children of six years where they attend the school for six years. After that they join the lower secondary schools (*Chugakko*) for another three years. The upper secondary schools admit students from the lower secondary schools at the age of fifteen who receive further education for another three years.

After schooling, students may go in for higher studies. Higher education is divided into four type of institutions. Universities (*daigaku*) offering four-year degree course, as well as post-graduate courses. At present, there are 523 universities. Some of these are private whereas others are established by the government. In addition to the universities, there are junior colleges; colleges offering technical education; special training colleges offering advanced courses in technical and vocational subjects; and teacher-training colleges. On 1 May 1997 there were 14,624 Kindergartens with 103,839 teachers and 1,789,523 pupils; 23,775 elementary schools with 420,901 teachers and 7,855,387 pupils; 11,185 junior high schools with 270,299 teachers and 4,481,480 pupils; 5,353 senior high schools with 276,108 teachers and 4,371,360 pupils; 595 junior colleges with 19,885 teachers and 446,750 pupils.

HEALTH

Hospitals on 1 Oct. 1996 numbered 9,490 with 1,664,629 beds. The hospital bed provision of 135 per 10,000 population was one of the highest in the world, physicians at the end of 1996 numbered 240,908; dentists 85,518.

TOURISM

Japan has many tourist attractions. Beautiful forests and mountains, temples and pagodas, classical Kabuki theater, traditional festivals and the ancient capital of Kyoto are some of the *musts* on the itinerary of the foreign tourists. Nearly 36 lakh foreign tourists visit Japan annually and generate foreign exchange of $ 3,585 million.

PUBLIC HOLIDAYS

1 January (New Year's Day), 15 January (Coming of Age Day), 11 February (National Foundation Day), 21 March (Vernal Equinox Day), 29 April (Greenery Day), 3 May (Constitution Day), 5 May (Children's

Day), 20 July (Ocean Day), 15 September (Respect for the Aged Day), 23 September (Autumnal Equinox), 10 October (Sports Day), 3 November (Culture Day), 23 November (Labour Thanksgiving Day), 23 December (Emperor's Birthday).

PART I

CONSTITUTION, GOVERNMENT AND POLITICS

1

Tradition and Modernity in Japan's Political Development

RAKESH HOOJA*

I

It would be appropriate to start with an analysis of the term "modernization" since modernity can be said to be the state of being modern or modernized. As Benjamin Schwartz has said[1], "following Weber. . . modernization involves the systematic, sustained and purposeful application of human energies to the 'rational' control of man's physical and social environment for various human purposes. I use the adjectives purposeful, systematic and sustained because it is quite obvious that the process of rationalization as such began long before the 'modern age' and is almost co-extensive with recorded human history". The effects and symptoms of rationality have been further explained as "mechanization and industrialization of the economy, bureaucratization in Government and social organization, the spread of the idea of progress and science in the intellectual sphere and a widening range of diversity in the area of social relations and values."

* Teaches in the Department of Political Science, University of Rajasthan, Jaipur.

Perhaps it would be better to adopt John Whitney Hall's broader concept[2] of modernization as "our ideas about the nature of modern society and the process by which it came into being". Hall describes there, how, starting with the essential features of modernity listed in Almond and Coleman's *Politics of the Developing Areas*[3], the Hakone Conference had evolved a "modernization syndrome", with the study of developing areas in mind, comprising of the following components:

1. Comparatively high concentration of population in cities and the increasingly urban-centredness of the total society.
2. Relatively high degree of use of inanimate energy, the widespread circulation of commodities and the growth of service facilities.
3. Extensive spatial interaction of members of a society and the widespread participation of such members in economic and political affairs.
4. Widespread literacy accompanies by the spread of a secular, and increasingly scientific, orientation of the individual to his environment.
5. An extensive and penetrative network of mass communication.
6. The existence of large scale social institutions such as government, business, industry, and the increasingly bureaucratic organization of such industries.
7. Increased unification of large bodies of population under one control (nation-states) and the growing interaction of such units (international relations).

If we accept these criterion then it is obvious that contemporary Japan is a highly modernized nation. The questions to be asked are: whether this modernization is the result of a break with tradition, whether Japan is still a traditional country in any respect, whether tradition and modernity are antithetical or not, whether tradition and modernity co-exist in Japan and if so to what extent and with what degree of inherent tension if any.

It would be interesting to see if Rajni Kothari's observations in "Tradition and Modernity Revisited"[4] correspond with the Japanese situation. Kothari holds that the two prevailing popular schools—of 'universalist modernization', which posits a common, determinate, end product, and of 'relativist modernization', which assumes a determinate starting point—are both erroneous and that "the point is that the content of 'modernization' varies from one period to another and the content of 'tradition' also varies from one society to another, the two aspects being closely related in the dynamics of change. Indigenous cultures differ markedly in their capacity to assimilate modernist impacts and whereas certain aspects of this 'modernity' may be too radical for some societies, for others they may not be modern enough. Much of this depends upon previous traditions, historical experience, structural and psychological variables, and the new opportunities offered by modern conditions of life so different from the old ones. . .the changes that are involved in 'development' are not directed from parochial to universal orientations as such, but rather from one set of universal parochial combinations to another". Kothari thus concludes that proper development necessitates the 'traditionalization of modernity' and the 'modernization of tradition.'

Before turning to the examination of Japan it will be useful to explain the term "political development", since different people tend to use it differently. As Lucian Pye has pointed out, the term has been taken to mean any one or more of the following political prerequisites of economic development; politics typical of industrial society; political modernization; the operation of a nation state; administrative and legal development; mass mobilization and participation; the building of democracy; stability and orderly change mobilization and power; and one aspect of a multi-dimensional process of social change (modernization). Developing on Parsonian variables, Almonds talks of structural differentiation, cultural secularization and sub-system autonomy as the essentials of political development. Huntington talks of a balance between institutionalization and participatory pulls, institutionalization being measured according to the degree of adaptability, complexity, autonomy and coherence. The Committee of Comparative Politics (Princeton volumes) implies that political development is the successful negotiation of the crisis of identity, legitimacy, penetration, participation, integration and distribution, while Organsky lists four stages: political unification, industrialization, national welfare and abundance; of political development. Pye asserts that the key ingredients of the 'political development syndrome' are equality, capacity and differentiation, but Riggs goes one step further and says that the balancing of the countervailing pulls of equality and capacity along higher levels of differentiation is the real index of the process of political development. Other writers like Vonder Mehden

[*Politics of the Developing Nations*] equate it with political modernisation and have set forth long list of developmental characteristics. One could go on like this at length but it is proposed to avoid polemics by stating that the spirit behind such constructs is similar and that therefore the trendwise changes that the Japanese polity has undergone from the Tokugawa era to the present day have been along the scale of political development, ups and down and the brief militarist era notwithstanding. Thus the term "Political Development" is being used non-technically to describe the evolution of the present day Japanese political system. Also it is maintained that the fact that consensus in Japan does not move along concentric circles and that there is a large body of perpetually alienated people in existence indicates that sufficient political development is yet to take place. Further, one tends to agree with Huntington that Political Development is not a time or era bound concept, and hence is different from "Political Modernization" and may even occur in the absence of modernization.

II

To return to our set of questions regarding the co-existence of tradition and modernity in the Japanese system, most people consider the country to be a case of "Continuity in Change". For example, Yanaihara Tadao[5], is quoted in Jansen[6] as saying: "modernization in Japan involves Japan's importation and assimilation of the institutions, technology, and culture of Europe and the United States. Simply stated it is equivalent to the Westernization of Japan's society and culture. . . but it is not the way of the world that Japanese society should become exactly like that of the West. World culture is to be enriched by the peculiar characteristics and differences of the culture of the various peoples in the world." Different generations of Japanese have felt differently about the elements of the West most worth emulating. Early flirtation with Christianity, vaccillation between *laissez faire* liberalism and militant statism, imitation of Hitlerian Germany, Fakuzawa's advocacy of equality, Kato's return to nationalism, the militarists' dream of an Asiatic empire, were all efforts to find the secret of the West's success, as is today's belief in democracy, nationalism and industrialization. However, Japanese traditions are still as strong as ever. As Dick Wilson says:[7] "the arranged marriage, the kimono, even the emperor himself, are having something of a revival". He then proceeds to conclude that "it looks as if Japan will absorb Westernization today just as expertly as she absorbed Chinese civilization and retained her own personality in ancient times''.

However Wilson has to admit that ''Japan is nevertheless a society in which there is a fundamental tension between the sense of group identity cultivated by its own tradition, and the sense of individualism encouraged by modern Westernism''. Thus he feels that the fundamental ''question is whether the superficially satisfactory mix of the traditional and modern in present-day Japanese life is a stable adaptation to modern conditions[8] or whether the survival of traditional elements merely identifies areas where modernization is lagging behind but will ultimately take over.''[9]

To do full justice to this question it will be necessary to examine Japanese roles, structures, processes, institutions and the like in detail. But before that, it would perhaps be appropriate to enumerate briefly the landmarks in the history of modern Japan.

III

The Meiji restoration of 1868 is often said to mark the beginning of the modern era in Japanese history. Though there are those, like Robert E. Ward[10] who feel that Tokugawa feudalism had sufficient modernist tendencies in existence for the later Tokugawa period to be considered modern; a view that gains great support from the assertions of Jon W. Hall.[11]

It is proposed to deal with present-day Japan's debt to the Shogun era, later in the paper at present starting with the restoration of 1868. It ''was not a social upheaval which brought about a transformation in the basic character of Japanese society, nor on the other hand, was it a mere palace revolution in which one elite replaced another . . [it] may be looked upon as a kind of revolution from above in that its leadership was supplied by a small group of young samurai . . . which were traditionally hostile to the Tokugawa house.''[12]

The motivations behind the Restoration were varied, ranging from calamities and dissatisfactions of the samurai at their deteriorating economic and social status, to a feeling of a threat to security posed by the consequences of the Perry Treaty (1854), which opened the country to foreign commerce and, it was feared, to Western imperialistic exploitation as well. The oligarchy that came to power was committed to modernize the country. They hoped to legitimize their ambitions by "restoring" to the Emperor his "rightful" position. Hence the emperor, who was "vested by right of divine descent with absolute power over the state", became the symbol of the new system.

The old Tokugawa system had succumbed to stresses generated by the introduction of a monetary system into the old rice-based economy; the commercialization and industrialization of the economy; the rigidity of the Tokugawa system in the face of cumulative challenges, growing dissatisfaction with the existing class system and relationships; the spread of urbanization and the consequent growth of new social and economic problems; and the development of a sense of nationalism amongst the Japanese. Thus it is not surprising that "old institutions were uprooted and new one introduced at an unsettling rate: the traditional four-class system of samurai, peasant, artisan and merchant, along with the rights and privileges of the samurai and the Tokugawa fiefs, as was the old land-tenure system, were abolished, in their place came mass public education, conscription, equality before law, rail-roads, modern industrial plants, technology, a merchant marine, and a modern army and navy. Politically the period [1868-1889] was marked by experimentation with various forms of government, with no particular one winning out. A professional bureaucracy was established to cope with the expanding needs of the state. A small number of educated Japanese gained their first insight into the political systems and philosophies of the West. Some, led by the Meiji Oligarchs, preferred the authoritarian strain in Western thought, perhaps best exemplified at the time by the Prussian state and the dominant Austro-Prussian school of constitutional law. "These [ideas] seemed, to the oligarchs, to be both more congenial to their native tradition and better suited to the urgent needs to the Japanese state for strong leadership and unchallenged national unity. Other political leaders. . . launched demands for limited suffrage, more representative government, and a national parliament".[13]

THE STATE AND ECONOMIC DEVELOPMENT

Analysis this "take-off period" from the point of view of *The Political Basis of Economic Development*[14], Holt and Turner feel that while Japan had already been undergoing changes in the structures of government and in the procedures of governing, "within a generation these changes had led to a great increase in the resolution of the authority structure of policy-making and to the development of a more reliable and effective mechanism for enforcing central decisions. These modifications made possible the most observable shift in the functions of government—the marked increase in the government's contribution to the satisfaction of the adaptive functional requisite''. This shift manifested itself through greater government involvement in resource allocation processes with the military establishment getting a larger share, and build-up of social overhead capital taking place. However, despite the take over of the ownership and management of some Japanese firms for a short time, there was little government involvement in the process of resource management, the only major government managed industry being the railways. The revenue collected by the Japanese government was high, for the times when measured against the gross national product and governmental involvement was great in the banking system, development of joint stock companies and, as has already been mentioned earlier, currency reforms. There was also a simultaneous increase in the contribution by government to the satisfaction of the ''pattern-maintenance and integration functional requisites'' as is evident from the creation of a professional police force, the repeal of laws defining social class, the payment of subsidies to individuals who had much to loose from widespread reform and who were in a position to resist changes, the fostering of public education, and the eventual introduction of welfare legislation designed to improve working and living conditions.

Thus one would not be going too far by maintaining that the proclamation of a new constitution on February 11, 1889 was but a logical step; the formalized proclamation of the evolution of a new system.

KOKUTAI THEORY OF STATE

The system of government thus established rested on a theory of state referred to by the Japanese as *Kokutai*. This meant that for both theoretical and legal purposes the emperor, as the successor of an unbroken line of divinely descended ancestors, embodied the Japanese state. The reigning emperor was thus the sole and ultimate repository of all state powers—executive, administrative, legislative and judicial. To this authority was added the spiritual authority that derived from his position as a lineal descended of the Sun-Goddess. He was thus the central figure in the nation's major religious cult—State Shintonism. In theory then, the Meiji Constitution set up a highly centralized state run by the Emperor.

In practice, however, the Emperor only lent legitimacy and an aura of sanctity to the political decisions of his ministers and advisors and simply authenticated their policies through ritualized acts. He also provided, and still does to some extent, the Japanese with their sense of historical continuity and serves as their symbol of national identification and the moral basis and justification of the existence and powers of government. Political power was, in reality, shared till 1932 among the following who were continually jockeying for a greater share of influence:[15]

1. The Meiji oligarchs and their direct successors in top civilian positions;
2. an increasingly distinct and professionalized group of military leaders;
3. the higher ranks of the civil bureaucracy;
4. leaders of the larger and more important conservative parties;
5. a big business group usually known as the *zaibatsu*; and
6. a hereditary peerage.

THE CHANGING POWER STRUCTURE

The political parties had gradually been improving their position and from 1924 to 1932 Japan witnessed a period of "*demokurashy*" in spite of the fact that the Meiji Constitution had originally been promulgated as a means of perpetuating the type of authoritarian rule with which the oligarchs were personally identified. This was because the constitution had made some minimal concessions to popular rights and representative government. However, things were soon to change. The army became disgruntled due to the need for retrenchment. The setting up of the Nationalist Government in China in 1928 threatened Japan's interests in Manchuria. The world-wide depression hit the Japanese countryside very badly, emphasising the need for firmer policies. The centuries old authoritarian tradition started reasserting itself. Army officers started attempting to strengthen their hold on government and got divided in to two groups.[16] The younger officers belonged mostly to the Imperial Way faction (*Kodoha*) and believed, drawing inspiration from Kita Ikki (executed 1936), in vague ideas of direct rule by the Emperor together with severe limitations on capitalist enterprise. From 1932 to 1936 they upset the tenure of Japanese political life through assassinations and small uprisings. They were opposed and eventually set down by the Control faction (*Toseida*) made up of senior, more conservative officers, who were less anti-business. The bureaucracy, *zaibatsu* and party leadership was forced to accept and adjust to the new situation and Japan was thus committed to war and eventual defeat.

THE IMPACT OF THE MILITARY OCCUPATION

The Military Occupation of Japan after the Second World War acted as a major catalyst for change. The army was disarmed and the famous renunciation of war clause added to the new "MacArthur" Constitution which was promulgated in 1946. The constitution was drawn up by Americans and the Japanese were persuaded, albeit with some degree of coercion involved, to accept it. The Emperor was reduced to being a symbol of the unity of the state instead of being the religious and governmental head as well as the head of state, under the previous constitution. Various officers were purged, the franchise expanded, labour granted the right to organize and bargain collectively, reforms carried out on the legal position of the traditional family system and in the educational system, powers of government decentralized, land reforms carried out, women given new legal and social status, localities given new rights of autonomy and home rule *vis-a-vis* the previously omnipotent national government and ministries, and attempts were also made to break up the *zaibatsu*. However, it has been noticed that the Japanese have undone a lot that was thrust upon them during the Occupation, even though the impact of the reforms has been great and has definitely led to the formation of a more democratic political culture.

IV

Commenting upon the process of modernization in Japan, Ward has noted two symptoms of continuity.[17] One is the "long drawn struggle between the authoritarian, although not totalitarian, tradition and the more liberal groups that stood for some form of constitutional and parliamentary government" and the other is "the country's attitude towards Western nations; since 1854, this attitude tended to swing through cycles of hostility and receptivity".

A.N. Eisenstadt[18] says that "Japan was possibly the only instance of modernizatian initiated by an autocratic oligarchy. . . was still able to direct and control the course of modernization for a relatively long time, absorbing many new social forces within the frameworks it established. This particularistic characteristic may perhaps be explained by the fact that this oligarchy was. . . in itself a revolutionary modernizing one, derived from the relatively autonomous tradition of Japanese feudalism, which became frozen in the Tokugawa regime, strongly committed to modernization of political administrative and economic fields, but at the same time basing itself on revival of traditional Imperial symbols. This continuity of the Imperial tradition was not purely symbolic, but it served as the major focus and content of the new national identity. . . ."

Eisenstadt further maintains that this elite while strongly emphasising innovation in the political field and most adept in political and administrative activity, was also very much oriented to the other social spheres, especially in education and economic activities. By virtue of these characteristics and because of the fact that it could rely to some extent on support from the wider social groups (such as some of the urban and peasant groups), it could channel (albeit after rather strong initial coercive measures) some of the traditional (feudal and national) loyalties of the wide strata, and through bureaucratic means draw these strata into the new central framework without really granting them, at least at first, full effective political rights.

Another reason Eisenstadt gives for the success of the oligarchy is that "on the whole it was the political change instigated. . . that formed the [new] class structure. The political and industrializing elite did not hold a large part of its property in land and did not have great interest in the protection of agriculture. From the very beginning this class was urban, bureaucratic (non-gentry like) and very strongly group and center-oriented. . . It was largely based on formal education criteria."[19] Thus the modernizing process did not have to fight the class structure.

A third reason Eisenstadt gives is that "in the rural and to some extent also in the industrial sector the process of social mobilization was affected in such a way as to assure the commitment of these groups to the new center, but at the same time, through the persistence or reorganization of various traditional-particularistic arrangements (such as the strong hold of family loyalties) it limited the development of new social and political aspiration".[20]

Eisenstadt goes on to point out that with the focus of political innovation and decision-making in Meiji Japan being concentrated in the oligarchy and the new bureaucracy, the articulation of demands and the orientation and organization of protest were still mostly couched in the traditional terms and patterns of organization. In fact, the articulation of demands in the beginning was minimal, the initial protest orientations and movements being aristocratic and peasant rebellions and outbreaks were of traditional types. Later with the growing stabilization and the extension of the modern framework, there also developed new types of articulation and protest which were, however, limited in their orientations and demands and contained a mixture of modernizing and traditional elements. The major cleavage of the time was between those groups that had aligned themselves with the army and those siding with the civilian parties and the bureaucracy, and the issues centered on the problem of access to the political center, on possibilities of political participation, and on the definition and redefinition of the national community and its symbols.

The major test of the ability of the Japanese system to adapt came in the Twenties when new groups and emerging elites (modern middle classes, professional and intellectual groups, and some workers organizations) developed more flexible political organizations and attempted to extend the scope of political participation. This led to the breakdown of the existing oligarchic-bureaucratic system and gave rise to the militarist regimes of the Thirties. This was because the rulers had attempted to stifle the new demands and to resist more flexible policies.

It was only under the impact of external forces (defeat in war) that Japan got a new start. Structurally it was characterised by the continuation of some of the former features; the combination of universalistic and particularistic criteria and organization. It was however based on widespread industrialization, urbanization and agrarian reform and changes effected in the symbolic sphere through the abolition of the divinity of the Emperor resulting in the institutionalization of a new parliamentary, constitutional regime.

ELEMENTS CHARACTERIZED BY CONTINUITY: POLITICAL CHANGE AND SOCIAL CONTINUITY

Study the *Social Origins of Dictatorship and Democracy*[21] Barrington Moore Jr. has drawn heavily from Robert N. Bellah[22], R.P. Dore[23], Robert A. Scalapino[24] and the writings of Thomas C. Smith among others to describe Japan from 1603 to the rise of pre-war quasi-fascism. Nothing the rise of the samurai-turned-bureaucrat and an allied mercantile class, Moore comments that *the most significant factor is the continuity of Japanese village life.* (We shall turn to this again later). He explains it thus: "the oligarchic structure, internal solidarity, and effective vertical ties with higher authority all survived, with little change, the transition to modern production for the market . . . the landlords maintained most of the village structure because through it they could extract and sell enough of a surplus to stay on top of the heap". In other words, unlike other countries, the ruling elite discovered that the traditional social structure continued to deliver the goods as far as they were concerned.

But Moore goes on to say that "the adaptability of Japanese political and social institutions to capitalist institutions enabled Japan to avoid the costs of a revolutionary entrance on to the stage of modern history. Partly because she escaped these early horrors, Japan succumbed in time to fascism and defeat. He gives the same reason for the rise of Nazism in Germany and implies that India is yet to undergo her "revolutionary entrance." This final hypothesis about the necessity of a revolution for political development on the ground that all structures have to become obsolete eventually, is questionable.

V

Having looked briefly at the process of modernization (which brings out the continued existence and influence of traditionalism) in Japan we can now profitably turn to analysing separately various Japanese institutions. It would be appropriate to start with the basic unit of human life—the family.

FAMILY AND AUTHORITY

Under the family system that prevailed after the fall of the Tokugawas the traditional concepts of the omnipotent paternal family head and of family supremacy over the individual had been studiously cultivated by the government as the core of an ideal and purely Japanese system.[25] These concepts helped buttress the authority of the state, the omnipotence of the Emperor and the primacy of the state over the individual. All this is now changing, albeit slowly. Constitutional provisions regarding respect for all people as individuals, equality under law and marriages based "on the mutual consent and essential equality of both sexes'' have helped in bringing about a more flexible attitude. For example, though arranged marriages have not been eliminated, a number of young couples who do make their owns decision to get married then get their parents consent, after which the traditional form of arranging the marriage through a go-between is observed. Thus the requirements of the individual get a slightly better hearing now. Another factor which has helped reduce parental authority is urbanization leading to children setting up separate homes. However, even now a lot of Japanese of all ages look upon these changes with some misgivings.[26]

However one should not get the idea that the omnipotent-family-head concept ever resulted in the complete throttling of individual ideas. This is because the decision-making process in Japan operate by ''unanimous consent.''[27] When an issue is posed before a group, the problem is discussed at length in a non-adversary manner, care being taken by talking around issues, to minimise open debate between sponsors of alternative solutions, until a compromise solution acceptable to all emerges. This is then formulated into a proposal which is accepted unanimously.While this traditional preference for decision by consensus has long been breaking down in Japan, it is surprising to see that even now this preference dominates at the local level and operates behind the scenes at the national level. Barrington Moore[28] quotes current examples of informal town meetings being held on the day preceding the formal one so that a consensus can be prepared and voting in the official gathering becomes a mere formality. This practice is further illustrated by opposition charges of ''tyrany by the majority'',[29] implying that majorities, even though acting legally (and legitimately from the point of view of competitive politics), have no right to over-ride minority views. Thus, it is quite possible that the violent protests for which Japanese politics is known derives from, among other reasons, the traditional belief of all views and opinions being awarded equal consideration, which is still stronger than the 'modern' democratic philosophy of majority-rule. Other implications of this collective decision-process are the group and faction-based style of politics and the usual absence of clear cut decisions due to blurred compromises.

Social change is of course taking place. As R.P. Dore has said,[30] ''An open competitive society in which the family plays no part in the economic productive activities of large sections of the population, in which codified law is a major element in social control and educational institutions outside the family play a major part in the training of new members of. . . society, in which a wide range of man's daily contacts are of an impersonal kind, and in which a rising standard of material well-being produces a constantly changing set of material values and has created an expectation of continuing change and continuing progress'' is gradually coming into being in the cities.

TRADITION AND INDUSTRIALISM

However, even today the Japanese worker in a factory, firm or government office is a member of it in the way that his Western counterpart would be a member of a family. ''The Japanese employee is part of a much more personal system, a system in which his total functioning as a person in seen as managements responsibility and in which his group membership transcends his individual privileges and responsibilities''.[31]

The question arises as to how such a traditional personalized social structure can sustain a modern industrialized economy. The answer given by one scholar is that the traditional, feudal economic structure was, like most other Japanese institutions, very flexible. As Norman Jacobs,[32] has written: ''One might even say, in the extreme, that the economic development of Japan had its origins in the failure of the Taikwa Reform of the Seventh century to establish the moral, substantive-rational political economy of China. By default, rather than by decision, this failure established or ratified, as an institutional assumption or choice, a pragmatic flexibility throughout the social order, including the economic order.'' This eventually led, he continues, to ''a collectivism or individualism which produces, respectively, productive co-operation and a willingness to accept personal responsibility and commitment so typical of Japanese behaviour [which] is conducive to development. And perhaps *one* way of explaining the measure of this difference is in terms of an institutional structure which emphasizes in the political realm, on the one hand, the kind of legal security and flexibility which grew out of the feudal relationships of Japan and of the developed West, and on the other hand, patrimonial grants of grace by superiors without redress of grievance by followers so typical of the long-range political institutions of the underdeveloped Asian societies''. Thus, collectivist-individualist dichotomies being completely lacking in Japan; there the traditional superior-subordinate relationships have been resilient enough to work under modern conditions also.

TRADITIONAL IDIOMS IN JAPANESE POLITICS

It should by now have become obvious that the personal factor of family type life runs throughout Japanese society. This tendency is more marked in the villages. "The rural character is a full, traditional, stable way of life. . . . The continuing importance of intensive agriculture gives this cultural tradition great durability today and makes it a living reservoir of traditional norms that are distinctively Japanese."[33] All this results in the real, as opposed to the formal, social and political leadership of Japan still being chosen according to traditional qualifications; ancestral status, age and family connections. Elections, the formal judiciary, the legislature—they just legalise what is being done. Of course, as time goes by they have started exercising an influence of their own also, but not so to a very significant extent.[34] For example, writing about the selection of a successor to Prime Minister Sato Michael Hornsby just before the event[35] said that "much in this cabalistic contest still remains shrouded. . . [for] the struggle for succession can be understood only in terms of the peculiar organization of Japanese political parties. These are invariably divided into numerous factions or Habatsu of differing size and importance, of which each has its own clearly identifiable leader."

"The relationship between the faction leader and his followers is one that is found throughout Japanese society in one form or the other. It testifies to the persistence beneath Western trappings of distinctively Japanese codes of fealty dating from pre-modern times."

"In Japanese terms, the leader plays the part of the *oyabun* (literally "parent role") and his followers take the *kobun* or child role. The former extends paternalistic aid and protection in return for the services and loyalty of the latter."

"The head of a Habatsu in the LDP (Liberal Democratic Party) makes it his business to look after the interest of his followers, to secure positions of importance for them within the party, and to see that they are financially well provided for at election time."

"Most of the substantial donations from business circles are channelled through the bosses of the three or four biggest factions who are regarded as potential party leaders and hence Prime Ministers. . . ."

"The rules of rank and seniority are such that it is almost impossible for the individual party member, however talented or ambitious, to move at move than a certain prescribed rate up the ladder of power. . . ."

"Each faction boss has. . . his own *Oyabun-kobun* relationship with the party leader and it is this that holds the whole together. . ."

". . . a faction like that of Mr. Takeo Miki, a former Foreign Minister, often behave[s] as if it were a separate opposition party."

"It is expected of a leader, either before death or retirement, that he should both indicate his chosen successor and prepare the ground for his acceptance by the rest of the members of the group."

These quotations from Hornsby's article serve the purpose of emphasising that the formal Western type meeting to elect a new party leader has no significance in Japan. What is important are the four or five big Habatsu who eventually manage to come up with a decision through "unanimous consent" keeping in view the fact that a split caused by voting would make it impossible for the new Prime Minister to become the *Oyabun*. The election of Tanaka has, of course, led to speculation that the traditional Japanese system may have gradually started moving towards self-extinction. But the traditional system has already withstood many changes and shocks and the chances are that it shall survive this one also.

THE EMPEROR

It would be fruitful now to consider the changing position of the Japanese Emperor, since he has served as a symbol of national and cultural unity in modern times. Ever since the end of the Tokugawa period, Japanese leaders have used the throne as a counterpoise to decentralizing tendencies and in doing so developed a kind of Emperor cult. The Emperor, pictured as heaven descended, divine, sacred, allwise, and virtuous was set apart from the nation, and period were forbidden to make him a topic of discussion or of derogatory comment. The exalted position of the Emperor was based on the political philosophy of *kokutai* or national polity. According to the *kokutai* doctrine, the Japanese nation is a large family ruled by the Emperor, who is its patriarchal father. Consequently, the relationship between the sovereign and his subjects was said to be similar to that existing between father and son and thus filial piety and political loyalty became one and the same thing. It was thus unthinkable for most Japanese that the relationship between Emperor and his subjects cold change.[36]

The Emperor was also the symbol of the Shinto-cult, which celebrated a revival in the Meiji era. Arthur Tiedmann[37] gives three basic principles of State-Shintoism:

"1. The Emperor is divine because he is the extension in time of the very bodies and souls of the great divine ancestors of the past and in particular of the physical and spiritual attributes of the Sun-Goddess;[38]

2. Japan is under the spatial guardianship of the Gods and therefore its soil, its people and its institutions are unique and superior to all others;

3. It is Japan's divine mission to bring the whole world under one roof and thus extend to the rest of humanity the advantages of being ruled by the Emperor."

Three of the first four articles of the Meiji Constitution also indicate the symbolic status of the Emperor:

Article 1. The Empire of Japan shall be reigned over and governed by a line of Emperors unbroken for ages eternal.

Article 3. The Emperor is sacred and inviolable.

Article 4. The Emperor is the head of the Empire combining in himself the rights of sovereignty.

Of course in reality the political role of the Emperor in the Meiji era had been to merely serve as a symbol and not to participate actively in the formulation and execution of policy. He, in fact, provided a rather convenient shield or smoke-screen for the small group that ruled in his name.

The new constitution however alerted all this by stating that "The Emperor shall be the symbol of the State and of the unity of the people, deriving his position from the will of the people with whom resides sovereign power" (Article I). This change has had two major consequences. It has become possible to discuss and write openly about the Emperor, both as a person and as an institution, even in a critical vein, without the risk of public censure or arrest. Concerted attempts have also been made to 'humanize' the Emperor and bring him closer to the people. In practice, however, the Emperor's political role has not changed much, being limited chiefly to performing ceremonial functions. The main difference is that, since ministers and advisors don't rule in his name any more, the lines of responsibility are now much more clearly drawn.

It had been believed that tampering with the myth of the Emperor as the exalted father of the nation would weaken the cement holding the society together and lead to social chaos; but the Emperor still enjoys considerable popularity and "the quotient of mass identification with the nation and its symbols remains very high in postwar Japan, [though] there has been a decrease in its intensity and an increase in the volume of principled dissent."[39]

THE TRADITIONAL ELITE

Now let us turn to the role of elites in Japan's transition. As Arnold Smith has pointed out[40] that contrary to usual experience the Japanese *Samurai* not only did not defend its established position but even took the lead in abolishing its own privileges and thus transforming the entire society.[41] It is suggested that this is so because the privileges of the *Samurai* were never really challenged by a rising democratic movement. One of the reasons for this was that the country was secluded from foreign ideational influences and thus ideological polarization was avoided and "private hurts were thus never raised to a great principle of struggle between right and wrong". Another reason for the *samurai* not resisting transformation was that they had already been removed, as a result of the civil wars that had brought the Tokugawa family to power, from the land three centuries prior to 1868. The civil wars had not only resulted in separating the warrior class from the land but also led to its "urban concentration, its anti-rural base, its relative demilitarization, or, conversely, its bureaucratization." Since the Tokugawa era was one of peace the Japanese *samurai* had not remained militarist but had increasingly turned its attention to the promotion of education and economic enterprise as necessary preconditions for the country's eventual renaissance.

The Tokugawa settlement had also resulted in a genuine class division within the aristocracy. A few thousand families of superior lineage monopolised the important offices, while several hundred thousand *samurai* families were cut off from all opportunities of employment. Thus when the consolidation of *daimio* power led to the bureaucratization of head-government the merit criterion for selection to offices in the head-bureaucracies was advocated so as to result in increased carrier opportunities for some of the *samurai.* Upward mobility based on achievement also become possible. An ideology of thus evolved 'merit' satisfied both the pride and aspirations of the *samurai,* and also intensified the invidious contrast between the daimio-domains and the corrupt and effect Shogunate in Edo. Simultaneously, or rather consequentially, the ideal of the warrior was gradually superceded by ideals more appropriate for a bureaucrat. Hence "the very rapid expansion of opportunities after 1868 was tailor-made for men who suffered from the acute discrepancy between their high social rank and their lowly economic position, who were free of bias against change since they had long since been severed from the land, whose educational preferment under the Tokugawa regime provided them with an immediate advantage over all competitors, and whose-traditional cult of action, habits of frugality, aristocratic aversion to money-making, and ideology of aspiration had prepared them psychologically for a bureaucratic career. In a society which heavily underscored status distinctions, the *samurai* could now hoped to rise to the highest positions. This hope, combined as it was with the collectivist ideal of national advance, outweighed the real deprivations to which they were at first exposed."[42]

CONTINUITY AND CHANGE IN LEADERSHIP

Thus in Japan the tension between tradition and modernity was limited because when all parties are more or less reformist and more or less traditional, the past does not appear as a barrier to progress, but rather as an obstacle in some respects and an aid in others. Prevailing attitudes of loyalty to the family, to the clan and above all to the Emperor also helped in avoiding conflict in the Japanese society and thus enabled the oligarch to act as a "modernizing autocracy".[43]

Writing about the same aspect, Bernard S. Silberman[44] says that "the new leadership, although recruited partially on the basis of achievement-oriented criteria, was also drawn almost totally from the traditional elite. The new leadership thus had a community of shared values with the former head officials who continued to wield both official and unofficial influence at the local level. Those *samurai* who remained behind saw no reason to challenge the leadership of men drawn from their own ranks. . . . Furthermore this continuity of leadership did not disturb the existing patterns of. . . hierarchical authority of village leadership. . . .The desire to make use of this traditional pattern of behaviour is reflected in the bureaucracy's deliberate maintenance of an unspecialized and functionally diffuse system of administration at the local level of government, one which resembled very closely the administration employed in the Tokugawa period. The use of family and the village community to perform the functions of control and socialization allowed the bureaucracy to avoid immediate investment of large amounts of scarce resources in new control and socialization structures.''

VI

We have already seen the role of various forces in Japanese politics between 1868 and 1945 as described above. So let us now turn as to how post-1945 Japan is governed.

The present constitution of Japan provides a system of government based essentially on a unique amalgam of British and American institutions and the Meiji Constitution. It preserves the monarchy but strips the Emperor of any semblance of political authority. It also retains a bicameral legislature, but completely reconstitutes the relationship and powers of the pre-war upper and lower houses. Superior legislative and financial powers are entrusted to the lower house. At the national level, executive and administrative authority is concentrated in a responsible cabinet, and an independent American style judiciary is vested with the power of Judicial review. The constitution places great stress on civil rights and introduces the principle of local autonomy to a much greater extent than prevalent previously.

However one find that a ''Triangular League'', consisting of leaders of the ruling party, senior government officials and big business circles that lead a host of conservative-inclined pressure groups, have taken over the decision-making functions from the Diet and Cabinet under what Fukuji Taguchi calls the ''Regime of 1955'',[45] Maki[46] describes it as: ''the conservative establishment: The Liberal Democratic Party (LDP) in power since 1955 as the successor of a series of post-war conservative parties; big business; the farmers; and most important of all, a plurality (till recently a majority) of the electorate to keep the L.D.P. comfortably in power.'' Though the socialists, J.S.P., J.C.P. and D.S.P. did slightly improve their position in 1971 House of Counsellors and city elections with even the opposition conservatives the Soka Gakkai-Komeito group suffering a set back;[47] the conservative do not seem to be seriously threatened. Tanaka's assuming office, however, also raises speculation of a possible conservative decline.

While it is understandable that party leaders are influential in a parliamentary system, the reason for big business and the bureaucracy being so, needs slight looking into. The bureaucracy in Japan is involved in politics because such involvement is a solidly entrenched part of

Japanese tradition, because the national legislature is week, because in modern times political decisions have become inextricably mingled with problems of administration and technology all over the world, and because upon retirement substantial number of the higher bureaucracy have successfully run for political office. (In fact the policy research committees of political parties and bureaucrats often jointly do the initial drafting of most bills). Big business influence drives not only from direct donations to party coffers and election campaigns and consequent access to the cabinet, but also from their practice of giving good jobs to retiring bureaucrats who have helped them in the past, and also through interest groups. The third factor is significant, since in Japan the relations between the Ministries, high administrative organizations of the national government and their organized public clienteles (interest groups) are apt to be very close and the three often act as one unit.

ALIENATION: ANARCHISM AND VIOLENCE

Fukuji Taguchi[48] feels that the groups that do not have access to power under the 'regime of 1955' have begun to feel alienated from the system (the rise of the *Zengakuren* being one symptom) and have turned to extremism. As Geoffery Ostergard[49] has pointed out, "the spirit of total negation (and thus indirectly of anarchism) can be traced to the influence. . . of Buddhism and Taoism." Barrington Moore[50] has described *samurai* drop outs detaching themselves from the system and touring the country as "ronin" and they can be considered prototypes of todays extremists. "Violence", says Ward[51] "and use of force to achieve political ends have long and not dishonourable histories in Japan. And the tendency of the people has often been not to denounce such recourses as ill advised or evil but rather to look to the announced motives and subsequent conduct of the users of violence as a key to judgement. If their motives and they individually were held to be sincere and, above all, if they showed a disposition to prove it and simultaneously to atone by some form of self-punishment—classically by *sepuku* or *hara-kiri*—then the initial act of violence was apt to be viewed with sympathy if not outright approval. Something of this sentiment undoubtedly survives in some quarters. . . " But on the other hand, speaking of today Geoffrey Ostergaard[52] writes that "there was frequent and outrageous violence which became really oppressive. . . . There were extravagances everywhere not only amongst students but also throughout the 'New Left'. . . . The militants strength began to collapse under the weight of their own provocations; especially under the pressure of legislation they had provoked.'' Anarchism in Japan is not opposed to parliamentary democracy but is trying to keep it from atrophying under conservative rule. Even traditionally extremism was never meant to smash the system but to preserve its purity and vitality. Thus when it because obvious that present day anarchism was threatening the existing democratic system it started loosing support. While still a major force, violence has for the time being been thrust to the background. It is conceivable that the Japanese mode of decision-making and their concept of status shall keep extremists from disrupting the policy once more.

THE REIGNING CONSERVATIVE IDEOLOGY

It would be interesting to digress a little and note Maki's assessment[53] of what the conservative ruling elite wants. ''In most simplistic terms the conservatives would like to see Japan strengthen or resuscitate what they regard as good and beautiful in its tradition: for example, some if not all aspects of the traditional family system; the priority of society over the individual; nationalism as manifested in history, tradition and culture; respect for the imperial institutions; and a military establishment as a mark of national power and dignity, if not as a manifestation of militarism.'' Thus it is obvious that the traditional pull is still very strong in Japan, so much so that, contrary to common experience, the progressives resist and the conservatives demand change in Japan. That Japanese traditions are not anti-modernist is demonstrated once more by the fact that even under the conservative regime of 1955 a lot of 'Progressive' and modern measures have been implemented.

VII

It may be appropriate to end by quoting some of the general propositions that Ward has elucidated:[54]

A. That with judicious management elements of a society's traditional political culture may be converted into potent agents of modernization.

B. That in the early stage of modernization firm political decisions of what sector of the population is going to bear the major share of the cost of development are necessary.

C. That where possible there is much to be said in favour of a strategy of development that confronts major political problems in sequence rather than concurrently.

D. That widespread fear of foreign intervention or exploitation can be a powerful stimulus to political modernization.

E. That if the quality of leadership is held constant, authoritarian and oligarchical forms of government may be superior to democratic forms in the earlier stages of political development. [A contention that author system finds disheartening to accept]

F. That despite the existence of an authoritarian political system to begin with, significant liberalizing tendencies may be inherent in the modernization process.

G. That the history of democratization of Japan emphasises the importance of gradual preparation and preparation in depth for the attainment of viable political system.

And one may add one more hypothesis, for Japanese experience suggest that society in the early stages of economic and political development may *require* a bureaucracy, and in fact the entire government system, that is recruited and organized, at least partially, on the basis of traditional pre-bureaucratic criteria and orientations.

It should be obvious by now that assertion of some writers that universalist and particularist (traditional and modern criteria co-exist in all societies and at all times is borne out by the Japanese experience.[55] In fact, in Japan, tradition itself has generated change, and modernization has taken place without destroying the traditional fabric in any way.

NOTES AND REFERENCES

1. "Modernization and its Ambiguities", *Hakone Conference Paper,* 190. Claude E. Welch in his reader *Political Modernization,* California, 1967, 1971 also takes a similar view but emphasises the diffusion of a "World Culture" and, in the political sphere, the concentration of power, along with a breakdown of traditional sources of authority (a point I do not fully agree with), the differentiation of political structures, and increased participation, coupled with greater identification of individuals with the political system.
2. From "Changing Conceptions of Modernization in Japan" in *Changing Japanese Attitudes Towards Modernization*, ed. Marius B. Jansen, Princeton, 1965.
3. Princeton, 1960.
4. *Government and Opposition,* Vol. 3, No. 3, 1968.
5. *Kindai Nibon Shoshi*, Vol. 1., Tokyo, 1952.

6. *Op. cit.*
7. *Asia Awakes: A Continent in Transition*, Weidenfeld & Nicolson, 1970.
8. E. Vogel, *Japan's New Middle Class*, Berkeley, 1963.
9. John W. Bennet, ''Japanese Economic Growth: Background for Social Change'', in R.P. Dore (ed.) *Aspects of Social Change in Modern Japan*, 1967.
10. ''Japan: The Continuity of Modernization'' in Lucian Pye and Sidney Verba ed. *Political Culture and Political Development*, Princeton, 1965 and also in ''Political Modernization and Political Culture in Japan'' Originally published in *World Politics*, Vol. XV, No. 4. (1963).
11. ''Feudalism in Japan—A Reassessment'', *Comparative Studies in Society and History*, Vol. V., No. 1 (Oct., 1962).
12. Cf. ''Japan'' by Nobutaka Ike in George McT. Kahin ed. ''*Major Governments of Asia*'', New York, 1963.
13. Robert E. Ward, ''Japan'' in Ward and Roy, Macridis (ed.) ''*Modern Political System: Asia*'', Prentice Hall, 1963.
14. New York, 1966.
15. Robert E. Ward, Modern Political Systems, *op. cit*,
16. Nobutaka Ike, *Op. cit*.
17. Ward and Macridis, *Modern Political Systems, op. cit*.
18. Modernization: *Protest and Change,* Prentice-Hall, 1966.
19. For a discussion of the role of education see R.P. Dore, ''The Legacy of Tokugawa Education'' in Jansen *op. cit.*, R.P. Dore, ''Education: Japan'' in R.E. Ward and D.A. Rustow (ed.) *Political Modernization in Japan and Turkey,* Princeton, 1964; and Herbert Passin's chapter on Japan in ''*Education and Political Culture*'', ed. James S. Coleman, Princeton, 1965.
20. Cf. R.N. Bellah ''Values and Social Change in Modern Japan'' in *Asian Cultural Studies*, No. 3, Studies on the Modernization of Japan, Tokyo, October 1962.
21. Boston, 1966.
22. *Tokugawa Religion: The Values of Pre-Industrial Japan*, Glencoe, 1957.
23. *Land Reform in Japan*, Oxford, 1959.
24. *Democracy and the Party Movement in Pre-war Japan*, Berkeley, 1953.
25. See Ward, in Pye and Verba (ed.) *op. cit.*, especially for the role of education in the process.
26. John M. Maki, *Government and Politics in Japan*, London, 1972.
27. Ward in Ward and Macridis (ed.) *op. cit.*
28. *Op. cit.*
29. Ward, *Ibid.*
30. *City Life in Japan: A Study of a Tokyo Ward,* Berkeley, 1958.
31. James C. Abbeglen, *The Japanese Factory: Aspects of its Social Organization*, Glencoe, 1958.
32. ''The Institutional Approach to Japanese Economic Development'' in *Asian Survey*, September, 1965, Vol. V., No. 9.
33. R.K. Beardsley, J.W. Hall and R.E. Ward, *Village Japan*, Chicago, 1959.
34. See *The Government of Japan*, A.W. Burks, 1964.

35. ''The Race for Leadership in Japan'' in *The Statesman*, July 4, 1972, quoted from *The Times*, London.
36. Nobutaka Ike in Kahin, *op.cit.*
37. *Modern Japan*, Van Nostrand, 1955.
38. Amaterasu-Omikami, considered to be the Emperor's ancestress, see for example, ''*Sources of Japanese Tradition*'' compiled by Ryusaku Tsunoda, Wm. Theodore de Bary and Donald Keene, Columbia University Press, especially page 17, ''The Sun Ancestress'' and page 520 Motoori Noringa ''The True Tradition of the Sun Goddess''.
39. Ward in Pye and Verba, *op. cit.* Cf. Theodore McNelly, ''The Role of Monarchy in the Political Modernization of Japan'' in *Comparative Politics*, Vol. I, No. 3, April 1963.
40. ''Japan's Aristocratic Revolution'', *Yale Review*, Spring 1961.
41. Cf. Eisenstadt, *op. cit* and Barrington Moore, *op. cit.*
42. Reinhard Bendix, *Nation-Building and Citizenship*, John Wiley and Sons, 1964.
43. A brief, simplified, analysis along these lines is also to be found in ''Japan: Modernization and Continuity'' by Ian Grossart in *The Politics of New States* ed. by Roger Scott, 1970.
44. ''The Bureaucracy and Economic Development,'' *Asian Survey*, Vol. V, No. 11.
45. ''Japan in Transition'' in Bernard Crick and William Robson (ed.) *Protest and Discontent*, Penguin, 1970.
46. ''Japan's Contemporary Conservatism'' and *Polity*, Vol. IV, No. 2, Winter 1971.
47. Lee W. Farnsworth, ''Japan: The Year of Shock'' in *Asian Survey*, Vol. XII, No. 1, Jan. 1972.
48. Crick and Robson (ed.) *op. cit.*
49. ''Anarchism in Japan'' in *Anarchism Today* (ed.) David E. Apter and James Joll, Macmillan, 1971.
50. *Op. cit.*
51. Pye and Verba (ed.) *op. cit.*
52. *Ibid.*
53. ''Japan's Contemporary Conservatism'', *op. cit.*
54. ''Epilogue'' in *Political Development in Modern Japan* ed. by R.E. Ward, Princeton, 1968.
55. One could thus agree with Joseph R Gusfield, ''Tradition and Modernity: Misplaced Polarities in the Study of Social Change'' in *The American Journal of Sociology*, Vol. LXXII, No. 4 (1966) where he lists seven ''fallacies'' regarding the belief that ''traditional'' and ''modern'' are incompatible on even internally consistent terms and emphasises their joint existence and contribution in the process of modernization'', or change.

2

The Imperial Institution in Japan

T.W. ECKERSLEY

Throughout Japan's long history no institution has shown greater capacity for survival in the midst of changing circumstances than the Imperial family. While its effective power often suffered virtual eclipse, particularly during the time of the Tokugawa Shogunate, it managed to keep itself intact and to assume in modern times an importance greater than it had ever had before. It is not necessary here to trace the vicissitudes of this institution through history, suffice it to say that it was around the person of the Emperor that the Japanese nation was unified at the time of the Meiji Restoration, and it was under a system of almost unquestioning Emperor-worship that the nation increased its industrial and military strength to the point where it plunged, in a seemingly 'make or break' effort, into the Pacific War on 8 December 1941.

The period of preparation for the Imperial revival was quite long and extended for the last hundred years of the Tokugawa regime. While it is probable that the Emperor system would have been revived by the trend of internal politics, there is no doubt that external events were responsible for the Imperial revival taking the form it did and at the time it did. Although the Meiji Constitution instituted a form of parliamentary government for Japan, the position of the Emperor in this Constitution was supreme. Article 1 embodied the concept of an unbroken line of emperors since the founding of the Empire by the first Emperor, Jimmu Tenno, in 660 B.C. It stated, 'The Empire of Japan shall be reigned over and governed by a line of Emperors unbroken for ages eternal'. Article 2 established the succession in accordance with the provisions of the Imperial House Law. Article 3 declared that the Emperor was sacred and inviolable, while Article 4 stated that he was 'supreme head of the Empire, combining in himself the rights of sovereignty, and exercising them in accordance with the provisions of this constitution'. Under Articles 5 and 6 he exercised the legislative power with the consent of the Imperial Diet and gave sanction to laws, ordering them to be promulgated and executed. Under Article 7 he convoked the Imperial Diet, opened, closed and prorogued it, and dissolved the House of Representatives. But it was under Article 8 that he exercised his extraordinary powers as the occasion might demand. This article stated:

> The Emperor, in consequence of an urgent necessity to maintain public safety or to avert public calamities, issues, when the Imperial Diet is not sitting, Imperial Ordinance in the place of law.
> Such Imperial Ordinances are to be laid before the Imperial Diet at its next session, and in case the Diet does not approve the said Ordinances, the Government shall declare them to be invalid for the future.

It is to be noted that the Government, not the Diet, had the power to declare ordinances invalid, and, as the Government was responsible to the Emperor, this power was rarely, if ever, exercised.

Article 9 extended the emperor's power by enabling him to issue or cause to be issued Ordinances necessary for the carrying out of the law, for maintenance of public peace and order, and for the promotion of the welfare of the subjects. While this article also stated that no ordinance should in any way alter any of the existing laws, the practice it meant that existing laws could be overridden if circumstances demanded it.

Article 10 gave the emperor wide powers over personnel of the Administration in that he was empowered to determine 'the organization of the different branches of the administration, and the salaries of all civil and military officers', and appoint and dismiss them. Under Article 11 the Emperor had supreme command of the army and navy, and under Article 12 he determined their organization and peace standing. Under Article 13 he declared war, made peace and concluded treaties. He conferred titles of nobility, rank, orders and other marks of honour under Article 15 and under Article 16 he ordered amnesty, pardon, commutation of punishments, and rehabilitation. While the personal exercise of all these powers depended greatly upon the personality of whoever was Emperor, and while they were exercised more in person by the Emperor Meiji than by either his son or the present Emperor, it was always possible for a small group to exercise dominant influence through him. It was not surprising then that when Japan was on the brink of defeat in the Pacific War, the only thought of those in authority in Tokyo was how to save the Emperor and the system he stood for from the consequences of defeat.

When on 26 July 1945, the Allied Powers called upon Japan to surrender unconditionally in terms of the Potsdam Declaration, the Japanese Government replied that Japan would surrender provided the Emperor's powers and position were left intact. No specific rejection of this conditional acceptance was made, and when the Allied Occupation Forces entered Japan to receive the surrender, the Emperor was still the supreme authority in the country, and it was through him that the Japanese people and Armed Forces were called upon to surrender. Nevertheless, within the framework of the terms of the surrender and occupation policies, the Japanese were themselves induced to make radical changes in the nature of the Emperor's office. The lead was given in this, too, by the Emperor himself, who, on 1 January 1946, issued the historic rescript renouncing his divinity. This rescript, which set the pattern for much that was to follow, was couched in plain terms and was different from the rescripts of preceding decades, which, using a special Imperial language, carried the weight of divine authority in Japan and was held in the esteem of Japanese soldiers and people alike in much the same way as the Holy Bible is in Western countries. While the new rescript, in a sense, invoked the Emperor Meiji, the fact that it was expressed in everyday language and renounced the concept that the Emperor was divine did much to undermine the authority of the rescripts which had been issued by him. A new tone was set in the Emperor's concern for and desire to share in the troubles of his people. 'The ties between us and our people have always stood upon mutual trust and affection. They do not depend upon mere legends and myths. They are not predicated on the false conception that the Emperor is divine and the Japanese people are superior to other races and fated to rule the world.' While many of the sentiments expressed in the rescript were in accord with tradition, the meaning of this passage was unmistakable; it was a clear break with the past and a disavowal of one of the basic concepts of the national faith. Though it would not be true to say that scepticism had been unknown in the period of nationalist revival, it had never before been pronounced with such authority, and this expression of it was symptomatic of much of the discussion which was to follow concerning the emperor and his place under the new constitution, the examination of which was already under way at this time.

It is not easy to determine the degree to which the changes that became apparent in Japan at this time were due to Allied Occupation policy or due to a desire for change or a calculated accommodation to change in the Japanese themselves. Without having undertaken exhaustive quantitative analysis, one can now only hazard a rough guess. It is certainly true that the atmosphere of defeat provided the right climate for Japanese heart-searching, just as it is probably true that this heart-searching would not have taken the form it did had not the Allied Powers initially launched upon a thorough-going policy of democratization and liberalization. It does seem, however, that where the Allied directives gave the lead there were hundreds of thousands, even millions of Japanese eager to follow. In nothing was this so apparent as the organization of the union movement in which, in a matter of months after the issuance of the directive granting freedom of association, the number of Japanese who were members of unions soon passed the 5 million mark. On the other hand, there was always a strong and influential body of Japanese that was resistant to change, and as the Occupation progressed this body was to grow stronger. Nonetheless, sweeping changes were introduced, and it is difficult to see them all being swept away by any reactionary movement. Apart from the desire for change from the bottom, there was movement in favour of change at the top, and the Emperor's rescript was compelling evidence of this. Many Japanese conservatives were aghast at the sweeping reform the Japanese Government was directed to carry out, but there is considerable evidence to suggest that some members of the Imperial family were happy to be freed of their divine attributes. The way in which they and some members of the aristocracy accommodated themselves to the changes of the times was remarkable.

It is in the revised constitution, which was passed by the Diet and promulgated by the Emperor himself on 3 November 1946, that the new status of the Emperor has been written into the law. Under the new

Article 'the Emperor shall be the symbol of the State and of the unity of the people, deriving his position from the will of the people with whom resides sovereign power'. With the exception of the vexed Article 9, no article of the revised constitution caused more controversy than this one, the description of the Emperor as 'a symbol of the State' causing a great deal of heart-burning amongst conservative politicians who declared that the whole basis of the 'national polity' (*Kokutai*) was being subverted, or at least changed. In a sense perhaps it was, but this did not appear to worry the Emperor himself as much as it did some of his supporters. Many years before his office had been described as an organ of the State', and the present Emperor had personally taken no great exception to it, although public opinion had long afterwards forced the resignation of the Professor who was responsible for this heresy. When proper account was taken of all that had occurred in the interim, the transition from being 'supreme head of the Empire, combining in himself the rights of sovereignty and exercising them in accordance with the provisions of the constitution' to 'organ of the State' and then to 'symbol of the State' seemed to be a natural progression. This was particularly so, when due recognition was given to the fact that present Emperor himself had always been disinclined to exercise his rights of sovereignty in any but a formal way, his real interest appearing to be in marine biology rather than in being Emperor. Nevertheless, the real cutting down of the Imperial institution to the proportions of a constitutional monarch was achieved in the new constitution not so much by altering the description of the Emperor but by simply deleting nine articles of the Meiji Constitution which embodied the extraordinary powers of the Emperor. What is left of these functions is now set down in Article 7 as a list of acts performed by the Emperor 'on behalf of the people with the advice and approval of the Cabinet,' and is largely formal in content.

It can be seen from the above that the position of the Emperor has changed considerably under the new constitution, and this constitutional change has been accompanied by various trends in the attitude and outlook of the Imperial Household, in the attitude and outlook of officials and of the Japanese people as a whole, which tend to confirm the impression that there is a fairly general belief that the new position of the Emperor not only conforms more with the requirements of the times, but is more acceptable to the mass of the Japanese people. The latest evidence of this change of attitude has been the way in which the members of the Imperial Family seem to have been almost glad to accept non-imperial status.

The changes necessary to transform the Imperial institution into a democratic monarchy have and are still taking place. It is evidence of the adaptability of the Japanese people and their institutions that these changes have had little effect upon the affectionate regard with which the Japanese regard their Emperor. There was a remarkable imperturbability in the way in which the present emperor weathered the post-war storm during which charges of his complicity in the crimes of the major was criminals were not infrequent, and there were proposals that he should take his place among the accused. This issue was not pressed, but for some time after the surrender there were a number of prominent Japanese who advocated the abdication of the Emperor, and, if the Crown Prince had been of age at the time, this suggestion would have been more likely to have won a greater degree of acceptance than it did. However, Emperor Hirohito stayed on and by 1952 Jean Stoetzel, the French sociologist, conducting an investigation on behalf of UNESCO found that 'not a few traces of traditional devotion (were) still to be found in the young.' By that time, too, the vast majority (78 per cent) of those questioned thought it reasonable that the Emperor should not be regarded as a war criminal while Tojo was sent to the gallows. As a result of the tests conducted and the questionnaires answered Stoetzel found that, notwithstanding its setbacks and political upheavals, attachment to the Imperial House remained strong in Japan, but it was a political or philosophical attachment rather than a personal one. Related to the question of the attitude towards the Emperor is the attitude of the people towards the revival of the *Kigensetsu*, the celebration of the foundation of the Empire which used to take place on the 11th February, but which was banned by the Occupation authorities. From time to time suggestions have been made for the revival of the *Kigensetsu*, but they have always been shelved because of the protests of a vocariferous minority. That this is a minority is adequately indicated by the answers given by the 85 per cent of those questioned by one of Stoetzel's assistants, who thought that the annual celebration of Empire Day should be restored. From their answers to this and other questions Stoetzel concludes that 'the youth of Japan has preserved intact its sense of continuity with the country's most distant past and retains a most lively awareness of Japanese history even in its mythological aspects'. This view of the Emperor system is supported by Professor Yanaibara in his *Short History of Modern Japan*, in which the view is expressed that insistence that the existence of the Tenno system is damaging to the democratization of Japan is not general, but that on the contrary, the Japanese people seem to feel a human respect in a new sense toward the Emperor who has cast off his divinity.

How deep and lasting is a loyalty based upon these less preferred emotions? It is hard to tell. It seems that the new patriotism is of a kind that may well flourish in easier times. How it will stand up to the pressures of world politics only the future will reveal.

3

Change of Leadership in Japan

P.A. NARASIMHA MURTHY*

In the rough and tumble of Japanese politics, the election of a new party leaders means an open war with no holds barred. More so in the case of the ruling Liberal Democratic Party which stands on a delicately built coalition of half a dozen or more factions. The factions throw everything at their command into a presidential contest, money, influence, persuasion, cajolery and even veiled threats, in fact, every conceivable means of getting votes for the candidate supported by each. The ruling party which has held the reins of power continuously since 1955, is always in a state of civil war: a presidential election brings to the surface the tensions, squabbles and clashes that normally remain hidden from the public. Especially after the 12th presidential election of 1972, which was won by Kakuei Tanaka, the in-fighting among the factions over the question of party leadership became both ferocious and endemic. The choice of Zenko Suzuki in June 1980 as a consensus candidate brought a temporary suspension of factional strife and averted a possible split in the party. Suzuki was accepted by the warring camps because of his known commitment to preserve harmony within the party and his singular ability to carry out behind-the-scenes mediation among

* Dr. Murthy is Professor in the Centre for East Asian Studies, School of International Studies, Jawaharlal Nehru University, New Delhi.

rivals. But the 16th presidential election held in November 1982 once again pulled the lid off the boiling LDP plot, and the in-fighting between the mainstream and non-mainstream groups erupted into the open.

ROLE OF FACTIONALISM IN PRESIDENTIAL ELECTIONS

Consensus and Election

In Japan the ruling party's presidential election is important because the winning candidate would not only head the party for 2 years under the provisions of the party rules (re-election is also possible under the rules), but also by virtue of his being leader of the majority party be the Prime Minister of the country under Article 67 of the Constitution of Japan.[1] Since April 1955 when the first President was chosen, the party has selected its leader through voting with some rare exceptions. Death or illness of an incumbent president has invariably been an occasion for the senior executives and advisers of the party to come together and choose a successor through consultation and negotiation instead of relying on the ballot. Consensus is also resorted to whenever the party elders fear an imminent confrontation or a split in the party. Thus, in November 1964, when illness forced Hayato Ikeda to resign, Eisaku Sato was chosen to succeed him and the party conference subsequently endorsed the choice. Two years later the party again chosen Sato as leader, but through formal election. Similarly, Suzuki, the 10th president of the party was chosen through negotiations following the sudden death of Masayoshi Ohira in June 1980.

The right to choose the party president was originally resticted under Article 3 of the party rules to *Diet* members of the party and one delegate each from the prefectural federations (two delegates prior to 1962). With such a limited electorate, the system naturally accentuated factional politics in the party as each faction tried hard to push its own leader for the presidency. In consequence, factional or committed voting became the rule and is still one of the notable features of the presidential election. The system also encouraged the prospective candidates to enlist support among voters on the basis of personal obligation and allegiance rather than the qualities of leadership. It was therefore inevitable that the successful candidate saw himself more as a *balancer of factions* than a *partly leader*. The collapse hence of intra-party balance often forced a party president to admit failure and quit.

In a society as strongly rooted in consensus as the Japanese, the ballot has only a limited role to play in the sense that the actual selection is not based on it but on the more informal methods of negotiation, consultation and accommodation. The ballot is used only to obtain confirmation of the selection already made through these formal methods. To the older members in the party, some of whom have lived through the three major epoches of modern Japan, viz., *Meiji*, *Taisho*, and Showa periods and have seen the gradual evolution of political processes in their country, voting has always been a disruptive force and should therefore not replace consensus altogether. The younger members, those born in the 1930s and 1940s, hold that it is a perfectly rational thing to choose the leader of a party through voting. All modern political parties do that. Nathaniel B. Thayer says in his study of the working of the Liberal Democratic Party that Eisaku Sato, Prime Minister and party president from 1964 to 1972, was himself of the opinion that election was ''the fair and proper way for a modern political party'' and that the evils of an election were fewer than the evils of selection based on consultation or consensus.[2]

For many years the process of presidential election has been the subject of adverse comments from several quarters. It has been considered, for example, a source of corruption that has eroded the foundations of the party and made access to funds and the ability to distribute political patronage the most important attributes of the leader. Several solutions were proposed in the past to overcome this, but none save a few minor ones have so far been tried. The more important among them were: (1) the abolition of secret voting and the introduction of open vote, (2) the separation of party presidency from the office of the Prime Minister, (3) election of the Prime Minister directly by popular vote, and (4) expansion of the base for presidential election.[3]

The last one found favour with the younger members as it held out the promise of giving the right to vote to a larger number of party members and a possible reduction in the role of personal allegiance. And so in April 1977 the party agreed to extend the franchise top members and associate members; in August, new election rules were written under which primaries were to be held in which the rank and file of the party participated. The first two winners in the primaries were then to go on to the second or final round in which only party members of the House of Councillors (Upper House) and the House of Representatives (Lower House) voted. The candidate getting the largest number of votes in the final round would be the party leader. The first primaries under these rules were held in November 1978 and they eliminated two out of the four candidates in the race. The final round of course ended up as a mere formality as the second candidate accepted defeat and withdrew from the contest.

Important modifications were recommended in March 1981 by an *ad hoc* panel of the party which virtually had the effect of leaving the primaries in a state of suspension. Headed by Hajime Tamura, head of the party's National Organization Committee, the panel proposed that: (1) a prospective candidate must be supported by at least 50 members, instead of only 20 as before, for filing his candidature; (2) there must be at least 4 candidates in the field in order to hold the primaries; and (3) the membership charges be raised to Yen 3000 per annum. These amendments took a heavy toll of party membership. As the amended procedures were stiffer than the earlier ones and had the effect of restricting or suspending the role of the primaries in the choice of party president, new members became chary of registering with the party because they were not likely to be given a chance to express their will in the choice of the party chief. The result was that party membership which had shot up to 3.1 million in 1979 dropped to 1.17 million in 1981 and subsequently to 1.04 million.

The amendments however, found favour with the three largest factions in the party, namely those led by Kakuei Tanaka (he is not a member of the party now but his group is still the largest and most active inside the party). Zenko Suzuki and Takeo Fukuda. One of the reasons why they supported the amendments is that only candidates sponsored by them could muster enough support for registration, given the importance of numerical strength of the factions in intra-party politics. Further, the revisions were welcome to them because they saw in them a means of freezing the primaries and strengthening the decision-making power of the party elders through consensus and consultation. It is obvious that if the primaries are bypassed the influence of the party elders remains strong; if they are held, that influence is reduced, if not totally eliminated.

The local chapters are in favour of the primaries being held because that gives them a chance to enlarge party membership. New membership means more revenue for them as under the existing rules they can retain a substantial part of the revenue from membership fees. Also, some of the non-mainstream factions, notably the one led by Toshio Komoto, opposed the reform plan as they felt it was aimed against them as well as the so-called "new leaders" in the party who had expressed themselves in favour of a change of leadership within the party. Komoto's followers had reason to feel "cheated" by the revisions because they were sure that his efforts to enlist new party members had placed a presidential victory within his research.

It was this and the preference of younger members in the party for going through the primaries, as much as factional bickering, that made the November 1982 elections inevitable. The party elders tried hard to reach a consensus but in the end they accepted failure and let the primaries decide as to who should be the leader of the party. Merely holding the primaries however has no meaning unless there is free vote in the second round and that is not likely to happen as long as party politics revolves around factions. Because the factions tend to be more powerful than the party as a whole, factional or committed voting still remains the most powerful instrument through which the primaries could be reduced to nothing more than a mockery. It is indeed surprising how the media and some commentators in Japan developed the myth of a Komoto victory if the primaries were held. It was clear along before the primaries that the leadership of orthodox factions in the party represented by the groups owing allegiance to Tanaka and Suzuki wanted Yasuhiro Nakasone to inherit the mantle of leadership. Their combined strength is almost two-thirds of the total number of party councillors and representatives. Given this numerical preponderance, these factions would certainly have reversed the verdict of the primaries, if that verdict had gone against the candidate backed by them. There was no need for them to resort to this as the primaries themselves chose to vote in favour of Nakasone.

Factionalism is the crux of Japanese politics. Remove the factions and Japanese politics becomes a meaningless exercise. They have a long history and their roots are firm in the Japanese social milieu. Factions in the ruling party multiplied under the peculiar circumstances in which political parties grew up in the immediate post-war period and became part of the political process after the formation of the Liberal Democratic Party. Factions are sustained by ties of personal loyalty, of a common political experience, a sense of fellow-feeling developed as a result of membership of the local or central bureaucracy and above all by the ability of factional leaders to collect money and distribute patronage. Despite sustained criticism against them and some half-hearted measures to do away with them, factions have not only come to stay but have also gained strength. The size of a faction is an important matter as on that depends the ability of its leader to make a bid for the party's presidency, win adequate representation for his group in the party machinery as well as the Cabinet and obtain a large share of the political funds of the party. The weight of numbers has always been decisive as was amply demonstrated in the November 1982 presidential contest. The Tanaka-Suzuki-Nakasone combination had as many as 169 representatives and 71 councillors and that made Nakasone's victory a foregone conclusion. (For factional strength and composition in the LDP, see Appendices II and III).

NAKASONE'S VICTORY

Whether Suzuki's successor should be selected through negotiations or voting became an issue long before the primaries were actually held on 23 November 1982. Four candidates, Yasuhiro Nakasone, Toshio Komoto, Shintaro Abe, and Ichiro Nakagawa, (he however died at Sapporo, Hokkaido on 9 January 1983, while on a visit to his constituency) all members of the Suzuki Cabinet, had decided to enter the field and none was willing to bow out of the race in order to avoid holding a primary. The balance seemed to be in favour of Nakasone from the start as he had been treated as heir-apparent by Suzuki and assured of support from the powerful Tanaka and Suzuki factions should a contest be forced upon him; they had demonstrated their intent by not fielding their own candidates. Given the state of mutual distrust and confrontation in the party between rival groups it was a foregone conclusion that no compromise was possible and the issue would have to be decided by the primaries. Yet an attempt was made by a negotiating team consisting of the Party President, the Secretary-General (Susumu Nikaido) and a former Prime Minister (Takeo Fukuda) to seek a formula which would tempt one or two candidates to withdraw. The negotiations sought to win over Komoto by offering to support him for the post of Deputy Prime Minister. Next, they resurrected an old plan of separating the office of Prime Minister from the office of party president. The former was to go to Nakasone and the latter to Fukuda who was not in fact a candidate. Proposed originally by Mikio Mizuta more than a decade ago to keep the Prime Minister's office outside the rough and tumble of election politics, the plan had never found favour in the party for the obvious reason that no one seriously thought that it was possible for the executive head of the nation to function effectively without a party base under his control. In 1980 too, a plan of this nature had been vaguely conceived with Eiichi Nishimura, a party elder, holding the office of party president and a younger party member taking over as Prime Minister. The plan came to nothing as Nishimura's constituency rejected him at the polls.

Contrary to pre-election forecasts that the Primaries would go in favour of Komoto, the final results showed that they had swung in favour of Nakasone. (See Table 1). The winner in fact had received more votes

TABLE 1

Results of LDP Presidential Primaries, 23 November 1982

Candidates	*Number of votes received*	*Number of votes received as per cent of total*
Yasuhiro Nakasone	559,673	57.62
Toshio Komoto	265,078	27.29
Shintaro Abe	80,443	8.28
Ichiro Nakagawa	66,041	6.80
Votes polled	971,235	
Invalid votes	2,915	
Number of eligible voters	1,045,714	
Rate of polling	93.16 per cent	

Source: *Asahi Shimbun* (Tokyo), 25 November 1982, p. 1

than Masayoshi Ohira, victor of the November 1978 primaries. The margin of votes between Ohira and his nearest rival Fukuda was 78,388; the margin between Nakasone and Komoto was a massive 294,595. As the first winner had received more than half of the votes polled, Komoto and Abe bowed out of the second round. That made the job of Takashi Hasegawa, Chairman of the Presidential Election Committee, very smooth. On 25 November the party Convention held at the Hibiya Hall, Tokyo, endorsed the electorate's verdict in accordance with party rules and the same day the party's councillors and representatives did the same. Thus, Nakasone became the eleventh President of the Liberal Democratic Party and the 71st Prime Minister of the country since it adopted the Cabinet System in 1886.

While the holding of the primaries has vindicated those who had advocated the selection of party leaders through voting instead of consensus, it is doubtful if it is going to be of any consequence in changing the nature of political choice made by the party. That choice still remains the prerogative of the more powerful factions in the party and will remain so as long as factions live. In a way the recent primaries were a victory by proxy for Tanaka and his faction. They demonstrated beyond doubt that the leadership groups, particularly those of Tanaka, are well entrenched and cannot be challenged. For the supporters of the former Prime Minister who is still fighting a legal battle in the court over his alleged involvement in the Lockheed bribery scandal, it was important not only to help the candidate for whom their leader had pledged support to win the election handsomely, but also demonstrate to anti-Tanaka groups that he continued to be powerful; and by inference, he was also innocent.

Their present ineffectiveness notwithstanding the primaries are likely to live and be accepted as an important part of the democratic process. They are no doubt expensive considering that, according to the *Asahi Shimbun*, party sources estimate the cost of the recent primaries at Yen 650 million, excluding the money which the candidates themselves may have spent. Ichiro Nakagawa, one of the presidential candidates, pleaded that the number of sponsorship members should be lowered from 50 to 30 in order to make it possible for smaller factions also to put up their candidates for the presidency. Some have suggested a revision in the schedule of holding primaries and a reduction in the campaign time allowed. Holding primaries earlier in order to ensure that they do not hamper the work of budget preparation for the following year and giving the candidates just about 2 or 3 weeks' time for campaigning are considered necessary to sustain voters' interest. Money and time were pointed out as important reasons why the primaries should be abolished by 40 per cent of LDP members questioned by the *Asahi* on the role of the primaries. But 51 per cent among them wanted the primaries to remain.[4]

A Long Carrier Crowned

For Nakasone, the November 1982 success is the crowning of a long and arduous carrier which began in 1947. The second son of a timber merchant of Takasaki, Gumma Prefecture, Nakasone went on to the Law Faculty of Tokyo University after schooling. Passing the higher civil service examination while still a student, he entered the Home Ministry after graduation but was soon conscripted into the navy and spent the war years in Taiwan. Repatriated in September 1945, he rejoined the Home Ministry. Within a year he decided to give up the bureaucratic carrier and returned to Takasaki where he formed the *Seiunjuku* (Blue Cloud

Academy) to propagate the ideal of national resurrection among the young friends around him. In 1947 he joined the Democratic Party of Japan and won a Lower House seat from the Gumma 3 constituency, a seat which he has retained till this day. His electoral success was facilitated by the Academy founded by him and which was transformed into an organization to work for him. That organization helped him to talk directly to the people during his election tours. Quoting one of his secretaries, Thayer says that Nakasone was one of the first to build an organization based on the people, and others have imitated him.[5] Over the next 30 years he rose steadily in the party hierarchy holding a variety of posts and was the party Secretary General when Takeo Miki was the party chief. He made his debut in the Cabinet under Nobusuke Kishi as Director General of the Science and Technology Agency and Chairman of the Atomic Energy Commission. He has held virtually all Cabinet portfolios excepting that of Finance and Foreign Affairs.

In the early 1950s he came under the influence of Tokutaro Kimura and later moved closer to Ichiro Kono together with Sunao Sonoda, Osamu Inaba and Yoshio Sakurauchi. When his political mentor Kono died in 1965, Nakasone inherited the mantle of leadership of his faction from him. That faction is the fourth largest in the ruling party.

Administrator, idealist, agitator and politician, Nakasone remains somewhat of an enigma to his friends and admires. His idealistic instincts compelled him to sponsor the Rising Sun Patriotic Movement at a time when the nation felt daunted by defeat and surrender. As a member of the Democratic Party he led a group of agitating Takasaki farmers against the new fiscal measures of the Yoshida Cabinet and successfully negotiated with Finance Minister Hayato Idea a tax exemption for farmers on their miscellaneous incomes.[6] Addressing a letter to John Foster Dulles, the American special envoy entrusted with the task of writing a peace treaty for Japan, Nakasone pleaded for the revival of civil aviation and freedom to pursue nuclear research. Yoshimasa Yamazaki, a veteran political commentator, writes that Nakasone was far from satisfied with the peace treaty. He quotes him: "The Security Treaty has overshadowed the Peace Treaty; and the Administrative Agreement has overshadowed the Security treaty."[7] At a party meeting Nakasone is said to have insisted: "We will have noting to do with such a shameful treaty. The United States inflicted enormous damage on the Japanese people by indiscriminate bombing. We ought to demand reparations from the United States."[8]

From his Democratic Party days Nakasone has evinced a keen interest in the peaceful uses of atomic energy, the process of selection of textbooks for use in schools and in the Constitution of Japan. In 1954 he organized a private research body to go into the question of constitutional amendments; the members of the group were: Iwao Takayama, Osamu Inaba, Joji Yabe, Hideji Kawasaki, Arata Sugihara and Tokuma Utsunomiya. He even wrote an "Ode to National Independence and Constitutional Change," and served as member of the Constitution Revision Committee set up by the Kishi Administration. As Director-General of the Defence Agency in the third Sato Cabinet (1970) he spelt out a 5-point programme which came to be known as *jishu boei* (autonomous defence) plan. Answering the Socialist member of Parliament, Sanshichi Hanyu, in the Upper House Budget Committee, Nakasone said that, (1) national defence would be strengthened within the constitutional framework, (2) defence and diplomacy would be integrated and brought in line with other national policies, (3) the principle of civilian control of the Armed Forces would be upheld, (4) the 3 non-nuclear principles, i.e. non-manufacture, non-possession and non-introduction of nuclear weapons by Japan, would be firmly followed, and (5) the Japan-United States Security System would be reinforced.

Within the party the zig-zag course that he has followed and the many turnabouts that he has taken have earned him the uncomplimentary description *Kazamidori* (literally weather-cock, generally apostate) but his justification for the shifting stances is that a political leader must always remain flexible and resilient; he cannot remain in politics if he fails to read the trend. Thus, when he wanted to move his support from Kishi to Tanzan Ishibashi in 1957, much to the displeasure of Kono, he justified his action on the ground that he could not possibly support someone who had a share in leading the country to war. Similarly, when he wanted to join the Sato Cabinet as Minister of Transport after consistently taking an anti-mainstream position he remarked: "It is difficult to function as an anti-mainstream faction by remaining outside the shooting range of the Administration." The most notable episode that left his followers and admirers wondering about his consistency and constancy was the manner in which he switched support from Takeo Fukuda of his own electoral district to Kakuei Tanaka in the July 1972 presidential contest. Tanaka then won, and ten years after he got a chance to repay Nakasone.

Nakasone's links with the world of Japanese business are tenuous though he has some powerful allies like Yoshihisa Ojimi (a former Industries and Trade Secretary), now Adviser to the Arabian Oil Company of Japan; Noboru Goto of the Tokyo Express Company; Koji Nakamura (a former Director of the Bank of Japan), now Deputy Chairman of Nomura Research Institute and Shoichi Akazawa. Nor is he altogether a stranger to the corporate world's leading lights. Over 10 years ago when he emerged as a possible presidential candidate the corporate world formed a small group to promote his cause. Sponsored by Shigeo Nagano (Japan Chamber of Commerce and Industry). Hiroshi Anzai (Tokyo Gas), Yoshizane Iwasa (Fuji Bank) and Hiroki Imazato (Japan Precision Instruments), the group consisted of Takeshi Sakurada (Federation of Employers' Associations), Shohei Mizuno (Arabian Oil Company of Japan), Hajime Sako (Taisei Construction Company), Kiichi Nochi (Shimizu Construction Company). Fumio Tanaka (Oji Paper), Goro Koyama (Mitsui Real Estate). Akira Miyazaki (Asahi Synthetics), Seiji Tsutsumi (Seibu Enterprises) and Yoshio Abe (First Industrial Bank).

The Nakasones are also connected through marriage with the Kajima (Kajima Construction), Saito (Dai Showa Paper) and Iwasaki (Mitsubishi) families.[9]

As in some other countries where political leaders find in the midst of their other responsibilities no time to have new ideas and gather around them a small group of informed men to do the thinking for them, Nakasone too has around him a similar coterie. In defence matters, it is Makito Momoi of the Tokyo Institute of Strategic Studies who is close to him. In other areas, the group that feeds him with ideas consists of Shumpei Kumon, and Seizaburo Sato (both of Tokyo University), Jiro Ushio (Ushio Electricals) and Kenichi Kayama (Gakushuin University). This group is said to have provided Nakasone with his election slogan: "Safety *(anshin)*, Stability *(antei)*, Security *(anzen)*."

In terms of political lineage, Nakasone is an outsider to the conservative mainstream or orthodox line which dominates the Liberal Democratic Party. Two of the largest factions at present belong to that tradition: the group which informally owes allegiance to Kakuei Tanaka and the group led by Zenko Suzuki. Both have descended from Shigeru Yoshida who guided Japan in its most difficult years after the war. The followers of Yoshida branched off into two streams after the veteran political leader withdrew from active politics, one branch represented by

Hayato Ikeda and the other by Eisaku Sato. The former was continued by Shigesaburo Maeo and then Masayoshi Ohira before Zenko Suzuki succeeded to it in 1980. Tanaka succeeded to the latter in 1971, with a sub-branch under Shigeru Hori moving away from his branch and joining Takeo Fukuda. A large number of leaders of the orthodox line have come from the bureaucracy, the two great exceptions being Tanaka and Suzuki. The levers of power in the party are firmly held by these branches and their representatives have provided the top level party leadership. When they are not at the top, their active support has always been necessary for other leaders to claim legitimacy and function effectively. Nakasone belongs to the heterodox or non-mainstream line in the party which includes factions that have descended from the Progressive and Democratic Parties as well as dissidents of the Liberal Party who were thrown out in 1954 for their criticism of Yoshida. A large number of leaders of this line have been party men; the notable exceptions being Nobusuke Kishi, Takeo Fukuda and Nakasone himself. Their rise and decline in the party has by and large depended on the degree of support and tacit understanding extended by the orthodox line. Given this, it is logical to raise the question whether Nakasone will be able to assert himself in the party and government or allow himself to be overwhelmed by the traditional leadership factions.

THE TASKS AHEAD

While the political, economic, diplomatic and defence problems inherited by Nakasone remain formidable, none is more complex than the need to contain the struggle between the mainstream and non-mainstream groups in the party through the maintenance of a balance. That balance is never perfect and successive party presidents and Prime Ministers have remained content with only an approximation. Rightly or wrongly, the Japanese media has created the impression that Nakasone cannot function independently and that his actions are controlled by the Tanaka elements in the Cabinet and party. A whole range of new compounds have been used—Tanakasone, Tanaka-managed, Tanaka-directed, to cite only a few—to strengthen this impression. It has gained further credibility by the fact that a slightly larger representation has been given to the group in the new Cabinet. (See Tables 2 and 3)

TABLE 2

Factional Balance: Ministers and (Parliamentary) Vice-Ministers

Faction	*Ministers*		*Vice-Ministers*	
	Nakasone	*Suzuki*	*Nakasone*	*Suzuki*
Tanaka	6	4	7	4
Suzuki	4	3	4	6
Nakasone	2	3	7	7
Fukuda	3	4	5	4
Komoto	2	3	2	3
Nakagawa	1	1	—	—
Independents	2	2	—	1

Source: Tokyo Shimbun, 1 December 1982, p. 8.

TABLE 3

Factional Distribution of Portfolios in the Suzuki and Nakasone Cabinets

Portfolio	*Nakasone*		*Suzuki*	
	Minister	*Vice-Minister*	*Minister*	*Vice-Minister*
Justice	Ind.	Komoto	Ind.	Komoto
Foreign Affairs	Fukuda	Suzuki	Nakasone	Komoto
Finance	Tanaka	Fukuda Suzuki	Ind.	Tanaka Tanaka
Education	Fukuda	Fukuda	Suzuki	Nakasone
Welfare	Tanaka	Nakasone	Nakasone	Suzuki
Ag. Forestry and Fisheries	Suzuki	Nakasone Fukuda	Suzuki	Fukuda Nakasone
MITI	Nakasone	Nakasone Tanaka	Fukuda	Suzuki Suzuki
Transport	Nakagawa	Nakasone	Tanaka	Fukuda
Postal Services	Nakasone	Tanaka	Tanaka	Nakasone
Labour	Ind.	Tanaka	Komoto	Suzuki
Construction	Tanaka	Tanaka	Fukuda	Tanaka
Autonomy	Tanaka	Fukuda	Tanaka	Nakasone
Chief Cabinet Sec.	Tanaka	Nakasone	Suzuki	Suzuki
PMs Secretariat	Komoto	Nakasone	Fukuda	Tanaka
Hokkaido Development	—	Suzuki	—	Komoto
Okinawa Development	—	Tanaka	—	Fukuda
Administrative Management	Suzuki	Suzuki	Nakasone	Nakasone

(*Contd.*)

TABLE 3 (*Contd.*)

	Nakasone		*Suzuki*	
	Minister	*Vice-Minister*	*Minister*	*Vice-Minister*
Defence	Komoto	Fukuda	Komoto	Nakasone
Economic Planning	Suzuki	Komoto	Komoto	Nakasone
Science and Technology	Suzuki	Tanaka	Nakagawa	Fukuda
Environment	Tanaka	Tanaka	Fukuda	Ind.
National Land Development	Fukuda	Nakasone	Tanaka	Suzuki

Source: *Tokyo Shimbun,* 1 December 1982, p. 8.

When a new leader takes over, the first order of business is to constitute his team to run the party and government. In view of the factional politics that prevails in the party, he usually tries to organize his team in such a way that it would give representation to all factions. It is however not uncommon for the leader to exclude from his Cabinet actions that opposed him and give larger representation to those which were allied with him or supported him. A Cabinet, representative of all factions is described as a "Cabinet of strong men," though more appropriately it could be termed "a balanced Cabinet." In the new Cabinet 15 out of the 20 ministerial positions and 23 out of 25 vice-ministerial positions have gone to the Tanaka, Fukuda, Suzuki and Nakasone factions. In the Suzuki Cabinet they held 14 ministerial and 21 vice-ministerial positions respectively. The more important portfolios of Finance, International Trade and Industry and Foreign Affairs have gone to the Tanaka, Nakasone and Fukuda factions. What is important is that the Tanaka faction, which played a decisive part in Nakasone's presidential victory, has obtained as many as 6 ministerial and 7 vice-ministerial positions in the new administration. The faction's position in the Cabinet is unassailable with the crucial Chief Cabinet Secretary's position going to Masaharu Gotoda, a member of the faction and the Ministry of Justice going to Akira Hatano, a member of the House of Councillors who has no faction but is known to the sympathetic to the former Prime Minister.[10]

Unlike the practice in other countries, the Chief Cabinet Secretary in Japan is not a civil servant but is a member of the ruling party. Usually this post is filled first before any other Cabinet appointment is made. The Chief Secretory has three important functions to perform: (1) to supervise and co-ordinance all matters coming under the Cabinet

Secretariat (such as preparation of agenda for Cabinet meetings, co-ordination of subjects calling for Cabinet decision, supervision of all important matters falling within the purview of the Cabinet and to look after research and collection of information by the Secretariat), (2) to serve as a link between the party and Cabinet, and (3) to act as spokesman for the Cabinet, particularly the Prime Minister. He has also a certain sum of money at his disposal which he is allowed to use at his discretion. Described as the Cabinet Secretariat Fund the money at the disposal of the Secretary in 1982 was estimated at Yen 1,200 million (or about US $ 5.2 million). The manner in which this money is used is never disclosed to the public. It has often been alleged that a large part of this goes to the nurturing of factionalism in the ruling party. When asked by Seiichin Inaba, a Socialist member of Parliament, how this money was being used, the former Chief Cabinet Secretary, Kiichi Miyzawa, told the Lower House Budget Committee (June 1982), that the information could not be revealed in public interest.[11] Because of the importance of the post, it was upgraded to the rank of Minister of State in June 1966. For the same reason, it was given as a matter of convention to a member of the Prime Minister's own faction. The speculation about Tanaka's influence has further gained respectability by his faction getting this important portfolio.

None of the important positions in the party is retained by the Nakasone faction. The leadership of the crucial Policy and General Affairs Committees has fallen respectively to the Suzuki and Fukuda factions, while the all-important post of Secretary General is with the Tanaka faction. The Secretary General is at the centre of all party matters in much the same way that the Cabinet Secretary is at the centre of all cabinet matters. As the number 2 man in the party he takes on behalf of the president all important decisions relating to the party and is often also taken into confidence in matters relating to government. Financial control, nomination of heads of various committees and the selection of official candidates at the time of election are some of his important prerogatives. He has the power to make or break the political careers of party members. At the time of presidential elections he is expected to throw his weight behind his own factional leader and ensure his victory. (This may not always work. For example, in June-July 1980, Yoshio Sakurauchi being the Secretary General did not help Nakasone improve his prospects; the party caucus preferred Suzuki as a consensus candidate). At the time new appointments are made to the top party positions all eyes are naturally on the selection of the Secretary General. The choice ordinarily falls on a man of the president's faction, though this practice has become weak in recent years. Successive Secretaries General in the past few years have been picked from factions other than the President's (See Table 4). While the relation of Susumu Nikaido[12] is in line with this trend, it nonetheless has lent support to the belief that the ruling party is unable to shake off Tanaka's shadow.

TABLE 4

Important LDP Functionaries Since 1972

Party Leader	*Secretary General*	*Policy Affairs Committee Chairman*	*General Affairs Committee Chairman*
Kakuei Tanaka July 1972-December 1974	Tomisaburo Hashimoto	Yoshio Sakurauchi	Zenko Suzuki
Takeo Miki December 1974-December 1976	Yasuhiro Nakasone*	Raizo Matsuno	Hirokichi Nadao
Takeo Fukuda December 1976-December 1978	Masayoshi* Ohira	Toshio Komoto	Masumi Esaki
Masayoshi Ohira December 1978-June 1980	Kunikichi Saito (Yoshio Sakurauchi)*	Toshio Komoto	Tadao Kuraishi
Zenko Suzuki July 1980-November 1982	Yoshio Sakurauchi* (Susumu Nikaido)*	Shintaro Abe (Rokusuke Tanaka)	Susumu Nikaido (Tatsuo Tanaka)
Yasuhiro Nakasone November 1982	Susumu Nikaido*	Rokusuke Tanaka	Kichizo Hosoda

* From factions other than the President's.

The unusually sharp reaction of the media and the Opposition to the new Cabinet and party leadership reflects the concern that has been expressed in recent years over what is seen as a surrender of the ruling party to "money power" and "corrupt elements" which have used the party machinery for dubious purposes. Within the party there is resentment towards the manner in which some factions have been exerting their influence derived from financial resources. Takeo Miki echoed the feelings of a cross-section of the party when he wrote in the August 1982 issue of the popular monthly *Bungei Shunju* that he could not bring himself to the level of accepting the dictum "politics is power;

power is money.'' In an editorial under the heading ''Running Counter to History?'' (*rekishi ni gyakko suru no ka*), written immediately after the presidential election, the *Tokyo Shimbun* commented that the Nakasone Administration seemed to be committed to defending and perpetuating ''money politics'' of the ruling party and sounded a warning that no reforms, fiscal or administrative, would succeed unless there was qualitative change in the nature of politics.[13] ''Money power'' and ''corrupt elements'' are obviously references to a number of scandals with which the names of important party members have been associated, the most serious scandal being the Lockheed bribery case. It is in the context of the Lockheed case that misgivings have been expressed: that with the influence it has acquired in the party and government, the Tanaka faction might attempt to create a climate of opinion in which it might become easier for its leader to get either a ''not guilty'' verdict or only light punishment.[14] While the atmosphere around Nagatacho (the district in which the LDP office is located) is full of speculation about the possibility of political or executive intervention in the case, Professor Hiroshi Itakura of Nihon University thinks that it is too late in the day to invoke provisions of Article 14 of the Law Concerning the Public Procurator's Office. Nor does he see any possibility of a Cabinet pardon. Political commentator, Takayoshi Miyakawa tends to agree with this.[15]

When a new Cabinet assumes office people generally entertain high hopes about it; those hopes are either fulfilled or destroyed by the Cabinet's performance. The Nakasone Cabinet however, has been received with great scepticism and doubt as some initial reactions show. The public seems concerned about issues relating to the Constitution, national defence and administrative reforms on which Nakasone's position is not free from controversy. Thus, the results of a survey organized by the *Tokyo Shimbun* in the Tokyo Metropolitan area on 27 and 28 November were suggestive of the mood of the people. While 30 per cent of the respondents supported the new Cabinet 32.6 per cent said they did not. And 59.4 per cent of them believed that Tanaka's influence on the ruling party and in the political world was bound to grow and not diminish. Among the important tasks which they wanted the Cabinet to take up earnestly were price stability and anti-recessionary measures (45.1 per cent), tax reduction (29.2 per cent), and fuller welfare measures (13.6 per cent).[16]

To the anti-establishment opinion, there is nothing ''new'' in the new Cabinet; it merely denotes yet another stage in the struggle by the conservative camp to consolidate power. Comparing the Nakasone Cabinet to that headed by Kiichiro Hiranuma (whose Cabinet was installed on 5 January 1939), the veteran Socialist leader Seiichi Katsumata cautions against a possible drift towards the "politics of oppression and suppression." To him centralization, administrative fiat and inefficiency are the great maladies that affect Japan; he does not see much hope of the new regime trying to cure them. On the contrary he fears that the fair name of administrative reforms might be used as a mere palliative to force wrong measures down the throat of the public.[17] Jiro Kamishima, Professor of Political Science, Rikkyo University, describes Nakasone as a "sail-with-the-wind type" and a "sub-leader" who will act as a cover to Tanaka. He too sees no possibility of Nakasone correctly discerning the direction of history and developing the political strength needed for mobilizing the confidence of the nation.[18] Daikichi Irokawa, Professor of Modern Japanese History, Tokyo University of Economics, emphasizes the utter cynicism with which politics is viewed today; he cites how one of his students twisted a famous remark of the Meiji political thinker Chomin Nakae on the qualities of political leaders of his time like Aritomo Yamagata, Masayoshi Matsukata and Tsugumichi Saigo, and applied the same to contemporary political figures like Fukuda, Suzuki and Nakasone.[19] Tokuma Utsunomiya, who left the ruling party some years ago in disillusionment, says that Nakasone will not last long as his administration pursues the policy of expanding the defence budget at the expense of people's livelihood.[20]

Shigeru Aoki, representative of the National Salarymen's League, says that his organization has three demands to submit to Nakasone and three litmus tests to measure his team's performance. The demands are: (1) a shift of focus from Mejiro (the locality where the former Premier Tanaka lives) towards the common people, (2) resist pressures for an increased defence budget, and (3) announce a clear schedule of administrative reforms. The litmus tests are: (1) whether welfare or defence will take the central position in the budget, (2) whether national economic problems will be solved through expansion of investment on public works or a reduction in the living standards of people, and (3) whether the G-card system will be introduced or not.[21] The powerful trade union federation *Sohyo* has vowed to launch a mass movement of the kind that was seen by the nation in 1960 against the revised Japan-US Security Treaty if the Administration fails to eschew Tanaka's influence from politics. Anticipating that the Constitution will be amended and there will be expansion of the defence budget, the federation has declared its total confrontation with the new regime and determination to seek the dissolution of the Lower House. The leading opposition party, the Socialist Party of Japan, has also sworn that it will confront the government on the question of defence expenditure and administrative reforms. Party Chairman Ichio Asukata has hinted that his party will seek to move a no-confidence motion against Nakasone in order to prepare the ground for the dissolution of the Lower House and holding of fresh elections.

These are the challenges to Nakasone's tact and skill. Obviously if he proves that he is a leader in his own right he might survive and consolidate his position. Whether he will be able to do this without displeasing those who have supported him and without throwing into disarray the factional balance in the party is the moot question. Not many who tried this in the past have lasted long. In his first interview given to the press after being elected party head he said that one of his endeavours would be to maintain party unity and at the same time refute allegations about Tanaka's influence; guardedly however, he also added that he could not remain indifferent to the positive role of the Tanaka group in the party.[22] That sums up the dilemma in which he finds himself as Party President and Prime Minister.

Notes and References

1. Paragraph 1 of Article 67 reads: The Prime Minister shall be designated from among the members of the *Diet* by a resolution of the *Diet*. This designation shall precede all other business.
2. Nathanial B. Thayer, *How the Conservatives Rule Japan* (Princetion, N.J., 1969), p. 177.
3. *Ibid.*, 174-6.
4. *Asahi Shimbun* (Tokyo), 24 November 1982.
5. Nathaniel B. Thayer, n. 2, pp. 90-91.
6. Yoshimasa Miyazaki, *No. 2 no hito: Jiminto no Kanjicho* (The No. 2 Man: Secretary General of the Liberal Democratic Party) (Kodansha, Tokyo, 1981), p. 321.
7. *Ibid.*, p. 322.
8. *Ibid.*, pp. 322-23.
9. Tomoyasy Saito, *Keibatsu* (Family Groups) (Rippusha, Tokyo), p. 315.
10. Described by the media as "Tanaka's pocket knife," Gotoda entered politics after retiring as head of the National Police Board. He was Deputy Chief Cabinet Secretary in the Tanaka Cabinet (1974-76) and unsuccessfully contested for an Upper House seat in July 1974 from Tokushima. As he contested against Kentaro Kujime, a member of the Miki faction, it became a source of friction between Tanaka and Miki ending finally in the withdrawal of the latter from the Cabinet.

    A former Superintendent General of the Police Agency, Hatano once contested the Tokyo gubernatorial election against the former Professor of Economics, Tokyo University of Education, Ryokicchi Minobe, and lost. Subsequently, he got elected to the Upper House from Kanagawa.

    It is interesting to note that Nakasone was also once head of the Police Department of Kagawa Prefecture and resigned when he was Inspector in the Metropolitan Police Department.
11. *Tokyo Shimbun* (Tokyo), 28 November 1982.
12. Nikaido, representing the Kagoshima 3 constituency, has been returned to Parliament 12 times since he made his political debut in 1946 on a Japan Co-operative Party (*nihon kyodoto*) ticket. A graduate of the University of Southern California, his name became known in the party when he joined hands with Kakuei Tanaka in June 1965, Tanaka was then Secretary General; Nikaido worked as his deputy. In 1972, Nikaido became the Chief Cabinet Secretary in the first Tanaka Cabinet and then for a brief 30 days or so remained Party Secretary General. Going out of circulation for 51/2 years, he emerged as Chairman of the Party General Affairs Committee after Suzuki took over. In the November 1981 reshuffle he was made Secretary General in place of Yoshio Sakurauchi who was moved to the ministry of Foreign Affairs.

    Nikaido's elevation to the second highest post in the party was a subject of adverse criticism in the Press as his name has been associated with the Lockheed bribery scandal as a "gray official." Public confidence in the party took a jolt. ("People Lash Appointment of Nikaido to LDP Post," The Daily Yomiuri (Tokyo), 1 December 1981; "Jimbutsu Haiken: Susumu Nikaidoshi," Asahi Shimbun, 14 December 1981; "Nagatacho Doings: Prime Minister Suzuki's Clever Strategy," The Mainichi Daily News (Tokyo), 9 December 1981; "Nikaido Kanjicho' ni hantai suru" Asahi Shimbun, 28 November 1981.

Nikaido has denied involvement in the affair and during 1977 and 1978 strongly resisted attempts at being summoned before the Diet for legislative investigation of the case. He feels that *Diet* investigation of the case would be a violation of human rights.

13. *Tokyo Shimbun*, 28 November 1982.
14. The Lockheed affair came in the limelight in 1974 as a result of revelations about payments that had been made by the Lockheed Corporation of the United States to important LDP leaders through the Marubeni (Trading) Corporation. The money was intended to facilitate the sale of wide-bodied Tri Star aircraft (airbuses) to the All Nippon Airways Company. According to those revelations, Tomisaburo Hashimoto was paid Yen 5 million. Takayuki Sato Yen 2 million, Kakuei Tanaka Yen 10 million, Susumu Nikaido Yen 5 million, Hideyo Sasaki, Mutsuki Kato and Kazuomi Fukunage Yen 2 to 3 million each. Tanaka is also alleged to have received an additional Yen 500 million, which in turn is said to have been distributed among other party members. When the Public Procurator's Office began investigating the case, Tanaka was arrested in 1976 and later released. Tanaka has repeatedly pleaded his innocence and the case is still before the court. However on 8 June 1982, the Tokyo District Court found both Hashimoto and Sato guilty and gave them suspended jail terms. Since then the public has come to believe that a Tanaka conviction is imminent.
15. *Tokyo Shimbun*, 28 November 1982.
16. *Tokyo Shimbun*, 30 November 1982.
17. *Asahi Shimbun* 30 November (''Viewpoint'' Column.)
18. *Ibid.*, 26 November 1982.
19. *Ibid.*, 27 November 1982.
20. *Ibid.*
21. *Ibid.*, 26 November 1982.

    The so-called G-card system (Green-card) is aimed at bringing out hidden or unaccounted wealth, eliminating inequalities in the tax system and encouraging small savings. There is considerable resistance within the ruling party to the introduction of this system and as a result no progress has been made in that direction.
22. *Ibid.*

APPENDIX I
LDP and Other Political Parties in the Diet

Party	*Number of Seats Held*	
	Lower House	*Upper House*
Liberal Democratic Party	287	134
Socialist Party	104	47
Komeito	34	27
Democratic Socialist Party	31	11
Communist Party	29	12
New Liberal Club	13	—
Shinsei Club	—	7
Ichi no kai	—	3
Second Chamber Club	—	2
Independents	7	3
Vacancies	6	6
Total	511	252

APPENDIX II

Strength of the various LDP Factions, House of Representatives

(1) *Tanaka Faction (Thursday Club) 64*

Name	*Age*	*Constituency*	*University/School*	*Number of times elected*
Adachi Tokuro	72	Shizuoka 3	Kyoto	11
Aichi Kazuo	45	Miyagi 1	Tokyo	3
Aino Koichiro	54	Saga (single)	Chuo	4
Arima Motoharu	62	Kagoshima 2	Tokyo	4
Esaki Masumi	66	Aichi 3	Nihon	14
Fukushima Joji	55	Kumamoto 2	Tokyo	3
Gotoda Motoharu	67	Tokushima (single)	Tokyo	3
Harada Ken	63	Osaka 3	Meiji (disconted.)	10
Hashimoto Ryutaro	75	Akita 2	Kyoto	13
Hata Eijiro	53	Oita 1	Musashi Industrial School (discontd.)	2
Hata Tsutomu	46	Nagano 2	Ibaraki	5
Hatoyama Kunio	33	Tokyo 8	Tokyo	2
Hayashi Yoshiro	55	Yamaguchi 1	Tokyo	5
Hori Kosuke	47	Saga (single)	Keio	2
Ishii Hajime	47	Hyogo 1	Konan	5
Imaeda Norio	57	Aichi 1	Army Aviation School	1
Kajiyama Seiroku	56	Ibaraki 2	Nihon	4
Kameoka Takao	62	Fukushima 1	Army School	8
Kanemaru Shin	67	Yamanashi (single)	Tokyo University of Agriculture	9
Kimura Morio	44	Aomori 2	Nihon	1
Kimura Takeo	79	Yamagata 1	Meiji	12
Kitamura Yoshikazu	56	Hokkaido 5	Hokkaido	1
Komiyama Jushiro	54	Saitama	Waseda	7
Kosaka Tokusaburo	66	Tokayo 3	Tokoyo	5
Kuno Chuji	72	Nagano 2	Middle School	13
Kyuma Fumio	41	Nagasaki 1	Tokyo	1
Maeda Masao	69	Nara (single)	Yamanashi Industrial High School	11
Matsuno Yukiyasu	73	Gifu 1	Commerce School	6
Minowa Noboru	58	Hokkaido 1	Hokkaido (Medicine)	6
Muraoka Kanezo	50	Akita 2	Keio	3
Nagata Ryoichi	70	Hyogo 2	Keio	10
Nakayama Toshio	57	Ibaraki 1	Nihon	4

(*Contd.*)

APPENDIX II (*Contd.*)

Name	*Age*	*Constituency*	*University/School*	*Number of times elected*
Nakamura Kishiro	33	Ibaraki 3	Nihon	3
Nakanishi Keisuke	41	Wakayama 1	Waseda	2
Nikaido Susumu	72	Kagoshima 3	University of Southern Calif.	12
Nonaka Eiji	62	Saitama 4	Keio	5
Obuchi Keizo	45	Gumma 3	Waseda	7
Ohara Ichizo	58	Miyzaki 1	Tokyo	2
Okuda Keiwa	54	Ishikawa 1	Waseda	5
Omura Joji	63	Okayama 1	Tokayo	6
Ozawa Ichiro	40	Iwate 2	Keio	5
Ozawa Tatsuo	65	Niigata 1	Tokyo	8
Sato Megumu	58	Osaka 6	Kyoto	5
Sato Moriyoshi	60	Hiroshima 3	Chuo	5
Sato Shinji	50	Yamaguchi 2	Keio	2
Saito Shigeyoshi	63	Shizuoka 2	Waseda	5
Someya Makoto	64	Chiba 4	Takushoku	4
Tahara Takeshi	56	Oita 2	Kyushu	2
Takatori Osamu	53	Niigata 4	Tokyo	5
Takeuchi Reiichi	55	Aomori 2	Tokyo	7
Takenaka Shuichi	64	Aomori 1	Tohoku	4
Takeshita Noboru	58	Shimane (single)	Waseda	9
Tamura Hajime	58	Mie 2	Keio	10
Tamura Ryohei	64	Kochi (single)	Waseda	6
Toida Saburo	64	Hyogo 4	Chuo (disconted.)	3
Utsumi Hideo	60	Miyagi 2	Chuo	6
Watanabe Kozo	40	Niigata 2	Waseda High School	4
Watanabe Kozo	50	Fukushima 2	Waseda	5
Watanuki Tamio	55	Toyama 2	Keio	5
Yamamoto Sachiv	71	Mie 3	Tokyo	5
Yamamura Shinjiro	49	Chiba 2	Gakushuin (disconted.)	6
Yamashita Ganri	61	Shiga (single)	Tokyo	6
Yamazaki Takesaburo	49	Kagoshima 1	Chuo	3
Yasuoka Akiharu	43	Amami-Oshima	Chuo	4
Abe Fumio	60	Hokkaido 3	Hokkaido	4
Aizawa Hideo	56	Okayama 1	Waseda	3
Amano Kimiyoshi	61	Tokyo 6	Tokyo	10
Aso Taro	41	Fukuoka 2	Gakushuin	2
Fukunaga Kenji	71	Saitama 5	Tokyo	13
Hamada Teijiro	40	Saitama 1	Tokyo	1

(*Contd.*)

APPENDIX II (*Contd.*)

Name	*Age*	*Constituency*	*University/School*	*Number of times elected*
Hamaono Takeshi	56	Tokyo 9	Chuo	2
Harada Shozo	59	Shizuoka 1	Tokyo	3
Hatano Chubun	65	Oita 1	Hosei	4
Hiraizumi Wataru	52	Fukui (single)	Tokyo	2
Horiuchi Mitsuo	52	Yamanashi (single)	Keio	3
Ikeda Atsushi	63	Chiba 3	Nihon	2
Ikeda Yukihiko	45	Hiroshima 2	Tokyo	3
Imai Isamu	63	Ehime 3	Tokyo	4
Ishikawa Yozo	57	Tokyo 11	Waseda	3
Ito Masayoshi	68	Fukushima 2	Tokyo	6
Kaneko Ippei	69	Gifu 2	Tokyo	8
Kaneko Iwazo	75	Nagasaki 2	—	9
Kasuya Shigeru	56	Tokyo 4	Nihon	4
Kawara Tsutomu	45	Ishikawa 2	Chuo	4
Kato Koichi	43	Yamagata 2	Tokyo	4
Kawasaki Jiro	34	Mie 1	Keio	1
Kikuchi Fukujiro	57	Miyagi 2	Waseda	3
Kino Haruo	63	Osaka 5	Tokyo	6
Kishida Fumitake	55	Hiroshima 1	Tokyo	2
Kitaguchi Hiroshi	51	Kumamoto 1	Chuo	2
Koga Makoto	41	Fukuoka 3	Nihon	1
Kondo Mototsugu	52	Niigata 1	Nihon	2
Koyama Osanori	77	Miyazaki 2	Tokyo	11
Kurihara Yuko	62	Shizuoka 2	Tokyo	3
Kuriyama Akira	61	Fukushima 1	Kyoto	2
Miyazaki Shigeichi	65	Kagoshima 1	Tokyo	4
Miyazawa Kiichi	62	Hiroshima 3	Tokyo	6
Mizuno Kiyoshi	57	Chiba 2	Tohoku	5
Morita Hajime	48	Kagawa 2	Tokyo	1
Murayama Tatsuo	67	Niigata 3	Tokyo	7
Niwa Yuya	38	Ibaraki 3	Keio	2
Ogawa Heiji	72	Nagano 3	Tokyo	12
Ohta Seiichi	36	Fukuoka 1	Keio	1
Okuda Mikio	54	Kyoto 1	Waseda	1
Osato Sadatoshi	51	Kagoshima 2	High School	2
Ozawa Kiyoshi	54	Tokyo 7	Middle School	2
Saito Kunikichi	73	Fukushima 3	Tokyo	9
Sasaki Yoshitake	73	Akita 1	Tokyo	8

(*Contd.*)

APPENDIX II (*Contd.*)

Name	*Age*	*Constituency*	*University/School*	*Number of times elected*
Sasayama Tatsuo	41	Akita 2	Keio	1
Shiozaki Jun	65	Ehime 1	Tokyo	5
Shirakawa Katsuhiko	37	Niigata 4	Tokyo	2
Sumi Eisaku	62	Toyama 1	Tokyo	4
Suzuki Zenko	71	Iwate 1	Fisheries Training Institute	14
Taido Sampachi	37	Chiba 1	Keio	1
Ianaka Rokusuke	59	Fukuoka 4	Waseda	7
Taniguchi Sen'ichi	70	Kyoto 2	Tokyo	8
Tazawa Yoshiro	64	Aomori 2	Waseda	8
Tosaka Jushiro	69	Ibaraki 3	Middle School	6
Toya Yoshiyuki	54	Kumamoto 2	Agricultural Technology Training Institute	2
Tozawa Masataka	63	Kanagawa 3	Tokyo	3
Tsushima Yuji	52	Aomori 1	Tokyo	3
Uetake Shigeo	51	Ibaraki 2	Anoyama Gakuin	1
Urano Yasuoki	40	Aichi 4	Gakushuin	2
Watanabe Shoichi	52	Hokkaido 4	Chuo	2
Yanagisawa Hakuo	46	Shizuoko 3	Tokyo	1
Yasuda Kiroku	69	Hokkaido	—	4
(3) *Fukuda Faction* 46				
Abe Shintaro	58	Yamaguchi 1	Tokyo	8
Akita Daisuke	76	Tokushima (single)	Tokyo	12
Fujio Masayuki	65	Tochigi 2	Sacred Heart	7
Fukita Akira	55	Yamaguchi 2	Commerce School	2
Fukuda Takeo	77	Gumma 3	Tokyo	12
Hayakawa Ogamu	65	Wakayama 2	Tokyo	14
Hosoda Kichizo	70	Shimane (single)	Tokyo	8
Ishibashi Kazuya	60	Chiba 3	Agricultural School	3
Kamei Shizuku	45	Hiroshima 3	Tokyo	2
Kano Akio	47	Ibaraki 1	Keio	2
Kano Michihiko	40	Yamagata	Gakushuin	3
Kato Mutsuki	56	Okayama 2	Himeji High School	6
Kokuba Kosho	69	Okinawa	Marine Aviation School	5
Koizumi Jun'ichiro	40	Kanagawa 2	Keio	4
Kubota Enji	78	Gumma 1	Industrial School	8
Kuraishi Tadao	82	Nagano 1	Hosei	14

(*Contd.*)

APPENDIX II (*Contd.*)

Name	*Age*	*Constituency*	*University/School*	*Number of times elected*
Matsumoto Juro	64	Hyogo 4	Tokyo	4
Mitsubayashi Yataro	63	Saitama 4	Youth Normal School	5
Mitsuzuka Hiroshi	54	Miyagi 1	Waseda	4
Miyashita Sohei	54	Nagano 2	Tokyo	2
Mori Kiyoshi	57	Ehime 2	Tokyo	2
Mori Yoshiro	45	Ishikawa 1	Waseda	5
Murata Keijiro	58	Aichi 5	Kyoto	5
Nakagawa Hidenao	38	Hiroshima 2	Keio	2
Nakajima Gentaro	53	Gumma 2	Waseda	4
Nakamura Shojiro	48	Chiba 3	Keio	2
Nakano Shiro	75	Aichi 4	Middle School (discontd.)	12
Nogami Tetsu	43	Toyama 1	Tokyo	1
Ochi Michio	53	Tokyo 3	Tokyo	4
Otsuka Yuji	53	Tokyo 1	Keio	3
Saigusa Saburo	69	Kokkaido 4	Tokyo Bunrika	3
Sano Kakichi	71	Shizuoka 1	Tokyo University of Commerce	3
Sato Ichiro	69	Kanagawa 4	Tokyo	3
Setoyama Mitsuo	78	Miyazaki 2	Meiji	11
Shirahama Nikichi	73	Nagasaki 2	Jikei Medical University	11
Shiseki Ihei	75	Chiba 1	Tokyo	9
Shoji Keishiro	71	Wakayama 2	Tokyo	8
Shiokawa Seijiro	60	Osaka 4	Tokyo	6
Tamazawa Tokuichiro	44	Iwate 1	Waseda	3
Tanabe Kunio	68	Yamanashi (single)	Waseda	5
Tanabe Masami	47	Aomori 1	Rikkyo	2
Tanaka Tatsuo	71	Yamaguchi 1	Tokyo	11
Tokai Motosaburo	67	Hyogo 3	Kyoto	10
Tomonou Taketo	67	Chiba 4	Tokyo	2
Tsukahara Shumpei	35	Ibaraki 2	—	3
Yamazaki Heihachiro	70	Fukuoka 3	Kyushu	5
(4) *Nakasone Faction* 43				
Amano Kosei	75	Fukushima 1		8
Eto Takami	57	Miyazaki 1	Miyazaki Agricultural School	5
Fujinami Takao	49	Mie 2	Waseda	6
Fukaya Takashi	46	Tokyo 8	Tokyo	3

(*Contd.*)

APPENDIX II (*Contd.*)

Name	*Age*	*Constituency*	*University/School*	*Number of times elected*
Hara Kensaburo	75	Hyogo 2	Oregon University (USA)	15
Hatsuta Sadayoshi	72	Fukushima 2	Nihon Medical University	9
Horinouchi Hisao	57	Miyazaki	—	3
Inagaki Jitsuo	54	Aichi 4	Waseda	3
Kamei Yoshiyuki	46	Kanagawa 5	Keio	2
Karasawa Shunjiro	52	Nagano 4	Tokyo	5
Kataoka Seiichi	71	Toyama 2	Tokyo	4
Kibe Yoshiaki	56	Shizuoka 2	Chuo (discontd.)	5
Kimura Takechiyo	72	Kagawa 1	Tokyo	6
Kumakawa Tsugio	51	Gumma 1	Waseda	2
Kuranari Tadashi	63	Nagasaki 1	Tokyo	9
Makino Takamori	56	Fukui (single)	Tokyo	2
Matsunaga Hikaru	53	Saitama 1	Waseda	5
Mizuhira Toyohiko	50	Aichi 6	Nagoya Industrial School	3
Morishita Motoharu	60	Tokushima (single)	Tokyo Higher Agricultural School	6
Nagano Sukenari	43	Kagoshima 1	Chuo	1
Nakamura Yasushi	50	Tokyo 5	Waseda	3
Nakao Eiichi	52	Yamanashi (single)	Aoyama Gakuin	6
Nakasone Yasuhiro	64	Gumma 3	Tokyo	14
Narahashi Susumu	48	Fukuoka 3	Keio	4
Noda Takeshi	40	Kumamoto 1	Tokyo	4
Ochi Ihei	61	Ehime 2	Industrial Technology School	5
Odo Saburo	56	Okinawa	—	1
Oishi Sempachi	46	Shizuoka 1	Waseda	4
Okonogi Hikosaburo	54	Kanagawa 1	Waseda	5
Sakurauchi Yoshio	70	Shimane (single)	Keio	13
Sato Fumio	63	Oita 2	Meiji	6
Sekiya Katsutsugu	44	Ehime 1	Chuo	3
Shimamura Yoshinobu	48	Tokyo 10	Gakushuin	2
Sunada Shigetami	65	Hyogo 1	Rikkyo	5
Tamou Takahisa	58	Toyama 1	—	3
Tani Yoichi	55	Hyogo 5	Commerce School	3
Uemura Sen'ichiro	70	Aichi 5	Waseda	8
Uno Sosuke	59	Shiga (single)	Kobe University of Commerce (disconted.)	8

(*Contd.*)

APPENDIX II (*Contd.*)

Name	*Age*	*Constituency*	*University/School*	*Number of times elected*
Watanabe Hideo	48	Niigata 3	Takushoku	3
Yamazaka Sadanori	61	Kagoshima 3	—	11
Yamazaki Taku	45	Fukuoka 1	Waseda	4
Yosano Kaoru	43	Tokyo 1	Tokyo	2
Yukawa Hiroshi	64	Osaka 1	Tokyo	3
(5) *Komoto Faction* 30				
Akagi Munenori	77	Ibaraki 3	Tokyo	13
Fujii Katsushi	67	Okayama 2	Tokyo	8
Fujimoto Takao	51	Kagawa 1	Tokyo	6
Hashiguchi Takeshi	68	Kagoshima 3	Tokyo	6
Ide Ichitaro	70	Nagano 2	Kyoto	15
Ishida Hirohide	67	Akita 1	Waseda	14
Ito Soichiro	58	Miyagi 1	Tohoku	7
Kaifu Toshiki	51	Nagano 3	Waseda	8
Kato Tsunetaro	77	Kagawa 2	Mukden School of Foreign Languages	12
Kawada Masanori	59	Hokkaido 2	Chuo	2
Kitagawa Ishimatsu	63	Osaka 7	Kansai University (discontd.)	3
Komoto Toshio	71	Hyogo 4	Nihon	13
Komura Masahiko	40	Yamaguchi 2	Chuo	1
Kondo Tetsuo	52	Yamagata 1	Hitotsubashi	5
Kudo Iwao	60	Iwate 1	Tokyo	2
Kujiraoka Hyosuke	66	Tokyo 10	Waseda	7
Mori Matsuhei	69	Ehime 3	Keio	9
Mori Yoshihide	62	Chiba 3	Tamagawa Gakuin	5
Moriyama Kinji	65	Tochigi 1	Tokyo	11
Niwa Hyosuke	71	Nagano	—	9
Noro Kyoichi	62	Mie 2	Tokyo Higher Normal School	7
Onishi Masao	71	Kochi (single)	Tokyo	7
Sakamoto Misoji	59	Ishikawa 2	Tohoku	6
Shibuya Naozo	65	Fukushima 2	Tokyo	8
Shiga Setsu	49	Iwate 2	Waseda	4
Suginami Shigeru	69	Fukushima 2	Showa Medical School	6
Tanikawa Kazuo	52	Hiroshima 2	Keio	7
Tsuji Hideo	63	Fukuoka 1	Tokyo	3
Usui Hideo	43	Chiba 1	Chuo	1

(*Contd.*)

APPENDIX II (*Contd.*)

Name	*Age*	*Constituency*	*University/School*	*Number of times elected*
Yamashita Tokuo	62	Saga (single)	Senshu	5
(6) *Nakagawa Group* 26				
Aoki Masahisa	59	Saitama 4	Tokyo	4
Eto Takami	See under Nakasone faction			
Furuya Toru	73	Gifu 2	Tokyo	6
Hasegawa Shiro	77	Gumma 2	—	13
Hasegawa Takeshi	70	Miyagi 2	Waseda	10
Hayashi Taikan	60	Chiba 2	Agricultural School	3
Hiranuma Takeo	42	Okayama 1	Keio	1
Horinouchi Hisao	See under Nakasone faction			
Ishihara Shintaro	49	Tokyo 2	Hitatsubashi	4
Kamei Shizuka	See under Fukuda faction			
Kano Akio	,,			
Kano Michihiko	,,			
Kokuba Kosho	,,			
Mitsuzuka Hiroshi	,,			
Miyashita Sohei	,,			
Mori Kiyoshi	,,			
Morishita Motoharu	See under Nakasone faction			
Nakagawa Ichiro	57	Hokkaido 5	Kyushu	7
Nakamura Kokai	57	Nagasaki 2	Kurume Medical University (disconted.)	5
Nakao Eiichi	See under Nakasone faction			
Nogami Tetsu	See under Fukuda faction			
Takahashi Tatsuo	53	Hokkaido 4	Chuo	2
Tamazawa Tokuichiro	See under Fukuda faction			
Uekusa Yoshiteru	43	Hokkaido 2	Waseda	2
Watanable Hideo	See under Nakasone faction			
Yamazaki Heihachiro	See under Fukuda faction			

(*Contd.*)

APPENDIX II (*Contd.*)

Name	*Age*	*Constituency*	*University/School*	*Number of times elected*
(7) *Uncommitted Members* 29				
Aizawa Hideyuki	63	Tottori (single)	Tokyo	3
Chikaoka Riichiro	55	Yamagata 2	Army School	1
Chisaki Usaburo	63	Hokkaido 1	Ritsumeikan (discontd.)	7
Fujita Yoshimitsu	70	Kumamoto 1	Tokyo	9
Fukuda Hajime	80	Fukui (single)	Tokyo	12
Funada Hajime	28	Tochigi 1	Keio	2
Furui Yoshimi	79	Tottori (single)	Tokyo	11
Hanashi Nobuyuki	53	Ibaraki 1	Hokkaido	6
Inamura Sakonshiro	65	Ishikawa 2	—	7
Inamura Toshiyuki	46	Tochigi 2	Waseda	5
Kamoda Toshitaro	52	Saitama 3	Waseda	2
Kimjura Toshio	73	Mie 1	Tokyo	12
Kosaka Zentaro	70	Nagano 1	Tokyo University of Commerce	15
Miike Makoto	81	Saga (single)	Kyushu	11
Miki Takeo	75	Tokushima (single)	Meiji	17
Murakami Isamu	80	Oita 1	Industrial Apprentice School	14
Muto Kabun	55	Gifu 1	Kyoto	6
Nadao Hirokichi	82	Hiroshima 1	Tokyo	12
Nemoto Ryutaro	75	Akita 2	Kyoto	13
Nishioka Takeo	46	Nagasaki 1	Waseda	7
Okuno Seisuke	69	Nara (single)	Tokyo	7
Sakata Michita	66	Kumamoto 2	Tokyo	15
Sakurai Shin	49	Niigata 3	Waseda	1
Sato Takashi	54	Niigata 2	Tokyo University of Agriculture	3
Shiina Motoo	51	Iwate 2	Nagoya	2
Shionoya Kazuo	62	Shizuoka 3	Waseda	6
Sonoda Sunao	68	Kumamoto 2	Osaka Dental University (discontd.)	14
Watanabe Eiichi	63	Gifu 2	Nagoya Higher Commerce School	7
Watanabe Michio	59	Tochigi 1	Tokyo University of Commerce	7

(*Contd.*)

APPENDIX II (*Contd.*)

Name	*Age*	*Constituency*	*University/School*	*Number of times elected*
(8) *Tatsumi Kai* 3				
Mihara Asao	72	Fukuoka 2	Meiji	7
Nakayama Masateru	68	Osaka 2	Kansai	3
Ono Akira	53	Gifu 1	Keio	1

Source: Kokkai binram (Parliamentary Guide) (65th edition, Nihon Seikei Shimbunsha, August 1982, Tokyo).

APPENDIX III

Strength of the Various LDP Factions, House of Councillors

(1) *Tanaka Faction (Thursday Club)* 40

Name	*Age*	*Constituency*	*University/School*	*Number of times elected*
Endo Kaname	66	Miyagi	—	2
Fujii Hirohisa	50	National	Tokyo	1
Fuiji Takao	39	Gifu	Seijo	1
Furuya Keiyu	60	Yamanashi	Middle School (discontd.)	1
Hasegawa Shin	63	Niigata	Waseda (discontd.)	2
Horie Masao	67	National	Army College	1
Hosokawa Morihiro	44	Kumamoto	Sacred Heart (Law)	2
Inoue Kichio	59	Kagoshima	Kumamoto Higher Industrial School	2
Inoue Takashi	57	National	Kyoto	1
Ito Ikuo	51	National	High School	1
Iwakami Jiro	68	Ibaraki	Kyoto (Law)	2
Kajiki Matazo	63	National	Kyoto (Agr.)	2
Kamei Hisaoki	42	Shimane	Gakushuin	2
Kanai Motohiko	78	Hyogo	Tokyo (Law)	2
Kawahara Shinjiro	64	Kagoshima	Agrcl. School	1
Kawamoto Kakuzo	65	Shiga	Hikone Higher Commerce School	2
Kimura Mutsuo	69	Okayama	Tokyo (Law)	4
Koga Raishiro	66	National	Kyushu (Engg.)	2
Kori Yuichi	80	Ibaraki	Tokyo (Law)	6
Maeda Isao	39	Wakayama	Keio (Law)	2
Masuoka Koji	57	National	Tokyo	1
Matsuo Kanpei	55	Aomori	Chuo (discontd.)	1
Matsuura Isao	59	National	Tokyo	1
Morishita Tai	60	Osaka	Tokyo	2
Natio Ken	50	Tokushima	High School	1
Nakagawa Yukio	65	Ehime	Agricultural School	1
Nakamura Taro	64	Yamanashi	Waseda	2
Nishimura Shoji	71	National	Tokyo (Law)	3
Ooki Hiroshi	55	Aichi	Tokyo	1
Osada Yuji	65	National	Tokyo (Law)	3
Ootaka Yoshiko	62	National	Higher Girls' School	2
Saito Juro	42	Mie	Keio (Commerce) London	2
Sakano Shigenobu	65	National	Tokyo	2
Sando Anzai	40	National	Bunka Gakuin	2
Seko Masataka	59	Wakayama	Nihon (Medicine)	2

(*Contd.*)

APPENDIX III (*Contd.*)

Name	*Age*	*Constituency*	*University/School*	*Number of times elected*
Shimura Aiko	65	National	Tokyo Music School	2
Sugiyama Reijo	59	Gifu	Ryutani	1
Totsuka Shinya	42	Shizuoka	Nihon	2
Tsukada Juichiro	78	Niigata	Tokyo University of Commerce	3
Ueda Minoru	68	Kyoto	Kyoto (Engg.)	4
(2) *Fukuda Faction 27*				
Ejima Atsushi	54	Yamaguchi	Tokyo	1
Fukuda Hiroichi	68	Gumma	Middle School	1
Furuya Keigi	61	Yamagata	Tokyo	1
Hara Bumpei	69	Tokyo	Tokyo (Law)	2
Hayashi Hiroko	49	National	Kobe Prefectural High School	1
Horiuchi Toshio	64	Nata	Nara Prefectural Normal School	2
Inoue Yutaka	54	Chiba	Tokyo Dental University	1
Ishimoto Shigeru	68	National	—	3
Kanemaru Saburo	68	Kagoshima	Tokyo	1
Kato Takenori	66	Okayama	Chuo	4
Katayama Masahide	68	National	Tokyo (Agr.)	2
Kumagai Tasaburo	75	Fukui	Kyoto (Econ.)	4
Machimura Kingo	81	National	Tokyo (Law)	2
Nakamura Keiichi	58	Hokkaido	Tohoku	1
Nakanishi Ichiro	67	Hyogo	Tokyo (Law)	3
Nakayama Taro	57	Osaka	Osaka Higher Medical College	3
Ozawa Taro	76	Yamaguchi	Tokyo	1
Suzuki Shogo	70	Fukushima	Tokyo (Agr.)	3
Suzuki Shoichi	63	Fukushima	Sericulture School	1
Tahara Takeo	71	Kagoshima	Army School	1
Takahira Kimitomo	68	Toyama	Commerce School	1
Tanaka Masami	65	National	Tokyo	1
Tanikawa Kanzo	62	Kochi	Tokyo	1
Tashiro Yukio	66	Kumamoto	Tao Dobun Academy	2
Tsuchiya Yoshihiko	56	Saitama	Chuo (Commerce)	3
Yamamoto Tomio	53	Gumma	Middle School	1
Yasui Ken	71	Tokyo	Tokyo (Econ.)	6

(*Contd.*)

APPENDIX III (*Contd.*)

Name	*Age*	*Constituency*	*University/School*	*Number of times elected*
(3) *Suzuki Faction* 25				
Endo Masao	59	Fukuoka	Tokyo	1
Eto Seishiro	41	Oita	Waseda	1
Fujita Masaaki	60	Hiroshima	Waseda (Comm.)	3
Fukushima Shigeo	64	National	Nihon	1
Goto Masao	69	Oita	Yokohama Higher Industrial School	2
Hayashi Yu	58	Kochi	Meiji (Pol. Economy)	2
Miyata Teru	60	National	Meiji	2
Inamine Ichiro	76	Okinawa	Waseda (Pol. Economy)	3
Isurugi Michiyuki	68	Iwate	Tokyo (Law)	3
Itagaki Tadashi	58	National	Chuo	1
Iwamoto Masamitsu	53	Hokkaido	Hokkaido	1
Kamijo Katsuhisa	71	Miyazaki	Middle School	2
Manabe Kenji	67	Kanagawa	Gifu	1
Masuda Sakari	69	Iwate	Kyoto (Law)	3
Miyazawa Hiroshi	60	Hiroshima	Tokyo	1
Nao Ryoko	65	Saitama	Chou (Law)	1
Okada Hiroshi	72	National	Tokyo	2
Otsubo Ken'ichiro	57	Saga	Tokyo	1
Sekiguchi Keizo	56	National	Tokyo Dental University	1
Shimazaki Hitoshi	59	Ishikawa	Tokyo (Law)	3
Shimojo Shin'ichiro	62	Nagano	Tokyo	1
Sonoda Kiyomitsu	62	Kumamoto	Hosei	4
Ueki Mitsunori	55	Kyoto	Tokyo (Law)	4
Yamauchi Ichiro	69	Fukui	Tokyo (Engg.)	3
Yusuda Takaaki	65	Ishikawa	—	3
(4) *Komoto Faction* 10				
Hatsumura Takichiro	68	Nagasaki	Middle School	2
Iwasaki Junzo	58	Tochigi	Nihon	1
Kita Shuji	57	Hokkaido	Agricultural School	1
Maruyama Masaya	55	National	Nihon	1
Moriyama Mayumi	54	Tochigi	Tokyo	1
Nakamura Teiji	79	Nagasaki	Agricultural School	1
Sakamoto Chikao	71	Miyazaki	Kyoto Higher Sericulture School	2
Tekeuchi Kiyoshi	61	National	Kyushu	1
Usui Shoichi	80	Chiba	Waseda	1

(*Contd.*)

APPENDIX III (*Contd.*)

Name	*Age*	*Constituency*	*University/School*	*Number of times elected*
Yoshida Minoru	72	Toyama	Tokyo (Econ.)	2
(5) *Nakasone Faction* 6				
Higaki Tokutaro	65	Ehime	Tokyo (Law)	2
Kurauchi Shuji	64	Fukuoka	Tokyo	1
Naito Yosaburo	70	National	Bunri	3
Naruse Zenju	66	Shimane	Keio	1
Oishi Buichi	73	Miyagi	Tohoku	1
Oshima Tomoji	65	Tochigi	Kyoto	2
(6) *Nakagawa Group* 1				
Takagi Masaaki	53	Hokkaido	Chuo	1
(7) *Uncommitted Members* 25				
Abiko Tokichi	78	Yamagata	Tokyo	2
Genda Minoru	77	National	Naval Academy	4
Fukuoka Hidemaro	72	Saga	Toa Dobun Academy (discontd.)	2
Hatano Akira	70	Kanagawa	Nihon	2
Hatoyama Iichiro	63	National	Tokyo	2
Hirai Teishi	60	Aomori	Aomori Medical School	3
Kajiwara Kiyoshi	60	National	Kyoto	1
Kamenage Tomoyoshi	61	Tokushima	Tokyo	1
Kobayashi Kokuji	74	Tottori	Tokyo (Agr.)	3
Kumagai Hiroshi	42	Shizuoka	Hitotsubashi	1
Kusunoki Masatoshi	61	National	Nihon (Law)	3
Miura Hassui	52	Kumamoto	Tokyo (Agr.)	1
Murakami Masakuni	49	National	Takushoku	1
Natsume Tadao	73	Nagano	Tokyo	2
Norota Yoshinari	52	Akita	Chuo	1
Okabe Saburo	55	National	Tokyo	1
Okawara Taiichiro	60	National	Tokyo	1
Saito Eizaburo	69	National	Waseda	2
Sasaki Man	56	Akita	Tokyo (Law)	2
Shintani Torasaburo	79	Nara	Tokyo (Law)	7
Takahashi Keizo	63	National	Takachiho Higher Commerce School	1
Tamaki Kazuo	59	National	Takushoku	3
Tazawa Tomoharu	49	National	Nihon	1
Yagi Ichiro	81	Aichi	Tokyo Sericulture School	4
Yamazaki Tatsuo	60	Aomori	Aomori Medical School	3

Source: Same as Appendix 1.

4

Hosokawa's Reform Government

SAVITRI VISHWANATHAN*

Morihiro Hosokawa, in his first address as Prime Minister in August 1993, proclaimed that his Cabinet represents "not just one stop in the passage of history but the starting point for a new history". He called his administration "the political reform government." He felt that it was the delay in enacting political reforms, which was the source of popular mistrust of politicians. He appealed for the break-up of the ties between politics, bureaucracy and business. Hosokawa said that his government would strive to create a national image of Japan as a "nation of quality," i.e., Japan would not wield its power over other nations and would create a substantial life-style of high quality and high culture at home.

On March 4, 1994, with the passage of the Bill on Political Reforms in the Diet, Hosokawa stated that this would be the basis of changes in the political system. The economic and administrative reforms would be the next on the agenda.

Hosokawa was an unknown figure in Japanese politics two years ago. What were the circumstances which led to his sudden rise? What ailed the Japanese political system and how would the present legislation reform the system and create credibility both within and outside Japan?

* Professor in the Department of Chinese and Japanese Studies, University of Delhi, Delhi.

A discussion of these issues might help in an understanding of the domestic politics of Japan.

1993 is a memorable year in the political history of Japan. The "1955 set-up", which ensured a stable political system in Japan was overturned. The Liberal Democratic Party for the first time had to sit along with the Japan Communist Party in the opposition. As is well known, the "1955 set-up" came into being with the merger of the conservative forces in the Liberal Democratic Party, in face of the threat of socialist unity. One of the factors which led to the 1955 set-up and its continuance is the US interest in securing a stable, pro-American, conservative government in Tokyo. The Liberal Democratic Party, a coalition of factions, constructed a framework for their perennial rule. The Opposition seemed to settle itself gradually into the "role of a supporting actor in the drama of political rule". It was a finely tuned political machine. The conservative and progressive forces put on a show of fighting on the stage, but behind the scenes, there seemed to be a consensus for the operation of the political system with efficiency. The political machine was designed to guarantee the parties steady supplies of money and votes. A mechanism was created that would benefit special interests. Ruling party legislators formed "tribes" (*zokuqiin*) along the lines of major interest groups and government organs, with jurisdiction over them. These members cultivates ties with bureaucrats of both the Central Government and the local governments, representatives of respective pressure groups and even organised labour. Through constant interaction among these groups, policies were formed, budget allocations made, contracts from the public sector granted, etc., in such a way that the constituents could be expected to reciprocate with votes and money, so that the power and influence of the politicians could be continued. This led to the emergence of a multi-faceted politico-bureaucratic and industrial complex. Over the years, this machine, aided by the prevailing international cold war situation, succeeded in maintaining peace, stability and prosperity within Japan and raised it to the level of a big economic power. The success of the LDP Government in this regard ensured its continuing support by the people. No viable alternative was offered by the Opposition to challenge the LDP dominance.

However, in course of time, this political framework led to various diseconomies and misgivings on the part of the people. The single-minded interest in increasing the Gross National Produce (GNP) led to the rise of another GNP (Gross National Pollution) as well, leading to environmental disruption, health hazards for the people, etc. The rights of the consumers were sacrificed in the interests of the producer. Provision of social amenities for the masses was given low priority. People's demands for quality of life could not be met. The "closed door" policy of Japan in the field of international economic relations, e.g., structural impediments to trade, its distribution system, *keiretsu* groupings and other features of Japanese working style, etc., came under serious criticism. The end of the cold war, with the collapse of the Soviet Union, demanded changes in the political system as well. Therefore, both at the domestic level and the international level, there was a call for cleansing and restructuring the political system, so that it was transparent and open.

The symptoms of "system fatigue" are most notable in the scandals involving politicians and businesses. This reached its first peak in 1976, with Prime Minister Kakuei Tanaka's involvement in the Lockheed scandal. This was followed by other scandals, such as the Recruit "Shares for Favours" scandal in 1989 and the Tokyo Sagawa Kyubin scandal in 1991. The Sagawa Kyubin scandal revealed large sums of money payments both to the ruling party as well as the opposition parties. However, in spite of the series of scandals, the people did not vote the LDP out of power. In fact, Kakuei Tanaka, after he was indicted, was voted back with a larger number of votes. Tanaka's constituency only looked upon him as a politician who brings money and benefits to his constituency from the Centre. The methods he used for retaining his power and influence were given scant consideration.

It was the Recruit "Shares for Favour" scandal in 1989, which sent shock waves in the LDP. Prime Minister Noboru Takeshita resigned in April 1989 on account of his involvement in the Recruit scandal. The Upper House elections in July 1989 clearly reflected people's anger against the LDP. It lost its majority in the Upper House.

The LDP had to take steps to restore the confidence of the people. It announced a three-pronged general framework for political reform, viz., reform of the electoral system, reform of the political fund raising system and reform of the LDP itself. The Sosuke Uno Government, which followed the Takeshita Government, set up a Council for Political Reform in June 1989. The next Prime Minister, Toshiki Kaifu, introduced a Political Reforms Bill based on the proposals given by the Council and as revised by the LDP in the Extraordinary Diet session in 1991. The Kaifu package was a system of single seat constituencies and proportional representation. But the Bill was defeated in September 1991. Kaifu took responsibility and resigned in October 1991. No doubt, if he had real power, he would have dissolved the Lower House and forced a general election.

The departure of Kaifu signalled that the LDP had failed to keep its promise of political reform, made in May 1989 after the Recruit scandal erupted and again during the Upper House elections in July 1989 and the February 1990 elections. Prime Minister Kiichi Miyazawa, who succeeded Kaifu, gave priority to the PKO Bill to allow Japanese forces to participate in the UN peace-keeping operations and showed no interest in reform.

The subject of reform re-emerged as a political issue in the end of August 1992, when the political world was rocked by the prosecutors proving the involvement of both Shin Kanemaru, the Vice-President of LDP, as well as Noboru Takeshita, former Prime Minister, in the Sagawa Kyubin scandal. Although Kanemaru finally accepted the charges and resigned both from his party post and from his seat in the Lower House, public indignation intensified against the leaders of the LDP for not undertaking any swift condemnation and the very light punishment meted out to Kanemaru. This was further fuelled by the revelation, during the investigations, that Kanemaru had sought the help of *Yakuza* (crime syndicate) for smoothening the way of political gain, particularly in setting up the Takeshita Government in 1987. This also signalled the end of the dominance of the Takeshita faction within LDP.

The Takeshita faction had emerged as the biggest faction after his defection from the Tanaka faction (Tanaka had been disabled by a stroke in 1985), taking most of the members with him. Four successive Prime Ministers, Noboru Takeshita, Sosuke Uno, Toshiki Kaifu and Kiichi Miyazawa owed their premiership to the support of the Takeshita faction. As an aftermath of the departure of Shin Kanemaru from the political scene, the infighting within the faction for leadership led to a chain reaction of realignment in politics, which will be discussed in detail in the context of the emergence of Hosokawa as a rising star in the political firmament.

Another spinoff of the Sagawa Kyubin scandal and the furore in the public was Miyazawa's determination to take up the political reforms in earnest. The business groups were also getting antagonised against the LDP for the kind of political turmoil in the nation, which went against stability and also the image of Japan. By May 1993, the opposition parties were ready to reach an agreement, but the LDP stalled. The LDP leaders (Yasuhiro Nakasone, Takayuki Sato, Koichi Kato, Seiroku Kajiyama) opposed the reforms. Within the Social Democratic Party of Japan (SDPJ) too a battle was on between the reform faction and the anti-reform faction. However, the reformers in the SDPJ emerged on top, leaving the LDP as the sole bastion of the anti-reform line. The Miyazawa Government was defeated by a no-confidence resolution in June 1993 and Japan went to the polls in July 1993.

The no-confidence resolution also revealed the division within the LDP. Forty members left the LDP to join the newly formed Japan Renewal Party and the New Harbinger Party. The leaders of the Japan Renewal Party were Tsutomu Hata and Ichiro Ozawa, who had been defeated in the leadership struggle within the Takeshita faction. Both were in favour of reforms.

In the July 18, 1993 elections, the LDP obtained only 223 seats, and even with the help of 10 independents could not get an absolute majority to form the government. The possibility of forming a coalition government with LDP as the core came to nought, when the Japan New Party, headed by Morihiro Hosokawa (present Prime Minister), and the New Harbinger Party (headed by Masayoshi Takemura, present Chief Cabinet Secretary) refused to succumb to the lure of the LDP and cast their lot with other opposition parties. The coalition arrangements made by the parties, which were break-always from the LDP, with parties at the other end of the spectrum such as the SDPJ as well as centrist parties such as the Democratic Socialist Party and Komeito, indicated a strong anti-LDP front bound by their resolve for reforms. It may be noted that the top leaders of the conservative parties including Premier Hosokawa, had started their political career in the Tanaka faction and this long association might also have been a binding force.

Hosokawa had been elected twice to the Upper House in 1971 and 1977 as a member of the Tanaka faction. In 1983, he had been elected Governor of Kumamoto Prefecture. The two terms he served as Governor gave him insights into the centralised system of the Japanese Government and the need for deregulation. In 1991, he resigned from the Governorship and the Takeshita faction gave him a berth as Chairman of the Sub-Council relating to quality of life in the Council for Promotion of Administrative Reform. In June 1992, he created the Japan New Party and this was greeted with derision by an LDP member. He is reported to have called Hosokawa "the President of a company on the verge of bankruptcy, who takes all that is left of the petty cash and bets it on a horse in a desperate gamble to stay in business''. The gamble paid off. The Japan New Party won four seats in the July 1992 election to the Upper House and 35 seats in the 1993 election to the Lower House. After winning his first election in the Lower House, Hosokawa was also catapulted to the post of Prime Minister, which is a record in Japanese political history. Both Tsutomu Hata and Ichiro Ozawa worked strenuously for the acceptance of Hosokawa as a consensus candidate of the coalition. Hata did not put forward his candidature to avoid the impression of his continuing the power struggle against the LDP leaders even after he had got his mandate from the people with his new party label.

The rise of Hosokawa is also symbolic of other changes in the Japanese political party scene. The young are wresting control from the older members in the Diet. Since the 1986 elections, the post-war generation in the Diet has risen, from 24 in 1986 to 146 in the 1993 elections. The average age of the members of the newly formed parties is in the range of forties and fifties. Younger members are succeeding to higher echelons of power as well. For example, even in the LDP, members rejected the veteran fashion leader, Michio Watanable (69) who had held important posts, such as foreign minister and deputy prime minister. They voted in favour of Yohei Kono (55) for the post of President. A new trend is also observed in the reduction of the influence of factions, which demand strict obedience to the faction leader.

The Hosokawa Government came to power at a time when the faith of the people in the government was at its lowest ebb. Leaders had been repeatedly implicated in scandals and corruption. Yet, there had been no clear change of government. The perception of Japan as a ''dirty'' country with no ethical values had been increasing among the international community. However, a survey by *Asahi Shimbun* in early September revealed 71 per cent approval rating for the Hosokawa administration. Fifty-two per cent of LDP backers voiced approval of the government, as did 47 per cent of supporters of the Japan Communist Party. As reasons for support, 37 per cent stated that the Cabinet provided some hope for change from politics as usual. Twenty per cent based their support on the readiness of the government to carry out reform. However, the people were not so optimistic about changes in the ties between politics, business and the bureaucracy. This should be taken as an indication of their realism.

Although the phrase 'political reform is used, the attempts since 1989 has been more in the direction of electoral reform, as it has been felt that it is electoral system which has led to money politics and prevented any change in the ruling party. In 1947, Japan adopted the single-entry ballot medium-sized constituency system, in which each electoral district is represented by three to five members. Periodic apportionment necessitated by population shifts has raised the total number of seats to 512 divided among 130 constituencies. The multi-member system leads to two or three candidates, sometimes even five, from the some party contesting elections in one constituency. This system gives little scope for debates on policy or political philosophy. Further, each candidate needs enormous sums of money to retain the support of his constituency. Thus it serves both money politics and factional politics.

In Japan, there has been legislation to limit campaign expenditures and to restrict corporate donations to political parties. For example, the revisions to the Political Funds Control Law in 1975 instituted provisions to restrict corporate and similar donations. This led politicians and factions to turn increasingly to fund raisers, whose proceeds are not connoted as political donations.

It is interesting to know that an average LDP Lower House Member is stated to use ¥134 million ($1.1 million). The member receives about ¥23 million ($190,000) from the government as an annual allowance, expenditure for legislative activities and transport and communication costs. The party and faction leader contributes ¥10 million ($80,000). The member still needs ¥70-80 million ($600,000), which he has to collect from somewhere. The main expenses of the politician are wages for 10 personal secretaries (apart from two secretaries paid from the national budget); ¥19 million for transport and communication costs; ¥12 million for office expenses and ¥40 million for public relations, publicity and ceremonial occasions. The root problem is excessive campaign spending, which has to be curbed.

What are the changes brought about by the new laws passed by the Diet recently? As regards electoral reforms, a combined single-member district proportional-representation (PR) system has been introduced with 300 single seats and 200 PR seats. The country would be divided into 11 blocks for counting of PR votes. Each voter would have two votes, one under each system. An advisory body would be placed in the PM's secretariat for delineating the new constituencies. This body would give its recommendations to the prime minister within six months. These would have to be approved by the Diet.

As regards contributions to political parties and their fund raising from companies and other organisations, lower ranges have been fixed for the maximum donations which can be made by each such organisation. In the case of individual politicians, the fund management organisation represented by the politician may receive an annual donation from companies but this would be limited to ¥500,000 per company. This would be limited to five years. However, all political organisations have to make public their source of funding, if it exceeds ¥50,000. Before this revision, the limit was ¥10 million. Hence the flow of funds from the sources will be more in the public eye and this will act as a check. Lower limits have also been laid on tickets for fund raising parties.

In order to encourage individuals to give donations to the politicians of their choice, income tax exemptions would be given for such donations. A public fund would be created at the rate of ¥250 per person, as given in the population census register, and would be distributed proportionately to all parties who have more than five Diet members or who have secured more than two per cent of the total vote, either in the Lower House or Upper House elections.

The Bill could not be passed without making some compromises with the LDP. The official Bill had been passed in November 1993 in the Lower House. It had been, however, defeated in the Upper House on January 21, 1994. Hosokawa had, therefore, to reach an agreement with the LDP, before January 29, 1994 when the Extraordinary Diet session was to end. The present Bill which has become law is a compromise formula.

In fact, Hosokawa had to accept a higher ratio of single-member seats division of the country into 11 blocks for proportional representation, as well as concede the right of individual politicians to receive corporate donations. No doubt, it was also in the interests of the LDP to save the reform Bill, otherwise its already tarnished image of practising money politics would have been further damaged. The Japan Communist Party has consistently voted against the Bill. There were "nay" votes from some members of the Social Democratic Party of Japan, as well.

There are misgivings that there was no wider debate on alternatives for reforms, and it was restricted only to the combined system of single-seat constituency and proportional representation. The experience of this system in other countries has not necessarily led to transparency or even curbs on money politics. The bigger parties would still be at an advantage.

However, *Asahi Shimbun's* public opinion polls, conducted at the end of February 1994, reveal that the percentage of support for the Hosokawa Cabinet is still high, though it is reduced to 57 per cent from 71 per cent last September. A high rate of support has come even from supporters of other opposition parties, including the JCP. The support extends from all sections of society and age groups. This is a hopeful sign.

The Hosokawa Cabinet has many more difficult tasks ahead, particularly in the economic field. In recent years, the declining voting percentage in various elections is being attributed not so much to distrust in political processes, but to a sense of pessimism about the revival of the Japanese economy. Support for the Hosokawa Cabinet would continue only if he succeeds in achieving an economic recovery.

The vitality of every democracy and the maintenance of high standards in public life depend upon the vigilance of the people and their timely intervention, on the basis of the rights given by the system and not by legislation alone. Japan is no exception.

5

Constitutional Developments in Post-War Japan

HANJI KINOSHITA*

As a result of World War II the *ancien regime* of Japan was destroyed and a new Japan has emerged from the ashes. The ultimate objectives of the Allied Occupation policy were the demilitarization and democratization of Japan. These objectives were indicated for the first time in the Potsdam Declaration of July 26, 1945. They were repeated (1) in the 'United States Initial Post-Surrender Policy for Japan', which was forwarded to General Douglas MacArthur by the United States Government on August 29, 1945; (2) in the 'Basic Initial Post-Surrender Directive to the Supreme Commander of the Allied Powers for the Occupation and Control of Japan', date November 8, 1945; and (3) in the 'Basic Post-Surrender Policy for Japan', which was adopted by the Far Eastern Commission on June 19, 1947, and was forwarded to the Supreme Commander for the Allied Powers on June 26, 1947.

As to demilitarization, the Potsdam Declaration stated as follows—

'There must be eliminated for all time the authority and influence of those who have deceived and misled the people of Japan into embarking

* Professor, University of Tokyo, Tokyo, Japan

on world conquest, for we insist that a new order of peace, security and justice will be impossible until irresponsible militarism is driven from the world (paragraph 6).

'Until such a new order is established and until there is convincing proof that Japan's war-making power is destroyed, points in Japanese territory to be designated by the Allies shall be occupied to secure the achievement of the basic objectives we are here setting forth (paragraph 7).

'The Japanese military forces, after being completely disarmed, shall be permitted to return to their homes with opportunity to lead peaceful and productive lives (paragraph 9).

'We do not intend that the Japanese shall be enslaved as a race or destroyed as a nation, but stern justice shall be meted out to all war criminals, including those who have visited cruelties upon our prisoners (paragraph 10).

'Japan shall be permitted to maintain such industries as will sustain her economy and permit the exaction of just reparations in kind, but not those which would enable her to rearm for war.'

With regard to democratization, the same Declaration stated:

'. . . The Japanese Government shall remove all obstacles to the revival and strengthening of democratic tendencies among the Japanese people. The freedom of speech, of religion, and of thought as well as respect for the fundamental human rights shall be established (paragraph 10).

'The occupying forces of the Allies shall be withdrawn from Japan as soon as these objectives have been accomplished and there have been established, in accordance with the freely expressed will of the Japanese people, a peacefully inclined and responsible government' (paragraph 12).

As is generally known, the Potsdam Declaration was issued by the three powers to give Japan 'an opportunity to end this war'. But the military cliques and other feudalistic ruling classes of Japan, sticking to the 'protection of the national polity' (*Kokutai-Goji*) or 'retention of the Emperor System (*Tenno-sei*)', naturally hesitated to accept it. To their astonishment, the Soviet Union entering the war on August 8, 1954, forced them to surrender, and on August 10, the government sent a message accepting the terms of the Potsdam Declaration 'with the understanding that the said Declaration does not comprise any demand which prejudices the prerogatives of His Majesty as a sovereign ruler'. Nevertheless, the reply of the American Secretary of State, (August 11), on behalf of the three powers stated only that 'from the moment of surrender the authority of the Emperor[1] and the Japanese government to rule the State shall be subject to the Supreme commander of the Allied Powers who will take such steps as he deems proper to effectuate the surrender terms', and that 'the ultimate form of the government of Japan shall, in accordance with the Potsdam Declaration, be established by the freely expressed will of the Japanese people.' On August 14, the Japanese Government sent the final communication accepting the Potsdam Declaration, that is to say, an unconditional surrender. On the same day, the Emperor issued to the Japanese people an Imperial Rescript regarding the surrender. On September 2, the Japanese delegates signed the Instrument of Surrender on the deck of the 'Missouri', an American warship.

Thus, the *ancien regime* of Japan came to an end and the pre-surrender form of the Imperial regime was abolished. Japan became a modern 'democratic' state, if not in fact, at least in form.

The two ultimate objectives of the Allied Occupation Policy were repeated in other documents. With reference to demilitarization, the 'United States Initial Post-Surrender Policy' (August 29, 1945) notes as follows: 'The ultimate objectives of the United States in regard to Japan, to which policies in the initial period must conform, are: (a) To insure that Japan will not again become a menace to the United States or to the peace and security of the world . . . . Japan will be completely disarmed and demilitarized . . .' (Part I—Ultimate Objectives). . . . 'Disarmament and Demilitarization are the primary tasks of the military occupation and shall be carried out promptly and with determination. . . . Japan is not to have and army, navy, airforce, secret police organization, or any civil aviation. Japan's ground, air and naval forces shall be disarmed and disbanded and the Japanese Imperial headquarters, the General Staff and all secret police organization shall be dissolved . . . .' (Part III—Political—I—Disarmament and Demilitarization). 'The existing economic basis of Japanese military strength must be destroyed and not be permitted to revive' (Part IV—Economic—I Economic Demilitarization.)

The 'Basic Initial Post-Surrender Directive' (November 8, 1945) is more precise on this point: 'The ultimate objective of the United Nations with respect to Japan is to foster conditions which will give the greatest possible assurance that Japan will not again become a menace to the peace and security of the world and will permit her eventual admission as a responsible and peaceful member of the family of nations. Certain measures considered to be essential for the achievement of this objective have been set forth in the Potsdam Declaration. These measures include, among others, the carrying out of the Cairo Declaration. . . . ; the abolition of militarism and ultra-nationalism in all their forms; the disarmament and demilitarization of Japan, with continuing control over Japan's capacity to make war . . . .' (Part I—General and Political—3. Basic Objectives of Military Occupation of Japan—(a)). Afterwards, the 'Basic Post-Surrender Policy' (June 19, 1947) confirmed this objective. (Part I—Ultimate Objectives. 1-a, 2-b, d, and Part III—Political—1. Disarmament and Demilitarization.)

With reference to another objective, namely Japan's democratization, the 'United States Initial Post-surrender Policy' states that one of 'the ultimate objectives of the United States in regard to Japan' is 'to bring about the eventual establishment of a peaceful and responsible government which will respect the rights of other states and will support the objectives of the United States as reflected in the ideals and principles of the Charter of the United Nations. The United States desires that this government should conform as closely as may be to principles of democratic self-government but it is not the responsibility of the Allied Powers to impose upon Japan any form of government not supported by the freely expressed will of the people.' The 'Initial Post-Surrender Policy' enumerates the principal means to achieve the ultimate objective of democratization as follows: '. . . .(b). . . The authority of the militarists and the influence of militarism will be totally eliminated from her political, economic, and social life. Institutions expressive of the spirit of militarism and aggression will be vigorously repressed. (c) The Japanese people will be encouraged to develop a desire for individual liberties and respect for fundamental human rights, particularly the freedoms of religion, assembly, speech, and the press. They shall also be encouraged to form democratic and representative organizations. . . ' (Part I—Ultimate Objectives). 'The Supreme Commander will exercise his authority through Japanese governmental machinery and agencies, including the Emperor. . . (But) this policy. . . *does not commit* the Supreme Commander *to support the Emperor* (italics the writer's) or any other Japanese authority in opposition to evolutionary changes looking toward the attainment of the United States objectives. The policy is to use the existing form of government in Japan, not to support it. Changes in the form of government initiated by the Japanese people or government in the direction of modifying its feudal and authoritarian tendencies are to be permitted and favoured' (Part II—Allied Authority—2. Relationship to Japanese Government). 'Democratic political parties with rights of assembly and public discussion shall be encouraged, subject to the necessity for maintaining the security of the occupying forces' (Part III—Political—3. Encouragement of Desire for Individual Liberties and Democratic Process). The 'Basic Initial Post-Surrender Directive' also mentions, among the measures considered to be essential for the achievement of the objective democratization such measures as 'the strengthening of democratic tendencies and processes in governmental, economic and social institution; and the encouragement and support of liberal political tendencies in Japan' (Part I—General and Political—3. Basic Objectives of Military Occupation of Japan). The same opinions are confirmed by the 'Basic Post-Surrender Policy' (Part I—Ultimate Objectives 1. (c), Part II—Allied Authority. 2. Relationship to Japanese Government, and 3. Encouragement of Desire for Individual Liberties and Democratic Process).

Thus the fundamental points decided by the Allied Powers as to the Constitution of Japan were:—

(1) Japan lost its independence. The sovereignty of Japan was subject to the Supreme Commander.[2]

(2) The ultimate form of government was to be decided by the freely expressed will of the Japanese people. Hence, popular sovereignty becomes the ruling principle of the new political *regime* of Japan, and the sovereignty of the Emperor is abolished. The political power of the Emperor is entirely eliminated.

(3) Japan was to be completely demilitarized and disarmed. She must not have any army, navy or air force. The authority of the militarists and influence of militarism must be totally eliminated. All the power to make war must be destroyed. The Secret Police Organization must be abolished. She must have responsible government pursuing a policy of peace.

(4) The Japanese people must establish individual liberties and respect for fundamental human rights, particularly the freedoms of religion, assembly and association, speech and the press. She must form democratic and representative organizations.

(5) Japan's sovereignty is limited to the islands of Honshu, Hokkaido, Kyushu, Shikoku and such minor outlying islands as the Allied Powers determine.

The old *Meiji* Constitution of Japan (the *'Meiji Kempo'*) was based on the principle of the sovereignty of the Emperor and on other feudalistic principles. It was promulgated in 1889 and was an imitation of the ancient Prussian Constitution of 1850; naturally it was diametrically opposed to the above mentioned objectives of the Allied Powers, and it was therefore necessary to draft a new Constitution.

Many elaborate drafts of the New Constitution were proposed and made known by various political parties and groups. Some of them, as that of the Communist Party, proclaimed the abolition of the Emperor System and required the establishment of a Republic. The Socialist Party demanded a 'Reformed Emperor System'. The drafts of the two conservative parties: the 'Liberal' Party (*Jiyu-to*) and the 'Progressive' Party (*Shimpo-to*) proposed to retain the old-fashioned Emperor System. Other groups, such as the Association for Study of the Constitution (*Kempo-Kenkyu-Kai*) and the Informal Talking Society for the Constitution (*Kempo-Kondan-Kai*), also made their drafts public.

On October 4, 1945, the Supreme Commander of the Allied Powers (SCAP) informed Prince Fumimaro Konoe, State Minister of the Prince Higashikuni Cabinet, that the Japanese Government would be required to revise the Constitution. On the same day, SCAP ordered the repeal of the Peace Preservation Law, the release of political prisoners, and the abolition of the Secret Police. On the next day, the Prince Higashikuni Cabinet retired and the Shidehara Cabinet was formed, to which on October 11 SCAP again issued an order to consider the revision of the Constitution. The Shidehara Cabinet therefore embarked on the task and established a Commission for Research into Constitutional Reform (*Kempo-Mondai Chosa-Kai*), the chairman of which was State Minister Joji Matsumoto. The Commission's aim, according to the order of SCAP, was the 'liberalization of the Constitution'. Its recommendations were: (a) to retain the sovereignty of the Emperor, and (b) to enlarge the power of the Diet, thereby limiting the Emperor's power. The general tendency of the draft was conservative.

While the Government was considering the draft of Dr. Matsumoto, General MacArthur, the Supreme Commander, finding the Matsumoto Draft inadequate for the democratization of Japan, asked his officials to prepare another draft, delivered it on February 13 to the Japanese government and asked the latter to adopt it.

It was known as the MacArthur Draft.[3] This draft provided for drastic changes in Japan's political regime. Firstly, it recognized the people's sovereignty, deprived the Emperor of his supreme authority and made him retain only ceremonial functions. Secondly, it renounced war and militarism. Thus, it was the most radical of all draft except that of the Communist Party. The Japanese Government was extremely surprised at its radical character. However, they could do nothing but translate it into Japanese, and, with some minor revisions aiming at mitigating its content, they published it as the Bill for the new Constitution (March 6, 1946).

On April 10, 1946, the first post-surrender general elections based on the new Election Law, were held, in which no overwhelming vote was given to any single party, but as the Liberal Party won the largest number of seats, the Yoshida (Liberal) Cabinet was formed.[4] The new Diet passed the Bill on October 7,1946, and promulgated it on November 3, 1946,[5] and thus the new Constitution became operative on May 3, 1947.

Meanwhile, the democratization of Japan's political system was pushed forward: (1) SCAP ordered the abolition of restrictions on the freedom of the press (September 29, 1945).[6] This measure was conceived as a means of destroying the Emperor's prestige in the eyes of the people. (2) The Imperial assets were 'fozen' and made subject to taxation (November 20, 1945), and later, all property of the Imperial Household was made the property of the State by Article 88 of the new Constitution. (3) Except for the families of the three Princes of the blood, who have been retained as members of the Imperial Household, all other Imperial Relatives were forced to join the ranks of commoners. (4) The most important step was that, on January 1, 1946, the Emperor renounced his deity status (of course, under the order of General MacArthur as initial implementation of the Allied reply). (5) Shintoism was shorn of its status as the national religion. (6) Lese-majeste was abolished as a result of amendments to the Criminal Code (November 11, 1947). (7) The peerage, which was the bulwark of the Imperil Household, was eliminated. (8) War criminals were punished (so-called A-class criminals were arrested on September 11, 1945, and were brought to trial on May 3, 1946; seven of them were sentenced to death by hanging and executed on December 23, 1948). (9) On January 4, 1946, purge orders were directed at anti-democratic and militaristic public office holders, and ultra-nationalistic organizations were dissolved. These measures were, in reality, the nucleus of the efforts to democratize Japan's government.[7] (10) Lastly, the financial cliques ('*Zaibatsu*'), which were as responsible for Japan's militaristic policy as the military cliques ('*Gun Batsu*'), were dissolved and the economic purge directed against their leaders, which was outwardly less striking, but basically more important than the political purge. In total, 288 persons were purged from the political and economic fields, and the number of organizations which were dissolved amounted to nearly 230 by the end of December 1951.[8]

Such was the political background of the new Constitution of Japan. The latter was the legal expression of the former. This made the Japanese people express themselves in the preamble of their Constitution as follows:

'We, the Japanese people, acting through our duly elected representatives in the National Diet, determined that we shall secure for ourselves and our posterity the fruits of peaceful co-operation with all nations and the blessings of liberty throughout this land, and resolved that never again shall we be visited with the horrors of war through the action of government, do proclaim that sovereign power resides with the people and do firmly establish this Constitution. Government is a sacred trust of the people the authority for which is derived from the people, the power of which is exercised by the representatives of the people the benefits of which are enjoyed by the people. This is a universal principle of mankind upon which this Constitution is founded. We reject and revoke all the constitutions, laws, ordinances, and rescripts in conflict herewith.'

'We, the Japanese people, desire peace for all time and are deeply conscious of the high ideals controlling human relationship, and we have determined to preserve our security and existence, trusting in the justice and faith of the peace-loving peoples of the world. We desire to occupy an honoured place in an international society striving for the preservation of peace, and the banishment of tyranny and slavery, oppression and intolerance for all time from the earth. We recognize that all peoples of the world have the right to live in peace, free from fear and want.'

'We believe that no nation is responsible to itself alone, but that laws of political morality are universal; and that obedience to such laws is incumbent upon all nations who would sustain their own sovereignty and justify their sovereign relationship with other nations.'

'We, the Japanese people, pledge our national honour to accomplish these high ideals and purposes with all our resources.'

The most fundamental change in the new Constitution as compared with the old *Meiji* Constitution, is that the Emperor is deprived of his supreme authority, and the sovereign power resides in the people. The Emperor is stripped of all the prerogatives provided for under the *Meiji* Constitution and is relegated to the *status* of a mere 'Symbol of the State and of the unity of the people, deriving his position from the will of the people with whom resides sovereign power[9-10] (Chapter I. The Emperor—Article I). With this step the ancient 'national policy' ('*Kokutai*') was abolished. The Japanese people are said to have 'chosen' to retain the Emperor System. But the Emperor has no political rights and does not represent the State to other nations. He is not the head of the State ('*Genshu*').[11]

The Emperor retains only ceremonial functions. He 'shall perform only such acts in matters of State as are provided for in this Constitution. Never shall he has powers related to government' (Article 4).[12] And 'the advice and approval of the Cabinet shall be required for all acts of the Emperor in matters of State, and the Cabinet shall be responsible therefor' (Article 3).

His functions are provided for as follows:—

(1) To appoint the Prime Minister as designated by the Diet (Article 6, paragraph 1).
(2) To appoint the chief judge of the Supreme Court, as designated by the Cabinet (Article 6, paragraph 2).
(3) Promulgation of amendments of the constitution, laws, cabinet orders and treaties (Article 7, No. 1).
(4) Convocation of the Diet (Article 7, No. 2).
(5) Dissolution of the House of Representatives (Article 7, No. 3).
(6) Proclamation of general elections of members of the Diet (Article 7, No. 4).
(7) Attestation of the appointment and dismissal of Ministers of State and other officials as provided for by law, and of full powers and credentials of Ambassadors and Ministers (Article 7, No. 5).
(8) Attestation of general and special amnesty, commutation of punishment, reprieve, and restoration of rights (Article 7, No. 6).
(9) Awarding of honours (Article 7, No. 7).

(10) Attestation of instruments of ratification and other diplomatic documents as provided for by law (Article 7, No. 8).
(11) Receiving foreign ambassadors and ministers (Article 7, No. 9).
(12) Performance of ceremonial functions (Article 7, No. 10).

Needless to say that the conservative and anti-democratic elements of the country are discontented with this new 'national polity'. As the 'reserve course' began to prevail in Japan subsequent to the cold war between the United States and the Soviet Union, especially after the Peace Treaty came into force, they began to try to relevant the Emperor from the status of 'Symbol' to the position of 'Head of the State', and to restore his former political prerogatives.

The second important subject in the new Constitution is the 'renunciation of war'. As the 'Preamble' states, the Japanese people resolved that never again will they 'be visited with the horrors of war', and they desire 'peace for all time', and are 'fully conscious of the high ideals controlling human relationship now stirring mankind', in short, they are determined to build a 'Peace State'. As far as the 'renunciation of war' is concerned, the new Japanese Constitution is singled out as being unique in the world. 'Aspiring sincerely to an international peace based on justice and order, the Japanese people forever renounce war as a sovereign right of the nation, or the threat of use of force as a means of settling disputes with other nations'[13] (Chapter II, Renunciation of War. Article 9, paragraph 1). The Japanese people renounce the use of all armaments. 'For the above purposes, land, sea, and air forces, as well as other war potentials will never be maintained. The right of belligerency of the State will not be recognized' (Article 9, paragraph 2).[14]

Notwithstanding these peace-loving provisions, the rearmament of Japan, under guise of the National Police Reserve, was urged by SCAP immediately after the outbreak of the Korean War (July 1950). This new little army was reorganized into the National Safety Force (October 1952). The Mutual Security Agreement being signed with the United States (March 1954), the Japanese Government adopted the policy of rapidly increasing the country's 'defence strength'. The National Safety Force was changed into the Self-Defence Force with its 'defence strength' considerably increased. Furthermore, its controlling administration, the National Safety Agency, was altered into the Defence Agency (June 1954).

The third essential subject in the new Constitution is respect for fundamental human rights. The *Meiji* Constitution was very defective in these matters. According to it, 'Japanese subjects' would enjoy their liberties only 'within the limits of laws', or 'within limits not prejudicial to peace and order, and not antagonistic to their duties as subjects'.[15] Moreover, the provisions concerning the rights of People 'shall not affect the exercise of the Powers appertaining to the Emperor, in time of war or in case of national emergency' (Article XXXI).

In contradistinction to the above, the new Constitution guarantees wholly and unconditionally the liberties of the people (at least, in form). Its provisions are:

(1) 'The people shall not be prevented from enjoying any of the fundamental human rights. These fundamental rights guaranteed to the people by this Constitution shall be conferred upon the people of this and future generations as eternal and inviolate rights' (Chapter III, Rights and Duties of the People. Article II).

(2) 'The freedoms and rights guaranteed to the people by this Constitution shall be maintained by the constant endeavour of the people, who shall refrain from any abuse of these freedoms and rights and shall always be responsible for utilizing them from the public welfare' (Article 12).

(3) 'All of the people shall be respected as individuals. Their right to life, liberty, and the pursuit of happiness shall, to the extent that it does not interfere with the public welfare, be the supreme consideration in legislation and in other governmental affairs' (Article 13).

(4) 'All of the people are equal under the law and there shall be no discrimination in political, economic or social relations because of race, creed, sex, social status or family origin' (Article 14, Paragraph 1).

(5) 'Peerage shall not be recognized' (Article 14, paragraph 2).

(6) 'No privileges shall accompany any award of honor, decoration or any distinction, nor shall any such award be valid beyond the lifetime of the individual who now holds or hereafter may receive it' (Article 14, paragraph 3).

(7) 'Marriage shall be based only of the mutual consent of both sexes and it shall be maintained through mutual co-operation with the

equal rights of husband and wife as a basis' (Article 24, paragraph 1).

(8) With regard to the most important rights, namely political and other liberties, the Constitution stipulates as follows:

(a) 'No person shall be held in bondage of any kind' (Article 18).

(b) 'Freedom of thought and conscience shall not be violated' (Article 19).

(c) 'Freedom of religion is guaranteed to all. No religious organization shall receive any privileges from the State, nor exercise any political authority' (Article 20, paragraph 1)....'The State and its organs shall refrain from religious education or any other religious activity' (Article 20, paragraph 3).

(d) 'Freedom of assembly, association, speech and press and all other forms of expression are guaranteed' (Article 21, paragraph 1). 'No censorship shall be maintained, nor shall the secrecy of any means of communication be violated' (Article 21, paragraph 2).

(e) 'Every person shall have freedom to choose and change his residence and to choose his occupation....' (Article 22, paragraph 1).

(f) 'Academic freedom is guaranteed' (Article 23).

(g) 'All people shall have the right to maintain the minimum standards of wholesome and cultured living' (Article 25, paragraph 1).

(h) Children shall not be exploited' (Article 27, paragraph 3).

(i) 'The right of workers to organize and to bargain and act collectively is guaranteed' (Article 28).

In summing up these provisions, the new Constitution provides as the 'Supreme Law' the following basic principle: 'The fundamental human rights by the Constitution guaranteed to the people of Japan are the fruits of the age-old struggle of man to be free; they have survived the exacting tests for durability and are conferred upon this and future generations in trust, to be held for all time inviolate' (Chapter X, Supreme Law—Article 97).

It is true that these provisions are excellent expression *in form*; nevertheless, *in fact*, these fundamental rights are being violated little by little by governmental agencies.

Be that as it may, the new Constitution is an epoch-making fact in Japanese political history. Besides these provisions concerning the liberties of the people, we must refer to other important democratic points in this Constitution. The Diet, which consists of the House of Representatives and the House of Count-sellers,[16] becomes 'the highest organ of State power' and 'the sole law-making organ of the State' (Article 41), the ultimate power residing in the House of Representatives (Article 59, paragraph 2, Article 60, paragraph 2, Article 61 and Article 67, paragraph 2). The Prime Minister is designated from among the member of the Diet by a resolution of the Diet (Article 67). He appoints the Ministers of State of whom the majority must be chosen from among the members of the Diet (Article 68, paragraph 1). All of them must be civilians, as mentioned previously (Article 66, paragraph 2).

The whole judicial power is vested in a Supreme Court and inferior courts established by law (Article 76, paragraph 1). The appointment of the judges of the Supreme Court is reviewed by the people at ten-year intervals in a general election (Article 79, paragraph 2). Whenever the majority of the voters favours the dismissal of a judge, he must be dismissed (Article 79, paragraph 3).

Amendments to the Constitution must be initiated by a two-thirds majority of all members of each House of the Diet and must be ratified by a majority vote of the people participating in a special referendum or in such an election as the Diet shall specify (Article 96, paragraph 1).

Thus, the new Constitution of Japan is democratic and liberal to an unheard of extent in Japanese politics. It can be said that for the first time Japan becomes, under this Constitution, a modern 'democratic' State. But, of late, business circles, the government, and especially the two conservative parties, the 'Democratic' party and the 'Liberal' party have proceeded to revise the Constitution. In doing so, they have two main objectives: to restore the political prerogatives of the Emperor and to rearm Japan thoroughly. They aim to make the 'Symbol' Emperor the 'Head of the State'. For the rearmament of Japan, the greater obstacle is Article 9 of the Constitution which they eagerly desired to abrogate. For this purpose, they brought before the Special Session of the Diet during the spring and summer of 1955 a Constitution Research Council Establishment Bill, which, however, proved abortive for the time being.

Meanwhile, they organized in May 1955 outside the Diet, a League for an 'Autonomous' Constitution with the participation of some right wing and conservative scholars and publicists, and inside the Diet they established the Diet Members' League for and Autonomous Constitution rallying some 300 conservative members of both Houses, which organization published in August 1955 a draft revision in the name of its chairman, immediately after the Session was closed. The draft aimed, besides the two above-mentioned objectives, at restricting the fundamental human rights. In a word, they are acting and thinking in the spirit which prevailed before the 'Summit Conference' at Geneva in July 1955, faithfully following a policy toward World War III. Such are the essential points of the late'reverse course' in Japan.

Against this 'reverse course' a united front names the People's Federation for the Protection of the Peace Constitution was formed by the democratic elements and the socialist parties. They include more than one-third of the members of the House of Representatives, which number is sufficient for preventing revision.[17] So, for the time being, the conservative and militarist Government's action is checked by the people's democratic energy. But whether their efforts have any prospect of success remains an open question.

Notes and References

1. At the end of the war, the various Allied Powers adopted different basic policies toward the Imperial regime in Japan. Some desired to retain that regime while others wished to destroy it. Upon this problem cf. Hanji Kinoshita, '*Purge Policy and After*' (Japan Paper No. 9, at the Twelfth Conference, Institute of Pacific Relations, Kyoto, Japan, Sept-Oct., 1954).
2. Independence was recovered at the end of April 1952 as the result of the Peace Treaty of September 1951.
3. The Draft was made known to the public in the 'Kokka Gakkai Zassi' (the Journal of the Association of Political and Social Science) of Tokyo University (September 1954).
4. Mr. Ichiro Hotoyama, the founder and president of the Liberal Party being purged immediately after the Election (May 3, 1946). Mr. Shigeru Yoshida, an old diplomatist, succeeded him.
5. This day is the ancient Anniversary of the Birthday of the Emperor of *Meiji*. This fact proves the conservative character of the Yoshida Cabinet.
6. This measure meant that the Japanese Press could publish the photograph of the Emperor with that of General MacArthur, which was taken when the former visited the latter. The Japanese Government thought that the photograph would damage the Emperor's prestige and prohibited the Press to publish it. SCAP counteracted the Government's order.

7. As to the 'Purge' system, see H. Kinoshita, '*Purge Policy and After*'.
8. By the change in the United States policy towards Japan since the cold war began, the purge and dissolution of organizations were extended to the communists ('Red Purge'). Hence, this total number includes leftists who were removed from public office.
9. The first MacArthur Draft stated: '....deriving his position from the sovereign will of the People, and from no other source, (Article I) and 'The people are the ultimate arbiters of their government and of the Imperial Throne' (Article XIV, paragraph I).
10. In the Peace Treaty of 1951, it is said as follows: 'The Allied Powers recognize the full sovereignty of the Japanese people over Japan and its territorial waters' (Chapter I, Article 1.)
11. The new 'national polity' was a step backward as compared to the policy of the statement approved by the Far Eastern Commission on July 2, 1946, based on a directive drawn up by the State-War-Navy Coordinating Committee early in 1946, and entitled 'Basic Principles for a new Japanese Constitution.' This document which was made known by the Dept. of State, April 18, 1947, states:

    '1. The Japanese Constitution should recognize that sovereign power resides in the people.....

    '2. Though the ultimate form of government in Japan is to be established by the freely expressed will of the Japanese people, the retention of the Emperor Institution in its present constitutional form is not considered consistent with the foregoing general objectives. Consequently the Japanese should be encouraged to abolish the Emperor Institution or to reform it along more democratic lines.

    '3. If the Japanese people decide that the Emperor Institution is not to be retained, constitutional safeguards against the institution will obviously not be required......

    '4. If the Japanese decide to retain the Institution of the Emperor, the following safeguards....will be necessary:

    a. ....

    b. The Emperor shall have no powers other than those to be conferred on him by the new Constitution.....

    c. The Emperor shall be deprived of all military authority such as that provided in Articles XI, XII, XIII, and XIV of Chapter I of the Constitution of 1889.....'
12. The MacArthur Draft states: 'The Emperor shall perform only such State functions as are provided for in this Constitution. He shall have no governmental powers, nor shall he assume nor be granted such powers' (Article III).
13. The MacArthur Draft states: 'War as a sovereign right of the nation is abolished. The threat or use of forces is forever renounced as a means for settling disputes with any other nations. No army, navy, air force, or other war potential will ever be conferred upon the State.'
14. With regard to demilitarization, we must notice that 'the Prime Minister and other Ministers of State must be civilians' (Article 66, paragraph 2). On account of this provision, ex-Admiral Kichisaburo Nomura could not become Minister of Defence in the Hatoyama Cabinet.

15. For example, Article XXIX (Chapter II, Rights and Duties of Subjects) states as follows: 'Japanese subjects shall, within the limits of law, enjoy the liberty of speech, writing, publication, public meeting and associations.
16. With regard to this problem, the MacArthur Draft provided for a Mono-Cameral System (Article XLI), but the Japanese Diet did not adopt it.
17. Article 96: 'Amendments to this constitution shall be initiated by the Diet, through a concurring vote of two-thirds or more of all the members of each House.....'

6

Local Government in Japan: An Analytical Review

RAJENDRA PAL GUPTA*

I

HISTORICAL BACKGROUND OF PUBLIC ADMINISTRATION IN JAPAN

If we have to understand well the administrative system of a country, we will have to go very deep into the history, culture, conventions, geography and economy of that country. As a result of the Meiji Restoration and emergence of the national state, public administration in Japan can be classified into three stages of development: First Stage (1867-1889), Second Stage (1889-1945), Third Stage (1945 to date).

First Stage (1867-1889): In 1868 a strongly controlled government system known as *Dajokan* was established. There were three ministers under the Emperor: Prime Minister, Minister of Left and Minister of Right. The Prime Minister was known as *Dajo Daijin* and he owned the overall responsibility for the government. The Minister of Left acted as an advisor on government ordinances. The Minister of Right supervised

* Research Scholar, Faculty of Law, Meijo University, Nagoye (Japan).

the operations of the ministries. The Minister of Left was known as *Sadaijin* while the Minister of Right was known as *Udaijin*. There were several Councilors, known as *Sangi* and they enjoyed the decision-making power regarding policies and their implementation.

The Supreme Court was established in 1875 and was known as *Dai-shin-in*. Unlike today the power of the State was not clearly divided between the executive, the legislative and the judiciary; rather the executive dominated the judiciary.

Imperial Ordinances: All activities of the government were based on Imperial ordinances, known as *Fukoku* and the proclamations of the *Dajokan*. The people were not allowed to criticize the government and agitations for democratic rights were prohibited by imperial ordinances. In brief, there was no law in the modern democratic sense.

Recruitment of Government Officials: Most of the government officials were recruited from the warrior class, known as *Samurai* and therefore the result was that a strong sense of *Kansoumimpi* was developed, which means that the government was placed above the people. Until 1887 the civil service did not have an open entrance examination and the posts in government offices were filled by several major and warrior clans who had contributed to the success of the Meiji Restoration. As a matter of fact the Emperor was the 'sovereign' and enjoyed un-briddled powers and there was no right vested in the people to criticize the government for its wrong policies.

The Second Stage (1889-1945): In 1889 the Meiji Constitution was promulgated and with it a limited monarchy was modelled on the pattern of Germany. After abolishing the *Dajokan* system the Imperial House and the Cabinet was established. The Imperial House consisted of the House of Peers and the House of Representatives. Although administrative power was divided into the legislative, the executive and the judicial organs, the Emperor still enjoyed the overall comprehensive ruling power over all the three organs. The judiciary was given an independent status, but still the courts were required to give judgements in the name of the Emperor.

Powers of the Emperor

During this period the Emperor had direct command of the armed forces and the Imperial House could not even discuss it, because it was supposed to be the prerogative of the Emperor who was the Supreme Commander of the armed forces. The Emperor could enact a law by issuing an Imperial Ordinance even without getting the prior consent and approval of the Imperial House. All the public administrators were generally referred to as 'the Emperor's officials' and were under strict regulations to remain loyal to the Emperor. It was the Emperor and not the Imperial House, who could make and approve the Budget.

Civil Service Examinations

For the first time two open civil service examinations were held for the services—one for higher and the other for lower grades. Legal knowledge of the candidate was given priority over his administrative ability.

During this period local governments were established in the prefectures, municipalities, cities, towns and villages, but these local governments were to a great extent under the control of the national government and enjoyed a very limited degree of autonomy.

In brief, a highly feudal character was retained during this stage, despite the introduction of constitutional monarchy.

The Third Stage (1945 to date): The new Constitution was promulgated in 1947, and this the Japanese public administration underwent various major changes. The new Constitution was based on the principles of democratic government and respect for fundamental human rights.

Superiority of the Legislative: The first major change was the superiority of the Legislative over the Executive. Now the National Diet, which is composed of the elected representatives of the people, has absolute powers to discuss the matters of the government, and the Cabinet is responsible collectively to the *Diet* for all its commissions and omissions, it being a parliamentary system.

Restructuring of Administrative Organizations: The second major change is the restructuring of the administrative organizations. The Ministries of Army, Navy, Home Affairs and Munitions were abolished, and two new Ministries of Labour and Construction were established keeping in view the new demands of the people. The remarkable change in this field is the creation of various Agencies, and most notably the Administrative Management Agency, which is in charge of research and planning regarding administrative organization and improvement of administrative efficiency.

Reform in Personnel System: The third major change was the establishment of the National Personnel Authority in order to bring impartiality in civil service appointments, keep party politics out of personnel administration, promote administrative efficiency and to democratize the old bureaucracy. It was established on the pattern of the Civil Service Commission of the United States.

The Authority is absolutely disaffiliated with both the Cabinet and other executive departments. It is headed by three members who are experts in the field of personnel administration, and are responsible for the introduction of various civil service examinations.

Autonomy to Local Government: The fourth change was to make the local governments autonomous bodies with less supervision by the national government and more participation by the local people in the administration of these local bodies.

Defence Administration: The fifth and final change was the amendment in the Constitution not to have a regular army. The new Constitution forbade armed forces; but after the Korean War a Police Reserve was established under the National Defence Agency, which has now been converted into the Self-Defence Forces.

After World War II many reforms were introduced in the local government system. The system of governing the prefectures, cities, towns and villages was, to a great extent, changed drastically in September 1946. According to these changes, women in Japan for the first time were allowed the right to vote. The Governors of the prefectures were no more nominated, but were elected by the people of the prefecture concerned.

While the pre-war system was modelled after that of Germany, the new post-war local government system was influenced by the American system of local government. The new system was oriented towards decentralization and contained the elements of 'direct democracy'. In the new Local Autonomy Law, which was enacted in the month of May 1947, the people of the prefecture were given absolute powers to enact laws for their own well-being and welfare and the national government had very little say in it.

Basic Principles of the Local Government System

If we go through the Constitution of Japan, we come to know that it has provided the basic principles of local government system in Chapter VII of the Constitution. The relevant Articles concerning the organization, operation, establishments of Assemblies, Chief Executive

Officer, Assembly members, local officials, their rights and duties, and the power of the National diet to enact a special law regarding these local public entities, are Articles 92, 93, and 95 of the Constitution.

Local Self-government

Article 92: Regulations concerning organization and operation of local public entities shall be fixed by law in accordance with the principle of local autonomy.

Article 93: The local public entities shall establish Assemblies as their deliberative organs in accordance with the law. The Chief Executive Officers of all local public entities, the members of their Assemblies, and such other local officials as may be determined by law shall be elected by direct popular vote within their respective communities.

Article 94: Local public entities shall have the right to manage their property, affairs and administration and to enact their own regulations within the law.

Article 95: A special law, applicable only to one local public entity, cannot be enacted by the Diet without the consent of the majority of the voters of the local public entity concerned, obtained in accordance with the law.

It is quite clear from the wordings of the above-mentioned Articles of the important role of the local governments in a democracy and provides for local government as per of the political system.

A local public entity has two principal organizations: 1. the Legislative Body or Assembly, and 2. The Chief Executive Officer.

III

Laws Governing Local Government

Within the framework of the Constitution, various statutes and regulations regarding the local government have been enacted. These statutes and regulations can be classified into two categories: (1) Statutes regarding the organization and management of local public entities, and (2) Statutes concerning their substantive powers and responsibilities.

The Statutes included in category 1 are as follows:

(a) Local Autonomy Law,

(b) Public Office Election Law,

(c) Fire Organization Law,

(d) Police Law,
(e) Local Public Service Law,
(f) Finance Law,
(g) Local Allocation Tax Law, and
(h) Local Taxation Law.

The second category includes Statutes, Regulations and Ordinances which deal with the functions of the local government. Since the duty of the local government is to conduct administrative activities directly related to the daily life of the people within its jurisdiction, these Statutes or ordinances are increasing day by day as the needs and requirements of the people are increasingly becoming complex and diversified. Particularly in recent years the enactment of such legislations has increased rapidly in Japan.

Enactment of Legislations by Local Public Entities

Under the Constitution the right is invested in every public entity to enact and adopt its own legislations. These legislations are of two types: By-laws and Regulations. By-laws can be enacted and adopted only by the local assembly, while the Regulations are independently promulgated by the chief of the executive body of the local public entity in respect of matters within its jurisdiction. Since both the chief of the executive body and the local assembly possess the characteristics of law and enjoy authority under the law, neither can be deemed as superior to the other, with only one exception that the By-laws enacted by the Assembly can even restrict individual rights and freedom, while the Statutes promulgated by the Chief Executive Officer must always be in accordance with the regulations as mentioned in the 'Agency Delegation Functions'.

IV

Kinds of Local Public Entities

The Local Public Entities can be classified into two types: 1. Ordinary Local Public Entities, and 2. Special Local Public Entities. These are general and pervasive in.terms of organization and functions. They are organized into two tiers: Regional Administrative Bodies, and Basic Local Public Entities.

Regional Administrative Bodies are at the top. They include

To (Tokyo Metropolitan Government), Do (Hokkaido Island), Fu (Osaka and Kyoto Prefectures) and Ken (Japan's 43 regular prefectures).

Basic Local Public Entities are at the bottom. They include Shi (Cities), Cho (Towns), and Son (Villages). These Shi, Cho, and Son are the municipalities and are much more important as local public entities.

Conditions to be Met to Become a City

A Shi or a 'city must' meet the following conditions:

1. It must have a population of 50,000 or more.
2. 60% or more of its houses must be located in the urban area.
3. 60% or more of its work-force must be engaged in industrial or commercial activities.
4. It should have a regularly appointed treasurer and a social welfare office.

Cities that have population of 500,000 or more and have been designated by special Cabinet order, are called 'designated cities'. At present there are 10 designated cities in Japan. They are Osaka, Nagoya, Kyoto, Yokohama, Kobe, Kita-Kyushu, Kawasaki, Fukuoka, Sapporo, and Hiroshima.

These cities have been given special attention in every field. They are given special treatment in respect of administrative supervion, functions and administrative organization. They have been provided much more financial assistance by the national government than the smaller cities. Their powers are far greater than those of smaller cities in all respects. To, Do, Fu, and Ken deal with the affairs requiring uniformity of performance, supplementary affairs and affairs related to liaision and coordination. The functions of To, Do, Fu, and Ken are the same, except that there exist special wards only in To.

Prefectures are intermediate bodies performing many functions on behalf of the central government. The boundaries of these prefectures are determined historically, and therefore areas and populations vary greatly from prefecture to prefecture. On the basis of the 1980 census, the population of these prefectures and their areas are given as under in order to show the vast difference between the prefectures.

The data clearly show how vastly the prefectures differ from one another in population and area because of their boundaries having been determined historically.

Prefectures	*Population*	*Area (km^2)*
Tokyo-to	11,615,069	2,145.51
Osaka-fu	8,473,412	1,862.27
Kyoto-fu	2,527,247	4,612.84
Hokkaido	5,576,110	83,514.54
	Data as per 1980 census.	
Total population of Japan	17,057,485	377,643.13

Special Local Public Entities

The public entities which are made to meet the administrative needs for special purposes are called 'special local public entities'. They are of four types: 1. Special Wards, 2. Property Wards, 3. Association of Local Public Entities, and 4. Local Development Corporations.

Special Wards

The wards of Tokyo Metropolis are called 'special wards'. These are expected to tackle the problems pertaining to the daily life of the people of the locality. But it cannot be said that the level of services is not uniform among these wards and other municipalities. However, if we compare these special wards with those of the city municipalities, we see that their role is restricted to some extent. There are the following limitations in the special wards:

1. They posses no statutory power to determine to basic city planning schemes and projects.
2. They have no power to construct the water supply and sewerage systems.
3. They have no power to deal with the fire system of the locality within their jurisdiction.
4. They have no power to levy taxes in order to meet their financial requirements.

All these powers are vested in the Tokyo Metropolitan Government which is an autonomous body.

Property Wards: Property wards are a part of a city, town, village or a special ward which owns property or public facilities. For the management of these properties, special public bodies are constituted. These public bodies are of two types:

1. Properties which were acquired or inherited by the city, town or village under the feudal system during the Meiji period, and

2. Properties which were transferred to the city, town or village at the time of the merger of the municipalities.

Association of Local Public Entities: In order to manage themselves in a more efficient and rational manner, two or more local public entities willingly merged themselves and formed associations. There are three types of such associations: 1. Total Affairs Association, 2. Partial Affairs Association, and 3. Office Work Association. Of these only the Partial Affairs Association exists, the other two are not visible at present.

Local Development Corporations: These corporations are established jointly by two or more local public entities in order to complete the planned projects and schemes. The functions of these corporations were the following:

(a) to acquire private land if utterly necessary to acquire it in public interest,
(b) to undertake construction of structures on such land for public facilities, and
(c) to develop these lands in accordance with the regional development programme.

These corporations are not permanent but temporary in character, because they are immediately dissolved as soon as the planned project and schemes are completed.

V

FUNCTIONS OF LOCAL PUBLIC ENTITIES

The functions performed by the local public entities can be classified into the following four categories:

Local Functions

The functions pertaining to the welfare and well-being of the residents are called local functions of the local public entities. These functions include the construction, management and maintenance of schools, hospitals, water-supply and sewerage and the promotion of industries. These functions include construction, management and maintenance of schools, hospitals, water supply, sewerage and also the promotion of industries. The conduction of election of the Chief Executive Officer and the Assembly Members is also included among these functions.

Mandated Functions: The functions entrusted to the local public entities by the Central Government, public corporations and others through statutes or cabinet orders are called 'mandatory functions'.

Regulatory Functions: In order to maintain law and order, and to provide safety, security and welfare to the residents, some functions are carried out by the local public entities and these functions are called 'regulatory functions'. Through these functions the local public entities can impose some restrictions on its citizen residents and can limit their freedoms and fundamental rights, that is why many legal luminaries are of the opinion that the conditions of enforcement of such regulatory functions must be stipulated by law.

Agency Delegated Functions: In this category are included functions which are entrusted to the Chief Executive Officer under statutory provisions or cabinet orders by the central government. These functions are carried out under the instructions of the Minister concerned in the case of delegation by the central government, and the local assembly has no right to interfere with these functions. These functions are mandamus in character. If any Chief Executive Officer fails to perform such functions, he can be dismissed from his post through legal proceedings.

VI

ORGANIZATION AND POWER OF LOCAL PUBLIC ENTITIES

Organization: The local public entity has its own assembly. Members of the assembly are elected by the people of the locality through direct popular vote. Every citizen who has acquired the age of 20 is eligible to cast his or her vote in the election of the members of the assembly.

Number of Assembly Members: In deciding the number of assembly members, the population of the local public body plays an important role. According to the *Local Autonomy Law* the number of assembly members is decided keeping in view the population of the local public body concerned. But the number of assembly members can be reduced by a by-law, enacted by the local public assembly concerned.

Tenure of Assembly Members: The term of office of an assembly member of a local public entity is 4 years.

Powers of Local Assemblies: The most important power of the local assemblies is 'the decision-making power'. But here one point needs to be made clear: the local assemblies are not invested with power to make all decisions of the local public entities. They are authorized to make decisions regarding matters of special importance only, while decisions pertaining to other day-to-day matters are within the jurisdiction of the power of the Chief Executive Officer and other executive organs.

Matters of Special Importance: Matters which are of special importance and require resolution by the local assembly are:

(a) Enactment of By-laws,
(b) Amendment in the By-laws,
(c) Repeal of the By-laws,
(d) Adoption of Local Budget,
(e) Disposition of important properties as provided by the By laws,
(f) Procurement of properties of general public interest as provided by the By-laws,
(g) Authorization of the settlement of accounts,
(h) Determination of the amount of indemnities, and
(i) Conclusion of important contracts as stipulated by the By-laws.

VII

EXECUTIVE ORGANS OF LOCAL PUBLIC ENTITIES

Two principles have been adopted for the establishment of the executive departments of local public entities. These principles are: 1. The Chief Principle or President Principle, and 2. Pluralism, or Parliamentary System.

Under the first the maximum powers are vested in the office of the chief of the executive, while under the second the local assembly enjoys sovereign powers and the chief of the executive is regarded as a mere head of the local public entity. The Local Autonomy System in Japan adopts both as adopted in the central government. That is why it is said that both the Chief of the Executive and the Assembly are inter-dependent and neither can be considered superior to the other, to ensure a fair administration.

Under Pluralism, the local public entity establishes various commissions which carry out the 'special affairs' independent of the Chief Executive Officer in a more democratic and efficient manner.

Administrative Commissions

There are the following administrative commissions:

1. Personnel Commission: This commission makes research, planning and programming and then submits its recommendations related to personnel administration, working conditions of the employees and examination of disadvantageous conditions, and action to be taken for the smooth-running of the administration.

2. Property and Health Commission: The management and maintenance of the public-property situated within the jurisdiction of the local public body, is controlled by this commission. The sanitary condition of the locality, management and maintenance of the hospitals, and looking after the hygienic facilities, are the primary concerns of this commission.

3. Finance and Education Commission: To prepare the budget for the financial year and to submit it in the Assembly and the efforts to get it passed by the local public body, is the main function of this commission. After receiving the demands of the various departments, the Finance Commission reconsiders the reasonableness of these demands and then, making adjustments in the inter-departmental requirements, submits a balanced budget in the local public assembly for approval. The main function of the Education Commission is to administer the primary, junior and high schools, falling within their jurisdiction, to appoint teachers and other staff members, to grant aid to the eligible private schools and to provide better educational facilities to the young boys and girls of the locality.

4. Road Construction and Environment Commission: The primary duty of this commission is to repair and maintain the roads and streets of the vicinity in proper condition and to construct roads and streets in areas where necessary. This Commission is also very careful about the problem of air-pollution; therefore it does not sanction licences to industries in the residential areas.

5. Water-supply and Fire-service Commission: The function of this commission is to provide better water service to the residents, and to maintain proper sewerage system. The construction and repairs of the water tanks and the drainage system are also a part of the function of this commission. The Fire Commission constructs, manages, and maintains the fire-stations and fire-brigades. It also ensures that every house has its own 'fire extinguisher'.

6. Construction and Public Transport Commission: This commission looks after the construction, repairs and proper maintenance of the public utility buildings, local government offices, and the residential apartments of the local government officials and employees. The Public Transport Commission is entrusted with the duty of providing regular and comfortable means of transportation to the residents of the locality. For that matter the proper maintenance of the transportation vehicles and employment and dismissal of the employees of the transport department is also within the power of this commission.

7. Agriculture Commission: The functions of this Commission are:

(a) Adjustment of various uses of agricultural land,
(b) Exchange and reapportionment of such land,
(c) Affairs related to agricultural land, and
(d) Agricultural administrative affairs.

8. Elections Administration Commission: The main functions of this commission are to conduct and supervise impartially the elections of the Assembly Members and also to manage all other affairs related the election.

9. Inspection Commission: The main duty of this commission is the inspection of the financial matters and give appropriate suggestions. This commission is also entrusted with the function of the management of the enterprises, operated by the local public body.

10. Public Safety Commission: This commission is the custodian of public safety and is therefore responsible for any lapse in the duty of the police personnel. This commission is vested with the power of overseeing the administration and operation of the police within the jurisdiction of the local public entity.

11. Local Labour Commission: This commission's duties are to

(a) check affairs concerning unfair labour practices,
(b) restrict and derecognize unconstitutional labour unions,
(c) mediate in conflicts between the management and the employees, and
(d) bring the employer and employees to the conciliation-table, and
(e) function as arbitrator and decide labour disputes.

VIII

THE LOCAL GOVERNMENT PERSONNEL SYSTEM

Today there are approximately 3 million local public service personnel in Japan. It is, therefore, desirable that the laws regarding personnel management should be the same and uniform throughout the nation. Keeping this in view the Local Public Service Law was enacted by the Parliament of Japan.

Local Public Service Law: The present Local Public Service Law came into effect in February 1951. It stipulates the status of the employees of the local public entities. It clearly explains the rules, regulations and procedure for the personnel management of the local public bodies.

Jurisdiction of the Local Public Service Law: The scope of the Local Public Service Law is very wide. It applies equally to all public employees without any distinction of caste, creed or religion. All the local, governments throughout Japan come within the ambit of this Law.

The Purpose of its Enactment: This Local Public Service Law was enacted with the purpose 'to ensure democratic and efficient operation of the public administration of the local public entities and thereby contribute to the realization of the principle of local autonomy'.

Amendments in the Local Public Service Law: It cannot be said that no amendments were made in this local public service law, but whatever amendments were made were not very drastic in nature. Several times in the past three decades this law was amended but with only minor changes, with one exception resulting from Japan's rectification of the I.L.O. Treaty No. 87 in 1966. However, the basic frameworks of this law has always been maintained since its enactment.

The Provisions of the Local Public Service Law: The Local Public Law defines the basic standards for the management of the local public entities. The provisions of the local public service law can be classified into two categories:

1. Provisions regarding the rights and duties of the local civil servants, and
2. Provisions concerning the requisite requirements of the local civil servants.

The provisions in category number one include the rights and duties, status and discipline and protection of interest of the local civil servants;

while the provisions in category two cover: (a) Appointments, (b) Compensation, (c) Working hours, (d) Working conditions, (e) Training, and f. Evaluation of the working performance.

In the Local Public Service Law only the fundamental standards of the personnel management are mentioned, and other matters are left to the discretion of the personnel organs of the local public entities. Particularly, such matters as employment, promotion, and training have been left to the voluntary judgement of the personnel organs of the local public entities.

IX

BASIC PRINCIPLES OF LOCAL PUBLIC SERVICE LAW AND SPECIAL LAWS

The basic idea of local public service law is to establish a democratic and efficient system of local public service. The following are the basic principles of the local public service law:

1. Promotion of the principle that the local public employees are servants of the entire community living within the jurisdiction,
2. guarantee of basic rights and status to the local public employees,
3. establishment of the merit system for promotion in service,
4. improvement in the efficiency of the public administration, and
5. the maintenance of public morality.

Special Laws: The following are the special laws enacted for various kinds of employees of the local public entities:

1. Special Laws for Public Educational Personnel,
2. Local Public Enterprise Law,
3. Local Public Enterprise Labour Relations Law,
4. Law concerning Co-operative Societies of Local Public Service Personnel, and
5. Law concerning Accident Compensation for Local Public Service Personnel.

Special law for public educational personnel is also called Law No. 1 of 1949. It was enacted for the purpose of smooth running of the educational institutions and therefore consists of all the rules pertaining to the service conditions of teachers and other educational employees.

Local public enterprise law is called Law No. 292 of 1952. The purpose of its enactment was to make rules for the smooth administration of the local public enterprises.

Local public enterprise labour relations law is called Law No. 298 of 1952. It consists of the rules regarding the rights, duties, and other benefits available to the employees of the local public enterprises so as to avoid unnecessary conflict in relations between the employees and the management.

Law concerning cooperative societies of local public service personnel or Law No. 152 of 1962 as it is called in brief, provides for the management of cooperative societies of local public officials. It also provides the stipulations for long and short-term benefit payments.

Law concerning accident compensation for the local public service personnel is known as Law No.121 of 1967. It has provided the rules and guidelines in cases where disease or injury or accident occurred during the course of duty.

All the above-mentioned provisions are applied to all local public entities throughout Japan irrespective of the size or population of the local public body.

X

AMENDMENTS IN THE LOCAL PUBLIC SERVICE PERSONNEL SYSTEM

The following have been the amendments in the local public service personnel system:

1. In 1979, an amendment was made in the system of cooperative societies of local civil servants. It was revised and, after the revision, the eligible age for pension was increased to 60 years.
2. In the same year 1979, an amendment was made on the recommendation of the National Personnel Authority to terminate and postpone pay raises for older employees.
3. In April 1981, there was an amendment made in the number of off-days. According to this amendment, a four-week-five-holidays system was adopted, under which local public officials have, by alternation, an extra day off every four Saturdays.

4. In November 1981, a law was promulgated fixing the retirement age at 60 in principle for all the employees of the local public bodies.

Besides this amendment, a variety of revisions were made in the personnel management and administration. These revisions include: (a) revision of compensation and retirement allowances, and (b) stricter observance of the predetermined number of employees in local public entities.

Reasons Behind the Amendments and Revisions: The various amendments and revisions in the local public service personnel system were largely the reactions to the rapid economic and social changes, which may be enumerated as under:

(a) Aging of the population,
(b) the rise in general education percentage,
(c) diversified life-style of the people,
(d) demands for varied services,
(e) a shift from high economic growth to a more moderate level, and
(f) tighter financial conditions.

Still attempts are to be made to reform the employment conditions of the local public bodies and the civil service system, to be reviewed further in order to meet the needs of the times.

XI

PRE-WAR RELATIONSHIP BETWEEN NATIONAL AND LOCAL GOVERNMENT

In the pre-war Imperial Constitution, known as the Meiji Constitution, there was no provision for local autonomy. However, here and there the words 'local authorities' were frequently used.

After the Meiji Restoration in the 1890s, the local autonomy system was established and the then Meiji Government promulgated four Local Autonomy Laws, which established the following systems:

(a) Fu-Ken-Sei (City system),
(b) Shi-Sei (City system),
(c) Cho-Son-Sei (Town and village system), and
(d) Gun-Sei (County system).

The gun-Sei was abolished in 1921, but the other laws remained in force until the reform measures adopted after World War II.

Limited Suffrage: All Fu and Ken as well as Shi, Cho, and Son did have local assemblies, but the members of these local assemblies were elected by popular vote of limited suffrage, which means that all the citizens of voting age were not allowed the right to vote and only the selected few were entitled to elect the members of the local assemblies.

Dominance of Imperial Ordinances: The Imperial Ordinances, which were known as *Chihoukan-Kansei*, clearly indicated that the Governors and other local officers appointed by the Emperor were subject to the supervision and control of the Minister of Home Affairs in respect of the personnel and organization of local authorities. In fact, the Imperial Ordinances made the Governors and other local officials the *Agents* of the national government. Although *Fu* and *Ken* were classified as local authorities, in reality they were no more than administrative regions of the national government, because the local assemblies of *Fu* and *Ken* were composed of the local magnates, who were elected by limited vote and were entrusted with the only right of approving the revenue and expenditure budgets. If the reality is to be exposed, the major role of these local assemblies was merely to agree to bear the expenses of the national administrative affairs.

Relationship between Fu or Ken with Shi, Cho or Son

Shi, Cho and *Son* were the subordinates of *Fu* and *Ken*; and the relationship between them was the same as that between the national government and *Fu* or *Ken*. The authorities of *Shi, Cho* or *Ken* managed most of the affairs under the supervision and control of the Governors of *Fu* or *Ken*.

Under such circumstances, inter-governmental relations, established in the 1890's were nothing more than a highly centalized administrative system wherein the national government had an upper hand in all respects,

XII

NATIONAL-LOCAL GOVERNMENT RELATIONS BETWEEN 1921 AND 1945

During the 1920s, Japan experienced rapid industrialization and urbanization. As a result of this development, the urban area governments faced the problems of housing, transportation and sanitation, while the rural area governments were confronted with the problems of poverty and stagnant tax revenue. Due to political awareness among the intellectuals which spread upto a wage-worker and farmers, political participation by the people in the administration of the local assemblies gradually increased, and the control by the national government shifted to the financial aspects.

Right to Vote

The right to vote, which was limited to a selected few or local magnates, was now expanded to the male citizens of the locality owing to a revision in the Local Autonomy Law in 1925. Due to this revision, some restrictions were imposed on the powers of the Minister of Home Affairs and Governors regarding the administration of local governments.

Law-Making Power to Local Assemblies

Till 1928 the role of the local assemblies was merely to agree to bear the expenses of national administrative affairs. In 1929 an epoch-making amendment was made in the Local Autonomy Law, according to which the assemblies of *Fu* and *Ken* were vested with the power to enact law for their own administration, i.e., the local assemblies for the first time in 1929 were vested with the regulation-making power.

The national government continued to exercise its power through financial control. From 1931 to 1934 the national government embarked on the subsidy programmes for the public works projects in rural areas. In 1936 and 1937 general revenues were granted with the establishment of the Special Subsidy Systems of *Shi, Cho, Son* and *Fu, Ken*. In 1940, the Local Apportionment Tax System was established, which has now developed into a local allocation tax grant system. The national government appointed governors as its 'local agents' to execute national administrative affairs, and thus reinforced and continued its control over the local governments through subsidies and grants.

In fact, during this period the financial management of the local governments became deeply intertwined with national finance, and as a result the relationship between the national and local governments become much closer.

Demand of Liberal Intellectuals

The liberal intellectuals were not satisfied with the grant of the right to vote only. They demanded that full local autonomy of *Fu* and *Ken* be provided through popular election of Governors. But the political impact of this demand was thought to be too drastic and hence their demand was not accepted until after World War II.

XIII

POST-WAR RELATIONSHIP BETWEEN NATIONAL AND LOCAL GOVERNMENTS

After accepting the Potsdam Declaration of August 15, 1945 Japan experienced various kinds of political, economic and social reforms under the direction of the occupying allied powers. As a result, the relations between the national and local governments also experienced many significant changes.

A chapter on local self-government was included in the Constitution of Japan. The Prefectural Governors and Mayors were no longer nominated by the national government, rather they were elected by the Direct Popular Election method, in which the people of the locality participated directly and elected people of their choice as administrators. This was a remarkable institutional change in the local government system of Japan.

The second note-worthy change in the local government system was that the Prefectural and Municipal Governments emerged as fully autonomous entities with the Dual Representative Organs of Chief Executive Officers and their local public assemblies—both elected by direct popular vote. Now the prefectural governors evolved from local agents of the national government to the Representative of the residents, and the prefectural entities ceased to be mere administrative regions of the national government.

The next remarkable change was the enactment of the Local Autonomy Law, which came into effect simultaneously along with the Constitution of Japan. In December 1947, the Ministry of Home Affairs was dismantled but has now again been revived with some allegedly restricted powers.

Although there was a visible impact of implementation of direct popular vote system for the election of prefectural governors, the prefectural governors enjoy the 'delegated power' to execute national administrative affairs, which makes them to a great extent independent of the jurisdiction of the local assembly, but directly responsible to the central minister concerned.

This system is now referred to as the *Kikan-Inin-Jimu* system, and invites criticism from the proponents of the autonomy for the local public assemblies. This *Kikan-Inin-Jimu* system, although a most controversial issue and full of contradictions, reallocates the jurisdiction and functions and forms the basis of relations between the national government and local governments.

XIV

THE KIKAN-ININ-JIMU SYSTEM

The focus of the post-war reforms in the Constitution was how to administer under the new constitution national administrative matters which were previously delegated to the prefectural governors and the mayors. The solution found out was to appoint prefectural governors, mayors and administrative agencies as 'agents' of the national government to delegate to them the power to deal exclusively with the national administrative affairs in accordance with the laws and ordinances.

The *Kikan-Inin-Jimu* (Agency Delegated-Functions) system is subject to various limitations and restrictions, which limit the autonomy of the local governments. The prefectural governors are under the control and supervision of the national government for the implementation of the directives and ordinances regarding the national administrative affairs. The competent minister directs and supervises, the governor in turn directs and supervises the heads or the municipalities, i.e., the mayor. That is why, this system is not fundamentally different from the *Chi-ho-kan-Kansei* system of the pre-war Meiji Constitution.

Beyond Local Assemblies' Jurisdiction

Although *Kikan-Inin-Jimu* activities are carried out with the organization, personnel and the budget of the local governments, the Local Assemblies don't have any decision-making power over these activities. They have neither the right to review the official papers nor the power to inspect or examine the execution of these administrative affairs. The only power they have is 'the right to demand explanation from the Chief Executive Officer and to express their opinions.'

Mandamus in Character

The *Kikan-Inin-Jimu* activities are mandamus by nature and contain the mandatory provisions. If the execution of these activities is deemed to be contrary to the provisions of law or the ordinance issued regarding them, the competent minister may order the governor to take appropriate action. But if the said governor fails to observe the orders of the competent minister upon approval from the High Court, the Prime Minister can remove such a governor from his office. The same procedure is applied between prefectural governors and mayors, and the governors are also vested with the same powers as the competent minister.

The Number of Kikan-Inin-Jimu Increasing Day by Day

The number of *Kikan-Inin-Jimu* laws has been increasing significantly in the post-war period. At the end of 1980, the number of such related laws was approximately 550 out of approximately 2200 laws in effect. Among the activities of the prefectural governments, nearly 70 to 80 percent are *Kikan-Inin-Jimu.*

To conclude, the *de-facto* control and supervision over the governors and mayors is observed by the national government through these *Kikan-Inin-Jimu* activities and laws.

XV
LOCAL AUTONOMY LAW

According to Article 2 Paragraph 10 of the Local Autonomy Law, the local governments have no jurisdiction over the following matters.

(a) Judicial matters,
(b) Punishment and national disciplinary actions,
(c) National transportation and communication,
(d) Postal services,
(e) National educational and training institutions,
(f) National hospitals and medical treatment,
(g) National navigation, meteorology and water-ways, and
(h) National museums and libraries.

Paragraph 3 of Article 2 of the Local Autonomy Law specifies 22 activities as illustrations of the scope of the responsibilities of the local governments:

Article 6 of the Local Autonomy Law specifies the following 4 criteria to be employed in determining the responsibilities of the prefectural governments:

1. Sphere of administration,
2. Necessity of unified administration,
3. Communication and adjustment among municipal government, and
4. Administration deemed not appropriate to be handled by the municipal governments.

This Article also provides that individual judgements should be based on these four criteria.

Article 158 of the Local Autonomy Law specifies in detail the internal organization of the prefectural governments. This Article has crearly specified that if a governor intends to create an organization which does not conform to the provisions of Article 158, he must consult the Minister of Home Affairs beforehand. It is also provided that the local governments must establish Administrative Agencies, as provided by ordinances for the purpose of administering delegated administrative activities, i.e., the local government should constitute Special Local Administrative Agencies for that purpose.

At present there are approximately 85 laws administered by 14 Central Ministries and Agencies, and probably the total number of special local administrative agencies amounts to 181. The number of special local administrative agencies was only 4 at the end of World War II, but by 1955 it had increased to 122.

This is really a new mechanism which, the national government introduced to control the local governments under the post-war Constitution.

7

Japan's Expanding Global Role

K.V. KESAVAN*

For about forty years, Japan had pursued what is known as the 'Yoshida Doctrine' which emphasised internal economic reconstructions, advocated a low-key foreign policy profile, encouraged only minimal defence capabilities and placed a premium on security alliance with the United States. The Yoshida Doctrine worked very well and Japan was a beneficiary of the cold war. In the uncertain post-cold war era, substantial sections of people, both in official and non-official circles, feel the need for Japan to made departures from the traditional line. The end of the cold war and the collapse of the Soviet Union have placed Japan at a crucial threshold in international politics. To be sure, Japan has been carefully nurturing an expanded political and economic role, especially in the last couple of years, and in the emerging new international order, it is certain to display greater activism.

What are the factors that give credibility to an expanded Japanese role? Japan's tremendous economic and technological power warrants a bigger role in global politics. It accounts now for about 18 per cent of the world GNP and 15 per cent of global trade. It has emerged as the biggest ODA donor. In 1991, it surpassed the US and contributed a total ODA of

* Professor of Japanese Studies, Jawaharlal Nehru University, New Delhi.

over $11 billion, Japan's overseas investments have not only grown sharply in volume, but have reached all corners of the globe. The total volume of its overseas investments during 1951-91 amounted to $352.3 billion. The shares of the different major regions are as follows: USA $148.5 billion, Europe $68.6 billion, Asia $53.4 billion, South America $43.8 billion, and Africa $43.8 billion. Japan's annual R & D expenditure has markedly increased in recent years. In 1975, Japan spent only $8.8 billion on R & D, but in 1990, the volume jumped to $90 billion accounting for 3.51 per cent of the GNP. Japan spends much more than any European country. As a percentage to GNP, Japan spends even more than the US.

Japan is the second biggest financial contributor to the United Nations. What is worthy of note is that its contribution is almost equal to the combined contributions of Britain, France and China, three of the five permanent members of the UN Security Council. Further, Japan's monetary contributions to multilateral financial institutions, such as the IMF, the World Bank, the Asian Development Bank, etc., are truly massive and second only to those of the US. These contributions remained big enough even prior to the end of the cold war. But in the 1990's Japan seems to have targeted these institutions to obtain greater voting shares. Japan knows that an active presence in these institutions, backed by formidable financial contributions, would inevitably help it deal with crucial issues leading thereby to an assumption of greater global responsibilities. The increasing role of Japan in these bodies has also made it stake its claim to some of the managerial positions. The ADB always has a Japanese as its President. In the post-cold war years when developing countries are increasingly opting for economic liberalisation programmes, their reliance on these financial bodies has become greater. Japan, by virtue of its strong position in these bodies, has opportunities to deal with their economic as well as political problems. Japan's use of political criteria for extending aid to East European countries and Russia is a case in point. Kaifu Toshiki, the then Japanese Prime Minister, had said, "Democracy, freedom and a market economy must be the framework for any country offered assistance."

Second, any projection of Japan's global role would depend upon the democratic situation. Politically, the reforms introduced by the Allied Occupation (1945-52) have taken strong roots and the present constitutional system has enjoyed a high degree of legitimacy. The political system is supported by a population which has recorded almost

100 per cent literacy. Public awareness of political and economic issues is maintained by a free and vigilant press, and popular rights are protected by the judiciary.

Notwithstanding the confusion created by the LDP spill in 1993, Japan has enjoyed a fair degree of political stability. Of course, the dominance of the LDP contributed to that stability. The cold war exerted its influence on Japan's domestic politics, in that political parties were branded either conservative or progressive mainly on the basis of the positions they took on such issues as the US-Japan Security Pact, the Constitution, and so on. But the conservative-progressive divide is no longer valid with the establishment of the present coalition government consisting of seven parties including the socialists, the moderate socialists, Komcito, labour elements and the erstwhile LDP politicians.

Though the LDP had been losing popular support for several years now, few could have anticipated its fall in such a dramatic way. Having failed to gauge the implications of its dismal defeat in the 1989 Upper House election, it did precious little to rid itself of the corrupt practices. What the electorate wanted was the restoration of ethics in public life. But Miyazawa Kiichi, the then Prime Minister, had refused to address the issue of political reforms earnestly. The upshot was that in the face of rising popular demand for such reforms, he could not hold together the different factions of his own party. The political reforms debate, in one sense, highlighted a basic generation gap, and the party split occurred because the younger elements could not relate to old-timers such as Kanemaru Shin.

Prime Minister Morihiro Hosokawa stated in his speech at the UN on September 27, 1993: "The post-cold war era opened not just a new page, but a whole chapter in Japanese politics." He is right, and Japanese politics is at an important transitional stage. Many issues which were long considered taboos are being discussed freely now. The Social Democratic Party of Japan (SDPJ, till recently the Japan Socialist Party), for instance, has come a long way in trying to shed many of its ideological inhibitions. It is an important partner in the coalition government and holds six portfolios. Assumption of power has brought a good deal of moderation to its attitudes. Its earlier positions on such issues as the Japanese flag, national anthem, the status of the self-defence forces, civilian nuclear programme, etc., have either changed or are in the process of review. It has built new bridges of understanding with South

Korea which it had refused to recognised earlier. Its previous stand of 'no constitutional amendment at any cost' has given way to a more realistic assessment of the need for Japan to change in tune with global circumstances.

In fact, with the exception of the Communists, no other party is totally opposed to constitutional amendments. Yamahana Sadao, former SDPJ Chairman and now a cabinet minister, expressed in April 1993 his willingness to join debates in defining Japan's role in world affairs under the Constitution. It was he who put forward his formula, known as Soken, which sought to implement the constitution pragmatically while maintaining its spirit. It is to the credit of the younger elements within the party, that they would have propelled a moment towards a review of its traditional policies and adoption of pragmatism in line with global trends. The traditional labour union base of the SDPJ has also eroded and the new labour federation, *Rengo*, is strongly inclined to align with the younger elements free from traditional ideological bonds. The *Zaikai* or such business groups as the Keidanren, the Keizai Doyukai and the Nikkeiren have quickly adjusted themselves to the political change and stated: "If the coalition government, excluding the LDP, is the answer to the public's desire for change, we must accept it."

Japanese politics, until recently, was so sharply polarised that it was almost impossible to think in terms of a coalition between the conservatives and the socialists (SDPJ). But a coalition government of seven parties of divergent viewpoints has come to power on the understanding that they would not change the basic policies of the previous government. Though the glue of power and the zeal for political reforms have held them together, it is still a challenging task for Hosokawa to reconcile their differences. For instance, he had to withdraw his proposal to increase the consumption tax, because of stiff resistance particularly from the SDPJ. Nor was it easy for him to get the political reforms passed by the Diet. Having faced defection within his own camp, leading to the defeat of the reforms bill in the Upper House, he was forced to make concessions to the LDP to have the bill endorsed by the Lower House. It was politically very risky for the LDP to oppose the reforms, lest it should incur the anger of the electorate. But before the LDP struck a compromise, it obtained major concessions from Hosokawa and, more importantly, succeeded in exposing the fragile base of the coalition.

Though Hosokawa has talked about political idealism in eloquent terms, he knows the ground realities only too well. He has to perform tight-rope walking to carry on the administration. How will it affect policy-making in Japan? Even during the years of LDP's rule, policy decisions took a long time due to the Japanese way of consensus-building. In the present fluid political situation, the formulation and implementation of policy decisions will be far more delayed. Now the Japanese Diet has become the central decision-making organ. This indeed has been so since the mid-1970's when, following the Lock-heed scandal, the political fortunes of the LDP started declining. The changes embodied in the electoral reforms are, therefore, important since they will ultimately have a great hearing on the complexion of the Diet after the next general election.

Neither the end of the cold war nor the collapse of the LDP has posed any immediate threat to the US-Japan alliance. The coalition partners in the Japanese Government have agreed to continue the broad lines of the foreign policy of the previous administration. Alliance with the US, therefore, continues to be the core of Japan's diplomacy. The two main aspects of the US-Japan bilateral relations—security and economic relations—need to be noted.

The end of the cold war naturally raised the question of the relevance of the alliance among the Japanese. The 1992 Diplomatic Bluebook admitted that the alliance, following the collapse of the cold war structures, has become "less persuasive" among the public. But opinion surveys conducted since then have indicated continued public support to the alliance.

On security, despite the elimination of the communist threat, Japan and the US have reiterated the need for maintaining the alliance in order to combat regional conflicts, arms race, ethnic and religions fundamentalism, etc. The Tokyo Declaration, signed by President George Bush and Prime Minister Miyazawa Kiichi in January 1992, talked eloquently about their shared security concerns. Later, president Bill Clindon, in his meetings with Miyazawa, emphasised the importance of the alliance and called US-Japanese relationship "the most important bilateral relationship in the world". In his three meetings with Hosokawa, he showed the same degree of interest in US-Japan security ties.

A strong convergence of interests continues to mark their security ties. One does not now hear of US complaints about Japan's 'free ride', because Japan has already fulfilled many of the American demands. The size of Japan's defence spending has been quite satisfactory to

Washington. Particularly Japan's expenditure of $5 billion by way of host-nation support to the US bases has been recognised by the US Congress and the Pentagon as very generous. Further, both countries have strengthened their mutual co-operation significantly in the field of defence technology.

Both have a shared perception that the North Korean nuclear programme poses a grave threat to the East Asian region. They have worked closely together to exert pressure on Pyongyang to submit its nuclear programme to international inspection. Hosokawa made a pointed reference to it in his UN speech in September 1993. Later, he discussed the issue with South Korea in order to promote tripartite understanding on the issue. Japan strongly supports the NPT regime and has categorically argued for its indefinite extension beyond 1995. Besides it has succeeded in bringing China under the NPT. It has held significant talks with both India and Pakistan to persuade them to join the NPT. Japan is also a strong supporter of the Missile Technology Control Regime (MTCR).

Both the US and Japan have shared concerns on a variety of problems affecting the Asia-Pacific region, the Middle East, Europe, etc. Japan desires continued American presence in the Asian Pacific, as a 'stabilizing factor'. It knows that a sudden American withdrawal would arouse the region's suspicion about Japan. The Asia-Pacific countries also consider the US a restraining influence on Japan. The APEC summit meeting held in Seattle in November 1993 demonstrated it.

One should also note how Japan's perceptions on certain issues have differed from those of the US. Japan's attitude towards China, since the Tiananmen incident, has been diametrically opposed to that of the US. Since the Houston G-7 meeting, Japan has resumed its economic assistance to China on the ground that it would be imprudent to isolate China. It has called upon the western countries to pay due consideration to China's sensitivity, instead of blindly applying western standards of human rights and democracy to assess the Chinese situation. In the case of economic aid to Russia too, Japanese and American perceptions have differed rather sharply.

The real source of bilateral irritation is seen in the economic sphere. US-Japan economic relations have become too massive and unwieldy. During the cold war years, the threat of a common enemy made the US take a benign attitude towards what it now considers "the narrow mercantilist policies of Japan". But now, as the Japanese economy has grown strong and its technology highly competitive, the US feels threatened. To be sure, serious economic frictions did occur even during the 1970s and 1980s, but were managed skilfully, by such mechanisms as voluntary export restrictions, etc.

Basically there is a glaring asymmetry in their bilateral trade and investment, and this imbalance has not been corrected for too long a time. In 1992-93, Japan enjoyed a trade surplus of $59.3 billion. Similarly, the cumulative Japanese investment in the US during 1951-91 was $148.5 billion, but US investment in Japan during the same period was only $9.9 billion. The usual American complaint is that, whereas Japan has full and free access to their market, the US does not enjoy the same privilege in Japan. They further believe that Japan makes no efforts to open its market unless strong external pressure (*gaiatsu*) is exerted.

In an effort to ease the situation, both Clinton and Miyazawa met in July 1993 at Tokyo and agreed to set up a specific framework to address a wide range of macro-economic, structural, trade and investment issues. Since the commencement of his presidency, Clinton has adopted a tough policy under pressure from US Congress and business circles. He has shown his keenness to set numerical targets in order to reduce Japan's trade surplus, and obtain results in "tangible forms". The US Trade Representative, Micky Kantor, stated: "We intend to use qualitative and quantitative measures in each and every sector to measure success." President Clinton warned: "We are going to try to pursue a much more aggressive policy now, which will actually open markets. We are going to try some different things to push that (Japanese) market open."

Japan is totally opposed to the policy of fixing numerical targets. In a democracy, it argues, numerical targets would means only managed economy. It was under the heat of these basic differences, that the Clinton-Hosokawa summit was held on 11 February, and expectedly, the meeting failed to produce any result. The US has now revived the use of Super 301 provision of the Trade Act of 1988. This is a major crisis situation in the bilateral relations since the end of the cold war, and calls for utmost tact and negotiating skill on both sides to manage it.

Two factors that will add considerable weight to Japan's role in global politics are: (a) its expanding role in the UN peace-keeping activities, and (b) its growing ODA.

(a) Japan's impressive financial contribution to the UN has already been noted. In addition, it has given full support to various UN measures in the sphere of disarmament. It has used the UN as an instrument for expanding its political role. It has participated in several UN peace-keeping operations by sending election monitors, volunteers, etc., to the countries concerned. In 1992, in the wake of the Gulf War, it passed the International Peace Co-operation Law and sent defence personnel for the first time along with civilians. But so far, Japan has not participated in peace-keeping operations involving the use of force, and in collective security operations, such as the Gulf War. It could not do so ostensibly because of Article 9 of the Constitution, which is interpreted as denying Japan the right to participate in collective security.

The important question that follows is: Since the UN Security Council is predicated upon the principle of collective security, can Japan, otherwise an eminently suitable candidate for permanent membership of the Council, hope to assume that conveted status? Japan's experience as a peace-keeper in Cambodia has enhanced its prestige. It played a major role in convening a conference for the economic reconstruction of Cambodia and contributed a substantial volume of assistance. In that process, it had numerous occasions to interact with the concerned factions involved in Cambodian peace and had been very much involved in political issues. The Japanese Government is getting the people prepared for a national debate on the question of Japan's participation in UN peace-keeping operations involving the use of force.

(b) Economic assistance is another important instrument used by Japan to bolster its global role. Japan's official aid flows to all parts of the world, truly in tune with the globalisation of its diplomacy. Asia which used to get a lion's share continues to be the biggest recipient with a reduced share of 51 per cent, followed by the Middle East (20.4%) and Africa (11.4%). Japan's aid is now flowing in a big way to Russia and the East European countries. Both the US and Japan consult one another on the distribution of ODA, and Japan's aid is soon likely to carry conditionalities. In April 1991, Tokyo announced its ODA guidelines outlining the criteria that would govern aid in future—(1) trends in military expenditure by the recipient countries; (2) trends in arms exports; (3) trends in the promotion of market economy; and (4) trends in human rights and environment. These conditionalities have still not been enforced by Japan. But in the uncertain post-cold war atmosphere, Japan could gradually put them into effect.

8

The First Phase of the Strategy of Japanese Rearmament: Some Intellectual Arguments**

S.J. NOUMOFF*

Is Japan, the only nation traumatized by the obscenity of nuclear weapons in the forefront of the struggle against nuclear militarism, or is Japan a pariah nation deprived of the natural right of self-protection and committed to the imperative of bringing military power into symmetry with her demonstrated economic power?

On this, the fortieth anniversary since the defeat of Japanese facism, Japan faces a cross-roads. Over these four decades one of the dominant features of Japan's political landscape has been a profound commitment to the portrayal of Hiroshima and Nagasaki as a surrealist glimpse into our own future, together, multiplied 650,000 times. While the Japanese peace movement in tandem with the political left have maintained the issue at the highest level of political consciousness, it is the thesis of this paper that we are presently at the cutting edge of a reversal of this momentum via a systematic multi-faceted campaign, with a patient time

* Department of Political Science, McGill University.

** Prepared for the International Symposium on the Reunification of Korea and Peace in Asia at the Yokohama International Conference Hall, Japan from July 6-8, 1985.

horizon cresting sometime before the end of this century, the consequences of which bode ill for the realization of both peace and justice in north-east Asia.

Nineteen eighty-five is a critical year, not as the consequence of the emergence of any totally new factors—all have been present as independent ones since minimally 1950—but rather owing to the convergence of a number of them, approaching critical mass. The most significant among them are: (1) the second term of Nakasone Yasuhiro as Prime Minister, (2) the second term of Ronald Reagan as President, (3) the intellectual character of 'revisionist historiography', (4) the concurrent strength and vulnerability of Japan's economy combined with shifting age distribution.

NAKASONE-ISM

The unanimous re-election of Nakasone Yasuhiro as President of the Liberal Democratic Party on 31 October 1984 is significant for two reasons; his long standing philosophy of right-wing nationalism, and the less than usual second term itself, as opposed to the more usual pattern of factional rotation of the Party Presidency and concurrent Prime Ministership.

The relevance of Nakasone's second term is that it represents the ultra right within the conservative movement with a commitment to the establishment of a new consensus. In an interview earlier this year he attacked the policies of the MacArthur occupation administration for 'foster[ing] communist by [adopting] measures advocated by the Japan Communist Party'.[1] Further in the interview he mocked the occupation administration's listing his own organization (Seiunjuku) as a 'rightist' movement.[2] Within two weeks of gaining the second term he outlined the goal of his administration as 'The promotion of a comprehensive security policy that would also guarantee the availability of food, energy and natural resources for the Japanese people'.[3] An almost banal statement for the head of a government to make, one which would go virtually unnoticed anywhere in the world but Japan. A periodic check of Nakasone's record would place his position unequivocally in context. In 1953 he began his public defence of the need to revise the Constitution. During the Prime-Ministership of Sato Eisaku, Nakasone's stewardship of the 'Self Defence Agency', begun in January 1970, resulted in two foreboding initiatives: (1) the prospect for the first time that Japan would acquire nuclear weapons, and (2) discussion of the need for buffer room in the form of a defense periphery.[4] By 1978 he had developed a full scale rationalisation of the current policy. In September of that year he penned an article for *Seiron*[5], the major points of which are as follows:

(1) As the superpowers' ability to directly intervene decreases, the prospects for small wars increases.

(2) Inadequate military capability may itself become the cause of conflict.

(3) The greatest danger to peace is the existence of a military vacuum.

(4) The military capacity of a state should be sufficient to make a potential enemy realize that an invasion cannot succeed, as their causalty rate would be too high.

(5) The defence mission changes with circumstances and developments, and 'at *this stage* [emphasis added] Japan will not posses ICBM's, aircraft carriers and other material that is clearly offensive in nature.....'

(6) The Japanese Constitution was drawn up by the occupation authorities and is not the expression of the 'complete free will' of the Japanese people.

(7) 83% of the population support the 'Self-Defence Force', with 48% being of the opinion that it did not violate the Constitution, 30% being uncertain and 20% believing it to be unconstitutional. (Even accepting these figures, 5% of the respondents supported the 'SDF' believing it to be unconstitutional). This runs totally in conflict with a survey conducted by Miyata Mitsuo to the effect that 80% of the population were in favour of unarmed resistance should an invasion take place.[6]

(8) Sometime between 1983 and 1988 the Japanese people should be asked if they are satisfied with the Constitution, and if they are not a two step amending procedure should be adopted: (i) Diet amendment, to be followed by, (ii) a national referendum.

It is clear from the last of these points that a five to ten year plan was envisaged in order to set the context for a reversal of the policies of these last forty years. Policies, especially ones as deep seated as the role of military policy within Japan, cannot be changed apocalyptically. It requires a carefully crafted scenario led by the maestro who first points to one actor to be answered in sequence by another. The intellectual content of the move towards reversal must be a questioning. To be followed by a rejection, of the premises which underlay the currently accepted Article 9 limitations. Is there evidence to suggest that the maestro has raised his baton? Clearly, the answer to this is yes. Can we dismiss the opening chords as merely the ratings of a maniacal fringe? If the answer to this was yes in the past, it is in my view no at this time. There is just a sufficient element of apparent truth in their position to make an argument of pseudo-credibility.

Prior to presenting this evidence, I would like to set the 1950 to 1978 period in context as a chronology.[7]

July 8, 1956—General MacArthur wrote to the then Prime Minister Yoshida Shigeru ordering the establishment of a 75,000 man police reserve. Simultaneously the U.S. effectively began to support Japan's rearmament.

October 4, 1952[8]—The U.S. Ambassador to Japan cabled Washington that Prime Minister Yoshida had agreed to amend Article 9 of the Constitution. Yoshida stalled and never attempted a formal constitutional revision.

March 1954—U.S and Japan signed four mutual security act agreements.

July 1954—The Japanese government announced that 'Article 9 of the Constitution prohibits the maintenance of war potential whether for aggression or self-defence. In this sense war potential means the ability to conduct modern warfare. It is not unconstitutional to maintain a force that does not amount to war potential.' The 'Self-Defence Force' was then organized out of the Police Reserve in a truly masterful stroke of Orwellian misuse of language.

June 16, 1955—Prime Minister Hatoyama Ichiro stated before the Diet Cabinet Committee 'it is not unconstitutional to maintain minimum war potential'. The Government then announced that 'it is possible to attack enemy bases for purposes of self-defense.'

May 1957—The National Defence Council announced that 'Japan will gradually improve its defense power to make it more efficient within the necessary limits of self-defense *in accord with national power and conditions'* (emphasis added). During the Kishi administration an official interpretation of Act 9 stated that the 'stationing of Japanese forces overseas and possessing nuclear weapons were not unconstitutional'.[9]

1960[10]—Revision of the U.S.-Japan security treaty and an oral understanding between the U.S. and Japanese governments whereby Japan approved the 'introduction' or 'transit' of nuclear weapons on American ships and planes in Japan. (This obviously ran totally contrary to the principle of prohibiting nuclear weapons on Japanese soil).

1964—Nuclear powered and armed submarine 'Sea Dargon' entered Sassebo naval station.

1968—Nuclear powered and armed air-craft carrier Enterprise entered Sassebo naval station.

—F-4 fighter adopted by the 'Self-Defence Forces' with the bomb sights and in-flight refueling capability removed. (Five years later in 1973, when the 'Self-Defence Forces' upgraded their air capacity by adopting the F-15, both the bomb sights and the inflights refueling capability remained on the air-craft).

January 1970—Nakasone Tasuhiro becomes Director-General of the 'Self-Defence Agency'. He introduces a two pronged programme: (1) Japan should adopt a self-reliant defense policy on the premise that each country should be responsible for its own defense; (2) in peace time Japan should command the air space and sea lanes proximate to the country, while in war time she should be prepared to extend this control to international air space and the high seas. (By October 9, 1972 these proposals had been rejected as policy by the government, and Nakasone's elevation to Prime Ministership was awaited in order to be repudiated.)

February 1972—Japanese government sources attribute remarks to Chinese Premier Zhou Enlai critical of the Japan Socialist Party proposal for 'unarmed neutrality'.

February 1, 1973—The Self-Defence Agency' announces a forces target of 13 Divisions (180,000 troops), four to five naval escort flotillas (280,000 tons), plus eight air-wings and one mixed corps (800 air craft).

December 1974—Officers within the 'Self-Defence Agency' begin to publicly argue that defence is necessitated by war not by peace, and that if Japanese military expenditures were maintained at the level of the 1% 'national consensus' an invading military force could not be defeated.

January 30, 1978—The Director-General of the Cabinet Legislation Bureau, Sanada Hideo, called for changes in existing limitations on 'self-defence' *in accordance with scientific and technological progress* (emphasis added).

March 9, 1978—The Japanese government declared that 'possession of [nuclear weapons] is not prohibited as long as it does not exceed the minimum requirements of self-defense'.

February 14, 1978—The 'Self-Defence Agency' declared that 'the only weapons prohibited by the Constitution were those intended exclusively [emphasis added] for the destruction of foreign territory'.

July 24, 1978—Chief-of-Staff General Karisu Hiroomi was dismissed after announcing that in case of invasion front-line commanders would have to take action prior to civilian authorization. By August of 1978 the government began to seriously consider approving this very same policy.

This chronology should clearly demonstrate two central features: (1) a pro-conventional armament core group has expanded to include nuclear armaments, and (2) the core group has gained incremental momentum with an exponential increase since the first stage of the Nakasone administration. Having thus achieved both minimum numbers plus political legitimacy the construction of the new consensus has begun. 'Nakasoneism' therefore means nothing more nor less than the legitimization of the new militarism.

THE NEW CONSENSUS

The strategy aimed at achieving the new consensus is multi-faceted, designed to crest, as previously indicated, some time between 1983 and 1988. The first stage of the process necessarily includes an attitude shift on both the causes and nature of World War II on the one hand, and on the other hand a reassessment of the entire 'Meiji' period. This preparatory stage is to be followed by a campaign aimed at shedding the Constitutional and psychological fetters imposed on Japan as a consequence of her 1945 defeat. It will likely be structured in the vocabulary of restoring Japan's authenticity which was emasculated during and subsequent to the occupation. The first line of attack will occur on the intellectual front, rather than as a direct government initiative. The government, for its part, will establish a hospitable and receptive cultural environment. Once this has been achieved, the public debate will 'naturally' begin on broad Constitutional change, to which the government will, in the discharge of its 'democratic' responsibility, simply respond with a referendum.

In the present period we are in a intellectual phase led by 'revisionist' historians, a group which henceforth I will refer to as the Yasekuni-ists. How have they crafted their argument?

Sanitization of Language—Rather than discuss the period of 1930 to 1945 in the language of aggression, imperialism or expansionism, the language of discourse itself is being changed. We now find a far more neutral vocabulary: 'The 100 Years War''[11], 'The 15 Year War'[12], 'The Manchurian Affair',[13] 'The China Affair',[14] 'The Greater East Asian War'[15] and 'The Pacific War'. All these terms share the common feature of removing any prejorative onus of Japanese responsibility for events which occurred during the period.

Redefinition of the Cause of World War II: Political Syllogisms-—(1) Japan, the Yasekune-ists argue, had two lofty objectives when the war began:[16] to safeguard herself, as do all countries as a matter of natural right; and to liberate Asia from the yoke of western domination. As all states recognize the right to self-defense, and virtually all of Asia, save some island nations, have been nominally freed from western colonialism, Japan has been historically vindicated. One application of this premise should suffice to illustrate its true character. If the premise is true, the Chinese people should be in the eternal debt of General Tojo: Japan's invasion of China permitted the Chinese to mobilize against the imperialists and even further permitted the Chinese Communist Party to dominate the anti-imperialism struggle. In this manner, Japan became the positive instrument of the Chinese revolution. The war, of course, had consequences for the colonialist system, but not the ones attributed to it by the Yasekuni-ists.

(2) Some have argued that Japan was confronted with only two choices in the 1930's: either to fight and perish or not fight and perish.[17] (Even if this were true rational choice would have dictated a far less severe cost if the latter option had been selected.) The imperative of survival left Japan with no choice but to fight, according to others. The U.S. had come to China's assistance and placed a noose around Japan's neck with the petroleum embargo and racist discrimination against Japanese exports. The Pearl Harbour air-strike by Japanese planes on the U.S. fleet consequently must be seen as a reaction to a U.S. initiation, and not first strike action.

(3) Three exemplary interpretations of the above referred language sanitization process instruct us in how to properly understand history.

(i) 100 *Years of War*[18]—The war in fact began in the last century, in 1863 and 1864, when Kagoshima and Shimonoseki were bombarded by the British and other westerners. The British had forced opium upon the Chinese and the Americans were stuffing the Indian population within its borders into cannons and blowing them up. Japan, cognizant of this reality, was determined not to permit comparable abuse of herself. Direct confrontation with the United States began at the turn of the century as a consequence of the American absorption of the Spanish pacific empire following the Spanish-American War. Pearl Harbor occurred as a consequence of the circumstances of the time when it became clear to Japan that the U.S. government had no intention of negotiating with her. Preceding this event, Japan's 'engagements' in China and Korea have been grossly over-simplified as aggression. Japan's goals were to free East Asia from British and American domination and establish the reality of self-determination and independence, and Asia was liberated. Even if the war was to be evaluated as hopeless from the outset, 'Yet the fight had to be fought, and Japan fought it'.

(ii) Greater East Asian War[19]—The abstraction of acts of war from the context of a given period, where an absolute standard is imposed divorced from the existence of an enemy, results in an erroneous conclusion that one's own troops acted in a barbarous and crazy fashion. Japan was humiliated by the Triple Intervention of 1895 when she was forced by Russia, France and Germany to return to Liaotung peninsula to China. This was nothing more than a gang-up by the established colonial powers on Japan, a kind of hazing of the colonial newcomer. International society is a bloody brutal jungle where the strong prey on the weak. All countries were living by this rule and it was unexplainable that Japan was singled out, save one: racism by European whites against Asian yellows. In the contemporary period, the failure by the entire Japanese nation to honour the dead who fought in defense of the country leaves their souls wandering in a state devoid of peace. A true Yasekunist argument.

(iii) Manchurian Incident[20]—Japan's behaviour in the 1930's bordered on the acceptable, given that of the other big powers of the period. The defeat by the Europeans, who dominated the League of Nations, of Japan's attempt to gain acceptance for an anti-racism clause was bitterly resented in Japan and persuaded the people that an international double standard was being employed. Exclusive responsibility for the outbreak of war cannot be placed at the feet of Japan, but rather blame must be shared by all powers. If we construct a moral/political balance sheet of the period we will find that while the allies had a slight advantage on the question of democracy versus fascism, Japan held the advantage on the question of equal application of a uniform standard against which action is to be judged. When we look at

the internment camps established by the American and Canadian governments for their own citizens of Japanese origin, even the democratic advantage of the west may be brought into question. Japan's sponsorship of the Indian National Army and the Indian Provisional Government enable India to achieve independence subsequent to the war.

How are we to evaluate these three positions? It is clear that there are elements of truth in the argumentation, but those truths are inserted as a facade behind which to provide legitimacy for absolving Japan from responsibility for the barbarism of Japanese imperialism. It is of course true that western imperialist nations ultimately bombed their way into Japan. A double standard in judging international behaviour combined with racism surely existed. Unquestionably, the expansion of United States economic and political power into the Pacific from the turn of the 20th Century brought a Japan-US. rivalry into closer proximity. But the truth of these statements does not transfer to the balance of the argument. The categorization of the occupation of Korea and the invasion of China as mere engagements is a surrealist rendering of history. As is the obfuscation of responsibility by employing the concept of complexity. Japan's strike against Pearl Harbor was not merely reactive to a *de facto* state of war declared by the U.S. nor did Japan launch the war as a regional war of national liberation. The existence of an enemy in wartime, both individual and national, does not *ipso facto* absolve either individual soldiers or national leaders for criminal culpability. This construction of an artificial equivalency can best be illustrated by expiating all accountability of those who fought in the military. We are witness to an attempt to resurrect the internal wartime propaganda in a vocabulary of respectability. A determinism which equates modernization with imperialism and war as the inevitable outcome of the historic process is, to say the least, a-historical.

Reassessment of the International Military Tribunal for the Far East (Tokyo War Crimes Trial)[21]—If the war itself has been totally misrepresented, it is clear from the Yasekune-ist perspective that Tokyo Trial must have been totally in error. The twenty-four members of the war government and the seven who were executed were merely victims of the victor's vengeance. The trial was both unfair and tinged with racism rather than justice. This unfairness was fanned by 'a succession of agitators and meddlers who wrote about all the terrible deeds that their countrymen had perpetrated'. The trial itself contained nine basic flaws.

(1) Unless there is a law there can be neither a crime nor a punishment. The juridical foundation of the trial, consequently, employed an *ex post facto* principle.

(2) No aggression was perpetrated against the USSR.

(3) Legitimate evidence was rejected (e.g., China was in a state of turbulence, Japan was fighting the expansion of communism, the U.S. declared *de facto* war on Japan on November 26, 1941, when Cordell Hull refused to assent to Japanese troops being stationed abroad, a situation inconsistent with the current U.S. policy of foreign bases).

(4) The Crimes Against Humanity Charge is hypocritical, as the U.S. bombed Japanese civilians which is an equal crime against humanity. Pearl Harbor on one side and Hiroshima and Nagasaki on the other side equalize on any reasonable balance sheet.

(5) The equation of Japan with Nazi Germany is inappropriate. Germany began with an ideology and committed aggression, while Japan with small incidents and then created an ideology. Japan also lacked systematic central control and a national core, being a democratic society. The Emperor failed to exercise his constitutional prerogative as he respected parliamentary democracy based on constitutional government.

(6) The attempt to impose a criterion of civilization upon the Japanese reflected nothing more than arrogance.

(7) Illegal acts were recognized under international law' individual criminal responsibility was not so recognized. While 'national leaders decided on acts of state and shipped up national support for their decisions they did not bear responsibility for the outcome of those decisions'.

(8) There was, simply put, a conspiracy to make Japan out as a villain.

(9) The court failed to call the most important witness, the Emperor himself.

In addition to these nine basic arguments, the proponents of this position further contend that international law itself was constructed by western powers as an instrument to serve their own interests, and therefore by extension could not be considered authentically international. History further teaches us that what is considered legal under international law during one period does not always coincide with justice.

How do these arguments measure up against an objective standard? Again, I contend, the record demonstrates an aspect of truth employed to mask a basic falsehood. International law was of course a European construction aimed at the regulation of their affairs to their mutual interest and revealed an arrogant ethnocentricism. It is also true that the coincidence of law and justice has always depended upon the viewer. Japanese civilian contributors to the war effort victimized by U.S. bombers, most especially the atomic incineration of those in Hiroshima and Nagasaki. Failure to call the Emperor as witness was clearly a political rather than a juridical decision; in order to spare him the fate of the seven.

Turning now to the fraudulently constructed arguments, even if we accept the legal paradigm presented, the concept of natural justice has always overrode the absence of specific legislation. The justification of aggression against China on the grounds that she was in a state of turbulence and communist expansion had to be combatted, borders on the profane. This twisted logic continues with the assertion that American failure to accept Japanese aggression against China was an American declaration of war against Japan. The forms which fascism took in Germany and Japan were of course somewhat different, but that difference was marginal and culturally specific, not representing a diverse political genre. Hitler, too, could have made the claim to democratic legitimacy based on his electoral victory. Remaining faithful to the pure logic of the argument, if Japanese imperialism was ''democratically'' and ''constitutionally'' authorized, then all Japanese should have been held criminally liable. Equally absurd is the argument that those who initiate acts are not culpably responsible for the consequences of those very acts.

In arriving at a judgement on the appropriateness of the Trial, it may be necessary to be reminded the activities of two units of the Kwangtung Army: 'The Water Supply and Prophylaxis Administration' and the 'Hippo-Epizootic Administration,'[22] after 1941, better known respectively as Detachment 731 and Detachment 100, commanded by Lt. General Ishii and Maj. General Wakamatsu. Minimally 3,000 Chinese, Korean, Russian and Mongolian nationals were systematically experimented upon until death, not to mention those experimented on in the field. Detachment 100 was charged with the production of bacteriological weapons, while 731 was responsible for the planning of bacteriological warfare. Fully operational, 731 had the capacity to produce 30 kg of plague bacteria monthly, in part to be carried on the rodent fleas produced in the 4,500 flea incubators and field tested in 1941 in the Changteh area of central China. Earlier in 1940 Detachment 731 experimented on Chinese troops with plague infected fleas disseminated through aircraft, bacteria saturated rain and water contamination. Branch 543 of Detachment 731 had approximately 13,000 rats prepared for this activity in the summer of 1945. 'Logs', or prisoners, were infected with typhoid, anthrax, plague and gas gangrene among other germs, sometimes by injection, other times through shrapnel fragments from infected bombs. In an attempt to improve prevention and treatment of frostbite, 'logs' had their limbs frozen prior to experimentation. When shrapnel bombs were employed the 'logs' had their heads and backs protected in order to prevent accidental death, while their buttocks and legs were left exposed. Starving Chinese prisoners were fed rolls which had previously been infected with typhoid bacteria. A partial further listing of experiments includes: extended X-ray radiation directed at the liver and other specific organs, the pumping of horse and monkey blood into prisoners to determine if these could be substituted for human blood as well as to test immunity to contagious disease, 'exploding' people within pressure chambers to determine the level of endurance to pressure, and the vivisection of live prisoners (without anesthetics) in order to compare healthy organs to diseased organs.

When one speaks of the failure to present evidence at the Tokyo Trial, it should be recalled that the U.S. Chief Prosecutor Keenan refused to submit evidence presented to him by the Soviet government on a sub-unit of the above detachments. The Nanking Epidemic Detachment Ei (also known as the Tawa Detachment).

As soviet citizens were victimized in the manner described above, surely there is no doubt as to 'an aggression' having been committed against the USSR. Praise of course must be extended to two Japanese authors, Morimura Seiichi and Shimozato Masaki, who in 1982 published their best selling account of Detachment 731, 'The Devils Gluttony'.

THE POST-WAR PERIOD

The record of post-war historic interpretation differs little from what we have seen above. The argument continues. Everyone recognized the error of restricting the development of a Japanese military as soon as the cold war broke out.[23] Article 9 simply fetters Japan in countering the Soviet menace.[24] On the cultural level a natural nationalism has inevitably emerged.[25] Japan must shed the institutions of the occupation administration, which impedes future development of the nation[26] and deprives the people of expressing proper gratitude to their ancestors and a pride in rather than a loathing of the past.[27] These institutions were imposed on Japan by the Jews, who attempted to do to Japan what they had earlier done in Weimar Germany. Hugo Press was the architect of the Weimar Constitution and Charles L. Kades of the Occupation Constitution, both Jews. This group has a historic antipathy to the state and are committed to its dismemberment.[28] Science must be learned in order to permit Japan to take revenge, as Japan was defeated by an atomic bomb[29] (read, more advanced science). Japan should follow the advise of one of President Reagan's friends, Lawrence W. Beilenson, who argued in 'Survival and Peace in the Nuclear Age' that the U.S. should withdraw from all foreign bases and permit each country to defend itself.[30] If this policy were adopted, Japan would reappropriate what is rightfully hers.

Let us again put to test the question of whether or not these views represent an ultra-right wing fringe, or are part of the dominant approach of Prime Minister Nakasone. In the summer of 1982 the well known 'text book' controversy broke out. The Ministry of Education approved a total historic reversal, by agreeing to the characterization of Japanese aggression against both Korea and China as mere 'advances'. While the government ultimately backed off, after severe protests from all of Korea and China, this situation must be seen as betraying the real views of the Nakasone administration, and as a probe in order to determine whether or not the timing was officacious. Later in that year, November of 1982, *The Washington Post* reported that Prime Minister Nakasone had set three objectives for his administration: (1) to develop a military capacity aimed at preventing penetration of Japanese air-space by the Soviet 'Backfire' bomber, (2) to develop the military capacity to block the passage of Soviet submarines through the straits of Japan', and (3) to secure and maintain the ocean lines of communication.[31]

In April of the following year, 1983, Japan held joint naval exercises with Australia and New Zealand,[32] followed in August by U.S. Defence Secretary Wineberger's urging, in a meeting with the Director General of the 'Japan Defence Agency', Tanikawa Kazuo, that Japan increase her defence budget to a level which would enable Japan to defend the sea-lanes.[33] The Soviet Union's inept shooting down of Korean Airliner 007 at the end of August fed the atmosphere of belicosity within Japan. The following is fairly representative of the official attitude: 'We (Japanese) must be prepared to confront the grim reality of a time when dialogue with the Soviets based in international law and morality may no longer be feasible...power. It is the only word to which the Soviets respond.'[34] (For a systematic and detailed analysis of what actually happened with 007, which the Japanese authorities certainly knew about, it is essential to read David Pearson's 'K.A.L. 007' in the August 18-24, 1984, issue of '*The Nation*'.) By early 1984 the strategic lines are drawn out even more clearly. Asao Shinichiro, Japanese Consul General in New York, wrote to the '*New York Times*' explaining new Japanese attitudes. Recent polls, he stated, revealed that in the 1950's barely 50% of all Japanese favoured the 'Defence Force' while in 1984 the figure had risen to 80% ; in the mid-1970's only 40% favoured the U.S-Japan Security Treaty, while in 1984, 65% were supportive. In the 1970's Japan had increased her per annum military expenditures by 7% while the NATO figure was 3% and the U.S. was flat. In 1984 the Japanese rate of increase would be 4.55% (6.9% in 1985,[35] the eighth largest military budget in the world) while domestic expenditures for welfare, education and public works would either be reduced or frozen Japan supports U.S. forces at a rate four times that of NATO countries, amounting to $ 1 billion per year. Ranked with the 15 NATO countries, Japan is fourth in naval tonnage, fifth in submarines and sixth in combat aircraft, with ground forces equalling the United Kingdom. Consul-General Asao placed all of this in the perspective of Prime Minister Nakasone's Williamsburg Summit comment about a 'new realism'. Shortly after the publication of this article, a back-bench member of the Liberal-Democratic Party, Kase Hideaki, referred to the 1% ceiling on Japan's defense expenditure as meaningless. In some sense, of course, he was correct, in 1984, employing the NATO formula, Japan was spending 1.6%[36] up from 1.5% from the previous year.[37] Kase's observation, however, was a call for the abandonment of even the fiction of a 1% consensus. Through the balance of 1984 and early 1985 the Liberal Democratic Party newspaper, '*The Liberal Star*', continued to echo the earlier arguments. Former Prime Minister Fukuda Takeo described Japan's path to World War II as springing from the economic instability of the 1930's.[38] Okuno Seisuke criticized the U.S. occupation authorities for arbitrarily branding Japanese value as feudal[39] and Former Minister of Education, and currently Deputy Secretary-General of the LDP, called for the teaching of manners and morals inherent in the Japanese since antiquity,[40] clearly implying that these were abandoned as a consequence of the occupation.

A final factor which must be considered is the changing age distribution within Japan. In 1983 approximately 50% of the population was born after the conclusion of the war, a figure which has climbed to 53% by 1985 and is projected to be between 56-57% by 1990.[41] This is clearly the more fertile target group for the right wing appeal. They are in no way responsible for the war, they are the beneficiaries of post-war prosperity, and have come to assume that prosperity by entitlement, and most importantly have been witness to more recent examples of war time bestiality by other societies. They will be encouraged to feel either guiltless or historically victimized. Either way, the Nakasone-ists are of the belief that they can craft 'the new consensus'. Japan, they will argue, the entitled to the same basic rights as all other nations, the right to self-defense and the right to exercise power consistent with the country's economic strength.

CONCLUSION

We have seen a systematic attempt over the last four decades to move Japanese society from the forefront of the struggle against nuclear weapons to the major proponents of a forward military posture, just one step short of total remilitarization. An ultra-nationalist post-war fringe has gained political support and legitimacy through the patronage of the office of the Prime Minister.

The Reagan regime has encouraged this movement partly out of a kind-red anti-communism, and partly out of an attempt to decelerate increasing Japanese economic competition by redirecting Japanese internal expenditures towards non-competitive military expenditures.

Three additional cautions are necessary; one of concern to the Japanese peace movement, the second to the People's Republic of China, and the third to the USSR. The Japanese Peace Movement, while retaining the strength built over the last 40 years, must add to this base with a supplemental approach direct to the post-war generation. A mere continuation of the previous approach will not address perceptions of this new constituency. There is the risk of loosing them to the militarist right. The Chinese must not be tempted to see their long-term strategic interest served by encouraging Japanese detachment from the U.S., even if the price were a remilitarized Japan. The Soviet Union's temptation to increase military pressure on Japan, and continue a hostile military posture towards China, both which troop and missile deployments, can only have the dual consequence of encouraging a pseudo-patriotism in Japan and a level of tension in northeast Asia inimical to a strengthened regional peace movement.

Who will be the first victims of a failed peace movement? The people of Korea. Those of us, therefore, concerned for a Korea reunited in peace and propriety must first turn our attention to combatting a remilitarized Japan.

Notes and References

1. Interview with Shinkichi Eto, *Liberal Star,* 1-10-85, Vol. 14, No. 156, p. 2.
2. *Ibid.*
3. *Liberal Star,* 11-10-84, Vol. 13, No. 154, p. 1.
4. Halliday, Jon, *Mr. Weathervane Takes Over in Japan, Marxism Today,* January 1983, p. 32.
5. Nakasone Yasuhiro, Waga soigo-teki anzem ho shoron, Seiron, September 1978, in *Japan Echo,* Vol. V., No. 4, 1978, Tokyo, pp. 32-39.
6. Miyata Mitsuo, Kuni o mamoru to wa nani ka, Sekai, August 1978, in *ibid,* p. 42.
7. Kaoru Murakami, Sengo boie mondai ronsoshi, Shokun, October 1978, in *ibid,* pp. 18-30.
8. Hata Ikuhiko, Rekishi, ni narihajimeta sengo, Bungei Shunjo, Oct. 1981, pp. 124-34, *The Post War Period in Retrospect,* Special Issue, p. 19.
9. Hata, Ikuhiko, *op. cit.*, p. 20.
10. Kugai, Saburo, The Nuclear Umbrella in East Asia, in Thompson, E.P. *el al* (ed.) *Exterminism and Cold War,* London, 1982, pp. 196-97.
11. Hasegawa Michiko, Sengo sedai ni totte no dai toa senso, Chuo Koron, April 1983, in *ibid.*, Vol. XI, Special Issue, 1984, p. 31.
12. Onuma Yasuaki, Bunmei no sbaki 'shosha no sasbaki' o koete, Chuo Koron, August 1982, in *ibid.*, p. 67.
13. Murakami hyoe, Gendai niuon o toinaosu, Chou Koron, 1983, in *ibid.*, p. 42.
14. Shimizu Hayao, The War and Japan: Revisionist Views, in *ibid.*, p. 5.
15. Hasegawa, *op. cit.*, p. 29.
16. *Ibid.*, p. 24.
17. *Ibid.*
18. *Ibid.*, pp. 31, 34.
19. Kobori Keiichiro, Showa shi no aru ketsuraku ni tsuite: wakai tomo eno tegami Shokun, June 1983, in *ibid.*, pp. 39-41.
20. Hasegawa, *Ibid.*, p. 34; and Murakami, *ibid.*, pp. 48-51.

21. Takeyama Michio, Showa shi to Tokyo saniban, Sieron, December 1982, in *ibid.*, pp. 55-62 and Onuma Yauaki, Bunmei no sabaki shosha no sabaki o koete, Chuo Koron, *ibid.*, pp. 63-69.
22. Material on the Trials of Former Servicemen on the Japanese Army Charged with Manufacturing and Employing Bacteriological Weapons, Foreign Language Publishing House, Moscow, 1950; Radio Moscow (English), 18 May 1985; *New York Times*, 3-22-83.
23. Shimazu, *op. cit.*, p. 8.
24. *Ibid.*, p. 10.
25. *Ibid.*, p. 9.
26. *Ibid.*, p. 7.
27. *Ibid.*, p. 11.
28. Irie Takanori, America ga tsukutta senga shinwa, Chuo Koron, August 1982, *ibid.*, p. 22.
29. Hata Ikuhiro, Rekishi ni narihajimeta sengo, Bungei Shunjo, October 1982, *ibid.*, p. 14.
30. Irie, *op. cit.*, p. 26.
31. Jones, Peter D., The Demilitarization of Japan, *New Zealand Monthly Review*, November 1984, Christchurch, New Zealand, p. 17.
32. *Ibid.*, p. 18.
33. *Liberal Star*, September 1983, Vol. 12, No. 140, p. 5.
34. Ito Kenichi, Kakunin sareta futatsu no koto, Shokun, November 1983, in *Japan Eecho*, Vol. XI, No. 1, 1984, p. 44.
35. *Liberal Star*, 3-10-85, Vol. 14, No. 158, p. 1.
36. Jones, o*p. cit*, p. 32.
37. Halliday, o*p cit*, p. 32.
38. *Liberal Star*, July 10, 1984, Vol. 13, No. 150, pp. 4-5.
39. *Ibid.*, p. 14.
40. *Liberal Star*, January 10, 1985, Vol. 14, No. 156, p. 15.
41. World Population Prospects: Estimates and Projections as Assessed in 1982, *Population Studies*, No. 86, United Nations, Department of International Economic and Social Affairs, New York, 1982, p. 404.

PART II

JAPANESE ECONOMY

9

Japan's Success Story: A Second Look

B.M. TANKHA*

The structure of Japanese unions, the relation of labour to management, the status of labour in society, are areas in Japan which are regarded as operating differently from the rest of the world. The success of Japanese competition focussed interest on these and other areas to try and explain the reasons for this success. Broadly it was felt that Japan's economic competitiveness depended either on a different organizational and management system or on a work ethic which ensured work for longer hours at lower wages. The debates carried on by those who argued that the peculiar characteristics of worker-management relations in Japan should be sought in its social structure, in the traditional Confucian ideas etc. and with those who saw these institutions as no different from those in the rest of the world, have defined the way we have looked at these areas. Our present interest is not only importing Japanese technology and goods but also Japanese techniques of management are based on the understanding that Japan has evolved techniques which have reduced tensions and conflicts and harnessed the energies of workers to national effort.

* Department of Chinese and Japanese Studies, University of Delhi, Delhi.

However, it is important to see these institutions in a proper perspective and evaluate their efficacy only after understanding the manner in which they actually operate within Japan. Rabindranath Tagore on his first visit to Japan saw the problem accurately. In answer to the criticism that the Japanese look down upon us because we are Asiatic, he wrote by replying that we look down on Japan. 'We close our eyes to her real self and see in her only a deformed Europe'. He went on to urge that we learn not just from Europe but from Japan, for he saw there a country which had learned to 'manipulate with skill and efficiency the entire assortment of intricate instruments that belong to European civilization.'

Here is the crux of the problem. If we continue to regard Japan in the image of Europe we will continue to misinterpret and misunderstand her history and institutions. We must reconsider her institutions and see their development and examine how they work in inter-relation within a larger social and political framework. In examining the question of labour relations, therefore, it is not enough to take some middle position between a class analysis and a view which looks at traditional elements as determining the characteristic organizational system but rather to see what manner of system has been created and how it actually works.

Here books like Satoshi Kamata's *Japan in the Passing Lane* are an invaluable guide. Kamata worked as a seasonal labourer in a Toyota factory 1972-73 and from his personal experiences he writes about the life of workers on the conveyor belt. The last sentence is a very suggestive end, for he writes of his experience: 'Whenever I come to this city and talk with workers. I feel as though I have strayed into some fantasy land. But this is a nightmare that I have lived, and the anger will not go away.' Kamata who has written other books is heir to an old traditions of what would now be called investigative journalism, or 'reportage' in Japanese and some of them have become classic accounts, such as Hosoi Wakizo's *Joko Aishi* (The Sad History of Women Workers) (1926) or the earlier Yokoyama Gennosuke's *Meiji Kaso Shakai* (The Lower Classes of the Meiji) (1900). This tradition is still alive and many examples can be given of reportage in a variety of fields, e.g. education, unions, etc. The intent however is not to review the existing literature but to suggest that there is available a wide variety of material which if used can help us determine the nature of modern Japanese society and redefine our categories and concepts.

When examining workers, there understanding of themselves, their relations with the management, we must consider the changes which have occurred in Japan after World War II and the American occupation. As in other developed societies class consciousness has been attenuated. Innumerable surveys show that most people feel that they are middle class and income differences have been reduced more than in most countries. Given the two major breaks in Japanese history, the Meiji Ishin of 1868 and 1945 inherited wealth plays a relatively minor role, as few families have survived with their fortunes intact. Therefore, the single most important way to advance socially, acquire property and wealth is through work and higher income. Access to jobs and attractive salaries is determined by performance in schools and universities. It is for this reason that the debates about the nature and continent of education have been so important and so persistent. It is for this reason also that, inspite of a continuous struggle for reform and change in the method of state approval of school text books in Japan, the Education Ministry continues to determine not only the content but the language of the text books. Here in particular books on history are the single most important category which have become the source not only of national but international controversy.

Education is not only accessible but enjoyed by most of the population, and as, it is the most important means of gaining entry into the elite system it continues to be regulated. An institutionally separate education for the elite has not been created. Since everyone has access to the same institutions, it builds up not only bonds of equality between the recipients but creates an ethos were, as work is the determinant of social success, failure is due not to institutional structures but to personal inability or incompetence. It is this pressure which accounts for the high suicide rate of school children of a ridiculously low age.

In the work place this general understanding is translated into the idea that there is no difference between the worker (*rodo*) and the management (*Kanri)* because the one can advance to the other given proper qualifications, that is, a university degree. As pay differentials are not wide it is possible to create an ethos in which there is no difference between the two, everyone is a 'worker' and both are responsible for ensuring that production proceeds in as efficient a manner as possible. The unity of society is reflected in the unity of a factory and in both context work is for the benefit to the larger whole, the nation or the factory.

In such a situation failure is not because of unequal relations but because of inability or lack of will to strive. Witness the slogans and songs which call for correct spirit. Secondly, ideological positions are motivated, selfish and disruptive. Not only this, but if guilt is admitted and a person recants from an ideological position, then forgiveness is extended and the person taken back as a number once again. The person becomes a fully functioning member of the society. Thus workers who confront the management can, if they recent, once again became trusted workers. But if they do not, they cannot hope to get back into the factory. Thus workers who win in court are given their wages but are told to stay at home.

It is this emphasis on the right spirit which also explains the peculiar amalgam of technologically advanced companies (e.g. Sony, Kyocera) using medieval ideas like Zen to inculcate the proper attitudes in their employees. Many companies, like Kyocera, have an education section which is concerned only with disseminating these house philosophies. Faced as we are with a resurgence of 'traditional' ideas, it would be instructive to analyse the limited change in religion and ethics even while there has been an immense transformation in knowledge and the way of life.

These brief comments are meant to suggest that in considering the means and methods by which social control is exercised in Japan we need to look at Japanese society concretely. That is, we need to examine closely the actual situation in areas which are of crucial importance to the social structure. We cannot confine ourselves to generalities but need to look at how these institutions function, how policies are implemented and what reactions they evoke.

The relations between workers and management is one such crucial area. The firm has come to be the spiritual centre of Japanese life. The family has become an adjunct of the firm. It is for this reason that the fundamental relations which govern life in Japan and which determine the mode of interaction are visible in worker-management relations and these form the bedrock of Japanese society.

The importance and meaning of *Jishu Seisan* (self-production) where workers have taken over factories and sought independence from capital are extremely important, for even though limited in scale and effect they offer a glimpse of the institutional pressure which shape the life of workers and to that extent they need to be studied carefully. They provide a way to understand the role of 'amoeba groups', 'equality control', 'relationalization' and other techniques of Japanese management which have gained currency, though their functioning remains obscure behind the great Kanji barrier.

10

Current Economic Issues Confronting Japan

G. BALATCHANDIRANE*

After the devastation and defeat in World War II, Japan rapidly built itself to join the ranks of the advanced nations in a brief span of time. On the way it managed to break a number of records. The economy reverted to the regular growth path in 1955, when it reached the pre-war peck production levels. From that year till the time of the first oil crisis it managed to notch up an average growth rate in excess of ten per cent per annum. Such a high and continuous growth record has so far not been seen in the history of the world; nor has it been replicated since.

In course of its rapid growth Japan became the world's largest ship-builder in 1956, overtook the British economy in size in 1962 and the West German in 1967, to become the third largest economy in the world. In the last decade it became the second largest economy in the world. If the present growth rates continue Japan should be the largest economy in the world by 2005, overtaking the United States. Japan has the world's largest per capita GNP. It is the largest holder of foreign assets and is also the largest holder of gold. Japanese banks and securities

* Lecturer in The Department of Chinese and Japanese Studies, University of Delhi, Delhi.

firm are among the world's largest. Today it is claimed that Japan is richer, more productive and more technologically advanced than any other nation in the world. It is the world's largest creditor, largest aid-giver, and accounts for close to ten per cent of world GNP.

Various internal and external reasons can be put forth to explain this impressive growth performance. The favourable external factors would include a very liberal trade regime that existed under the auspices of GATT, the easy availability and cheap price of a wide spectrum of technology, the low and stable price of raw materials till about the time of the first oil crisis, etc. Among others, some of the networthy domestic factors that aided Japan in its rapid growth are a highly literate and willing work force, new management methods, the dynamic role of the state, large increases in labour productivity and capital stock, and increasing economies of scale, which were viable as access to foreign markets was easy. The benign occupation policies were important in no small measure.

The period from 1955 to 1973, when the first oil crisis took place, is regarded as the period of high speed growth of the Japanese economy. The growth rate of the Japanese economy preceptibly slowed down after the first oil crisis but still remained respectable compared to the growth rates of other advanced nations. As a response to the oil crisis, Japan implemented a set of policies targeted at energy saving and fuel efficiency, which was called "Operation Scaledown." There was significant saving of energy due to these policies, as for example, in 1980 the amount of oil expended to produce a ton of steel was just half of what was needed in 1973. The second major response of industry to the oil crisis was a change-over to low-energy using industries, such as mechatronics and micro-electronics that produced high value-added items.

In the decade following the first oil crisis, the Japanese economy grew on an average around 4.3 per cent per annum. The role of exports continued to be important, accounting for 40 per cent of growth during this period. By the mid-eighties, the cost of energy in Japan had gone up eight times compared to the what it had been in 1970, and this slowed down growth. Large scale investments targeted at pollution control and infrastructure building also contributed to the fall in growth. Slow growth was one reason why Japan's trade surpluses, which her trading partners found to be major irritants, continued. In 1985, the Plaza Accord was arrived at to counter this, by letting the yen appreciate against other currencies. It was expected that a high yen would reduce Japan's exports and hence its trade surpluses. While the yen did appreciate, from 260 yens to 130 yens to the US dollar between 1985 and 1987, the trade surpluses did not reduce. Exports did not slow down, as Japanese industry became even more competitive by raising its productivity levels further, through technological innovation and a move to more value added products.

As Japan entered the nineties it had to contest with a number of issues. Trade friction was a continuing problem, the economy entered a recession, its agricultural protectionism was being increasingly questioned and labour shortage was creating difficulties for domestic industry. The strong yen forced the Japanese to shift their production centres for relatively lower value-added industries overseas. The formation of NAFTA and the European Union has only strengthened this trend, as Japan is worried about the increasing difficulties of exporting to both North America and Europe.

To see some of the major issues confronting Japan in detail we could start with agriculture, where the peculiar aspects of Japanese agriculture have led to a situation where, despite being one of the largest importers of agricultural products. Japan has had to face tremendous international, particularly American, pressure to open up its protected agricultural sectors. The Americans have been particularly incensed over the closed nature of the rice market in Japan. At the risk of oversimplification, their argument would run as follows: Japan managed to have significant trade surpluses with the US because the Japanese were able to export to the US products in which over the years the US had lost out in terms of productivity, which affected the competitiveness of the product. Namely, the Japanese product was of higher quality at a lower price. Thus, the comparative advantage in specific industrial products helped them benefit under a free-trade regime. Whenever the US raised the issue of huge bilateral trade surpluses with Japan, one of the consistent arguments put forth by the Japanese was what every nation would tend to export products in which it had a comparative advantage and import products in which it had a comparative disadvantage.

Thus, when the same argument was put forth to the Japanese that they should import rice in which their is no comparative disadvantage (the price of Japanese rise is about five to ten times the international price), the Japanese were hard put to make the world understand their problem. The high degree of protectionism that exists in Japan today had been necessitated by the small scale of production which farmers practise; there is no way this problem can be overcome, as consolidation of land into viable economic units is unthinkable with the astronomical rise is land prices. This aspect, coupled with the fact that the agricultural lobby in Japan is very powerful, would ensure that the protected nature of Japanese agriculture would throw up important social, economic and political problems.

On the industrial front, Japan today finds that it would not be able to repeat the fantastic performances of yesteryears. This is because of the fact that the technology gap between Japan and world, which it had been trying to bridge at a furious pace since 1955, is much narrower today. However, access to high-level technology has become difficult today for Japan with the western reluctance to part with it; the West obviously does not want to see a reply of what happened to a number of consumer durables, whose technology Japan borrowed from them to only capture large shares of their own market in these products. Thus Japan has to depend on its own efforts. That the Japanese are not invincible leaders of technology has recently been made clear by the high definition television and the fifth generation computers. When the Japanese started their research into both these areas they had a clear lead over their main competitor, the US; and the world was so used to seeing Japan get the better of the West in one technology after the other, that it was taken for granted that the US would lose out in the long-run. In the event, the Japanese have declared that they have given up their fifth generation computer project and the high definition television technology, which is found to be inferior to the one developed by the Americans.

Turning to international economic relations, Japan has been consistently having a trade surplus. The excess of exports over imports stock at 2,000 billion yen in 1981. This rose to a peak of 13,700 billion yen in 1986, after which it started to fall. Now it is approaching the earlier peak level with the figure for 1992 being of the order of 13,500 billion yen. In this period Asia has emerged as the leading market for Japanese exports pushing the North American market to the second place. Europe, which figures in the third place, has also increased its importance as a regions absorbing Japanese exports. With respect to imports, we find that while in relative terms, Asia's share in the total imports of Japan has fallen, it has continued to remain the top exporting region to Japan. Asia had accounted for over half of Japan's imports by 1985, and the figure today is around 45 per cent. North America and

Europe are the second and third most important regions accounting for Japan's imports.

In Asia, it is the Association of Southeast Nations and the Asian Newly Industrialising Economies that are of critical importance to Japan. In the immediate post-war years, this region was very important as a source of raw material for Japan as it no longer had the colonies to depend on. With the rapid growth of industry, the demand for raw materials grew at a hectic pace and the nations of Southeast Asia were and still are important suppliers of raw material to Japan. The economic miracle of Japan depended in no small measure on the ready availability of raw materials and a huge market at the backyard of Japan. Today, however, it is the countries of this region which are dependent on Japan and it has a trade surplus with almost all of them.

Japanese investments in this region had been just trickle in the immediate post-war years, but has risen significantly over the years and Japan is the largest investor in this region today. The motive of the Japanese in investing in this region is to get under the tariff wall which might come up in future against Japanese goods. But there is a much more important consideration that has been prompting the Japanese to invest in various countries of this region.

The strengthening of the yen in the mid-1980s and the increasing trade friction has spawned a new trend of Japanese production facilities being shifted overseas. This is qualitatively different from the similar process that had been going on even earlier. The former shift of production overseas had been unco-ordinated in the sense that the investments would be made in one country and production done exclusively in that country. Now investments in-various countries are made with a comprehensive game plan. Specific parts are sourced from these countries, assembled at another and exported to the West. The considerations of Japanese industry, while investing in Southeast Asia earlier had been (a) the development of natural resources required by Japanese industry, (b) getting under the tariff wall, (c) exploitation of low-wage rates in the recipient countries, and (d) export of polluting industries, etc.

Now the clear intention is to get round the various trade barriers erected by the West, to cope with NAFTA and the European Union, and to overcome the problem of the strong yen which would impede exports. The shifting of production facilities triggered off by these considerations has been going on since around 1986. Typically, a Japanese company would set up operational headquarters in Singapore and then set up international centres, which link Japan, the Asian Newly Industrialising Economies, and the ASEAN. Simultaneously, facilities related to physical distribution, such as land and marine transportation, warehousing, etc., have been created. The setting up of an extensive physical distribution network system is expected to translated into a comprehensive international distribution system, and the formation of a centralised management of a multi-country-based production system.

With respect to aid, it might be useful to start with the fact that in the annual report in 1958, the Ministry of International Trade and Industry clearly talked of the linkage between Japan's aid policies and the goal of trade promotion. There was a clear understanding that trade was to be promotion through aid and that trade was to secure materials that Japanese industry would need for rebuilding the economy; nor was the development of external markets for Japanese products lost sight of. The adoption of resources diplomacy as a basis of aid started after the first oil crisis. The huge bilateral trade surpluses that Japan notched up in the late 1970s was one reason why the Americans insisted that Japan contribute a fair share to the collective security arrangements in Asia. Thus, we find that aid, in addition to being an international economic tool, started assuming the mantle of a foreign policy tool.

The Asia-Pacific region was absorbing almost all the Japanese aid around the time of the first oil crisis. While this is no longer true, the Asian region continues to take the lion's share of Japanese aid. In 1991, the top five and seven of the top ten aid recipients were from Asia. India was the second largest recipient of Japanese bilateral Official Development Assistance. About three-fifths of all Japanese aid goes to Asia today. However, the Asian countries have a number of criticisms against Japanese aid. First, the aid is more in the way of loans than grants. Second, a high percentage of Japanese aid is tied. Namely, there are conditionalities written into the aid agreements which force the recipient to utilise a specified percentage of the aid to buy goods and services from Japan or from Japanese companies. The common refrain is that buying from Japanese companies is not cost-competitive. Third, the overall level of aid is claimed to be low. While in absolute terms Japanese aid is the largest in the world in terms of ODA/GNP ratio, it ranks a lowly thirteenth among the major aid givers.

Despite the various recriminations, distrusts, etc., the Asia-Pacific region is where the Japanese feel that their economic stake is the highest and for the countries of this region too, their economic future is tied more with Japan then with the West. Already their economies are greatly intertwined and all the indications are that this trend will continue. Some of the countries' ardour in adopting the ''Look East' policy—namely using the Japanese development experience as a model to follow—might have cooled a bit with what they feel is a let-down by the Japanese. However, on the positive side, Japan probably has more to teach them in terms of technology, management techniques, etc., than the West. And the formation of NAFTA and the European Union is making the Japanese realise more and more the value of this region, not just as a market but also as a huge production base.

On the domestic front, the recession in Japan might have taken a heavy toll of the economy. The earlier shocks, such as the oil crisis of 1973, etc., were easily weathered by Japan. The image that Japan is a country with extreme resilience has persisted, because in the past, compared to other nations, Japan usually emerged relatively unscathed from various crises. However, one common feature of the earlier shocks was that they originated from outside Japan. This time the source of the economic crisis is easily located within Japan and it is believed that Japan will not be able to weather this crisis, as it could the earlier ones. The cause of the present crisis is directly attributable to the 'bubble economy', the bursting of which has led to the recession.

In the late 1980s there was a rapid expansion of domestic credit for industry at favourable terms. This was made possible through asset-inflation in securities, banking and real estate markets. Low interest rates, a booming Tokyo stock market, and fast increases in property values combined to give rise to the bubble. The rising asset prices and bank lending and financial activities mutually reinforced each other. As people expected that the price of land and equities would always rise, they borrowed to invest in them, leading to further demand and hence price rise. Firms also did much the same thing. The increasing value of assets was used to borrow even more, thus leading to the ballooning effect. The bursting of the bubble resulted in a calamitous downturn.

Some of the pressing problems for the Japanese of the domestic front today include: keeping agriculture a viable sector and without sacrificing food security; coping with labour shortage; facing the ever-rising cost of energy; keeping the technological lead which is being increasingly threatened; taking care of the increasing percentage of the aged population, particularly when social security is at a low level, etc. The

Japanese after all are human and, despite all their spectacular successes, have been making mistakes. Now it is apparent that they bet on the wrong horse when they embarked on the much publicised and expensive high definition television project which had to be given up.

A recent study by the Harvard Institute of Economic Research has come out with some startling revelations regarding the much-vaunted intelligent management of Japanese industry in the post-war years. First, there was no co-ordinated, unified approach in the way industrial policy was formulated targeting various priority sectors; hence, the way Japanese built their industry is probably not all that efficient cost-wise. Secondly, despite what much of the literature has been giving us to believe, the government did not always make the right choice of industry. Too many times it supported industries that ultimately proved to be slow-growers. In other words, there were massive inefficiencies in resource allocation.

For far too long the literature on Japan has been glossing over the negative features of modernisation and the inherent tensions in Japanese society. Now that the initial fascination of learning from Japan is tempered with the current understanding of the problems faced by Japan and the realisation that even the Japanese did go wrong, a completely fresh look at the Japanese economic performance might be in order.

11

Sovereignty and Liberalisation: Indo-Japanese Economic Ties

G. BALATCHANDIRANE*

While considering the various dimensions of economic relations between India and Japan, one finds that trade, investment and aid are the important aspects. Trade relations existed between these two countries even before 120 years when India exported cotton and imported copper from Japan. Since then the quantum and composition of trade have undergone tremendous changes. The rapid economic growth of Japan which was triggered off after the restoration of the Emperor Meiji in 1868, had created the needs for various kinds of imports. Broadly they can be classified as raw materials and industrial technology. For the latter, Japan turned to the then advanced nations in the West. For the former, nations in Asia were the natural choices. Since India was under British rule and since industrial growth in India was not significant before independence, the trade relations between these two countries were confined to a few commodities like raw cotton, cotton manufacturers and silk manufacturers, etc. This composition changed after World War II. In what follows we will see some major trends in the trade between the two countries in the post-World II period. Some

* Lecturer, Department of Chinese and Japanese Studies, University of Delhi, Delhi.

attention would also be given to the recent issue of Japanese investments in India. We will try to see how the Japanese dealt with foreign investments when they imported technology.

There was an explosion in global trade since the 1950s. Japan after its defeat in 1945, was occupied by the Supreme Commander of Allied Forces (SCAP). SCAP had adopted a punitive policy *vis-a-vis* Japan till about 1949. From then onwards international political considerations made the US, the main if not the only active member of SCAP to take a benign policy towards Japan. The primary considerations were to build Japan on strong capitalist lines to ward off communism in Asia, and building a future market for US exports. Japan went on a rapid industry-building spree while borrowing technology from the West. Raw material needs soared during the high growth phase that ensued starting in the mid-1950s. India after independence tried to build herself so that a degree of self-reliance could be achieved. The industrial base of India was then not very significant. So she had to rely on primary commodity exports as the main source of foreign exchange.

Thus in the period since 1950s, we find that the chief characteristic in the trade between the two countries has been that while Indian exports were non-manufactures the imports have been mostly manufactures. Further a few items like iron ore, frozen shrimps and diamonds have been taking up a major share of Indian exports to Japan. For example a single item iron ore has been accounting for one-third to one-half of the total Indian exports to Japan in this period. This despite the fact that Indian iron ore has been facing stiff competition from Australia and Brazil. These countries have technologically sophisticated port loading and transportation facilities which has helped them offer iron ore at a price lesser than India's. If iron ore continues to hold a large share of our exports in spite of this, it is not because India has found ways of overcoming the competition. This rather implies that first, the total quantum of trade is low and secondly that India has not succeeded in diversifying its exports.

The problem with shrimp exports has been that we are not able to meet the demand. In the past decade shrimp exports have been stagnant at around $225 million a year. This is a potential area for growth as no fall in Japan's demand can be seen in the foreseeable future. Deep sea-fishing and prawn culture are the areas that need modernizing to increasing our exports of this commodity. Diamond exports of India has rapidly increased of late. It was $6 million in 1970 and gradually rose to over $200 million by mid-1980s. India managed to increase its share in Japan's total imports of diamonds of over 20 per cent.

Overall, if one sees the performance of various export commodities and trend is erratic. But one characteristic that is easily discernible is that the traditional items have been losing their place in Indian exports to Japan. These have been replaced by the non-traditional items. In fact, this is believed to be one of the contributory factors for India's trade deficit with Japan. Two things need to be done on the export front. Export of non-traditional items has to be increased. At the same time export of traditional items have to be shored up as they have been slipping recently. For example, the explosive demand for iron ore because of rapid growth of Japanese steel industry in 1960s and 1970s may have passed the peak by 1980 or so. But since the base of steel industry in Japan is still huge, there is scope for progress on this front.

Turning to imports from Japan, by 1950 cotton textile manufactures and other consumer goods were predominating Indian imports from Japan. By 1965 their importance declined. They were replaced by machinery and equipments. Of late close to three-fourths of the imports from Japan are accounted for by finished products. These include machinery (general and electrical), transportation and handling equipment, iron and steel and telecommunications equipment. There have been no smooth progression in the way the various items imported from Japan have behaved over the years.

A brief analysis of the commodity structure of Indian imports from Japan reveals the following features. Just three items — general machinery, electrical machinery and transport equipment — have been predominating. Their share in total Indian imports stood at close to 30 per cent in 1960. This share increased to close to 60 per cent by 1986. Over the years they have been edging out items like metal goods, chemical goods and textile goods.

To see the India-Japan trade in a larger perspective, between 1960 and 1986, in terms of value, the total trade increased fifteen-fold. For, India, Japan has been an important trading partner, accounting for over 10 per cent of the total trade. For Japan, trade with India has been an insignificant 1 per cent or less of its total trade.

India's trade with Japan has been increasing over the years. India had a negative balance of trade with Japan in the 60s which turned positive in the 70s. But since 1981 India has been registering a negative balance of trade with Japan. The liberal trade policy of India has led to rapidly increasing imports from Japan. These have not been matched by exports to Japan. Imports of iron and steel, industrial machinery and infrastructure-related equipments etc., have risen loading to the deficit. The second reason is the narrow base of Indian exports to Japan. As regards Japanese investments in India we will not go into the history of Japanese investments in India but will confine ourselves to the recent focus on the issue of the 21-point list of "requests" for further policy reforms presented by the high-level Japanese economic mission that visited India towards the end of January 1992. This mission has come to be called as the Ishikawa mission as it was led by Dr. Rokuro Ishikawa. It wanted specific changes in India's investment, trade and fiscal policies as a precondition for increasing Japanese investments in India. The tacit assumption was that technology transfer from Japan would be facilitated. Dr Ishikawa said that a number of countries have already offered attractive conditions as trade and investment partners to Japan. Therefore, he expected India to provide a competitive policy environment. He told the Indo-Japanese business cooperation committee that these "requests" might sound harsh. But he was convinced that India too had its own "requests" for Japan.

The "requests" he listed wanted the abolition of foreign equity participation which now stands at 51 per cent. Profit repatriation has to be delinked from export earnings. Restrictions on capital goods imports for new joint ventures has to be removed. FERA has to be revised soon to include recent policy changes. Provisions governing commercial activities of foreign corporations and real estate acquisitions have to be liberalised. An exit policy has to be formulated soon. Restrictions on "emergency imports" were to be remove. Import tariff was to be reduced. Import licensing was to be relaxed. In budgetary allocations priority should be given for improving industrial infrastructure such as power and telecommunications. Restrictions on industry location has to be relaxed. Protection for small-scale industry was to be reduced and restriction on banking activities was to be abolished.

The amazing thing that followed these "requests" was not that no protests were raised against this sort of blatant terms — dictating in the guise of "requests"; it was the unbelievable spectacle of our leaders falling over each other trying to convince the Japanese that our environment was indeed conducive to Japanese investments and that more favourable changes were on their way. Newspapers talked of Indian leaders assuring the team that "most of the policy reforms suggested by Dr. Ishikawa were very much on the agenda of the government''. The next day the government assured the mission that it will ''accommodate its requests for further trade and fiscal policy changes to facilitate investment in India''. The mission was assured that FERA was soon to be revised. Tariff structure for capital goods imports would be rationalized. With regard to other points like for example the exemption from export commitment the government said this was a purely temporary restriction. The Japanese were ''requested to bear with this inconvenience'' which was forced on India because of its balance of payment difficulties. Significantly the long awaited amendments of FERA coincided with the arrival of the Ishikawa mission.

Since it is technology that India is wanting to borrowing from Japan, let us pause a bit to see the Japanese experience in technology imports in the 1950s and 1960s, when it imported large numbers of technologies from the west to rapidly build itself after the second world war. The authoritative study on this available in English is Terutomo Ozawa's *Japan's Technological challenge to the West: Motivation and Accomplishment* (MIT Press, 1974). While discussing about Japan's acquisition of technology he talks about the Foreign Investment Law of 1950 and draws implications from the preamble. ''The phrase 'limiting the induction of foreign investment to that which will contribute to the self-support and sound development of the Japanese economy' seems to imply that *without appropriate government controls, the acquisition of the foreign capital and technology will lead to the domination of the Japanese economy by foreign interests.* Indeed as will be discussed....*this is the basic assumption held by the government in formulating its policy for the acquisition of foreign capital and technology*''.

If the Japanese during their technology borrowing phase believed government controls were necessary to avoid domination of their economy by foreign interests, why should India feel different to do so? If it was their basic assumption that the lack of controls would lead to foreign interests to dominate the Japanese economy and they kept this in mind while formulating their policy for the acquisition of foreign capital and technology, why can we not do the same?

Ozawa goes on to discuss another phrase 'providing for remittances arising from foreign investment'. He talks of how ''guaranteed remittances of investment earnings were emphasised as a primary justification of the controls''. He further quotes the speech of then Japanese Prime Minister Hayato Ikeda in New York city in 1950 to show it as a reflection of this attitude. Sections of the speech are reproduced as they are quite revealing and should certainly be read by our leaders and policy-makers.

''As to the first point of assuring transfer, our dollar position does not allow us to serve every Tom, Dick and Harry and let them exchange their yen earnings and take dollars home. We are bound to be selective in this respect...When the Government commits itself to a certain amount of transfer, the Government is legally obligated to incorporate the commitment in its running dollar budget. Then there will be no default. This checking system is by no means intended to create red tape. It is a device of a poor but honest borrower who does not want to cheat creditors. The related law clearly states that these checkings and restrictions will be removed one by one as our dollar position warrants the removal.'' (pp. 17-18)

Thus in their haste to import technology Japanese did not do away with the controls. Rather they made their position clear to the world on where they stood.

If this does not provide us with enough pointers, let us see the experience of the Southeast Asian nations. In the 1980s many of them sought to develop rapidly on the pattern of Japan by borrowing technology from Japan. They had romantic notions of modernising rapidly. In the event, their ardour has cooled now. They have found that Japanese have been investing in fields which they believe are beneficial to Japan and not where the recipient countries feel they have a dire need. Technology transfers from Japan have neither gone on large-scale nor have they rapidly modernised the recipient nations.

This is not to cavil at the way Japan invests or transfers technology. This is just to point out that if the Japanese believe what they do is rational from their point of self-interest, we should have the conviction that what we do is rational from the point of our self-interest. And the courage to say so.

12

Trade Competitiveness and Management Technique—Aspects of US-Japan Business

R. NIGAM* AND RAJ KUMAR GUPTA**

I

It is worthwhile to quote here the observations made by Ms. Joanna Shelton, Special Assistant to the US Treasury Secretary, made at a briefing organised in the last week of October, 1983 by the John Hopkins School of Advanced International Studies. "The fundamental cause of concern in that Japan has been perceived to have become such a strong international competitor, and this is coupled with perception that the Japanese markets are closed to imports." Inspite of a long series of trade measures aimed at blunting Japanese competitive edge not much could be achieved by the US. After running through a list of bilateral trade issues, ranging from various products and high technology goods to agricultural goods and tobacco over the past years very little movement has taken place in reducing trade deficit of US with Japan. This can mainly be attributed to the fact that on account of advanced technology

* Dr. Nigam is Professor of Commerce, Delhi School of Economics, Delhi University.

** Dr. Gupta is Lecturer of Commerce, Delhi School of Economics, Delhi University.

and management techniques built on high degree of motivation and life-long commitment, cost competitiveness of Japanese goods is always higher than those anywhere in the world. US administration has been saddled with the responsibility of looking after "decaying industries such as still convalescing ones like cars and high technology industries which are increasingly feeling the heat of Japanese competition." A situation has reached when it appears something like a humiliation for a country (USA) which sees itself as the world's leading industrial nation and growing source of concern to supporters of free trade.

"While there is continuing economic and political concern about the immediate implications of the bilateral trade deficit, there has also been growing recognition that a defensive posture aimed at limiting damage to uncompetitive industries is inadequate and potentially dangerous approach to the industrial challenge posed by Japan." This can be seen in part in the increased emphasis, which for example, car manufactures like Ford have put on quality in their production. But its most striking concern is the field of high technology products. Prof. Robert Reach of Harvard University, a man who has been leading the industrial policy debate in the USA puts it as "The fear has been expressed repeatedly by the White House scientific staff that we cannot afford to let a foreign country especially not Japan dominate in any technology which could be strategically important." What Japan is doing in high technology field has also been underlined in a recent report by the General Accounting Office of the US under the title "Assessment of bilateral telecommunication agreement with Japan". The report analyses the progress which has been made under a three-year agreement which came into effect in the beginning of 1981 and which was designed to open up Nippon Telephone and Telegraph (NTT), Japanese government-owned telephone company. While the study makes it clear that the progress has been slow, what comes out most clearly is the intense interest within some of the most advanced US companies in getting into the NTT procurement system which in part is put down to the prospective $120 billion programme which NTT has announced for the modernisation of its network, upgrading it into a broad band digital system. US tele-communication sales to NTT are running at not more than $38 million a year (1982) compared with 10 times that volume of Japanese sales to US telecommunication companies. The study makes it clear that "access to the NTT procurement is important to the international competitiveness of the US tele-communication industry." Because

"NTT is a generator of important technology for Japanese firms in the compute and semi-conductor as well as telephone industries." Here lies the answer to the problem. It is partly in this context of a growing admiration in the US for Japanese technology, the US pressure for greater access for Japanese market needs to be seen.

II

Both economists and policy-makers have been treating US-Japan problem as one of international economic relations the main reason for various arrangements to bring about orderliness lies in the high degree of international competitiveness of Japanese industry which, as put by one write "is a shocking indictment of American mediocrity". For the last years a number of American industrial management experts, from the topmost captains of the industry down to the humblest segment have been flooding across the Pacific to Japan in a bid to steal their manufacturing secreta and put them to the desperately needed use back home. After all the studies, books and articles that have appeared in the last years, and with all the science with so-called Japanese, and with management techniques already starting to make a dramatic impact on the quality and productivity on some US manufacturers from car and locomotive producers to the makers of semi-conductors—one would have thought that the US has started winning battles in the economic war with Japan. Recently a new study called "Quality on the line" which documents the generally appealing quality of one of the simplest and most common American manufactured product, i.e. the domestic air-conditioner has revealed some eye-opener fact. It constitutes a damning indictment of the production and general management in US firms comparing the defect rates of Japan and US air-conditioners. This report concludes "two exercises are in entirely different leagues—the worst air-conditioners from any Japanese company at a failure rate of less than half of the best American manufacturers."

The researcher, Prof. D. Garvain, when he first compiled the results of his intensive two year study whose summaries were published in the *Harvard Business Review*, himself got a surprise and shock. He suggests that the implications of his findings reach far beyond the narrow bounds of the air-conditioner industry, into US manufacturing as a whole. It is here that the inter-factory comparisons are more valid and can give the true state of affairs of American industry and its management. He emphasises (No apples *vs.* oranges here), "the comparison is firmly grounded . . . the shocking doubts for which nothing had prepared him, is that the failure rates of products from the highest quality producers (in Japan) were between 500 and 1000 times less than those of products from the lowest (in the US)." He came up basically with two major findings:

(1) that in the production process itself the Japanese defect rate was almost 70 times lower than the US, and

(2) that in the first year after the air-conditioners had been sold, the Japanese defect rate (measured by number of service calls) was normally 17 times better than the Americans.

III

It has been demonstrated in this study that it is best to invest in public quality. Not only the Japanese were the highest quality-producers with the highest output per hour (a finding independent of any differences in production technology or capital intensity), but the Japanese manufacturers incurred warranty cost, averaging only 0.6 per cent of sales against a range of between 1.8 per cent and 5.2 per cent for the Americans. He also calculated "Total cost of quality" in theory. Low warranty costs might be off-set by higher expenditure on defect prevention. But Garvain's results produced the opposite conclusions: costs the Japanese incurred by ensuring quality were less than the failure costs incurred by the best US companies—just 1.3 per cent of sales against 2.8 per cent. According to Garvain the reason is clear: failures are much expensive to fix after a unit has been assembled than "The cost of extra-hour spent, per-testing a design. Similarly, field service costs are much higher than those of incoming inspection."

IV

The traditional scheme that Japan is full of miracle workers and managers while Americans are merely human has also been examined by Garvain. Far from it, apart from him, US academic opinion does not like that. It if just that Americans have made virtually every obvious mistake in the book while the Japanese exercise their frightening ability to master every detail of the production and marketing process. According to him the two countries' managerial practices differ mainly in the following ways:—

(1) The quality-control function tended to have a higher status and the more direct access to top management, in the Japanese companies.

(2) The Japanese companies reviewed defect rates in daily meetings. The US plants with the lowest loss plant employee line defect rates averaged 10 such meetings per month; at all other US factories average was only 4.

(3) Every Japanese company used a group of employees as topical consumers, to test and evaluate consumers, with final authority over their releasing but at 9 of the 11 US plants, first-line supervisors told Garvin that their managers attached far more importance to meeting production schedules than to quality or in other jobs. This accords with one of the most common findings in comparative research on US and Japanese manufacturing.

(4) Only 3 US plants set annual target for reducing failures in the field; between 1979 and 1981, these were only once cut their service call rates by more than 25 per cent yet all the Japanese companies consistently improved their quality in several cases by as much as by 50 per cent and they all had elaborate company-wide systems of goal-setting.

(5) The Japanese not only collected the field failures information, that their US counterparts ignored, they also insisted on extreme precision in reporting. "It was not unusual for Japanese managers to be able to identify the 30 different ways in which switch has failed"—reports Garvin.

(6) Nor did the Japanese have to wait for such information. In the US, service call statistics took anything from a month to one year to get from the field to the factory; in Japan it was only between a week and month.

(7) The Japanese all used reliability engineering, particularly sophisticated technique applied in the US Aero Space industry for over two decades—for analysing the weaknesses of new product designs. Only one American maker of domestic air conditioners practised this approach and its defect rates were among the lowest.

(8) At most of the Japanese companies new assembly-line workers were trained, in all jobs on the line for about six months. US

workers received only several hours or days of instruction usually just for a single task. It is because of this that the Japanese workers are much more adept in tracking down quality problems originated at work stations and for better equipped to propose remedial action.

(9) Every Japanese plant made extensive use of so-called "statistical quality-control technique" (including the heavy use in controling its production process. Only one US plant—the one with the lowest defect rate—made a comparable effort, Japanese gave their workers much more information before they introduced a new model line which they did far more often than Americans. This appears to be a key factor in Japanese export drive whether in air-conditioners, cars or consumer electronics.

According to Professor Kennith Andrews of the Harvard Business School who edits the *Harvard Business Review* this study constitutes "shocking and irrefutable evidence to mediocre American performance... our quality problem must be worse than we thought." The achievements of Japanese are not to be taken as miracles. Even some of the American firms like IBM, Hewlett-Packard and Ford are currently demonstrating that it is not impossible to make the extraordinary improvements in quality levels. "What is needed is a long term commitment to fundamentals—working with vendors to improve their performance, conducting the work force, developing an accurate and responsive quality information system, setting targets for quality improvement, and demonstrating interest and commitment at the very highest levels of management."

V

As pointed out earlier the main issues in US-Japan business relations are not of economic diplomacy and international economics but are those of productivity, quality and competitiveness; all of which depend upon the management techniques and employee motivation, such as *quality circle* approach, concensus *decision-making*, and the like. Most of the literature and more straight-forward Japanese technique is of securing the maximum employee performance by offering enormous and almost company-wide financial incentives in the form of bonuses tide of corporate performance and profitability which can double a worker's salary and perquisite package. This has been demonstrated in a recently published book "*The Threat of Japanese Multinational*" (published by

John Wiley & Sons, as part of a series of books from Wiley and the German Post Institute for Research and Information on Multinationals) by Lawrence Franko of Tufts University. Franko summarises much of the two myth-breaking analysis about Japanese management which has emerged since the late 1970s from western and Japanese academic in this handy volume.

VI

There is little magical inscrutable about the way Japanese companies are running; in many cases they are much simply applying with extraordinary attention to many of the management practices which the Japanese have learnt from the west but which the west has tended to forget. He has made out an inventory of points of comparison between Japanese and western management practices. These include:

1. The crucial advantage gained in our mature industries by Japan's very early development of what calls *global logistics system*. Not only did Japanese invest much earlier than the west, in developing countries—in Latin America as well as Asia—even now its *third world* industrial sites are "far more oriented to export markets". Only in electronics and particularly semi-conductors has the west followed a similar pattern.
2. The west has been cramped by its own narrow view about the likely profitability of certain market segments. Franko says that Japanese firms "Were power-fully helped in achieving world market dominance in many (socalled) 'down-market' segments by neglect of, disdain shows for, be western producers. A misleading 'up-market/down-market' vocabulary. This reflected the negligence and was even abandonment to many segments by western makers of cars, motorcycles, TV set and machine tools and so on.
3. Franko quotes a popular Japanese catch phrase "high, thin, short and small" has been a far more positive way of viewing of what the west still seems as *'down market'* products. It is this approach which partly account for Japanese domination of so many mass markets in consumer electronics and such other goods.
4. Franko maintains that the west would be "very wrong" to think that "the Japanese only copy our technology." Such a view is at

> least ten years out of date. In any case it is abased on "a perverse view of creativity which has much to do with finding new uses of and markets for existing technology and as with making new technological break throughs. Franko also points to the alarming disparity between Japanese and US spending levels on industrial research and development. According to his calculation the Japanese consumer electronic firms spent four per cent of their sales on *research and development* in 1982, which is almost twice the US rate for the year.

In conclusion one may say that the US-Japan trade dilemma for the last few years is not one of dismantling trade barriers, revaluing Japanese currency, promoting imports in Japan and restricting production of certain types of goods and protecting US home producers. It is much more than that. These aspects of tariff and non-tariff barriers can very well be sorted out through bilateral negotiations and use of GATT institution and mechanism but the crux of the problem lies in the areas of management techniques, employee motivation and productivity, cost effectiveness, product-quality, etc. all of which have given considerable edge to Japan in competitiveness. There are limits to protectionism and the sooner the western world realises it the better. The endeavour of US should be to increase its productivity, cost effectiveness and international competitiveness so that both US and Japanese manufacturers are able to compete in an open trade system worldwide. The role of economic diplomacy and international negotations should not be confined to creating or removing various types of tariff and non-tariff barriers and put various types of pressures on trade policy. They should also pay adequate attention to research and development, innovative technology and its commercial application at a fast rate. USA and Japan can work out mutually beneficial sharing arrangement and joint ventures for their manufacturing firms so that the research and development results of each are made available to both. Effort should be to ensure uninterrupted and uninhibited flow of managerial, financial and technological resources all over the world for the benefit of the all countries. This way the two industrial gains can play their positive role in not only minimising the economic tensions between them but also in bringing up a just and equitable economic, financial, managerial and technological international order, for which the whole world has been clamouring in the last 25 years.

13

India's Exports to Japan: Problems and Issues

BADAR ALAM IQBAL*

The emergence of Japan as one of the leading economic super powers as well as one of the trading surplus nations in the world has been possible due to an interaction between economic, social and political factors in the decade of the 1980's. There are certain vital factors namely inductive planning for the economy, restrictions on possible competition between two most important facets [firms and imports], low interest rates and minimum controls on the firms and industry which have made Japan as a global force.

In recent years, Japanese Planners have initiated a market-oriented policy to deal with economic issues based upon trade liberalisation, increasing privatization and reducing fiscal deficits. As a result, Japanese manufacturers constitute one-third of the Japanese total Gross Domestic Product (GDP)[1]. This has been possible because of the ability of Japanese to adapt quickly to the fast changing business environment all over the World.

---

* Dr. Iqbal is visiting Associate Professor, Indira Gandhi Institute of Development Research, Bombay. He is Reader, Commerce, A.M.U., Aligrah (U.P.).

In recent times it has been noticed that Japan's imports are dominated by food and raw materials [particularly minerals and fuels]. This situation is of great advantage to major producing nations of food and minerals. Added to this, Japan has also reduced some tariffs and non-tariff barriers. Hence developing economies should capitalise the existing trends and situation for enhancing their exports to Japan in a big way. India should also come forward with action-oriented policy for increasing exports to Japan especially traditional items or farm exports for earning substantial amount of foreign exchange which is badly needed by India to overcome its BOP problem. With this background, the present paper reviews critically trends in Indo-Japanese Trade in the decade of the 1980's and will also suggest a strategy for increasing exports to Japanese market which has great potentials to absorb India's goods. This paper has three sections. First section reviews trends in Indo-Japanese Trade in the decade of the 1980's. Second section highlights the major constraints standing in the way of increasing exports to Japan. Third section suggests an action plan or strategy for increasing exports to Japanese market.

I

India's trade relations with Japan are traditional, diversified, and strategic. They need continuity and diversity in the decade of the 1990's. This section deals with the brief historical perspective and most recent trends in Indo-Japanese trade in the decade of the 1980's.

HISTORICAL PERSPECTIVE

India's trade relations with Japan were established in old times. "The teaching of Buddha which contributed much to shape India's social and cultural attitudes reached Japan in the middle of the Sixth Century" [Coelho, Commerce, Bombay, December 4, 1971; p. 30]. "Indian textiles was first introduced into Japan with Buddhism around the Seventh Century".[2] However, the modern commerce began much later when Japan come out of isolation at the end of Tokugawa era. Trade then came up with the start of Meiji Restoration period. During the seventh decade of the Nineteenth Century, trade relations between India and Japan were confined to exports of cotton, twist, the yarn from India and imports were limited to copper of Japan. Exports of cotton yarn were gradually substituted by raw cotton which Japan began to import due to the rising demand of raw cotton from domestic industry. Trade between 1887 and 1898 showed ups and down in quantitative terms.[3]

Trade between India and Japan continued to grow since the beginning of the Twentieth Century. Since 1902 and till 1919 most important commodities were cotton and silk manufactures. This period was more productive for Indo-Japanese trade as the same recorded regular growth. The most revealing aspect of the said period has been not only Japan's share in India's foreign trade increased, the composition of Indo-Japanese trade also went a radical change and new items namely jute, rise, iron, oilcakes etc., had emerged on the scene of major imports from India. On the export horizon new goods such as rubber manufactures, paper glass and glassware were added in the list.

On the resumption of normal trade relations, after the end of the World War I, with continental and empire countries, the steep rise in Indo-Japanese trade halted [Agrawal, 1974, p. 53]. India, had been enjoying a favourable balance of trade with Japan due to higher exports and the same continued till 1936-37. Since the inception of Indo-Japanese Trade Agreement of 1937 India had started facing unfavourable balance of trade and the same trend continued till its trade with Japan came to halt during the World War II.

After the Second World War, India's trade with Japan revived at a gradual pace. In the early fifties trade with Japan was small but began to pick up since 1951. Re-emergence of Japan as a dominating trading nation of the World during sixties and onwards has been phenomenal. But India's trade with Japan has not been able to take advantage from this situation and as a result, the flow and the total trade turnover between the two nations have been at the low ebb.

Most Recent Trends

Japan has been for the last few years one of the top three trading partners of India. But there is a basic asymmetry in the bilateral trade relations in the 1980's in the sense that "while Japan accounts for about 10 per cent of India's foreign trade, India's share in Japan's foreign trade is less than 1 per cent."[4] This trend should not be continued in the decade of the 1990's. For this India has to make all out efforts to increase export to Japanese market in a big way.

However, during the last two years, Japanese technology and aid and investment have made a distinct and discernible impact on Indian economy, especially in the automobile, electronics, electrical and engineering sectors. Japan is among the world trade leaders of today and India must hope to strengthen and expand the economic relations and the two-way trade which is the need of the hour.

The most significant development in regard to Indo-Japanese trade in the last two year has been a declining trend in India's trade deficit with Japan. Table 1 indicates trends in Indo-Japanese trade between 1980-81 and 1989-90.

Data set out in Table 1 reveals that India's exports to Japan went up by more than 3.6 times or recorded an annual average compound growth rate of 15.3 per cent between 1980-81 and 1988-89. India's Imports from Japan increased by 3.5 times or registered an annual average compound growth rate of nearly 15 per cent. India's total trade with Japan has gone up by 3.5 times or recorded an annual average compound growth rate of more than 15 per cent which is slightly lesser than the annual average compound growth rate registered by India's export to Japan. Trade deficit went up by nearly 3 times or recorded an annual average compound growth rate of more than 13 per cent during the same period. This means despite of the better annual average growth rate in India's exports, India has been facing trade deficit with Japan. Chart 1 shows trends in Indo-Japan trade.

TABLE 1

Trends in Indo-Japanese Trade Between 1980-81 and 1989-90

Year	*Exports*	*Imports*	*Total Trade*	*Balance of Trade*
1980-81	597.8	748.8	1,346.6	– 151.0
1981-82	690.0	886.0	1,576.0	– 196.0
1982-83	833.9	1087.0	1,921.8	– 254.0
1983-84	825.7	1446.9	2,272.6	– 621.2
1984-85	1029.4	1240.0	2,269.4	– 210.6
1985-86	1164.4	1774.0	2,938.4	– 609.6
1986-87	1340.9	2555.2	3,896.1	– 1214.3
1987-88	1614.9	2114.3	3,729.2	– 499.4
1988-89	2161.9	2622.0	4,783.9	– 460.1
AACGR	15.3	14.9	15.1	13.2

Note: AACGR stands for annual average compound growth rates.

Source: Report on Currency and Finance, RBI, Bombay, [Various Issues], DGCI&S, Calcutta.

CHART 1
Trends in Indo-Japan Trade

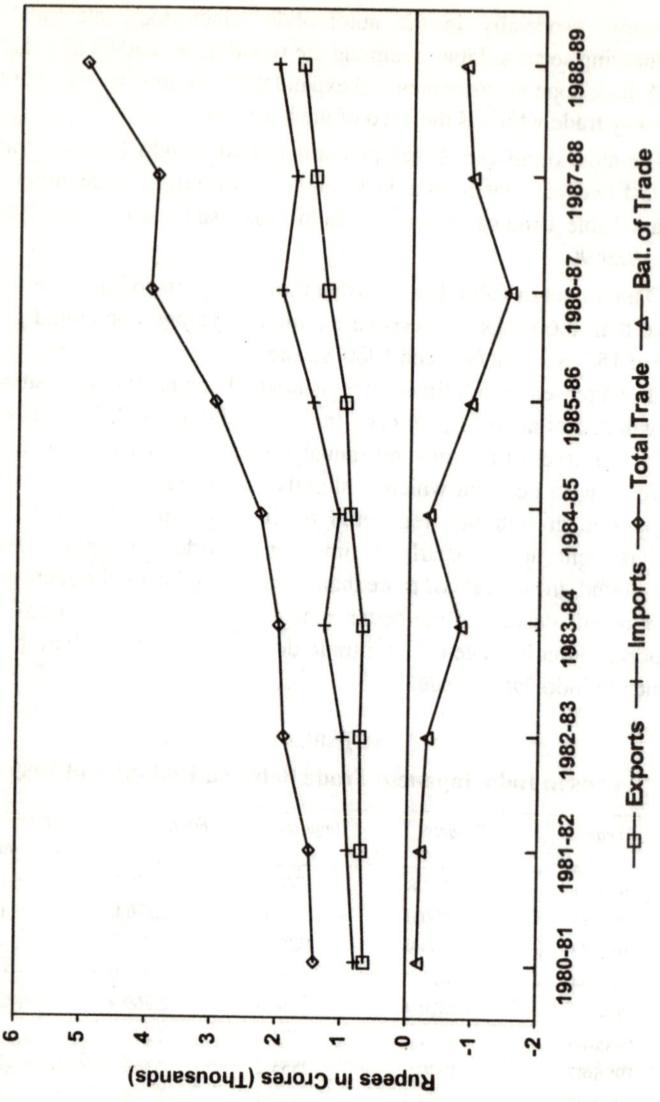

It is pertinent to point out here that "India had enjoyed a favourable trade balance with Japan up to 1979-80. Since then the balance of trade has turned against India" [Bhattacharyya, 1990, p. 38]. The trade deficit between India and Japan was the highest in the year 1986-87 amounting to Rs. 1,214 crores which constituted 90 per cent of India's total imports to Japan in that year. It is heartening to point out that "the downward trend in the trade deficit witnessed since 1986 has been maintained and in the year 1988-89, the trade deficit was amounting to Rs. 460 crores"[6] in 1988-89, the trade deficit as percentage of India's total exports to Japan stood at 21 per cent [Bhattacharyya, 1990, p. 38].

A Comparison

Table 2 gives a comparison in trades in India's foreign trade and Indo-Japanese trade between 1980-81 and 1988-89.

From the Table 2 it is clear that Indo-Japanese trade has done fairly well as compared to India's Foreign trade during the period of 9 years, i.e from 1980-81 to 1988-89 [Chart 2] as the annual average compound growth rates in regard to India's exports to Japan. India's imports from Japan, India's total trade with Japan have been much better as compared to India's total exports, India's total imports and India's total foreign trade during the period under reference. However, in regard to trade deficit, annual average compound growth rate of Indo-Japanese trade has been much higher than annual average compound growth of India's total trade deficit. Chart 3 gives much better picture regarding a comparison of different facets of India's foreign trade and Indo-Japanese trade during the period of 1980-81 and 1988-89 by comparing the annual average compound growth rates during the said period.

The appreciation of the $ in terms of the Yen has also reversed the earlier trends in bilateral trade, wherein the growth was considerably negated by the appreciation to the Yen. As a result, for the first time trade trends in Yen were higher than in dollars [The *Shipper Digest*, July 1990, p. 2]. Table 3 gives some comparative trends in Indo-Japanese trade in terms of Yen and Dollars.

Table 3 proves that for the first time Indo-Japanese trade in Yen were higher than in dollars and as a result, Indo-Japanese total trade recorded an increase of nearly 11 per cent in terms of Yen and 6 per cent in terms of dollar Exports registered a rise of 16 per cent in terms of Yen and nearly 11 per cent in terms of dollar. Imports showed a rise of 6.4 per cent

TABLE 2

Comparative Figures on India's Foreign Trade and Indo-Japanese Trade between 1980-81 and 1988-89

INDIA'S FOREIGN TRADE

(Rupees in Crores)

Years	*Exports*	*Imports*	*Total Trade*	*Balance of Trade*
1980-81	7610	12549	19259	−5838
1981-82	7803	13607	21410	−5801
1982-83	8803	14292	23095	−5489
1983-84	9777	15831	25603	−6060
1984-85	11743	17134	28877	−5390
1985-86	10895	19658	30553	−8763
1986-87	12452	20201	32653	−7748
1987-88	15741	22340	38081	−6599
1988-89	20281	27693	47974	−7412
AACGR	11.50	9.191	10.67	2.68

INDO-JAPANESE TRADE

Years	*Exports*	*Imports*	*Total Trade*	*Balance of Trade*
1980-81	598	749	1347	− 151
1981-82	690	886	1576	− 196
1982-83	834	1088	1922	− 254
1983-84	826	1447	2273	− 621
1984-85	1029	1240	2269	− 210
1985-86	1165	1774	2938	− 610
1986-87	1341	2555	3896	−1214
1987-88	1615	2114	3727	− 499
1988-89	2162	2622	4874	− 460
AACGR	15.34	14.93	15.12	13.1

Source: Same as Table 1.

CHART 2

Trends in India's F. Trade and Indo-Japanese Trade

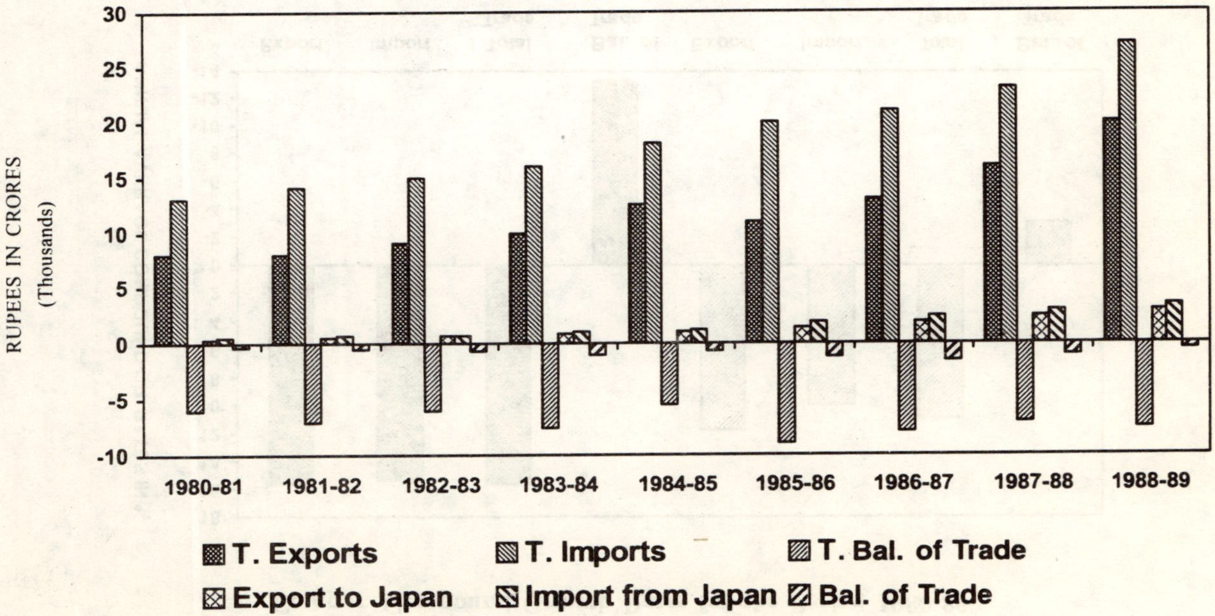

CHART 3

Compar. Compound Growth Rates for the Period 1980-89

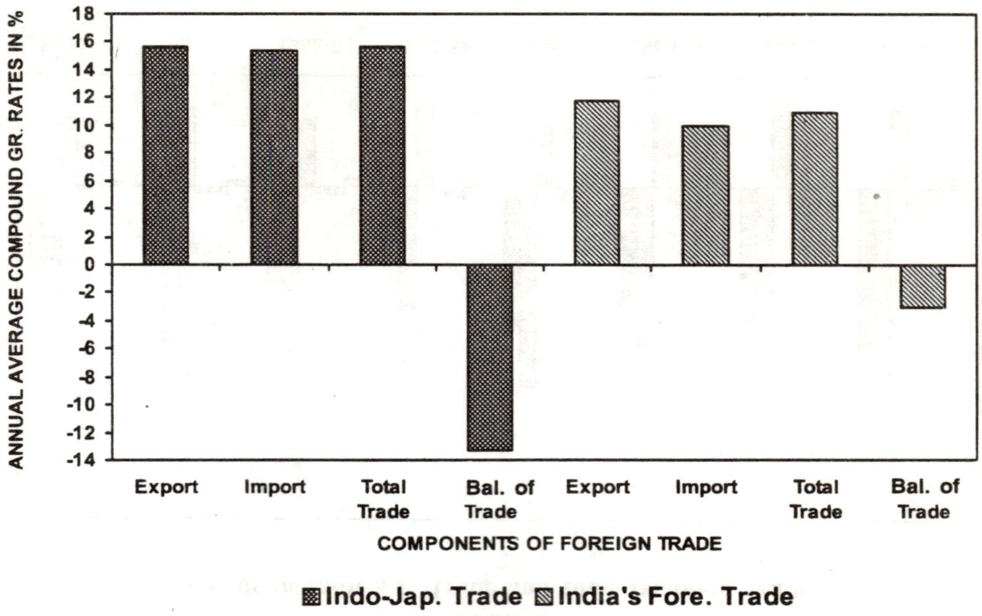

TABLE 3

Indo-Japanese Trade in Terms of Yen and Dollars 1986-89

Particulars	*1986*	*1987*	*1988*	*1988*	*1989 Jan.*
					(In Million US $)
Total	3396	3487	3886	2552	2707
India's Exports	1296	1530	1804	1195	1322
India's Imports	2099	1957	2082	1357	1385
Trade Balance	–802	–427	–278	–162	–63
					(In Billion Yen)
Total	576	509	498	326	362
India's Exports	223	227	231	152	177
India's Imports	223	258	267	174	185
Trade Balance	–130	–61	–36	–22	–8

ANNUAL RATE OF GROWTH (%)

	1986/ 1985	*1987/ 1986*	*1988/ 1987*	*1989 (Jan.-Aug.) 1988 (Jan.-Aug.)*
Total Trade				
In terms of US$	+21.0	+2.7	+11.4	+6.0
In terms of Yen	–13.0	–11.6	–2.2	–10.9
Exports				
In terms of US$	+9.1	18.1	17.9	10.6
In terms of Yen	–21.8	+0.7	+1.8	+16.0
Imports				
In terms of US$	+31.5	–6.8	+6.4	2.1
In terms of Yen	–6.4	–19.4	+3.5	+6.5

Source: The Shipper Digest, Bombay, July 1990.

in terms of Yen and 2.1 per cent in terms of dollar. These trends also confirm that they "are consistent with the program initiated by Japan to contain its trade surplus and balance of trade with the trading partners" [Shipper Digest, *op. cit.*, p. 2]. A clear trend in regard to these facets can be seen from Charts 4 & 5.

Trends in 1990-91

Indo-Japanese trade during the first ten months [April-December] of the current financial year amounting to Rs. 4,492.7 crores against Rs. 3,893.5 crores in the corresponding three quarters of 1989-90 which certainly a healthy trend keeping in mind the present trade and payments crisis.

According to the latest figures issued by the Ministry of Commerce, Government of India. India's exports during (April-December) of 1990-91 stood at Rs. 2,113.5 crores and India's imports from Japan valued at Rs. 2,379.2 crores as against of Rs. 1,903.6 crores and Rs. 1,989.9 crores exports and imports respectively during the same period of 1989-90.

Some Revealing Facts

The most revealing aspect of India's trade with Japan which is of concern, has been India's "inability to diversify significantly its export basket, despite serious efforts being made during the last decade" [Bhattacharyya, 1990, p. 38]. This does not mean that no new export items have been enlisted into India's major exports to Japan but that overall impact on the export structure has so far been marginal. The most recent item which has penetrated into Japanese sophisticated market has been dyes and dye intermediates. Other non-traditional items which have also gained considerably are leather goods, garments, textile fabrics, engineering goods including auto parts and machine tools, fresh fruits and vegetables, chemicals, household furnishing floorings, software and sport goods, however, there are certain traditional times and as also iron ore and marine goods which have recorded considerable decline in 1990-91.

Another fact has been that India's export basket to Japan is dominated by traditional goods. It is amusing that only three goods namely—iron ore, marine goods and diamonds constituting nearly 75 per cent of the India's total exports [Bhattacharyya, 1990, p. 39].

It is also important to reveal that about a dozen goods account for more than 90 per cent of India's total exports to Japan. They include readymade garments, leather, granite, fruit and vegetables, cotton and cotton fabrics. The export of these items to Japan has been the outcome of India's efforts to diversify the items to enter into Japanese market.

Products which have provided good possibilities for increasing exports to Japan in 1990-91 include light engineering goods, gold jewellery, carpets, bicycles and bicycles components and computer software. These trends show that there has been gradual and steady diversification of exports to Japanese market.

CHART 4

Indo-Japan Trade in $ and Yen

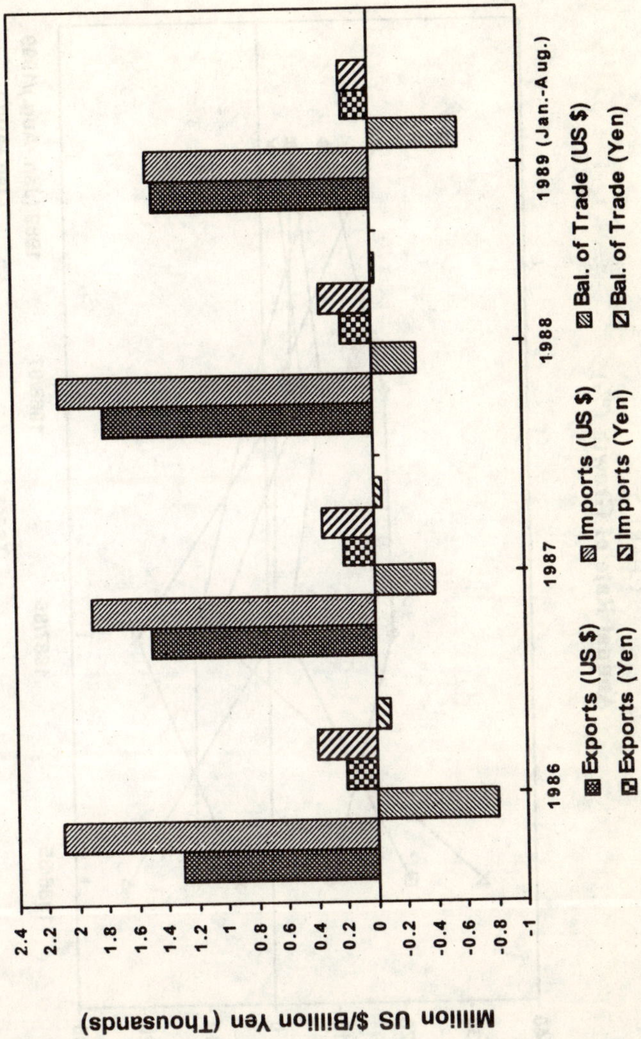

CHART 5
Annual Rate of Growth (%)

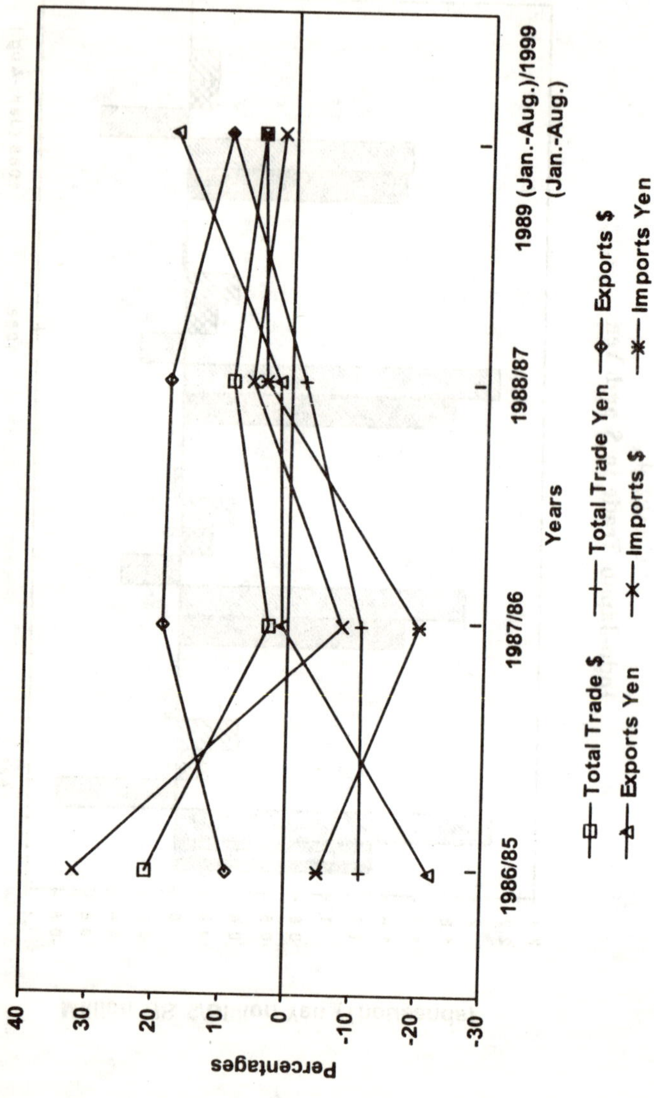

However, these efforts are modest and India has to go a long way in diversifying exports to Japan as there has been enormous potential of penetration of Indian goods into Japanese market.

Very recently, the Japanese ambassador to India [*Mr. S. Kobayashi*] has rightly suggested that "the potential Indian exporters should explore every possible measure to offer highest quality products as there has been enormous scope of Indian goods to enter into Japanese market". Hence India must strengthen its foreign exchange earning capability for its economic growth and this could be possible when India would "improve further the international competitiveness of its manufacturing industry as Japan has great potential to absorb Indian manufactured goods in a big way in year to come" [The Independent, Bombay, May 10, 1991, p. 8]

Confirming the worst fears, India's trade gap for the year 1990-91 has crossed the Rs. 10,000 crore mark to finish at Rs. 10,500 Crore, showing an alarming rise of nearly 36 per cent on the figures of last year, i.e. 1989-90 amounting to Rs. 7,731 crores. Under such situation India has to come out with all out efforts to increase exports to those nations where there is an enormous scope of absorbing Indian goods such as Japan, Germany and EEC countries. If concerted efforts are made India could increase exports to Japan in a big way and then ease out the alarming trade gap.

India will commit a "fundamental mistake in its export strategy if it does not take note of rapidly changing global market conditions especially in Japan, Germany and the EEC" [*The Independent,* Bombay, May 10, 1991, p. 8]. If India seriously wanted to promote its export expansion, the Japanese market should not be underestimated. Keeping in mind the existing trends in India's foreign trade, India-Japan Standing Committee (IJCS), has formulated an action-oriented strategy for increase exports to Japan at the rate of 17 to 18 per cent. Table 4 gives projections in regard to India's exports to Japan for 1995.

From the foregoing analysis it has been brought out that though Indo-Japanese trade has done fairly well in the decade of the 1980's, there has been much left to be achieved as existing potential has not been tapped fully. With recent liberalisation undertaken by the Government of Japan there has been enormous opportunities for Indian exporters to capitalised the situation and should bring India out of the alarming trade gap. However, it is not easy to penetrate into Japanese market as there are "too many constraints" in the way of attaining an appreciable increase

TABLE 4

Commodity-wise Projections of Export to Japan

(US $ Million)

Items	*Exports in 1988*	*Projected Exports in 1995*
Foodstuffs	322.7	630
Raw materials	662.5	2015
—Textile materials	24.0	25
—Iron ore	473.0	1800
—Chrome ore	7.0	30
—Other non-ferrous metals	7.0	200
Mineral fuels	46.1	50
Manufactured goods	748.5	2765
—Chemicals	21.9	185
—Machinery & equipment	3.8	10
Textiles [garments]	103.9	600
—Metal goods	3.9	300
—Diamonds	556.1	1500
—Leather & Leather goods	20.9	170
Total [including others]	1804.4	15500

Source: IJBC, New Delhi.

in India's exports to Japan. Section II deals with major handicaps standing in the way of Indian exporters to increase exports to Japanese market. If major constraints are solved then it would not be difficult for India to attain the projections for India's exports to Japan amounting to 5500 million US dollars the end of 1995.

II

Japan has emerged India's third largest trade partner after the USSR and the USA. It accounts for nearly 10% of India's total trade. There has been diversification with products such as textiles, leather and leather goods, shrimps, prawns and lobster, non-metallic mineral goods and diamonds partly replacing an export-mix mainly of agricultural commodities. However, more sophisticated items such as engineering goods, electronics, garments and chemicals, which seemed to have had a promising start, have not really performed to a desired level. This is due to lack of desired international competitiveness of Indian manufacturing industry because without increasing the export of manufactured products, there is no way to achieve this target. Lack of exposition to greater international competition has also been attributed to this level and structure. Hence this section brings to light the major factors responsible for exporting less to Japan and how they showed be overcome.

Constraints to be Looked into

(a) All trade policy is ultimately concerned with exports. However, some regulation have a more immediate effect. Hence, bilateral matters should be given much attention as compared to multilateral issues. One of the major defects in India's approach is that we do not use the linkage available from our big purchases abroad to promote exports. This aspect should be tackled effectively and a suitable machinery should be set up for the purpose. India has done well with Japan under GSP arrangements in the past. It is important to note here that further enlargement of the existing GSP concessions is not likely to make much difference. But values, volume and quotas require regular revision keeping in mind the long-term perspective. There is also a need to study the availability of GSP for new exports entering into the Japanese market. For instance, a case can now be made for reduced tariffs or GSP quotes for certain tropical agricultural products, namely shrimps, where the ACP get reduced duty and where there is no history of their being traditional exporters. India also needs to get reductions in the tariff on processed agricultural commodities or goods supplied in consumer packs. This areas has got lesser attention in trade policies. Hence, the trade policy should by dynamic and result-oriented in the long-term perspective.

(b) Export promotion is a broader term divided into three parts namely, product development, marketing and infrastructure improvement. There are a number of organisations dealing with promotion and product development, which do not involve any individual producer. Similarly, there are inadequate incentives for producers to undertake exports themselves as these producers do not have necessary resources at their command to get involved in the needed expertise. This trend leads to speculative sales and resulting into defaults, price instability, commercial disputes and eventually a setback to the entire export promotion effort. Hence, the need of the day is to give more emphasis on the participation of the individual producers and they should get urgent need for decentralisation of promotion efforts. The present setup of export promotion organization should be gradually democratized and permitted to develop, so that they can undertake a major effort in export promotion. These organizations should have a capacity for self-policing. The Government's paternalistic approach may not go a long way in export promotion. If resources are pooled by the exporters (producers) for export promotion, only then will they feel really involved. It is also observed that there are too many export promotion councils and organisations with much overlapping of jurisdiction and effort. There should be a self-sustaining, self-governing export community for each major export commodity for Japanese market.

(c) Fluctuations in exchange rates has also hampered India's exports to Japan during the last 15 years. From 1971 to 1975 the Indian rupee was depreciated in real terms mainly because of the sharp depreciation of the Nominal Exchange Rate (NER), which resulted from the fact that the rupee was for most of the time pegged to pound sterling, which was itself falling very sharply. Between 1973 and 1974, inflation in India was quite rapid and somewhat faster that inflation abroad. During the 70s Indian exports grew at a remarkable rate of 8 points per year in real terms, largely due to the depreciation of the real exchange rate. The period beginning from 1979 tells an entirely different story. This period began with a world oil prices increase. The need to increase non-oil exports and the adverse international trade and aid climate suggested that our Real Exchange Rate (RER) be brought down. In fact, it rose in the third quarter of 1985 the RER was higher than in 1979 by 15%. Only in the last quarter of 1985, it came down sharply. It was however still higher than in 1979.

(d) Infrastructure problems, namely transport, freight costs and packaging, having hampered the flow of goods from India to Japan. Hence, they require much more attention. Not only are freight rate often more expensive than those of competitors elsewhere, but transport arrangements are also primitive, cumbersome and slower. Shipping and ports are the backbone of Indian exports to foreign markets. Indian shipping services are inadequate and wherever available arè infrequent. Indian ports are also ill-equipped to handle the large-sized ships effectively and efficiently. It is essential that we stay up-to-date as regards, in our ports, airports and all types of handling facilities. Regrettably even State Corporations, such as the Shipping Corporation and Air India, sometimes utilise their monopoly position to increase export freight rates. The port charges are also disproportionately high, being 3/4 times more than those prevailing in Asian ports such as Colombo, Hong Kong, Singapore and South Korea. What is urgently needed is to provide for efficient container vessels at least for most of our identified destinations. These services must be competitive in quality, cost and frequency.

Packing is getting better, but improvement is slow, particularly on packaging for retail distribution. Which is where there is most value addition. Serious consideration needs to be given to allowing exporters to do this in India or Japan depending upon where it can be done in a better way and economically.

(e) Despite India's relatively cheap manpower and endowment of large resources, India is rated as one of the high cost nations in the world. This trend has done irreparable damage to India's export structure. India has also lost much share in world trade and the trend is still persisting. The high cost trend is persisting due to the heavy burden of taxes, direct and indirect, and their cascading effect, and the high cost of finances, inputs, and raw materials. These factors keep the quality at a low level. Hence, the need of the hour is that these impediments have to be overcome at all cost. Commodity taxes should be so rationalized as to make Indian exports competitive. Despite the recent reduction in the interest rate on export credit (pre- and post-shipment) India is still nowhere near the major exporting countries for instance Switzerland, where export credit is available at 7% and Japan where it is available at 6%. Malaysia provides export credit at 5% and Pakistan provides export credit at the lowest level, i.e., 3%. But in India the rate of interest on export credit is as high as 9.5%. How Indian exporters can keep the cost and quality constraint at a low level and make themselves competitive? Prices of raw materials and inputs are also on the high side as compared with other major exporting countries such as South Korea, Japan and Taiwan. This aspect also needs rethinking and materials should be made available to exporters on internationally competitive rates. Excise and customs duties must be reduced and exemption on machinery and equipment required for export must be given so that expansion, modernization and technological upgradation could be made possible which are the only alternatives for keeping cost and quality at a competitive level.

(f) Erratic power supply and sudden cuts as well as high cost of power also have far reaching adverse effects on Indian goods competitiveness in the Japanese market. By and large units are not able to have optimum utilisation of their capacity on account of these constraints, raising their overhead costs. Labour remains idle leading to increase in the wage bill without contribution to production. In fact, the exporting units should be insulated against power cuts and power shedding. Power tariffs for export units should also be rationalized. Some sort of rebate on the consumption of power should be made available to export-oriented units. In a recent issue of *Fortune* (Bombay, April 1991) it is mentioned that "power tariffs changes are also responsible for the resign prices of Indian goods in Japanese market and our dilemma is that it is not possible to pass on these extra cost to the consumers in the Japanese market because of stiff competition, nor can we absorb them. The power tariffs are ten times more than what are charged to the steel industry in Brazil and Mexico". These observations have to be taken seriously by the concerned authorities and such existing disparities in regard to power tariffs must be minimized at all costs.

(g) Indian exports to Japan are also lacking in marketing infrastructure and marketing techniques. Indian exporters are not able to either negotiate or offer competitive terms, invest in the creation of distribution channels nor indeed keep constant track of business opportunities in Japan and provide essential after-sales service. Counter trade and barter deals are assuming significance as effective trading techniques. But India has not made such dealings so far. However, there is an urgent need to adopt these techniques of marketing so that the flow of trade could be increased. The private export and trading houses, which account for bulk of the export trade, are not allowed to enter into such trade transactions. This comes in the way of export expansion to the Japanese market. Hence the need of the hour is that both governmental agencies as well as private sector exporting organisations should have access to this modern method of export promotion. To start with, a few sectors should be identified for the purpose. There is also an urgent need for entering into marketing collaborations with Japanese firms and setting up joint trading companies specially for promoting exports of Indian traditional goods in particular and non-traditional goods in general. In a recent study of India-Japan Business Cooperation Committee (IJBCC) certain items have been identified wherein there will be great potential of exports to Japan. These items are equipment and machinery, metallic ores and food goods and the demand of these items will be increasing keeping in mind Japanese global imports liberalisation till 1993. Such opportunities must not be missed out by the Indian exporters and a çoordinated policy of resources and efforts must be the necessity of the decade of the 1990.

(h) It is rightly said ''no risk, no gain''. Indian exporters are not taking any risk of entering into the Japanese market with their new products. They are afraid of losing their capital due to the sensitivity of the Japanese market. They know that nothing dies faster than a newly launched product. They also know that more than 80% of the new products develop face leakages at an early state of their development, meeting a premature death in their marketing adventure. Such a high mortality rate of a new product shocking for as it involves a tremendous wastage of human effort and materials. This fear keeps Indian exporters away from exporting their goods to the Japanese market. But for increasing exports to Japan risk will have to be taken at all cost. Government agencies and other export promotion agencies should come forward and motivate the new entrants to export goods to the Japanese market. They should extend moral support and should also make efforts to take out the persisting fear from the minds of the new exports. They should also provide all possible information on the movement and consumer trend in Japan to these exporters.

(i) While the Government of India's intentions to boost export by granting of various incentives to exporters are to be lauded, the implementation of such incentive leaves much to be desired. This situation also bumper the flow of goods from India to the Japanese market. It is often observed that the incentives meant for genuine exporters either do not reach them at all or reach them so late that their advantage is nullified. There are numerous occasions when these incentives have gone to wrong hands (*The Hindustan Times*, May 8, 1989) while genuine exporters have faced harassment. This situation should be avoided and the incentives must go to the need exporters so that they could contribute much for the promotion of exports to Japanese market in a big way.

Sometimes it happens that Indian exporters face un-necessary delays in getting incentives for the promotion of exports to the Japanese market. They also lose their time, money and energy in getting the incentives. In the case of the cash assistance schemes, it is often found that in the last two months of the financial year the applications form the exporters for cash assistance are not accepted at the counter of the joint CCI & E for some reason or the other. If at all the application if found complete in all respects the authorities say that they do not have cash to pay and thus ask the exporters to submit the same at a later date. This means that exporters do not get assistance in time. Hence, it may be said that "assistance delayed in effect is assistance denied."

Similar fate is encountered in the case of International Price Replenishment Scheme (IPRS). The benefit under the said scheme to exporters is also frequently delayed. Once it is done with great difficulty and inconvenience, the export promotion council might not have the money to make the payments of IPRS. Hence, the hardship in securing incentives and other benefits must be minimized. They could be minimized with some flexibility in the procedures and by gearing up the administrative machinery. If these trends continue then whatever efforts are to be made will all go in vain.

(j) All goods in general, and engineering goods in particular, require selective approach for exports to Japanese market. This is due to the fact that there is severe competition in the Japanese market. The time has come to think in terms of not only creating the right type of "Winner" but also to find out "root of competitive ability" [*Business Express*, Bombay, May 16, 1991, p. III]. They should also be assured of that resources are not spread too thinly. It is thus high time to be selective in strategy and approach. Looking on the exports of engineering exports, the concept of selectivity becomes all the more important. Those items which are gaining a market in Japan must get all sorts of help and encouragement so that they could attain "economies of scale" and emerge as leading items in India's engineering exports effort. The significance of caring for customers can be understood from the golden ruled "do unto others as you would have them do unto you" [Sastry, VVR, *Business Express, op. cit.*, p. III]. These things should be kept in mind while exporting India's leading items to Japanese market.

In the Japanese market there has not been an image of India as an industrial country, though India has been among the 10 most industrialised countries of the world. As a result, in the Japanese market there is an impression that Indian goods are not qualitative and hence have not penetrated into the Japanese market. But India is the producer of quality goods and has an ability to compete in the Japanese market. India's competitive ability should be boosted "competition grows and makes more attractive and innovative products available to customers. Therefore, to survive and grow, affirm needs to keep itself on the toes, ever looking for newer and more creative ways of meeting the changing customer needs''. This should be translated into reality if India want to penetrate into Japanese market in a big way. There is an urge for projecting India's image as an industrial country capable of producing the sophisticated industrial goods and having technology in several lines of industrial output comparable with best available anywhere. The Government of India should encourage and sponsor trade fairs and exhibition in major cities of Japan in which Industrial goods, including machinery and various descriptions of engineering goods, figure prominently. Japanese importers still believe that Indian engineering goods, lack quality. Building up capabilities in this respect makes it possible for Indian companies to face international competition and exposure of various sorts. Such exposure may have far reaching effect on the product (its design, specification, performance, operational life and productivity, supply schedule (maintenance of regular supply, assembly in foreign countries, installation of machinery, etc., quality, pricing, packaging, in a big manner. Very recently Japan has shown keen interest in a sustaining publicity in regard to India's investment policy, export incentives, 100 per cent Export Oriented Units, etc. This is a welcome effort and India should come out with a comprehensive plan in the said respect.

Exporter's strategies and policies as also tactics matching those of competitors and, to some extent, substitutes, specifications and technical quality requiring high technical excellence and responsiveness. Princing must be aimed at long-term interest of customer retention rather than immediate profit, even though the market can bear higher prices in the short-run; and packaging with all its variety and sophistication in conditions where the packages seem to sell the contents will come in the way of Indian export to do all out efforts in expanding exports to Japan.

Exposure would be a real test of strength which many organisations would like to face. There are other rewards that go a long way with exporting which may be big enough compensation, for instance, protection from recession in the domestic market causing large scale under utilisation of capacity, acquaintance with foreign market (Japan), knowledge of competitor and its way of handling issues, improvements in designs and more upto date knowhow all of which would involve high cost if procured from other channels. Hence all out efforts be made to boost the image of India in general and of Indian goods in particular. It is pertinent to suggest here that both the Governments [India and Japan] should consider a possibility of Government to Government agreement for the programme of publicity as publicity in Japan is quite expensive. Negotiations in this respect should be taken as early as possible.

(k) The tendency of the Government for plundering instead of concentrating and consolidating known pastures has given rather poor results while wrong commodities, wrong countries, and wrong organisations have all created an unnecessary rush of activities in different circles. Not only that, the quantitative results have been poor but also that the returns have not been quite economical considering the cost of promotional activities involved (*Commerce*, Bombay, May 30, June 5, 1989). The major factors standing in the way of developing export obligation concept are: (i) cumbersome producers creating credibility gaps; (ii) delay in getting clearance from the governments at the Centre and the States as also various agencies controlled by them; (iii) restriction of their freedom to sell in the domestic market even when the export markets have remained subject to recessionary forces, and (iv) non-availability of other incentatives. Similarly, the requirements of market promotion and market maintenance are different in the sense that once a market has been developed, it requires sustained efforts to retain it. This is not easy in conditions dictated by the other competitors and substitutes. The existing trends have been affecting India's exports to Japan in a big way. These should be simplified in the light of Abid Hussain Committee appointed by the Government of India in the 1980's.

(l) Although launched aims and objectives in the later part of the decade of the 1980's, export performance of the export-oriented units (EOU's) has been dismal. Out of the 780 units approved by the end of 1989, only 150 units have become operative. Against the original target of earning foreign exchange worth Rs. 5,000 crores in five years, the actual cumulative earning of these units has amounted to a meager sum of Rs. 1000 crores by the end of 1989 and was far behind the set target. The surprising aspect is that many units have shown their inclination for desbending or, in other words, for opting out of the scheme. Hence, it is necessary to review and restructure the entire scheme so that it could become more productive and economically viable. The Japanese have shown the keen interest to have more information about EOUs on sustained basis and as a result, IJBCC is drawing up a programme for export seminars and continuous public in Japan regarding these units and it is hoped that this step will give a lot of benefits for EOUs for expanding their exports to Japan.

The Foreign Exchange Regulation Act (FERA) enforced in the beginning of the 1970's and the same has outlived its utility so it must be recast to promote exports and to enable Indian business to compete in the Japanese market. This is of paramount significance in the sense that the conditions in which business operates now are entirely different from what they were when the original legislation was framed. Time changes very fast and is of vital importance for the expansion of International business. Decision-making at times, has to be done quickly and on the spot. But the existing procedure is time consuming and delay in getting clearance from the Reserve Bank of India (RBI) makes the decision unproductive. This situation has affected Indian goods export to foreign markets in general and Japanese market in particular. Hence the need of the day is to make the procedure more effective, flexible and productive so that the entrepreneurs have the freedom to operate according to the circumstance of the business. It would be better if the same is modified in the light of the suggestions given by the Raunaq Singh Committee.

(m) Lower Unit Value realisation is another major constraint affecting the flow of goods from India to Japan. There are many commodities, although physical targets have been achieved, the unit value realisation has declined as in case of tea, raw cotton, iron ore, jute, cashew nuts and tobacco. This has been due to severe competition India has been facing from major exporting countries of these items in the Japanese market. A comprehensive plan must be chalked out in this respect so that India could enhance its unit value realisation on an increasing scale. In this respect, various Boards and Export Promotion should be assigned a greater role.

(n) A major factor for India's poor export performance in relation to Japan is the heavy pressure on exportable surplus form domestic demand and supply constraints, making export promotion yet more formidable and challenging. In recent years, this pressure has become more alarming due to the higher domestic demand. Therefore, efforts must be made to stabilise production base of India's items entering into Japanese market. If production base is not stabilised then there is a great possibility of giving away its share to other rivals in Japanese market as it has shaped in case of shrimps.

(o) Notwithstanding the inroads made by Indian traditional and non-tradition items in the Japanese market, it is surprising to note that Indian exporters have not been able to add value to their product lines. There are a number of cases in which India has failed to obtain value-added realisation in regard to specific goods. . .goods ranging from agro-based items such as cashew, marine products, species, tea and coffee to .lothing and engineering goods. The Government of India has also laid stress on technology upgradation in several key export sectors which is reflected in adequate measures in our recent import policy. It is high time for Indian exporters to capitalise on the situation and to develop higher-value realization in specific goods such as engineering goods, leather manufactures and readymade garments in the Japanese market.

(p) Apart from the value addition problem there is a problem of establishment of warehousing/storage facilities at important commercial centers (Tokyo, Osaka, Hiroshima and Kyoto) in Japan. Such warehouses can be set up jointly with some of the leading processors, packers or the distributors in Japan for joint marketing arrangements. The most advantageous aspect of warehousing in Japan's commercial cities is that, apart from ensuring prompt deliveries, it establishes a strong market presence in Japan. This may serve as a key for capturing the Japanese market. But unfortunately none of the major commercial cities of Japan have warehousing facility for Indian goods and this is why Indian non-traditional items such as engineering goods, textiles, gem and jewellery and carpets have failed in making any dent in the Japanese market.

(q) One of the reasons responsible for the narrow base of Indian goods is that India's export promotion efforts are too short-term in nature and are also spread too thinly over too many goods at one and the same time. The essence of marketing in Japan is that competition requires a concentrated campaign possibly over the years, to establish a market for a particular products or even a brand or product. The campaign has to be directed at wholesalers, distributors or consumers, possibly varying the projection and techniques. Once launched, it should not be subject to sudden variations even for financial reasons, added to this, there has to be constant follow-up which itself will cause adjustments in the campaign and development in the product. One big promotion by itself is often wasteful and ineffective. The time-frame within which we expect to develop a market is usually too short and we try to sell to much at the same time. These tendencies will hamper India's export efforts to Japan and will also not last long. Therefore, these steps must be avoided at all costs. There should be a regular exchange of buying/selling missions between the two countries on specific goods [IJBC].

(r) The lack of knowledge as to know, how to enter into Japanese market is another important constraint standing in the way of widening the export base of Indian goods in the Japanese market. The exporters do not have adequate knowledge about exporting to the Japanese market and the procedures to enter the Japanese market. Every Indian exporter should know the basic regulations and procedures to be followed while exporting goods to Japan. They must know the currency requirements and exchange regulations, trade policy and trade regulations [tariff-rate quota system (TRO) and GSP Scheme such as CCCN], structure of duties, and taxes on exports and imports, documentation, trading channels, etc. The knowledge of these basic requirements may go a long way in expanding India's exports to Japan.

From the foregoing analysis it has been brought out that there has been a lot of factors which have hampered India's exports to Japan and due to these factors India has failed in widening her export base in the Japanese market and as a result, India accounts for even less than 1 per cent of Japan's total trade [Bhattacharyya, April-June 1990, p. 38]. These factors have to be tackled on war footing so that India could capitalise the opportunity of liberal import policy [tariffs reductions, simplification of import testing procedures, expansion in import quotas on agricultural goods, and more open Government procurement arrangements (Saxena, S.S., April-June 1990, p. 10] of Japan announced recently.

As India has been passing through critical juncture of depleting balance of payments [BOP] and seeking Japan's help to overcome the crisis. It is heartening to note that Japan is keen to help India to improve its balance of payment position in a big way. Hence, the need of the hour is to remove the major handicaps and Indian exporters "must explore every possible measure to offer best quality goods" [Kobayashi, S., Japan's ambassador to India]. It is true that there is growing tendency among consumers in Japan to attach greater importance to quality than to price in their buying decisions. For this, India has to strengthen its foreign exchange capabilities through improvement in its international competitiveness of the goods in a big way which needs an action and result oriented strategy. With this background, Section III suggests a package of guide-posts for better and effective export performance of India with Japan in the decade of the 1990's.

III

Japan is a land of opportunities for exporters. However, it is a formidable task to capitalise the opportunities as Japanese standards are very high in qualitative terms. This could be possible through greater exposure of Indian industry producing manufactured goods to greater international competition. This requires innovative approach and strategy which would base on the effective solution of certain issues which are being discussed in the III section in the following pages.

Issues to be Tackled on War Footing

There are certain key and vital issues to be looked into for having a sound and action oriented strategy for Japanese market. They included: (1) uncompetitive Export Prices; (2) poor quality; (3) non-fulfilment of delivery schedules; (4) commercial feasibility; (5) sales promotion; (6) lobbying; (7) institutional support; (8) strengthen territorial division; (9) empowered committee; (10) development of export culture; (11) production for export; (12) inductive targets; (13) exchange of information; (14) follow up of basic principles for negotiations; (15) trade fairs and exhibitions; (16) constant vigilance; (17) professional approach; (18) long-term policy; (19) publicity; (20) storage facilities; (21) and training for maintaining high quality. The said issues will go a long way in widening India's export base in Japanese market which is the need of the day.

(1) India is basically a high cost economy. This has been due to a number of factors such as: (a) high cost of inputs namely steel, cement, power and oil; (b) low level of productivity due to low efficiency of labour, capital and technology; (c) high incidence of commodity taxation; (d) uneconomic size of production units; (e) lack of spirit on the part of the entrepreneurs for the attainment of 'optimum size'; and (f) high cost of credit. These constraints lead to higher prices for Indian goods entering into Japanese market and thus, they become uncompetitive already lost international competitiveness. Hence there is an urgent need to reduce the cost without tampering with quality in order to survive in the savagely, very competitive Japanese market. Japan can also play an effective and efficient role by transferring new technologies to India enabling her to reduce costs to the minimum possible extent. Trade-related investment could serve a better cause in keeping the cost checked and also in the acceleration of India's exports to Japan. Very recently, the Japanese have suggested "a model industrial town to be set

up jointly by the private and Government sectors of the two countries where export-oriented and import substitution ventures could be set up'' [IJBCC]. The should be accepted by the Indian Government without any further delay as it will serve as a ''spring board'' in Indo-Japanese trade in a big way.

(2) The Japanese consumers are very sensitive to the quality. Indian exporters should not take risk in compromising on quality control if they wanted to have a major share of Japanese market. Hence, it is of paramount significance to apply innovative techniques in the manufacturing process so that a new dimension could be given to the consumer goods. Indian manufactures and exporters must keep themselves abreast with the latest developments in technology and should also endevour to implement the ''marketing game' of international trade. Products of 'super quality' only are likely to sell. Japan also has stringent quality and testing standards for imports. Therefore, support sectors for exports are of paramount significance and they could ensure that products meet Japanese standards and would solve many of the problems of packaging, cold chain, quality testing and were housing which Indian goods have been facing in these days. Scope for increasing cooperation in the said areas between the two nations is the need of the hour.

(3) Indian export to Japan is affected due to non-supply of goods in time to the main outlets. Strict adherence to time schedule is an important factor in marketing goods particularly in Japan. In the absence of time schedule exporters may loose their credibility and reliability. These two facets are the missing links in India's exports to Japan. It is generally said that delays make the product to loose 80 per cent of its sales. This sort of loss of sales could be averted by offsetting the delays through prompt acceleration of production schedules timely by appraisal of the market situation. Exporters should maintain enough buffer stocks so that goods could be delivered in time.

(4) Products are exported for earning larger profits. If a product can not be manufactured on a large scale and sold at profit, it has little commercial value. Certain industrial and consumer goods which involve highly advanced engineering technology and specialised skill in their production do not, at time, qualify the test of commercial feasibility and seldom succeed in marketing. In regard to certain items namely—carpets, engineering goods and non-metallic goods an assessment of commercial feasibility is of vital importance in Japanese market. Indian

exporters of these goods should carefully assess the commercial feasibility before evolving an export strategy to Japanese market.

(5) Japan is an open and highly competitive market, where the consumer can be won over through publicity media like, T.V., radio, newspapers, specialised trade Journals, bill boards, etc. The Japanese Government has been very active in encouraging imports through various promotion schemes and using booklets providing details on how the market has become more open. Indian exporters should capitalise on these schemes for expanding exports of their items. The Japan External Trading Organization is one of the organizations, which help importers to get required trade information Indian exporters, should establish effective and efficient links with such organizations so that they could know what and how to export to Japanese market.

(6) Lobbying is a powerful tool, through which necessary influence can be exerted on high-ranking decision-markers in Tokyo. Lobbyists offer a wide range of services, utilizing their contacts, influence and rapport with the Government officials which goes a long way towards expanding trade and economic relations between India and Japan. Since it is an accepted act of intervention and plays a vital role in not only promoting trade interest but also averting undesirable decisions, it is desirable to create a special fund in India for lobbying in Japan. This could be done by earmarking a nominal portion of export earnings from Japan. Some matching grant should be provided by the Government. This may prove as an effective tool for expanding trade and economic relations between India and Japan.

(7) As Japan is the third largest trade partner of India after USSR and the USA, it needs a special treatment and thrust. It immediately requires an institution for: (a) supplying information on changes in Japan's trade policies and practices and tools of effective and efficient marketing in Japanese market; (b) analyzing the impact on India's trade from changes in Japanese trade policies and providing necessary feedback; (c) identifying export opportunities; and (d) giving specific recommendations to Government on changes needed in export promotion policies and incentives to respond to the marketing opportunities. These tasks must be assigned to a Special Task Force for the purpose. It should work in collaboration with India-Japan Committee for Business Cooperation, Institute of Foreign Trade of India and Indian Council for Research on International Economic Relations. In this regard also the recent request of Indian Government to establish a special office

at Tokyo to expand India's export base must be translated into a reality. The modalities should be worked out at the earliest as it will pay positive and increasing dividends to Indian export community.

(8) As India's trade relations with Japan are traditional, strategic and vital for both the countries, it is of paramount significance to establish a territorial division for trade with Japan in the Ministry of Commerce or if desirable to make it a separate division. But the division must be headed by a senior official who has vast knowledge of Japanese economy. The main thrust would be to provide necessary help to manufacturers and exporters to capitalize the identified opportunities and also to provide protection against the perceived threats. These divisions are also of vital importance as they may be very useful in translating the huge potential of this market into a reality. This division should also play double role firstly to provide all sorts of information to Japanese importers on exportable items and exporting companies and secondly to locate Indian partners and Indian exporters desiring to explore the Japanese market.

(9) Japanese market will remain a very important trading destination for India in the years to come. Hence, it is desirable to appoint or from an Empowered Committee under the control of Cabinet Secretary. The main purpose of this committee would be to give guidance on the working of territorial/Japan's division in the Ministry of Commerce. It would monitor the export expansion policies. Plans and programs for various products meant for Japanese market. It would also adopt selectivity criteria and will evolve the concept of strategic targeting at micro-level. The feedback will be the responsibility of the territorial/Japan's division. This Committee may also serve as a coordinating agency for avoiding duplication of various organizations working on trade relation between the two countries.

(10) The recent trends in Indo-Japanese trade are undoubtedly causing concern. A balance between imports and exports should be brought as early as possible. This may be possible if necessary thrust is being given to promote exports on one hand and on the other hand to attain a high rate of growth in the economy. We should take a lesson from Republic of Korea which has secured a trade surplus in 1985. For this an effective export culture should be developed. It is correct to say that the lingering India's trade deficit is due to "lack of an export mentality" on the part of the Government as well as on the exporters. In all nations of the world, exports are the result of 'group activity' involving Government on the one hand, and industry and trade on the other. In Indian economic setting

this link is missing. India must take lesson in this regard from south Korea, Taiwan, Singapore and Hong Kong, which are the best examples of excellent export performers. These nations have developed export culture and there has been the closest possible coordination between the Government, industry and trade. Export promotion also needs an effective structure of its own. Japan has set up Japan External Trade Organization (JETRO) and Korea has established Korea Trade Promotion Corporation (KOTRA), which are serving great cause for their respective economies by providing infrastructural facilities which export trade requires. India has no such organizations which can inflow the information of JETRO and KOTRA pattern. India do have IFTI and TDAI but the purpose and functions are different. India should also set up an organization of JETRO and KOTRA pattern after making indepth study of the organisation and management of the said organisations. This step will really give a boost to India's pattern of exports to Japan and this project should be undertaken without further delay.

(11) In India, the question of achieving stability in production and improvement in productivity are of vital importance specially in the context of export development. India's major traditional exports have been shown ups and downs. This state of affairs has been to the fluctuations in the domestic production of traditional items. In these situations, exporting countries may give up her share in favour of other countries. Expanding exports cannot be sustained on fluctuating production and low productivity. It has, therefore, to evolve a sound production base to undertake export development activities, and this should not be a long drawnout process as India cannot afford any delay. In this respect India should ask all help from Japan through transferring technology to India on an increasing scale specially through foreign direct investment. This step will certainly bring the desired improvements in the level of production and productivity.

(12) Inductive targets may serve useful purpose in expanding exports to Japan. Product-by-product targets may also be set in regard to items being exported to Japan. They will facilitate and encourage the development in a planned manner. A sector-by-sector approach may also serve a useful purpose in trade expansion with Japan. There may be a strategy for wider economic cooperation between India and Japan.

(13) There is also a need for regular exchange of information among trading organizations of India and Japan. This flow of information would promote trade effectively and will also evolve various forms of

14

Japan-US Economic Relations and Their Impact on ASEAN

IPPEI YAMAZAWA*

A PRIORITY ISSUE FOR ASIA AND THE PACIFIC

All ASEAN countries have achieved rapid economic growth throughout the 1970s and their potential for continued growth in the future gave a great momentum to the activity of Pacific economic co-operation. However, in the 1980s, most ASEAN countries have experienced a very slow or negative growth, resulting in an economic growth slump in Asia and the Pacific. Restoration of the economic vitality of the ASEAN economies is certainly a priority issue in our region.

Many economists agree that the main factors causing the slowdown of the ASEAN economies include the rapid fall of oil prices and prices of other primary products and the stagnant growth and protectionism in the developed countries. A metaphor of two elephants, the United States and Japan, walking on the grass of ASEAN represents a popular perception among ASEAN countries of their present situation. Whether the two elephants struggle or make love, the grass of ASEAN suffers.

* Prof. Ippei Yamazawa, Hitotsubashi University.

This allegory conveys a tue element of the economic relations among the US, Japan, and the ASEAN countries, but does not represent the entries picture. I would like to add two other elements; *first*, the two elephants are being drowned by the tidal waves of economic fluctuations and they were treading on the grass unintentionally; *second*, the two elephants have to co-operate to calm down the waves and the grass could also participate so as to bring about co-prosperity in the region.

The purpose of this paper is first, to explain the present situation of the ASEAN economies and to understand the forces affecting it. Since the ASEAN economies are open to the outside world, their present depression should be understood in the context of the fluctuation of the world economy. The present depression is the final phase of a long swing which began with the rapid oil and other primary products price increases in the late 1960s and early 1970s and is ending with the recent rapid decline of those products, which was exaggerated by the ill-managed policy responses by developed countries to the price increases. Big imbalances and economic conflicts still remain among trading partners and the present economic difficulties of the ASEAN countries has been aggravated by them, especially by those between Japan and the United States, and between the United States and the Asian NICs.

The seconds purpose of this paper is to find a way out of those difficulties and to suggest a way to restore the vitality of the ASEAN economies. Market economies are subject to fluctuation of prices and production. Developed economies are mainly responsible for the fluctuation, but developing economies have to learn how to adjust to it.

WORLD-WIDE ECONOMIC FLUCTUATIONS OF THE 1970-1980s

The present state of ASEAN economies should be understood in a broader context of world-wide economic fluctuations since the late 1960s.

Growth Disparity between Developed and Asian Developing Countries

Let me start with a quick review so the growth performance of individual countries in Asia and the Pacific. In the 1970s, especially after the first oil price hike, most developed countries continued slow growth after their rapid growth of the 1950s and 1960s (Figure 1). Japan's

FIG.

Changes in Major Variabl

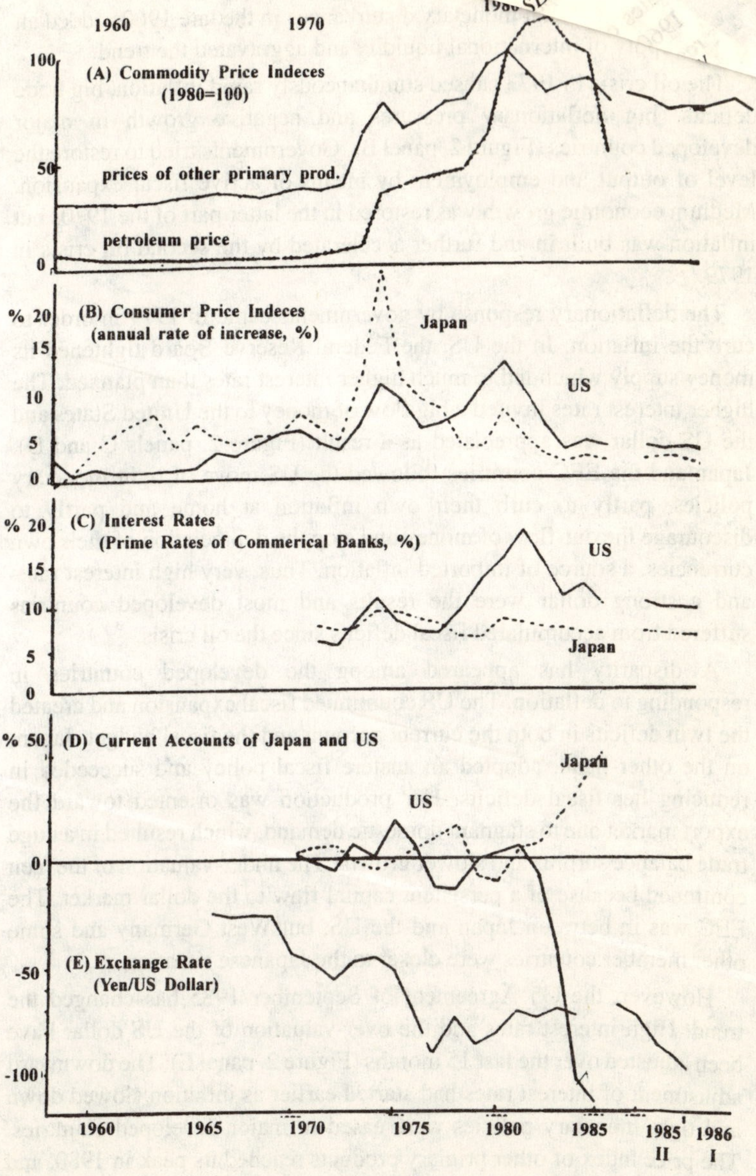

increase in most developed countries throughout the ... They all resulted from the excess demand for productive ... at the end of a rapid growth and accelerated inflationary ...ure. International monetary disturbances in the late 1960s added an excess supply of international liquidity and aggravated the trend.

The oil crisis in 1973 caused simultaneously rapid inflation, big trade deficits, big deflationary pressures and negative growth in major developed countries (Figure 2, panel B). Governments tried to restore the level of output and employment by means of active fiscal expansion. Medium economic growth was restored in the latter part of the 1970s but inflation was built in and further accelerated by the second oil crisis in 1979.

The deflationary response by governments came in 1979 in order to curb the inflation. In the US, the Federal Reserve Board tightened its money supply which led to much higher interest rates than planned. The higher interest rates invited a big flow of money to the United States and the US dollar was appreciated as a result (Figure 2, panels C and D). Japan and the EEC countries followed the US move of tight monetary policies, partly to curb their own inflation at home and partly to discourage the out-flow of money and stop the depreciation of their own currencies, a source of imported inflation. Thus, very high interest rates and a strong dollar were the results and most developed countries suffered from accumulated fiscal deficits since the oil crisis.

A disparity has appeared among the developed countries in responding to deflation. The US countinued fiscal expansion and created the twin deficits in both the current account and the fiscal budget. Japan, on the other hand, adopted an austere fiscal policy and succeeded in reducing her fiscal deficits. Her production was oriented toward the export market due to stagnant domestic demand, which resulted in a huge trade balance surplus and slower growth. The under-valuation of the Yen continued because of a persistent capital flow to the dollar market. The EEC was in between Japan and the US, but West Germany and some other member countries were closer to the Japanese situation.

However, the G5 Agreement of September 1985 has changed the trend. High interest rates and the over-valuation of the US dollar have been adjusted over the last 15 months (Figure 2, panel E). The downward adjustment of interest rates had started earlier as inflation slowed down and tight monetary policies were eased in major developed countries. The price index of other primary products reached its peak in 1980, and turned down since then, reflecting the slackened demand for raw materials in developed countries. The decline of oil prices came more drastically. It began with a small decrease in 1983 but dropped sharply since December 1985. The long swing is now finishing its final phase, although big imbalances between developed economies still remain unresolved (Figure 2, panels A, B, C and E).

Continued Growth of the Asian Developing Countries

On the country, the economic performance of Asian developing countries differ from that of developed countries over this long swing. These developing countries took off in their economic growth in the 1960s. They provide typical examples of the "spread of industrialisation" in Alexander Gerschenkron's terminology. Modern industrialisation started earlier in the Asian NICs in the late 1950s, and was spread to the ASEAN countries in the late 1960s.

These Asian countries have a common strategy, i.e., outward-looking industrialisation, versus the inward-looking strategy of their Latin American counterparts. The Asian NICs succeeded in their export-led growth, and benefitted from the unprecedented expansion of world trade before the oil crisis. The growth of the ASEAN countries, on the other hand, came later but it benefitted from the favourable prices for their main exports, such as petroleum and other primary products. They implemented ambitious development programmes and continued having a rapid growth throughout the 1970s.

However, the world-wide depression in the early 1980s hurt badly the Asian developing countries for the first time (Figure 1). Their exports to developed country markets stagnated and their export earnings decreased drastically. Their imports for development continued to grow and they incurred big trade deficits. In order to avoid further accumulation of foreign debts, many countries reduced their development programmes. The ASEAN countries have thus been trapped in a serious depression. On the other hand, Korea and Taiwan have been spared from this final phase, partly because of the decreased costs for energy and raw material imports, and partly because of accelerated exports due to their under-valued currencies served by the exchange rate alignment. Some ASEAN countries with less reliance on primary product exports, such as Thailand, have been affected less by stagnant commodity markets and have maintained a medium growth.

ECONOMIC CONFLICTS BETWEEN JAPAN AND THE UNITED STATES

The biggest issue at present between Japan and the United States is the economic conflict between the two. Trade conflicts occur between close trade partners. The United States is the biggest trade partner of Japan and Japan is the second biggest partner of the United States after neighbouring Canada. No trade conflicts occur in the absence of trade. Trade occurs since both partners gain from it. However, a trade conflict starts when one partner or both partners complain about the distribution of trade gains between the two. There are always causes of complaints and it is hardly possible to eliminate trade conflicts between trading partners. It is, however, feared that the trade conflict has escalated so much that policy measures are taken by one or both sides restricting trade or other economic relations between the two. Since we are in the world of multilateral trade, trade conflicts between two countries easily affect other countries. Furthermore, they may become a political problem and affect non-economic relations as well. Although we cannot eliminate the causes of a trade conflict, the escalation and politicisation of trade conflicts should be avoided.

From Sectoral to Over-all Conflict

The Japan-US trade conflicts occurred in the process of Japan's catching up with the United States. Japan's export structure changed drastically during her rapid growth period. New exports were shipped to the US market and competed with American producers. American producers demanded protection and the conflict and concluded with voluntary restriction by Japanese exporters. Textiles provides a classic example.[1] It was followed by iron and steel, TV sets, cars, machine tools, and semi-conductors and most of them are still under voluntary export restriction. There are conflicts between Japanese exporters and American producers in individual sectors.

However, in the 1980s, there has emerged a new aspect of Japan-US conflicts. It focuses on the over-all imbalance between the two countries, and new solutions are searched for. Bilateral balances of trade and current accounts have turned in Japan's favour and have expanded since 1981. Further liberalisation of the Japanese market and the reduction of the bilateral imbalance to a certain percentage of the liberal imbalance have been demanded by the US side.

Japan responded with a series of trade liberalisation programmes. Indeed, there have been complaints about complicated distribution channels in the Japanese market and commercial practices preventing access by foreign exporters. In July 1985, the Japanese government announced the Action Programme to further reduce those barriers and promote imports. It was the seventh in a series of trade liberalisations since 1972. It includes the reduction or elimination of tariffs on over 1,800 items from January 1986, a package of liberalisation and simplification measures in standards and certification procedures, and government procurement procedure. It departs from preceding trade liberalisation programmes in its principle and scale, and it is expected to increase imports and reduce the trade surplus in a long-run.

On the other hand, trade negotiations have continued on sectoral problems. Existing voluntary restraint agreements have been re-negotiated (textiles, steel, TV sets, machine tools, automobiles and animal skins and leather) and MOSS (Market-Oriented Sector Specific) talks started on four new sectors (tele-communications medicine and medical equipment, electronics, and forest products).

Macro-economic Imbalances

The bilateral trade imbalance recorded in the trade between Japan and the United States reflects imbalances within each country. That is, a big total import demand in the United States has resulted in large imports from most competitive Japan, and a small total import demand in Japan has resulted in few US exports to Japan. The United States has similar imbalances with West Germany and some other EEC member countries. As was shown in Section 2, the huge surplus of Japan and the huge deficit of the United States have resulted from different responses by the two countries over the long swing.

As is shown in Table 1, Japan reduced her fiscal deficit (under strict administrative reforms) from 4.0 per cent of the GDP to 1.7 per cent between 1981 and 1985, while the United States expanded her fiscal deficits (relying mainly on tight monetary policy) from 2.8 to 5.2 per cent during the same period. Japanese exports expanded, circumventing stagnant domestic demand, and Japan has had a slow growth and a huge trade surplus. The United States, in contrast, adopted a less austere fiscal policy and experience a boom in 1983 and 1984, but she has incurred huge twin deficits. A clear solution to both Japanese and American economists is that the two countries should correct their own over-all imbalances individually.

TABLE 1

Macro-Economic Performance of Japan and the USA

(Billion US Dollar)

	1981	*1982*	*1983*	*1984*	*1985*	*1986*
JAPAN						
1. Exports	151.5	138.4	147.0	169.7	177.2	209.2
(rate of change, %)	(16.1)	(–8.7)	(6.2)	(15.4)	(4.4)	(19.1)
2. Imports	142.9	131.5	126.4	136.2	130.5	125.5
(rate of change, %)	(1.1)	(–8.0)	(–3.9)	(7.7)	(–4.2)	(–2.3)
3. Balance of trade	20.0	18.1	31.5	44.3	56.0	82.7
4. Current account	4.8	6.9	20.8	35.0	49.3	
(CA/GDP, %)	(4.0)	(6.9)	(1.8)	(2.8)	( )	
5. Fiscal deficit and surplus						
(FD or S/GDP, %)	(–4.0)				(–1.7)	
6. Growth rate of real GDP (%)	3.7	3.1	3.2	5.1	4.5	2.3*
USA						
1. Exports	233.8	212.3	200.5	217.9	213.1	
(rate of change, %)	(5.8)	(–9.2)	(–5.6)	(8.6)	(–2.3)	
2. Imports	273.4	254.9	269.9	341.2	361.6	
(rate of change, %)	(6.3)	(–6.8)	(5.8)	(26.4)	(5.9)	
3. Balance of trade	–28.0	–36.5	–67.3	–112.5	–124.5	159.1**
(BT with Japan)		(–19.0)	(–21.7)	(–36.8)	(–49.7)	(–54.7)**
4. Current account	6.4	–8.0	–47.0	–106.5	–117.8	–141.0
(CA/GDP, %)	(0.2)	(–0.3)	(–1.4)	(–2.9)	(–3.0)	
5. Fiscal deficit and surplus	–78.7	–125.7	–202.5	–178.3	–207.1	
(FD or S/GDP, %)	(–2.8)	(–4.2)	(–6.3)	(–5.1)	(–5.2)	
6. Growth rate of real GDP (%)	2.2	–1.9	5.0	8.5	2.8	2.3*

* 1985 III (July-September)—1986 III.

** 1986 January-November.

Source: IMF, *International Financial Statistics*, Yearbook 1986.

In the United States, however, especially in Congress, they focus on the bilateral balance and seek a political solution. Trade bills submitted to the Congress include import restrictions on American side and requests for Japanese concessions. The 1987 Trade Bill submitted recently demands trade surplus countries to reduce bilateral imbalances by 10 per cent every year and proposes to retaliate against them by means of selective import surcharges if they fail to do so.[2] However, some policy measures requested by the United States contradict with GATT rules, and few economists expect the bilateral imbalance to be corrected by those measures.

Co-operation for Macro-economic Adjustment

What have Japan and the United States done for their macro-economic adjustment? The Bank of Japan reduced the official re-discount rate four times last year; from 5.0 to 4.5 per cent in January, to 4.0 per cent in March, to 3.5 per cent in April, and to the record low of 3.5 per cent in November. In the Overall Economic Measure announced last September, the government implemented a policy package including a public investment programme of 3 trillion Yen in order to boost domestic demand and to achieve a 4 per cent growth target. However, the annual growth rate of the real GDP turned out to be as low as 2.3 per cent to September 1986, and many demanded more active fiscal expansion. On the other hand, the wholesale price index declined by 9.9 per cent to the year ending last December, and the consumer price index remained unchanged for the same period.

On the other hand, the US Congress enacted the Gramm-Rudmann Act in 1985 which obliged the government to eliminate fiscal deficits by 1991. However, the scheduled budget cuts have been difficult due to a struggle between defence and social security priorities and tax revenues have fallen short of expections. Money supply has been eased to lower interest rates and stimulate investment in productive capacity. The real GDP grew by 2.3 per cent for the past year (to September 1986). The wholesale price index declined by 1.9 per cent in the year to November 1986 and the unemployment rate was 6.7 per cent in November 1986.

The two countries have resorted to exchange rate adjustment after the G5 meeting in September 1985. The US Dollar was over-valued in 1981 to 1985, due to the very high interest rates and capital inflow to the United States. It weakened the competitiveness of American products and aggravated her trade imbalance. In contrast, Japan was annoyed by the undervalued Yen and welcomed the appreciation of the Yen up to 190-200 Yen per Dollar, although no target zone was agreed upon in G5. However, the appreciation proceeded further than expected. In March 1986 when the Yen fell short of 180 Yen per Dollar, the Bank of Japan intervened by reverse transaction, that is, by selling Yen and buying Dollars, but the appreciation did not stop and the Yen fell short of 160 Yen per Dollar by August. It stayed at the 160 Yen level for three months after the Miyazawa-Baker Agreement in November 1986, but it started to rise rapidly again since the middle of January. The Dollar depreciated rapidly against the German Mark as well, down to a record low. International capital movement has been very active in the present liberalised financial markets, and since the interest rates have decreased to the record low, the US Government seems to urge a further depreciation of the Dollar by affecting market expectations.

However, in spite of the drastic exchange rate adjustment over the past 16 months the trade imbalance of Japan and the United States has not been corrected. The Japanese trade surplus with the United States has decreased in terms of the Yen since April 1986, but it has continued to increase in terms of the Dollars. That is because of the J-curve effect, and too rapid appreciation tends to discourage the recovery of domestic economy. Export competitiveness has deteriorated so much that it cannot be restored by cost reduction through rationalisation, which tends to discourage investment by exporting industries and thus delays the recovery of the domestic economy. Rather, concerted actions for macro-economic adjustments are needed. Although monetary policies change in parallel under high capital mobility, fiscal policies tend to be independent and left to the discretion of individual governments. Concerted efforts are needed for fiscal policy expansion.[3]

ASEAN ECONOMIES IN THE 1980s

The overall imbalance of Japan and the United States and the economic conflict spurred by the bilateral imbalance between the two have effected the Asian developing countries seriously. There are economic conflicts between the two countries, and Asian developing countries, also some ASEAN countries suffer from trade conflicts as well. Let us start with a quick overview of the present state of the ASEAN economies and their relations with the United States and Japan.

Serious Setback in 1985-86

The economic situation differs among the ASEAN member countries, reflecting different export structures and some *ad hoc* factors specific to individual countries. Table 2 shows changes in major macro-economic variables for individual countries.[4] Both Indonesia and Malaysia have been affected most seriously by the drastic decline of petroleum and other primary product prices as well as by the stagnant demand for their products in developed countries.

In Indonesia, export earnings have decreased badly due to the decrease of both prices and volumes of their major exports, such as oil and agricultural materials. Both mining and agriculture have stagnated and industrial production for export has also decreased except for plywood and textiles. Domestic and foreign investment have been inactive. The real GDP growth was less than 2 per cent in 1985 and pessimists predict a negative growth in 1986. The government announced an over-all economic remedy in May which included the promotion of non-oil exports and encouragement of foreign investment. The government devalued the Rupiah by 31 per cent in September, and has maintained high interest rates in order to prevent capital flight. However, the economy has not looked up yet and there is concern about accelerated accumulation of external debts due to persistent current account deficits.

Malaysia has suffered from similar difficulties; a big reduction of export earnings due to the reduced exports of oil, rubber, and palm oil, the negative growth of industrial and mining production, and decelerated private consumption and construction activities. Exports of textiles and electronics have been encouraged by the depreciation of the Ringgit, but not enough to relieve the entire economy. Real GDP growth was estimated to be 1.1 per cent for 1985 and around zero for 1986.

On the other hand, the Thai economy has been performing better, partly because of its non-reliance on oil exports. It suffered from a reduction of its main export of rice, which, through curtailment of production and shutting down of many rice mills, has stagnated domestic demand. However, exports of textiles, shoes, toys, and agro-industrial products have been active and their production has increased. The economy has maintained a 4-5 per cent growth recently. Since imports of industrial material and investment goods have decreased, its trade balance has improved and the government's concern has shifted from persistent trade deficit to the boosting of domestic demand through fiscal expansion and lower interest rates.

Negative growth in Singapore and the Philippines have been caused mainly by their own *ad hoc* factors. Singapore experienced a minus 2 per cent growth in 1985 after 8 per cent growth in the previous year. Its serious setback resulted originally from the depression of its two neighbouring countries, Malaysia and Indonesia, but it was also aggravated by the sudden end of a construction boom and the decrease of

TABLE 2

Macro-Economic Performance of ASEAN Countries

(Unit %)

	1971	*1972*	*1973*	*1974*	*1975*	*1976*	*1977*	*1978*	*1979*	*1980*	*1981*	*1982*	*1983*	*1984*	*1985*
INDONESIA															
1. Change in export		44.0	80.7	131.3	4.4	20.3	27.0	7.3	33.9	40.5	1.6	0.1	–5.1	3.5	
2. Change in investment		39.5	41.0	48.7	43.1	24.6	19.4	14.6	1.8	40.6	20.9	11.3	17.0	–7.7	
3. Growth rate of real GDP	7.0	9.4	11.3	7.6	5.0	6.9	8.9	7.7	6.3	9.9	7.9	2.2	4.2		
4. Investment/GDP	15.8	18.8	17.9	16.8	20.3	20.7	20.1	20.5	20.9	20.9	21.4	22.6	29.4	26.3	
5. Change in consumer price index	4.4	6.4	31.0	40.6	19.1	19.8	11.0	8.1	20.6	18.5	12.2	9.5	11.8	10.5	4.7
6. Current account balance/GDP	–4.0	–3.0	–2.9	2.3	–3.6	–2.4	–0.1	–2.7	1.9	4.0	–0.7	–5.9	–7.8	–2.5	
7. Change in exchange rate		–5.6	0	0	0	0	0	–6.2	–29.1	–0.7	–0.8	–4.5	–27.3	–11.4	–7.7
MALAYSIA															
1. Change in export		4.7	77.1	38.9	9.3	37.8	14.8	21.8	49.6	16.8	–9.1	2.2	17.2	16.9	–6.5
2. Change in investment		20.8	67.5	55.3	–15.3	5.7	24.5	39.3	40.8	23.2	17.0	13.6	8.8	4.1	–19.2
3. Growth rate of real GDP	7.1	9.4	11.7	8.3	0.8	11.6	7.8	6.7	9.3	7.8	7.1	5.6	5.9	7.3	
4. Investment/GDP	20.9	21.3	23.6	29.6	25.5	22.8	23.8	26.7	28.9	30.7	35.2	37.4	47.0	33.5	29.3

(*Contd.*)

5. Change in consumer price index	1.6	3.2	10.5	17.4	4.5	2.6	4.8	4.9	3.6	6.7	9.7	5.8	3.7	3.9	0.3
6. Current account balance/GDP	–2.6	–4.9	1.4	–5.7	–5.3	5.2	3.3	0.7	4.4	–1.2	–9.9	–13.4	–11.6	–4.9	–2.1
7. Change in exchange rate		7.6	14.8	1.4	0.5	–5.9	3.2	6.2	5.8	0.5	–6.0	–1.4	0.6	–1.0	–5.7
PHILIPPINES															
1. Change in export		0.2	71.4	44.6	–15.8	11.4	22.4	8.8	34.3	25.7	–1.5	–12.1	–1.6	7.9	–12.6
2. Change in investment		4.4	27.7	60.7	37.9	21.0	8.7	16.5	33.1	18.6	10.9	0.4	–14.9	–26.2	–10.7
3. Growth rate of real GDP	4.9	4.8	9.2	5.0	6.4	8.0	6.1	5.5	6.3	5.2	3.9	2.9	1.1	–4.5	–3.7
4. Investment/GDP	21.1	20.8	20.3	25.1	29.6	31.3	29.0	29.0	31.0	30.7	30.7	28.8	27.5	18.7	17.1
5. Change in consumer price index	15.1	10.0	14.0	33.5	8.2	6.1	7.9	7.6	17.5	18.2	13.1	10.2	10.0	50.3	23.1
6. Current account balance/GDP		0.1	4.4	1.4	–5.8	–6.1	–3.6	–4.5	–5.1	–5.4	–5.4	–8.1	–7.9	–3.9	
7. Change in exchange rate		–3.7	–1.3	–0.5	–6.4	–2.6	0.5	0.5	0.2	–1.8	–5.0	–7.5	–23.2	–33.5	–10.3
SINGAPORE															
1. Change in export		24.3	66.9	59.0	–8.6	22.5	25.1	23.0	40.4	36.1	0.9	–0.9	5.0	10.2	–5.2
2. Change in investment		33.3	33.4	33.0	2.8	5.2	3.9	23.5	23.1	35.6	27.0	21.9	13.8		

(Contd.)

TABLE 2 (*Contd.*)

	1971	1972	1973	1974	1975	1976	1977	1978	1979	1980	1981	1982	1983	1984	1985
3. Growth rate of real GDP	12.5	13.4	11.5	6.3	4.1	7.5	7.9	8.6	9.4	10.3	9.9	6.3	7.9	8.1	
4. Investment/GDP	40.2	41.1	39.2	44.6	37.6	37.7	33.4	37.6	41.8	45.3	44.5	45.2	45.1		
5. Change in consumer price index	1.7	2.3	19.5	22.4	2.6	−1.9	3.2	4.8	4.0	8.5	8.3	3.9	1.2	2.6	0.5
6. Current account balance/GDP	−32.4	−17.1	−12.5	−19.8	−10.4	−9.6	−4.5	−5.8	−7.8	−13.3	−10.1	−8.1	−4.9	−4.0	
7. Change in exchange rate		7.8	14.4	0.8	2.7	−4.1	1.2	7.2	4.5	1.5	1.3	−1.3	1.2	−1.0	−3.1
THAILAND															
1. Change in export		30.1	44.7	56.3	−9.7	35.0	17.1	17.0	29.7	22.8	8.1	−1.2	−8.3	16.4	−4.0
2. Change in investment		5.6	29.5	35.4	11.9	10.7	34.6	18.7	23.3	22.3	0.2	−9.7	14.5	8.1	−13.3
3. Growth rate of real GDP	4.7	4.8	9.4	5.4	7.1	8.7	7.2	10.1	6.1	5.8	6.3	4.1	5.8	6.2	4.0
4. Investment/GDP	22.9	23.4	28.1	27.9	27.7	24.4	26.6	27.0	28.8	27.2	24.7	21.0	23.0	23.9	22.7
5. Change in consumer price index	0.4	4.9	15.5	24.3	5.3	4.1	7.6	7.9	9.9	19.7	12.7	5.3	3.7	0.9	2.4
6. Current account balance/GDP	−2.5	−0.6	−0.4	−0.7	−4.3	−2.7	−5.7	−5.0	−7.7	−6.2	−7.1	−2.7	−7.2	−5.0	−4.0
7. Change in exchange rate		0	1.3	1.3	−0.1	−0.2	0	0.3	0.5	−0.3	−6.2	−5.2	0	−2.8	−13.0

KOREA															
1. Change in export		52.1	98.6	38.3	13.9	51.8	30.2	26.5	18.4	16.3	21.4	2.8	11.9	19.6	1.1
2. Change in investment		1.1	49.3	48.7	13.2	29.9	44.5	54.5	37.2	−7.6	−0.8	10.6	11.9	4.4	
3. Growth rate of real GDP	9.2	5.9	14.4	7.9	7.5	12.7	10.8	10.1	7.3	−3.0	6.9	5.5	9.5	7.9	
4. Investment/GDP	25.1	22.1	25.5	31.4	29.6	25.6	28.1	31.5	35.7	30.7	28.5	26.4	27.2	29.0	
5. Change in consumer price index	13.4	11.7	3.2	24.3	25.3	15.3	10.2	14.5	18.3	28.7	21.3	7.3	3.4	2.3	2.5
6. Current account balance/GDP	−8.7	−3.4	−2.2	−10.8	−8.9	−1.1	0	−2.2	−6.4	−8.5	−6.8	−3.7	−2.1	−1.6	
7. Change in exchange rate		−1.7	−1.4	−1.6	−16.5	0	0	0	0	−20.4	−10.9	−6.9	−5.8	−3.8	−7.4

Footnotes: 1, 2: Changes in export and investment at current prices.

6: Positive figures show surplus, while negative figures show deficit.

7: Change in US Dollar per national currency, positive figures showing appreciation and negative figures depreciation of the national currency concerned.

Source: IMF, International Financial Statistics.

TABLE 3

Exchange Rate Adjustment of Asian Countries

	1985				1986								
	Sep.	*Oct.*	*Nov.*	*Dec.*	*Jan.*	*Feb.*	*Mar.*	*Apr.*	*May*	*June*	*July*	*Aug.*	*Sept.*
Japan	237.0	214.7	203.7	202.8	200.1	184.6	178.9	175.6	166.8	168.0	158.6	155.0	153.6
		10.3	16.3	16.8	18.4	28.3	32.4	34.9	42.0	41.0	49.4	52.8	54.2
Germany	2.84	2.64	2.59	2.51	2.44	2.33	2.26	2.27	2.23	2.24	2.15	2.05	2.03
		7.5	9.6	13.1	16.3	21.8	25.6	25.1	27.3	26.7	32.0	38.5	40.0
Korea	892	892	891	891	891	886	884	886	887	888	885	881	887
		0	0.1	0.1	0.1	0.6	0.9	0.6	0.5	0.4	0.7	1.2	1.7
Hong Kong	7.73	7.71	7.72	7.72	7.72	7.71	7.71	7.70	7.70	7.70	7.70	7.68	7.80
		0.2	0.1	0.1	0.1	0.2	0.1	0.3	0.3	0.3	0.3	0.6	–0.9
Taiwan	40.4	40.1	39.8	39.9	39.3	39.1	38.8	38.5	38.2	38.1	38.0	37.0	36.7
		0.7	1.5	1.2	2.7	3.3	4.1	4.9	5.7	6.0	6.3	9.1	10.0
China	2.96	3.06	3.20	3.20	3.20	3.20	3.21	3.21	3.19	3.20	3.64	3.69	3.71
		–3.3	–7.5	–7.5	–7.5	–7.5	–7.8	–7.8	–7.3	–7.5	–18.7	–19.8	–20.0
Singapore	2.23	2.14	2.11	2.12	2.13	2.14	2.16	2.19	2.22	2.22	2.19	2.15	2.17
		4.2	5.6	5.1	4.6	4.2	3.2	1.8	0.4	0.4	1.8	3.7	2.7
Indonesia	1,122	1,122	1,122	1,125	1,127	1,127	1,127	1,124	1,126	1,130	1,130	1,132	1,633
		0	0	–0.3	–0.5	–0.5	–0.5	–0.2	–0.4	–0.8	–0.8	–0.9	–31.3
Malaysia	2.45	2.43	2.43	2.43	2.45	2.47	2.53	2.60	2.60	2.63	2.64	2.59	2.62
		0.8	0.8	0.8	0	–0.9	–3.2	–5.8	–5.8	–6.9	–7.2	–5.5	–6.5

Thailand	27.1	26.5	26.2	26.7	26.6	26.5	26.4	26.4	26.4	26.4	26.2	25.8	26.1
		2.2	3.4	1.4	1.8	2.2	2.6.	2.6	2.6	2.6	3.4	5.0	3.8
Philippines	18.6	18.7	18.7	18.9	19.0	20.5	29.8	20.5	20.5	20.6	20.5	20.5	20.5
		–0.6	–0.6	–1.6	–2.2	–9.3	–10.6	–9.3	–9.3	–9.8	–9.3	–9.3	–9.3

Notes: upper row: monthly average exchange rate in terms of individual national currencies per US Dollar.
lower row: appreciation (+) or depreciation (–) rate from G5 (September 1985) (IMF formula, change in US Dollar per national currency).

Source: IMF, *International Financial Statistics,* supplemented by Bank of Tokyo's data.

exports of petroleum products. It has also been affected adversely by weakened competitiveness of its industrial products due to wage rate increases over previous years. However, electronics exports have resumed and the steady growth of that service sector contributes to the revival of its growth. Real GDP growth continued to be negative between 1985/II and 1986/I, but it turned out a small positive, 0.8 per cent in 1986/II. It is estimated to be 1-2 per cent for the whole year 1986.

The Philippine's growth has decelerated since 1981 due to political instability and it was negative in 1985 and 1986. The new President Aquino has succeeded in obtaining supplementary financing from the IMF and has eased monetary and fiscal policies. She has also benefitted from good crops in 1986. However, both consumption and investment have stagnated, and foreign investment and exports have not resumed yet. Many strikes continue and the unemployment rate is very high. Real GDP growth was minus 2.2 per cent for the first half of 1986. NEDA expects a 1.5 per cent growth for the latter half of 1986 and a 5 per cent growth for 1987, but economists predict the resumption of growth will be delayed.

On the contrary, the Korean economy has looked up in 1986, partly because of the decreased import prices of oil and raw materials and partly because of the quick resumption of industrial exports after the exchange rate re-alignment. Table 3 shows the monthly changes (accumulated change since G5) per US Dollar rate of Asian countries since September 1985. The Japanese Yen and German Mark were appreciated by 54 and 40 per cent respectively for a year, while the Korean Won was almost pegged to the US Dollar. The new Taiwan Dollar was appreciated by 10 per cent and the Hong Kong Dollar, Singaporean Dollar, and the Thai Baht have also been almost pegged to the US Dollar, while the Chinese Yuan, the Indonesian Rupiah, Malaysian Ringgit, and the Philippine's Peso were depreciated. Korea and other Asian NICs exports have benefitted from the strengthened competitiveness against Japanese and German products and they certainly contributed to their resumed rapid growth in 1986. The better performance of Thai exports resembles that of Asian NICs because of its greater reliance on industrial exports than other ASEAN member countries.

Figure 3 depicts changes in both exports and investment for the ASEAN five and Korea (see Table 2 for precise figures). It shows almost a parallel fluctuation of the two variables and their downward trend in the 1980s for all countries. Table 2 shows that investment/GDP ratio were

FIG. 3

Increase in Investment and Export (%)
Percentage Increase Over Previous Years)

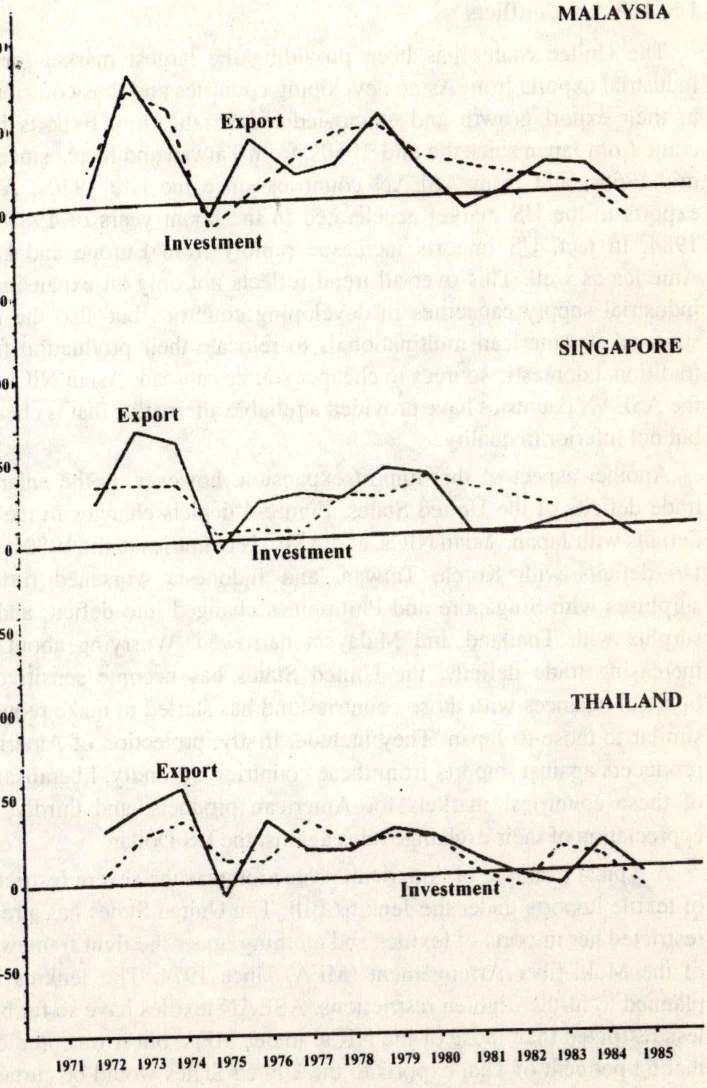

much higher than average for these countries, implying their rapid economic growth in the 1970s. However, the ratio also has declined recently. The worsened environment for export expansion has severely affected ASEAN's growth in these years.

US-ASEAN Conflicts

The United States has been providing the largest market for the industrial exports from Asian developing countries and thus contributed to their export growth and export-led industrialisation: Exports have come from Japan since the mid-1950s, from Taiwan and Korea since the mid-1960s, and from ASEAN countries since the late 1970s. Asian exports to the US market accelerated in the boom years of 1983 and 1984. In fact, US imports increased rapidly from Europe and Latin America as well. This over-all trend reflects not only an expansion of industrial supply capacities in developing countries but also the new strategy of American multinationals to relocate their production from traditional domestic sources to cheaper sources abroad. Asian NICs and the ASEAN countries have provided a reliable alternative that is cheaper but not inferior in quality.

Another aspect of this import expansion, however, is the enlarged trade deficits of the United States. Figure 4 depicts changes in the US deficits with Japan, Asian NICs, and ASEAN countries in the 1980s. The US deficits with Korea, Taiwan, and Indonesia worsened further, surpluses with Singapore and Philippines changed into deficit, and its surplus with Thailand and Malaysia narrowed. Worrying about the increasing trade deficits, the United States has become sensitive to bilateral balances with those countries and has started to make requests similar to those to Japan. They include, firstly, protection of American producers against imports from these countries, secondly, liberalisation of these countries' markets for American products, and thirdly, the appreciation of their exchange rates against the US Dollar.

A typical example of American protection was the severe restriction of textile imports under the Jenkins Bill. The United States has already restricted her imports of textiles and clothing under the tight framework of the Multi-fiber Arrangement (MFA) since 1974. The Jenkins Bill planned to further tighten restrictions. ASEAN textiles have so far been less restricted than those of the NICs' under MFA, but it was predicted that 64 per cent of Thai exports to the United States would be curtailed by the new bill. Textile workers and college students demonstrated in

FIG. 3 (*Contd.*)

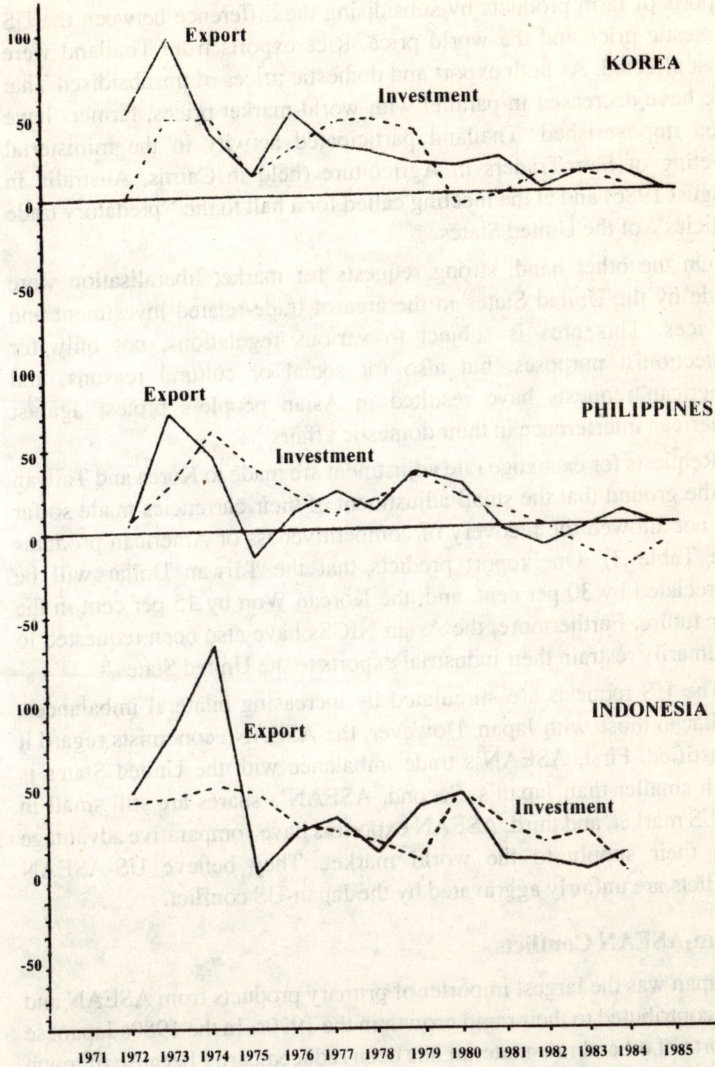

100
50
0
-50
Export
Investment
KOREA
100
50
0
-50
Export
Investment
PHILIPPINES
100
50
0
-50
Export
Investment
INDONESIA
1971 1972 1973 1974 1975 1976 1977 1978 1979 1980 1981 1982 1983 1984 1985

protest before the American Embassy in Bangkok. The bill was eventually rejected by President Regan but it contributed to the renewal of the MFA in July 1986.

Another example is the Farm Bill 1986, which promotes American exports of farm products by subsidising the difference between the US domestic price and the world price. Rice exports from Thailand were most affected. As both export and domestic prices of unsubsidised Thai rice have decreased in parallel with world market prices, farmers have been impoverished. Thailand participated activity in the ministerial meeting of Fair Traders in Agriculture (held in Cairns, Australia in August 1986) and at the meeting called for a halt to the "predatory trade policies" of the United States.

On the other hand, strong requests for market liberalisation were made by the United States in the area of trade-related investment and services. This area is subject to various regulations, not only for protectionist purposes, but also for social or cultural reasons, and American requests have resulted in Asian people's protest against American interference in their domestic affairs.[5]

Requests for exchange rate adjustment are made to Korea and Taiwan on the ground that the small adjustment of their currencies made so far has not allowed the recovery of competitiveness of American products (see Table 3). One report predicts that the Taiwan Dollar will be appreciated by 30 per cent, and, the Korean Won by 15 per cent in the near future. Furthermore, the Asian NICSs have also been requested to voluntarily restrain their industrial exports to the United States.[6]

The US requests are stimulated by increasing bilateral imbalances, similar to those with Japan. However, the ASEAN economists regard it unjustified. First, ASEAN's trade imbalance with the United States is much smaller than Japan's. Second, ASEAN's shares are still small in the US market, and third, ASEAN exporters have comparative advantage with their supply to the world market. They believe US-ASEAN conflicts are unfairly aggravated by the Japan-US conflict.

Japan-ASEAN Conflicts

Japan was the largest importer of primary products from ASEAN and thus contributed to their rapid growth in the 1970s. In the 1980s Japanese imports of oil and raw material has been reduced partly because of much slower growth in Japan, and partly because of reduced consumption of these materials per unit of production. On the other hand, Japanese exports of machinery and parts grew rapidly to meet their development needs and the increase resulted in a bilateral balance with those countries. Figure 5 depicts the change in bilateral balance between Japan and the Asian NICs and the ASEAN countries. Japan incurred trade deficits with oil exporters such as Indonesia, Malaysia, and Brunei, and persistent trade surplus with such industrial exporters as the NICs and Thailand.

Export promotion to Japan has been a major issue raised by the ASEAN side in the Japan-ASEAN Forum, an annual series of Official consultations since its start in 1977. Bilateral trade imbalances with Thailand and Singapore caused economic conflicts here too, and official commitment to export promotion was strongly requested by the ASEAN side. They include improved market access for their major exports such as boneless chicken, bananas, plywood, and so on, through improved GSP (Generalised System of Preference) and simplified standard and certification procedures. The Action Programme announced in July 1985 includes some official measures responding to these requests.

It should be noted that a new type of request has emerged recently. It is best represented by the White Paper on Structural Adjustment of Thailand-Japan Economic Relations, authorised by the Thai Government in August 1985.

It requested Japanese co-operation in such areas as trade, private investment, and official development aid, and aimed to promote the joint adjustment of the structure of economic relations between the two countries.

Similar ideas appeared in the requests made by Indonesia and Malaysia. Although they maintain persistent trade surpluses with Japan, and Japan continues to be the biggest importer of their primary products, they wish to explore new industrial exports to Japan and seek Japan's co-operation in that direction.

CONCERTED EFFORTS TO IMPROVE THE TRADE ENVIRONMENT

To summarise my analysis of economic changes in Asia and Pacific, the industrialisation of ASEAN should be viewed in the global context of a long swing of the world economy in the 1970s and 1980s. It is characterised both by a big swing in commodity prices and by awkward policy responses of the developed countries. Both commodity prices and high interest rates/over-valuation of the US Dollar have been adjusted

FIG. 4

US Balance of Trade by Country and Region, 1975-1985

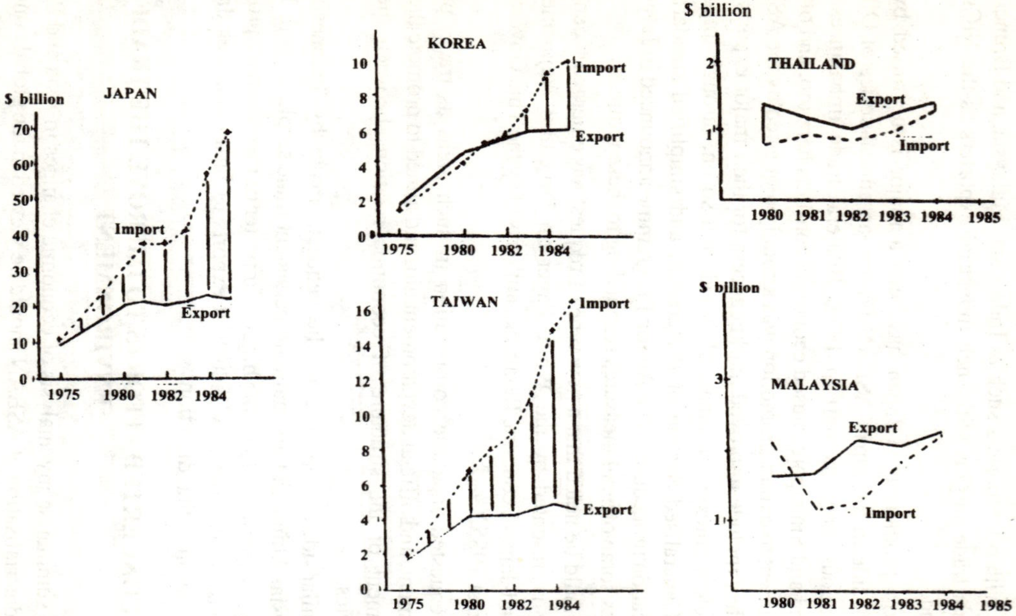

Source : US Department of Commerce, *Highlights of US Export and Import Trade.*

recently, but what still remain unsolved are the big macro-economic imbalances, Japan's slow growth with huge trade surpluses and the American huge twin deficits. The ASEAN countries started their modern economic growth in the upward phase of the long swing, benefited from serious increase of their export earnings, but have suffered from a big setback in the downward phase in the 1980s. Their difficulty has been aggravated further by economic conflicts between the two big economies in the region.

There are, of course, some areas to be improved by the ASEAN countries. The vulnerability of mono-culture economies is seen in their present difficulty. The diversification of their export structure, especially the exploration of possible new industrial exports, seems to be inevitable. Thailand has partly succeeded in that direction and other countries are oriented in the same direction. Secondly, the regional vulnerability should also be reduced, decreasing high dependence on the American and other developed country markets, and they should diversify their export destination to other areas. A major promising alternative is their own ASEAN market with its growth potential. Further promotion of intra-regional co-operation is required in order to achieve that goal. Thirdly, economic fluctuation is inevitable in market economies. Contrary to the famous Prebisch contention, there has not been any long-run trend of declining prices of primary products *vis-a-vis* industrial products, but a long swing in the term of trade. It is imperative for ASEAN countries to become able to manage their economies through the fluctuation of their main production and export earnings.

ASEAN countries have been much freer from the debt service problem than many Latin American NICs. It does not mean, however, that they have been less affected by it. Latin American countries, after having faced insolvency problems, were obliged to depress their economies under conditional loans from the IMF and World Bank. In contrast, ASEAN countries have been very sensitive to the accumulation of foreign debt, and have been quick to take restrictive measures to stop its further accumulation. They all suffer from potential debt accumulation. Recently, there has emerged a new approach to this problem, as is represented by the "Baker Plan" proposed for the World Bank last year. Instead of forcing developing countries to take austere policies and to give up their growth, it helps them to continue medium growth and take advantage of their high growth potential.

The high growth potential of ASEAN countries has given a big momentum to the activities for Pacific economic co-operation. Concerted efforts are needed to realise this growth potential, and Japan is expected to play a leading role in it. Some urgent measures should be taken to relieve present payment difficulties and to prevent fatal setback in major development projects. In the short-run, successful co-ordination of macro economic policies of Japan and the United States is imperative. But the fundamental and long-run solution should be the improvement of the trading environment and the promotion of a harmonious division of labour in the Asian and Pacific region.

It is hardly possible to eliminate all possible causes of trade conflicts among close trading partners, especially in Asia and the Pacific, where trade and industrial structure has been changing drastically. However, it is most undesirable that major countries pursue begger-my-neighbour policies as have been observed recently. The trade environment should be improved so as to include built-in measures for solving trade conflicts. This task is being pursued now in the new Uruguay Round of GATT negotiation.

Efforts for strengthening the GATT system will help us to get rid of trade problems in the region. However, resistance by vested interest groups gaining from current protection should never be under-rated. The real difficulty in reaching an international agreement exists in reaching domestic agreement within individual countries. The commitment to "stand still," that is, exact no more protectionistic measures, may sound like a modest approach, but it will serve to tie the hands of domestic protectionists with international commitment.

Domestic adjustment should be promoted in parallel with the negotiation of individual issues. Trade liberalisation alone will not work well without adjustment assistance in the switch-over from declining sectors to growing ones. Domestic adjustment is not confined to developed countries, but developing countries are also advised to remove gradually protectionist measures benefitting domestic producers. Trade liberalisation is often requested reciprocally but it is also needed for improving the efficiency of domestic production.

Objections by vested interests cannot be neglected and it takes time to promote structural adjustment within individual countries. Initiatives for trade liberalisation and structural adjustment cannot be taken unilaterally

FIG. 5

US Balance of Trade by Country and Region, 1975-1985

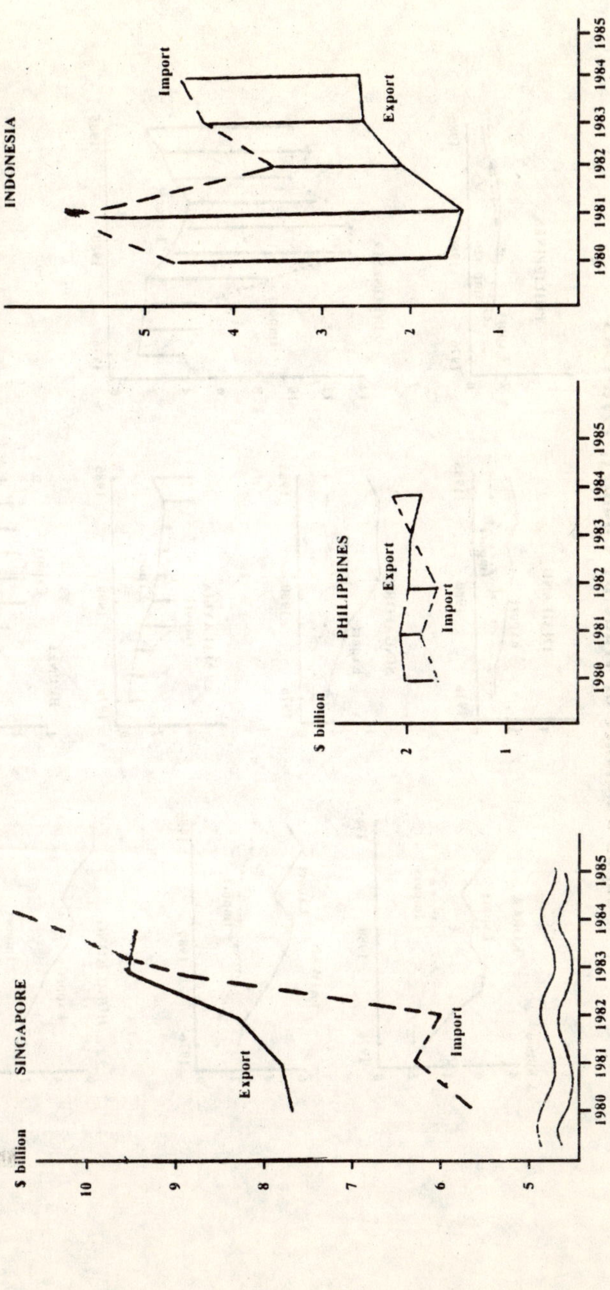

Source : US Department of Commerce, *Highlights of US Export and Import Trade.*

FIG. 6

Japan's Balance of Trade by Country, 1976-1985

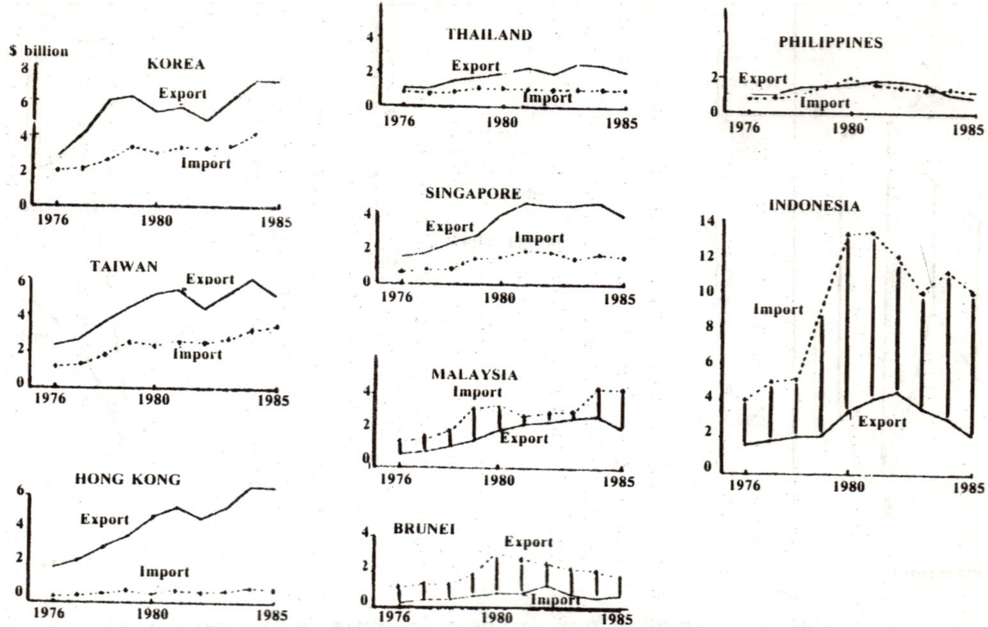

Source : MITI, *White Paper on International Trade*, 1986, (J).

in reality. International commitment on gradual liberalisation and structural adjustment helps to promote slow but steady adjustment. Co-operation for the joint promotion of structural adjustment in Asia and Pacific is desirable.

In July 1986, the Japanese Government published a report by the Economic Structure Study Group, an informal advisory group attached to the Prime Minister. Its report, known as the *Maekawa Report*, suggested the restructuring of Japanese industries by promoting the national decline of major industries at their maturity stage. But the redirection of the Japanese economy and business behaviour will take time in yielding sufficient adjustment. Trade surpluses will continue for sometime and the present GATT system needs to be improved so as to accommodate long-lasting imbalances and trade friction. And it is important to understand each other's problems with structural adjustment in our concerted effort.[7]

NOTES AND REFERENCES

1. Trade disputes over textiles between the United States and Japan in 1969-71 activated similar disputes between the United States and Korea, Thailand, Taiwan, and Hong Kong and was finally concluded with the full-fledged framework of managed trade in textiles, the Multi-fiber Agreement in 1974. See I.M. Destler, H. Fukui and H. Sato, *The Textile Wrangle: Conflict in Japanese-American Relations, 1969-71*, Cornell University Press, 1979.
2. *Nippon Keizai Shimbun* (The Japan's *Economic Journal*), January 14th, 1987.
3. At the end G5 meeting in Paris (February 21-22, 1987), the five Finance Ministers agreed on a package of macro-economic policy co-ordination so as to maintain their currency exchange rate at the present range. It includes the reduction of the BOJ's re-discount rate (down to 2.5 per cent) and further stimulation of domestic demand through fiscal expansion by Japan, stimulation of domestic demand through tax reduction by West Germany, and the improvement of the balance of payments through the reduction of its fiscal deficit by the United States. *Nippon Keizai Shimbun*, February 23, 1987.
4. This section relies on the survey, published in *Asia Trends* 1986 I-IV, Institute of Developing Economies.
5. Complaints about the American requests in Asian developing countries was occasionally reported in newspapers. *Nihon Keizai Shimbun*, February 17th, and April 25th, 1986.
6. The Korean Won appreciated against US Dollar by 3.2 per cent during the year 1986 under the deliberate guidance by the Bank of Korea. It has been accelerated this year, apparently in consideration of its increasing trade surplus with the United States (4.2 billion dollars in 1985 and 7.4 billion dollars in 1986). The Won was appreciated from 860.8 Won on January 5th to 855.9 Won on February 18th. Taiwan has continued to appreciate the NT Dollar as she has accumulated foreign exchange reserves of 50 billion

Dollars, almost as much as West Germany and Japan. The NT Dollar rate on February 18th was 34.99 per US Dollar. *Nippon Keizai Shimbun*, February 19th, 1987.

7. See for further detail Ippei Yamazawa, *Review of Pacific Economic Co-operation: Trade and Structural Adjustment*, Mimeographed, February 1987.

15

Japan's Economic Impact on ASEAN Countries

RUPERTO P. ALONZO*

INTRODUCTION

The economic interdependence of ASEAN member countries with Japan may have been initially occasioned by post-war geopolitical considerations, but it has certainly grown in importance over the last few decades. Especially with the onset of the first oil crisis in the early 1970s, Japan looked to some ASEAN countries as sources of its vital energy needs. Increased international capital mobility that came with the recycling of the Petrodollars allowed many ASEAN economies to expand and diversify, further stimulation trade with Japan.

This interrelationship looms large not only in terms of trade flows but also in the form of capital flows, although the direction in the latter case

* Ruperto P. Alonzo, Associate Professor, School of Economics, University of the Philippines. Professor Hiroshi Kakazu of Ryukyu University, presently Visiting Professor at the University of the Philippines, gave helpful comments and lent valuable materials for this paper, including his own study on the topic (Kakazu 1982). The research assistance of Teresita de Leon is also gratefully acknowledged. Important suggestions from Conference participants, especially Professors Ippei Yamazawa and Kimimaru Yoneda, have been incorporated in the revision of this paper.

has been expectedly one-way. Japan has been, and continues to be, a major source of direct foreign investment and official development assistance for ASEAN member countries. ASEAN as a regional bloc has also been involved in direct dialogues with the Japanese Government in seeking Japan's economic cooperation, as exemplified in the Second ASEAN Summit Meeting in August 1977, and more recently in the Second Japan-ASEAN Economic Ministers' Meeting in June 1985, where ASEAN member countries expressed interest in availing of Japan's active help in their pursuit of industrial development.

Changes in the world economic environment in the 1980s, however, have had strong repercussions on the performance of the ASEAN economies and on their relationship with Japanese economy. The recession that hit the industrialised countries in the early 1980s led to a contraction in world trade and a nurturing of protectionist sentiments. Prices of primary products that constituted a huge share of developing countries exports declined with the recession and have been slow in picking up. As world interest rates soared in the early 1980s, countries that relied on foreign borrowing to finance their growth in the 1970s found themselves squeezed by the debt burden, the Philippines being the prime example within the ASEAN bloc. On the other hand, the recent appreciation of the Japanese Yen *vis-a-vis* the US Dollar, triggered by the huge budgetary and trade deficit of the US and the huge trade surplus of Japan, is viewed positively by many ASEAN countries as a step towards the opening up of the huge Japanese domestic market.

This paper attempts to trace the changing economic relationships between the ASEAN countries and Japan since the beginning of the 1970s, in view of gaining some understanding of how recent world developments, particularly in the economic sphere, are likely to affect these linkages. Brunei, a recent member of the Association, is left out of the study, not because it is considered unimportant, but because the sources used for this paper have not yet included it in the statistics. Section II begins with an overview of the economic characteristics of ASEAN economics in relation to Japan, where the diversities in the structure and performance of ASEAN economies are highlighted. Section III then looks at the trends in ASEAN-Japan commodity trade, drawing not only from official statistical sources but also from the analytical studies of specialists in the field. Capital flows, both official and private, are discussed in Section IV, together with other forms of economic co-operation. The Final section summarises the paper and evaluates the likely directions of ASEAN-Japan economic relationships.

AN OVERVIEW OF ASEAN ECONOMIES

With a combined area more than eight times bigger and a combined population at least two times larger than Japan's, ASEAN countries as a group maintain an important economic presence in the region, even though their total Gross Domestic Product (GDP) is only one-sixth of Japan's gross output (see Table 1). The composition of GDP shows agriculture comprising 20 per cent to 26 per cent of their output and 42 per cent to 70 per cent of employment in four countries, underscoring the developing nature of these economies.

As Table 1 shows, the economic performance of these ASEAN countries over the past two decades has also been noteworthy. Before the first oil crisis, the regional economy was already growing at about 8 per cent per year, although only Singapore's 13 per cent could outpace Japan's 10 per cent average annual growth for the period 1965 to 1973. For the ensuing period 1973 to 1984, which saw two rounds of major oil price increases, all the ASEAN countries have grown even faster than their richest neighbour, managed to move only at 4 per cent per year. In spite of the high output growth rates, however, per capita incomes remain low in some countries; in 1984, Indonesia's per capita GNP was only one-twentieth of Japan's, while that of the Philippines, saddled with political problems and a bulging debt burden, had declined to only one-sixteenth of Japan's.

In general, ASEAN member countries maintain very open economies, as shown by their high exports/GDP and imports/GDP ratios. Such openness has rendered many of these economies vulnerable to world price fluctuations. The decline in the world prices of primary products in the early 1980s translated into declining terms of trade for the ASEAN countries (except Indonesia) from 1980 to 1982, but 1984 saw the relative prices of their exports picking up again. Still, by 1984, the Philippines, Singapore, and Thailand were suffering deficits in their trade balance, although Indonesia and Malaysia with their fuel exports managed to run surpluses.

Despite the adverse world trends in the early 1980s, the export sectors of most ASEAN countries have remained buoyant, perhaps because of the proper mix of internal and external economic policies. Thailand, in particular, has shown a remarkable two-digit annual growth rate in exports over the period 1973 to 1984, in spite of erratic movements in its terms of trade in the 1980s. Domestic inflation was kept at single-digit

TABLE 1

Major Economic Indicators of the ASEAN Countries and Japan, 1940

Indicator	*Indonesia*	*Malaysia*	*Philippines*	*Singapore*	*Thailand*	*Japan*
Population (Million)	158.9	15.3	53.4	2.5	50.0	120.0
Per Capita GNP($)	540	1,980	660	7,150	860	10,630
Annual Growth Rate,						
1965-1984 (%)	4.9	4.5	2.6	7.8	4.2	4.7
Inflation Rate (%/year)						
1965-1973	63.0	1.2	8.8	3.1	2.5	6.0
1973-1984	590	6.2	12.9	4.4	8.2	4.5
GDP ($ million)	80,590	29,280	32,840	18,220	41,960	1,255,006
Average Annual Growth						
Rate of GDP (%)						
1965-1973	8.1	6.7	5.4	13.0	7.8	9.8
1973-1984	6.8	7.3	4.8	8.2	6.8	4.3[a]
Composition of GDP/						
Employment (%)						
Agriculture	26/57	21[b]/42	25/52	1/2	20/70	3[b]/11
Industry	42/13	25[b]/19	34/16	39/38	28/10	41[b]/34
Services	34/30	44[b]/39	41/33	60/61	52/20	56[b]/55
Exports ($ million)	21,888	16,407	5,391	24,055	7,413	170,038
Exports/GDP (%)	27.2	56.0	16.4	132.0	17.7	13.5
Imports ($ million)	13,882	14,060	6,365	28,565	10,581	134,257
Imports/GDP (%)	17.2	48.0	19.4	156.8	25.1	10.7

Average Annual Growth of Exports (%)						
1965-1973	11.1	8.0	4.2	11.0	6.9	14.7
1973-1984	1.4	7.5	5.6	7.1	10.4	7.5
Average Annual Growth of Imports (%)						
1965-1973	14.0	4.4	3.0	9.8	4.4	14.9
1973-1984	10.5	8.9	2.3	7.1	5.9	1.6
Terms of Trade (1980 = 100)						
1984	101	93	101	101	81	109
1982	105	85	89	100	77	103
Gross International Reserves ($ million)	5,730	4,441	844	10,416	2,688	33,899

Notes: a. Growth rate is for 1973-1983.

b. Values are for 1983.

Source: World Bank, *World Development Report*, 1986.

levels in Malaysia, Singapore, and Thailand between 1973 and 1984. Indonesia's 17 per cent annual inflation, while the highest in the region, was nevertheless a substantial improvement from the annual rate of 63 per cent during the previous period. A prime example of economic mismanagement in the 1970s and 1980s was that of the Philippines, where domestic expansion through foreign borrowing and inflationary government spending, mixed with an unrealistic exchange rate policy which penalised the export sector, have led to severe balance of payments difficulties. By the end of 1984, all the ASEAN countries, except the Philippines, had gross international reserves covering at least two-and-a-half months' worth of imports.

ASEAN-JAPAN TRADE RELATIONS

The Magnitudes and Directions of Trade Flows

The 1970s witnessed a substantial growth of ASEAN exports to Japan, growing at 28 per cent per year between 1970 and 1980 (see Table 2). ASEAN's share in the total imports of Japan increased from 10 per cent in 1970 to 15 per cent in 1980. Since then, however, Japan's imports from ASEAN as well as from the rest of the world have begun to decline, such that by 1985, the Dollar value (in nominal terms) of Japan's import from the region was only 86 per cent of its 1980 value of US $21 billion. Nevertheless, with Japan's imports from the rest of the world declining as well, the ASEAN region's relative share dropped only slightly, to 14 per cent of Japan's total imports.

A basically similar pattern may be observed of Japan's exports to ASEAN. Between 1970 and 1975, ASEAN imports from Japan grew at 27 per cent per year; this growth rate declined to 17 per cent per year between 1975 and 1980. After a peak of US $15 billion worth was reached in 1981, Japan's exports to ASEAN began falling in absolute terms, although total world exports of Japan recovered in 1984 and 1985. Thus, by 1985, the share of the region in Japan's total exports was only 6 per cent, down from the 10 per cent level experienced in the early 1980s. ASEAN has maintained a trade surplus with Japan throughout these periods, in contrast to the tremendous surplus of Japan with the rest of the world. From the point of view of Japan, therefore, ASEAN has been more important as a source of its imports than as a destination for its exports.

TABLE 2

Trade between ASEAN and Japan, 1975 and 1980-1985

(In Million US$)

	1970	*1975*	*1980*	*1981*	*1982*	*1983*	*1984*	*1985*
Exports to:								
Indonesia	320	1,850	3,460	4,120	4,260	3,550	3,100	2,170
Malaysia	170	570	2,060	2,420	2,500	2,770	2,900	2,170
Philippines	450	1,030	1,680	1,930	1,800	1,740	1,100	940
Singapore	420	1,520	3,910	4,430	4,340	4,410	4,600	3,860
Thailand	450	960	1,920	2,250	1,910	2,510	2,400	2,030
ASEAN Total	1,810	5,930	13,030	15,150	14,810	14,980	14,100	11,170
Imports from:								
Indonesia	640	3,430	13,170	13,300	12,000	10,430	11,200	10,120
Malaysia	420	690	3,470	2,930	3,010	3,130	4,400	4,330
Philippines	530	1,120	1,950	1,730	1,530	1,310	1,400	1,240
Singapore	90	400	1,510	1,930	1,810	1,450	1,800	1,590
Thailand	190	720	1,120	1,060	1,040	1,020	1,000	1,030
ASEAN Total	1,870	6,360	21,220	20,950	19,390	17,340	19,800	18,310
Balance:								
Indonesia	–320	–1,580	–9,710	–9,180	–7,740	–6,880	–8,100	–7,950
Malaysia	–250	–120	–1,410	–510	–510	–360	–1,500	–2,160
Philippines	–80	–90	–270	200	270	430	–300	–300

(Contd.)

TABLE 2 (*Contd.*)

	1970	*1975*	*1980*	*1981*	*1982*	*1983*	*1984*	*1985*
Singapore	330	1,120	2,400	2,500	2,530	2,960	2,800	2,270
Thailand	260	240	800	1,190	870	1,490	1,400	1,000
ASEAN Total	–60	–430	–8,190	–5,800	–4,580	–2,360	–5,700	–7,140
Japan's World Trade								
Exports	19,320	55,730	129,810	151,910	138,580	146,800	170,100	175,600
Imports	18,880	57,860	140,530	140,830	130,320	125,020	136,500	129,500
Balance	440	–2,130	–10,720	11,080	8,260	21,780	33,600	46,100

Note: Figures for 1984 are rounded off to the nearest US $100 million; all other figures are founded off to the nearest US $10 million.

Source : 1970, 1975 & 1980: MITI, *White Paper on International Trade*; 1981-1983: UN, *Yearbook of International Trade Statistics: Japan Customs Statistics*, cited in Sakuta (1986).

The overall trade balance picture, however, hides the different trends experienced by the individual member countries (see Table 2). In the 1980s, Indonesia and Malaysia, as major sources of raw materials and fuel, accumulated huge surpluses, while Singapore and Thailand ran huge deficits. The pattern for the Philippines has been mixed with the relatively small deficits of 1981 through 1983 turning into small surpluses in 1984 and 1985.

Among ASEAN countries, Indonesia remains as the most important exporter to Japan, accounting for 55 per cent of Japan's imports from ASEAN in 1985. The Philippines, which was the second biggest ASEAN exporter to Japan in the 1970s, has dropped to a poor fourth, with only 7 per cent of the regional share in 1985, compared to 18 per cent ten years before and 29 per cent fifteen years before.

In terms of use of Japan's merchandise exports, Singapore has been the biggest ASEAN importer in the 1980s, with more than 30 per cent share of the region's imports. The Philippines, once the biggest regional importer with a 25 per cent share in 1970, hugged thc bottom in 1985, with only an 8 per cent share. Indonesia, Malaysia, and Thailand each accounted for almost 20 per cent of ASEAN imports from Japan by 1985.

Trends in Economic Interdependence

The pattern that emerges from the broad overview of ASEAN-Japan trade is that of a diversification of the exports and imports of Japan within the ASEAN market, with the changing roles of the different member countries in their trade relationships with Japan. The expansion of Japan's trade with ASEAN in the 1970s was accompanied by a similar expansion with other less developed countries. The share of exports to LDCs in total Japan exports rose from 41 per cent to 46 per cent between 1970 and 1980, while the corresponding import share increased from 40 per cent to 60 per cent, as Japan's industrial structure became more competitive with the industrialised countries and more complementary with the developing countries (Kakazu, 1982).

This complementarity, however, was not fully exploited in the 1980s when Japan's imports began to decline. Even as the ASEAN countries' exports continued to grow (although at slower rates), the 1980s saw a decreasing share of Japan in total exports of the region (see Table 3). For the Philippines, Singapore and Thailand, the United States has become the dominant export destination by 1984, perhaps with the stimulation brought about by an overvalued Dollar. Japan nevertheless remained as the major source of imports for the region, as the ASEAN member countries continued to rely on the industrialised economies for their intermediate and capital goods requirements.

TABLE 3

Share of Major Trading Partners in ASEAN Countries' Trade, 1975, 1980 and 1984

(*In Per Cent*)

	Imports			*Exports*		
	1975	*1980*	*1984*[a]	*1975*	*1980*	*1984*[a]
Indonesia						
Japan	31.0	31.5	23.8	43.9	49.3	47.3
USA	14.0	13.0	18.4	26.2	19.6	20.6
EEC	19.7	13.4	14.9	5.7	6.4	4.7
Singapore	7.2	8.6	12.9	8.9	11.3	9.7
Malaysia						
Japan	20.1	23.0	25.4	14.5	22.8	19.7
USA	10.7	15.0	16.1	16.1	16.3	13.2
EEC	20.4	15.5	14.1	23.3	15.2	14.6
Singapore	8.5	11.7	13.9	20.3	19.1	22.5
Philippines[b]						
Japan	27.9	19.9	13.6	37.4	26.6	19.4
USA	22.2	23.6	27.4	29.8	27.5	38.0
EEC	12.5	10.6	10.8	16.0	18.5	13.4
Saudi Arabia	10.3	10.0	6.9			
Singapore				1.4	1.9	6.0
Singapore						
Japan	16.9	17.8	18.2	8.7	8.1	9.3
USA	15.7	14.1	14.6	13.9	12.7	20.1
EEC	13.0	10.8	10.0	14.0	12.3	9.7
Malaysia	11.6	13.9	15.0	17.2	15.0	16.1
Thailand[b]						
Japan	31.5	20.7	26.9	27.8	15.1	13.0
USA	14.4	16.6	13.4	10.6	12.7	17.2
EEC	17.1	12.8	12.1	16.1	25.8	20.5
Saudi Arabia	9.0	9.0	8.5			
Singapore	2.0	2.0	7.9	9.1	7.7	8.4

Notes: (a) Figures for Malaysia are for 1983.

(b) For the Philippines, Singapore is not a major supplier of imports and Saudi Arabia is not a major buyer of exports. For Thailand, Saudi Arabia is not a major buyer of exports.

One good summary measure of intercountry trade relationships is the "co-efficient of economic interdependence," defined as the ratio of the sum of two countries' exports to each other to the sum of the two countries' gross output (Kakazu, 1982). The results of such calculations for the ASEAN countries and Japan are reported in Table 4.

TABLE 4

Co-Efficients of ASEAN Economic Interdependence with Japan, 1970, 1979, and 1984

(In Per Cent)

	Co-efficients			*Per Cent Change*	
	1971	*1979*	*1984*	*1971-1979*	*1979-1984*
ASEAN	1.442	2.284	2.325	158.4	1.8
Indonesia	0.484	1.037	1.071	114.3	3.3
Malaysia	0.218	0.468	0.568	114.7	21.4
Philippines	0.366	0.312	0.194	–14.8	–37.8
Singapore	0.236	0.411	0.503	74.2	22.4
Thailand	0.252	0.281	0.262	11.5	–6.8

Source: Figures for 1971 and 1979 are from Kakazu (1982); those for 1984 are calculated from Tables 1 and 2.

Table 4 confirms quantitatively the earlier discussion where the strong links of Indonesia, Malaysia, and Singapore in the 1970s have been pointed out, together with the generally deteriorating trade relations between ASEAN and Japan in the 1980s. For the ASEAN region as a whole, whereas the co-efficient of economic inter-dependence grew at an average annual rate of 6 per cent between 1971 and 1979, the change in the index was less than 1 per cent per year from 1979 to 1984. Only Malaysia and Singapore have managed to sustain a reasonable degree of trade interdependence with Japan.

The Composition of Trade

The commodity composition of ASEAN trade with Japan (Table 5) highlights the exchange of resource-based exports from developing countries for the industrial products of the developed country. More than 80 per cent of ASEAN imports from Japan are heavy industrial goods. In particular, between 1975 and 1982, the share of machinery in total imports from Japan expanded from 44 per cent to 55 per cent for Indonesia, from 52 per cent to 62 per cent for Malaysia, and from 52 per cent to 59 per cent for Singapore. Meanwhile, ASEAN exports to Japan

TABLE 5

Japan's Trade with ASEAN, By Major Commodity Group: 1975, 1980 and 1982

(In Million US Dollars)

	Japan's Exports to:						Japan's Imports from:				
	Indonesia	*Malay-sia*	*Philip-pines*	*Singa-pore*	*Thai-land*		*Indonesia*	*Malay-sia*	*Philip-pines*	*Singa-pore*	*Thai-land*
1975						*1975*					
Foodstuffs	5	9	29	32	9	Foodstuffs	123	28	631	9	456
Raw Materials & Fuels	18	4	13	5	4	Raw Materials	528	396	463	8	154
Light-Industry Goods	238	75	130	219	75	Textiles	—	—	4	—	2
Textiles	113	39	83	111	39	Metals	110	21	267	1	2
Heavy-Industry Goods	1,556	473	847	1,253	473	Mineral Fuels	2,725	130	—	295	—
Chemicals	264	55	121	67	55	Processed Goods	51	134	26	83	111
Metal	476	122	195	388	122	Chemicals	3	4	7	33	18
Machinery	816	295	531	797	295	Machinery	—	25	3	36	2
Total Exports	1,850	566	1,026	1,524	566	Total Imports	3,430	691	1,121	399	724
1980						*1980*					
Foodstuffs	75	27	30	52	13	Foodstuffs	335	61	526	27	333
Raw Materials & Fuels	42	10	24	23	25	Raw Materials	1,852	1,632	1,207	40	511
Light-Industry Goods	318	161	225	529	157	Textiles		14	10	—	1
Textiles	143	66	101	227	79	Metals	345	128	883	14	17
Heavy-Industry Goods	3,004	1,848	1,388	3,233	1,705	Mineral Fuels	10,779	1,315		1,111	
Chemicals	363	125	180	199	175	Processed Goods	195	455	194	241	270
Metals	749	428	366	745	513	Chemicals	12	15	42	84	31
Machinery	1,892	1,295	842	2,289	917	Machinery	11	59	74	120	4
Total Exports	3,458	2,061	1,683	3,911	1,917	Total Imports	13,167	3,471	1,951	1,507	1,119

1982					
Foodstuffs	12	25	36	58	18
Raw Materials & Fuels	45	9	33	13	20
Light-Industry Goods	373	207	260	675	168
Textiles	127	72	112	235	73
Heavy-Industry Goods	3,780	2,235	1,460	3,553	1,678
Chemicals	373	130	177	187	226
Metals	1,083	551	398	800	417
Machinery	2,324	1,555	885	2,565	1,035
Total Exports	4,260	2,502	1,803	4,373	1,907

1982					
Foodstuffs	327	65	431	38	467
Raw Materials	769	1,576	867	29	322
Textiles	—	17	10		1
Metals	261	93	554	125	5
Mineral Fuels	10,728	995	22	1,464	
Processed Goods	169	353	195	257	229
Chemicals	9	26	63	86	37
Machinery	1	76	40	130	6
Total Imports	12,005	3,010	1,576	1,826	1,041

Source: MITI, *White Paper on International Trade*.

show the bulk being in the form of foodstuffs (for Thailand), raw materials (for Malaysia and the Philippines), and mineral fuel (for Indonesia and Singapore). There has been an increase in the export of processed goods from the Philippines and Thailand; but with a low base to start from, the share of processed goods in total exports to Japan remains low.

A more detailed breakdown of Japan's major imports from ASEAN countries (for 1985) is given in Table 6, where the highly concentrated nature of member country exports is seen. For Indonesia, Malaysia and Singapore, oil-based and liquefied natural gas exports constitute more than half of their exports to Japan. Exports from the Philippines and Thailand are more diversified, but bananas for the Philippines (with a 20 per cent share) and natural rubber for Thailand (with a 27 per cent share) stand out nevertheless. Table 5 also reveals the importance of ASEAN to Japan, as the region provides a huge share of the latter's imports of certain specific raw materials (71 per cent of liquefied natural gas, 67 per cent of natural rubber, 61 per cent of unwrought tin).

Trade and Growth Relationships

While the discussion has thus far focused on the magnitude and composition of ASEAN-Japan trade flows, the implications of changes in these trade relationships on the future performance of the individual ASEAN economies are more difficult to trace, as they require serious econometric modeling efforts. The broad macro-economic directions are clear: a slowdown in the Japanese economy would generally lead to a contraction of its imports from its trading partners. The drop in exports of the trading partners would in turn lead to a contraction in their output and employment. The problem lies in estimating the likely quantitative dimensions of these effects.

An early study of MITI (1976), cited by Kakazu (1982), estimates these effects to be substantial. Measures of the elasticities of Japan's imports from individual ASEAN countries with respect to Japan's GNP, covering the period 1960 to 1974, were as follows: Indonesia, 1.89; Malaysia, 0.74; Philippines, 0.90; Singapore, 1.73; and Thailand, 1.12. In other words, a 1 per cent drop in Japan's output would lead to a 1.89 per cent drop in its imports from Indonesia (or a 1.89 per cent drop in Indonesia's exports to Japan). Trade multipliers, on the other hand, measuring by how much a country's output would expand when its exports expand, were estimated as follows: Indonesia, 2.133; Malaysia, 1.944; Philippines, 2.768; Singapore, 1.973; and Thailand, 2.518.

TABLE 6

Japan's Major Imports from ASEAN Countries, 1985

	Imports from ASEAN Country ($ Million)	*(Per Cent)*	*Total Imports of Japan ($ Million)*	*Share of ASEAN Country (Per Cent)*
Indonesia				
Total	10,119	100.0		
Liquefied Natural Gas	3,995	39.5	7,200	55.5
Crude & Partly Refined Oils	3,889	38.4	34,599	11.2
Heavy Fuel Oils	598	5.9	2,019	29.6
Malaysia				
Total	4,330	100.0		
Wood	1,179	27.2	3,700	31.9
Crude & Partly Refined Oils	1,157	26.7	34,599	3.3
Liquefied Natural Gas	1,122	25.9	7,200	15.6
Unwrought Tin	144	3.3	333	43.2
Philippines				
Total	1,243	100.0		
Banana (fresh)	247	19.9	297	83.4
Iron Ore	151	12.1	1,228	4.9
Copper Ore	133	10.7	1,209	11.0
Wood	122	9.8	3,700	3.3
Unwrought Copper	93	7.4	550	16.8
Singapore				
Total	1,594	100.0		
Petroleum Products	1,015	63.7	5,975	1.9
Chemical Goods	150	9.4	8,073	1.9
Electrical Machinery	95	6.0	3,881	2.5
General Machinery	70	4.4	4,728	1.5
Thailand				
Total	1,027	100.0		
Natural Rubber (raw)	273	26.6	408	67.0
Fish & Shellfish	179	17.4	4,610	3.9
Unwrought Tin	60	5.8	333	18.0
Flows (fresh, frozen)	58	5.6	143	40.3
Vegetables	53	5.2	693	7.6

Source: MITI, *White Paper on International Trade, 1986*, as cited in Yamazawa and Adachi (1986).

The net effect of a contraction in the Japanese economy on a given country would depend not only on the above measures but also on the ratio of Japan's imports from that country to Japan's GNP. The results of the MITI simulation showed that, given the trade and domestic output structure in 1975, Indonesia would be the ASEAN country most adversely affected by a Japan slowdown, while Singapore would be the least affected. The effects, of course, cut both ways: positive developments in the Japanese economy would benefit Indonesia the most and Singapore the least.

A recent study by Yamazawa, Nohara, and Osada (1986) uses the 1975 international input-output tables reconstructed by the Institute of Developing Economies (1982) to derive at an indicator referred to as the "mutual inducement ratio," which is defined as country A's value-added induced by country B divided by B's value-added induced by A, where the inducement effect is measured using input-output relationships. The results showed basically the same pattern found in the MITI study: Indonesia would be most sensitive to changes in the Japanese economy, followed by the Philippines, Malaysia, and Thailand, with Singapore coming last.

While such simulation studies may be helpful in clarifying possible policy actions in the event of different scenarios materialising, their actual use in policy formulation has to be approach with caution. These simulations often rely on a host of centers paribus and "what if" assumptions; the data bases used in the studies cited above cover only up to the mid-1970s, and the applicability of the co-efficients and parameter estimates to the economic conditions prevailing in the 1980s may be questioned, especially in the light of the second oil price shock in the late 1970s, the world economic recession in the early 1980s, and the major currency re-alignments in the mid-1980s.

The projected scenarios coming from such studies may also influence the course of the economic policy, whereby a concrete action is taken to counteract any expected adverse trends. Some of the steps that may be taken, such as non-tariff measures, are difficult to build into such models, giving rise to charges of unfair trade practices when observed trade flows do not follow the models' predictions.

Thus, with the world recession in the early 1980s, although Japan's tariff barriers were lowered, an increase in complaints could nevertheless be heard from many trading partners about Japan's non-tariff barriers.

Balassa-(1986) cites a long list of official complaints from Korea and Singapore. The Federation of ASEAN Economic Associations chose for the theme of its annual conference in December 1986 the topic, "Barriers to ASEAN Market Access to the US, Japan, and the EEC" (see, for example, the Guina 1986 for a representative listing of ASEAN member country complaints). Bilateral negotiations between Japan and the ASEAN countries, either individually or as a bloc, are regularly taking place to look into these perceived problems. Ultimately, of course, much of a country's growth also depends on its handling of its own internal and external economic policies, as the varied experiences of the individual ASEAN nations bear out.

Economic Assistance and Private Investment Flows

As mentioned earlier, the predominantly one-way flow of capital funds from Japan to ASEAN countries is another major venue of interaction between Japan and the region. The flow of funds may come by way of Official Development Assistance (ODA) or through private direct investments.

The past decade has witnessed a substantial increase in Japan's ODA to ASEAN member countries (Table 7). The share of ASEAN in the total of Japan's ODA, however, has shown a dramatic decline: between 1975 and 1984, the share in grants fell from 30 per cent to 26 per cent, while that in loans likewise fell from 45 per cent to 34 per cent.

The distribution of Japan's ODA among the member countries is also uneven. ODA cumulated from 1980 to 1984 was highest for Indonesia, followed by Thailand. In per capita terms, however, Indonesia appears to have received the lowest, although it is the poorest among the member countries. In fact, there seems to have been a negative association between per capita incomes and the level of per capita assistance over this period.

It may be argued that looking at official development assistance in terms of bilateral flows is "unfair," since much foreign aid is really determined multilaterally, as developed countries meet to discuss their respective allocations to the LDCs. Aid flows, however, do allow the identification of the individual donor countries, so that discussions of how much assistance one is getting from which country cannot be avoided.

TABLE 7

Japan's Bilateral Official Development Assistance to ASEAN

(In Million US Dollars)

	Annual Flows			*Cumulated*		*Per Capita*
	1975	*1980*	*1984*	*1975-1980*	*1980-1984*	*1980-1984*
ASEAN						
Grants	59.5	183.9	270.8	2,029.8	1,094.3	3.91
Loans	321.2	519.4	562.5	2,925.1	2,653.0	9.47
Total	380.7	703.3	833.3	5,954.9	3,747.3	13.38
Indonesia						
Grants	10.8	59.2	73.7	130.8	301.9	1.90
Loans	187.1	290.8	94.0	870.5	1,045.7	6.58
Total	197.9	350.0	167.7	1,001.3	1,347.6	8.48
Malaysia						
Grants	3.3	12.7	35.8	33.1	109.7	7.17
Loans	60.1	52.9	209.3	216.3	433.3	28.32
Total	63.4	65.6	245.1	249.4	543.0	35.49
Philippines						
Grants	36.3	35.7	57.7	133.8	245.5	4.60
Loans	34.1	58.7	102.4	198.3	502.4	9.41
Total	70.4	94.4	160.1	332.1	747.9	14.01
Singapore						
Grants	1.4	6.1	13.2	14.6	43.5	17.40
Loans	6.3	–2.3	15.2	12.6	10.8	4.32
Total	7.7	3.8	28.4	27.2	54.3	21.72
Thailand						
Grants	7.7	70.2	90.4	100.4	393.7	7.87
Loans	33.5	119.3	141.6	319.4	640.7	12.81
Total	41.2	189.5	232.0	419.8	1,034.4	20.68
All Countries						
Grants	201.7		1,063.9			
Loans	648.7		1,363.5			
Total	850.4		2,427.4			
ASEAN's Share (%)						
Grants	29.5		25.5			
Loans	48.1		41.3			
Total	44.8		34.3			

Note: Per capita figures are based on mid-1984 populations.

Source: Japan Ministry of Foreign Affairs, *Japan's Official Development Assistance (ODA) 1985.*

TABLE 8

Japan's Private Direct Investment in ASEAN Countries

(In Million US Dollars)

	1975	*1980*	*1981*	*1982*	*1983*	*1984*	*1985*
Indonesia	589	529	2,434[a]	410	374	374	406
Malaysia	52	146	31	83	140	142	79
Philippines	149	78	72	34	65	46	60
Singapore	52	140	266	180	322	225	339
Thailand	14	33	31	94	72	119	49
ASEAN	856	926	2,834	801	973	906	935[b]
World	3,280	4,693	8,931	7,703	8,145	10,155	12,218

Share in ASEAN Total

(In Per Cent)

	1975	*1980*	*1981*	*1982*	*1983*	*1984*	*1985*
Indonesia	68.8	57.1	85.9	51.2	38.4	41.3	43.4
Malaysia	6.1	15.8	1.1	10.4	14.4	15.7	8.5
Philippines	17.4	8.4	2.5	4.2	6.7	5.1	6.4
Singapore	6.1	15.1	9.4	22.5	33.1	24.8	36.3
Thailand	1.6	3.6	1.1	11.7	7.4	13.1	5.2
ASEAN/World	26.1	19.7	31.7	10.4	11.9	8.9	7.6

Notes: a. Indonesia received US $1,838 million in equipment funds and loans for Pertamina LNG Project and US $181 million in equipment funds for Asahan aluminum project in 1981.

b. The ASEAN totals for 1984 and 1985 include Brunei, where Japan's investment for FY 1984-1985 amounted to US $5 million.

Source: Finance Ministry Reports, as cited in Sakuta (1986).

Private direct investments from Japan to ASEAN countries have similarly shown a decreasing trend, at least as a proportion of Japan's total private direct investment (Table 8). As of 1985, the bulk still went to Indonesia, followed by Singapore. For Indonesia in 1981, US $2 billion was accounted for by only two projects (the Pertamina LNG Project and the Asahan Aluminum Project). The Philippines, which had 17 per cent of the ASEAN pie in 1975, had its share down to only 6 per cent by 1985. A 1977 study by Japan's Ministry of Finance (cited in Kakazu, 1982) showed that as of that time, more than half of outstanding investments by Japan in ASEAN went into mining of Indonesia and the Philippines. For Malaysia, Singapore, and Thailand, over half of

Japanese private investments were in the manufacturing sector, with textiles dominating in Malaysia and Thailand, and transport equipment significant in Singapore. Most of these flows, of course, depend much on Japanese private investors' perceptions of the investment climate in the host country, but close consulations between the private investors and the Japanese Government do allow some latitude for bilateral negotiations.

CONCLUDING REMARKS

This overview of the economic impact of Japan on the neighbouring ASEAN countries has dealt extensively on trade relations and touched only briefly on other forms of economic interactions, as the historic record weighs heavily on the trade aspects. With the recent appreciation of the Japanese Yen, many observers are hoping that the slackening of Japan's imports observed in the first half of the 1980s would be reversed. At the same time, it is expected that, with the recent currency re-alignment making domestic investment opportunities less attractive, Japan's private investors would seek out opportunities in other countries more aggressively and step up their pace of foreign investments, keeping prospects bright for ASEAN member countries.

REFERENCES

Balassa, Bela, "Japanese Trade Policies towards Developing Countries," *Journal of International Economic Integration*. Vol. I, No. 1 (1986), pp. 1-19.

Guina, Carol, "Trade Barriers from the U.S., Japan, and the EEC." Paper presented at the 11th Annual Conference of the Federation of ASEAN Economic Associations on Barriers to ASEAN Market Access to the U.S., Japan, and the EEC, Bangkok, Thailand, 27-29 November, 1986.

Institute of Developing Economies, *International Input-Output Table for the ASEAN Countries, 1975*. IDE Statistical Data Series No. 39, Tokyo, 1982.

Japan, Ministry of International Trade and Industry, *White Paper on International Trade*, Various issues.

Kakazu, Hiroshi, "The Economic Interdependence between Japan and ASEAN," Ryukyu University, Economic Study No. 23, 1982.

Sakuta, Eiji, "Japan-ASEAN Economic Relations," *Journal of Japanese Trade and Industry*, 5 (1986), pp. 10-14.

United Nations, *Yearbook of International Trade Statistics*, Various issues.

World Bank, *World Development Report, 1986*.

Yamazawa, Ippei, and Adachi, Fumihiko, "Patterns of Japan-ASEAN Trade." Paper presented at the 11th Annual Conference of the Federation of ASEAN Economic

Associations on Barriers to ASEAN Market Access to the U.S., Japan and the EEC; Bangkok, Thailand, 27-29 November, 1986.

Yamazawa, Ippei, Nohara, Takashi, and Osada, Hiroshi, ''Economic Interdependence in Pacific Asia: An International Input-Output Analysis,'' *The Developing Economies*, Vol. XXIV, No. 2 (1986), pp. 97-108.

16

Peace, Stability and Prosperity in Southeast Asia: An Indonesian View

MOCHTAR KUSUMAATMADJA*

Speaking on peace and stability in Southeast Asia before a largely Japanese audience in Tokyo is not so strange as it seems because Japan can play an important role in efforts to establish a peaceful, stable and prosperous Southeast Asia. As peace and political stability are a prerequisite for prosperity, it can be said with justification that Japan is closely linked to the future prosperity of the region.

The Southeast Asian region has not known peace since before the start of the Great Asia War, the Asian theater of World War II, more than 40 years ago. Even now when most armed conflicts have ceased, hostilities of a limited nature still continue in Cambodia, and all the countries of Indochina, Cambodia, Laos, and Vietnam, are suffering from the ravages of war and economic underdevelopment.

THE DEVELOPMENT OF ASEAN

Indonesia has since 1966 abandoned its policy of "confrontation" with its neighbours and in 1967 helped to establish the Association of

* Prof. Mochtar Kusumaatmadja, Minister of Foreign Affairs.

Southeast Asian Nations, thus laying down the basis for a stable, peaceful and prosperous Southeast Asia through co-operation with its neighbours in economic, social and cultural fields. The end of the war in Indochina between the United States and Vietnam in 1975 raised hopes for a peaceful future for Southeast Asia.

The ASEAN Summit Meeting in Bali held in early 1976, which reflected this optimism, produced two documents of great importance in the history of ASEAN, namely, the ASEAN Concord and the ASEAN Treaty of Amity, Friendship and Co-operation. These documents contained principles and provisions for ASEAN co-operation beyond the economic, social, and cultural fields, laying the basic foundation for closer political co-operation.

It was not unit the end of 1978 or the beginning of 1979 that political co-operation between the ASEAN member countries became a reality. The impetus was provided by the invasion of Cambodia by Vietnam.

The Bali Summit of 1976 was important because it was at this meeting that the philosophy of ASEAN regional co-operation as proposed by Indonesia's President Soeharto was endorsed by the other ASEAN heads of state and government.

The basic philosophy of ASEAN co-operation is the attainment of regional resilience through the enhancement of the respective national resiliencies of the ASEAN member countries.

This philosophy of regional co-operation contains two principles or concepts which need further clarification, namely, the nature and form of co-operation among the member states and the concept of national resilience.

In ASEAN the nature of regional co-operation between the member states is rather a loose one, a truly voluntary co-operation between sovereign nations with no supranational bodies or institutions. As to form, it is therefore truly an *association* of nations, *not* an organisation.

National resilience refers to the strength of the member nation states and their capacity to withstand threats to their national existence and survival, both from external and internal sources, and it is therefore a broader concept than national defence. It encompasses the economic, political, social and cultural aspects of national life. Of these the economic aspect is the one most susceptible to international co-operation, the other aspects being more properly matters of national concern.

Since the ASEAN member countries are for the most part economically underdeveloped, assistance to their development is, therefore, the first priority. The more so since most of them suffered from colonial exploitation followed by the sufferings of war and internal political instability. It is thus not surprising that in varying degrees the ASEAN member countries have required considerable infusions of foreign economic assistance and investment. As their economies improve and their capacities for international trade increase, there is a tendency for the issues of trade and access to foreign markets to replace economic assistance and aid.

ASEAN-JAPAN RELATIONS

Since the ASEAN countries are basically free-market-oriented economies eschewing rigid economic planning, it is the free market economies of Europe, America and Asia that are the ASEAN countries' natural trading and economic partners.

Japan takes an important place among the economic and trading partners of the ASEAN member countries. It is against this general background of economic and trade relations between the ASEAN countries and Japan that I wish to discuss some aspects of ASEAN-Japan economic and trade relations.

The point to be made clear at this juncture in this: By assisting Indonesia and the other ASEAN member countries, whether by providing economic assistance or access to its own markets, Japan is thereby assisting the enhancement of the ASEAN countries' national resiliencies. This indirectly helps bring about political stability in the Southeast Asian region. An enlightened policy of economic assistance and co-operation through trade with the ASEAN countries provides Japan with an opportunity to play a constructive role in enhancing political stability in Southeast Asia through means that are essentially non-political.

The question whether such a policy is in keeping with Japan's self-interest can be answered in the affirmative. Strictly from an economic point of view, the strengthening of one's partner in an interdependent relationship makes good sense. The stronger Japan's trading partners in Southeast Asia become, the better it is for both sides in the long-run. From a long-term political point of view such an enlightened economic and trade policy *vis-a-vis* the ASEAN countries is at least harmless to Japan's political interests and may even be beneficial in the long-term.

As I have just stated, both the ASEAN countries and Japan are basically free-market-oriented economies. Neither side threatens the other since neither side has imperialistic designs, nor does either attempt or aspire to impose a certain political or economic system on the other. Both sides aspire to a peaceful world free from interference and intervention from outside forces. Most ASEAN countries, along with Japan, share a common concern about the threat of nuclear war and the danger of nuclear testing.

After reiterating the political rationale for close economic and trade cooperation between the ASEAN member countries and Japan, it remains to be said that such co-operation must absolutely be based on the principle of mutual benefit and mutual respect for the interests and national integrity and sovereignty of both sides.

ASEAN-JAPAN ECONOMIC ISSUES

Having stated the case for long-term economic and trade co-operation between the ASEAN member countries and Japan and the long-term benefits such co-operation will bring for the stability of Southeast Asia, I will now review the economic and trade relations between the ASEAN member countries and Japan in the 1980s. I will then offer some thoughts on some problems which merit our special attention if this co-operation is to bring long-term benefits for both the ASEAN countries and Japan.

The first half of the 1980s has witnessed some discouraging trends in the economic relations between the ASEAN countries and Japan.

Trade relations who some worrying developments as can be seen from various indicators. Although Japan's total trade with the world soared from US $295 billion in 1981 to US $305 billion in 1985, total trade with ASEAN fell from US $36 billion to US $31 billion in the same period with no sign of immediate rebound in sight. In fact, while total trade with the world continued to show signs of vigorous expansion, trade with ASEAN is likely to stagnate or even decline further.

ASEAN's share in Japan's total trade has been experiencing a continuous decline since 1980, falling from 12.7 per cent in that year to only 9.0 per cent in the first half of 1986. These developments are of particular concern to Indonesia, whose exports to Japan in 1985 were 24 per cent lower than in 1981, while imports in the same period declined by no less than 47 per cent. Although the balance of trade remains in favour of ASEAN, this cannot be a consolation in view of the weakening overall trend of ASEAN-Japan trade relations.

Equally discouraging from the viewpoint of the ASEAN countries is the trend of Japanese direct investment abroad which, in the wake of Japan's huge current account surplus, is growing in importance among the elements of Japan's economic presence in other countries. The last few years have witnessed a staggering growth of Japan's direct investment abroad. Annual investment rose for US $4.7 billion in 1980 to US $12 billion in 1985. Yet Japan's direct investment in the ASEAN countries stagnated at US $0.9 billion annually, meaning a steep decline in the ASEAN countries' share in Japan's annual overseas direct investment from 19.7 per cent in 1980 to 7.7 per cent in 1985.

As far as development assistance is concerned, ASEAN countries continue to enjoy a high priority in Japan's assistance policy. As of 1985, nearly 36 per cent of Japan's total financial assistance went to the ASEAN countries of which Indonesia, with a share of 17 per cent, is by far the biggest recipient.

Without this financial assistance the ASEAN countries' efforts to adjust the new global economic environment might have turned out to be much more costly in terms of the scaling down of development efforts. It will continue to be of crucial importance to future economic development of the ASEAN countries. Therefore, the willingness of Japan to increase its development assistance is an encouraging sign.

REASONS BEHIND THE DECLINE IN TRADE

One of the reasons for the decline of ASEAN-Japan trade is its vulnerability to the instability of commodity trade. Depressed commodity prices as a result of the declining resource intensity of Japan's economic growth, on the one hand, and over supply, on the other, have hit the exports of ASEAN countries around 90 per cent which consist of primary commodities. This abrupt decline in turn affected Japan's exports to the ASEAN countries.

The concentration of Japan's investment in ASEAN in resource and import-substitution sectors is another reason. As commodity prices decline, investment in the resource sector becomes less and less profitable. Similarly, as growth performance deteriorates, ASEAN countries become less and less attractive to import-substitution investment.

Should the two trends persist, Japan may also finally find the attractiveness of ASEAN countries as borrowers declining.

The new position of Japan is a factor. To be sure, Japan's main export markets are not found in the ASEAN countries. It is the United States, the European Community, and several newly industrialising countries that absorb the lion share of Japan's exports. These markets are increasingly protectionist, however, and this trend is forcing Japan to concentrate its trade policy agenda on maintaining access to them and to divert its foreign direct investment to these large markets as a way of penetrating them from within.

Barriers to Japan's market for manufactured products are a cause. The barriers are certainly the lowest as far as border protection is concerned. However, consumers are to be found inside rather than at the border of a customs area. There is a long distance between the border and consumers and it is in this distance that problems lie.

The inability of the ASEAN countries to improve their supply conditions so as to be competitive with South Korea and other more advanced developing countries is a problem. Further domestic adjustments are necessary, and the possibility of using intra-ASEAN liberalisation as an adjustment vehicle is being seriously considered.

Differences in diagnoses may continue to exist. Even so, the decline in ASEAN-Japan economic relations needs to be halted before they become irreparable.

ASEAN AS AN ADJUSTMENT MECHANISM

Representatives of ASEAN countries have repeatedly proposed adjustment measures, both bilaterally and in the context of ASEAN. The key word is restructuring. The combination of Japan's declining reliance on some "simple" manufacturing activities, a tightening labour shortage in Japan, the continuously appreciating Yen, and rising current account surpluses provide a favourable environment for Japan to relocate some industries abroad. The factor endowments of ASEAN countries are particularly suitable for some of the industries.

In addition to trade liberalisation, fiscal stimulation, and an expansive monetary policy, a restructuring programme appears to be necessary. This programme would involve not only funds, but also the transfer of knowledge and technology that would open up new opportunities for Japan's investment in the ASEAN countries. The basic idea of the

"Fukuda Fund" is still valid. While designing the restructuring, ASEAN countries should rediscover the merits of co-ordinated adjustment as a way of reaping economies of scale, including less closely protection *vis-a-vis* the rest of the world.

Undoubtedly, support from other developed countries is necessary. Trade liberalisation and fiscal and monetary policy co-ordination are issues of global concern. In other words, ASEAN-Japan Dialogue is not a substitute for global efforts such as the new GATT round. Nor will the Pacific-wide efforts become redundant. These forums are complementary.

To face the new environment, the ASEAN countries are aware of the need to reinvigorate ASEAN economic co-operation. As the twentieth anniversary of ASEAN approaches, various activities aimed at formulating new approaches to ASEAN economic co-operation are under way. The next summit is expected to come up with substantial agreements that would help re-establish the attractiveness of ASEAN as a "growth centre."

17

*Japan's Security and Military Role in Pacific Asia**

Juwono Sudarsono**

Observations of Japan's recent military and security outlook in the Pacific Asia region must necessary take into account three basic factors. The first and traditionally the most important, is the nature of Japanese and American military co-operation. The second and in the main the most incipient element in the equation, is the changing domestic political balance within Japan, especially after the election of Mr. Yasuhiro Nakasone as prime minister in late 1982 and, more recently, his re-election in late November, 1983. The third element, Japan's external dimension, has to do with the perceived threat perception within Japan of the Soviet Union's increased military capabilities in Pacific Asia, more especially in Northeast Asia.

Other elements in the analyses can, of course, be taken into account but these (and especially the economic dimensions of the Japan-United States trade and business balances) are beyond the immediate focus of this essay.

---

* Paper presented at the Fourth Indonesia-India Conference, Jakarta, August 19-20, 1985, sponsored by CSIS (Jakarta) and IDSA (New Delhi).

** Dr. Juwono Sudarsono is a lecturer at the Faculty of Social Sciences, University of Indonesia.

A number of treatises has been published about the changing nature of the Japan-United States military and security co-operation as well as its implications for the security of the western half of the Pacific Asia region.

The nature of Japanese and American co-operation in the field of security reaches back to the early 1950s, and to 1960 in particular, when the Japan-United States Security Treaty came up for a review. As the Japanese economy grew in the 1960s and Japanese goods and services began to make inroads into American markets, pressure began to build up within the United States Congress to reassess the nature of co-operative efforts between the two nations.

By 1976, as Japan's trade surplus begin to have telling effects to the many important constituencies in the United States and with the Vietnam War receding into the background, American pressure for an increased share of Japan's defence expenditure began to grow into an open controversy.

In the same year, the Japanese government issued its National Defence Programme Outline (NDPO) which subsequently became the major document in presenting Japan's future military and security posture. The NDPO was conceived at a time when Soviet military capabilities in Northeast Asia was considered to be marginal and when American defence expenditures worked under considerably less restraint than the previous five years. More importantly, "burden-sharing," though already a watchword among American political and military circles, had not become an issue of immediate spill-over from America's deteriorating trade balance with Japan.

In addition, the NDPO was devised on the basic assumption that Japan's military and security role would remain constricted to its islands and territorial water, resulting in an essentially "defence posture" with heavy reliance on land defence. Although the United States had long pressed for an increase in the Japanese Maritime Self-Defence Force capabilities since the early 1970s, the prevailing strategy was to safeguard commercial traffic between Japan and its sources of oil in the Gulf area in the Middle East.

There remains, as an authoritative publication has reaffirmed, a philosophical divide between Japan's proper role in the context of changing American security perceptions in the region. Notwithstanding the Reagan administration's appreciation of Mr. Nakasone's more assertive role in projecting Japan's political and diplomatic profile, the

Japanese have in the main viewed the issue in the framework of self-defence.[1] The ambiguity of Japan's non-nuclear stipulations may have facilitated co-operation with respect to visits of American nuclear-powered or nuclear armed vessels to Japanese ports, but it has at the same time sustain the psychological aversion to over identification with American military objectives in Northeast Asia.

As pressures within the American Congress began to be increasingly felt in Japan, the Japanese defence establishment began to issue statements pertaining to Japan's future "comprehensive" and "monodirectional" strategic outlook. Understandably, there followed a series of interpretations of the practical effects of the new strategic initiative, with the United States at one time suggesting that if Japan were to increase its burden in the defence of sea lanes outside of Japan's territorial waters, the United States navy could more effectively swing its forces westward to the Indian Ocean and the Gulf region.

As things now stand, the recent publication of the Japanese White Paper on Defence suggests that though the magic figure of 1 per cent of GNP allocated for defence might have been broken. Actual expenditures for the five year plan throughout fiscal year 1983-1987 may still be below the equipment levels committed in the NDPO.[2] This suggests that despite Prime Minister Nakasone's declarations on Japan's efforts to assume responsibility for extending the defence of the sea lanes up to 1,000 nautical miles from its shores, the practical implications of that commitment remain ambiguous. Moreover, although there has recently been increased Japanese-American joint military exercises in Northeast Asia (more particularly joint naval and air surveillance over the Straits of Tsushima, Tsugaru and Soya), joint military plans in further forms of co-operative effort has emerged only after the June, 1984, United States-Japan defence talks in Honolulu.

These efforts, the result of prolonged negotiations dating back to 1978, established firmer ties between the two countries. Guidelines were established to prepare joint actions in the event of an armed attack against Japan, the deterrence of aggression and co-operation in case of a crisis situation that may arise in the Korean peninsula.

Despite these efforts, the Japanese government continues to try to secure whatever room for political manoeuvre it can retain from a decidedly uncomfortable psychological predicament. Fears of over-reliance on the United States and involvement in a conflict situation may not be an original party that resulted in protracted negotiations over

Japan's sea-lanes defence and of the Japanese strategic and logistical support to United States forces.

By early 1984, in the wake of the September, 1983, Korean Air Lines incident and the attendant climate of tension in Northeast Asia, co-operation between Japan and the United States improved markedly. An assertive Reagan administration anxious to flex its muscle over an incident from which it could reap full propaganda benefit, made it easier for the Nakasone government to press for increased defence expenditure. Although the Defence Agency and the Ministry of Finance could not agree on the scope and intensity of Japan's defence requirements, a growing number of joint United States-Japan military exercises with infantry and land forces were conducted complementing those previously established between the air and maritime services.

These joint security and military co-operative endeavours were assisted by several agreements reached between the two countries in the field of trade and commerce. Since April, 1984, Japan has agreed to increase its import of beef and citrus products from the United States for a period of 4 years. In May of the same year, Japan opened her domestic financial market by internationalising the yen. By December, 1984, amidst strong pressure from American unions, Japan decreased her steel exports from 7 per cent of the American market to about 5.8 per cent.[3]

The one remaining more concerns the United States trade deficit, which in 1984 reached US $36.8 billion and which in 1985 is expected to total US $55 billion. Nevertheless, these figures do not seem to adversely affect the continued co-operation between Japan and the United States, now entering into areas of military technology unforeseen even in the wake of the Korean Air Lines incident.

Under a memo of understanding signed in November, 1983, Japan has begun to export its technology to the United States. The United States has succeeded in procuring the Japanese-made "image seeking" missile-guidance system, despite some misgivings in Japan that such weapons system if developed might come under restrictions and that any spin-offs from such advanced technology will work against the interests of Japan-made goods.

Beyond Prime Minister Nakasone's vision of collective security projected to within 1,000 nautical miles, closer co-operation in military and security matters may help to reduce frictions over the trade surplus that Japan enjoys over the United States. In mid-July, 1985, the United States House of Representatives passed a bill calling on Japan to accelerate its military and defence build-up to "fully carry out" its regional security responsibilities. Coming as it did only weeks after a similar bill passed in the United States Senate, the implication has been made clear that henceforth Japan's increased burden-sharing will come under closer scrutiny. Although Reagan administration officials deny that defence and trade issues are directly linked, both houses of Congress have made it clear that legislation and resolutions concerning the two issues would be worked out in a joint House-Senate conference within the coming weeks.[4]

DOMESTIC DIMENSIONS OF SECURITY

The uneasy balance within the Liberal Democratic Party, which surfaced after the election of Mr. Nakasone as prime minister, continued to influence the nature of the push and pull between domestic and international issues. In December 1983, Mr. Nakasone survived an election setback only by forming a coalition with a minor party from the opposition, the New Liberal Club. The ill-health of Mr. Kakuei Tanaka, who suffered an heart attack in February, 1985, further complicated the already intense world of factional politics within the LDP.

Prime Minister Nakasone was therefore under heavy pressure to consolidate his position within the party, one measure of which was a gradually implement his foreign and defence initiatives rather than to expanding them as promised soon after he first took office in late 1982.

In addition to incipient factionalism, Mr. Nakasone was also publicly committed to streamline the government, cut public spending and elevate ethics of governmental propriety among public servants. These domestic declaratory obligations at the same time worked against his inclinations to increase Japan's share of the defence burden in and around Japan's defence perimeter. Moreover, since the cutting of allocations on social security and public works resulted in increased tensions within the prevailing factions of the LDP while Japan's ability to project a comprehensive and coherent security posture abroad became very limited.

One result of the LDP's rancorous factionalism has been a relative strengthening of the Japan Socialist Part (JSP). The JSP has come under new leadership since 1983. Under its new chairman, Masashi Ishibashi, the party began to reconstruct its foreign and defence policy priorities, hoping to project a more "realistic" (right of centre) approach in these two areas. The New JSP leadership has also softened its line on the role of the Self-Defence Forces, contending that it was unrealistic to do away with the Self-Defence Forces if the JSP could in the future come to power.[5]

Prime Minister Nakasone in the meantime is running considerable risk by maintaining that his special relationship and rapport with the current American president would allow him to maintain his high priority on defence spending. Despite his past successes in committing weapon system orders up from 26 per cent of the defence budget in 1981 to about 33 per cent in 1984, in the final analysis, the Japanese political public may not care too much about his public relations accomplishments abroad and much prefer that bread and butter issues be addressed to with more serious attention.

TABLE 1

Trends in Japan's Defence Expenditure

(in per cent)

Fiscal Year	*1980*	*1981*	*1982*	*1983*	*1984*
Nominal Increase	6.5	7.6	7.8	6.5	6.5
Real Increase	2.0	3.9	4.6	4.3	4.6
Defence Exp. % of GNP	0.90	0.91	0.93	0.98	0.99

TABLE 2

Indicators of Defence Spending

	NATO	*Japan*
(1) Ability to procure Weapons from USA relative to exchange rates, social pressures on budget.	Multinational "spread"	Bilateral "burden sharing"
(2) Indirect economic and social costs (e.g. conscription), military use of public facilities and land.	Important esp. in West Germany	Less prominent
(3) Operations, maintenance and capital costs.	Relative to independent European nuclear forces	No Japanese nuclear deterrent

Within these broad parameters of Japanese domestic politics, it is conceivable that a sustained challenge from the JSP might towards the beginning of 1986 lead towards a new format in Japanese politics. Despite its idealistic thrust in the past, the new JSP has undertaken initiatives previously not pursued by any of its leaders since 1966. Assuming that the factionalism within the LDP may not result in a clear cut victory for one or a coalition of factions, and also assuming that apart from Mr. Ishibashi, the JSP can lend greater credence of the refurbished party platform, the change in mood may affect the nature of Japan's collaborative effort with the United States and other allies in the Pacific region.

As things now stand, however, and given past experiences of factionalism within the LDP, no major military or security initiatives can be pursued any stronger than currently undertaken by the current prime minister. In other words, chances are that a re-alignment within the LDP should quickly take the initiative in grasping the public mood in Japan and subsequently undercut whatever political gains the new JSP leadership may have achieved within the past few months.

The election of Mr. Nakasone to the prime ministership changed the terms of the defence debate with Japanese society. In essence, the most dramatic policy statement of the incoming government was the prime minister's open commitment of Japan being an unsinkable aircraft carrier for the United States.

Understandably, Mr. Nakasone wanted to reap full benefit from the prevailing rhetoric coming from the White House during the first term of the Reagan administration, apart from sensing that the time had come for Japan to play a higher profile in international politics and diplomacy.

The climate of the new cold war enabled Mr. Nakasone to commit Japan's defence more strongly with a Western strategic outlook. Throughout 1983 and 1984, despite French and German resistance, Mr. Nakasone clearly wanted strategic issues in Europe to be linked with the overall Japanese-United States alliance in Northeast Asia. The issue over the deployment of Soviet SS-20s in Siberia reflected the Japanese prime minister's mood that a strategic link be clearly established between the two theaters, thereby making Japan a linchpin of Western defence.

Whatever the motive, the hard-line stance was fortuitously assisted by the September 1, 1983, shooting down of the Korean airliner. This incident, skilfully used by both Japanese and American military establishments, helped to create the right conditions within each country's domestic political setting to justify increased spending for defence. It marked the second international incident (after the invasion of Soviet forces into Afghanistan) which gave an impetus to the growing popular perception that Soviet military behaviour constituted a threat to Japanese security interests.

Previously, within the mainstream of Japanese political and defence establishments, Japanese security policy had been divided among essentially three lines. The first grouping tended to link increased Soviet military power in the Pacific with decreasing American relative power and credibility, especially during President Carter's term of office. For this group the only solution was to create Japan's autonomous defence and to jettison its traditional subordinate role to American security policy.

The second view, reflected in the celebrated Masamichi Inoki Report of July 1980, takes the view that Japanese defence spending should gradually increase within the context of the Japanese-American alliance, an alliance that it deemed vital to Japanese national interests. This formulation gained support among politicians and bureaucrats who gauged that the level of Japanese defence spending could be adjusted to the prevailing public opinion in Japan and in the United States within the context of three balancing issues: the bilateral trade balance, negotiation over burden-sharing and, increasingly, the joint response toward growing Soviet military and naval capability.

The third group, one which has strongest support within Japan's ministries of finance and international trade and industry, argues for a minimal response. It leans to the view that the main threat to Japan's overall national interests do not come from the Soviet Union, but from the structural dependence of Japan's perennial need for food, energy and raw materials from abroad.[6]

Despite Afghanistan and the Korean Air Line's incident, however, the balance has not resulted into any marked and effective change towards the view adopted by advocates of autonomous defence. There is, according to most observers of Japanese domestic politics, a clear difference within the Japanese political hierarchy, between openly advocating a more assertive role for Japan in diplomatic and security matters and spending more money to put these inclinations into practical steps. There is little evidence to support the thesis that Japanese politicians, however aware they are of Japan's economic dependence on the United States, can be pressured to considerably allocate more expenditure for its defence that it currently plans to do.

Moreover, notwithstanding Japan's deep-seated aversion of the Soviet Union, many influential Japanese politicians feel that they are already making more than substantial effort to increase its level of defence expenditure. The real rate of increase in defence spending over the past ten years has been higher than that of America's Western European allies and that the increase in defence spending from 1980 on was always higher than the increase in the budget as a whole. Japanese observers are also keen to emphasise that the absolute size of the Japanese defence budget is large and that the proportion spend for procurement of new weapons and other equipment has risen considerably faster than the increase in the total defence budget.

By other standards, however, Japan's American partners feel that defence efforts, even after Afghanistan and the Korean airliner incident, seem less than adequate. While recognising that in absolute terms defence spending has made Japan number 8 in the world in terms of absolute expenditure, the amount in terms of percentage of the GNP usually hovers below 1 per cent. Likewise, though in absolute terms the Japanese defence budget has quadrupled, defence spending as percentage of the national budget has been held steady in the 1970-1980. The share to defence spending relative to the general budget has increased from 5.13 per cent in 1981 to about 5.8 per cent in 1984. But, as has been outlined above, these increases must be taken into account relative to spending in other areas of the budget, in particular allocations for social welfare and in view of the high Japanese budget deficit in recent years.[7]

Recent events tend to confirm the view that as a result of the convergence of several factors, the Nakasone government has made attempts to break the 1 per cent barrier imposed by a politically inspired Japanese decision to restrain defence allocations relative to the gross national product. The advisory commission of the prime minister's office and the LDP's sub-committee group has publicly made known its preference to lift the ceiling. The report was not endorsed by the LDP executive council in December 1984, but there is little doubt that towards the end of 1985 heated debate over the 1 per cent ceiling will continue in Japan.

The implications of the Japan-United States military co-operation, its domestic political dimension and the up-and-down of the perception of threat from the Soviet Union have not been all too clear to Japan's Asian neighbours. One argument, prevalent among Southeast Asian strategists, is that a major expansion of Japan's military capabilities would constitute a major reordering of the power balance in Northeast-Asia. It would not only create strong reaction from the Soviet Union and heighten its sense of being increasingly encircled by a coalition of formidable powers, but will also result in intense apprehension in Southeast-Asia.

The major consensus among most observers, however, is that Japan is not keen to play the kind of activist regional role that the United States would like it to pursue. During the years of the Carter presidency, the general prevailing opinion was that advocates for Japan's autonomous defence could only gain support if American power and credibility would further decline.

Now that the Reagan administration has restored confidence to America's allies of its commitment to a strong defence posture, the nature inclination within the Japanese political and bureaucratic hierarchy is to emphasise its stand between minimal response and gradual assertiveness within the Japanese-American alliance format. In this context, Japan has improved its capabilities in mining, petrol, surveillance and anti-sub-marine warfare capabilities in addition to the increase in the number of joint air and naval exercises its forces conduct with American forces in Japan, the Philippines and Guam.

For the foreseeable future, even in the remaining years of the Reagan-Nakasone "special relationship," the main contribution that Japan can economically and politically press for is in non-military engagements. Japan has provided increased concessional aid to Thailand and Pakistan, two of America's regional allies that receive increased military assistance from the Reagan administration over the past two years. It seems very likely that for the foreseeable future, "autonomy" and "alliance" will continue to be the watch-words in the continuing debate over Japanese security and military policy.

Notes and References

1. *Strategic Survey, 1984-85* (London: IISS, 1985), pp. 94-95.
2. *International Herald Tribune*, August 10, 1985.
3. *Asian Wall Street Journal*, June 13, 1985.
4. *Far Eastern Economic Review*, August 1, 1985.
5. *Strategic Survey, 1984-85*, p. 94.
6. Gerald Curties, "Japanese Security Policies," *Foreign Affairs*, Spring, 1981.
7. *Strategic Survey, 1983-84* cites that Japanese defence spending as % of GNP thoroughout the years 1980-84 has been 0.90%, 0.91%, 0.93%, 0.98%, 0.99% respectively.

18

The Outlook for Pacific Co-operation and the Role of Japan

SABURO OKITA*

At the end of World War II, the American journalist Walter Lippmann declared that the Atlantic Ocean had become an inland sea, thus inaugurating the "Age of the Atlantic." Since then, great strides in transportation and telecommunications have expanded cultural, economic and scientific and technological exchange among the nations of the Pacific. This progress has begun to turn the vast Pacific Ocean into another inland sea, setting the stage for the "Age of the Pacific."

THE ADVENT OF THE "AGE OF THE PACIFIC"

The major factors facilitating the advent of the Age of the Pacific are the rapid growth of the Asia-Pacific region's market economies, the deepening of their economic interdependence, and their growing share of world trade. This region, which 30 years ago was one of the poorest in the world, is now undergoing a dramatic transformation.

There have been two great waves of economic development in the Asia-pacific region since 1960, and a third wave is now about to break.

* Dr. Saburo Okita, Chairman, Institute for Domestic and International Policy Studies.

The first wave was Japan's rapid growth in the 1960s, when it achieved annual economic growth rates of more than 10 per cent; today Japan, together with the United States, is a major pillar of the world economy. The second wave, in the 1970s, was the first growth of the region's newly industrialising nations: Hong Kong, Singapore, South Korea and Taiwan. Despite the global recession caused by the two oil crises of that decade, the Asian NICs have succeeded in maintaining a tempo of economic growth greater than that of most advanced countries.

The third wave of growth will occur in China and the countries of the Association of Southeast Asian Nations (Brunei, Indonesia, Malaysia, the Philippines and Thailand; as noted above, Singapore, the sixth ASEAN member country has already joined the ranks of the NICs). Although global recession and protectionism in the advanced countries has slowed growth in Asia and the Pacific for the past several years, the countries of the region, stretching from Northeast Asia through China to Southeast Asia, will maintain their growth potential and dynamism into the twenty-first century.

From the end of World War II to the 1960s, the advanced industrialised nations of Europe and North America were the engines of world economic growth. The United States' economic growth and the European Community's rapid increase in both intra- and extra-regional trade reflected the fact that the Atlantic region was the centre of global economic and trade expansion. Subsequently, however, growth fell off rapidly, and the region was beset by a malaise that lowered productivity growth and weakened economic vitality. The centre of growth shifted to the oil-producing countries and to the Latin American and Asian NICs.

The countries of the Asia-Pacific region overcame the second "oil shock" of 1979 by skillfully implementing economic adjustment policies; thus, with the recovery of the global economy in the early 1980s, the dynamism needed for regional development re-appeared and they were able to continue their remarkable growth. In contrast to Latin American countries, whose development is impeded by their heavy burden of external debt, the countries of Asia and the Pacific are today facing new growth opportunities.

One of the key factors promoting economic growth in these countries has been the effective economic management. Their governments have promoted active private-sector domestic investment and adopted a development strategy of actively fostering export-oriented industries. The saving rate has risen with the standard of living, enabling these countries to raise the funds needed for development domestically. In addition, the private sector has skillfully utilised the market mechanism to promote vigorous business activities. Finally, improved agricultural production has provided a solid foundation for their continued growth.

Though government and private-sector efforts have made development possible, we must also note the existence of certain conditions facilitating such efforts. The region's pattern of development has been likened to the V-shaped pattern of a formation of flying geese, a pattern reflecting the unique character of Pacific developments. The United States, the first Pacific nation to achieve rapid growth, became the leading country. Next, Japan achieved dramatic developments in consumer goods, followed by consumer durable and capital goods. The Asian NICs and ASEAN are now following in Japan's wake.

In addition to their varied stages of development, the countries of Asia-Pacific region differ in natural-resources' endowments, religion, culture and history. This very diversity has facilitated the flying-geese pattern of development. Each country has achieved growth by building on its unique strengths in the context of its own stage of development. This pattern of development, free of the rigid traditional North-South relationship of exploiter and exploited, offers proof that it is possible for North and South to grow and develop simultaneously, thus opening a new chapter in the history of North-South relations.

A DYNAMIC DIVISION OF LABOUR

Next is a brief description of the circumstances of the countries participating in the region's development.

Access to its enormous market is one of the United States' major contributions to the establishment of a harmonious division of labour within the region. The US market, the largest in the world, is among the world's most open. The United States absorbs about 60 per cent of the manufactured exports of the region's developing countries. American capital, technology and management know-how have also made a great contribution to Pacific development. In addition, US military might has played a stabilising role, thus indirectly aiding the region's economic growth.

Japan has contributed high-quality, low-priced capital goods. Japanese machinery has enabled the NICs and the ASEAN countries to improve the international competitiveness of their industries. In recent years Japan has also begun to provide more industrial co-operation, capital exports and development assistance. Above and beyond this, Japan's success is proof that Asian countries can develop along the lines of Western models.

Industrialising through aggressive export promotion, the Asian NICs have also contributed to the region's economic development. Although Japanese and American capital is still moving chiefly into the NICs' labour-intensive industries, the NICs themselves have begun to increase the production of consumer durable and capital goods.

ASEAN countries, rich in labour and natural resources, have been utilising these resources to increase the international competitiveness of their labour-intensive industries. The centre of production in such industries is now shifting from the NICs to ASEAN. Southeast Asia, along with the Middle East, used to be called the world's tinderbox. But the formation of ASEAN, an active organisation for regional co-operation, has demonstrated that the countries of the Asia-Pacific region can enjoy stability and economic development.

Australia, Canada, and New Zealand have also aided the region's development, both as manor exporters of foodstuffs, coal and ores and as advanced industrial countries that have built up complementary trade relations with such countries as Japan, South Korea and Taiwan.

THE REGION'S PROSPECTS

We have seen that economic development in Asia and the Pacific has followed a flying-geese pattern, with the United States and Japan leading the way. What course will the region follow in the future?

The most important factor to be taken into account when considering the prospects of the Pacific economy is the direction of the US economy. After World War II the United States contributed to the revitalisation of the world economy by providing massive aid to Europe through the Marshall Plan, and at the same time bore most of the cost of the free trade system, exemplified by such institutions as the International Monetary Fund and the General Agreement on Tariffs and Trade. Though America's strength is not what it used to be, neither Japan nor West Germany has the wherewithal to take America's place. The United States still has tremendous potential, and will remain the major determinant of the direction of international politics and the world economy for the foreseeable future.

US productivity declined in the 1970s but began to recover in the 1980s. Plant and equipment investment has risen and the quality of the labour force is starting to improve. Wage restraint, efforts to streamline management and other factors have had a beneficial impact.

Nevertheless, the US economy cannot stand up indefinitely under the heavy burden of its huge current-account deficit; reducing this deficit has become an urgent priority. In this regard, the September 1985 Agreement of the Central Bankers and Financial Authorities of Britain, France, Japan, West Germany and the United States to lower the value of the Dollar *vis-a-vis* that of other key currencies represented a hopeful development for the US economy and for the world economy as a whole.

As stated above, the United States is the largest market in the world. Nevertheless, in many areas US business is losing international competitiveness and protectionist pressure is mounting. For the sake of the world's economic vitality, it is hoped that the United States will not try to reduce its current-account deficit through protectionism but instead will increase efforts to improve its balance of payments through policies designed to facilitate industrial restructuring and enhance competitiveness.

The Asian NICs have achieved rapid growth through a combination of export-oriented economic policies and vigorous private-sector investments. South Korea and Taiwan have recently recovered from recessions and show signs of renewed growth, though Singapore's economic problems continue. In addition to further expanding their exports, the NICs as a whole need to create greater economic stability by expanding their domestic markets on the one hand and promoting regional trade by opening up their markets on the other.

ASEAN member countries are now at the take-off point in their economic development, but their growth rates have been slowing as a result of the global recession and growing protectionism in advanced countries, not to mention the stagnant oil and primary-product markets. The fall in the prices of oil in particular has created a "reverse oil shock" for oil-producing countries like Indonesia and Malaysia, burdening them with serious budget deficits and a worsening balance of payments. Meanwhile, the Philippines' huge external debt and political instability, as well as the stagnation of such key export markets as copper and lumber, necessitate difficult decisions in economic management. Vigorous efforts to maintain political stability have been continuing since February 1986, when Corazon Aquino took office as president, and economic reconstruction would have a beneficial effect on this process.

Despite these setbacks, ASEAN countries retain the development potential afforded by their abundant labour and natural resources. These countries face brighter prospects than many other developing countries and should not scale down their development strategies on the basis of unduly pessimistic projections. Their international competitiveness in labour-intensive industries will continue to grow, and with this will come the need for a shift from import replacement to export-led directed industrialisation. The promotion of economic development will also require technology and capital from advanced industrial countries.

When assessing the future of the Asia-pacific region, we must also carefully evaluate China's open-door economic policy, since this is one of the major variables affecting the region. If China followed the example of Hong Kong, Singapore and Taiwan, its modernisation policies would lead to both the growth of labour-intensive industries and the possibility of direct competition with ASEAN. However, in view of China's stage of development and its stock of natural resources, not to mention the potential size of its domestic market, trade relations between China and the rest of the region are more likely to be complementary. The steady development of China's economy should make a large contribution to trade expansion and economic growth in the entire region. It may take some time for economic relations with China to become closer, in view of the wary attitude toward China of the other countries in the region. Nonetheless, the dominant trend is toward greater economic interdependence.

Within China itself, the problem of reconciling the open-door policy needed for modernisation with the requirements of domestic political discipline has yet to be resolved. Nonetheless, as long as China's national goal of the "four modernisations" remains paramount, an open-door policy is inevitable. Though there may be occasional swings, it is hard to imagine a return to the earlier inward-looking stance.

Since China's participation in the Asia-pacific economy would not only add a new dimension to the region's trade and economy but also exert a major influence on its future, it would behoove us to create an environment that allows China to play an active role in the region's interdependence system.

One other factor that should be examined when considering the region's future is the direction of Soviet policy. Since Mikhail Gorbachev came to power in March 1985, the Soviet Union, recognising the urgent need for domestic economic reform, has become increasingly interested in the growth potential of Asia and the Pacific. In a speech in Vladivostok in July 1986, Gorbachev defined the Soviet Union as a "Pacific power" and made its intention clear of participating actively in the future development of the Pacific. The Soviet Union's request to take part in the Pacific Economic Co-operation Conference indicates its growing interest in the region.

At present some within the Soviet leadership are questioning the traditional emphasis on political and security concerns in Soviet policy toward Asia and the Pacific and are advocating a shift to a policy emphasising economic priorities. We must closely watch the Soviets in order to discern their intentions. Meanwhile, it would be unwise to slow the present momentum for change by rebuffing Soviet interest in Pacific co-operation on political and strategic grounds. Peace and stability in Asia and the Pacific cannot arise from exclusionary principles but must spring from a form of co-operation that includes all countries concerned.

A JAPANESE MARSHALL PLAN

How should Japan respond to the above-mentioned developments?

The two oil crises of the 1970s have adversely affected Japan's trade balance, but it quickly recovered and is now recording a massive surplus. The major reason for this phenomenon is that Japan's industrial structure has shifted from one centred on resource-intensive heavy industries to one reliant on industries that feature high technology and low natural-resource consumption. Another reason is that in such products as automobiles and consumer electronics Japan is internationally competitive in both quality and price. Finally, we can cite, Japan's high saving rate.

Several factors could reduce the trade surplus. It is projected that the saving rate will fall as the proportion of elderly people in the population grows and social security payments rise. In addition, imports of manufactured goods will increase owing to the rising wages and the resultant loss of international competitiveness in manufactured products. Nevertheless, for some time Japan probably will continue to run a trade surplus and will remain a net capital exporter. Of course, at a time when the United States has become a net capital importer, Japan's continued ability to use its excess domestic savings to satisfy the capital needs of the United States and other countries is desirable seen from the viewpoint of global economic growth. The problem is how best to use Japan's enormous saving surplus to contribute to this end.

In April 1986 I delivered a report entitled "The Potential of the Japanese Surplus for World Economic Development" as a representative of the United Nations University's World Institute for Development Economics Research in Helsinki. I proposed devoting a portion of Japan's saving and current account surpluses to the growth of the developing countries.

In September that year, the Minister of Finance, Kiichi Miyazawa, announced that Japan was prepared to make a special contribution of SDR 3 million (approximately US $3.6 billion) to the IMF to allow a more flexible response to the developing countries' needs. In December the Japanese Government announced a special contribution of US $2 billion to the World Bank.

Whatever the method chosen, it is becoming increasingly important to utilise Japan's huge savings and current-account surpluses to promote the growth of the world economy. In the Asia-Pacific region alone, the developing countries urgently need to improve their infrastructure, such as roads, ports, electric power supply, telecommunications and so forth. The provision of capital through such institutions as the World Bank, the Asian Development Bank and the Overseas Economic Co-operation Fund of Japan, as well as private financial institutions, could contribute to the dynamic growth in the region.

More concretely speaking, China's seventh five-year plan (1986-90) requires US $40 billion in foreign capital to meet the annual growth target of 7.5 per cent. Indonesia needs US $2.5 billion a year in foreign capital to fulfil its development goals. Altogether, the countries of Asia, including South Asia, require no more than US $20 billion annually in foreign exchange for their economic development plans. In view of the fact that Japan's net long-term capital outflows in 1985 totalled US $65 billion, Japan could provide the major part of this sum on its own.

What I am proposing is a Japanese version of the Marshall Plan. I strongly hope that the Japanese Government and people will realise that it lies within their power—and is their responsibility—to take the initiative in aiding the growth of the developing countries.

At present almost all the capital leaving Japan is being invested in US bonds, securities and real estate. Diverting some of this money to the developing world would contribute significantly not only to Asian development but also to the global economy. Economic growth in the developing countries would raise their purchasing power, creating a larger market for the exports of advanced countries, including Japan. Thus the economies of advanced countries would also grow, establishing a "virtuous circle" of growth.

At the same time, Japan must continue its efforts to import more primary products and, more important, more internationally competitive manufactured products from other Asian countries. I myself believe that Japan should aim at doubling imports from the rest of Asia over the next five or six years. If Japan opened its market further and developed a horizontal division of labour with other Asian countries, economic relations between Japan and the rest of Asia would expand dramatically.

PACIFIC CO-OPERATION: PROBLEMS AND PROSPECTS

Regional Interdependence and the Need for Co-operation

The economic development of Asia and the Pacific over the past 20 years has increased the economic interdependence of the countries in the region. Our task now is to manage and develop this interdependence in such a way as to foster a better balance among countries and ensure the region's stability and prosperity. The most important aspects of this task are the maintenance of an open international economic system and industrial restructuring.

Strong economic growth is causing dynamic changes in the international division of labour among the countries of the region, and comparative advantage is shifting; the development of the NICs is part of this process, but so is trade friction, and protectionism often strengthens in countries that wish to maintain the status quo.

Industrial restructuring is unavoidable if we are to protect the free trade system that has fostered the region's export-oriented economies and promote the development of economic and trade relations based on the free trade principle. We must also expand trade within the region. In 1985 trade within the western Pacific region, including Northeast Asia, Southeast Asia, and Oceania, accounted for only 15 per cent of the region's total trade, while trade with the United States was close to 40 per cent. In contrast, trade within the EEC accounted for about half of all EEC trade, while trade with the United States amounted to only 10 per cent.

Increasing interdependence is leading to a growing recognition that some form of regional co-operation is the most effective way of dealing with issues of common concern. Close consultation on shared problems and on the implementation of co-operative measures to identify and resolve economic disputes before they develop into political crises will promote the region's resilience and stability.

Steady Progress in Pacific Co-operation

The concept of economic co-operation among the countries of the Pacific has been debated among scholars, business people, and government officials for the past 20 years. The first person to articulate the issue was Professor Kiyoshi Kojima of Hitotsubashi University. As early as 1965, he sought to define Pacific co-operation, calling for a Pacific free trade zone along the lines of the EEC. A group of Japanese scholars interested in this issue have explored regional economic co-operation since 1968 in the Pacific Trade and Development Conference. Meanwhile, the Pacific Basin Economic Council, initiated by a group of business people in 1968, has helped deepen understanding of the region's interdependence.

The Pacific Economic Co-operation Conference was established in September 1980, on the occasion of the Canberra Seminar convened at the behest of Prime Minister Masayoshi Ohira of Japan and Prime Minister Malcolm Fraser of Australia. The founders of the PECC understood the need to focus on existing problems in a pragmatic and flexible way. The PECC searches for areas in which there is a recognised potential for co-operation and seeks formulas for successful co-operation. The PECC's tripartile competition—government officials, academics and business leaders—is an appropriate one for promoting Pacific co-operation at the present stage of development.

As it broadens its scope of activities, the PECC is becoming one of the most authoritative bodies promoting Pacific co-operation, and its work will become increasingly important as time passes. The PECC considers and recommends policy measures to enhance co-operation, policy planning and the prevention of friction through free and frank exchanges of views, at the same time maintaining close links with the governments of the participating nations. Task forces comprising specialists from each participating country explore concrete methods of co-operation in such areas as trade, investment, finance, technology transfer, energy, fishing, livestock and animal feed.

One indication of the progress made in Pacific co-operation over the past several years was the decision made at the July 1984 meeting in Jakarta of the ASEAN foreign ministers and their dialogue partners from other Pacific region's countries and the EEC to establish a "six plus five" formula for inter-governmental talks on economic development in the Pacific region. In accordance with the proposal of Indonesian Foreign Minister Mochtar Kusumaatmadja, the six-plus-five formula was included, in addition to the six ASEAN foreign ministers, the foreign ministers of Australia, Canada, Japan, New Zealand, and the United States. It was agreed that six-plus-five consultations would be held once a year and would cover topics in two general areas: economic developments affecting the Pacific region and proposals for specific co-operation projects. The first such project designed had to do with the development of human resources. Working-group meetings in Jakarta in the fall of 1984 were followed by a conference of representatives of the 11 participating governments and the ASEAN secretariat in 1985.

Major Issues Facing the PECC

It is still too soon to predict the final outcome of the Pacific co-operation initiative. At present, consensus among the participating countries forms the basis for activities, and it would be counter-productive to force the pace of progress. At this point we must concentrate on strong and persistent efforts to increase real co-operation, with faith in our ultimate success. It is most important to expand activities gradually on the basis of shared interests, procedural flexibility, and decision by consensus. The importance of ASEAN initiatives cannot be over-emphasised. Pacific co-operation must also promote the private-sector activities that have played a central role in producing the dynamism of Pacific economic development, at the same time remaining open to the rest of the world.

Three points regarding our future efforts deserve emphasis. *First*, we must deal with the problem of turning ideas into actual policies. We can see from the activities of the PECC task forces that concrete plans for Pacific co-operation are materialising. Government-level consultations among the participating countries are desirable to determine how each country is to formulate specific policies and how the cost associated with policy implementation are to be distributed. In raising this point, attention is to be paid, to the proposal to establish a Pacific Co-operation Research Fund, made by the delegation of the Japan National Committee for Pacific Economic Co-operation at the fifth general meeting of the PECC, held in Vancouver in November 1986. This proposal will be discussed at the sixth general meeting, to be held in Osaka in May 1988.

Second, although Pacific co-operation has focused mainly on trade and economic issues, we must also promote cultural and educational co-operation. Understanding of one another's history, culture and present circumstances is a prerequisite for smoother relations among the nations of the Pacific. While recognising that money and goods are the main forms of exchange among the Pacific nations at present, we must also reaffirm the importance of comprehensive co-operation, which includes the exchange of people, information and culture. Stress is to be made on the need for governments to make conscious efforts to promote cultural, educational and personal exchange rather than limit themselves to the economic area, where to some extent the market mechanism works automatically.

The third point has to do with the issue of "open regionalism" and the extent of national participation. Our ideal is a form of Pacific co-operation that is open to all countries. Nevertheless, the political realities of the region complicate the automatic application of this principle. In the circumstances, the only way to realise open regionalism is to endeavour to include all countries that share the objective of regional interdependence and co-operation and wish to contribute actively and constructively to this end.

TOWARD DYNAMIC PACIFIC CO-OPERATION

In conclusion, an emphasis should be made on three points that have an effect on the achievement of true pacific co-operation.

The *first* is that the export-oriented economies of Asia and the Pacific, which are responsible for the region's economic dynamism over the past 20 years, are now facing difficulties because the free trade system on which they depend is under assault by new waves of protectionism from the advanced industrialised countries. Protectionist measures of any kind impede the functioning not only of bilateral trade but also of the entire global trading system.

In today's economic environment of growing interdependence, a co-operative approach to trade and economic problems aimed at upholding and further developing free trade is the only way to ensure mutual long-term benefit. Trade and economic problems should be resolved according to rules established by multilateral consensus rather than by bilateral negotiations. The Pacific co-operation framework facilitates the creation of such rules. If the nations of the pacific co-operative to uphold an open and free trading system, they will be in a position to offer international leadership.

The *second point* is that because the countries of the region are at different stages of development, Pacific co-operation provides a golden opportunity to address the North-South problem at the regional level. This problem has been debated at the global level in such forums at the United Nations, but the diversity of the economies of the South and the conflicting interests of the countries of the North have made a global approach difficult. A North-South Dialogue at the Pacific-region level could afford a new springboard for a fruitful international dialogue.

The Asian NICs have already achieved an economic take-off, and the ASEAN countries have begun the take-off process. Since the international competitiveness of ASEAN's labour-intensive industries will strengthen as wages continue to rise in the NICs, the ASEAN countries can expect to develop export-led economic growth. Japan, the United States, and the other advanced nations of the region can facilitate ASEAN's take-off by providing capital and technology.

In addition, the advanced countries should help the South Pacific nations to develop their economies, providing aid in such areas as fishing, agriculture and tourism. There is also a great need for aid to improve transportation and communications between island nations. Such co-operation could help make the Pacific region a model for solving North-South problems.

The *third point* is that though the region has untold potential for development, various political problems still stand in the way. The problem of Cambodia is one such hindrance to stable development. US-Soviet tensions also affect the region deeply. The region's potential wealth could make it a bone of contention between the superpowers.

It is unrealistic to expect that conflicts rooted in ideology or political systems can be resolved by economic means alone. Nonetheless, economic strength can contribute indirectly to the gradual relaxation of tensions. Though the region's development so far has been limited to trade and economic transactions, this has formed a firm foundation for fruitful exchanges in other areas, as well. For the first time in history the nations of Asia and the Pacific have a common basis upon which to build comprehensive exchanges. This common ground provides an excellent opportunity for pursuing the long-term objective of widening and deepening interdependence among countries of differing cultures, systems and beliefs.

PART III

FOREIGN POLICY

19

Recent Trends in Japan's Foreign Policy

LALIMA VARMA*

Japan's decision to allow its Self-Defence Forces to participate in the United Nations peace-keeping operations in 1992 was a clear indication of its keenness to activate its foreign policy. It seems to be determined to play a more visible role in resolving various conflicts facing the international community.

During the Gulf War (1990-91) Japan's 'cheque book diplomacy' came under severe criticism. Its contribution of $12 million towards the war effort received little appreciation from its allies. On the other hand, Japan resented paying for a war which it had neither started nor escalated nor was it consulted. The Gulf crisis, as Shijuro Ogata, Deputy Governor of the Japan Development Bank, stated in a public lecture, was "in a sense a blessing in disguise". It has left the Japanese, he said, with a "feeling of powerlessness, a feeling of foreboding". (*The Japan Times*, May 5, 1991). It was time for it to make a serious effort to invigorate its foreign policy and policy-making process which would enable it to make expeditious and independent decisions.

---

* Associate Professor of Japanese Studies, Jawaharlal Nehru University, New Delhi.

The collapse of the Soviet Union and the formation of the Commonwealth of Independent States, developments in Eastern Europe, the formation of exclusive economic groupings in Europe and North America, have further compelled Japan to search for a new global and regional role in the post-cold war era.

For an economic power, such as Japan, the growing inter-dependence among nations, caused by the massive flow of goods, money and information across national borders, setting up of joint ventures and offshore manufacturing bases, is a matter of great importance. Interdependence broadens both the areas of conflict and co-operation and a time threatens the very existence of the multilateral trade system. Being an important beneficiary of the free trade system Japan realises that it must play an active and positive role in resolving the problems confronting this system. Japan's decision to open its long-protected rice market is to be viewed in this context.

This new emphasis requires Japan to reorient and restructure its foreign policy goals. Its efforts to carve out for itself a role in the post-cold war era, first requires that Japan reassess its relations with the US and the West European countries, with whom it conducts almost 50 per cent of its economic activity.

Close relations with the US have been and will probably continue to be the "cornerstone" of Japan's foreign policy. This fact has been time and again reiterated by successive Japanese leaders. In his speech to the Diet in January 1992, Japanese Prime Minister Kiichi Miyazawa, while repeating this point, said that Japan has also accepted that it has benefitted from its relations with the US and, at the same time stated that, "it would be no exaggeration to say that Japan would not have achieved its post-war prosperity had it not been for the good-hearted support of the US" (*The Japan Times,* January 25, 1992).

Nevertheless, for decades Japan's relations with the US have come under severe strain. Most of the problems are in the economic sphere. They are restricted not only to bilateral trade but to other areas of economic activity as well. Japan has made inroads into several spheres of the US economy. The US attributes the strains in the reactions between the two countries to Japan's domestic institutions, economic structures and strict import laws which pose numerous difficulties for the foreign countries to penetrate into Japanese markets.

Even though there have been regular dialogues to sort out these problems, not much success has been achieved. Sharp differences between the two countries have come out in the open, at the recent summit between Prime Minister Morihiro Hosokawa and US President Bill Clinton, held in February 1994. The Japanese Prime Minister very emphatically refused to submit to US demands, and accused the US Administration of violating General Agreement on Trade and Tariff (GATT). He also went to the extent of saying that Japan would refer its grievances to the World Trade Organisation. Differences between the two countries have deepened so much that the US Administration has declared its intention of reviving Super 301 against Japan.

The present state of US-Japan relations is not a sudden development. The Japanese perception of the US has been undergoing a change for some time. A large section of the Japanese are not happy with the image of their country as a "follower" of the US. At an international symposium on the "Changing World Order and the United Nations System", held in Yokohama in March 1992, Motofumi Asia, Professor of International Relations at Nihon University and former diplomat and foreign ministry official, clearly stated that the Japanese Government should come up with its own specific ideas and measures to improve the international community rather than just follow the US. In an interview with *The Japan Times* he also expressed the belief that "Japan should have the courage to tell the US that if it tries to remain the world's policeman, the military budget will continue to burden its economy and prevent it from recovering" (*The Japan Times*, April 1, 1992).

However, there are limits beyond which Japan cannot go against the US. It is aware of its own vulnerability *vis-a-vis* the US. With practically no fuel or mineral resources of its own, Japan imports a large part of it either from the US or countries closely allied to it. Similarly, the US and countries friendly to it constitute the main market for Japanese finished products.

For its national security too, Japan is dependent on the US. With the collapse of the cold-war structure and the disintegration of the Soviet Union, Japan's dependence on the US should have been reduced considerably. However, according to the Japanese point of view, the threat to its security has not diminished much with the end of the cold war. Its relations with Russia continue to be strained with the territorial issue still unresolved. The Korean peninsula still remains divided. The restoration of diplomatic relations between the People's Republic of China and the Republic of Korea has brought in a new alliance in the region. Japan is disturbed by this development. China's army of over two million is also a source of apprehension for the Japanese.

Nevertheless, in the changing world context, the necessity of the continuance of the Security Treaty, the basis of Japan-US relations, is an intensely debated subject within and outside Japan. The foreign ministry continues to hold the opinion that the "formal defence ties between the two countries are as important as ever, even if the global context has changed. The existence of the treaty, it is argued, guarantees the non-emergence of Japan as a military power. East and Southeast Asian countries in particular need to be continuously assured of this fact, having suffered the wrath of Japanese militarism during the pre-world war period.

At the same time the demand for a review of the Security Treaty is also gathering momentum. One of the objections to its continuance is that it perpetuates Japan's image as a power secondary to the US. The Japanese also resent sharing the expenses of maintenance of the bases in Japan ("Whither the Japan-US alliance", *Japan Echo,* Autumn 1988, p. 37). The "high handed" behaviour of the US at times has created a public opinion in Japan, which is critical of the US. The "superpower status" of the US is also doubted at times. President George Bush, during his visit to Japan in January 1992, was described by many Japanese as a salesman whose main purpose was to sell cars—an image unbecoming of a President of a superpower.

Emergence of a unified Europe, in the form of a European Community, has also made Japan apprehensive of its interest in the West. Trade imbalance between the two has increasingly become a source of tension. Whereas Europe attributes this imbalance to Japan's trade practices, on its part it has taken serious exception to the European anti-dumping law as essentially directed towards Japan. In a way the present phase represents serious tensions between Japan and the G-7.

It is due to these developments that Japan is increasingly shifting its attention towards the Asia-Pacific region. Its interest in the region can be traced to the oil crisis and certain reversals in US-Japan relations in the early 1970s. Since then, and especially during the 1980s, Japanese investments and aid directed towards this region has increased rapidly. In particular, East Asian countries, such as, South Korea, Hong Kong, Singapore, Taiwan and China, and some of the Southeast Asian countries have been the main beneficiaries.

The Asia-Pacific region is attractive not only as a market and for its huge reservoir of raw materials, but it is also regarded by Japanese companies as "production bases to service the global market". In comparison to the Japanese overseas manufacturing bases in other parts of the world, where almost 50 per cent of the output is sold in the local markets, in Asia a much higher percentage of the output is exported. Investments in Asia have acquired an added importance, because the manufacturing bases which had been set up in Europe and the US to avoid import restraints have almost reached a saturation point.

In Asia too, the East and Southeast Asian countries, which have been the destination of a large part of Japanese aid and investment, are also now reaching a stage of development where some of them are in a position to compete with Japan for markets and overseas investments. From this point of view, it is likely that in the next decade or so Japan, in its quest for new areas of investments, might seriously explore other regions, such as South Asia.

Japan's growing interest in the Asia-pacific region has constantly brought to the forefront the question of it emerging as a leader in this region. Japan, however, is keen to gain the trust of its Asian neighbours, who had suffered the wrath of Japanese militarism in the pre-war period. Consequently, such proposals, as Malaysian Prime Minister Mahathir Mohammad's idea of creating an East Asian Economic Caucus in which an important role is visualised for Japan, did not receive an enthusiastic response.

However, an interesting paradox of Japan's foreign policy is that, while it is quite reluctant to assume the leadership role in the Asia-Pacific, it is equally apprehensive of letting any other country, be it the US, EC, or for that matter even China, dominate in the region. In fact, Japan feels that China is gradually moving towards establishing itself as a powerful country which it will be difficult to ignore. Consequently, the emphasis of Japan's foreign policy in the Asian region is, and will continue to be, maintenance of strong and friendly ties with all the countries. In its calculations, this strategy would not only benefit it economically, but would also be the best guarantee of its own security.

It is in keeping with this strategy that Japan has tried to maintain friendly relations with China, in spite of the problems which have cropped up off and on. Even after the Tiananmen Square incident, Japan was not only the first amongst the developed countries to resume ties with China, but it also took the initiative of convincing other of the necessity of lifting sanctions against China. It was as opportunity which Japan used not only to assure China of its friendship, but also to strengthen it further. The first ever visit by a Japanese Emperor to China in October 1992 could not have been better timed.

Another way by which the aspirations of any other country to assume a dominant position in the region can be curbed, Japan feels, is by strengthening the role of a collective forum, such as the Asia-Pacific Economic Co-operation (APEC). Japan is also not likely to be very averse to the idea of expanding the role of APEC from being a purely economic forum to one which will consider political and security issues as well. A proposal of this nature was made by the Australian Prime Minister during his visit to Tokyo in 1992. Japan did not reject it outright. Instead it was agreeable, provided the other countries shared the same view.

One of the major strategies of Japan, to enhance its role and influence is Asia, and in the world as a whole, is aid. In recent years Japan has emerged as the foremost aid donor and intends to continue to be so. In fact, aid has become an important pillar of Japan's foreign policy concerns. It is, hence, not surprising that Japan is not in agreement with the other aid-donor countries who have adopted a posture that, with the end of the cold war, the strategic reasons for providing aid no more exists. Another important factor, which has compelled the aid-donating countries to take recourse to such an attitude is that many of these countries themselves are facing serious financial crises at home.

At a meeting of the Development Assistance Council, held in December 1993, many of the members supported cutting short the list of aid-receiving countries on the basis of per capita gross domestic product of more than $8,355. Japan opposed the proposal, and ultimately a compromise was arrived at.

The importance attached to ODA in Japan's foreign policy calculations is more than clear in the 1993 White Paper on ODA. For the first time, ODA is linked with the national interests of the country. ODA, the paper states, will enhance the international community's confidence in Japan and will help it to build close and friendly relations with the developing countries.

Japan, whose economic interests are best served in a peaceful environment, is a strong advocate of disarmament. It is a signatory to the Nuclear Non-Proliferation Treaty and continues its effort to urge other countries, such as India and China, to sign it. Thus, Japan's aid policy, since 1991, is also formulated so as to enable it to influence the aid-recipient countries from manufacturing and exporting destructive weapons, including nuclear weapons. Even though Japan has not been able to adhere strictly to this aspect of its aid policy, it still is in possession of a weapon which places it in an advantageous bargaining position *vis-a-vis* the recipient countries.

Aid is also linked to the recipient countries' policies towards promotion of the democratisation process; move towards a market-oriented economy; and its human rights record. Japan has been at the forefront in providing aid and economic assistance to the East European countries, which are in the process of democratising their political and economic structures.

For Japan, which now intends not only to play an active role but also to make its presence felt in the world community, the UN becomes a forum of increasing importance. Since its admittance to the UN in 1956, Japan has maintained a more or less low profile. However, over the years it has emerged as one of the major contributors to UN funds, and consequently feels that it deserves a permanent seat in the Security Council. Japan is also a vocal supporter of the deletion of Articles 53 and 107 of the UN Charter referring to the "enemy nations" of World War II which, it argues, is irrelevant in the changed international scenario. Adoption of the peace-keeping bill in 1992, enabling the Japanese Self-Defence Forces to participate in the UN peace-keeping operations, is an expression of Japan's keenness to change its "contribution policy" to more active participation.

Japan realises that in order to assert itself and influence policies, it must be well represented in such world bodies as the World Bank, International Monetary Fund, etc. The presence of Japanese personnel in these bodies currently is not in consonance with its financial contributions. In the UN itself Japan can have double the number of Japanese working there. It has become imperative that Japan enhance its staffing in the multilateral organisations where it has gained important positions. To rectify this situation it has not only to train personnel for this purpose but also bring about changes in its employment structure and wage system, etc.

It is evidently clear that Japan's foreign policy has undergone significant shifts and changes in recent years. It is desirous of playing an active role in world politics, while excluding military ambitions. Instead, it envisages a peaceful international order, where it can compete with other nations to enhance its economic interests. The Asia-Pacific region will increasingly occupy a central place in Japan's foreign policy concerns.

20

South Asia in the Evolving International Context: The Role of Japan**

IFTEKHARUZZAMAN*

The dawn of the decade of nineties has been marked by happy notes on the emerging pattern of international relations. Confrontation between the superpowers and their respective blocs that dominated the post-World War II era is by all indications giving way to an unprecedented degree of mutual cooperation. A new global order, analysts largely agree, is on the horizon while nations tend to leapfrog each other in getting out of the long nightmare of cold war. The 'new order' is expected to be one in which military options are to make room for political accommodation and dialogue, a change under which negotiations and cooperation are to prevail over conflict and tensions.

In a "trickle-down" process the lessening of global tensions is also showing signs of resolution—partial if not total—of some of long-standing disputes in various regions of the Third World. On a closer

* Senior Research Fellow, Bangladesh Institute of International Studies, Dhaka, Bangladesh.

** An earlier version of the paper was presented at the 35th International Conference of Orientalists in Japan held in Tokyo on 11-12 May 1990.

focus, nevertheless, the winds of change are far from refreshing many other 'hot-beds' of tension. Strifes persist in the Middle East, Cambodia, Afghanistan and many parts of Africa. In few regions, however, deadlocks against peaceful inter-state relations seem as astounding as in South Asia. The principal burden of what follows here is to present a framework of understanding of the challenges and opportunities facing South Asia, a region long bedevilled by mutual mistrust, endemic tensions and occasional hostilities on the one hand and massive poverty and chronic under-development on the other. The paper also seeks to examine in this context the possible role of Japan, South Asia's largest donor and a leading trade and economic partner.

The political implications of the global changes for South Asia are examined in the first section. The second part of the paper deals with economic implications, while the final section attempts some conjectures on Japan's possible role in the region.

I. POLITICAL IMPLICATIONS: PERSISTENT MISTRUST AND INSTABILITY

One of the striking aspects of the emerging global order is that there would possibly be less willingness on the part of the global powers to get embroiled in crises and conflicts in various parts of the Third World, and by implication, more incentive on the part of the regional powers to play increasingly assertive role in respective regions. Domination of the two superpowers in global affairs is by all indications giving way to a diffusion of power to greater number of power centers. The trend is towards increase in the significance of so-called middle powers like Germany in a new Europe, Japan in East Asia and the Pacific, and powers like India, Indonesia, Brazil and Mexico in their respective Third World regions. What essentially appears to be in the offing in regional contexts is that the proxy-power policy of the past few decades is being revised into a free-for-all game which by all means is likely to provide renewed impetus to regional powers.

Winds Favouring India's Long-nourished Goals

In the context of South Asia the powerful winds of the global change is blowing all in favour of the regional superpower India offering it a renewed opportunity to assert its regional supremacy. What has occurred as a fortuitous event for India has added to the tensions and suspicions in inter-state relations in the region in general and to the perception of insecurity and vulnerability of India's smaller neighbours. This is evidenced by recent Indian actions and postures towards most of its small neighbours, geared apparently to fulfil its long-nourished strategic and security goals.[1]

The changing global political climate may reasonably be perceived to have provided some grounds for lessening of tensions in the South Asian region and improvement of inter-state relations. The South Asian sub-system as a component of the international system cannot of course be insulated from the overall global scenario. Developments in superpower relations in the past, particularly in the context of East-West confrontation have influenced regional events. To that extent of East-West confrontation of US-Soviet tensions can be viewed to be capable of removing some of the external inputs to South Asian conflicts. Similarly, the process of Sino-Soviet and Indo-China rapprochement may also contribute to improvement of relations between South Asian states. It would be simplistic, to hastily conclude that improvement of inter-state relations in South Asia has been greatly facilitated. Such a perception would tend to fallaciously treat inter-state relations in South Asia as simply a function of external inputs.

South Asian politics indeed has a dynamics of its own and most, if not all, of the problems that bedevil inter-state relations in the region are created within the region, by its history, its geo-politics and its economics and ecology. The troubles of the region of South Asia, its endemic tensions, mutual mistrusts and occasional hostilities are essentially the products of contradiction of India's security perception with that of the rest of the countries. India's neighbours perceive threats to their security coming from India which for its part considers its neighbours as an integral part of its own security.

Quest for Regional Pre-dominance

To be sure, an unusually disparate pre-eminence rendered to India in the South Asian regional configuration by facts of geography, demography, economics and ecology is something about which neither India nor its neighbours can do much but accept.[2] The Indian pre-eminence in South Asia is hardly a problem for its neighbours; problem arises when pre-eminence is used as the justification for pre-dominance. The past few years saw intensified Indian quest for regional pre-dominance. Indian military build-up in various phases in past four decades has essentially been a function of the perceived dictates of the need for regional supremacy. India of course partly justifies its arms build up by its perceived compulsions out of Pakistan's acquisition of advanced weapons and concern over growing security links between Pakistan and US CENTCOM forces.

With or without the bogey of a threat from Pakistan—which but for its nuclear card constitutes hardly any match—Indian military buildup in the Indian Ocean region has been monstrous.[3] One notable dimension of the Indian quest for regional military predominance in recent times has been its two-pronged approach to the superpowers. On the one hand New Delhi's collaboration with the Soviet Union in the field of production of weapons was significantly strengthened, and on the other hand, India went for considerable degree of fresh openings with the West. Thus while India continued expanding its import of Western technology, Moscow's role as India's pre-eminent partner in defense buildup has been carefully preserved. The exercise has therefore, been essentially to chart ways of balancing both which India has been doing most successfully to attain the military superiority over its counterparts.

In any event, what is significant in our context is that Indian expansion of its military power, particularly naval strength in the Indian Ocean zone has significantly enough, coincided with the ongoing process of superpower detente. The level of Indian military power and its projection causes concern to its neighbours and has certainly establishing implications.

Security Doctrine

The Indian thrust for regional dominance is clearly drawn from New Delhi's defense and security perception which is essentially inherited from that of British India, a continental security strategy. Contrary to the realities of post-colonial period, this old conception of Indian defense and security strategy has been regarded in India as a pride heritage of the Indian colonial past.[4] Nehruvian vision of India was a 'closer union', a confederation of independent states with common defense and economic possibility.[5] A unity of South Asian defense and strategic unity as perceived in India in one or other modification,[6] has rendered the smaller states of the region virtually buffer status.

India's interest in territorial inviolability of her small neighbours in the region has come to be known as the Indian version of the Monroc Doctrine. The essential theme of the doctrine is that South Asia is to be regarded as an Indian backyard. The critical factor is a combination of the comprehensive power potential of the country with a great-power-psyche nourished by Indian political elites and politico-strategic thinkers. The reference point for India in relation to its international posture is clearly the type of role assumed by great powers. India under such perception is to be viewed as a dominant country in the region just as the US, Soviet Union and China in their respective areas.[7]

It is more than coincidental that the doctrine appeared in renewed prominence in Indian writings at the height of Indian involvement in the ethnic crisis in Sri Lanka. The doctrine, it is claimed, is a product of a series of conversations between the incumbent and opposition political forces so that it reflects an Indian national consensus.[8] Operationally the Indo-Sri Lanka Accord of July 1987 accompanying the controversial Indian Peace Keeping Forces (IPKF) operations in Sri Lanka and the Maldives operation of November 1988 have been viewed to be real life test cases for the India Doctrine.[9] Indeed, the doctrine provided the conceptual *raison d'etre* for Indian military moves in Sri Lanka and Maldives. Thanks to its role in these two neighbouring states India has emerged as an interventionist regional power. New Delhi confidently manifested that it would not have any hesitation in physically intervening in internal developments of a South Asian state if such intervention is regarded as within India's means and promoting Indian national interests.[10]

Confrontation not Cooperation

Other recent developments also manifest further worsening of inter-state relations in the region. Little progress has been achieved in the resolution of the host of largely Indo-centric problems in the Indo-centric region. South Asia's problems are indeed enormous. These include perennial Indo-Pakistan rivalry which has its origin in the very creation of the two countries and which has been nurtured over the years largely by mutual mistrust and suspicion. Problems between Nepal and India, no less age-old in nature, have surfaced recently and quickly took the relation between the two to its lowest ebb. The second half of the past decade has witnessed particularly steep deterioration in the South Asian political climate as India's relation with its neighbours sharply worsened leaving the region unaffected by winds of global change.

Hopes raised by possibilities of Indo-Pakistan rapprochement with the change government in Islamabad failed to sustain and over the age-old

Kashmir dispute the two have now reached the lowest ebb of their relations ever since they fought their third successive war. War on words have transformed into trading of fire for lives in the border. Neither India, nor Pakistan would possibly like to go to another war on the issue despite high tempo on both sides. Both have however weak and unstable governments, so neither can afford to sound anything but stern, thereby sustaining the mutual antagonism and regional instability.

The new Indian government's promise to improve relation, with the rest of the region also failed to turn into reality. Little substantive progress has been achieved between Bangladesh and India over major issues of dispute including water-sharing, maritime boundary and insurgency problem which define Dhaka's continued vulnerability. The latest round of talks on trade and transit dispute between New Delhi and Kathmandu ended in failure leaving the tiny Himalyan Kingdom under persistent economic blockade by India. Nearly three years of Indian military presence in Sri Lanka has ended while the basic issues related to, and left behind by the intervention remain unresolved. With lingering disunity between the militant Tamil Tigers on the one hand and the other groups that collaborated with the Indian forces on the other, the prospect of lasting peace is not given a good chance. It may also be not too easy for India to disengage from the problem even if it wanted to particularly as it has entrapped itself with it too closely. And as the Sri Lankan Foreign Minister recently blamed India for acting to "destabilize" his country[11], it may be long before the new wave of mistrust between the two can be washed off.

India in a word has been following an over-assertive policy towards its neighbours as a part of its design to ensure itself as the regional superpower which is the source of threats to the rest. New Delhi's policy of striving for influence by pressure rather than gaining cooperation through understanding has contributed to continued estrangement in South Asian relations. Progress in the South Asian Association for Regional Cooperation (SAARC) has been frozen since its fifth summit was postponed due to controversies over Indian postures and actions to throw its weights around. The current tension between India and Pakistan has dealt yet another blow to any hopes for holding the delayed summit in the immediate future.

Regional Arms Race

All these imply a growing mutual threat perception leading to massive defense buildup in the region. Military expenditure in South Asia during

starvation and under-nourishment. Recent estimates show some 270 million chronically malnourished and 450 million in acute poverty.[19]

South Asia is constrained greatly in terms of social development by the instability of the respective political systems and weaknesses of economic management. On top of the problems of domestic origin, the international impediments have in recent years been getting more severe. The world economy in the 1980s was dominated first by sharp recession, then with steady and prolonged growth in industrial countries associated by high interest rates, declining commodity prices, massive exchange rates movements and sharp decline of soft lending for developing countries. While some of the developing countries did well in terms of economic growth—in several the GNP grew at 6-10 per cent annually—the South Asian countries continued to suffer. The developing countries that achieved better performances like the NICs of East Asia did so by sound macro-economic policies and more importantly by maintaining competitiveness of exports. For South Asia, while domestic policy failures and political and economic mismanagement contributed to low growth, excessive indebtedness and continued losses from external economic shocks of the past decade accounted for a major part of the problems.

The most depressing fact is not that the countries have made so little progress, but that situations are growing increasingly worse. In some of these countries real income per capita had already flattened in the 1970s to the level of the previous decade while in case of others fell in the 1980s. Most of these countries have been revaged by natural disasters as their economies continued to shrink. For lack of resources most governments are forced to spend less on health, education and infrastructure.

South Asia has a population of over one billion,[20] about a fifth of the world population. All the countries belong to the World Bank classification of low income economies. An average South Asian earns a per capita GNP of $290 and is born with a life expectancy of 57 years. Comparable figures for Japan are $15,760 and 78 years. The total GDP of South Asia is only about 12 per cent of that of Japan. The GNP in the South Asian economies grew during 1965-87 at an annual rate of 1.8 percent as against 4.2 percent in Japan. The region had a negative trade balance of over $13 billion in 1988 whereas Japan's trade surplus of $77 billion for the same year was much more than the combined GDP of all South Asian countries minus India. Export composes only about

8 percent of GDP and external borrowing, accumulated outstanding and disbursed amount of which in 1987 stood at $61 billion is the main source of funding for growing exports and the substantial portion of development activities.

Debt Situation as the Critical Area

Thus if a country's external relations is a function of its domestic compulsion, few other factors can be as critical in South Asian external relations as economic imperatives. And as a corollary, no compulsion other than aid dependence can be as overriding in determining its external economic diplomacy. The pre-eminence of the aid factor is dictated by the fact that unlike many other developing countries South Asia's exposure to the global economy is very low in terms of other aspects of external economic interaction like trade and investment. As already indicated, export accounts for very low share of the region's GDP while import continues to be overwhelmingly credit-financed. Foreign investment for its part, is at a very low level—picking up only in recent years—and remains out of international commercial lending. On the other hand, the quantum, nature and terms of inflow of external resources are the most critical aspects of economic interaction with the outside world. Annual inflow of ODA has reached by 1987 upto $5.1 billion annually and the region's total outstanding debt currently accounts for nearly a quarter of the GDP. The share of aid in ADP provisions has been increasing steadily and there is little scope of any significant reversal in the foreseeable future. There is hardly any two opinions today that South Asian economies cannot be effectively managed without assurances of aid inflow. Thus, while anomalies in the global trading and related structures do influence the South Asian economies, their priority area remains the issue related to international debt situation.

The moot question in this context is whether the emerging global order augers any significant change in the environ in which South Asian states are to operate their aid-dependent external economic policy. There is hardly any denying that economics is invariably related to politics and to that extent it is possible to anticipate some general positive movements arising from growing interdependence of nations and increased globalisation, the main theme of global change. Lessening of tensions, possibility of decrease in global arms spending, reduced compulsion for extending aid for political influence, and above all, an apparent global consensus on enhanced importance of multilateral institutions including the UN bodies are among the factors that might call for some optimism. Moreover, to the extent that domestic economic imperatives—growing budget deficit and mounting external borrowing in case of the US, and economic restructuring and modernization needs in case of the USSR—are among the factors leading to the global changes, there is a possibility that all states, big or small would gradually recognize the need for ensuring the symmetric rights and obligations of all rather than unilateralism in the world economy.

East Bloc Participation

The positivism is however obscured by some critical considerations. Firstly, the present global economic order, essentially a creation of the post-World War II Bretton Woods system has remained virtually as align world for the Soviet bloc economies. The Soviet Union and its allies have so far kept themselves immune from this system and deliberately avoided any responsibility for its anomalies although most of them had benefited from the international financial resources. The on-going process of *perestroika* in Soviet Union and corresponding reforms in other socialist countries indicate possibility of greater degree of linkage and interaction with the global economy, but there is little possibility of their substantive integration with it. In relation to the international debt problem as such the Soviet leader Michael Gorbachev of course announced at the UN the Soviet preparedness to institute a moratorium of upto 100 years on the repayment of the LDC debt and in some cases to write off the same completely. He also proposed that debt-service payments of developing countries should depend on economic performance of each individual country. This Soviet offer, however, has little, if any substantive significance for the overall Third World debt problem since the overwhelming proportion of the debt is owed to the West. Moreover 90% of whatever amount of aid the Soviets offer are directed to their developing communist allies. Other than its rhetoric and political value—party as an effort to win Third World friends at low cost—the offer seems to have little practical value for the Third World. So long as the East bloc does not demonstrate the will and commitment to share the responsibility for global economic imbalances and come forward with practical measures to remedy the same like participating in the North-South process, there will be little to be expected by way of its contribution to the economic aspect of the new order.

The Shrinking Pie

Secondly, the global community, particularly the developed West, appears to be caught up in a euphoria of "new era" in East-West relations. The developed nations, particularly the West are rushing to reward the peoples of East Europe for what they did to cause the fall of communism. Now that Marx and Engels have been thrown to the garbage and Lenin faces disgrace for the decades of socialist misrule, the East Europeans, the West feels, deserve to be assisted politically, economically, financially, technologically and in all other conceivable ways in their new journey to democracy—a journey to establish the reign of Western democratic values. Nearly all the developed countries are reciprocating the opening of the iron curtain by opening their own doors to the East flooding investment, finance, high-tech and what not. Following the decision of the Paris summit of the top seven, the Foreign Ministers of the 24 industrialized nations pledged determination to step up aid to Poland, Hungary and other East European countries. Besides billions of dollars of assistance to meet the immediate needs a European Bank for Reconstruction and Development (EBRD) is to be set up to coordinate long-term assistance programs. Japan is also following up with millions of dollars of offer of low interest aid and with much more to come.

There is hardly any thing wrong in all these. What appears striking are the developments taking place parallel with these in relation to assistance to the Third World. A World Bank report revealed that debt relief arranged in 1989 for the Third World countries amounted to little over half of what was in the previous year. Winds of change is far from changing the global financial trading and economic structure which is so organized as to promote the interests of the advantage at the expanse of the disadvantaged. Third World's advocacy for a new international economic order has failed to produce any impact. The irony is that while decades of negotiations could not help develop appropriate specialized institution to finance and coordinate long-term Third World development, the EBRD is already going to be launched before the changes in East Europe are unfolded clearly enough. The continued shrinkage of funds, particularly soft-lending for LDCs may not yet be linked to the steady rise in flow of funds to East Europe. The indications, in any case, are breeding some skepticism. Analysts are predicting diversion of institutional funds away from the Third World needs towards East Europe. There is already evidence that international capital flows are changing directions in response to opportunities emerging in East Europe.[21]

New Frictions

Another feature of the global economy in the 1990s will be the frictions that are likeky to be created by the economies of East Europe in their efforts to develop free market and to integrate with global economic structure. Political motivations in this context may not be readily matched by economic realities. The most likely vehicle of growth and recovery to be opted by these economies will be boosting of exports to repay the huge amount of debt already accumulated and still pouring in, and to generate surplus for development. This may not be easily achieved as they would find it too difficult to penetrate into the extremely demanding and competitive markets of the developed West. They may, therefore, need to focus on the market of developing countries opening in either case new phase of challenges for the nascent manufacturing industries of the countries like South Asia.

Increased Losses

Tracing the trend in the global economy in last about a decade—the period which actually witnessed the process leading to the global change indications appear to be far from encouraging. The period has witnessed unprecedented growth of protectionism on the one hand and fall of commodity prices on the other leading to further deterioration of prospects of Third World development. Problems of reduced exports and growing deficit in balance of payments, high unemployment, low investment, high inflation and low growth of these countries have accompanied further contraction in international financial liquidity. Instead of addressing these issues most of the 'gain economies', have resorted to further stringencies including various protectionist measures. The threat of a new phase of trade war looms large with 'Euro-protectionism' in sight in 'Fortress Europe' of the 1990s. The implications of EEC Project 1992 are disquieting for the Third World countries from the point of view of trading, investment and financial prospects.[22]

Macro-Economic Policy Coordination

Imbalances and anarchy in global economic order are likely to continue, while efforts for reducing them within occasional and narrow macro-economic policy coordination among the major developed market economies have so far failed to produce the desired results. The Baker Plan and subsequently the Brady version of the US proposal to face the debt problem, for example, are aimed more at ensuring the continued reverse flow of funds from debtor to donor than at reducing Third World debt burdens. Moreover, the focus of these proposals are mainly on relatively larger debtor nations and those borrowing from Western commercial banks like countries of Latin America, so that least developed countries like the South Asian ones are to benefit, if at all, only marginally.

One notable dimension of the recent movements in global economic scenario is a growing role of Japan not merely as the new 'economic superpower', but also as the initiator of what may turn out to be a relatively more substantive effort aimed at adjustments. Mention may be made of the Okita Proposal[23] for recycling the financial surpluses of countries like Japan and F.R. Germany to finance development of Third World countries. It involves recycling of US $ 125 billion in five years from 1988 to help the developing countries break the vicious circles of lagging economic growth. The Japanese government's own commitments include provisions for untied funds of US $ 65 billion over the period 1987-92 and in addition doubling of its ODA in five years. Before extending the point further we briefly review some aspects of Japan's economic ties with South Asia.

III. JAPAN'S ROLE IN SOUTH ASIA

Japan is a leading economic and trade partner for South Asia. In 1988 more than 10 per cent of South Asian exports were directed towards Japan while over 11 percent of the region's imports came from this country. The balance, as expected is of course in favour of Japan which had $ 1.8 billion worth of trade surplus with South Asia. South Asia's trade deficit with Japan is indeed about a quarter of the region's deficit with the industrialized countries. Needless to mention, trade balance with Japan is negative for all the South Asian countries, the ratio of value of import of these countries being in most cases many time that of exports. For Japan South Asia is, however, a relatively less significant region as a partner for trade with only 1.46 percent of its exports directed to South Asia while only 1.37 percent of imports come from that region. Japan's trade with countries like China or Korea are several time more than its trade with all South Asian countries taken together. South Asia's exports to Japan is about one-tenth of what Tokyo imports from its ASEAN neighbours while the value of Japan's exports to South Asia is little more than one-fifth of that to ASEAN.

Important Development Partner

In terms of economic aid, however, South Asia appears to be a much more important region from the view point of Japan. The total value of Japanese ODA to the region increased from $ 477.17 million in 1979 to $ 1,109.47 million in 1988. In terms of its share in overall Japanese ODA, with 17.3 percent of the total disbursement, South Asia is the second most important region for Japan after Southeast Asia (which includes countries of ASEAN). In 1987, 18.49 percent of Japanese ODA flew into South Asia whereas the corresponding ratio for the US was 4.7 and that for all the DAC countries taken together was 9.57. Japanese ODA to the region in that year was $ 970.22 million as against the US figure of $ 329 million. The value of Japanese ODA was also about equal to the combined flow from West Germany, U.K., France, Netherland and Sweden, the other largest donors for the region.

Four of the seven South Asian countries figure amongst the top ten Japanese ODA recipients in recent years, while Japan is the largest donor for all of them. In 1987, 36.1 percent of inflow of public debt to Bangladesh came from Japan while the corresponding figures for Bhutan, India, Maldives, Nepal, Pakistan and Sri Lanka were 36.9, 31.8, 40.6, 28.8 and 36.6 respectively.[24]

The above analysis indicates that Japan's relationship with South Asia is of profound mutual significance. The figures also define the extent of leverages available at the Japanese end and thus the type of a role that Japan may assert in its dealing with these countries. In a significant coincidence, while delivering a policy statement in Dhaka on Japan's Relations with South Asia, Tadashi Kuranari, then Foreign Minister of Japan announced in 1987 his government's willingness that in implementing its external economic commitments Japan will "naturally take fully into account the needs of the South Asian countries since they are Japan's important partners for economic cooperation."[25] He also reiterated Japan's commitment to make "utmost efforts" to pursue Japan's relations with these countries further.

Nota bene, there are now growing realization and indication that the emerging international order is unlikely to be one where Japan would (or could) continue with its so-called low-profile and passive role. To say that Japan's international role is growing to become commensurate with economic and industrial power is to state the obvious. The global extent of Japan's interest and compulsions is also likely to open and widen the political dimension of its international role.

Expanding International Role

Partly in responding to growing international pressure and partly in pursuance of its own national interest, Japan has been expanding its international role through it 'International Cooperation Initiative', the main contents of which include expansion of ODA, promotion of cultural exchange and cooperation for peace.[26] Japan has indeed manifested, slowly and discretely though, that it follows a policy of using its economic assistance for political objectives and for goals that are considered to promote its national interests. Using economic aid and cooperation as an important instrument of attaining its 'comprehensive security' Japan has been exhibiting greater international activism and assertiveness since the late 1970s.

To protest Soviet invasion of Afghanistan Tokyo boycotted Moscow Olympic and imposed economic sanctions against the Soviets. The Vietnamese Invasion of Kampuchea prompted Japanese aid freeze to Hanoi. Economic sanctions were also imposed on Iran in the wake of the taking of US hostage in 1979. Tokyo refused economic aid to Poland for the latter's suppression of the trade union movement. Japanese assistance to Philippines was greatly increased after the fall of Marcos in 1986. Japanese economic aid was also used as an instrument of pressure for political objectives in case of China after the Tiananmen square incident. Experience therefore suggests that Japanese aid has been used as an instrument of positive incentive as well as negative sanction. By the same token in the wake of political liberalization in East Europe most of the countries of the region have been receiving increased flow of Tokyo's economic assistance. Similar approaches have been noticed in relation to Tokyo's aid policy towards some of the South American countries including Nicaragua. Thailand, Turkey and Pakistan have on the other hand benefited from increased economic assistance by virtue of being classified as 'countries bordering areas of conflict'. Japan is also committed to strengthen its assistance to 'those areas that are important to maintenance of peace and stability of the world.[27]

Political Dimension

Japan's interest in a similar role in South Asia was indicated in Kuranari's statement. He said, "I also believe it important to make active contributions, cooperating with other peace-loving nations in Asia, to the relaxation of tension and peaceful settlement of conflicts, by promoting dialogue. Needless to say, one must take into account the situation in South Asia when considering the peace and stability of the whole Asia. From this point of view, Japan wishes to further strengthen its efforts for promoting political dialogue with countries in South Asia''.[28] During more recent visit to some of the countries of the region the Japanese Prime Minister Toshiki Kaifu said, ''I would like to pronounce clearly Japan's intent to continue its vigorous support for the political stability and economic development of the South Asian countries as well as the rest of the world by engaging in dialogue and cooperation.''[29]

Problems that South Asian political scene are basically of regionaj origin and are rooted in the region's history, geo-politics, economy and ecology which the outside powers can hardly eliminate. But they need to do what they can, namely, to use their leverage to influence developments that may diminish prospects of further catastrophes and improve the overall climate. The role of Japan as a ''donor superpower'' becomes critical in this context. Japan's new international responsibility, as it includes help establish global peace, cannot be confined to extending money in the name of economic assistance irrespective of developments in the political arena.

It is not intended to suggest here that Japan should or could jump headlong into South Asia's political problems. Japan may possibly assert itself instead as a partner in political dialogue on specific issues that relate to peace and stability in the region. Our analysis on the South Asian political scenario has indicated that time is possibly ripe for following up what Japan has already indicated through political pronouncements. During his visit to New Delhi Prime Minister Kaifu urged upon India and Pakistan to sign the nuclear NPT to ensure regional peace and stability.[30] Japan may, in this context, in cooperation with the US and possibly USSR facilitate an agreement between India and Pakistan on nuclear restraint in the region.

Aid as a Tool for ''Positive Sanction''

Referring to recent tensions between India and Pakistan over the disputed territory of Kashmir, the Japanese Prime Minister urged India and Pakistan to ''exercise self-restraint and try to resolve the issue peacefully through talks.[31] Tokyo's continued economic assistance may indeed be used as an instrument of positive sanction to induce such favourable developments in the region as cuts in defense budgets and other measures for reducing tensions, like use of dialogue instead of confrontation in interstate relations.

Economic aid without accountability tends to be spent on purposes not necessarily desired by the donor, nor by the real targets, namely the vast majority of the people who are in need. To ensure that Japanese loans effectively promote development financing needs to be subject to strict scrutiny and continued streamlining on the basis of specific guidelines.

Effective Use of Aid

Effective utilization of resources, borrowed or otherwise, defines the extent of improvement in the management of the economy and hence the way South Asia's reach to a take-off can be telescoped. Japan as the world's leading donor nation can indeed assume an increasing role in the shaping of overall priorities of its aid recipients, particularly in the way aid is to be utilized. This is in accordance with a widely held view that the world's largest donor has a responsibility to guide its recipients, as and when applicable, "on a smooth path of development by giving them advice on development strategies and macro-economic policies."[32] There seems to be an appreciation in Tokyo of both imperatives and leverages leading to such role. Foreign ministry officials accompanying the Japanese Prime Minister during the recent visit to the region was reported to have said that they "want to improve the quality of Japanese economic assistance in a region where the country's aid policy has come under criticism". One official said, "we have reviewed Japan's policy of money gift giving and want it tied to more constructive projects."[33]

Target-Oriented Aid

Japan's aid has so far focused basically on large-scale projects which do contribute to the development of the recipients' infrastructure. The relative effectiveness of such projects in promoting the economic well-being of the vast majority of people, however, needs to be carefully assessed. The needs of millions of the deprived masses may be better served by providing such assistance as would increase their own capability to mitigate their sufferings. The overwhelming majority of these rural farmers and small-scale entrepreneurs lack the capital to build up economic footing. So does the bulk of unemployed urban and rural labour force. And their needs are surprisingly small and critically immediate. It may be more useful to provide assistance to projects that would support say, a few hundred small-scale low-interest loans of few hundred dollars each to such vulnerable but potential work force than pouring millions to big prestigious projects whose benefits drain out into vested hands long before filtering down to the target population.

The need for Japanese ODA for humanitarian purpose in the region, torn by recurrent natural disasters is likely to remain as pressing as ever. Cooperation for infrastructure development will also be needed, but assistance in specific target-oriented projects would be more useful in terms of concrete benefit. In addition to small loan for productive activities, education and human resources development are further areas that need Tokyo' increased attention.

Opening of Market

On the trade front, there is now a growing recognition that unless Japan open up its market more and expands its imports further, it will not be possible for the developing countries to grow out of their debts and develop their economies.[34] Trade balance in case of South Asia, as already indicated, continues to be grossly in favour of Japan, it needs to be considered that in 1988 for example, Japan exported to South Asia 1.78 times more than what was imported. With the US on the other hand, the balance in the same year was on the positive side for the region. One can argue over the competitiveness of South Asian products in the Japanese market. But the comparison indicates the potentials for improvements that can be made with more liberal trading practices adopted by Japan. Textiles and clothing which occupy the largest proportion of South Asian manufacturing exports to OECD markets are examples in which Japanese import from South Asia may be expanded.

Risk-Sharing in Investment

Another area that needs Tokyo's increased focus is some risk sharing between the capital market in South Asia with that of its own. Foreign direct investment remains relatively under-explored in the region and it can be an important additional source of financing development. Labour in South Asia is abundant and wage levels are very low. There are immense opportunities for viable investment in areas of labor-intensive manufacturing sectors.

This may be an effective way for reducing the dominance of the public sector in Japanese cooperation with the region. Since the vast majority of Japan's surplus funds are in the hands of private enterprises, promotion of such channeling of funds may be mutually beneficial. South Asia will be particularly attractive to small and medium sized Japanese investors who in the face of severe competition elsewhere may find their ventures economically viable in the region. Opportunities exist in export-oriented industries as well as in production geared to meet the demands of huge local markets. In addition to cheap labour such industries may often use locally available raw materials. Existing institutional arrangements at both ends in this regard would need to be strengthened.

Political Limitations

Politically, however, needless to stress, most of the challenges and limits to options are essentially defined by the problems within the South Asian region, and more specifically by the designs and postures of the big neighbour India. India seems to be in a dilemma. Overwhelmed with the unprecedented rise of its power parallel with the fortuitous blessings of global changes, it seems to be too incapable and inexperienced as to hos to exercise this power in its neighbourhood without playing a regional bully. It is thus behaving like a superpower-in-being with a tiny heart, harassing smaller neighbours by coercive means. By all indications, India is opting for short-term gains without due emphasis on long-term implications of show of force as against diplomatic and political options. With its undeniable pre-eminence in the region India could very well opt for compassion and goodwill which could generate mutual confidence and promote regional stability.

Development in SAARC, as already mentioned have been frozen shattering the expectations raised by the launching of the first ever attempt towards regional cooperation. Japan, like most other outside nations as well as regional and international organizations has offered to cooperate with the association, viewed to be potentially catalytic in promoting economic progress and political harmony. But mainly because of India's resistance SAARC has yet to make use of such offers. New Delhi considers external cooperation on the part of SAARC to be detrimental to its own leverages *vis-a-vis* neighbours with whom it prefers to deal bilaterally rather than multilaterally, even on issues that are multilateral in nature. The Japanese offer to cooperate with SAARC came once again during the visit of the Prime Minister who proposed that Japan could become a "dialogue partner" for SAARC in line with Tokyo's relation with ASEAN which has proved to be very constructive.[35] India's response, as could be expected, was cool, as the Indian Prime Minister was reported to be rather positive.''[36] Substantive progress on such areas is likely to remain hostage to the inability of the states in getting out of their paralyzing past and age-old attitudes of mutual mistrust and suspicion.

Need for Home-Work

Finally, it is relevant to observe that most of the problems of South Asia get accelerated incidence as these relate to domestic politico-economic weakness of the states. Stability and progress in South Asia depend to a great extent on successful modernization and development of individual countries, a process for long obstructed as much by divisive forces and unresolved issues within as by diminishing options in the hierarchical international economic, financial and trading structure.

The fact that the countries are so resource-poor, so marginally poverty-stricken, so underdeveloped in terms of growth of socio-political institutions, and so polarized on matters of shared interests add to the vulnerability of the states and weaken the bargaining chips *vis-a-vis* the outside world. What therefore, is essentially needed is to organize the homework whereby the state system—the polity and economy—will be stronger. And in the ultimate analysis it is through building a strong nation-state—socially, politically—that long-term responses to the challenges may be found.

NOTES AND REFERENCES

1. For detailed discussion on the Indian Strategic and security objectives, see, Shelton U. Kodikara, *Strategic Factors in Inter-state Relations in South Asia*, (New Delhi), 1984; K.M. Pannikar, *Problems of Indian Defence* (Bombay) 1960; K. Subrahmanyam, *Indian Security Perspectives,* (New Delhi); Baldev Raj Nayar, ''A World Role: The Dialectic of Purpose and Power'', in John D, Mellor(ed), *India: The Rising Middle Power*, (New Delhi), 1981: and Iftekharuzzaman, 'The India Doctrine: Relevance for Bangladesh'', in M.G. Kabir and Shaukat Hassan, (eds.), *Bangladesh Foreign Policy: Challenges and Options* (Dhaka) 1989, pp. 19-43.
2. The disparate power configuration is discussed in further detail in Iftekharuzzaman, *op. cit.*
3. Particularly notable in recent years were the increases in Indian naval forces which are now reportedly equipped with a nuclear-submarine. In mid-1987 a second aircraft carrier was obtained from Britain and two diesel-electric submarines were under construction as were four Covettes. An Indian built frigate was completed and two

minesweepers, a guided-missile destroyer and two diesel-electric submarines were obtained. In April of 1988, Tu-142M bear F Maritime reconnaissance and ASN aircrafts were acquired. The army received some of its Swedish howitzers and a program to modernize its armored vehicles was underway.

4. See for example, K.M. Pannikar, *Problems of India Defence,* Bombay, 1960, p. 23.
5. Quoted in S.D. Muni, ''South Asia'', in Mohammad Ayoob (ed.), *Conflict and Intervention in South Asia*, (London), 1980, p. 48.
6. Pran Chopra, for example, builds his concept of SAARC Route to Security on the same premise, see his ''From Mistrust to Cooperation'', in Pran Chopra, *et. al. Future of South Asia.* (Macmillan, Dhaka) 1986, pp. 13-17.
7. K. Subrahmanyam, *op. cit.*
8. Bhabani Sengupta, ''The India Doctrine'', *India Today*, 31 August 1983.
9. The Indo-Sri Lanka Accord and the Maldives intervention have been separately examined elsewhere. See for example, Iftekharuzzaman and Humayun Kabir, ''The Indo-Sri Lanka Accord: An Assessment'', *Biiss Journal,* Vol. 8, No. 4, and Iftekharuzzaman, ''Maldives: Small, Beautiful and Vulnerable,'' *Dhaka Courier*, 11-17 November, 1988.
10. Bhabani Sengupta, ''Maldives Confirms India's Lead Role in South Asia'', *Dhaka Courier*, 18-23 November 1988.
11. *The Japan Times*, 16 February, 1990.
12. World Bank, *World Development Report*, 1989, Table 11.
13. US Congressional Research Service Study titled ''Trends in Conventional Arms Transfers to the Third World by Major Suppliers, 1980-87'', quoted in *Strategic Digest,* (New Delhi), February 1989.
14. *Inquilab* (in Bangla, Dhaka), 2 June 1989.
15. *Far Eastern Economic Review,* 29 March 1990.
16. K. Subrahmanyam, ''India's Security: The North and North-east Dimension'', *Conflict Studies,* No. 215.
17. *FEER Asia Yearbook, 1989,* (Bankok, 1989).
18. *International Herald Tribune*, 22 February, 1990.
19. Findings of a study by Prof. Buchanon of Ottawa University, conducted in India, quoted in *The Dawn* (Karachi), 26 February 1989.
20. Data quoted in this and subsequent sections are taken, unless otherwise mentioned, from Tables 1-7 annexed with this paper.
21. *The Japan Times*, 27 February, 1990.
22. For details see, M. Iqbal Karim, ''Towards a Single European Market: Problems, Prospects and Implications'', *Biiss Journal*, Vol. 10, No. 2, 1988.
23. The Okita Proposal was contained in Saburo Okita, *et.al.*, *Mobilizing International Surpluses for World Development—A WIDER Plan for a Japanese Initiative,* World Institute for Development Economics Research, Helsinki, 1987. See for excerpts, UN ESCAP, *Economic and Social Survey for Asia and the Pacific*, Bankok, 1987.
24. *Outlook of Japan's Economic Cooperation,* Economic Cooperation Bureau, Ministry of Foreign Affairs, Japan, February 1990, p. 27.
25. Tadashi Kuranari, ''Japan's Relations with South Asia: A Golden Chance'', Speech delivered at a Seminar organized by *Biiss*, Dhaka, 14 August, 1987.

26. See for details, *Diplomatic Blue Book 1989*, Ministry for Foreign Affairs, Japan.
27. See for details, Dennis T. Yasutomo, *The Manner of Giving: Strategic Aid and Japanese Foreign Policy,* Lexington Books 1986, and Juichi Inada, Japan's Aid Diplomacy: Increasing Role for Global Security'', in *Japan Review of International Affairs,* Spring/Summer 1988.
28. Tadashi Kuranari, *op. cit.*
29. *The Japan Times*, 1 May 1990.
30. *Ibid.*
31. *Ibid.*
32. *Japan's Official Development Assistance Annual Report 1988,* Ministry of Foreign Affairs, Japan, p. 29.
33. *The Japan Times,* 2 May 1990.
34. Hiroaki Fukami, ''The International Debt Problem and Japan's Response'', in *Japan Review of International Affairs*, Fall Winter, 1989, p. 211.
35. *The Japan Times,* 1 May 1990.
36. *Mainichi Daily News,* 1 May 1990.

TABLE 1

Basic Indicators of South Asian Countries and Japan

Indicator	*Bangladesh*	*Bhutan*	*India*	*Maldives*	*Nepal*	*Pakistan*	*Sri Lanka*	*Total SA*	*Japan*
Population (mid-1987 millions)	106.1	1.3	797.5	0.196	17.6	102.5	16.4	1041.6	122.1
Area (thousand sq. km.)	144	47	3,288	—	141	796	66	4,482	378
GNP capita									
—US $ (1987)	160	150	300	300	160	350	400	290	15,760
—Av. ann. growth rate (1965-87)	0.3	—	1.8	1.9	1.4	2.5	3.0	1.8	4.2
Life expectancy at birth (year 1985)	51	48	5.8	59	51	55	70	57	78
GDP (million $ 1987)	17,600	250	220,830	—	2,560	31,650	6,040	278,930	2,376,420
Trade (1988)									
—Exports	1,291	—	15,324	66	261	4,509	1,463	22,915	264,961
—Imports	2,989	—	24,310	126.2	544	6,589	2,211	36,768	187,483
Balance	—1,698	—	—8,986	—60	—282	—2,079	—748	—13,853	77,478
Terms of Trade (1980 = 100)	91	—	114	—	93	99	96	94	153

External Public Debt (million $ 1987)									
—Outstanding and disbursed	8,851	—	37,325	—	902	13,150	4,109	64,337	—
—Net ODA receipt	1,637	—	1,852	—	345	858	502	5,194	—
Long-term debt service as % of: (1987)									
—GNP	1.8	—	1.3	—	1.2	3.4	5.2	—	
—Export	24.2	—	18.9	—	9.7	25.9	19.2	—	

Source: World Bank, *World Development Report 1989*, Tables 1, 3, 14. IMF, *Direction of Trade Statistics Yearbook 1988-89*.

TABLE 2

Trade Statistics of South Asian Countries

(Figures in million dollars)

Country/Trade	*1981*				*1988*			
	World	*Ind. Countries*	*U.S.*	*Japan*	*World*	*Ind. Countries*	*U.S.*	*Japan*
Bangladesh								
Exports	791.3	268.2	80.1	27.1	1,291.1	879.8	335.6	74.1
Imports	2,651.4	1,021.9	155.9	288.5	2,988.9	1,270.4	476.3	
Balance	—1,860.1	—753.7	—75.8	—261.4	—1,697.8	—390.8	202.4	—402.2
India								
Exports	6,827	2,984	769	557	15,324	8,727	2,879	1,642
Imports	14,550	6,272	1,370	880	24,310	14,493	2,748	2,291
Balance	—7,723	—4,378	—601	—323	—8,986	—5,766	131	—549
Maldives								
Exports	10.4	4.6	—	2.7	66.2	31.2	14.7	2.0
Imports	38.0	10.8	—	3.7	126.2	24.1	—	11.9
Balance	—28.4	—6.2	—	—1.0	—60.0	7.1	14.7	—9.9
Nepal								
Exports	94.8	23.9	2.4	1.9	261.6	159.9	55.6	2.0
Imports	213.3	75.9	8.2	48.4	543.8	264.1	70.9	68.2
Balance	118.5	—52.0	—5.8	—46.5	—282.2	—104.2	—15.3	—66.2

Pakistan								
Exports	2,880.8	1,008.8	197.3	201.5	4,509.3	2,615	506.9	515.8
Imports	5,630.5	2,671.7	470.7	655.0	6,588.6	4,055	855.6	971.7
Balance	—2,749.7	—1,662.9	—273.4	—443.5	—2,079.3	—1,440	—348.7	—355.9
Sri Lanka								
Exports	1,023.8	428.7	145.7	34.2	1,463.4	856.3	366.8	83.8
Imports	1,905.7	811.7	129.3	260.9	2,210.9	977.6	152.7	305.1
Balance	—881.9	—393.0	16.4	—226.7	—747.5	—121.3	214.5	—221.3
Total South Asia								
Exports	11,628.1	4,618.2	1,194.5	824.4	22,915.6	13,269	4,158.6	2,319.7
Imports	24,988.9	10,846.0	2,134.1	2,136.5	36,768.4	21,084.2	3,690.4	4,124.5
Balance	—13,360.8	—6,245.0	—936.6	—1,312.1	—13,852.8	—7,815.2	198.2	—1,804.8

Source: IMF, *Direction of Trade Statistics Yearbook 1988-89*.

TABLE 3

Japan's Trade with South Asian Countries

(Figures in million dollars)

Country/region	*Japan Exports*		*Japan Imports*		*Balance*	
	1981	*1988*	*1981*	*1988*	*1981*	*1988*
World	151,500 (100.00)	264,961 (100.00)	142,868 (100.00)	187,483 (100.00)	8,632	77,478
—Industrialized Countries	70,283 (46.39)	159,135 (60.06)	49,370 (34.56)	29,499 (49.33)	20,370	66,636
—Developing Countries	70,099 (46.27)	101,962 (38.48)	88,553 (61.98)	91,456 (48.78)	—18,454	10,506
—South Asia	2,395 (1.58)	3,878 (1.46)	1,379 (0.09)	2,562 (1.37)	1,016	1,316
—ASEAN	15,245 (10.06)	21,399 (8.08)	23,784 (16.65)	22,621 (12.07)	—8,539	1,222
—China, P.R.	5,076 (3.35)	9,486 (3.59)	5,238 (3.70)	9,861 (5.26)	—207	—375
—Korea	5,640 (3.72)	15,442 (4.83)	3,395 (2.38)	11,827 (6.31)	2,245	3,615

Figures in Parentheses indicate percentages.

Source: IMF, *Direction of Trade Statistics. Yearbook, 1988-89.*

TABLE 4

	1979	1980	1981	1982	1983	1984	1985	1986	1987	1988
Asia	1,331.15	1,382.51	1,604.51	1,624.30	1,613.80	1,594.17	1.731.77	2,493.54	3,415.83	4,334.35
Northeast Asia	48.07	81.69	320.77	374.02	359.32	344.61	331.91	459.57	577.17	724.64
Southeast Asia	791.74	860.93	929.03	793.06	811.35	932.13	902.15	1,100.49	1,805.88	2,100.50
(ASEAN)	(572.06)	(730.38)	(799.68)	(684.12)	(727.12)	(833.95)	(800.01)	(914.47)	(1,670.50)	(1,920.21)
Southwest Asia	477.17	434.93	350.29	449.70	410.02	308.31	375.02	830.95	970.22	1,199.47
Others	14.17	4.96	4.42	7.52	1.10	9.12	2.69	3.54	–2.61	3.54
Middle East	203.45	203.61	190.07	193.64	200.53	249.48	201.02	339.82	526.00	532.52
America	186.72	222.91	210.53	268.23	261.41	210.83	252.25	418.46	515.72	833.93
Central & South America	165.97	118.47	176.52	184.45	240.66	229.03	224.93	316.54	417.99	399.29
Oceania	13.60	11.58	19.42	22.63	17.95	25.10	24.09	54.69	68.02	93.07
Europe	**2.22	**1.46	**2.28	**2.91	**2.43	1.31	1.02	2.31	2.13	3.00
Unallocable	22.55	23.18	61.64	76.99	93.35	117.48	121.84	220.85	301.82	424.75
Total	1,921.22	1,960.80	2,260.40	2,367.33	2.425.27	2,427.39	2,556.92	3,846.21	5,247.63	5,421.87

Share (%)

	1979	1980	1981	1982	1983	1984	1985	1986	1987	1988
Asia	69.3	70.5	71.0	68.6	66.5	65.7	67.7	64.8	65.1	62.8
Northeast Asia	2.5	4.2	14.2	15.8	14.8	14.2	15.3	12.7	11.0	11.3
Southeast Asia	41.2	43.9	41.1	33.5	34.8	38.4	37.6	30.4	35.6	34.2

(Contd.)

TABLE 4 (*Contd.*)

	1979	*1980*	*1981*	*1982*	*1983*	*1984*	*1985*	*1986*	*1987*	*1988*
(ASEAN)	(29.8)	(35.9)	(35.4)	(28.9)	(30.0)	(34.4)	(31.3)	(23.8)	(32.0)	(29.9)
Southwest Asia	24.8	22.2	15.5	19.0	16.9	12.7	14.7	21.6	18.5	17.3
Others	0.7	0.3	0.2	0.3	0.0	0.4	0.1	0.1	0.1	0.1
Middle East	10.6	10.4	8.4	8.2	8.3	10.3	7.9	8.8	10.0	9.1
Africa*	9.7	11.4	9.3	11.3	10.8	8.7	9.9	10.9	9.8	13.8
Central & South America	8.6	5.0	7.8	7.8	9.9	9.4	8.8	8.2	8.0	6.2
Oceania	0.7	0.6	0.9	1.0	0.7	1.0	0.9	1.4	1.3	1.4
Europe	**0.1	**0.1	**0.1	**0.1	**0.1	0.1	0.0	0.1	0.0	0.1
Unallocable	1.2	1.2	2.7	3.3	3.8	4.8	4.8	5.7	5.8	6.6
Total	100.0	100.0	100.0	100.0	100.0	100.0	100.0	100.0	100.0	100.0

Notes: 1. As the figures in the table are rounded off, they do not necessarily add up to the totals.

2. "——" indicates no achievements, '**' indicates excess of returning money.

3. "Unallocable" includes ODA for dispatching of survey teams to several areas and Administrative Gosts of JICA's activity, etc.

*4. Sub-Saharan African Countries excluding Sudan.

Source: Outlook of Japan's Economic Cooperation, February 1990, Economic Cooperation Bureau, Ministry of Foreign affairs, Japan.

TABLE 5

Geographical Distribution of Japan's ODA by Types

(Net Disbursement Basis, Million Dollars)

Type / Area	ODA (1987) Grants: Grant Assistance	ODA (1987) Grants: Technical Assistance	ODA (1987) Grants: Total	ODA (1987) Loans	ODA (1987) Total	ODA (1987) Share (%)	ODA (1988) Grants: Grant Assistance	ODA (1988) Grants: Technical Assistance	ODA (1988) Grants: Total	ODA (1988) Loans	ODA (1988) Total	ODA (1988) Share (%)
Asia	654.37	451.10	1,105.47	2,310.42	3,415.89	65.1	683.92	001.74	1,285.66	2,748.69	4,034.35	62.8
Northeast Asia	54.53	12928	183.81	393.36	577.18	11.0	52.35	177.40	229.75	494.90	724.64	11.3
Southeast Asia	273.01	257.52	535.52	1,330.35	1,865.88	35.6	200.69	342.58	603.27	1,593.32	2,196.59	34.2
(ASEAN)	(207.77)	(244.95)	(452.72)	(1,226.84)	(1,679.56)	(32.0)	(166.84)	(325.75)	(492.61)	(1,427.63)	(1,920.21)	(29.9)
Southwest Asia	321.83	61.69	383.52	586.70	970.22	18.5	370.88	78.13	449.01	000.47	1,109.47	17.3
Others	—	2.01	2.01	—	2.61	0.1	—	3.64	3.64	—	3.64	0.1
Middle East	107.90	52.03	159.93	366.08	520.00	10.0	127.10	72.55	199.65	382.87	582.52	9.1
Africa*	272.98	89.74	302.72	153.00	515.72	9.8	525.96	110.41	636.37	247.55	883.93	13.8
Latin America	79.24	152.77	232.01	185.99	417.99	8.0	96.30	185.62	281.92	117.37	399.20	6.2
Oceania	36.09	20.05	26.15	11.87	68.02	1.3	46.00	28.98	75.04	18.03	93.07	1.4
Europe	0.34	2.67	3.01	**0.82	2.18	0.0	—	4.28	4.28	10.32	3.96	0.1
Unallocable	3.13	298.69	301.82	—	301.82	5.8	3.85	420.90	424.75	—	424.75	0.6
Total	1,154.06	1,067.04	2,221.10	3,026.53	5,247.63	100.0	1,483.19	1,424.49	2,907.68	3,514.19	0,421.87	100.0

Notes: 1. As the figures in the table are rounded off, they do not necessarily add up to the totals.

2. "—" indicates no achievements, "**" indicates excess of returning money.

3. "Unallocable" included ODA for dispatching of several areas and Administrative Cost of JICA's activity, etc.

*4. Sub-Saharan African Countries excluding Sudan.

Source: As of Table 4.

TABLE 6

Geographical Distribution of DAC Countries' Bilateral ODA in 1987

	Bilateral	Asia							Africa				
	ODA	Total	North-east Asia	South-east Asia	(ASEAN)	South-west Asia	Others	Middle East	Africa	incl. Sudan	Central & South America	Oceania	Europe	Indo-nesia
U.S.A.	7,007.00	643.00	–27.00	304.00	200.00	329.00	37.00	2,636.00	767.00	810.00	1,440.00	174.00	1.00	1,352.00
France	5,316.32	269.88	52.01	74.67	57.27	143.20	—	519.61	2,415.64	2,420.56	929.57	625.82	20.00	535.11
Japan	5,247.63	415.88	577.17	1,865.88	1,679.56	970.22	2.61	526.00	515.22	503.47	417.99	63.02	21.00	301.82
West Germany	3,000.07	521.53	46.80	177.27	120.79	321.32	4.27	785.04	912.60	950.96	523.78	14.41	72.00	–260.11
Italy	1,877.88	203.00	104.94	28.37	27.25	57.10	0.05	247.10	1,113.30	1,192.86	160.50	0.000	10.00	134.77
Netherlands	1,397.87	414.55	4.16	177.27	173.31	227.76	5.36	121.99	457.99	516.92	217.18	1.41	3.55	180.37
Canada	1,259.47	338.32	35.45	90.94	89.97	208.56	3.37	55.73	356.85	368.91	141.00	2.15	0.01	365.40
U.K.	1,001.53	232.22	5.60	30.76	22.99	195.65	0.11	57.13	351.79	383.06	65.08	40.04	15.50	200.53
Sweden	896.69	174.73	5.34	57.96	5.07	110.99	0.44	28.46	391.51	383.92	56.64	—	0.99	246.34
Australia	534.97	182.58	28.65	137.75	123.50	15.71	0.47	9.46	34.95	35.01	0.67	275.13	0.11	31.47
Norway	527.55	121.03	8.38	11.73	10.79	98.13	2.79	3.73	309.18	312.32	79.81	0.03	2.00	01.66
Denmark	459.01	115.81	23.05	9.80	9.56	82.90	—	52.61	224.24	233.39	14.09	0.01	—	57.29
Belgium	425.13	41.52	25.57	10.97	8.56	4.45	0.53	12.97	272.69	275.00	22.70	0.15	0.012	74.98
Switzerland	388.49	77.03	5.67	13.74	11.97	53.78	3.84	19.02	102.00	103.47	57.93	0.10	0.00	70.87
Finland	262.70	47.26	2.12	16.77	3.04	28.36	0.01	15.51	138.08	145.11	12.84	0.28	—	48.73
Austria	155.34	12.86	4.32	2.20	2.08	6.34	—	103.92	13.40	13.80	5.98	0.47	4.34	14.37
New Zealand	00.10	6.85	0.25	4.57	4.55	0.54	1.40	—	0.82	0.82	0.28	45.82	—	12.39
Ireland	27.34	0.01	0.08	0.20	0.20	0.33	—	2.40	14.25	16.58	0.22	0.04	—	9.82
DAC Total	29,941.21	6,818.72	904.74	2,986.63	2,640.84	2,865.01	62.34	5,107.58	8,452.10	8,895.18	4,007.02	1,250.68	133.11	3.991.98
DAC Average	1,003.40	378.82	50.26	165.92	146.71	159.17	3.46	288.75	460.56	494.18	227.61	69.43	7.40	221.78

U.S.A.	100.0	9.18	–0.39	4.34	4.14	4.70	0.53	37.62	10.95	12.42	20.55	2.51	0.10	19.29
France	100.0	5.08	0.98	1.40	1.03	2.09	—	9.77	45.44	45.53	17.40	11.17	0.30	10.07
Japan	100.0	65.09	11.00	35.56	32.01	18.49	0.05	10.02	9.83	11.31	7.97	1.30	0.04	5.75
West Germany	100.0	16.88	1.52	4.82	3.91	10.40	0.14	25.41	29.53	31.07	16.95	0.47	2.35	8.42
Italy	100.0	10.81	5.69	1.51	1.45	3.61	0.00	13.16	59.29	03.52	8.55	0.00	1.01	7.18
Netherlands	100.0	29.66	0.30	12.68	12.40	16.29	0.38	8.73	32.76	36.98	15.59	0.10	0.25	12.90
Canada	100.0	26.86	2.81	7.22	7.14	16.56	0.27	4.42	28.33	29.29	11.20	0.17	0.00	29.01
U.K.	100.0	23.19	0.57	3.07	2.30	19.53	0.01	5.70	35.12	38.25	6.50	4.00	1.58	23.91
Sweden	100.0	19.49	0.00	6.46	0.57	12.38	0.05	3.17	43.66	43.53	6.32	—	0.11	27.47
Australia	100.0	34.13	5.36	25.75	23.09	2.94	0.09	1.77	6.53	6.54	0.13	51.54	0.02	5.88
Norway	100.0	22.94	1.59	2.22	2.05	18.60	0.53	0.71	58.01	59.20	5.65	0.02	0.39	11.69
Denmark	100.0	25.23	5.02	2.14	2.03	18.07	—	11.46	48.85	50.85	3.06	0.00	—	11.39
Belgium	100.0	9.77	0.01	2.58	2.11	1.05	0.12	3.05	94.14	94.70	5.34	0.04	0.03	17.04
Switzerland	100.0	19.83	1.40	3.54	3.08	13.84	0.99	5.13	41.70	42.03	14.91	0.05	0.15	18.23
Finland	100.0	17.99	0.81	0.38	1.19	10.80	0.00	5.90	52.56	55.24	4.89	0.11	—	18.55
Austria	100.0	8.29	2.78	1.42	1.33	4.08	—	66.90	8.63	8.88	3.85	0.30	2.79	9.25
New Zealand	100.0	10.35	0.38	6.91	0.88	0.82	2.25	—	1.74	1.24	0.42	69.20	—	18.73
Ireland	100.0	2.23	0.29	0.73	0.73	1.21	—	8.78	52.12	00.04	0.80	0.15	—	35.97
DAC Average	100.0	22.77	3.02	9.97	8.82	9.57	0.21	17.36	28.28	79.71	13.68	4.18	0.44	13.33

Note: As the figures in the table are rounded off, they don't necessarily add up to the totals. Data on 1988 are still unknown.

Source: As of Table 4.

TABLE 7

Ten Major Recipients of Japan's Bilateral ODA

(Net Disbursement Basis. Million Dollars, %)

Rank	1984			1985			1986		
	Country	Amount	Share	Country	Amount	Share	Country	Amount	Share
1	2	3	4	5	6	7	8	9	10
1	China	389.35	16.04	China	387.89	15.17	China	496.95	12.92
2	Malaysia	245.14	10.10	Thailand	264.10	10.33	Philippines	437.96	11.39
3	Thailand	232.02	9.56	Philippines	240.00	9.39	Thailand	260.41	6.77
4	Indonesia	167.69	6.91	Indonesia	161.33	6.31	Bangladesh	248.47	6.46
5	Philippines	160.07	6.59	Burma	154.04	6.02	Burma	244.14	6.35
6	Bangladesh	123.28	5.08	Malaysia	125.59	4.91	India	226.71	5.89
7	Burma	95.40	3.93	Bangladesh	121.48	4.75	Indonesia	160.83	4.18
8	Egypt	81.47	3.36	Pakistan	93.31	3.65	Pakistan	151.56	3.94
9	Pakistan	67.03	2.76	Sri Lanka	83.74	3.28	Sri Lanka	126.91	3.30
10	Sri Lanka	63.77	2.63	Egypt	73.01	2.86	Egypt	125.70	3.27
	Total Above	1,625.22	66.95	Total Above	1,704.49	66.66	Total Above	2,479.63	64.47
	World Total	2,427.39	100.00	World Total	2,556.92	100.00	World Total	3,846.21	100.00

(Contd.)

TABLE 7 (*Contd.*)

Rank	1987			1988			1984-88 Total		
	Country	*Amount*	*Share*	*Country*	*Amount*	*Share*	*Country*	*Amount*	*Share*
1	*11*	*12*	*13*	*14*	*15*	*16*	*17*	*18*	*19*
1	Indonesia	707.31	13.48	Indonesia	984.91	15.34	China	2,501.01	12.20
2	China	553.12	10.54	China	673.70	10.49	Indonesia	2,182.02	10.64
3	Philippines	379.38	7.23	Philippines	534.72	8.33	Philippines	1,752.13	8.55
4	Bangladesh	334.20	6.37	Thailand	360.62	5.62	Thailand	1,419.59	6.02
5	India	303.94	5.79	Bangladesh	341.96	5.32	Bangladesh	1,169.39	5.70
6	Thailand	302.44	5.76	Pakistan	302.17	4.71	Myanmar (Burma)	925.18	4.51
7	Malaysia	276.39	5.27	Myanmar (Burma)	259.55	4.04	India	753.62	3.68
8	Burma	172.00	3.28	Sri Lanka	199.83	3.11	Pakistan	740.76	3.61
9	Turkey	162.39	3.09	India	179.46	2.79	Malaysia	709.72	3.46
10	Pakistan	126.69	2.41	Egypt	172.90	2.69	Sri Lanka	592.51	2.89
	Total Above	3,317.87	63.23	Total Above	4,009.82	62.44	Total Above	12,745.93	62.18
	World Total	5,247.63	100.00	World Total	6,421.87	100.00	World Total	20,590.02	100.00

Source: As of Table 4.

21

*Japan's Growing Role: An International Perspective**

KIICHI SAEKI

An important and fundamental change takes place in the world today, the systems for international politics, economy and security which have developed over the post-war years are losing the fundamental to effectively deal with emerging realities, a situation that strongly requires reforms and turnabout. An attempt to discover a new approach, including the building of a new order, should require strenuous thinking and study from the comprehensive, long-term and global perspective.

Discussion in this paper will focus on three points: First, the profound impact of the international economic imbalance on the world's politics and economy. Second, the new development that seems to promise an improvement of US-Soviet relations through dialogues and negotiations with regard to the issues of peace and disarmament, and the outlook and impact of the new development. And third, the remarkable economic development in the Asia-Pacific region and a concept on the desirable economic, cultural and academic co-operation in this region.

---

* This article is originally a paper presented at the Thirteenth Indonesia-Japan Conference, Bali,

INTERNATIONAL ECONOMIC IMBALANCE

The international economic imbalance which has a serious impact on the world economy and politics is dramatically symbolised by the fact that the United States which created the post-war international economic system and reigned as the key currency-nation has become the world's largest debtor nation, while Japan which started as a defeated and underdeveloped country after the war has become the world's largest creditor nation.

Indeed, the American current account deficit stood at US $170 billion in 1987 and its net external debt balance exceeded US $400 billion at the end of 1987. There will be some improvement in the US trade balance in the coming years, but the external debt balance will continue to expand, and will likely reach US $800 billion toward the end of the 1980s. Throughout most of the 1990s, the United States will remain a debtor nation.

In contrast, Japan's current surplus amounted to US $87 billion in 1987. At the end of that year, Japan's net external credit balance ran to US $240 billion. By the early 1990s, Japan will have a net external credit worth US $400 billion.

The international economic imbalance will reach proportions of greater complexity and seriousness due to the accumulated debt of developing countries which is expected to increase from US $1,190 billion at the end of 1987 to US $1,245 billion at the end of this year.

This international economic imbalance, particularly between two economic superpowers—the United States and Japan—should not be left as it is for long. If the world economy is to be managed smoothly, balance must be restored through some process of adjustment. What constitutes a major challenge is whether this adjustment can be achieved by avoiding international economic dislocation or collapse such as the dollar's continuing fall, the explosion of protectionism in the United States, the bloc formation of the world economy and debt crisis of the Third World resulting in a serious worldwide recession.

This is the most important economic issue that should be coped with, not by the US and Japan alone, but through co-operation among all the countries of the free world. It is hoped that this problem will be solved constructively through accelerating domestic demand-led growth in Japan and Western countries excluding the United States, and stabilising exchange rates including their orderly changes. There is a great possibility for the situation to turn to this direction. However, if a wrong step is taken and effective international co-operation for economic measures fails, it may rekindle inflation in the United States to the degree that induces a Third World credit crisis and worldwide.

The greatest factor which has enabled the Free World to maintain advantage over the East has been the high industrial productivity and efficiency and the economic prowess sustained by the market economy. However, if inappropriate measures are taken in the process from recovery from the international economic imbalance, international security may be threatened by economic collapse rather than by military threat. The international economic imbalance also raises the question of reviewing the defence burden sharing or the burden sharing in comprehensive security, between the United States and its allies.

Can the world's largest debtor nation continue to play the role as a world leader? Can the world's largest debtor nation continue to bear the cost of defending the world's largest creditor nation by borrowing from that creditor? Should the United States involve itself in the defence of its allies even at the cost of the quality of American life? Should the United States endure the heavy burden of defence of the West, while its allies share relatively light defence burdens and strengthen their economic competitiveness against the US? Will the United States continue to bear the heavy defence burden for its allies even when they disturb American efforts to restore economic balance or even when they take advantage of American economic weakness? When a country finds it increasingly difficult to assure the implementation to the great external commitments it has made, will its allies offer sufficient co-operation to that country for the maintenance of their alliance?

The United States must appreciate what Walter Lipmann wrote in 1943: "Foreign policy consists in bringing into balance with a comfortable surplus of power in reserve, the nation's commitments and the nation's power." It would be the natural course that the American people have determined to ask their allies for fair burden sharing in order to bring their commitments and their power into balance.

However, the problem raised here is more complicated and has broader implications. The demand for burden sharing should be based on the assurance of proper sharing in the decisions on common defence policies and comprehensive security policies. Must we regard the weakening of American leadership as the lack of world leadership and as the beginning of an end of Pax Americana, and must we consider the construction of a new international management system that replaces it? Will it be sufficient to consider local reorganisation while maintaining the basic framework of the alliance system led by the United States? These questions must be answered. In fact, however, the American economy is strong enough to overcome the twin deficits and revitalise itself, and for now it is realistic to set aside any concept transcending the framework of complementing US leadership as an approach beyond our immediate concern.

NEW DEVELOPMENT IN US-SOVIET RELATIONS

Regarding the second issue and disarmament, I would like to consider new encouraging developments that are emerging in the relations between the United States and the Soviet Union; that is improvements of the relations through dialogues and talks.

The present situation seems to justify a view that new promising changes are taking place to stabilise and improve US-Soviet and East-West relations through dialogues and talks. Already there have been three summit meetings between US President Ronald Regan and Soviet Secretary General Mikhail Gorbachev, and as many as 26 talks between US Secretary of State George Shultz and Soviet Foreign Minister Eduard Shevardnadze. The INF (intermediate-range Nuclear Forces) treaty was signed late last year between the two superpowers, and their defence Minister talked for the first time in March this year. On April 14, the Afghan peace treaty was concluded through mediation by the United Nations. From May 29 to June 2, the 4th US-Soviet summit was held and there is a possibility of a fifth summit within the year.

The INF treaty aims to reduce only 4-5 per cent of nuclear weapons, but nevertheless it can be evaluated as an epoch-making agreement that makes a breakthrough in disarmament talks. The treaty does not stipulate control of future weapons but abolition of one type of existing nuclear weapons. It is an asymmetrical reduction including major cuts on the part of the Soviet Union and it contains revolutionary and broad verification plans, including spot inspection and continued surveillance.

We should also properly evaluate the strong leadership of Gorbachev who aims to introduce a ''new way of thinking'' in foreign policy and security policy in regard to the pullout of Soviet forces from Afghanistan.

There is little possibility for an agreement to be signed for the 50 per cent reduction of strategic nuclear arsenal at the 4th summit. However, it is certain that the ratified INF treaties will be exchanged, and preparations for various special statements and conclusion of agreements have been made to assure continued efforts for maintaining the disarmament momentum that has been created through the signing and ratification of the INF treaty. Some progress is expected in the talk on regional conflicts and the human right issue. The bilateral relations on the working level including the trade issue will also be improved.

Be that as it may, sufficient significance can be found in the fourth US-Soviet summit as it demonstrates the progress of efforts being made to promote mutual understanding and stabilise and improve bilateral relations through dialogue and talks and confirm this as something irrevocable. It is significant that by visiting Moscow for the first time in 16 years, the US President gave a strong impression to the world about the actual stabilisation of the bilateral relations and expectations for their improvement. We should also note that President Reagan, who once branded the Soviet Union as an "evil empire," has changed his view so as to see Gorbachev as a real friend with whom he can discuss anything without personal malice. We should also note the British Premier Margaret Thatcher's positive assessment of Reagan's Moscow visit and of the Soviet reform initiated by Gorbachev, which will greatly benefit not only the Soviet people but also the peoples of other countries.

We should also pay attention to the fact that the recent developments in US-Soviet relations are strongly influenced by Gorbachev's new approach, and that a new way of thinking should be introduced to the issues of international relations and security. In his political report to the 27th Soviet Communist Party Congress in 1986, Gorbachev emphasised the following points:

1. No country can defend itself only by means of military technology. Security is a major political problem that can be resolved only by political means.
2. Security is only relative as far as US-Soviet relations are concerned. It is not the best wisdom to think of oneself at the disadvantage of others.
3. There is no victory in nuclear war or arms race. Nuclear war, arms race or search for military predominance will bring about no political benefit to any country.
4. The present level of nuclear power balance on both conflicting sides which is extraordinarily high, assures equal danger to both

sides. The level of military confrontation should be sharply lowered.

5. There is no effective alternative to co-operation and joint action by all countries concerned under the present circumstances. Objective conditions have arisen in which even conflicts with capitalist countries can continue only in the forms of peaceful competition and peaceful rivalry.
6. The Soviet Union opens its doors for verification and is interested in verification as much as other countries. Comprehensive and strict inspection is probably one of the most important factors in the process of disarmament.

At the International Forum held in Moscow in 1987, Gorbachev also called our attention to the following points:

1. The Soviet Union's foreign policy is affected by domestic policies more than before. We need, therefore, continued peace and it is important for international relations to take a predictable and constructive course.
2. In its international aspects, perestroika represents a socialist call for peaceful competition with all types of government. In order to conduct and develop such competition in a civilised form befitting mankind in the 21st century, we need a "new way of thinking" (*novoye myshlenye*).
3. The comprehensive, specific political manifesto on the international security system that was clarified at the Communist Party Conference a year before is based on the principle that one's own security cannot be established at the cost of others.
4. The new structure of international security cannot be built-up unless it is based on trust. Everyone feels the lack of a new way of thinking as well as the lack of trust.

The introduction of a new way of thinking in such international relations should be followed by changes in the Soviet Union's military doctrine. At the International Forum held in Moscow, Gorbachev emphasised that his country's military doctrine is obviously oriented toward self-defence, that it advocates exclusion of massive weapons from its arsenal and restriction of war potential within the rational framework and that the Soviet Union has repeatedly declared that the Soviet Union does not aim at greater security than other countries "but will not be content with security less than others.'' Soviet Defence Minister, Yazov pointed out in his book that the Soviet military doctrine regards defence as its mainstay. Thus the Soviet Union emphasises that it discards predominance in arms and seek rationally sufficient military power for defence.

I am not naive enough to believe that all of these words will be put into action, but it would be wrong to take all these words as only propaganda. The Soviet concessions in the IMF treaty negotiations, Gorbachev's decisions that led to the pullout of Soviet forces from Afghanistan, the Soviet Union's expression of its intention to participate in the Olympics in Seoul and the cooperative attitude towards Middle-East problems and at the United Nations lead us to admit that the introduction of a ''new way of thinking'' contains something more than mere rhetoric and propaganda.

Even if Gorbachev's intention to promote *perestroika, glasnost* and *novoye myshlenye* is serious, it does not appear that sufficient conditions to realise his aims exist in the Soviet Union. There are oppositions and insubordination to Gorbachev's perestroika as domestic reforms among the top echelon of the Soviet leadership, in the middle-level bureaucracy and even among the general public. If glasnost is excessive, it is that it runs the risk of exploding ethnic movements in the Soviet Union beyond control. If his domestic reforms are pushed too rapidly, it may develop into a crisis in which the Soviet system may collapse. If it is moved too slowly, the momentum for reform will be lost.

The introduction of a ''new way of thinking'' in foreign policy to accelerate domestic reforms will inevitably suffer the same fate as perestroika and glasnost if they fail. In the long-term, successful domestic reforms, rather than their failure, may bring about a crisis in the Soviet domination of Eastern Europe.

However, it is certain that at the bottom of Gorbachev's thinking there is a sense of crisis that the Soviet Union may tumble down from its position as a superpower unless domestic reforms are carried out energetically to correct its serious economic and social stagnation. And if he assumes that perestroika is necessary to revitalise the Soviet economy and that a serious pursuit of lasting peace, predicable and constructive international relations are needed to concentrate on perestroika, it appears that the Soviet Union does not have any alternative but to pursue his domestic reforms, particularly perestroika, and the introduction of a ''new way of thinking'' in its foreign and security policy. Even if the

Soviet leader fails in these attempts and loses his post, the Soviet Union does not seem to have room to choose a return to a path of military expansion as pursued in the Brezhnev era.

We should consider that even if Gorbachev's domestic and foreign policies especially the introduction of a "new way thinking," may be halted or decelerated, fundamentally they are unlikely to be reversed, we should thus aggressively respond to new situations and opportunities.

However, in dealing with the Soviets, we should bear in mind the following three points:

First, the Soviets have not given up trying to outcompete the United States and the Western world in the type of government. They are attempting to introduce a "new way of thinking" into their diplomatic and national security policy and orient their military doctrine toward self-defence because they wish to preserve their standing as a superpower rivalling the United States in the 21st century, and because they perceive such measures to be in their best interest for maximising the benefits of the nation. They have not shed their strong dependence on and tendency towards power. The closed nature of the Soviet government, its secrecy and heavy-handedness with regard to human rights, remain disquieting. Admittedly, the nature of the threat posed by the Soviets is changing, but still it will not disappear.

Second, we should not be overly optimistic about the speed with which the Soviets shift their policy in the direction we hope. Reform of society and the introduction of new thinking cannot proceed quickly, given the ingrained habits of the Russian people, entrenched tradition, rigidities of the system and conflicts within the military and leadership. We must make sure that Soviet leaders match their words with deeds and respond to seemingly promising developments with much caution. We should take the process of trust while verifying the facts rather than "trust but verify". If being accustomed to democratic ways, we let our optimism go too far, and if the Western world overestimates the extent and speed of reform in the Soviet Union and relaxes its guard, the actual military balance might tilt in disfavour of the West to the extent that it jeopardises the strategic military balance. However, proper understanding of the significance of the new Soviet approach should not allow excessive caution to prevent us from seizing a good opportunity for establishing a stable East-West relationship.

Third, while improving its relationship with the United States, the Soviet Union may take advantage of problems besetting the relations between the three centres of power in the West, namely the United States, Western Europe and Japan. We must cope with this possibility with due caution. As Secretary General Gorbachev's speech delivered at the 27th Soviet Communist Party Congress indicates, he does not believe that flaws in their mutual relations will easily undermine the economic, military and political bonds uniting the United States, Japan, and that Western Europe and Japan will act in concert with the United States at the expense of their own interests. Gorbachev is also aware of the possibility that the emergence of another centre of power will aggravate the distortions of the relations between the three major powers.

Western countries must prepare proposals that will strengthen solidarity in the West and must be ready to actively assume leadership in negotiations to build desirable East-West relations so that a schism among the Western countries will not deepen by passively responding to Soviet proposals, not to mention arms reduction negotiations.

If US-Soviet relations are stabilised and move steadily, if not rapidly towards improvement through dialogues and negotiations, US counter-measures to the Soviet threat and the strategic value of China as a buffer state will decline. For China, the need to depend on the US to counter the Soviet threat will decline. China may consider that the "new way of thinking" in Soviet foreign policy will promote an improvement of Sino-Soviet relations. The three major obstacles that stand in the way of improving Sino-Soviet relations are thought to be ceased and headed towards a resolution.

However, there are no signs that it will progress to the degree that enables the withdrawal of Vietnamese troops from Kampuchea in the near future. Ultimately, the structure of the coalition government after the withdrawal of the Vietnamese troops and strong mistrust of Vietnam on the part of China are making the solution difficult. China does not intend to improve Sino-Soviet relations at the expense of Sino-US relations. It will persist in its independent path with regard to the US and the Soviet Union. China understands fully that the US, which is located far away from China compared with the neighbouring Soviet Union, will bring about more economic benefits and fewer military threats.

Part of the three major obstacles in Sino-Soviet relations may be maintained for the time being even after the Soviet withdrawal from Afghanistan as it is China's advantage to pursue benefits from an improvement of relations with the Soviet Union without losing benefits from maintaining friendly political and economic relations with the West.

An improvement of US-Soviet relations may calm America's sense of alarm over the improvement of Japan-Soviet relations and will provide possibilities of promoting to some extent economic exchanges between Japan and the Soviet Union through trade and investment. However, the US may continue to watch Japan closely regarding technology transfers in fields which may be used militarily even if remotely. Unless the Soviet Union shows its sincerity towards resolution of the territorial issue, there will be limits to the improvement of economic exchanges between Japan and the Soviet Union. A foothold for a basic improvement of Japan-Soviet relations including the territorial issue will not be realised before the visit to Japan by Secretary General Gorbachev. The Soviets do not seem ready to determine to introduce a "new way of thinking" into a improvement of Japan-Soviet relations including the territorial issue. It appears that Japan has time to come up with a "new wisdom" to induce the Soviets to come up with a "new way of thinking" on this issue.

ECONOMIC DEVELOPMENT IN THE ASIA-PACIFIC REGION

With respect to the third subject, economic development in the Asia-Pacific region, the important problems are how to harmonise economic development in this region to the global development of the world economy while maintaining its vigorous dynamism and what kind of institutional backing will be necessary to support economic, cultural and academic development and co-operation in this region.

For economic development in the Asia-Pacific region, optimistic views are predominant. It is thought that the V-shaped formation in which the advanced countries of Japan, the US, and Canada are followed by newly industrialised countries (NICs), which in turn are followed by the ASEAN countries and China and that spill-over effects of development will continue to expand. Despite an adjustment in the world economy, which has been shaken by the twin deficits in the US, wide fluctuations of foreign exchange rates, sharp increases and declines in crude oil and other primary commodity prices and a stock market crash, the Asia-pacific economy did not lose its dynamism.

South Korea, Taiwan and Hong Kong kept on growing sharply cashing in on "three lows": low exchange rates, low crude oil prices and low interest rates. Although the growth rates of Malaysia, Singapore and Indonesia declined in 1985 and 1986, their economic performance improved in 1987. Due to the cheap dollar and the strong Yen, imports from NICs and Thailand to Japan shot up, while the share of Japan in investment in Asia surged from 10 to 19 per cent. Taiwan's direct investment in the ASEAN countries is increasing sharply.

At the sixth general meeting of the Pacific Economic Co-operation Conference (PECC) held in Osaka from May 18 to 20, 1988, it was forecasted that economic activity in this region in the 1990s will remain dynamic and that economic growth rates would be 3 per cent for North America, 4 per cent for Japan, 6-7 per cent for the Asian NICs and China and 5 per cent for the ASEAN countries.

However, the fact that the target amount of the "PECC Fund," which is needed to spread the scale and scope of PECC activities in the region without relying in advanced countries' initiatives, is only one million dollars seems to suggest limitations of PECC activities.

Newspapers report that there were many misgivings and oppositions to former Prime Minister Nakasone's call through video tapes to make the PECC into a Pacific version of the OECD. In view of the sensitive reactions of the Asian countries which fear that the US and Japan, superpowers in the PECC and members of the OECD, a rich nations' club, may dominate the PECC, leadership by the superpowers in the PECC should be carefully avoided.

In the Asia-Pacific region, there are advanced industrial countries like the US and Canada, which are to be joined by a free trade agreement, and other advanced industrial countries like Japan, Australia and New Zealand. It also includes the NICs, the ASEAN countries, the island nations of the South Pacific, China with its huge economic potentials and the USSR, which stated that it was an Asia-Pacific as well as a European nation.

There are economic, political, cultural and religious gaps and diversities among these countries. It will be difficult to adopt OECD-type common policies among these nations but some form of co-ordination of co-operative relations will be necessary. However, at present co-operation in the Asia-Pacific region should be promoted with the following priorities:

1. To focus on economic co-operation and market opening, and on cultural and academic co-operation;
2. To avoid exclusive and closed regionalism. The danger of the development of a bloc to cope with the US-Canada free trade

agreement and formation of an integrated market by EC should be strictly avoided;

3. To aim at forming free and open relationship of mutual dependence from a global perspective;
4. To focus on functional rather than organisational integration of regional co-operation and not make haste to build an international agency by related governments;
5. To minimise to the bare necessity the changes of superpowers taking leadership. Japan should be ready to take necessary initiatives but should care fully avoid assuming leadership; and
6. To decide on whether to PECC, a co-operative setup of government, business and academic circles, should allow the Soviet Union to become an official member after judging what kind of contribution it can make in economic co-operation of this region.

JAPAN'S INTERNATIONAL ROLES

Japan's international roles may be summarised as follows:

Basic Posture

1. Japan should clearly indicate its posture as "a Japan which contributes to the world."
2. As an economic superpower and the world's largest creditor nation, Japan should make maximum efforts to promote smoothly the adjustment process to recover balance from international economic inequilibrium. Aggressive efforts could be made for the sustained growth of the world economy, prevention of protectionism and solution to the North-South problems, especially the problem of cumulative debts.
3. In order to build a peaceful and stable world, Japan could undertake a fair burden-sharing in a comprehensive security framework in addition to paying a political role as an important member of the free world.
4. With the realisation that the international political and economic system which prevailed after the Second World War is now undergoing a transition process, Japan should search for new policy measures including the building of a new world order from a long-term, comprehensive and global perspective.

Economic Issues

The Macro Economy and Currencies

Japan should make efforts to shift its economic structure into one led by domestic demand so that simultaneously the large external imbalances are corrected and people attain a living standard comparable to their nation's affluent status and so that such a society can be maintained. It should keep on making efforts for economic policy co-ordination among the major advanced countries to stabilise foreign exchange rates. For this purpose, the summit countries should conduct mutual surveillance of their economic performances and continue co-operation in the foreign exchange markets including joint intervention. Furthermore, they should search for measures for long-term stabilisation of the international currency system.

Trade Issues

Japan should actively promote the Uruguay Round to prevent protectionism and division of the world economy into block and to maintain and expand free trade. Contributions of the NICs to the revitalisation of the world economy should be given their due respect while it is expected that these countries will be further integrated in the free international economic system and they will play roles commensurate with their economic power.

The Cumulative Debt Problem

Based on the assumption that debtor nations will help themselves, the flow of funds to the developing countries should be secured in co-operation with international agencies. For the time being, economic adjustment and the development of the debtor nations could for example, be supported on a case-by-case basis.

Political Co-operation

Measures for the Post-INF Situation

Japan may support US initiatives to reduce strategic nuclear arms and conventional arms following the reduction of intermediate nuclear forces (INF). In doing so, Japan could pay due attention to Western European fears. At the same time, efforts could be made to correct imbalance on a global scale without sacrificing Asia, while launching studies on a comprehensive strategy which will meet the needs arising from new developments in East-West relations.

Afghanistan

A democratic government may be established based on the principle of national self-determination after the withdrawal of Soviet troops from Afghanistan. For this purpose, an international watchdog organisation could be established centering on the United Nations and Japan may participate in it. At the same time, a structure for international co-operation should be built for the economic reconstruction of Afghanistan. Through such an organisation, Japan may actively aid Afghan reconstruction.

Other Regional Conflicts

Japan could, for example, co-operate for an early resolution of the Iran-Iraq War, and regional conflicts in Cambodia and Central America and aid reconstruction following the termination of conflicts.

UN Peace Keeping

It appears that for a fair burden-sharing as an ally, Japan does not contemplate shouldering new defence roles in addition to the continuous build-up of Japan's defence capabilities. Instead it will be necessary for Japan to share an increased portion of expenses for US troops stationed in Japan. At the same time, Japan could be ready to actively participate in and co-operate with the United Nations' international peace-keeping operations in addition to what I have stated so far.

Aid to Developing Countries

Japan may make efforts to enhance aid to developing countries as a major part of a fair burden-sharing from the view point of comprehensive security and from consideration of importance of the North-South problems. Present official development assistance (ODA) may be increased steadily and conspicuously, while efforts could be made to upgrade its quality. Effective measures could be taken for economic assistance to the Philippines which requires special political considerations. For economic assistance to Indonesia, a record figure of US $2.3 billion was agreed upon between the two countries at the end of May as capital assistance in the current year. (US $300 million has already been decided upon, and US $1.4 billion in Yen loans and US $600 million in united loans from the Export-Import Bank have been added.)

Promotion of Cultural Exchanges

Mutual understanding among nations, Japan may make efforts to further promote cultural exchanges including student exchanges.

CONCLUDING REMARKS

The forthcoming Economic Summit in Toronto is unlikely to produce real and concrete results. This is because president Reagan is a lame duck while new regimes have just taken office in France and Italy, and Canada, the host country, is likely to have an early election. Consequently, discussions among leaders will likely focus on medium and long-term issues. In this sense, the leaders should try to build relations of trust among themselves rather than aiming at immediate results or domestic public relations effects.

22

Japan's International and Regional Role: An Indonesian Perception*

JUSUF WANANDI

INTRODUCTION

Since the last Japan-Indonesia colloquium, about 3 years ago, there have been a lot of changes and new developments in the Asia-Pacific region, in Japan and in Indonesia, as well as in Japan-Indonesia relations. It will not be easy to capture all those developments here, but one — and perhaps the most — important development has been Japan's changing regional and global role.

The changes that have occurred and continue to unfold are almost total, namely in all aspects of life. The focus here, however, is on Japan's role in the political, security and economic fields. The aim of this examination is to understand, anticipate and provide some successions on Japan's future strategic role in the Asia-Pacific region. The term ''strategic'' is used here not in its narrow sense, namely confined to the military security realm, but in its broadest sense as implied in the idea of

* This article is originally a paper presented at the Thirteenth Indonesia-Japan Conference, Bali, June 6-8, 1988, sponsored by CSIS and JIAA (Tokyo).

"comprehensive security," which has been proposed initially in the report of a study commission established by Prime Minister Ohira and chaired by Prof. Inoki. The discussion of Japan's international role in this paper is centered on its role in the Asia-Pacific region where such role is given emphasis by Japan.

Japan's economic position, as the second economic power in the world, has global implications, and the industrialised world, particularly the US, indeed expects Japan in perform a global economic role. In the security field, however, an expanded role by Japan will be confined to the Asia-Pacific region, in particular in sharing the burden with the US for the defence of Japan. Similarly, in the political field it will initially be centered on the Asia-Pacific region, but gradually this may be extended to other regions, such as Central America and Mexico. Its implementation will probably be closely linked to Japan's economic role and in close co-operation with the US. Thus Japan's international role should be appreciated in the context of international burden sharing with the US and as a consequence of shifts and changes in the power configuration among the major powers, particularly between the US and Japan themselves.

JAPAN'S INTERNATIONAL ROLE IN THE SECURITY FIELD

Lately, a lot has been written and said on Japan's evolving role in the security field, including in Japan itself. While the more open discussions and debates in this field are healthy, they easily lead to misunderstanding and misperceptions, especially on the part of outsiders.

One fact, however, stands out unambiguously, namely the continued strong hesitation and resistance on the part of the Japanese public to accept a drastic and sudden change of Japan's security role and responsibility. Commitment to and belief in Article 9 of the Constitution remain strong. This article denies Japan the use of military force in resolving international conflicts. It also prohibits Japan to build-up an armed force. It was only after the outbreak of the Korean War that a small self-defence force (SDF) was created, but the defence of Japan's security remains in US hands.

The new international and regional environments in the 1970s led to a gradual change in the attitude of the Japanese people towards SDF. The Japanese became concerned with US-USSR strategic balance and the credibility of US umbrella and they observed with greater anxiety the

Soviet naval build-up in the Pacific. More directly, they felt helpless in the face of the 1973 oil embargo.

The existence of SDF is today already accepted as a fact and it has become easier now to recruit its officers. Although as a percentage of GNP, Japan's defence expenditures remain low, in absolute terms such expenditures have increased rapidly. The people also have come to accept a build-up of SDF's defence capabilities and the defence treaty with the US has received increased public support.

Significant efforts to strengthen SDF have been undertaken only since the early 1980s, partly as a reaction to increased pressures from the US, which could no longer accept Japan's "free ride." First and foremost among those efforts is the division of tasks and missions in co-operation with US armed forces. This involves an increase in SDF capabilities to defend the Japanese homeland and its surrounding water from an attack from the Soviet Union, at least until the US comes to the rescue. It is also meant to increase control over and to prevent the use of the three vital straits of Japan by Soviet strategic submarines for access from the Okhotzk Sea, so that they could be neutralised more readily by Japan in case of an open conflict with the Seventh Fleet. Such control has been extended to 1,000 nautical miles to the South and the Southeast, and will in the future be further extended to the East in order to limit the degree of manoeuverability of Soviet submarines. These capabilities support US "maritime strategy" which is aimed at the destruction of Soviet naval bases in the Pacific and its strategic submarines in the Okhotzk Sea in case of a US-USSR open conflict, as well as US "horizontal escalation strategy," namely in opening up a new front in the Pacific to serve as a counterbalance in case the US or its allies in Western Europe are under attack.

To this end, joint exercises between US forces and SDF have been undertaken since 1979. The capabilities of the Maritime and Air SDF continue to be strengthened. Today the Maritime SDF deploys over 50 destroyers and by 1990 will have 60, including two to be equipped with the Aegis Air Defence System and 100 P-3CS for anti-submarine warfare (ASW). The air SDF now deploys 100 F-4 "Phantoms" and by 1990 will have approximately 200 F-15 "Eagles." In 1990 it will also have 100 F-16's which will be equipped with the most modern Japanese made avionics.

All those efforts are in accordance with the Mid-term Defence Review 1987-90 defence plan, to achieve the targets set for 1991. It was those targets which enabled Prime Minister Nakasone to steadily increase Japan's defence expenditures by 5 per cent annually in reall terms throughout 1983-85 while other expenditures — except ODA — were reduced. In 1987 the defence budget surpassed 1 per cent of GNP, and for the first time in 1988, under Prime Minister Takeshita, it is larger than each of the defence budgets of Britain, France and West Germany.[1] This makes Japan's defence expenditures the third largest in absolute terms after the US and the Soviet Union.

In the context of defence co-operation and the sharing of defence burden between Japan and the US, one needs to include Japan's financial contribution to US troops stationed in Japan covering facilities and local personnel amounting to US $2.5 billion or about 40 per cent of the total costs.

In addition, preparations are made for the prepositioning of arms and ammunition and other logistics in Japan to be used by US troops in case of an attack on Japan and conflicts around Japan. The capabilities of Land SDF are also being strengthened to deal with a Soviet attack on Hokkaido.

The second effort on the part of Japan is in the area of transfer of hightech to the US in the field of defence and armaments, which began with technology co-operation in the SDI programme. Such technological co-operation remains limited to co-operation with the US, since under Prime Minister Miki Japan has set a constraint to itself in transferring defence-related technologies.

The third aspect of the burden sharing scheme is the provision of so-called strategic assistance by Japan for certain countries that face security problems, such as Pakistan, Turkey, Egypt, Thailand, the Philippines, and in the future perhaps also Central America. It is in the form of economic assistance meant to help those countries that have strategic significance to the US and the Western world, to cope with internal political and security problems or conflicts with other countries.

The fourth aspect, which is much in the spirit of "comprehensive security" is the increase of Japanese official development assistance (ODA), which has surpassed US ODA this year, as well as the so-called recycling programme, as originally pledged in the Venice Economic Summit in 1986, the amount of US $30 billion, of which the allocation of US $2 billion to ASEAN has been agreed on. The recycling programme is not directed only to public sector financing but involves participation of the private sector, and therefore should be seen as complementing rather than substituting ODA.

Thus far, most countries in the Western Pacific, namely China, South Korea, ASEAN, Australia and New Zealand, are of the view that efforts to strengthen SDF's capabilities and the increase of Japan's defence budget in the context of burden sharing with the US are already sufficient. Further increases would arouse suspicions in the region. The current Reagan Administration is also of the opinion that the military strength of SDF will be sufficient with the competition of the Defence Mid-term Review 1986-90.[2]

Apparently some consensus has been reached in the US on what this burden sharing should imply. Previous amendments in the US Congress to force Japan to increase its defence expenditures to 2 to 3 per cent of GNP were rejected by the majority in the Congress in early May 1988. The Reagan Administration seems to be worried that a further push in this direction could lead Japan to take a go-it-alone attitude, which certainly is not in the interest of the US itself.

There is also the prevailing concern in various countries of the Western Pacific over a possible resurgence of militarism in Japan. Vocal statements by extreme rightist groups, including from within the LDP as represented by former ministers Okuno and Fujio, on Japan's role in World War II tend to reinforce the fear about Japan's future role in regional security and defence. Indeed, such fears are not well founded and have largely been caused by a lack of understanding of Japanese society.

Essentially, however, the countries in the Western Pacific are quite comfortable with the current Japanese defence strategy and security role as well as with the level of its defence capabilities. This is due to two factors. *Firstly*, it is the prevailing strongly anti-militaristic attitude of the Japanese public which will oppose any attempt to make the SDF an independent military force. *Secondly*, the defence alliance with the US has become transparent and the strategy and role of the SDF in the joint missions with the US armed forces have been defined more clearly.

Nevertheless, one could discern some subtle undercurrents in Japan that demand further examination on the costs and benefits of greater independence in Japan's ability to defence its own homeland and the surrounding waters, albeit still within the alliance with the US. It is a fact that all of the new weaponry for the SDF, from the PC-3 Orion to the Aegis anti-missile system and the production of FSX fighters, are determined by the US as part of the US military mission. It is in the light of these developments that perhaps one should interpret Prime Minister Takeshita's statement at the Defence Academy on 21 March 1988, suggesting that Japan should develop a defence capability proportionate to its national power. One also notes other developments: the members of the Zoku, the defence forum in the Diet, have increased in the past few years to about 20 per cent of the total number of deputies and the Japanese industries have increased pressure to produce the FSX themselves.

From the outside, one could detect a greater desire in some quarters in Japan for the SDF to have more independent conventional capabilities for the defence of Japan against an eventual Soviet attack, namely involving surface-to-sea missiles, advanced helicopters and fighters and Japan's own reconnaissance capabilities. Therefore, the debate between LDP politicians and the Self Defence Agency (SDA) no longer revolves around the issue of whether aircraft carriers are necessary for the defence of Japan, but around the type of carrier to be procured.

Nonetheless, the debate remains quite obscure to outsiders. There is therefore the additional uncertainty and concern that at the end Japan may build up its military capability without a clear strategy and become a military power without knowing what the power is to be used for. Indeed, the question is why Japan would wish to have a more independent defence capability. Is it because the Soviet threat has been perceived by the Japanese public in the past few years as a real one even though it is doubtful that the Soviets have the capability to attack Japan? Is it because Japan is concerned that some day it could be drawn into a US-USSR conflict by the maritime and horizontal escalation strategies of the Americans? Or is it because Japan perceives China, or North Korea, as a long-term threat although relations with both countries are excellent today? Thus in view of the possible misperceptions that such a debate could create among Japan's friends in the region. It is crucial that institutionalised consultations on these issues do take place.

The other problem which continues to have an influence on the direction of Japan's security policy is the pressures from the US, especially in regard to burden sharing. It is known that the pressures mainly comes from US Congress and US public opinion. Congress has amended the State Department Authorisation Bill and the Defence Authorisation Bill by stressing the need for US allies, namely Japan and NATO members, to increase their defence expenditures in the context of burden-sharing. Although no official figures were stipulated, the talk among some members referred to 2 to 3 per cent of GNP in the case of Japan. Those amendments have been overruled by a large margin recently, but the pressures will persist in the future.

Therefore, this problem needs to be dealt with more systematically and in close co-ordination by both the US and Japan so as not to lead to non-sensical burden-sharing programmes. The implications of a 3 per cent of GNP Japanese defence budget would be unthinkable. At the current levels, this would amount to about US $90 billion or one-third of the US defence budget and larger than the combined defence budgets of Britain, France and West Germany.

In the context of burden sharing, many other proposals have been made. Suggestions were made in the Trilateral Commission Meeting in Tokyo in April 1988 that the burden sharing should including an increase of the Japanese ODA; a joint undertaking with the US to provide a kind of "Marshall Plan" to Mexico and Central America; or to establish a free trade area between the US and Japan — extended perhaps to Canada and Mexico.

The Asia-Pacific region would certainly welcome an increase of Japanese ODA, direct investment from Japan to the Asian NICs and ASEAN, further opening up of the Japanese market to exports from the Asian NICs and ASEAN, as well as an increase in the so-called strategic assistance. In regard to the last mentioned assistance, Japan could consider supporting the US proposal for a "Marshall Plan" for the Philippines as a way to diffuse nationalistic sentiments in the Philippines on the issue of US bases. The bases are of important to the security of sea lines of communication (SLOC) which are vital to Japan. Japan could also play a role in the resolution of the Kampuchean conflict by providing the necessary economic assistance following a political settlement. Japan could offer humanitarian assistance to Vietnam to cope with its current food shortage and in so doing contributes to preventing the flow of large waves of refugees that could cause instabilities in the region.

However, beyond those suggestions Japan, and indeed the Asia-pacific region as a whole, should address some more fundamental questions: should Japan continue with the pace of increasing its defence capabilities as experienced in the last few years that has led to a doubling in real terms within 8 years? Should this be accompanied by other diplomatic efforts such as negotiating for a disarmament in the

Asia-Pacific region or "confidence building measures" including the promotion of economic and political relations with the Soviet Union?

The following issues should also be addressed: will the nature of threat to the US-Japan alliance and to the stability of the Asia-Pacific region be different in the future or will it be the same as currently perceived? Finally, how would the US-Japan alliance and regional stability be affected by a more independent Japanese defence capability?

So far, security and defence issues between Japan and the US have been dealt with fairly well, and this is often seen to be compensating the increased tensions in their trade relations. However, the security relationship between the two countries should not be linked to their economic and trade relations. US-Japan economic relations are in themselves a source of conflict and should not complicate relationship in other fields. From the regional perspective, a stable and sound US-Japan relationship is the most important cornerstone of regional peace and stability.

JAPAN'S INTERNATIONAL ROLE IN THE POLITICAL AND ECONOMIC FIELDS

Japan's political role has been manifested mainly in the economic field. This is in accordance with Japan's idea of comprehensive security and very much in line with Indonesia's concept of national resilience. Indeed, from the point of view of the developing countries in the Asia-pacific region, economic development is the most important factor of internal political stability as well as regional peace and stability. Therefore, Japan's assistance in this field would greatly contribute to the maintenance and promotion of peace and stability in the region.

In addition to the above policy, Japan could consider a more active participation in the resolution of conflicts in the Asia-Pacific region. With regard to the Kampuchean conflict, it can do so, for instance, by providing signals that Vietnam can count on economic assistance from Japan if it is willing to make real political compromises to resolve the Kampuchean problem as early as possible. The conditions for progress have never been more promising than today. All parties involved seem to be better disposed to seriously negotiate a political solution, but Vietnam seems to need additional incentives to come forward.

Japan could immediately provide humanitarian assistance for Vietnam, which is currently facing severe food shortages. This assistance could be given through and administered by international agencies. If the international community fails to provide the necessary assistance for Vietnam, the regional implications — in the form of new large waves of "refugees" — could be estabilising. Japan could also play a constructive role in the reduction of tensions in the Korean peninsula because of its relations with the US and China and its economic position *vis-a-vis* both South Korea and North Korea.

However, Japan's principal political and diplomatic task is to stabilise its relations with the US, because this is the most important relationship in the Asia-Pacific region as it provides the foundation for regional peace and stability. The main problem here is how to bring together these two great and advance nations that have such great difference in values and cultures.

Japan-US relations have developed to such an extent as to outgrow mere interdependence. The two nations and societies are essentially in the process of integration in various fields of life, economic, political and security-wise. Their social relations have become more extensive and deepened. But because of the great differences between these two societies, these process is likely to be full of tensions. If this process of integration proceeds smoothly, Japan-US relations in the future will become stronger. This will greatly enhance their role and ability to contribute positively to the maintenance of international peace and stability, especially in the Asia-Pacific region.

In this regard, the coming years will be most critical for that relationship and, therefore, also for the entire region. What is expected from Japan is to hasten the process of internationalisation. In the economic field, this would involve more extensive structural changes as proposed in the Maekawa Report, which in part would be reflected in changes in the structure of its imports. In the political field, this may involve a change in political processes within the LDP and a shift in political constituencies from the dominance of rural framers towards that of the urban middle-class.

Those changes require a strong political leadership and a bureaucracy which could rapidly adapt itself to those changes. The issue is no longer that of whether Japan should change or not, but how faster the change could take place. Politicians are not at the forefront in advocating change, but they have given greater attention to the calls for change. The business community and the academic world are among those that are eagerly promoting the internationalisation of Japan.

The world, one could observe, is impatiently waiting for the necessary adjustments on the part of Japan that would allow her to fulfil an "international role." Indeed, each nation is unique in a sense, and the Japanese are also a unique nation. However, this argument can no longer be used as a pretext for delaying the necessary steps to be taken by Japan. Not only are those changes important for the regional and the world at large, but they are essential to Japan's own survival that is so much dependent on the international environment. Unless Japan becomes a military superpower and possesses all of the most advanced technologies that would allow her to become economically self-reliant and self-sufficient, which is unlikely even in the distant future, it continues to have a great stake in the maintenance of an international order.

Japan-US political relations, as discussed earlier, will continue to be put to the test. Thus the management of this relationship requires more intensive political consultations and co-operation. This will all contribute to the implementation of more effective joint efforts in dealing with the overcoming crisis in various parts of the world such as Korea, Indochina, South Pacific, the Persian Gulf, Middle East and Central America.

In managing Japan-US relations, the Japanese side has the institutional in infrastructure and the various agencies involved are well co-ordinated. This is not the case on the US end, in spite of the very intensive relations and interactions, at the ministerial level (over 30 meetings the last year), between the Diet and the US Congress, among their academics and business. This intensity is to be found even in the relations between the Japanese prime minister and the US president; until the end of his term in 1989, President Reagan is expected to meet prime Minister Takeshita a total of 6 times. However, the weak co-ordination in the American policy making mechanism and institutional infrastructure as well as its global rather than regional orientation have all contributed to the *ad hoc* approach in dealing with specific country issues.

It should come as no surprise that the need for a rather permanent "wisemen committee" of representative from both sides was urgently felt, as proposed for instance by George Packard (SAIS). However, its proper functioning would still depend on the co-ordination on the US side. Perhaps, this requires the establishment of a team under the US President in charge of inter-agency co-ordination on all matters relating to Japan, and which receives bipartisan support from the US Congress and other sectors in society, e.g. labour unions.

Japan's political relations with other countries in the Asia-pacific region are next in the order of importance, because the region constitutes its immediate security environment. The countries in this region are also Japan's important political and economic partners. These relations have been overwhelmed by the intense nature of Japan-US relations in the past few years. However, the importance of nurturing these "other relations" should not be overlooked by Japan as a way to counterbalance its relations with the US, which have been colored by so much "Japan bashing."

To those "other countries" Japan is an important partner as a source of capital and technology as well as in trade and, therefore, Japan can count on their friendship. Perhaps Japan needs more sustained efforts in promoting relations with these other Asia-pacific countries. Within the government, the Gaimusho is certainly the focal point, but greater attention needs to be given by other ministries, e.g. the Ministry of Education. In the Diet, the focus is on China and Korea and interest in ASEAN is still very little. Relations between the mass-media and the youth are still very superficial, often contributing to greater mutual misperceptions rather than eliminating them. There is also need for efforts to promote exchanges among scholars and academics as well as of scientific and technological know-how.

Among these "other countries," Japan's relations with the Soviet Union and with China deserve some further examination here. The past few years have seen efforts to normalise US-USSR relations, and indeed, the level of tensions is now much reduced compared to the 1970s and the early years of President Reagan. High-level and substantive dialogues on disarmament, INF, START and on chemical and conventional weapons have taken place and have reached the stage that ensure their continuation. This process may have influenced other negotiations, including perhaps on the Soviet withdrawal from Afghanistan.

Nonetheless, this process of normalisation of relations will not be an easy one, because of the different and opposing ideologies and systems of the parties concerned. However, we are given evidence or how powerful economic realities and pressures could be in forcing those two countries to enter into the process. It is likely that this process will also be extended to USSR's relations with other Asia-Pacific countries, especially since the Vladiwostok speech of Mr. Gorbachev two years ago.

In contrast to the process of normalisation in US-USSR relations, the relationship between Japan and the Soviet Union has remained cool, and there are no sign as yet of improved relations. This may be because Soviet diplomacy towards Japan remains inflexible as far as the issue of the Northern territories is concerned. On the part of Japan, the obstacle may lie with the fact that the Soviet Union has become identified as the country's main and concrete threat. In addition, Japan's interest in Soviet natural resources has significantly diminished, while communication gap at the working level may still be significant.

Japan should also test the intentions of the Soviet Union in becoming an active and constructive participant in regional Asia-pacific affairs and development. Indeed, the regional eagerly waits more concrete steps by the Soviet leadership, for instance, in encouraging Vietnam to accept a political settlement of the Kampuchean problem, to discuss with Japan the issue of the Northern territories, in actively promoting regional disarmament and confidence building measures. The USSR should also participate in the economic activities in the region. An impetus to such participation could be given by fully involving the Soviet Union in the existing non-governmental regional co-operation structure such as the PECC (Pacific Economic Co-operation Conference).

The past year have seen improvements in Japan-China relations which earlier have suffered from the emergence of a number of problems, bilateral and otherwise. These problems include, among others, the unfavourable trade balance for China, the low level of Japanese investments coming into China – less than those to Taiwan — the increase in Japan's defence posture and defence expenditures, and the rewriting of the history textbook. The importance of Japan-China relations lies not only in the fact that these two major, neighbouring countries need to co-exist peacefully, but also in the need to bring China into involvement in regional and international affairs in accordance with the accepted rules so that it may contribute to regional and international peace and stability. Since China is a big country, Japan's relations with it will always need to be counterbalanced. While the world hopes that Deng's modernisation efforts will succeed, which will strengthen China's constructive international involvement, the country's complex internal problems do not rule out possible policy changes in the future.

In addition, China is still seen as a potential threat by a number of countries in the region, in ASEAN particularly. Therefore, Japan needs to manage its relations with China by taking that factor into account.

China itself may become Japan's major competitor, the two being the largest countries in the Wester Pacific with different systems.

Japan's economic role cannot be limited to the Asia-Pacific region. With a GNP of US $3 trillion and a trade surplus of US $90 billion in 1987, Japan's economic impact is global. Japan's economic posture and policy have been criticised on many fronts, namely that its markets are relatively closed, that its policies are merchantilistic, that it provides too much protection for its farmers, that its tax system leads to too large savings, that its distribution system acts as a non-tariff barrier and so on.

One should acknowledge, however, that the past few years have seen so many policy changes introduced by the Japanese economy, if often seen as "too little and too late." The effects of the Yen appreciation have been rather powerful and have let to a much faster pace in the economy's structural adjustments than foreseen in the Maekawa Report.

Japan's economic relations with the Asian NICs and ASEAN are also changing very rapidly as a result of those developments. The large flows of foreign direct investment from Japan to these countries have also led to increased intra-industry trade as manifested in the growth of components and part imports into Japan. Imports of consumer durables are also on the increase. The Asian NICs have opened the way also for the ASEAN countries to follow. It remains to be seen whether this process would be sustained and that the above changes were not merely a one-shot phenomenon. Further efforts by Japan, especially in the area of agricultural protection, which is also recognised by outsiders as a difficult and politically sensitive issues, are seen as the ultimate test of Japan's determination to change.

CONCLUSIONS

The above discussion suggests the importance of regular and continuous consultations and communications among all countries in the Asia-Pacific region which are greatly affected by the dramatic changes and dynamic developments over the past few years. This is a task that Japan and Indonesia should undertake in all seriousness. Consultations between the two countries should not be limited to governments or the business community, but should be extended to politicians, academics, the media, and the youth. Both sides must give greater attention to each other.

The recent shifts in international relations have wide-ranging implications. While the military strategic relay and its developments greatly influence the region's stability and security environment, economic factors and economic relations have become the priority area. For the ASEAN countries, the immediate threat is the many economic challenges they are currently faced with. Domestic economic development in these countries has become so intertwined with international economic development.

In view of this, ASEAN's immediate threat no longer refers to either the Soviet Union or China, but is focussed on developments in the international economy which is greatly affected by developments in US-Japan relations. ASEAN's main agenda in meeting this challenge is to structure and promote mutually beneficial relations with the industrialised world with which it has intensive economic relations.

Glasnost and *Perestroika* may open up new opportunities which may be beneficial for the Asia-Pacific region and may promote ASEAN-USSR relations. However, this will depend a lot on the concrete steps taken by the USSR in the years to come. Similarly, China's modernisation offers new opportunities for international and regional co-operation and will have a profound impact on China itself. This will also contribute to the creation of a healthy regional environment beneficial to ASEAN.

Political developments in the Philippines, South Korea and Taiwan, and in other ASEAN countries, all add to the more encouraging regional picture today compared to a few years ago. The South Pacific region has becomes somewhat unstable today, but there are no reasons to believe that such instabilities are a permanent feature of the region. All in all, the Asia-Pacific region is relatively healthy. But its health will depend to a larger extent on improvements in US-Japan relations. This implies a larger burden on the part of Japan, which is to be manifested primarily in a more extensive and active economic role.

Notes and References

1. NATO's estimates of defence expenditures for 1987 are as follows: US $288.4 billion for the US; US $40 billion for Japan; US $34.5 billion for France; US $34.2 billion for West Germany, and US $31.8 billion for Great Britain.
2. Statement by R. Armitage, Assistant Secretary of Defence (ISA), US DOD at the National Defence University Pacific Symposium on "Patterns of Co-operation and Pacific Basin Security," Washington, D.C., February 25, 1988.

23

Japan as a Regional Power

CHULACHEEB CHINWANNO*

Japan, a major external power in Southeast Asia, is often seen as a one-eyed giant because its interest has been mainly economic and it seems to play only an economic role in Southeast Asia while avoiding political or security roles. Japan's predominant concern with economic activities in the region is quite understandable because Southeast Asia is Japan's major source of essential raw materials as well as substantial market for her manufactured goods.

However, various changes have occurred in international politics at the global and regional levels over the past forty years since the Second World War. Japan, now a leading economic power second only to the US, has to face these realities and may have to become a more than one-eyed giant in the future. Japan has to play other roles in addition to an economic one as a regional power, not only to commensurate its economic status but also to contribute to the prosperity and stability in the Southeast Asian region.

This paper is an attempt to look at Japan's relations with Southeast Asia, especially ASEAN, and its roles as a regional power.

---

* Dr. Chulacheeb Chinwanno, Director, Center for Asian and Pacific Studies, Thammasat University.

POST-WAR JAPAN AND SOUTHEAST ASIA: ECONOMIC DIPLOMACY

In order to understand Japan's relations with Southeast Asia, one has to look at the post-war Japanese foreign policy, as well as the international conditions in East and Southeast Asia, especially the strategic policy of Japan's major ally, the United States *vis-a-vis* the region.

After the defeat in the Second World War, Japan became reluctant to get involved in international as well as regional politics. It appeared that the main theme of Japanese foreign policy in the post-war period emphasized the separation of economic considerations from political ones (*seikei bunri*).[1] This policy not only contributed significantly to the economic growth of Japan, but also enabled Japan to keep a low profile in international political and security affairs.

The international environment in the 1950s also facilitated Japan's foreign policy, because the global politics was dominated by the United States and its rivalry with the Soviet Union. In addition, the victory of the Chinese Communist Party on mainland China in 1949 and the subsequent Korean War in the early 1950s led the United States to extend the containment policy to Asia. Consequently, the United States decided to boost the recovery of Japanese economy and to make Japan an anti-communist bastion in Asia. Both the United States and Japan[2] also realised that Southeast Asia was strategically and economically important not only because of its location, but also because of the food and raw materials it supplied to Japan as well as to many other countries.

Japan's enthusiasm about the prospect of doing business with Southeast Asia can be seen in the June 16, 1953 statement of Prime Minister Yoshida Shigeru:

> I do not think it is necessary to dwell upon the importance of our relations with Southeast Asia, since we can not expect much from trade with China. The government desires to extend every possible co-operation for the prosperity of the countries of Southeast Asia in the form of capital, technique, service or otherwise in order thus to advance further the relations of reciprocal benefit and common prosperity.[3]

At the same time, several leaders in Southeast Asian countries perceived their countries confronting the problems of communist infiltration, and decided to take on an anti-communist policy. Moreover, they thought of the economic development and industrialisation as a means to cope and contain these problems. Japan was thus looked upon as another country besides the United States which could provide what was needed for their economic development.

Japan then negotiated and concluded the reparation agreements with various countries in Southeast Asia, for example, with Burma in 1954, the Philippines in 1956, Indonesia in 1958, and South Vietnam in 1959. The reparation payments were in the form of goods, equipment and services, and it appeared that "the programme (of war reparations) served to recondition the people of the region to Japanese goods, Japanese spare parts and Japanese practices. . .in brief to a resurrected and refurbished Japanese presence."[4] The reparations payment not only allowed Japan to normalise the relations with Southeast Asian nations, but also paved the way for Japan's expansion of economic activities in the region.

Japan saw the economic viability and political stability of the region as essential for her economic activities. Thus, Japan, for the next two decades began a vigorous pursuit of what Foreign Minister Shigemetsu Mamoru called "economic diplomacy" (*keizai gaiko*); the promotion of trade and economic co-operations in order to stabilise the region.[5]

In addition, Japan also intensified its economic aids to Southeast Asia and had by the early 1970s became the principal aid donor for Indonesia and Malaysia exceeding the United States, and also became the primary donor to the Philippines and Thailand. Japan's economic aids seemed to facilitate the sale of Japanese manufactured goods and to promote trade expansion with Southeast Asia. Moreover, Japanese private investment also poured into the region in search for cheap labour, and by the early 1970s Japan became one of the leading investors in the region.

Japan throughout these years concentrated only on her economic role and avoided the involvement in the politics of the cold war. In fact, Japan left it to the United States to play the "World Policeman" role. As long as the United States remained present in Asia and Southeast Asia, Japan did not have to worry or want to change its rather successful foreign policy of economic diplomacy.

However, it had become increasingly obvious to the people in Southeast Asia that Japanese "economic diplomacy" towards the region was dictated by commercial motives and was mainly concerned with profits from trade and with obtaining natural resources for her industries. As Japan continued to expand her economic activities into the region, anti-Japanese feeling and criticism began to surface.

In Thailand, students, led by the National Students Centre (NSC), organised an anti-Japanese goods movement, boycotting Japanese products at various department stores in Bangkok for 10 days.[6] The students cited the issues of trade imbalance and Japanese economic and cultural aggression and domination as the causes for launching the movement.

The anti-Japanese feeling in Southeast Asia also manifested itself when Japanese Prime Minister Tanaka made a goodwill trip to the region in mid-January 1974. A stormy welcome, including street riots in Indonesia and anti-Japanese demonstrations in Malaysia and Thailand, greeted him and shocked Japan.

These anti-Japanese activities could be seen as a nationalistic reaction to perceived economic "domination" but Japan, as a result of the influx of Japanese goods and the conspicuous presence of Japanese businessmen and economic activities. Moreover, the Japanese trade, aids, and investment patterns were strongly criticised by many people including scholars in Southeast Asian countries.[7]

In the field of trade, the Japanese were criticised for practising restrictive and protectionist policies through tariff and non-tariff barriers, resulting in increased exports from Japan and fewer purchases and imports by the Japanese. This was especially notable in the case of Thailand which had since 1957 suffered a chronic trade imbalance with Japan.

The Japanese aid programme was also criticised as essentially serving Japanese economic interests more than those of the recipients, because much of the aid was tied and structured to benefit Japanese firms. Similar criticism was voiced against Japanese investment practices, which were seen as means of gaining access to minerals and agricultural products needed by Japan at low cost.

Another important factor often cited as a cause of anti-Japanese sentiments was certain behaviours of the resident Japanese businessmen. A leading Indonesian politician once complained, "The Japanese are too exclusive. . .They don't want to mix with our people. . .They have their own clubs, their own restaurants, their schools. It brings back memories of the Japanese occupation."[8] These criticism—valid or not—seemed to be in the minds of many in Southeast Asia at that time.

The anti-Japanese movements in Southeast Asia had a lot of impact on Japanese leaders as well as the public; and Japan started to realise that it could not pursue only economic interests without regarding other considerations. Japan had to improve its image and its relations with Southeast Asia and was in need of a new foreign policy, a new direction. Concurrently, several changes also occurred in the mid-1970s at the international and regional levels, and these new realities forced Japan to consider playing other roles in addition to the economy one.

JAPAN'S POLITICAL ROLE: FUKUDA DOCTRINE

Until the end of the Vietnam War in 1975, the Unites States, Japan's formal ally, played extremely active political and military role in maintaining security and stability in the Southeast Asian region. However, since then there had been a vast change in global and regional politics. The three Indochinese states — South Vietnam, Kampuchea, and Laos — had fallen under communist control. Moreover, the United States had reduced its previously overwhelming influence in the region, while the Soviet Union and China had engaged in fierce competition for incluence in the region.

The five non-communist countries in Southeast Asia, formed a regional organisation called ASEAN since 1967 to enhance economic co-operations, felt a pressing need in 1975 to co-operate closer and to overcome the diverse national interests. Such co-operations, economic as well as political, were considered essential to the growth of national and regional resilience in order to co-exist peacefully with the Communist Indochinese states and to maintain peace and stability in the region.

Japan was also concerned for the future of Southeast Asia because it had enormous stakes. Japan, perceiving ASEAN as a stabilising force in the region, began to involve itself more fully with ASEAN, on the multilateral basis as well as with each individual member country. Japan also tried to improve its economic relations with ASEAN and expanded the cultural and academic exchanges to improve its image.

At the same time, Japan also felt concerned with the future development of the three Communist states in Indochina, as these states were seen as "an integral part of Southeast Asia," Japan, seeing economic potentials in these countries, wanted to have friendly relations with them and proposed to help them rebuild their countries. The Japanese argued that this would eventually not only have beneficial effects on the stability of the area but would also affect the degree of independence the Indochinese states were able to manifest in their relations with the Soviet Union and China.

In fact, Japan wanted to be friendly with all, communist as well as non-communist states in Southeast Asia. Japan was also looking for a political role to play in the region because it gradually realised it was becoming a regional power in Southeast Asia in the post-Vietnam War era. Japan was nonetheless somewhat reluctant and played its new role cautiously.

The attendence of Prime Minister Fukuda at the Second ASEAN Summit Conference in Kuala Lumpur, held to celebrate the tenth anniversary of ASEAN in August 1977, was quite significant because this was the first meeting ever to be held jointly between a Japanese prime minister and ASEAN heads of governments. During the following visit to ASEAN countries between August 9-18, 1977, Prime Minister Fukuda announced in Manila what was later known as the "Fukuda Doctrine." This could be seen as Japan's attempt to clarify its intention and roles in Southeast Asia.[9]

Three basic principles were set forth in the "Fukuda Doctrine" as follows:

> *First,* Japan, a nation committed to peace, rejects the role of a military power, and on that basis is resolved to contribute to the peace and prosperity of Southeast Asia and of the world community.
>
> *Second*, Japan, as a true friend of the countries of Southeast Asia, will do its best for consolidating the relationship of mutual confidence and trust based on "heart to heart" understanding with these countries, in wide-ranging fields covering not only political and economic areas but also social and cultural areas.
>
> *Third,* Japan will be an equal partner of ASEAN and its member countries, and co-operate positively with them in their own efforts to strengthen their solidarity and resilience, together with other nations of the like mind outside the region, while aiming at fostering a relationship based on mutual understanding with the nations of Indochina and will thus contribute to the building of peace and prosperity throughout Southeast Asia.

In addition, Fukuda also promised in his Manila speech to respond to ASEAN's request by providing a loan of Yen totalling US $1 billion to the ASEAN member countries to be used for five major industrial projects, one in each of the member countries. The Fukuda Doctrine and the Yen loan represented a firm commitment of Japan towards the prosperity and stability of ASEAN. It also represented Japan's serious effort to articulate explicitly her political role and policy towards Southeast Asia. Japan came to believe that to maintain stability, Japan must play a dual role, economic as well as political, by helping to promote economic development and by contributing to the strengthening of ties between ASEAN and the three Communist Indochinese countries while avoiding the role of a military power.

Japan thus established diplomatic relation with Vietnam, and in 1976 concluded an agreement to extend ¥0.5 billion in grant aid to Vietnam, in addition to the ¥8.5 billion in grant aid previously given to Hanoi as reconstruction aid. This grant would be used by Vietnam to purchase from Japan various equipment and materials necessary for her economic development.

The Fukuda Doctrine provided the framework for Japan to get involved in Southeast Asian regional politics, and Japan attempted to play a positive political role in bridging ASEAN and communist states in Indochina, and to bring both sides into peaceful co-existence. But this policy had proved increasingly difficult to maintain as a result of the recurrence of armed conflicts in Indochina in late 1978. Japan had to abandon this even-handed policy when Vietnam invaded and occupied its neighbouring communist state, Kampuchea, in January 1979. The Vietnamese occupation created tensions along Thai-Kampuchean borders as well as between ASEAN and Indochinese states.[10]

JAPAN AND SOUTHEAST ASIA IN THE 1980S: AN ACTIVE REGIONAL POWER

The political-military environment in Southeast Asia had experienced radical changes by the end of the 1970s. The security and stability of the region remained threatened by perennial conflicts, while the United States continued to reduce its role and had became increasingly passive. At the same time, the Sino-Soviet competition for regional influence intensified and greatly affected the relations and conflicts between two Communist states, Vietnam and Kampuchea.

Vietnam, suspicious of China and Kampuchea collaboration, decided to turn on to the Soviet Union by joining the Comecon and signing the Treaty of Peace and Friendship with the Soviet in 1978. Then Vietnam launched an invasion and occupied Kampuchea in January 1979. A month later, China attacked Vietnam so as to "teach them a lesson."

ASEAN was very much alarmed by these military actions, especially the Vietnamese military aggression against Kampuchea. Moreover, the continuing presence of large Vietnamese forces in that country and Laos, as well as the close alliance between Vietnam and the Soviet Union caused grave security concerns for ASEAN, especially Thailand. ASEAN denounced the aggression and called for the immediate and total withdrawal of Vietnamese troops from Kampuchea so as to allow the Kampuchean people to exercise their rights of self-determination from outside influence. ASEAN had called all their friends, the United States, Japan, China and other peace-loving countries to support their stance.

As for Japan, her response to the Vietnamese invasion of Kampuchea was similar to that of the United States, by endorsing the ASEAN position on this issue in the form of support for the ASEAN sponsored UN Resolution, calling for the withdrawal of Vietnamese troops. Japan continued to maintain its diplomatic ties with Vietnam, hoping that such ties were necessary to promote Vietnam's independence from the Soviet Union. However, Japan's hope had not been realised so far.

In general, Japan's image in Southeast Asia, especially in ASEAN in the 1980s had improved significantly, since the anti-Japanese movement a decade ago, and its economic and cultural relations with ASEAN had greatly expanded, quantitatively as well as qualitatively. In the economic realm, Japan in the 1980s continued to be the biggest investor[11] and trading partner for all the ASEAN countries and continued to be the biggest aid donor to ASEAN. Such forms of economic co-operations and transactions in the areas of trade and investment have benefitted ASEAN as well as Japan. In such complex relationships, disagreements and conflicts of interests were expected to arise, but both ASEAN and Japan seemed to be able to find ways to solve these problems together without straining their relations. Japan and ASEAN have become closely interdependent. Japan has been viewed by ASEAN as an important economic power in the region and is expected to play an active economic role in helping ASEAN to develop their economies. ASEAN countries want more direct investment from Japan, especially in the export-oriented industries, and also more transfer of technology. In addition, ASEAN countries also want access to the Japanese market with less tariff barrier, and want to be treated fairly and equally.

To compliment these positive role in the economic arena, Japan should also play some political roles. As a regional power Japan has the responsibilities to maintain stability and security in Southeast Asia. It is understandable that while Japan supports ASEAN on the Kampuchean issue, Japan does not want to alienate Hanoi too much. Japan also tries to bridge the ASEAN countries and the Communist Indochinese states and to bring them into a peaceful co-existence.

Japan also provides some creative proposals to bring about the political settlement in Kampuchea. At the ASEAN Ministerial Conference with the Dialogue Partners held in June 1984, Shintaro Abe, then Foreign Minister put forth a three-point proposal intended to give additional thrust to the joint appeal advanced in 1983 by the ASEAN Foreign Ministers. The proposal reads as follows:

1. When partial withdrawals of Vietnamese troops from the Thai-Cambodian border area in the west of Cambodia, the establishment of safety zones in that area, and the introduction of peace-keeping forces to ensure the respect for and the safeguarding of the zones have all been realised with the consent of all countries concerned, Japan will be prepared to make a countribution in bearing the expenses for such peace-keeping activities as may be required by an international arrangement and to extend humanitarian assistance to the Cambodian people in the safety zones.
2. When the Vietnamese forces have completely withdrawn from Cambodia and free electrons are to be held under international supervision, Japan will be prepared to extend cooperation in sending personnel for election supervision and supplying materials and equipment of a non-military nature, including the means of transportation necessary for holding elections.
3. When true peace has been restored in Cambodia, Japan will be prepared to render as much economic and technical co-operation as possible for reconstruction in Vietnam, Laos and Cambodia.

Japan's support on the Kampuchean issue and its initiative and "Creative Diplomacy"[12] have appreciated by ASEAN. Moreover, ASEAN also hopes that Japan would continue to play an active political role, because Japan has been seen as a stabilising force in the regional politics of Southeast Asia.

In the meantime, Japan has been under pressure to move into the military/security area.[13] This trend may be inevitable as a result of at least two factors. One is the increasing presence of the Soviet force near Japan in the Pacific, especially in the four islands north of Hokkaido. Moreover, the Soviet Far Eastern Fleet has been greatly enhanced by the availability of facilities in both Danang and Cam Ranh Bay in Vietnam.

The Soviet could choke off Japan in times of a crisis. Another factor is the pressure from the United States on Japan to shoulder a grater defence burden, as well as to protect the Sea Lanes of Communications (SLOC). These two factors would push Japan to increase its defence budget close to the 1 per cent limit or beyond that in the near future, and to expand its military/security role as well. On the other hand, Prime Minister Nakasone has repeatedly stated that Japan would not become a military power.

ASEAN leaders seem to take the words of the Japanese Prime Minister, and have not been much concerned with the increase of the deference budget, as long as the increase in gradual and with the approval of the United States and on the condition that Japan will not go nuclear in the future. As for the defence of the Sea lanes of Communications it is understood that the one thousand nautical mile radius would not include the ASEAN seas. Moreover, it is the impression that there may not be any consensus among ASEAN on the expansion of Japan's security role in the future. For Thailand, some form of Japanese security role in Southeast Asia may be welcome if it complimented the US's role and is not objected by other ASEAN members. Malaysia and Indonesia seem to object to Japan's direct military role in the region, especially Malaysia may objected because it goes against the concept of the Zone of Peace, Freedom and Neutrality (ZOPFAN). Indonesia may tolerate a gradual military buildup under some conditions. Jusuf Wanandi of the Centre for Strategic and International Studies in Jakarta wrote in 1979: "A gradual buildup of Japan's military capability can be accepted by ASEAN, granted that Japan would take the efforts to consult ASEAN on a regular basis and granted that this buildup would be pursued within the framework of the defence treaty between Japan and the US."[14] It appears that ASEAN countries, for the time being, do not entertain the idea of Japan's security role in the region. In fact, ASEAN seems to be more comfortable with Japan's concept of "comprehensive security." This concept, representing an attempt at a more comprehensive definition of security, does not mean only the military aspect of the security, but also the political and economic aspects. In fact, the emphasis is on the latter, which seems to correspond to ASEAN's concept of resilience. Japan and ASEAN can co-operate on this "comprehensive security."

CONCLUSION

Japan has a major role to play in Southeast Asia. In fact, the decade following the end of the Vietnam War can be viewed as a watershed in

Japan's relations with Southeast Asia, a period during which the economic and political ties developed and matured. Japan is regarded as a major regional power and is expected to play active roles in the economic and political arena, so as to bring about the development, prosperity and stability in Southeast Asia.

NOTES AND REFERENCES

1. This concept was conceived in the 1950s as a means for Japan to trade with Communist China. See Masahide Shibuzawa, *Japan and the Asian Pacific Region: Profile of Change* (London: Croom Helm for the Royal Institute of International Affairs, 1984).
2. See J.W. Dower, *Empire and Aftermath: Yoshida Shigemaru and the Japanese, 1878-1954* (Cambridge: Harvard University Press, 1979).
3. Cited by K.V. Kesavan, *Japan's Relations with Southeast Asia, 1952-60* (Bombay: Someiya Publication, 1972), p. 123.
4. Raul S. Manglapus, *Japan in Southeast Asia: Collision Course* (New York: Carnegie Endowment for International Peace, 1976), p. 4.
5. Donald C. Hellmann, *Japan and East Asia: The New International Order* (New York: Praeger Publications, 1972), p. 68.
6. David Morell & Chai-anan Samudavanija, *Political Conflict in Thailand* (Cambridge, Mass.: Oelgeschiager, Gunn & Hain, 1981), p. 141.
7. For Thailand, see Khien Theeravit, *Khwam samphan tang settakit rawang thai loe yeepoon* (The Japanese-Thai Economic Relations), (Bangkok: Social Science Research institute, Chuialongkorn University, 1974).
8. Cited by Manglapus, *Japan's Relations*, p. 48.
9. On Fukuda Doctrine, see William W. Haddad, "Japan, the Fukuda Doctrine and ASEAN," in *Contemporary Southeast Asia,* 2:1 (June 1980), pp. 10-29, and also Yano Toru, "The Fukuda Doctrine and Its Implications for Southeast Asia: A Japanese Perspective," in *Southeast Asian Affairs 1978* (Singapore: Institute of Southeast Asian Studies, 1979), pp. 60-64.
10. See Chulacheeb Chinwanno, "The Prospects of Security for ASEAN," presented at the Asian Dialogue Second Odawara Symposium on the ASEAN-Japan Relationships in a Global Context, Sponsored by the Japan Center for International Exchange and the East-West Seminar, Odawara, Japan, March 3-4, 1979.
11. On the Japanese investment in ASEAN, see Sueo Sekiguchi (ed.), *ASEAN-Japan Relations: Investment* (Singapore: Institute of Southeast Asian Studies, 1983); and in Thailand, see Chulacheeb Chinwanno and Somsak Tambunlertchai, "Japanese Investment in Thailand and Its Prospects in the 1980s," *Ibid.*, pp. 181-226.
12. Shintaro Abe, *Creative Diplomacy: Japan's Initiative for Peace and Prosperity* (Tokyo: Ministry of Foreign Affairs, Japan, 1985).
13. Frances Lai Fung-wai, "Japan's Defence Policy and Its Implications for the ASEAN Countries," in *Southeast Asian Affairs, 1984* (Singapore, Institute of Southeast Asian Studies, 1984), pp. 56-60.
14. See Jusuf Wanandi, *Security Dimensions of the Asian-Pacific Region in the 1980s* (Jakarta: Centre for Strategic and International Studies, 1979).

24

Indo-Japanese Relations in Changing World Scenario**

HARCHARAN SINGH JOSH*

Our Prime Minister recently paid a visit to Japan. He declared on his return that both India and Japan will now forge a new relationship in the post-Cold War period. He emphasized that "important countries like India and Japan have to define their future roles in this scenario both in Asia and the rest of the World."

Shri Narasimha Rao was happy with the discussions he held with the Japanese leadership and a cross-section of the industry. It is a matter of great satisfaction that his talks with the scientists and intellectuals had given him the opportunity to explore new avenues to cooperation. Indeed there is large scope for cooperation between the Universities of Japan and India on specific areas of research. Prospects of Indo-Japanese economic cooperation appear bright after Prime Minister's visit.

Shri P.V. Narasimha Rao's visit to Japan has opened a new chapter in relationship between the two countries. It is, however, clear that the Prime Ministers of India and Japan have for the first time initiated political dialogue which may given an added dimension to what has

* President, Indian Council of World Affairs, New Delhi.

** Address delivered at the symposium on "Indo-Japanese Relations in Changing World Scenario" at Sapru House, New Delhi, July 3, 1992 hitherto been a limited relationship. Japan is keen on extending areas of cooperation between the two countries in view of fast changing international scene. Both wish to work together for reshaping the U.N.'s structure to reflect current realities.

There is a growing realization in Japan on India's stand on NPT. India is against the presence of nuclear and other weapons of mass destruction anywhere, and calls for the dismantling of existing arsenals and halting of production and testing of nuclear weapons.

The bilateral talks that the Indian and the Japanese Prime Ministers have agreed to assume importance in this context.

Japan now has a better appreciation of India's economic needs and has welcomed steps taken for liberalization of economy.

The Indian Prime Minister Shri P.V. Narasimha Rao's visit to Japan comes seven years after the last visit by a Head of the Indian Government, viz. that of late Shri Rajiv Gandhi in 1985. In many ways Shri Rao's visit must be regarded as being of much greater significance for fostering an Asian view on World developments.

The dramatic change in the world situation during the last couple of years including the disintegration of the Soviet Union leading to the end of Cold War as well as radical reforms introduced in India by the Indian Government last year have had a direct impact on the entire course of Indo-Japanese relationship.

In the immediate post-war period the Japanese were immensely pleased when the Indian Judge in the International War Crimes Tribunal pronounced that Japan was not guilty of any War Crimes of which it was accused. India was further admired by Japan when Nehru refused to accept the 5% reparations from Japan. Visit of Shri Jawaharlal Nehru and President Rajendra Prasad laid foundations for stable friendship between Japan and India.

Japan is now super-power in economy and is increasingly playing vital role in the Councils of the World. In industry it is giant which has dwarfed the West. India has taken bold initiative and is pursuing its economic policies with vigour and determination. Japan promises to contribute vitally to India's economic development.

The government and people of India attach great importance to bilateral ties—historical, cultural and religious—between India and Japan.

Political events of the recent past in India has demonstrated the viability of its democratic institutions and stability of its polity.

Apart from trade with Japan, India and Japan have set up Joint Sector Projects both in the public and private sector in India. Japan is India's biggest bilateral donor. This position has been consistently maintained for the last five years.

The Indian Prime Minister Rao's visit to Japan has taken place at a time when India and Japan are celebrating the 40th anniversary of the signing of bilateral Treaty of Peace and Amity (9 June 1952). Earlier in 1951 India declined becoming a signatory of San Francisco Peace Treaty with Japan because the Indian government objected that the Security Pact with the US should be negotiated after the US occupation of Japan ended. The Indo-Japanese Treaty of Peace and Amity was the first one Japan signed on terms of equality after gaining its sovereignty.

Thus ever since India became independent in 1947, the two nations have enjoyed friendly relations continuously. Historically, the bond originates from Buddhism which came to Japan in the 6th Century. India and Japan thus share common spiritual and cultural heritage. With the end of Cold War now, it is time that both the countries engage in a meaningful relations in view of the changing global context.

India and Japan can gain immensely from each other's experience.

There is a need to develop closer understanding of each other policies and explore ways and means of developing common approach to world events.

25

India and Japan: The Partnership is Forty Years Old**

P.A. NARASIMHA MURTHY*

The 40th anniversary of the formal opening of diplomatic ties between India and Japan is being observed this year. A number of events have already taken place in Japan to mark this occasion and more are planned to be held in India between August and December, including the raising of an Indo-Japanese Friendship Cherry Garden with saplings and seeds specially flown from Japan for this purpose. Thus to remember and celebrate is to provide fresh nourishment to a relationship that has been cordial, steady and free from dramatic twists and turns. More so at a time when attention world-wide has shifted from military relationships to those which are built on cultural and economic foundations.

NO INDIAN REPRESENTATIVE AT SAN FRANCISCO

In 1971 one of Japan's highly-respected dailies, the *Asahi Shimbun*, carried a series of articles on Japan's relations with the United States of

* Professor & Chairman, Centre for East Asian Studies, School of International Studies, Jawaharlal Nehru University, New Delhi.

** Adapted and enlarged from an address delivered at Tokyo on 9 June 1992.

America. One of them covered the San Francisco Peace Conference of 8 September 1951, and made a very pertinent reference to the notable absence of China at the conference. What the article forgot to add, due to oversight no doubt, was that another important Asian country was also absent at the San Franscisco Opera House where the peace treaty was signed by 49 nations, including Japan. That country was the Indian Republic.

India was invited to join the conference, but chose to stay out because it believed that the peace-making process reflected the division of the world into two antagonistic camps, and participating in it would run counter to its endeavour to create a climate of peace in the world a climate which million of war-weary Japanese people themselves hoped for. In Asia, in particular, peace was of paramount importance as large parts of this vast continent were achieving national independence after countries of political subordination and lopsided economic growth, and needed an environment in which the hopes of material improvement that swayed the minds of millions of people could be fulfilled. Furthermore, India's decision to abstain from joining the San Francisco gathering accorded well with its determination not to precipitate the division of the world into "we" and "they" but work for the spread of a spirit of co-operation, equality, friendship and tolerance among nations based upon full respect for national freedom and national pride. Peace and friendship were also the goals sought by the people of Japan.

It is not necessary, nor is it desirable at this juncture, to dwell at length on the complex situation which then existed in Asia and the world. Suffice it to say that feelings were still running very high over the unfortunate events which took place between 1931 and 1945. There was a sense of despair, gloom and isolation in Japan, while the urge for vindictive action was strong elsewhere. Having just then attained freedom from 200 years of British rule, India sought to create a sense of optimism and an atmosphere in which the unfortunate experience of the past did not come in the way of thinking and planning for the future. It was in this spirit that representatives of India at the Tokyo Tribunal, the UN Commission for Asia and the Far East (now the Economic and Social Council for Asia and the Pacific), the International Labour Organization and the World Health Organization, to mention only a few instances, took the position that the sad events of the recent past should not deny Japan and the Japanese people a place of honour, equality and contentment in the comity of nations. It was in the same spirit that it chose to conclude a separate bilateral accord with Japan to establish peace and diplomatic relations.

It is appropriate at this point to recall that as early as June 1948 the Indian representative to the Plenary Session of the International Labour Organization (held at San Francisco) moved a formal resolution proposing Japan's readmission into the organization. In like manner, Japan's admission to the Economic Commission for Asia and the Far East was not only supported by India but advanced by one year due to the helpful role played by the then Indian Executive Secretary of the Commission. Dr. Saburo Okita, who then represented Japan at the ECAFE, makes an appreciative reference to this in one of his writings, and records that the Executive-Secretary was also instrumental in getting representation for Japan on the Commission's staff. India also put its full weight behind Japan's application, first submitted in 1952, for membership of the UN, though alone it was not in a position to do much in that world body. It may sound boastful to dwell on these little details, but the purpose in recalling them is to stress the point that it was not expediency, nor matters of the moment, but a genuine concern for a representative world system which led India to support Japan's integration with the family of nations.

THE TREATY OF PEACE: A SYMBOL OF PERPETUAL AMITY AND FRIENDSHIP

The Treaty of Peace between India and Japan was signed in Tokyo on 9 June 1952 after brief negotiations were held alternatively in New Delhi and Tokyo. The instruments of ratification were exchange in New Delhi on 27 August 1952. In fact, diplomatic relations between the two nations had been opened a few weeks before the formal signing of this accord. In May 1952, the Indian Liaison Mission in Tokyo and the Japanese Overseas Agency in New Delhi were elevated to the status of Embassies, with K.K. Chettur as the first ambassador of free India to Japan, and Ichiro Kawasaki as Japanese Charge d' Affaires in New Delhi, pending the arrival of Tsutomu Nishiyama as ambassador.

The bilateral accord was based on a long-term vision of bringing together the people of India and Japan in a bond of warm friendship and co-operation. The eleven-article accord opened with the declaration: "There shall be *firm and perpetual peace and amity* between India and Japan and their respective peoples." (Emphasis added.) In articles

VI(a)(b) and IX(a)(b) both sides demonstrated wisdom in giving up their claims, including compensation for damages caused by action taken against the nationals of each other during the years 1941-45. In brief, it was a simple, straight-forward accord in which little scope was left for any problem to arise between the two countries and become a source of friction or misunderstanding between them. The treaty was indeed a landmark in so far as it established a "new pattern of international reconciliation" among nations. It was the first such bilateral accord that two Asian nations concluded after the San Francisco Treaty, barring the Japan-nationalist China (Taiwan) Peace Treaty of 28 April 1952.

OTHER BASIC ACCORDS: CREATING AN ECONOMIC PARTNERSHIP

The foundations of friendship, good will, and mutual respect having thus been laid, the two countries initiated steps to conclude such other agreements as were required to widen the basis of their relationship in accordance with the spirit of Article II(a) of the Treaty of Peace. Let me briefly touch upon four important agreements which were concluded within the first decade of the coming into force of the Treaty of Peace.

(1) On 26 November 1955 an agreement on civil aviation was signed, the purpose of which was to (*a*) open direct air services between India and Japan, (*b*) save the flow of precious foreign exchange on travel by Indian and Japanese nationals between their two countries, and (*c*) encourage the national airlines of each country to secure its legitimate share of the growing international air traffic market. In addition, the agreement helped mutual extension of airport facilities such as the availability of fuel, lubricating oils and equipment needed by aircraft as well as MFN treatment in respect of customs duties and inspection charges. (The agreement was replaced by a revised one, signed on 28 September 1973.)

(2) The next to come was a cultural accord which was signed on 29 October 1956. The preamble to the Cultural Agreement between India and Japan says that the signatories to it were inspired by a desire to, (*a*) cement "centuries of cultural relations between the two countries" (*b*) "promote and develop closer cultural relations in the future," and (*c*) also promote and deepen "in every possible way . . .the relations and understanding between the two countries." Schemes for regular exchanges in wide-ranging fields such as education, science, sports,

library materials, the theatrical arts, and audio-visual media like radio programmes, television features and films, were contemplated in the agreement. In order to monitor these exchanges the agreement provided for the creation of a Mixed Commission consisting of representatives from both sides. The cultural accord was initially to be effective for a period of ten years, and indefinitely thereafter unless one of the contracting parties wanted its termination. As neither party desired to terminate it, the agreement is still in force and provides a framework for cultural exchanges between the two nations.

(3) An agreement on commerce was signed on 4 February 1958, which laid the foundation for the growth of bilateral trade, and economic and industrial co-operation. The agreement guaranteed (*a*) *equality* in respect of entry, residence and internal travel by the nationals of each side in the territory of the other and also in respect of navigation and entry of merchant marine of each in the ports and harbours of the other; (*b*) *reciprocity* in matters concerning customs duties, internal taxes and charges levied on imported goods; and (*c*) most-favoured-nation treatment in regard to access to law courts and the right to property and contracts. It also contained a clause on the exchange of scientific and technical knowledge in order to promote economic development and improvement of the living standards of the citizens of India and Japan.

(4) One of the last basic accords was the agreement on avoidance of the double taxation, signed on 5 January 1960. Tax sparing treaties are an important instrument of economic policy, especially in creating the right kind of investment climate and guaranteeing prospective foreign investors that the value of their investment is not eroded through taxation in both the source and host countries. The Indo-Japanese Agreement on the Avoidance of Double Taxation covered taxes on profits, salaries and remuneration earned by companies, corporations and individuals. It was of special interest to India in the context of extending incentives to foreign, particularly Japanese, investment and technology flow into its economy. (On 8 April 1969 some of the provisions of this agreement were modified by mutual agreement, in order to make them harmonious with the amended tax legislation in India.)

MORE AGREEMENTS

These basic accords were further supplemented by a number of other private and quasi-official agreements like (1) the agreement between the

Federation of Indian Chambers of Commerce and Industry and the Japan Commercial Arbitration Association, regarding the use of arbitration facilities in trade, May 1955; (2) the first yen credit agreement, 4 February 1958; (3) the first long-term agreement (10 year) on the export of iron ore to Japan, 19 March 1958; (4) the Hindu-Hitachi agreement on training Indian students in Japan in engineering and technical fields, 20 October 1959; (5) the agreement on the establishment of a prototype production and training centre for small-scale industries at Howarh, 25 January 1960; (6) the second long-term agreement (15 years) on export of iron ore to Japan, 8 March 1960; (7) the agreement with Citizen Watch Company for the establishment of a watch factory at the Hindustan Machine Tools Limited, Bangalore, 25 March 1960; (8) the agreement on setting up a training centre for processing marine products at Mangalore (Karnataka) to help India conserve and increase its fisheries resources in and around its costal waters, 31 March 1962; and (9) the first agreement on creating agricultural demonstration farms with Japanese support to train Indian farmers in the techniques of multiple cropping, intensive cultivation and scientific use of chemical fertilizers, 23 April 1962.

The peace treaty and other accords were intended to be proof of good intentions and were meant essentially to lay down a framework within which bilateral economic relations were to be conducted. This was necessary for two reasons: (1) Both India and Japan gave precedence to economic over other matters as they both faced the daunting task of providing food, clothing, shelter and other amenities to their citizens. (2) Some ground rules were necessary in order to march two economic systems which followed different paths — one choosing the path of planning and the other relying largely of the market mechanism. Using the complementary nature of their economics, they sought to link them closer together through these agreements and accords. And some of them have had a critical role in providing strength to the partnership. Thus, for example, the yen credit agreement of February 1958 was the beginning of Japan's commitment to India's economic progress and industrial development. The thirty-three yen credits which have so far been extended have made Japan the largest provider of bilateral economic assistance to India. It is not the size, nor even the number of instalments, that is very important. What is of significance is the fact that this assistance has gone into both public and private sectors and to fields like energy, fertilizers, power, railway modernization, expansion of port and harbour facilities, and health and family welfare schemes. The yen credits have indeed played a vital role in changing India's economic profile.

The agreements on the development and export of iron ore, all of them private as far as Japan is concerned, and quasi-official from the point of view of India as they were concluded by public sector entities like the State Trading Corporation and the Minerals and Metals Trading Corporation, had a slightly different kind of role to play. They literally forged an "iron nexus" between India and Japan. By offering an assured market the steel industry of Japan helped India develop its wealth hidden in the form of iron ore and convert it into precious foreign exchange which went into the implementation of numerous industrial projects. Iron ore hewn from ridges like the "ox Hump" (Bailadilla) and "horse face" (Kudremukh) fed the blast furnaces of Japan's steel industry which converted into steel and steel products, and exported them in large quantities. It was no accident that precisely when exported iron ore was the top foreign exchange earner for India, exported steel and steel products had the same status in Japan's international trade transactions.

EXCHANGE OF VISITS: OFFICIAL AND NON-OFFICIAL

Outside the framework of these accords and agreements, what added further strength to the yet fragile Indo-Japanese relationship was the exchange of visits by political leaders, statesmen and captains of industry. Broadly speaking, this exchange fell into two categories. (1) There were visits by goodwill delegations to promote people-to-people understanding, goodwill-*cum*-economic delegations to study and explore economic opportunities, parliamentary delegations to foster closer relations among legislators, and arts and theatrical groups to foster links between Indian and Japanese artists and theater persons. Of these, there was high frequency of visits by goodwill-*cum*-economic missions throughout the 1950s and the early 1960s. They observed, studied and assessed the opportunities generated by economic development in the two countries and tried to match the requirements of the two economies in such manner as to make bilateral co-operation most effective and mutually beneficial. These early missions laid the foundation for co-operation in agriculture, health care, medicine, mining and industry. From Japan came missions led by prominent men like Taketora Ogata, Taizo Ishizaka, Heitaro Inagaki, Shin Ichi Takasugi and

Shigeo Nagano, to recall only a few. The Inagaki and Nagano missions made gestures which eventually resulted in the creation of a Leprosarium in Agra, and a small Japanese cultural monument in the form of a tea pavilion in the precincts of the Japanese Embassy in New Delhi. From India went delegations led by captains of industry like M.J. Vaidya, J.V. Somayajulu and M.R. Ruia to study the economic partnership. It was during this period that Professor P.C. Mahalanobis, adviser to the Indian Prime Minister on economic planning and also a member of the Planning Commission, went to Japan to initiate talks on joint studies on economic development and exchange of information and experience in economic planning. That visit resulted in the birth of the Committees for the study of Economic Development in India and Japan, later re-designated as the India-Japan Study committees.

(2) Then there were visits by statesmen and heads of state or their representatives which were largely ceremonial, formal and symbolic. In October 1956 Vice-President S. Radhakrishnan, in October 1957 Prime Minister Jawaharlal Nehru, and in September 1958 President Rajendra Prasad went to Japan, taking with them the message of resurgent India and good will of the people of India towards the people of Japan. These were reciprocated by visits to India by Prime Minister Nobusuke Kishi in May 1957, the then Crown Prince and Princess, and now the Emperor and Express of Japan, in November-December 1960, and Prime Minister Hayato Ikeda in November 1961, all representing Japan's sturdy pragmatism and determination to build a new social order as well as carrying with them the warm feelings of the people of Japan towards the Indian nation and its citizens.

The then Crown Prince paid a ceremonial and symbolic visit to India in November-December 1960, and on 30 November laid the foundation-stone of India International Centre (at Lodi Gardens, New Delhi), which was being raised as an important cultural and intellectual centre on the model of the International House of Japan, established in 1952 in the Azabu district of Tokyo. the President of the Board of Trustees of the IIC, C.D. Deshmukh observed on the occasion that India and Japan had begun to revive their old relations blurred by the "unpredictable and erratic course of history."

Exchange of Prime Ministerial visits has been useful in creating an opportunity for the highest political leaders of the two countries to hold a dialogue not only on bilateral issues but on regional as well as global problems. Since 1957 eight rounds of the Prime Ministerial dialogue have been held (not counting the talks held during Prime Minister Indira Gandhi's brief stay in Tokyo, August 1982, on her way back from the United States and Prime Minister Rajiv Gandhi's talks with his Japanese counterpart, October 1987, when he stopped briefly at Tokyo on his way to Canada to attend the Commonwealth Premiers Conference, including the Rao-Miyazawa talks held in the last week of June this year.

PRIME MINISTER NEHRU IN JAPAN: SENSITIVE APPRECIATION

It is pertinent here to add a few words about Prime Minister Jawaharlal Nehru's visit to Japan. He was there from 4 to 13 October 1957, and was the first Asian statesman of stature to visit Japan after the end of the war. He went there, he saw, and he conquered the minds and hearts of the Japanese people.*

Nehru in turn was conquered by what he saw here. In a note which he circulated among chief ministers of the Indian states immediately upon his return from Japan, he candidly said: "Some of my previous impressions I have had to change as a result of closer acquaintance." What we see in that note is a very sensitive understanding of, and appreciation for, the endeavour which the Japanese people were making to overcome the adversity which had overtaken them in the recent past; an admiration for the fortitude with which people submitted themselves to discipline in order to strengthen the nation and its economy, for their artistry, and for their skill to make small things go far.** Comparing India's experience with that of Japan in respect of ideas and institutions received from the West, Nehru noted that Japan had not blindly copied them but adapted them to suit its requirements and that had resulted in a good deal of saving. India, in contrast, had tried to reproduce the European and American models in administration and industry which was providing very expensive and far removed from Indian conditions of life.

---

* I was then a casual student attached to the Department of Agricultural Economics, Tokyo University, and vividly remember the spontaneous welcome Nehru received wherever he went. My friends in Japan who admired the Indian leader used to remind me that Nehru represented the spirit of New Asia, not just India.

** Nehru's fascination for Japanese landscape gardening provided the stimulus for the design of the Buddha Jayanti Park on the ridge in New Delhi according to Japanese principles.

INSTITUTIONAL ARRANGEMENTS TO CONDUCT INDO-JAPANESE RELATIONS

In the 1960s some long-term arrangements were made to conduct bilateral relations and monitor their progress. The Indian "Committee of Three", for instance, was increased in 1962 with a view to promoting interest in Japan's economic development and study the usefulness of that country's experience in our own development. Located in the Planning Commission, the Committee was expected to (*a*) maintain close liaison with its Japanese counterpart which had been created four years earlier, (*b*) collect and disseminated information relating to the state of the Japanese economy, (*c*) organize periodical roundtable conferences to review the state of bilateral relations and make suitable recommendations for their improvement, and (*d*) initiate basic studies which might add to the areas of understanding between the two countries. Complementing this, the business communities of the two nations agreed, in February 1966, to create a joint forum for the purpose of strengthening bilateral trade and economic relations. Meeting alternately in India and Japan, the India-Japan Business Cooperation Committees have played an important role in the expansion of Indo-Japanese trade, Joint venture and technology transactions. (The 23rd joint assembly of the two national committees was held in New Delhi in January 1992.) The foreign service bureaucracies of the two countries also set up in November 1966 the annual Secretary Level conference to exchange views on bilateral matters as well as global problems of mutual concern. In 1978 the Conference was raised to the level of Foreign Ministers.

CULTURAL RELATIONS

The long journey of *mahayana* Buddhism from India to Japan some fourteen hundred years ago and its influence on Japanese life are well-known facts. Being more pragmatic and this-worldly than the ascetic *theravada* branch, *mahayana* Buddhism went well with the Japanese temperament; with it also went many elements of ancient Indian culture and mythology. In modern times, particularly in the last quarter of a century or so, there has been a reverse flow of cultural influences from Japan to India. A reference was made earlier to the tea pavilion standing in the precincts of the Japanese Embassy in New Delhi.

That was donated in 1958 by the Japanese steel team which came to India to negotiate the purchase of iron ore. It was went to be a symbolic if event to mark the beginning of bilateral relations and also create an interest among Indian people in the finer aspects of Japanese culture. A tea pavilion was chosen for this gesture because it represents the essence of *zen* Buddhism. The pavilion is made of three elements: its immediate environment represents evanescence; the garden in which it is generally built represents the selflessness of *dharma*; and the pavilion's interior stands for *nirvana*. The pavilion's external environment suggests that life is constantly changing. It is all transitoriness outside, while inside it is absolute peace. Nothing could have been a more fitting gift than this pavilion to build a cultural bridge between the two countries.

In the years since then many other aspects of Japanese culture have begun to register their presence in India and make an impact on wider sections of the Indian people. Ikebana, Kabuki and Noh are more widely known today among Indian than, say, 25 years ago.

The cultural agreement of 1956 provided a vast scope for developing exchanges in a wide area, ranging from education to the visual arts. New schemes were added to the ongoing exchanges by a decision of the Mixed Commission in 1973. Co-operation in joint research, promoting short- and long-term facilities for teaching the Japanese language in India, arranging visits by Indian students to attend courses of study in Japan, gifting of books, increasing the number of fellowships and a host of other activities have now been brought under the purview of Indo-Japanese cultural exchange. The Festival of India and the Japan Month celebrations which were organized a couple of years ago in Japan and in India respectively reflect the growing cultural interaction between the two countries and their growing interest in the history, culture, institutions and traditions of each other.

THE TASK AHEAD

There have been years of anxiety and concern about the health of the relationship. Between 1970 and the early 1980s, developments extraneous to this bilateral relationship cast their shadow on it and threatened to leave it damaged. It is, however, a measure of the wisdom and maturity of the leadership of the two countries that this was not allowed to happen, and the relationship remained insulated against those developments. As a result, trade continued to expand, though at a much slower pace than the depth and versatility of the Indian economy could support, yen loans continued to be extended at a steadily rising level, and joint venture arrangements were continued to be made between Indian and Japanese enterprises. In the early 1980s, new strength was sought to be given to the relationship through frequent exchanges of high level delegations, holding of cultural events, continuing contracts at different levels, and creating a "fast channel" to process proposals for business tieups with Japan.

India and Japan have stepped into the last decade of the century with a relationship that is correct, largely economic in content, and is a little away from the main current of world politics and the changing balance of power. Since they started building up their bilateral relationship at the beginning of the 1950s, the world has passed through great changes. Gone is the Cold War and with that the domination of the world by rival military blocs; gone also is the premium commanded by unbridled military power. The Soviet Union has disappeared into history. Old conflicts are getting resolved with the countries and regions engaged in them turning their attention towards rehabilitation and reconstruction. Nations which until yesterday were firmly committed to rigid planning are rapidly moving to a market and incentive-based economy. Every where the magic expression used is "economic reforms". No wonder, therefore, that the world community eagerly looks for new and constructive initiatives to countries which are not prisoners of their own military might, but have distinguished themselves through their economic capabilities and performance. Asia itself is slowly developing an awareness on oneness, not in the Tagore-Okakura sense of abstract spirituality, not even in the sense of leadership or domination, but in the sense of a common economic destiny. These events make it imperative for India and Japan to take a closer look at their relationship, consolidate it still further, and make it an important feature of the 21st-century global landscape. Indo-Japanese relations must have a relevance and a role not only in the Asian context but also in the broader world context.

Beyond bilateral interests there are problems which concern the world community as a whole. Neither India nor Japan can keep aloof from them. These problems are related to: (1) the widening gap between the developed and developing countries, (2) competition and antagonism within the developing world, (3) diminishing resources of multinational organizations which support economic development and poverty alleviation programmes in the Third World, (4) environmental degradation, (5) imbalance in the flow of surplus resources from the developed to the developing countries, (6) exchange rate volatility and its adverse effects on weaker economies, (7) formation of rival trading blocs, and the spectra of protectionism, (8) regional tensions caused by proxy interests, (9) compliance with NPT and reduction of military expenditures, and (10) regional economic cooperation. On many of these problems India and Japan have identical views. On others, they have different perceptions, approaches, and assessment. How to harmonize those differences and at the same time enlarge and strengthen their bilateral partnership and cooperation will remain high on the agenda for the leadership of the two countries in the 1990s and beyond.

Taiki Bansei is a wise, old Japanese saying. Great tasks are never accomplished in one day. Therefore, the task of building solid, sound and mutually beneficial Indo-Japanese relations needs to be seen as a long-term task. What is required is a renewal of faith in the vision, the spirit and the ideal which motivated the singing of the Treaty of Peace. It would be prudent not to let these be distorted by considerations of the moment.

26

India and Japan: An Unrequited Affair

ARJUN ASRANI*

Throughout their long histories, India and Japan, until modern times, had heard of each other only through third countries. The Japanese had always had a tremendous curiosity about the world and have generally been receptive enough to imbibe foreign culture. Historically, Japan was so much influenced by Chinese culture that it is still called China's cultural sister. India, on the other hand, has always been culturally self-sufficient. It might have absorbed some foreign elements but had never been overwhelmed by them, e.g., the Greek and British influences.

The Japanese first came to know about India in their travels along the Silk Route and voyages around maritime southeast Asia, especially Cambodia. Many Japanese Buddhist scholars spent years seeking and gaining first-hand knowledge of Buddhism from Indian priests who had come to China to translate the Sutras.

The Japanese hunger for knowledge was so keen that they undertook perilous voyages and journeys to China at great expense and discomfort to meet Indian scholars who were learning Chinese in order to translate the Sutras. This had been happening when Buddhism was ceasing to

* Indian Foreign Service (Retd.), Former Ambassador to Japan.

flourish in India itself. Konjaku Monogatari's Buddhist stories, with 12th century settings, popularised India as the origin, China as the communicator, and Japan as the recipient of the great message of Buddhism. These stories constituted the literary development of Buddhism in Japan.

In the Kamakura Period (1086 to 1220 AD) news of the disappearance of Buddhism from India and the destruction of the great seat of Buddhist learning at Nalanda by invaders was slow to reach Japan. But when it did, it shocked the Japanese. As a result, old India-centred Buddhism began to make way for neo-Buddhism, following abortive Mongolian invasions of Japan in 1274 and 1281. The yearning for India, the longing to get to the source of Buddhism, faded away. Then came the European era from 1542.

During the 1603-1866 Edo Period, Confucianists rose in prominence and their criticism of Buddhism also tarnished the image of India. Classical scholars on their part were equally opposed to both Buddhism and Confucianism, as both were regarded as alien doctrines. One result was that the concept of India was freed from the concept of Buddhism. However, two books on India, based on information obtained from Italian missionaries, did come out during the early 18th century. It was from the Dutch that the Japanese were shocked to learn of the colonisation of India in the early 19th century. The lesson they learned was that a nation could isolate itself only at its own peril.

During the Meiji Era, starting in 1868, Japanese scholars had no particular love for India or Asia. In 1885, Yukichi Fukuzawa, a Meiji ideologue and passionate advocate of modernisation, suggested that Japan should get out of Asia and cited India as a bad example, which Japan must avoid. But other scholars, such as Tenshin Okakura wrote: "Asia is One" and "Ideals of the East", in which India and China were exhaustively treated with great sympathy and concern. After the Russo-Japanese War there was a wave of Indian students coming to Japan; some of them were political workers running away from the British. Some of them went underground there.

If we go over the history of India-Japan cultural contacts we find that the two did know of each other. There was even affection between them. But that affection was one sided, and unrequited love. When Japan was ready and found time to make an approach India was looking the other way. And when India was willing, Japan's heart was somewhere else. It was a problem of timing. A history of missed opportunities.

The story after World War II has not been very different. Soon after the War, the Japanese were touched by Pandit Nehru's thoughtful gestures, such as sending a baby elephant called Indira to the children of Tokyo. Even more gratifying for the Japanese, including those who were against the War, was Justice Pal's dissenting judgement at the Tokyo War Crimes Tribunal. Many Japanese at that time were also in inarticulated sympathy with Nehru's idealism and ideas on non-alignment. With the Chinese market closed, there appeared to be vast prospects for doing business with India.

In many ways the period of the 1950s, right upto 1961, had been the best period in our relationship so far. The Japanese at that time had felt gratitude for whatever India or Indians had done for their morale in the immediate post-war years. Indian nationalists, who had always admired Japan's prowess in modernisation, had once again been awed by the rapidity with which Japan had overcome its war-time devastation and the speed at which it had been marching ahead to a fresh economic miracle. As early as 1954, India was amongst the western and Asian countries that Prime Minister Yoshida had been planning to visit in an extended tour. For some reason the trip to the Asian countries was dropped completely. Within weeks of his accession to power, in 1957, Prime Minister Kishi announced a tour of six countries of South and Southeast Asia, including India, immediately before a visit to Washington. According to Prof. Shiro Saito, in his book, "Japan at the Summit", the Asian tour had been planned in order to strengthen Kihi's bargaining position in Washington by Demonstrating a convergence of interest between Japan and the Asian region, which could be usefully combined in a triangular association with the United States. Apparently, Kishi's scheme for an Asian Development Fund had met with a cool reception from some Asian countries, including India, because the non-aligned countries were reluctant to become involved in a western-oriented scheme.

Otherwise, however, Kishi's trip had been a complete success and Nehru had returned the visit within the same year. Nehru received a rousing welcome from the government and the people of Japan, way beyond his expectations. Soon thereafter, in 1958, India became first country to be extended Japanese yen credits.

Japanese business and industry had also realised the potential of a huge market in India, especially when they were not allowed to develop fully their pre-war traditional market in mainland China. Long-term agreements on supply of iron ore from India had been concluded some industrial joint ventures and technical collaborations had taken place and agreements had also been reached on the avoidance of double taxation.

Within a year after Nehru's visit President Rajendra Prasad of India had also visited Japan at the invitation of the Emperor. In return for this visit Emperor Showa had sent the then Crown Prince Akihito and Princess Michiko to India in November, 1960. The young and charismatic royal couple had captivated the hearts of the Indian people. In his welcome address, the President of India had said: "To us in India, Japan is a striking example of a rapidly changing society in which traditional patterns are gracefully adapting themselves to modern requirements. Your country's attempt to preserve and maintain a balance between the old and the new, the rising tempo of your economic development that affect all levels of society and your rapid recovery from the tragedy of war are surely sources of inspiration for other Asian countries." I believe this still remains the uppermost impression of Japan among the Indian people.

Once again, in 1961, India was amongst the first Asian countries to be visited by Prime Minister Ikeda. According to Prof. Shiro Saito's book quoted earlier, Ikeda's Southeast Asian trip was part of Japan's "economics-centred" diplomacy. It is possible that he did not find Nehru satisfactorily responsive. A Japanese acquaintance, who travelled to India with Ikeda, told me that the Japanese delegation had left India somewhat disappointed with Nehru. It is conceivable that had Nehru reacted positively to Ikeda's proposal for jointly developing Southeast Asia, India might eventually have become a founder-member of APEC. Be that as it may, the fact remains that relations between India and Japan, while always cordial and trouble-free, ceased to have the warmth of the 1950's for the next two decades. Form 1960, Japan became firmly entrenched in the western security system, while India continued to remain non-aligned and, after 1971, increasingly close to the Soviet Union. After 1961, it was to take 23 years before a Japanese Prime Minister could travel to India. Moreover, given Japan's anxiety over its relations with China, the Sino-Indian border war also did not help matters. Nor did the India-Pakistan wars of 1965 and 1971 or the Indian peaceful nuclear explosion experiment of 1974. Above all, India's increasingly inward-looking economic policies disappointed the Japanese.

This does not, however, mean that India-Japan relations remained entirely uneventful in the 1960s and 1970s. The Foreign Ministers of the two countries continued to exchange visits at regular intervals, Prime Minister Mrs. Indira Gandhi visited Japan in 1969 and the Foreign Ministry consultations continued to take place more or less annually. Japan continued to extend yen credits to India. Technical collaborations continued to grow but without much Japanese financial investment. The India-Japan Committee for Studies on Economic Development, constituted in 1962, as a kind of think tank comprising eminent people from both sides, continued to meet. Joint meetings of the India-Japan Business Co-operation Committee commenced from 1967. India participated in a big way in the World Expo at Osaka in 1970. Indian food at the Indian pavilion at the Expo proved so popular that the number of Indian restaurants has continued to grow ever since all over Japan.

In 1984, Prime Minister Nakasone, the first world-class Japanese statesman in a long while, visited India after a gap of 23 years in terms of prime minister level visits. He did so presumably because he felt that the time had come for Japan to play a prominent role on the world stage, and relations with India, a large Asian country and a leader of non-aligned and developing countries, needed to be bolstered. He had also probably come to the conclusion that although India's special relationship with the USSR was unfortunate from the western viewpoint, India had intelligently used it in its given situation and that, in any case, India's foreign policy was at least consistent and predictable. In a memorable address to our Parliament he declared, "I have come to build a new co-operative relationship befitting the coming centuries, between the two most powerful democracies in Asia: Japan and India. I have come to forge closer Japan-India relations, which will promote the development of our two countries, and will contribute to the peace and prosperity of Asia and the world."

Prime Minister Rajiv Gandhi's visit to Japan in 1985 was also a success in as much as Japanese aid to India, which had long stagnated at about 30 billion yen per annum, was doubled in 1986. It has continued to increase and is now around 120 billion yen ($ 1.15 billion) a year. In 1987, Japan gave a special loan of nearly 30 billion yen for importing wheat and fertilisers from the USA for dealing with the drought situation. Prime Minister Kaifu came to India in 1990 on his first Prime Ministerial visit to an Asian country and chose India's Parliament as the venue for making a policy speech on Japan and South Asia. Former Prime Minister Takeshita attended Rajiv Gandhi's cremation in 1991. Earlier, in 1988, when Rajiv Gandhi had come to Tokyo to inaugurate the Festival of

India in Japan, Mr. Takeshita, as Prime Minister, had observed that he considered relations with India as one of the pillars of his foreign policy.

When our balance of payments position was under severe pressure in 1991, Japan was the foremost in coming to our assistance with quick-disbursing bilateral aid, as well as through the ADB, the World Bank and the IMF. This was done at a time when we had obviously only a temporary government. In 1992, the Japanese Government was quick to mount a 100-member Economic Mission to India, under Dr. Ryokuro Ishikawa, after our announcement of drastic economic reforms. It has hopefully opened the way for much greater Japanese business interest in India. Certainly, it made the subsequent visit of out Finance Minister a greater success. Perhaps we cannot expect the Japanese to invest in India as much as they have done in the ASEAN countries. But our vast market should prove to be attractive, now that we have considerably opened it up.

India too has taken several initiatives to strengthen the relationship in recent years. Prime Minister Rajiv Gandhi visited Japan thrice between 1985 and 1988. A three-day official mourning was declared in India on the occasion of Emperor Showa's demise. The President of India attended both Emperor Showa's funeral and, later, Emperor Akihito's enthronement ceremony. Over the last three years, we have, for the first time conferred Padma Bhushan awards on two Japanese dignitaries: Mr. Y. Sakurauchi and Mr. Goro Koyama. In addition the Indira Gandhi prize for 1992 went to Dr. Saburo Okhita, the well-known development economist of Japan. We mounted a six-month long very successful Festival of India all over Japan in 1988. We have been supporting Japanese positions in international fora to the maximum extent possible. The Emperor and the Empress have been invited to India. When Japan sent its minesweepers to the Gulf after the Gulf War, India readily acceded to Japan's request to afford facilities at Indian ports in case of need. Government land was provided at the concessional institutional rate to the Japanese Embassy in New Delhi for constructing a Japanese school. In response to the Japanese residents' complaint that they could not obtain Japanese foodstuffs in India, the Indian Government has recently enhanced the quota of duty-free import of foodstuffs by foreigners in India from Rs. 5,000 to Rs. 50,000 per head per annum. These are small gestures but hopefully they are indicative of our inclination.

Most welcome to the Japanese, has been a series of radical policy changes in India which are designed to integrate India into the world economy, and to open India's economy to the world. These changes have liberalised India's foreign investment policy, our import-export policy, and our industrialisation strategy, while at the same time bringing the rupee ever closer to full convertibility. The strategic shift in India's economic policies, in response to the world's changes, has truly been very great.

In Southeast Asia, India has become a sectoral dialogue partner with ASEAN. For the present the dialogue is to be restricted to the spheres of trade, tourism, investment and science and technology. It is to be hoped that the new status would give India the scope and the incentive to expand its economic relations with this region and extend them, in due course, to the Asia-Pacific region as well. Looking East is very much part of the new orientation in our policies. We have already applied to APEC for being associated with it.

It was in these propitious circumstances that Prime Minister Narasimha Rao's visit to Japan took place in June 1992. His meeting with Prime Minister Miyazawa was particularly friendly and belied the expectations of some sceptic that the Japanese would try to tie aid to our stand on the NPT. The Japanese, for several reasons, would certainly like us to sign the NPT, but they now have at least a better appreciation of our stand. Equally successful was the Prime Minister's luncheon meeting with businessmen, two hundred of whom paid handsomely from the lunch ticket to attend the meeting. Among the Prime Minister's speeches, his philosophical address to the Japan Institute of World Affairs, attended by scholar, and diplomats, was the most remarked upon. Overall, the success of this visit was enough to make foreign diplomats in Tokyo sit up and ask questions, some of them having received urgent queries from their capitals. Although the offer of Japanese aid was also enhanced to nearly a billion dollars, it would be a mistake to judge the significance of the visit merely in aid terms.

In 1992, India and Japan celebrated the 40th anniversary of their bilateral Treaty of Peace and Amity signed in 1952. Apart from cultural programmes and symposia, held in the two countries, the Japanese sent the charming young couple, Prince and Princess Akishino on a goodwill visit to India to mark the occasion.

In the economic field, the Japanese continue to provide India its largest aid package at about $1.15 billion. Our bilateral trade with Japan is second only to that with the USA. Over the last three years, the two-way trade has continued to hover between $3.5 and $4 billion.

Actually, our exports have continued to grow slowly but steadily, while our imports from Japan have been dropping. As a result we have a favourable balance of about $500 million. The stagnation in trade has been the result of the three-year recession in Japan combined with the rise in the exchange rate of the yen.

It is in the field of private direct investment in India that Japan has so far proved a disappointment, after showing great promise in 1992. In 1991, such investment had been only Rs. 52 crore. In 1992 it increased to Rs. 610 crore but in 1993, it fell back to Rs. 257.4 crore. It is a fact that the Japanese economy has been going through its worst post-war recession and the Japanese Foreign Direct Investment worldwide has come down to half of what it was in 1989. Another important factor is that with the opening up of China and Vietnam, the Japanese considered it expedient to give priority to investment in these countries which are more important to Japan economically and strategically. Meanwhile, the Japanese companies are using this delay to study thoroughly the Indian market and situation. I believe it is merely a matter of time before the Japanese feel confident enough to enter India in a big way.

Much more remains to be done to add depth and breadth to the relationship. There is virtually no dialogue between the two countries in the field of security and strategic thinking, for example. Burdened with their constitutional constraints, the Japanese defence establishments have been understandably shy hitherto. It would now be useful to exchange high-level visits in the defence field and have our defence personnel attend each other's courses. This kind of activity is helpful in increasing transparency and avoiding misconceptions.

The Soviet Union and Japan: A New Era of Friendship

NIRMALA M. JOSHI*

The forthcoming visit of President Mikhail Gorbachev to Japan in April 1991 will be of historic significance not only because he will be the first Soviet Head of Government to visit Japan since the Bolshevik Revolution in 1917 but also because it is taking place in a radically altered environment, both at the global as well as regional levels. At the global level, the Cold War has just come to an end. Conflict is yielding place to cooperation in the relationship among most nations. In the Post-Cold War situation every nation in the World is busy readjusting its relations with others. Technology, industry and commerce are emerging as the major determinants of relationship among nations. At the regional level, Sine-Soviet relations have been completely normalized. Soviet interaction with other countries in the region such as South Korea is improving considerably. The Soviet image among countries of Southeast Asia has improved significantly. The conflict in Indo-China is being peacefully sorted out. The Soviet-Japanese relations cannot be kept isolated any longer from these healthy developments.

* Dr. Joshi is in Centre for Soviet and East European Studies, Jawaharlal Nehru University, New Delhi.

Therefore, Gorbachev's visit is expected to impart a fresh stimulus to Soviet-Japanese relations. Eversince the Second World War a serious dispute over the territorial issue has divided the two countries and hampered the growth of meaningful ties between them. It is anticipated that Gorbachev visit may well bury the past history of hostility and pave the way for a new era in their relationship.

The proposed visit to Japan is taking place at a time when Perestorika has entered its most difficult phase. The transition to market economy is causing enormous hardship and the Soviet Union requires massive assistance from every possible quarters. Unrest in the Soviet Republics is increasing with all kinds of demands being put forward, compounding Gorbachev's difficulties. The only bright spot is the easing of the international situation. The Cold War is formally over and this has paved the way for a sound and a stable relationship with the United States and Europe. Now the Soviet Union has placed the normalisation of its relations with Japan on its foreign policy agenda. Soviet approach to its relations with Japan was rightly stated by Foreign Minister Edward Shevardnadze in his press conference in Tokyo in December 1988. He said, "Even if there remains something painful between the Soviet Union and Japan, Moscow intends to adopt a fresh approach on the basis of new thinking".[1] Today there is greater keenness on the part of the Soviet Union to improve its relations with Japan. The Soviet Union no longer views Japan in simplistic terms of East-West rivalry. It has recognised Japan as a global economic power. In its perception, Japan is one of the core countries of the Asia-Pacific region. Consequently, any success of its regional policies in the Asia-Pacific region the Soviet Union would have to count on Japan's support and cooperation. It is against this background of internal compulsions and the changing priorities in the Asia-Pacific region that Soviet relations with Japan can be understood.

In this article an attempt has been made to understand the evolving Soviet policy towards Japan. In order to do so it would be necessary for us to analyse the Soviet compulsions for a change in its policy.

SOVIET COMPULSIONS

Soviet compulsions *vis-a-vis* Japan are at two levels: regional and bilateral. At the regional level, Soviet concerns are strategic and the security environment in the Far East. While at the bilateral level, compulsions are especially the economic development of the Far East and Siberia. First, the Soviet strategic concerns.

After Gorbachev assumed the office of the General Secretary of the Communist Party of the Soviet Union in March 1985, he was confronted with a highly tense and a militarised situation the Asia-Pacific region. The region was the main theater of the New Cold War in the eighties. Earlier, the Soviet response to the escalating Western military presence in the area was to change its own military strength. Such a policy proved counter-productive. It was not only a drain on scarce Soviet resources but was also fraught with a danger of war - including nuclear war. Gorbachev's strategy to alter this highly militarised situation began to unfold with his famous speech at Vladivostosk in July 1986. Subsequently, the New Delhi Declaration of November 1986 on Principles for Nuclear-Weapon Free and Non-Violent World, and Gorbachev's speech at Krasnoyarsk in September 1988 further elaborated the Soviet thinking on this subject. In a nutshell, the focus of this strategy is three-fold. Firstly, the Soviet aim is to halt the proliferation and build up of nuclear weapons in Asia, lessening of naval activity in the Pacific and the Indian Ocean and reduction of armed forces in the region. This region was perceived as having become the second largest area after Western Europe where the US had undertaken large scale military build up. According to Soviet estimates, the United States had concentrated over 300 military installations near the Far Eastern border of the Soviet Union. There were 12 naval and 12 air force bases in Japan, South Korea and the Philippines.[2] Hence the aim of Soviet strategy is to lower the level of military presence here. The second aim is to promote constructive bilateral relations with all the important countries of the region particularly those like China, Japan, Indonesia, etc. with whom the Soviet Union did not enjoy friendly relations. Linked with this objective is the Soviet goal of setting regional conflicts in the Asia-Pacific region on the basis of national reconciliation. Thirdly, Soviet aim is to further Soviet participation in the regional economic groupings of this region with the objective of seeking preferential treatment for Siberia and the Far East. For instance, the Soviet Union is hoping to join the Pacific Economic Conference on Cooperation, the Asian Development Bank etc. In order to achieve these goals the Soviet Union has suggested several measures including the convening of an All Asian Forum on the pattern of the Helsinki Conference. The All Asia Forum could discuss all the issues concerning the region's security environment. What is of importance in Soviet view is to initiate a dialogue at any mutually acceptable level.

On its part the Soviet Union has taken several measures to meet the above mentioned objectives. In order to reduce the level of military confrontation in the Asia-Pacific region, the Soviet Union has begun pulling out its troops from Mongolia. This process would be completed by 1991. It is planning to cut the size of its armed forces stationed in the country's Asia part by 200,000 troops. Recently Shevardnadze said: "The process of eliminating medium and shorter range nuclear missiles is close to completion. In the Far East 12 land divisions are slated for reduction, 11 air force regiments will be disbanded and the Pacific Fleet will deactivate 16 warships including 9 large surface vessels and 7 submarines."[3] He also reiterated Soviet resolve to remove in the near future Soviet military presence outside the country; in Asia and other parts of the world. However, in order to achieve a peaceful environment it is necessary to seek the cooperation of the countries in the region. The Soviet Union has already initiated a process of active diplomacy here. It is also initiating measures in the Far East and Siberia so as to qualify for the membership of regional economic groupings.

In the above mentioned regional strategy Japan could play a pivotal role. In Soviet perception Japan has been one of the pillars of American military strategy in the Asia-Pacific region. Japan shares not only a military security arrangement with the United States, but since the late seventies it has also been an active partner in the American military plans. The Council for National Defence of Japan approved a new programme of modernisation of the armed forces for the period 1986-90.[4] In the autumn of 1982, a decision was made to deploy at the Misawa naval base 48 F-16 fighter bomber with longer range and capable of carrying nuclear weapons thereby exposing Soviet maritime territory and Sakhalin to any attack from Japan. In 1978, Japan signed a treaty with China which contained the anti-hegemony clause, directed at the Soviet Union. Japan has also opened its ports to American ships of the Seventh Fleet which were equipped with the Tomahawk *cruise* missiles. Y. Nakasone, the then Prime Minister of Japan while on a official visit to Britain in 1983, proudly proclaimed that Japan would serve as an unsinkable air-craft carrier. This could hardly have been re-assuring to the Soviet Union. In fact, Soviet leaders apprehended that Japan was gradually giving a go-by to its constitutional stipulation on nuclear weapons. In his Vladivastok speech Gorbachev gave expression to these Soviet fears. He said, "the three non-nuclear principles as well as peaceful provisions of Japan's constitution are being circumvented over more openly". Besides Japanese cooperation of the FSX missile technology have added to Soviet apprehensions. In 1987, Japan formally agreed to participate in the Strategic Defense Initiative (SDI) research programme of the United States. These developments made the Soviet Union to perceive that a Washington-Tokyo-Seoul Axis had come into existence. In fact, Gorbachev assumed that an eastern version of NATO had come into existence. While speaking at a dinner in honour of visiting North Korean leader Kim II Sung, Gorbachev said that the United States was seeking to set up an eastern military alliance grouping Japan, South Korea and other Asian states in a bloc similar to NATO''.[5] Thus Japan was perceived as a crucial link in the American military presence in the Asia-Pacific region. Hence the goal of the Soviet Union at the minimal level would be to elicit the support of Japan in lowering the military presence in the region, while at the maximum level it would aim for an independent or a neutral Japan in this regard.

At the same time, the Soviet Union has evinced a keen interest in joining the regional economic grouping of Pacific Economic Cooperation Conference (PECC), and the Asia-Pacific Economic (APEC). It is also keenly pursuing the Australian proposal for setting up a regional economic grouping the Asia-Pacific Economic Forum. The Soviet Union has accepted the outlook of these groupings and is willing to carry out the necessary structural changes in its economy so that its candidature is not opposed by other members. Measures like the transition to market economy, broader access to Soviet market and the introduction of mutually beneficial foreign economic relations are expected to pave the way for greater economic involvement in regional economic cooperation. The Soviet goal in the words of Shevardnadze is ''to work for a partnership relationship and for making the economy of Soviet Far East and Siberia a part and parcel of the emerging economic structures in Asia and the Pacific''.[6]

Thus, a peaceful environment in the region would not only reduce Soviet threat perception but it would also be conducive to the economic development of the Far East and Siberia. It can then concentrate its energy and resources on the development of its Far Eastern region. In his famous Vladivostok initiative Gorbachev had focussed attention on the region's disappointing growth rate and the need to promote the regional industrial potential. According to a Soviet scholar ''the available data shown that in 1986 the Far Eastern Economic Regions' share in the country's overall industrial output amounted to three per cent almost remaining at the 1968 level (2.8 per cent). This means that the regions accelerated development had not taken place''.[7] Further, he added: ''No matter how deplorable we must full realise the fact of the Soviet Far East gravely lagging behind other countries in the Asia-Pacific region. The thrust of the Soviet development plans is to make the Far East and Siberia more autonomous and give it a larger role in the processing of its raw materials. In order to convert the region from merely being a source of raw materials to a processing zone it will be necessary to construct new industries especially in areas like machine building, metallurgy, etc. It will also be necessary to refurnish the existing industrial and make them highly sophisticated and modern if the Far East and Siberia is to play a more dynamic role in the Asia-Pacific region keeping with its economic potential. Moreover, the transition to market economy is indeed a very difficult task and will entail tremendous hardships and sufferings. The deplorable state of its economy and the ambitious scheme for the development of the Far East and Siberia require massive resources in terms of aid and investment. Japan, a highly industrialised and a wealthy nation could help the Soviet economy.

JAPANESE RESPONSE

Ever since Gorbachev came to power there has been an unmistakable change in Soviet attitude towards Japan. It has already reconsidered its earlier hostile and rigid attitude and adopted a friendly and flexible approach towards Japan. This trend was evident in his Vladivostok speech in 1986 when Gorbachev referred to Japan as a great country. Even in his *Krasnoyarsk* speech in September 1988 Gorbachev repeated his earlier assessment of Japan. It was as part of policy of befriending Japan that Shevardnadze became the first high level Soviet dignitary to visit Japan (15-19 January 1986) after a gap of ten years. The visit marked the resumption of a political dialogue in an effort to normalise relations between the two countries. In May 1986 (29-31 May 1986) Japanese Foreign Minister Shintaro Abe was in Moscow to continue the political dialogue initiated earlier. The only positive outcome of the visit was that for the first time a Cultural Agreement between the two countries was signed. The Soviet Union has also permitted Japanese citizens to visit ancestral graves in the Habomais island group, Shikotan and Sakhalin. Since then the foreign ministers of the two countries have been holding bi-annual meetings alternating between Moscow and Tokyo. They have also continued their meetings at international meets including the session of the U.N. General Assembly. Similarly, there have been high level exchanges of ruling party leaders and politicians of the two countries. During Shevardnadze's visit to Japan in December 1988 (20-22 December 1988) an important step was taken with a view to improving relations between the Soviet Union and Japan. Three permanent working groups were set up to deal with the major issues confronting the two countries. The areas covered by these working groups were bilateral relations, regional situation and signing of a Peace Treaty. In spite of these developments, there has been no further progress in the relationship between the two countries.

Even at the economic level, the regular exchanges of foreign ministers of the two countries have not provided any stimulus to Soviet-Japan trade. The two way trade is not large and actually fell 6% in the first half of this year (1990) to U.S. $2.77 billion because of Soviet payment problems. Japan is an equally modest investor, committing itself to only 33 joint ventures with Soviet partners.[8] These joint ventures are in low tech-areas like fisheries, timber and processing. Soviet-Japanese and Japanese-Soviet economic committees have also been set up and the level of annual inter-governmental consultations on trade and economic issues has been raised. In October 1986, a Japanese industrial fair was held in Moscow. Giver Japan's economic potential and the opportunity available in the Soviet Union, the economic interaction between the two countries is marginal.

Despite Soviet efforts to improve its relations with Japan, Soviet-Japanese relations have not been able to achieve a breakthrough. For underlying Soviet-Japanese relations are serious differences on a territorial issue, which the Japanese refer to as the Northern Territories issue. Linked with the territorial dispute is the conclusion of a space treaty between the Soviet Union and Japan. The peace treaty would formally end the state of Second World War between the two countries, which so far has not been signed by them. To date the territorial issue has proved to be the most serious obstacle to a fundamental improvement in Soviet-Japanese relations. In Japanese view resolution of the territorial issue and the signing of the peace treaty as absolutely necessary before any basic improvement in the reactions can take peace. At dispute are four island; the Habomai island group, Shikotan, Kunashiri and Etorofu. These islands known as the Northern Territories were never considered as part of the Kurile chain of islands. Japanese refusal to concede that these four islands are a part of the Kurile islands has given rise to the territorial dispute. Since then both the Soviet Union and Japan have made conflictual claims and disagreed over the definition of the Kurile islands. During the 1955-56 negotiations the Soviet Union offered to vacate to islands, that is, the Habomai group and Shikotan which were closer to Japan. Initially the Japanese side acquiesced with the Soviet officer, but later rejected the offer on the plea that the Soviet Union must return all the four islands. In the sixties the Soviet Union also withdrew its offer, after the period of the US-Japanese security agreement was extended. Meanwhile, failing to reach an agreement on the territorial question, the Soviet Union and Japan put off the signing of the Peace Treaty of 1951. But the two countries restored diplomatic relations after signing a Joint Soviet-Japanese Declaration of 1956. At the same time it was agreed that negotiations on the conclusion of a peace treaty would be continued. The peace treaty could be signed only in conjunction with the settlement of the territorial issue.

Since then, both the sides have put forward conflicting claims and have adopted an uncompromising stand on the Northern Territories issue. Successive Soviet governments have vacillated in their approach to this contentious issue. At time the Soviet Union has adopted a conciliatory approach by admitting that certain difficulties exist between the two countries. This was evident during Prime Minister Tanaka's visit to the Soviet Union in 1973. The joint statement issued at the end of the visit talked about "yet unresolved problems". From the Japanese perspective this was an acceptance by the Soviet Union of the existence of a territorial dispute between the two countries. At other times, the Soviet Union has adopted a hardline approach, whereby it denied the existence of a territorial disputing by stating that the issue had already been solved by internationally recognised agreements. Such an approach was discernible in the late seventies and the eighties when Japan whole-heartedly allied itself with the United States during the New Cold War, and became an integral part of the American strategy of containment in the Asia-Pacific region. The result was that the Soviet Union also stepped up its military presence in the region and in the process two of the disputed islands, namely, Kunashiri and Etorofu were fortified. Since then the Soviet Union has been maintaining two squadrons of MIG-23 aircraft and around 10,000 troops there. The question however, is not whether the Soviet Union has adopted a soft or hard approach to its problems with Japan. What is of importance is the acknowledgement of the territorial dispute?

So far all governments have refrained from admitting this problem. The reason being that the Soviet Union would not like to touch the results of the Second World War. In his meeting with foreign minister Abe in May 1986 Gorbachev unequivocally said: "Soviet-Japanese relations can be successfully cultivated only on the basis of reciprocity provided nobody encroaches on the results of the Second World War and the inviolability of the existing borders.''[9] The Soviet fear is that any concession on the post-war settlement of boundaries could set a dangerous precedent both within and outside the Soviet Union. Another reason could be that Japan had already shelved its territorial disputes with China and South Korea, and has normalised its relations with them, while it has shown reluctance to postpone the territorial problem with the Soviet Union. The then Foreign Minister Sosuke Uno pointed out that Japan's claims to the Soviet occupied 'north territories' are 'totally different' in nature from Japan's dispute over sovereignty of Takeshima Island with South Korea and Senkhu Island with China.

This does not, however, mean that the Soviet Union is unwilling to solve its dispute with Japan. Importantly, during an earlier visit to Japan, Shevardnadze once again reverted to the earlier soft-line approach towards Japan. The joint statement issued at the end of the visit talked about ''unresolved problems'' an allusion to the Northern Territories issue. Again during his recent visit, he talked about the geographical aspect of the problem. In short, under Gorbachev's leadership the Soviet Union has adopted a conciliatory approach and appears to be willing to resolve the territorial issue.

The Japanese response to Soviet overtures for normalisation relations had been tenaciously the same for decades. In Japanese Perspective, it is essential to first resolve all the outstanding issues left over as a result of the Second World War. At every opportunity Japanese leaders, politicians and officials have unfailingly raised this issue and have sought the return of the four islands. They have maintained that until the four islands are returned to Japan and the peace treaty signed there can be no fundamental improvement in Soviet-Japanese relation. This Japanese stand was aptly put forward by the present foreign minister Tare Nakayama. In a recent interview he said that Japan and the Soviet Union would be able to engage in the full range of dynamic economic relations including development projects in Siberia and elsewhere in the Far Eastern region. Further, he added, ''Such Japanese-Soviet relations would also contribute to peace and stability in Asia and the Pacific, and to further improvement of East-West relations. Before this can be done, however, it is essential that we resolve the Northern Territorial issues and conclude a peace treaty.[10]

In fact, persistent advocacy of this stand provoked an angry retort from Gorbachev. In his meeting with a Japanese parliamentary delegation in Moscow in July 1999, Gorbachev remarked that the Northern territories was not a subject for negotiations because Moscow had no territory to spare.[11] What must have irritated the Soviet leader is not just the mention of the issue, but its internationalisation by Japan. During his meeting with Gorbachev in May 1988, President Reagan of the United States raised this issue and urged the Soviet leader to adopt a more flexible stand. Later at the Toronto summit of major capitalist countries in June 1988, Prime Minister Takeshita said that its territorial problem with the Soviet Union was an international responsibility. Japan has also rejected the Soviet approach of shelving the territorial dispute until a mutually acceptable solution is evolved. In Soviet view developing relations in other areas especially economic relations could help in creating a congenial atmosphere which in turn would be beneficial for solving the territorial issue. But the Japanese authorities have rejected such an approach and have staunchly adhered to the principle of "Unity of politics and economics". Former Japanese Foreign Minister Abe declared: "Our economic policy in respect of USSR will be tougher than that of the West European countries. Japan will use its economic might as a weapon against the USSR".[12] The result of this rigid stand is that Soviet-Japanese relations have reached an impasse.

In a message to Prime Minister Nakasone, Gorbachev expressed the hope that the Japanese Government will give due attention to the recently advanced proposal to draw up a comprehensive approach to Asian security problem...".[13] Although there was no official reply to the Soviet proposal the Japanese newspaper *Tokyo Shimbum* asserted "our country cannot reply positively to the Soviet proposal, if it is aimed at perpetuating the post-war borders".[4] Even the Soviet suggestion for convening a Helsinki type conference to discuss the problems of security in the Asia-Pacific region is unacceptable to the Japanese side. According to T. Kuranari, former foreign minister "Japan will not take part in the Asia wide process unless the territorial problems are solve—The Soviet Union wanted to transplant the Helsinki principles to Asian soil, that is to maintain the existing borders."[15] Similarly, Japanese perception of Soviet military presence in the region has hardly undergone a change. Japan still considers the Soviet Union to be its chief adversary. In Japanese assessment there is not yet any significant reduction in Soviet military presence. To some extent, Japanese assessment of Soviet military presence is linked with its (Soviet) occupation of the Northern Territories. As long as the Soviet Union continues its occupation of the four islands, Japanese perception is not likely to undergo any major shift.

Even on the question of Soviet entry into the regional economic groups, the Japanese response has not been encouraging. Japan and the United States have been opposing Soviet membership of the PECC, although the latter has expressed full support for the philosophy of PECC. Japanese position was put forward by Nakayama who said that "...an economy should lean toward free and open exchange and be engaged in wide ranging activity in the region. Given that the Soviet Union does not fully satisfy these criteria at this point".[16] Thus, on the whole, the Japanese response to Soviet overtures is negative. In view of this approach the question to be asked is: how will the issue of Northern Territories be solved? Now that Gorbachev's visit to Japan has been announced what are the changes for a basic improvement in Soviet-Japanese relations?

GORBACHEV'S VISIT

Gorbachev's forthcoming visit to Japan will undoubtedly give a powerful stimulus to Soviet-Japanese relations. It is probable that the high point of the visit will be the signing of the peace treaty which will formally end the Second World War between the two countries and pave the way for improved relations.

On the question of signing a peace treaty the Soviet leaders have always showed a willingness to sign it and end the state of abnormal relations with Japan. Gorbachev has vigorously talked of a compromise, balance of interests and a pragmatic approach. Shevardnadze agreed that a territorial dispute sharply divides the two countries. However, it was during Alexander Yakovlev, a close aside of Gorbachev, visit to Japan in November 1989 that the Soviet solution to the issue was put forward in an indirect manner. In his press interview Yakovlev hinted at a 'third way' as a possible way of solving the problem. As pointed out by Hiroshi Kimura, a noted Japanese expert on International relations, the third way rejects the first and the second way, that is, previously proposals advocated by Japan and the Soviet position had been to simply reject *toto* the Japanese position. The third way we assume offers a compromise solution.[17] Thus there is a possibility that a compromise formula may be evolved which could reconcile the differences.

A compromise formula could be along the following lines. Firstly, it is exportant, as suggested by Boris Yeltsin, that the Soviet public should be made aware of the existence of a territorial dispute with Japan. In the second stage, the Soviet Union should straight away offer to return two islands Habomai island group and Shikotan to Japan, to which it had even agreed earlier in 1956. If the trend in Soviet-Japanese relations appears positive in the coming months, the Soviet Union may even hand over these two islands before Gorbachev's visit to Japan. However, regarding the other two islands Kunashiri and Etorofu the Soviet Union is expected to announce a firm date for their return. It could be between 3 to 5 years, according to observers. But what is of importance is the announcement of a firm data for their return to Japan. The reason why the Soviet Union needs items is that certain issues are yet to be resolved. One such issue is the Soviet concern for the security. During his recent visit to Japan in September 1990 Shevardnadze hinted at a possible demilitarisation of the islands at some stage settlement process. Japan would be asked to accept demilitarisation of the islands, curtail naval activity in the Sea of Okhotsk, not hinder free passage for Soviet ships and initiate confidence building measures in the North West Pacific. Such a measures would make the Soviet Union feel more secure. The following remark of Shevardnadze indicates that on the question of security the two sides appear to have reached an understanding. He said that the two sides have reached a common understanding that their security should not be damaged.[18] Other related issues that need to be sorted out before the two islands are stand over to Japan are demarcation of the boundary between the two countries, the question of nearly 10,000 Russian inhabitants settled on these islands, agreement on fisheries and defining the economic zone of the two countries. These issues can be sorted out by joint committees of the two countries within a fixed time limit. The Soviet Union would exercise sovereignty over these two islands till their final return to Japan. Meanwhile, the Soviet Union should permit Japanese citizens to freely travel to these two islands. From the Soviet perspective, such an arrangement would not constitute on infringement of the post-war settlement of boundaries. In return Japan would be expected to sign the peace treaty and not demand compensation from the Soviet Union.

On other hand, it is increasingly being felt in Japan that it should also adopt a flexible stand on the Northern Territories issue. Many important Japanese leaders are coming round to the view that a compromise on this issue is necessary. Ichiro Ozawa, General Secretary of the Liberal Democratic Party and an influential leader of the ruling party is in favour of reaching a compromise with the Soviet Union. It is being felt that Japanese demand for the immediate return for all four islands is not realistic. Although all the four islands must become Japanese territory, the Japanese leaders are inclined to wait for some more time. Another compelling reason for Japan to adopt a conciliatory attitude is that it can no longer ignore the positive trends in Soviet foreign and domestic policies. If the Soviet Union sharply reduces its military spending and there is a settlement of the Northern Territory issue, then a Soviet threat would no longer dominate Japan's strategic thinking and planning.

It may be pointed out in this context that Japan's security perception was largely dominated by Soviet occupation of the four islands and Japan considered the Soviet Union to be its main adversary. Today the fact is that Japan is beginning to realise that the Soviet Union may not be its any security concern in the future.[19] Reduction in Japanese threat perception *vis-a-vis* the Soviet Union has coincided with its own aspiration to play a prominent role in the Asia-Pacific region. Japan's active diplomacy in the region, increase in the budget of its Self Defense Forces and greater willingness to take on military burden in the name of burden sharing indicate that it would like to be more assertive. If Japan is nurturing the ambition to play an assertive role in the region, it is necessary that other countries perceive it to be independent power. In that context improved relations with the Soviet Union will help Japan to project an independent image. Moreover, Japan cannot isolate itself from world trends. The Soviet Union has already buried its adversarial relations with the United States and Europe and Japan would not like to be the add mad in these world trends.

The above mentioned factors indicated that Japan is likely to adopt a conciliatory attitude. Hence the possibility of arriving at a settlement of the Northern Territories issues is bright. This means that the two countries are likely to sign the peace treaty.

But at the regional level, Soviet attempts to secure Japanese endorsement for its numerous proposals for the Asia-Pacific will not be forthcoming. This is because the Japanese are still wary of Soviet intentions. Shevardnadze rightly understood the Japanese attitude when he said, "they (Japanese) suspect that there are hidden meanings to each word and phrase of a Soviet statement, or they suspect that the Soviet Union is seeking its own treats which are disadvantageous to Japan. It is hard for us to understand why they act like this.''[20] To some extent, Japanese suspicion is legitimate. The long years of Soviet occupation of the Northern Territories have made the Japanese wary of Soviet intentions. Japan's close relationship with the United States may have also been responsible for Japanese suspicions about Soviet intentions. The fact is that Japan considers its relations with the United States as the cornerstone of its foreign policy. Japanese Foreign Minister Nakayama stressed that even in the present changing would relations, the United States would continue to be of fundamental importance for Japan. In his words: ''The US-Japan security treaty is a firm bond linking our two nations in this time of continuing uncertainty and instability. Along with making it possible to pursue peace through deterrence and dialogue it also functions as an indispensable framework for peace and stability in the Asia-Pacific region''.[21]

Similarly, the United States a major power in the region has no intention of decreasing its military presence in the Asia-Pacific while rejecting the Soviet proposal for a collective security system on the model of Conference on Security and Cooperation in Europe as unsuitable for Asia. Mr. Richard Solomon, Assistant Secretary of State for East Asian and Pacific Affairs felt that it is preferable to adopt existing proven mechanisms to meet the challenge of changing circumstances before creating new ones.[22] In other words, American strategy continue to be based on forward deployed forces, overseas bases and bilateral security ties. These elements would remain essential in American perspective for maintaining regional stability, deterring aggression and preserving U.S. interests. The reason for such a strategy is that continuing force modernisation efforts of Soviet air and naval assets in the Pacific have not reduced their capability. In such strategy the role of Japan is useful and the American endeavour would be to enlist the cooperation of Japan.

On the other hand, the Soviet Union has been trying to convince Japan that military confrontation at sea is a common threat to both the countries. Since both the countries are neighbours in the Far East, military confrontation can be detrimental to both of them. In this regard the most urgent task in Shevardnadze's view is ''giving a fillip to a curbing of the continuing dangerous militarisation of this region''.[23] The Soviet Union has suggested to Japan several confidence building measures like familiarization with each others military doctrines, reciprocal information about major exercises, to establish contracts between the USSR Ministry of Defence and the Japanese National Security Agency, exchanging visits by military delegations etc.

So far Japan has reacted cautiously to Soviet proposals for tripartite talks between the United States, Japan and the Soviet Union on the question of lowering military presence here. The Soviet Union has not been able to wean Japan away from the U.S. For Japan its relations with U.S. are of primary importance. Hence the prospect for significant changes at the regional level appear dim at the moment. It is reported that Gorbachev may announce a drastic reduction of Soviet troops from the Far East and propose measures for Asian disarmament. Whether the Soviet will be able to elicit an appropriate response from Japan is difficult to say.

However, the importance of the visit will lie at the bilateral level. It is reported that agreements covering seven areas are likely to be signed during Gorbachev's forthcoming visit. The areas are: Inter-governmental dialogue, Japan's technical assistance for the Soviet Union's Perestroika reforms, and relating to the Chernobyl disaster, bilateral trade and payments, trade with the Soviet Far East, environmental protection and cultural exchanges. The areas converted are indeed comprehensive and could means a breakthrough in the existing impasse in Soviet-Japanese relations.

CONCLUSION

The end of Cold War is the result of Gorbachev's imaginative and innovative foreign policy initiatives. He has brought about revolutionary changes in the international and regional environment forcing all countries to readjust their relations on the basis of cooperation. This makes a change for the better in Soviet-Japanese relations imperative. Equally important is the fact that there is a perceptible change in the threat perceptions and attitudes of both the countries. Apart from changes in international environment, the democratization and marketization of Soviet system have contributed to this changed perceptions and attitudes. There are now more people in the leadership of the two countries who favour flexible approach to the outstanding territorial dispute. They desire substantial improvement in their relations. In the Soviet case, there seems to be an element of competition among leaders who are seeking improved relations with Japan.

A public opinion poll jointly conducted by TASS and Kyodo Tsushin with participation of USSR Centre of Public Opinion Studies in October

1990 clearly show that increasing number of people both in the Soviet Union and Japan support flexible approach to territorial dispute and prefer friendly relation between the two countries.[24] In both the countries, expectation from Gorbachev's visit are high. These factors will certainly influence the Soviet and Japanese leaders when they meet in Tokyo.

However, Gorbachev's visit is not going to result in complete disappearance of the territorial problem and dramatic shift in Soviet-Japanese relations. It is likely to constitute a decisive step in direction of solving the problem gradually. We may also reasonably expect that a peace treaty will be signed during Gorbachev's forthcoming visit to Japan in April 1991. The conclusion of the Treaty will herald a basic improvement in Soviet-Japanese relations.

However, the main thrust of Soviet-Japanese relations would be at the bilateral level primarily in the economic field. The Soviet economy is on the brink of collapse and desperately needs aid and investment. Japan has been promising large scale assistance provided the Soviet Union settle its Northern Territories issue. Now that a solution appears to be in sight it remains to be seen to what extent Japan is also likely to contribute to help Gorbachev out of his present difficulties.

At the regional, however, Soviet objective of eliciting Japanese cooperation for its initiatives may not succeed. The Soviet Union may find that it is not easy to wipe out long years of mistrust. Consequently, Japanese strategic thinking will hardly differ from that of the United States, its security partner in the region. Although military rivalry in the Asia-Pacific is receding and competition shifting to political and economic spheres American relationship with Asia, including Japan remains heavily grounded in its rivalry with the Soviet Union at the time of writing this essay.

Notes and References

1. Summary of World Broadcasts (SWB), FE/0341 A2/4, 22 December, 1988.
2. *Far Eastern Affairs* (Moscow), No 1, 1985, p. 4.
3. Eduard Shevardnadze's Statement at Conference on "Asia-Pacific Region—Dialogue, Peace Cooperation" held at Vladivostok on 9 September 1990.
4. No. 2, p. 6.
5. *Times of India* (New Delhi), 26 October, 1986.
6. No. 3.
7. B. Klyuchnikov, "The Soviet Far East in the Pacific Century", *Far Eastern Affairs,* No. 4, 1988, p. 10.

8. *Far Eastern Economic Review* (Hong Kong), 30 August 1990.
9. *Pravda* (Moscow), 31 May 1986.
10. *Far Eastern Economic Review*, 30 August 1990.
11. *Ibid.*
12. *International Herald Tribune* (Singapore), 6 August 1990.
13. Y. Stolyarov, Soviet-Japanese Trade and Economic Relations'', *Far Eastern Affairs*, No. 5, 1987, p. 35.
14. L. Kutakova, ''Japan and Contemporary Key Problems'', *Far Eastern Affairs*, No. 1, 1988.
15. *Ibid.*
16. K. Sarkosov, ''A New Channel of Soviet-Japanese Dialogue'', *Far Eastern Affairs*, No. 4, 1988.
17. *International Herald Tribune*, 6 August 1990.
18. *Japan Times* (Tokyo), 1 January 1990.
19. S.W.B., FE/0863 CI/2, 7 September 1990.
20. *Ibid.*, FE/0865 CI/2, 10 September 1990.
21. *International Herald Tribune*, 6 August 1990.
22. *Indian Express* (New Delhi), 1 November 1990.
23. S.W.B., S.U./0451 A3/3.5, May 1989.
24. *Izvestia*, 25 November 1990.

28

Japan, Germany and the UN Security Council

RAJARAM PANDA*

1. INTRODUCTION

The Persian Gulf War clearly demonstrated that the United Nations has been a very powerful and effective instrument of conflict control and resolution of international conflicts. The war also demonstrated the inadequacies of UN functioning in certain areas and reinforced the arguments that the world body needs reforms. Japan which has carefully shunned taking part in any regional and international conflicts after its disastrous experiences in World War II was dragged into the Persian Gulf War by the United States. The Gulf War in turn gave adequate impetus to Japan's quiet re-evaluation of its foreign policy. And this reorientation and redefining a greater independent foreign policy role in global events also demands a greater active role in the affairs of the United Nations and therefore Japan has demanded, and justifiably so, for a permanent seat in the UN Security Council because it feels that it needs to have a stronger voice international affairs. However, despite proforma American support, Japan's long-standing hope for a permanent Security

* Dr. Panda, Ph.D., Jawaharlal Nehru University, New Delhi, Asahi Foundation Fellow, August 1992-August 1993, Reitaku University Chiba, Japan.

Council seat, which it surely deserves, seems doomed unless there is a broad-ranging reform of the Security Council and creation of a class of permanent members without veto power. Like Japan, similarly Germany has also very valid claims for a UN Security Council seat.

II. UN NEEDS REFORM

Any discussion on whether Japan deserves a seat in the UN Security Council must precede a discussion on whether the world body is without flaws and whether it needs any reforms. In a speech in November 1991 to the UN, U.S. President George Bush declared that he world needs a ''Pak Universalis'' centered on the United Nations, rather than a Pax Americana centered on Washington. This affirmed the rising status of the world body, as people and governments recognize grown interdependence in every field from arms control, drug enforcement and the environment to refugees, poverty and disaster relief. While this is duly acknowledged, it is also felt that there must be a central means of coordinating such multinational efforts. Those who talk of reforming the world body see this as the only forum but also acknowledge that it does not reflect present realities and that it is inefficiently organized and caught up in intergovernmental rivalries for top posts. They also criticize its structure as lacking fairness and therefore call for substantial reforms.[1]

In the Gulf crisis, the United Nations was seem as finally coming of age. The developments in Yugoslavia again put the spotlight on the United Nations. But many countries in the Third World fear that the United States which dominates the Security Council, seeks to hijack the UN to promote its own version of a new world order. If the United Nations is to function more democratically, the Security Council structure needs re-examination.

Given the high profile of the United Nations during the Gulf crisis, it seems strange that its lack of involvement in the Madrid Middle East peace conference was barely noticed. After all, the conference was based on UN Resolutions 242 and 338 and concerned with finding answers to the biggest challenge to international diplomacy—the Arab-Israeli conflict. The United States acquiesced in Israel's insistence that the UN should have only observer status, while at almost the same time, the UN played a significant part in reaching a settlement in Cambodia.

After the Cold War, many Third World countries sense the emergence of an expanded Northern bloc in the UN, dominated by the United States.

They fear that this could be detrimental to the interests of the developing countries if they do not toe the US line. During the Cold War, the Eastern block countries stood by the Non-aligned countries on all major issues. Now with the end of communism in the Soviet Union, many in the developing world feel that, as the only remaining superpower, the US will use the UN to promote its own version of a new world order. The extent of US domination of the UN system was seen in September 1991 when the head of the team inspecting Iraq's nuclear capability, David Key, faxed his team's findings not to the International Atomic Energy Agency's headquarters in Vienna, nor to the UN in New York, but to the US State Department in Washington.

The Gulf crisis brought the role of the UN in solving world problems into international focus. Diplomats, especially in the West, congratulated themselves on the level of international solidarity against Iraq's invasion of Kuwait. Some in the Third World were alarmed by the power of the US to set the international agenda. Then UN Secretary General Javier Perez De Cuellar himself called the war a US rather than an UN action. If it had been a genuine UN operation, the other 130 UN members outside the "coalition forces" should have contributed, however modestly, to the UN effort.

Despite the prominent UN role before the war began, the Security Council did not meet in the first four weeks of the coalition bombing of Iraq-among the most intensive in history—because of US insistence. And why was the UN General Assembly not convened? Could it have been because the Non-aligned countries have a majority there? Critics of US foreign policy charge that Washington has a bleak record as far as the UN is concerned. In its 46-years of existence the UN has been used more often than not as a tool for Western—shall we say US—foreign policy goals. UN ineffectiveness over the years cannot be blamed entirely on Cold War divisions. An overwhelming majority of the UN Security Council resolutions were vetoed by the US and Britain. Most had little or nothing to do with the Cold War, but were supporting anti-colonial struggles in the Third World. In addition, American intransigence towards ILO, UNESCO, International Court of Justice and World Health Organization has helped undermine the UN system. Together with the client states, the US has consistently used the UN to justify military interference in Vietnam, Grenada, Libya, Panama and covert subversion in Iran, Lebanon, Guatemala, EL Salvador, Nicaragua, Angola and Mozambique. With the UN under the spotlight, many analysts are beginning to question permanent memberships of the UN Security Council, a framework which dates from the Allied victory in World War II.

The UN Security Council is still based on the "ally-enemy" designations of World War II, and economically powerful countries such as Japan and Germany as well as the entire Third World, are excluded from permanent representation. Such a decision-making structure fundamentally defeats the purpose of fostering global cooperation and representation. Also, the value of a system where a single veto can override any initiative is being increasingly questioned. The five permanent members of the UN Security Council, namely the US, Britain, France, the Soviet Union (now Union of Sovereign States) and China have the power of veto. Until 1971, one-fifth of the world's population living in communist China was not even represented in UN while the so-called nationalist China (Taiwan) was a permanent member of the Security Council. Nearly fifty years later, with the unification of Germany and end of the Cold War, the post-War era has finally ended. Why should the entire continents of Africa and Latin America be excluded from being permanently represented? What about Japan (World's biggest creditor nation), and Germany (Europe's biggest economic power)? The dubious qualification of a nuclear capability is no longer valid; India exploded a nuclear device back in 1974. The other question is whether Britain and France should continue to be permanent members. While claiming independence from US foreign policy, France's voting pattern in the Security Council has generally been pro-US.

Moreover, France has done its best to prop up dictatorship in Francophone Africa. The most recent example was dispatching French troops to the dictator Mobuto's Zaire. No one has called for an emergency session of the UN Security Council to discuss French intervention in Zaire. Britain's foreign policy has shown even less autonomy from its Trans-Atlantic ally. In the past decades, especially since the Suez debacle, British policy has seemed little more than playing second fiddle to the US. No democratic new world order can be achieved until the UN addresses Third World demands for a more just and humane international order. For years, the East-West conflict effectively blocked fundamental UN reforms. As a result, the system grew steadily more unwieldy. Now, the expanding UN role in world and greater demands on its resources have given reform efforts new impetus.

Founded by 50 countries in 1945, the UN currently has 179 members. Initially it employed 1500 people. Now the UN system counts more than 51,600 employees around the world, nearly 14,000 of them are attached to the New York-based secretariat and its dependence is. In addition, at least 9600 consultants were employed by UN agencies in 1991.

Critics also decry the UN's bloated structure. Its present unwieldy form is a product of constant addition to the original framework everytime a new global issue, such as environment, has been recognized. There has been no effective mechanism to coordinate the various activities while just such a central ''neve centre'' has become more and more vital since most global problems are interrelated. The UN secretariat may be restructured to make it more responsive to changing needs by creating four major departments: (*a*) political and security affairs; (*b*) humanitarian and human rights issues; (*c*) development and environmental questions; and (*d*) management and finance. If this is done, this will eliminate the old practice of certain powerful governments dominating top posts and make comprehensive decision-making easier.

The United States, long the UN's greatest contributor, has a central role to play in the organization's future. Joseph Nye, director of the Center for International Affairs at Harvard University and author *Bound to Lead—The Changing Nature of American Power*, believes the US should still be a world power, but in the context of a new, cooperative approach. Japan, another large UN contributor, has not has many problems. But as one of the non-permanent members of the Security Council, Japan is facing many expectations from the world, while being embroiled in domestic political controversies about its role in peace-keeping.

The UN faces the difficult task of reforming itself to strengthen its functions. Specifically, the composition of the all-important Security Council must be changed to better tackle problems arising in the post-Cold War global community which is greatly different from what it was at the time of the establishment of the world body. Permanent membership to the Council does not properly represent the present day diversified distributions of responsibilities, contributions and strengths. The non-aligned movement at its conference in Indonesia in September 1992 appropriately called for democratization of the UN and the world body to be better representative of the Third World. Critics have dismissed the UN as a mere debating society. In order not to give room for such criticism, the UN must carry out further financial and structural reforms to assume a central position in the world affairs. The new UN General Assembly President, Stoyan Ganev of Bulgaria, has indicated that he also favours expansion of the UN Security Council that reflects international change.

III. BACKGROUND

The United Nations was created in 1945 as the linear descendant of the League of Nations, itself founded in the aftermath of World War II according to the tenets of an ideology developed in the 19th century. The League was essentially a permanent conference of colonial powers which, unhappy at the dangers inherent in the imperial scramble for Africa and appalled by the breakdown in international order represented by the World War I, sought to codify international norms and control nationalist excesses. It secured widespread support, from progressive imperialists who perceived it as a useful mechanism for settling inter-imperial disputes, and from socialists who could portray it as a way-station on the road to world government. When the League effectively collapsed in the 1930s, its failure was widely ascribed to two things; the absence of the US and the failure to establish any mechanism to cope with the international breakdown of economic order. The United Nations was designed to address both the problems, though the second proved to be more difficult than the first.

The Americans have had a curious love-hate relationship with UN from the very beginning. Essentially an isolationist country, its involvement in the outside world has always been problematic. But in spite of much vocal opposition, successive administrations in Washington have liked the UN and found it useful. The US has never paid less than 25 per cent of the UN budget, a far larger share than any other country. It is an American institution from the start, founded in San Francisco and later established permanently in New York. The Americans gave the UN its atmosphere of moral uplift, its aura of sanctimoniousness. The idea of a great power veto is also a peculiarity familiar American notion. In spite of the isolationist sentiments that kept the US out of the League of Nations, the UN has remained a solid element in the formation and execution of American foreign policy for nearly half a century.[2]

IV. UN NEEDS CASH

It has almost become fashionable these days to talk of reforms but different groups want different things. The great powers want efficient peace-keeping operations and a trim secretariat. The developing countries want a new economic deal. The middle-range countries want a renewed commitment to multilateralism. Almost all the arguments revolve around money. How does it come? The UN's regular budget is relatively small—about $ 1 billion. About eight countries contribute 75 per cent of the budget—the Group of Seven leading capitalist states plus the former Soviet Union.

Roughly, the US pays 25 per cent; Japan 12.45 per cent; the former Soviet Union 11 per cent; Germany 9 per cent; France 6 per cent; Britain 5 per cent; Italy 4 per cent; and Canada 3 per cent. Most of the other members of the UN subscribe less than 1 per cent each. At present, 44 per cent of the member states pay the minimum assessment of one hundredth of 1 per cent, and the shares of 16 new members have yet to be determined. The US traditionally has been the strongest critic of wasteful UN spending, much of which inevitably comes out of the pockets of American tax payers. At least 70 per cent of the secretariat's regular, assessed budget, which stands at $ 2.4 billion for 1992-93, pays for salaries and other "staff costs". Of late, there has been a marked hesitancy in the US not to fulfil its full commitment of payment. Consequently, it is now the most serious defaulter in its regular payments.[3] What makes the picture gloomier is the demise of the Soviet Union. As of October 1991, Moscow owed $ 46 million in regular dues and $ 173 million for peace-keeping.

The American delinquency springs partly from policy, partly from book-keeping. Congress has periodically withheld funds to promote fiscal reforms and deny support for controversial reforms like aid to Palestinians. With the end of the Cold War, the major threats to peace are local and regional—like the fighting in Croatia and Georgia. Yet if the US continues to remain in the default list, it can hardly expect Boris Yeltsin to pay a fair share of UN costs.[4] Member states are reportedly in arrears for $ 908.5 million in regular dues and $ 844.4 million in peacekeeping contributions. One of the worst offenders is the United States, which is $ 731 million behind, although Washington has promised to reduce its debt by some $ 300 million before the end of 1992. The UN Secretary General has offered some bold proposals to get the

UN's books out of the red. For example, he wants to charge interest on late payments by members and to borrow from banks when the need arises, as well as to establish a $ 50 million reserve fund for peacekeeping activities. Almost certain to be rejected by the General Assembly is a proposal to levy UN taxes on international air travel and arms sales.

V. A CASE FOR JAPAN

Soon after coming to power, Prime Minister Kiichi Miyazawa pledged "the greatest possible contribution to the United Nations". He also expressed a strong desire to do away with the "superpower" structure perpetuated by the permanent member countries of the Security Council. Japan's professed "UN-centered" approach to world affairs has not up to now been taken at face value abroad. What probably brought this state of affairs into the open was the response to the issue of whether Taiwan or the People's republic representing the "true" China. Though many countries one after another started transferring their support to mainland China, Japan along with the US persisted until the very end in efforts to have Taiwan maintain its seat. Then after China was admitted to the UN, Japan followed the US lead in moving to resume diplomatic ties with China. What was utmost behind Japan's policy was to giving priority to Japan-US ties and accommodating hawks at home.

The "UN-Centered" philosophy was first enunciated under the Kishi government in 1957, the year after Japan joined the world body. The twin pillars of Japanese diplomacy at that time were "cooperation with the countries of the free world", and "resolutely upholding an Asian standpoint". However, in 1969 Japan announced that its ties with the United States is more important than with any other country. Finally in 1974, all references to the "UN-centered" concept were dropped.

As the confrontation between the US and the Soviet Union Heated up, Asian and African nations and the non-aligned countries jumped on the Soviet bandwagon. The General Assembly became a platform for denunciation of the developed Western countries over such issues as redistribution wealth, Middle Eastern and South African problems, and so on. As the United States started distancing itself from the United Nations, Japan decided not to interfere in any way with America's global strategy.

Japan's conduct on the world stage in the past on decade and beyond reflected its feature to evolve an independent policy. Japanese diplomacy continues to cling to crumbling Cold War structure. It has failed but beginning now to come to grips with the emerging new world order.[5] On the other hand, Japan has displayed initiative in other areas: by inviting the UN University to set up its headquarters in Tokyo in 1973, by proposing a conference of luminaries to inquire into administrative and financial reform of the UN in 1986, by introducing a resolution that the 1990s be the UN Disaster Prevention Decade. Since 1986 the US has drastically cut back its financial support of the UN and Japan's willingness to step up the breach has won it considerable gratitude. It is now felt that with the Cold War over, the time has come to tackle problems of global scale. These include the deteriorating North-South issue, hunger, refugees, environmental destruction and so on. The world expects a good deal of Japan because attention is focused on the role Japan is capable of fulfilling in assuring the right to a peaceful life. This calls for Japan's place as a permanent member of the Security Council.

The new role that the UN has assumed upon itself—namely the peacekeeping role—helps define the members' attitude to the world body. For example, the UN effort for ending the 20 years of civil war in Cambodia was indeed extraordinary. And then came the question of deploying peacekeeping forces. However, the members were more interested in expanding the UN's peacekeeping role than in paying for it. The risk of renewed war in Cambodia demanded an urgent infusion of funds and more reliable system of contributions from any military role in maintaining the post-Cold War peace, have the enormous responsibility of carrying a bigger financial burden. The current popularity of UN peacekeeping reflects its effectiveness. Peacekeeping does cost money, though very little compared to a war. It must be paid for.[6]

Peacekeeping assessments reflect the economic strengths of member states. But the formula assigns extra payments to the Security Council's permanent members. For reasons of history, Japan and Germany do not have permanent seats. Their present power justifies their inclusion and the larger contributions that would accompany it.[7] The US has fallen inexcusably far in arrears and Russia, heir to the Soviet Union's obligations, has also slipped behind and therefore economic realities may soon force the issues. An increased contributions from Japan and Germany would undoubtedly entitle them to an increased policy role and consequently a re-evaluation on their future status in the Security Council would be inescapable.

The UN has two tasks: to provide a system for maintaining international peace and security, and to devise means of managing essential global problems. The agenda for strengthening a system for maintaining international peace and security demands further strengthening of the UN Security Council. The classical definition of security means maintenance of a system that contains conflicts and deals with, or preferably prevents, war. The concept of security during the post-Cold War era, however, carries a broader connotation: environmental problems, social justice, population planning, economic equality and so on. The truth, however, is that the traditional concept of peace and security—avoiding war and controlling conflict—is still in vogue. The world's bill for armaments is still of the order of $ 1000 billion a year, an unimaginable sum of money and a huge waste of resources. There is great instability in many areas of the world, and it is often fuelled by the flow of arms. A curious irony of the current situation is that the five permanent members of Security Council, on whom so many hopes for peace are now placed, are also the world's five largest arms exporters. American's recent decision (September 1992) to sell advanced F-16 aircrafts to Taiwan, much to the annoyance of China, is only a worrisome reminder to the fact that the builders of a system for maintaining international peace and security are also working for its destruction. If Japan and Germany with their constitutional restraints are allowed to become permanent members of the Security Council, they may be able to some extent contribute to the halting this process towards global annihilation.

The notion of these addition members in the Security Council has some merit, but it leaves open the question of whether the new comers should also have veto. The existing permanent members argue that too many countries with a veto would hamstring the Security Council when it comes to vote on peacekeeping operations and other crucial issues as and when they arise. The Japanese quite justifiable have expressed their desire to joint the Council on a permanent basis. The presence of Japan as a permanent member of the Security Council would undoubtedly enhance the credibility of organization. Germany's position is different from that of Japan's. Germany has at the moment a number of problems: reunification, and their special relationship with France. Italy has suggested that all EC countries should be represented with one veto. Then there would be one vacancy for Japan. Italy thinks that the 50th anniversary of the UN in 1995 would be a good opportunity for Japan to be included in the Security Council on a permanent basis with veto power. However, Western countries are reluctant to engage in a revision of the UN Charter, not because of Japan, but because of the more important and more explosive demands of the Third World.

More than a hundred countries have gained independence since 1945. The existence of this two-thirds of the membership was not taken into account when the Charter was signed. Any substantial change now would trigger a number of other demands from many Third World countries. However, one needs to realize that the world now is not the same as that obtained in 1945 and therefore changes are inevitable to meet the changing realities of today.

The British are the most nervous and the most unwilling to speculate about possible changes in the Security Council. The French do not like the idea of making the Security Council larger or giving it more permanent member. They believe some countries are better suited to playing a significant international role than others. according to the French, there are three prerequisites for maintaining global pretensions: a planetary vision, a significant military capability and readiness to make a commitment. They say neither Japan, nor Germany, nor other aspirant countries like India, Brazil and Nigeria fit the mold. The French at the UN also have a firm belief, not shared by the Anglo-Saxons, that financial power should be subordinate to political power. This sets them apart from the majority of the G-7 countries who believe the reverse. One French diplomat said: "It is a mistake when layers and bankers run the world. Intellectuals make better decisions."

Japan believes that by being a permanent member of the UN Security Council, it can do its world duties as it is able with a share in that core of power. Japan reasons that since it is the second largest payer of the UN bills and an economic superpower, it deserves a role equal to its status. Critics suggest this gross economism is apt to be wrongly taken as an atavistic reappearance of militarism in a different garb. Not only the Chinese and Koreans and some Southeast Asians are wary of this development, some highly respected Japanese scholars and critics, besides socialists and communists in the Diet are cautioning the business-backed government against souring up Japan's developing Asian relationships and causing antagonism and distrust where cultivation goodwill and trust is essential. Professor T. Kamo of Tokyo University opines that Japan must not press any claims at the United Nations based on its economic power. He suggests that there are many areas, such as technology and expertise where Japan can make effective contributions to the UN efforts towards maintenance of peace and promotion of development.

Japan has been elected a record number of seven times as a non-permanent member of the Security Council but obviously it is not satisfied. It expects that grant of a permanent seat on the UN Security Council would close that ignominious chapter of history which many post-War Japanese and leaders are working hard to revise by repeating or recalling the wartime complaints that Japan was rather a victim than the sole instigator of a war. Japan feels that a permanent veto-endowed seat will give it a share in the final say in running the world. Japan's concept of a revamped United Nations is different from many others who also want to renovate the organization. While most non-aligned, Third World, and some European leaders want the UN to be more reflective or representative of the present-day world with its post-Cold War and post-Soviet realities on more democratic lines, some advocate even the abolition of veto power of the few and to make the Security Council a broader council of equals. But since there is opposition to making any structural changes in the Security Council from the veto-wielding members, Japan proposes the establishment of a Special Council that will include major contributors. Japan introduces economic strength of a nation as qualification for UN role in peacekeeping in the world. An economic power is the only justification of Japan's claim to leadership of the world, an image of this power-base being deplored as at home as in Japan's Asian neighborhood.

VI. AMERICA'S STAND ON THIS ISSUE

Although the United States agreed to Russia's assuming the permanent seat of the Soviet Union, it does not see this the right time to reshape the Council to allow Japan also to become a permanent member. During his visit to Japan in January 1992, President Bush told the Japanese that Washington "in principle" would be ready to support Japan's taking a permanent seat on the Security Council with veto powers equal to that of China, Russia, Britain, France and the United States but that such a move right now raises several legal, political and possibly even strategic problems from the US point of view. So far, Japan has not made a formal request to the US for support of their becoming one of the permanent members of the Security Council, but it is something they are seriously considering.[8] There still is not a consensus in Japan on playing such a role.

Washington's support in principle for Japan's assuming a permanent seat on the Security Council was first expressed by President Richard M. Nixon. Since then every US President has endorsed the position but without wanting to do much about it. This is especially true for the Bush Administration, which feels that the UN Security Council is now finally operating in an effective manner and therefore now is the worst time to be tampering with it. The only way for Japan to become a permanent member of the Security Council is if the United Nations Charter is amended, which requires a two-thirds of the General Assembly and the backing of all five current permanent members of the Security Council. It is felt in the US that if the Charter is reopened, it will lead only to trouble. For one, some members will begin pushing for the creation or abolition of other UN institutions. In particular, US officials recall that the granting of veto power to the five permanent members of the Security Council was one of the most contentious issues when the United Nations was founded at the end of World War II, and there are many countries that would push to abolish veto powers if the Chapter were reopened. Moreover, if Japan is brought into the Council as a permanent member, Germany, Brazil, India and Nigeria could all be expected to press similar cases. US Administration officials also argue that the Japanese clearly are not yet ready to take part in UN peacekeeping missions, though Japan dispatched its first peacekeeping troops to Cambodia in September 1992. In the past, the permanent five members of the Council normally did not take part in peacekeeping missions, but this has been changing in recent years. Japan, however, has realized this and despite strong public opposition and outcry in the Diet from the opposition, passed the peacekeeping operation bill, authorizing the dispatch of Japanese Self-Defense Forces under UN command for peacekeeping purposes in trouble spots in the world. This makes the Japanese case strong.

If this was the last signal from the United States to its Asian ally to end Japan's demilitarized status as a condition for Tokyo's Security Council membership; Tokyo has already, in a sense, fulfilled the requirements. But this has brought up another problem: all four of the other permanent members of the Security Council, particularly China, firmly opposes Japan joining their ranks. This has already raised many eyebrows in neighboring South East Asian nations and Korea who read that any reversal in Japanese policy would be pregnant with the possibility of

Japanese militarism revisited. Consequently, Washington now tells Japan that if it really wants to be a permanent member of the Security Council, it will have to take the lead in lobbying for such a move within the UN itself to lay the political groundwork. Tokyo has also been told that it should look on this as a ''five or ten year'' project and not something that is going to take place overnight. It will be better in Japan's interest if it shuns any hasty move and adopts a gradualist approach to this issue because it will only create expectations and potential opportunities for others to demand that it should do more than what it might be prepared to do right now.

Japan's election to the Security Council as a non-permanent member in October 1991, the seventh time so far and first time in three years, carries with it enormous responsibilities. In the post-Cold War international community in which ideological confrontation has disappeared, there will still be frequent clashes of interests between the big and small nations but also between developed and developing countries. In such disputes, if Japan, representing Asian nations, were to respond solely to the wishes of Western countries and cooperate only with permanent members of the Security Council, the support for Japan may change into despair.[9] During the Cold War, marked by severe US-Soviet confrontation, Japan as a member of the West camp, cooperated throughout with the US. It is predicted that in the post-Cold War era, now that ideological dissent has crumbled, there may be more confrontations than before involving the different interests of the developed and developing countries, and between large and small countries. At such times, if Japan, after being elected as a non-permanent UN Security Council member and representative of Asia, looks only towards European countries, and the United States, or seeks cooperation only with the UN Security Council permanent members, the support now being given to Japan will turn into disappointment.[10]

Japan's case nevertheless for a permanent seat in the Security Council is strong, though it requires patience to pursue for such a policy. While Japan has been exhorted to assume a significant political international role commensurate with its economic status, it is unfairly denied the forum to project its policies with equal political power in the Security Council. Japan is sick of hearing that it is an economic giant but a political dwarf. In response to the demands from the US and other nations, Japan had to wither enormous domestic controversies in passing legislation allowing Japanese troops to take part in future UN peace-keeping missions. It is for the first time since World War II that Japan has deployed soldiers overseas to Cambodia. The government met fierce opposition in 1990 over a similar bill designed to send troops to Saudi Arabia in a non-combatant role alongside the United States and allied forces pitted against Iraq. It was eventually scrapped after opponents said the plan would violate the US-drafted "peace" constitution, which prohibits Japan from using the military to settle international disputes. Public opinion drastically changed since and Diet passed the bill in September 1992 enabling the government to dispatch troops to Cambodia.

Thus, it is clear that Japan is restructuring its policies to meet the changing needs of time.

VII. FUTURE

The moves by Germany and Japan to secure seats for themselves in the UN Security Council have triggered alarms within the developing countries that the possible expansion of the most important organ of the UN may risk retaining its exclusive character. The two nations have been holding talks with each other and the US since Japan expressed its desire for a permanent seat in the Security Council. Developing nations see the inclusion of these economic giants as a move to make the Council a replica of the G-7, an elite gathering of militarily and economically dominant nations. In an understanding that seems to have been struck between Japan and Germany, the former would be the one to make all the public gestures while the latter would manoeuvre behind the scenes to lobby the memberships. Germany is hesitant to pitch its claims too strongly as its efforts to increase its clout are viewed with suspicion in European capitals.

Nationals like India and Brazil hope that when the Council is expanded, it will give due representation to the burgeoning economies in Asia and South America. They feel that there is much wisdom in UN Secretary General Boutros Ghali's suggestion that the five new members include India, Brazil and Nigeria, besides Japan and Germany. In January 1992, the Indian Prime Minister, P.V. Narasimha Rao, suggested in New York that the UN should introduce reforms in keeping with the vastly changed scenario since its inception nearly 50 years ago. He suggested that in order to assure the world that the Council had not become a play thing in the hands of the US and the United Kingdom, the

Council should be expanded. While he did not pitch for India, he felt that there should be a larger representation. Those not in favour of an expansion argue that more members with veto powers would hamper the functioning of the UN body. But, in recent years none of the five members have used their powers. In the past the erstwhile Soviet Union and China have used the veto.

"Preventive diplomacy" and "collective security" on a global scale are the new catch words in international politics. But both these concepts are highly ambiguous and need to be defined at the UN forum itself. The veto right of each of the five permanent members of the Security Council is not in conformity with the UN's own principle of "sovereign equality of all its members". Yet, no country has chosen to give up its UN membership. One reason no doubt is the growing inevitability of international inter-dependence. Also, the system of superpower check and balances that the Cold War had occasioned did ensure that the sovereign rights of each member states has been observed.[11]

The Cold War equations are no longer valid. Some Third World countries have already expressed fears that the emergence of a weak-kneed Russia as a successor to the Soviet Union may now ruin the reasonably efficacious systems of checks and balances that had worked in the Cold War period. The general perception in the Third World is that Russia will be soft in its political attitude towards the United States and that the United States and that the United Kingdom and France could still be expected to toe the US line. On the other hand, China, beset with domestic problems, does not possess the diplomatic will to play godfather to a Third World country that may be threatened in the exercise of its sovereign equality in the UN forum. Therefore, the question arises as to whether the existing veto rights cannot be abrogated or whether, as an alternative, more countries could be given permanent membership with similar veto rights. In the UN, there is no constitutional procedure by which the existing permanent members could be disfranchised of their status without their own consent.

There is also a school of thought that advocates the enlargement of the permanent membership of the Security Council but without veto rights for the potential candidates. This will be an arrangement of no consequence to the interplay of power politics in the Security Council. The potential candidates are unified Germany and Japan, which, as the vanquished powers in World War II, were even viewed as "enemy states" in the UN Charter itself. However, the phenomenal events of the subsequent Cold War and the general political mood of the unfolding post-Cold War period have made both these countries highly respected members of the world community today.

The war in the Persian Gulf was a test case for Japan. It gave further impetus to Japan's quiet re-evaluation of its foreign policy. Most Japanese felt that their vast monetary contribution was not appreciated by the United States. Most Japanese tax payers did not approve of the government's giving away $ 13 billion towards the Gulf war funds under pressure from America. The United States was perceived as having bullied Japan into making such a heavy financial sacrifice. Indeed, most Japanese did not see their vital interests threatened by Saddam Hussein's takeover of Kuwait and were sharply divided about the wisdom of supporting the coalition. But the point is Japan does not have strictly an independent foreign policy until probably the Gulf War that has compelled it to evolve one. It's formulation of foreign policy has been heavily influenced by the decision-makers in Washington. Nevertheless, despite such an impressive contribution to the Gulf War efforts, Americans felt the Japan's support of the coalition was slow, grudging and inadequate, especially since three-fourth of Japan's oil comes from the Middle East. What the United States failed to appreciate was that Japan's political style requires that major changes in its foreign policy be worked through a methodical, consensus-building ritual that Westerners often find frustrating and confusing. The rapid American timetable for assembling the Desert Shield coalition did not fit that process. American public support for Japan dropped during and after the war. Japan learnt a lesson and begun to realize that it should not allow itself to be placed in a position where the US could drag it into a goreign policy adventure without adequate prior consultation.[12]

The Gulf war initiated in Japan a re-evaluation process in its foreign policy posture which will make its case for a seat in the Security Council strong. The government devised a new plan to deal with future crises, which would allow up to 2000 troops from Japan's SDF to participate in a future UN peacekeeping force.

The issue of UN peacekeeping forces has emerged as an important element of international politics and diplomacy during the post-Gulf war period. But with the Gulf war over, do you need world policemen? The answer is clearly 'Yes'. Carnage and atrocities inflame Bosnia, anarchy and famine afflict Somalia, defiance and renewed threats rise from Iraq's rogue regime, Cambodia's unease peace teeters. Wars in Central Asia are no less grim. This turns out to be the agenda of the post-Cold War world.

these developments have put pressure on the world's major powers to reassess and jettison the benign neglect they have traditionally adopted towards UN peacekeeping efforts.

The United States is the leader and it has required major changes in American thinking to structure a foreign policy program that would turn the UN into an effective agent to restrain regional conflict. Regional efforts are ideal ways to resolve regional conflicts but such things have not happened. The case of Yugoslavia is a test case as was the case in the Gulf. But Yugoslavia is not Iraq. The US has no endangered vital interests that justified sending an American invasion force. The Balkans did not provide the providing ground for Operational Desert Storm II. Neither was Yugoslavia necessarily a new Vietnam or Lebanon. It was unlikely that America's political and military leaders were automatically to repeat the mistakes they made in the 1960s. And despite the unflinching support of American public for their country's world leadership role, in the case of Bosnia, they felt that European powers should intervene. But Britain is a prisoner of its costly experiences in Cyprus and Northern Ireland and was hesitant to go to Yugoslavia. Germany is prisoner of the history of the Nazi occupation of the Balkans and was not willing to go. France, traditionally allied with Serbia, was politically limited, as was Russia. The consensus in America in the post-Cold War era is that it should not bear any burden or pay any price to halt others' conflicts. On the other hand, consensus has built up in America in shoring up an international system that would prevent rogue states from carrying out massive human rights abuses or punish them if they do. And that system has to be run through the UN Security Council.[13]

It is in this context that Japan's and Germany's interests to be permanent members of the Security Council need to be appreciated. The euphoria it generated in Japan when the peacekeeping operation bill was passed enabling the government to send Self Defence Forces in non-combat role to Cambodia speak of the massive public opinion against such a policy. The government in Japan, however, has been aware that if it has to protect its global interests, it has to respond to the demands of international change. Strictly speaking, such a dispatch of Self Defense Forces overseas, albeit for peacekeeping operations, clearly violates the country's constitution but government has made flexible interpretation of Article 9 of the constitution to suit its argument that these Self Defense Forces will be doing only peacekeeping duties without any combat role. Indeed, to sustain such operations under UN command requires nations with worldwide interests, money and manpower and there are not many. The list always comes down to the United States, Britain and sometimes Italy and France in conjunction with a regional state or two.

The American demand that Tokyo and Bonn should start carrying on their share initiated a debate both in Japan and Germany to re-evaluate their policies, the passing of the peacekeeping operation bill in Tokyo has raised a storm in Tokyo. Many Japanese view it as a slippery evasion of the constitution. The government, however, realized that genuine collective security has to mean that Tokyo is prepared to fight and finance. And to scotch any apprehension of a possible future unilateral action, the government has agreed to integrate Japanese forces into a large multilateral force.

The debate also in Germany to speak for its own interests as a full-fledged member of the UN inner circle stems from the fact that Germany is the world's their largest economic power, the UN's third largest financial contributor and that it is being asked more and more, since the end of the Cold War, to take its share of political and military responsibilities, albeit under the UN leadership, worldwide.

Officially, Germany is not, at this time, seeking a permanent seat at the UN Security Council. It finds expedient to let Japan break open the gates of the selected club of permanent Security Council member with veto power and plans to be not on Japan's train when it gains its admission, now expected by 1994 or 1995. The *Bild am Sonntag* quoted an important government member as saying "Germany's position has changed and it will seek a permanent seat at the United Nations Security Council as soon as Japan has obtained its own."[14] Speaking to the General Assembly in September 1992, Germany's foreign minister Klaus Kinkel said the Security Council is not representative of the economic and political balance in the world body and that it does not reflect the international order today. He pleaded for a permanent seat on the powerful Security Council.[15]

Those who are opposed to modifying the present Security Council *status quo* and suggest it would be equivalent of opening a Pandora's Box, conveniently forget that the UN Charter has been changed to add four new non-permanent members in the past. The truth of the matter is the United States does not feel concerned by such a change. A superpower like the United States will always do what it wants with or without UN blessing. Britain, like France, would prefer to maintain its present privileged Security Council would prefer to maintain its present privileged Security Council status but as always will end up siding with the United States. Russia will be, for years to come, in the US pocket and will not stand in the way. That leaves China. China seems to be the only permanent Security Council member that might possibly side with France and block the move for enlarging the Council. However China might be no more enthusiastic about Japan's admission into the inner circle than France over Germany's possible promotion. Both Japan and Germany have argued that a situation where a major power is not allowed to take part in decision touching on its own interests and is obliged to keep a low profile, is unhealthy and generally stirs right-wing, nationalist reaction. This compels them to make their own claims.

Both Japan and Germany faced similar issues in deciding UN troops roles. Germany's neighbouring countries fear the future German military roles. Hilter's Germany started World War II on September 1, 1939 in an attempt to conquer Europe from the Ural Mountains to the Atlantic coasts. Many Europeans have not forgotten the tremendous human and material losses in Poland, the non-defunct Soviet Union, France and other European countries during the World War II. The German people must convince neighboring countries that they are "fully democratized" when the government changes its policies on sending troops abroad. Germany's constitution prevents German soldiers from missions outside NATO territory. The conservative government of Chancellor Helmut Kohl wants the constitution changed to allow German participation in UN peacekeeping. Similarly, Japan has striven sincerely to convene its Asian neighbours that it has no future military intentions. Japan's Asian neighbors have not forgotten Japanese atrocities before and after World War II. China, and North and South Korea as also the countries in South East Asia have expressed concern about Japan's dispatch of military personnel to Cambodia. However, both Japan and Germany are now restored as international powers, but they come to that status trailing an unforgettable history.

The present UN Security Council members have argued that if both Japan and Germany revise their constitution enabling the military to participate in multinational forces in peacekeeping operations, their case for permanent seats in the Security Council would be strong. The long-term projection of the Japanese government's passing of the peacekeeping operation bill is believed to be aimed at this historic deal.

Japan has realized that if it aims to continue its uninterrupted economic success, it has to emerge from its narrow cocoon world of self-pity and inward-looking and assume a wider global role that would be commensurate with its economic status. A permanent seat for Japan, as also for Germany, the UN Security Council with veto right will not only assuage the pride of both Japan and Germany but also inevitably lead to their exercising a political power that when combined with their economic strength, will be a stabilizing factor in international politics and help contribute to the establishment of a new world order.

Notes and References

1. *The Japan Times* (Tokyo), 30 November 1991.
2. *The Guardian* (London); 28 December 1991.
3. *Ibid.*, 31 December 1991.
4. *The New York Times*, editorial, 24 December 1991.
5. *Asahi Evening News* (Tokyo), 1 January 1992.
6. Brian Urquhart, ''The United Nations in 1991: Problems and Opportunities'', *International Affairs* (London), Vol. 68, No. 2, April 1992, p. 317.
7. *The New York Times*, 31 January 1992.
8. *Ibid.*, 8 January 1992.
9. *Mainichi Daily News* (Tokyo) 21 October 1991
10. *Ibid.*
11. *The Hindu* (Hyderabad), 2 February 1992.
12. Richard Holbrooke, ''Japan and the United States: Ending the Unequal Partnership'', *Foreign Affairs* (New York), Vol. 70, No. 5, Winter 1991-92, p. 51.
13. *International Herald Tribune* (Singapore), 13 August 1992.
14. *The Japan Times* (Tokyo), 5 September 1992.
15. *Mainichi Daily News*, 25 September 1992.

29

Japan and the Gulf Crisis: An Appraisal

RAJARAM PANDA*

The end of the Cold War brought the first glimmer of hope for peace in the world. Japan which was not involved in any armed conflict for the past four decades has enjoyed unaffected peace and spectacular economic success in the most favourable economic environment during the post-World War II period. However, the swift developments in international politics and rapid global changes in power alignment compels Japan for a greater global role. The post-Cold War Period is more challenging for Japan than ever before. The price of the new found tranquility is the corruption around the world of threats to peace on a small scale. The collapse of Eastern Europe means of demise of Communism; it meant the Soviet Union and communism are no longer enemies. But if there are no real enemies in the world, there are no real friends either and it is extremely difficult to predict where and when the next enemy will appear.

Since the outbreak of the Persian Gulf crisis triggered by the Iraqi invasion of Kuwait on August 2, 1990, the United States and Iraq fought a bitter war. This was the first major crisis in the first post-Cold War

* Dr. Panda is Assistant Editor, *Newstime*, Hyderabad (A.P.).

period. Until just a few years ago, the main adversary in the region was Khomeini's Iran. Though it could not be called an ally, Iraq was a friendly country. The Soviet Union enjoyed the same kind of relationship with Iraq. At the time of the outbreak of the Gulf crisis, as many as 5,000 Soviet citizens were staying in Iraq, including military advisers. In their attitude towards Iraq, the Arab countries are divided too. However, relations between countries in the Middle East are extremely volatile and it is impossible to anticipate at a given time whether nations will become friends or foes. It is extremely likely that in the post-Cold War era, international relations will become more complex with new power realignments and it is possible that today's friends will become tomorrow's foes and *vice-versa*. How does Japan response to this changing global changes is the question that needs to be answered.

It is still believed in Japan that its friendly relations with the United States must serve as the cornerstone of its diplomacy. It is also believed in Japan that it must maintain lasting friendly relations with China and must build close cooperative ties with South Korea. Japan's relations with Southeast Asia alone has a similar reasoning. It also hopes to develop a lasting friendly relationships with the Soviet Union once the Northern territorial issue has been settled, a peace treaty concluded and economic cooperation advanced. Though the goal of Japanese diplomacy has been to develop friendly cooperation with all corners of the globe, but this still falls short of developing a sense of the real world. It is extreme likely that this will be the major defect of Japanese diplomacy in the post-Cold War era. The risk is that Japan may lose sight of the harsh realities of international politics.

Japan does welcome the developments that took place in breath-taking rapidity and the recent changes in the Soviet Union because they open up new vista of economic opportunities. What Japan fails to realise is that these global changes mean decreased political opportunities. These changes will make it difficult for Japan to define its position in the world. At the turn of the decade academics and scholars opined that the 21st century would be the Pacific Century. This author tried to make a very persuasive argument a decade ago in his book *Pacific Partnership: Japan-Australia Resource Diplomacy*, based on the tremendous economic activities taking place in the Pacific region. But the developments of 1989 and 1990 compels one to re-examine the global political change that would impinge considerably on the global economic scene. If the world moves away from the projected 'age of the pacific' towards the second 'age of the Atlantic', Japan would unlikely to be playing a central role in the next century. It would not only lose its ability to speak out internationally but there is every possibility of the old situation of the West against the rest of the world returning to the forefront of the global scene.

The revitalisation of the Eastern Europe could become a nightmare for Japan. Japan's responsibility within such a scenario would be enormous. It needs to stress the designers of the new order in Europe that a new Europe cannot be built up efficiently without Japanese economic, technical and political cooperation. The Collapse of East European and Soviet communism left a waste-land in which now grow all sorts of weeds. Similarly, the end of the Cold War revealed more ancient sources of conflict. Iraq's invasion of Kuwait was a grab for underfended wealth, the oldest form of imperialism. The cost of reversing the invasion reveals the difficulty of maintaining order in a world of countries divided by differences in wealth and religion, but united in their ability to obtain the most lethal weaponry. As has been true for most of the century, the only western power capable of meeting a challenge on this scale is the US. But the US is no contracted global policeman. It is increasingly inwardlooking and distracted. It wished to have a greater sharing of the burden, but resents any dilution of its authority. The ending of the Cold War has created a difficult challenge for the Western world powers. It is to cooperate in the absence of a threat, to provide a global order where there is no unquestioned leader. It is against this background that Japan's role in the world stage as an important ally of the West attains significance.

Regardless of the future development of the situation, the Gulf crisis from the onset hand immense significance for Japan, as it forced Japan to force squarely the issue of security, which it had managed to evade throughout the post-War period. Although the Cold War structure had begun to break down following the thaw in superpower relations and the sweeping changes in the Eastern Europe, the process of the end of the Cold War was far from completed. Enormous military capability accumulated during that period remained virtually intact. It is also feared that the frozen unresolved issues such as ideology, nationalism, ethnic and religious animosity, economic discrepancy etc., may flare up against at any moment.

THE PAST

The situation facing the world today is still far from the advent of peace. The suggestion of a peace divided, which has been highly hailed, entirely misses this reality of international politics. A peace dividend comes from the fact that war has been effectively deterred and peace will be maintained. In the sense, the world has already received the dividend. The real issue, however, is to discover and construct a system to ensure the humanity all of continuous delivery of the dividend in the future. The Cold War structure provided Japan with a comfortable and favourable environment until very recently. At the start of the American Occupation after World War II, the US policy towards Japan was the total demilitarisation and dismantling of the heavy industry of the nation that sustained the military structure. But with the advent of the Cold War, this policy gradually changed. The birth of communism in China and the Korean war began to dwarf the fear of a possible revival of militarism in Japan. The United States decided to project Japan as a frontline state in the Far East to protect and further American strategic interests in that part of the world. Consequently the US allowed Japan to rebuild its industry to ensure an economically strong Japan not to fall prey to communism and urged Japan to rearm itself. Thus the Self Defence Forces was born, of course with constitutional limitations.

The Japanese, by nature diligent, and also prompted by the dire need for survival, eagerly started working on rebuilding industry. But Japan only reluctantly and stingily went along with the reconstruction of its armed forces, partly because of the general sentiment of aversion to war stemming from the memory of abhorrent experiences of the War, and partly because of an unwillingness to spare extra resources for the military from a drained economy. This Japanese approach—to remain as lightly armed as possible while concentrating as much energy and resources as possible on the economic form—is often called the Yoshida Doctrine, after Shigeru Yoshida, the Prime Minister at that time. In the immediate aftermath of the War, many Japanese intellectuals literally believed in the ideal of the Utopia promised by communism (this has been provide by the collapse of communism in Vietnam in the 1970s and subsequently in Eastern Europe in the 1989-90), and the argument that Japan would be dragged into an unworthy war by having a security arrangement with the United States received wide popular support. Even today, long after people were disillusioned with the promise of communism, remnants of this way of thinking persist in Japan, most typically, in the neutralistic editorials of major newspapers. While it is not suggested here that Japan must cast off this kind of obsession completely, it is suggested that such an absession must not come in its way from forming articulate political views which is why Japan has been criticised as a rich, selfish nation ever busy in furthering its economic prosperity while remaining unconcerned about developments outside its shores. In other words, it must play a more positive and constructive and if need be an assertive role in international politics.

The greatest luck has been however, that Japan has been involved in any armed conflict in the post-War period, while reaping all benefits of the Cold War period. On the economic side, the country was able to stay away from—in fact forced to stay away from—the Asian landmass and concentrated its economic activities in areas where the market principles thrives. These conditions were the product of the post-War international situation and Japan luckily benefited from them. Japan's remarkable economic performance in this favourable post-War economic environment did entail an element of luck as the Korean War immediately after the War gave a swift change to the US policy and the US encouraged Japanese heavy industries to increase production to meet the American war needs in the Korean peninsula.

When Japan regained its independence in 1952 after the Occupation period, it did so by agreeing to a so-called "majority peace treaty", to which the Soviet Union was opposed and hence did not become a party. Thus, Japan clearly expressed its national will to become a member of the Western camp. This fundamental policy decision is what opened the way for Japan's post-War success. It was a highly political decision and it was this political act which enabled the Japanese economy to enjoy smooth sailing thereafter.

Such a conscious political decision led to a significant enhancement of Japan's international stature. The alliance with Japan came to be critical importance to the US in its efforts to counter the growing threat of the Soviet Union in the Western Pacific and East Asia. The Security Treaty with Japan became the Lynchpin of American strategic policy in the Far East. Japan's policies also contributed to the maintenance of this favourable environment. The steady build-up of Japan's defence capability throughout the 1980s alleviated the deterioration of the US military balance in East Asia that occurred in the 1970s. The continuing increase in Japan's Official Development Assistance also contributed to stability in Asia.

Due to these decisions, the Western nations, especially the US, took generous attitudes towards Japan. Reconstruction and development of the Japanese economy were welcomed as evidence that the US had adopted the right policies towards Japan after the War. The success of democracy in Japan was received favourably by public opinion in the US. All these conditions allowed Japan to enjoy a state of moratorium for nearly half a century. The peculiar phenomenon of the ''warship for the United Nations'' in Japan is a product of this state of moratorium.

A majority of the people seem to have forgotten the historical fact that while the San Francisco Peace Treaty was concluded in 1952, Japan's membership in the United Nations was realised only towards the end of 1956 in the General Assembly, after having repeatedly been barred by vetoes in the Security Council. In other words, Japan owed much of its post-War development to its position as a member of the West but not particularly to its membership in the UN, which nurtured the illusory idea that Japan should be equally friendly with every country of the world, and its still prevalent in Japan and hinders the Japanese peoples' understanding of real international politics.

The political environment and the strategic scenario surrounding Japan have undergone profound and fundamental change. The perceived Soviet threat no longer exist, thanks to President Gorbachev's policy of glasnost and perestroika and his peace offensive towards China and South Korea. The Soviet Union is no longer perceived as the 'evil empire' and regional conflicts elsewhere are no longer perceived in Japan as a result of conspiracies hatched in Moscow. Japan has grown too big economically for other countries to keep being generous to it. Japan's economic strength has endowed it with a status from where the conventional post-War policies are viewed no longer adequate and relevant and are much less effective. This puts Japan at a major crossroads. The swift changes in international political and strategic environment demands an adequate Japanese response an adjustment. Japan finds to urgency to accelerate this adjustment process.

The international system prevailing during the immediate post-War period was relatively simple structure supported by two pillars. One was the pillar of security derived from the East-West confrontation, the other was the pillar of economy, which was *ipso facto* the economy of the West. Now that this structure has begun crumbling, alliance relations in the West are beginning to change subtly. A re-examination of the alliance—re-assessment of who are truly worthwhile allies and who are not—is now in order as part of the global trend. It is highly plausible to believe that the pattern of autocratic bi-polarisation of the world will not be maintained in the future. The pattern of global change that witnessed in the 1990s and whose peace was accelerated during the closing months of 1989 demonstrate that the fixed alliance relations over the last 40 years were a kind of aberration from customary historical practices. This means for Japan the end of unfettered use of complementary benefits provided by the international system. Pressures have built up on Japan to pay a proper price in order to continue enjoying these benefits.

A realignment of alliance relations has already started. While some in Japan hold the view that Japan need not react hastily because it is not clear yet where Europe is heading, others opine that Japan can not afford to just sit and wait, especially when the pace of international change has been accelerated by the Gulf crisis, triggered by the Iraqi invasion and subsequent annexation of Kuwait in August 1990. Indeed, the Gulf crisis is the first major crisis confronting the world leaders during the post-Cold War period.

The Gulf crisis presented as the first major test to Japan's foreign policy and diplomacy. While there were some in Japan who saw the Gulf crisis was a clear case where the use of force was absolutely necessary in order to maintain peace and order, there were others who voiced against Japan getting involved in a military conflict in a region with which it has very little historical linkage. The exponents of a military role for Japan argued that a country which would not participate in the efforts of its allies in such an extraordinary crisis has to be regarded as a second class citizen however wealthy it may be. From now on, it is going to be a matter of survival for Japan for it duly undertake its responsibility in international society, especially its responsibility as a member of the West. An image created at a time of a dramatic crisis does not easily leave peoples' memories. It would not be appropriate for Japan to underestimate the consequences of the public perceptions formed in the US Japan's sole ally in the West.

If the US breaks its ties with Japan because of the Gulf crisis—a remote possibility at time present moment—it will not only hurt Japan but the United State's own self-interest as well. It would totally destabilise the Asian region and inflict tremendous damage on the entire world. Japan need to realise that it is not the appropriate time to argue about the reasons after such a possibility becomes a reality.

As regards Japanese response to the Gulf crisis, three things seem to be the possible areas where Japanese response could be conceived: dispatch of SDF personnel, sharing the cost of the multinational forces, and provide financial support for those countries which suffer by participating in the economic sanctions against Iraq But what appeared to be most critical for Japan was the issue of dispatching SDF personnel to the Gulf and demonstrate the nation's willingness to share not only financial burdens but hardship and risk with other countries. It was in this perspective, the participation of the SDF, if not in a combat role, was seen essential.

Japan imposed upon itself very strict constraints about the use of its military forces. It was definitely within the country's discretion to give up its inherent right. However, to escape from its duty was not. It is the duty of a responsible modern state to contribute to the maintenance of peace and order of the world. When Prime Minister Kaifu announced the evening of August 29 his initial Persian gulf package, which included no financial contribution to multinational forces there, he referred to it as the "maximum" effort his government could make. But less than 24 hours later, following a phone call irom Kaifu to the US President George Bush which revealed that the US was unimpressed by Japan's weeks of soul-searching, the aid package to the forces jumped from zero $1 billion. Given Japan's primarily US-oriented foreign policy, the government's reaction to a lack of American enthusiasm, could be considered typical. But the government's continuous failure to set its own international agenda, especially on the Gulf crisis, seems to have left both Japanese and foreign policy-makers exceptionality discouraged about that possibility of Japan's taking action befitting its newfound economic status.

In late 1989, Japan's Vice Foreign Minister, Takakazu Kuriyama, wrote about the necessity for Japan to set its own international agenda in a controversial essay entitled "New Directions for Japanese Foreign Policy in the Changing World of the 1990s". Japanese Foreign Policy in the Changing World of the 1990s". Kuriyama argued that Japan's economic strength has too much influence on the future direction of the world for it to maintain a passive foreign policy based on an international order maintained by the US. He wrote: "Japan, as an important member of the industrial democracies can no longer conduct a passive foreign policy. Japan's foreign policy must outgrow as soon as possible, from that of a minor power to the foreign policy of a major power." Unfortunately, even today, that essay seems to remain the only major piece of concrete evidence of present domestic policy-makers' determination to work out an independent foreign policy. Foreign ministry official still readily admit their policies are based on a wait and see attitude towards other Western nations, in particular the US. Some even justify this stance by saying the public's negative reaction to the now-defunct UN Peace Cooperation Bill which indicates that Japan is still not ready to be a major player in the international arena.

The public debate that the UN Peace Cooperation Bill generated demonstrated the near general public consensus that Japan should play a more active role in the international community—a consensus that must be acted upon quickly in order for Japan to make a positive contribution to solving the crisis in the Gulf. However, as long as foreign policy remains in the hands of domestic goal-oriented politicians, any sincere efforts to set forth an independent diplomacy will be in vain. If Japan ever wishes to be a responsible member of international society, the dispatch of SDF personnel is an inevitable step. To discharge an international obligation in the sphere of security is definitely a governmental responsibility. If the Japanese government tries to depend upon and shifts the responsibility to the private sector to fulfil this obligation, instead of a legitimate governmental body, the SDF, the credibility of Japan as a nation will simply be destroyed. The American analysts of the Gulf issue suspect that Japan may be looking at the Gulf crisis only as a ''not imminent'' incident happening in a remote area, and basically a conflict between the US and the Arabs and that Japan may be regarding its response to the crisis as something which it offers as a nice gesture to the US. Their frustration was further exasperated as they see no awareness on the part of the Japanese of their partner's feelings.

But Japanese reluctance to play a major global role has caused concern to its major ally—the United States. Analysts from Japan's major think-tank, the Japan Institute of International Affairs are of the opinion that Japan is unlikely to play a major political role even in the long-term. But it is to be seen how Japan can escape this for, a major economic role in the global politics does entail a commensurate political role. Japan has often stated a willingness to play a more active role in the areas of Official Development Assistance or the protection of the world's environment but it is still not making a great effort to present substantial independent international agenda.

As mentioned earlier, it was the Yoshida Doctrine that influences Japan's inward-looking policy at a global stage. It suggested that Japan confine itself to economic activities, and eschew any political role in global affairs. As a result of following the Yoshida Doctrine for 45 years, Japanese officials have become too comfortable and can no longer think in political and military terms. And even if policy-makers come up with alternatives to an American agenda, few political leaders are courageous enough to implement a policy different from that of the US. The failure of Japan to come up with any concrete view on the Gulf crisis was a failure of the internationalists in Tokyo; they just lack sufficient political clout.

The consequences of Japan's present inability to present its own international policy could be very damaging for Japan's future political and economic relations with the rest of the world. The general pattern of Japan-US relations of today is reminiscent of the years preceding World War II. As now, Japan did not openly pass judgement on American foreign policy in the twenties. As a result, following the Depression, when the nation finally expressed its discontent, the US was taken aback. The Gulf crisis showed that unless Japan makes its own judgement on world issue and acts according to it, rather than to the American stance, the international community will not appreciate its efforts to assume more responsibility. The fact that Japan was not consulted before the US sent troops to the Gulf was an example of how Japan's failure to set an international agenda and this is what puts strain on Japan-US bilateral relations. Opinions are advanced in Tokyo that if the US thought Japan was a country with its own opinion and can take its own stand on certain aspects of international developments, like Germany, it would have consulted Tokyo before because it would have wanted to hear a good advice. But it did not feel it was necessary because it expected Japan just to follow the US position. If Japan sincerely wanted to make an international contribution suitable for an economic superpower, it must realise that a global political role has become increasingly inescapable. Japan continues to be the lynchpin to stability in the Pacific. now the US emphasises on developing its bilateral relationship with Japan into a global partnership. Japan is already a global power, not a regional power, and this entails responsibilities beyond Asia where its foreign economic relations are predominantly focussed.

The policy of Japanese government has been to build up a generation of Japanese who can help their country assume a leading role in international affairs. The Keio High School in New York is just doing that. Apart from the emphasis on learning English Keio School encourages the students' assertiveness and non-conformity. It hopes that their individualism will influence their follow students when they return home. The concern it not so much to train business leaders because the Japanese are competitive enough with an educational system that emphasises group achievement and discourages self-expression. But the

Japanese is not just an economic animal. What is needed is that Japan should become more relative, both as individual and as a society as a whole so that it could play a suitable role as a world leader in non-economic areas. In 1989, there were 17,877 Japanese around the World studying in Japanese day schools to the 9th grade, plus another 19,816 weekend pupils. In 1980, there were 12,365 students at Japanese day schools and 7,736 weekend schools.

The work habits of the Japanese has severely affected the social fabric in Japan. Consequently, the government has come under tremendous pressure to improve the quality of life and the United States has consistently exhorting Japan to undertake this restructuring programme. This restructuring issue would involve an expenditure of $ 3 trillion over ten years by Japan to improve quality of Japanese life. While many agree that Japanese life has to be improved none accept any American role in it. Some even criticise it as American interference with what is purely a Japanese affair. On the Gulf issue, though Kaifu committed $ 2 billion to help the American Gulf forces with logistics, it was not domestically accepted. This as well as the handling of the UN Peace Cooperation Corps Bill demonstrated that Japan is still not prepared to have a matured foreign policy.

Japan's foreign policy did show sign of maturity on the issue of whether to continue to deny China Western aid suspended since repression of a democratic movement in Beijing in June 1989. Japan did play a policy of its own and went its own way. Kaifu at the Houston G-7 summit in June 1990 had forcefully championed China's cause on grounds that the West must not do anything to isolate Chinese and later resumed aid releasing nearly a billion dollar in aid that was frozen in 1989. Kaifu with some help from President Bush effectively blocked a coordinated G-7 aid programme for Gorbachev on grounds that what the Soviet Union needed was not massive aid on ground that what the Soviet Union needed was not massive aid but management lectures from the West on how to run a market economy. But the Japanese policy towards the Soviet Union was projected differently at Japan, probably to assuage the Japanese' feelings as well as to soft-pedal a policy to protect the ruling party's political base. Kaifu said for the consumption of general public in Japan that Japan would not participate in any large scale economic aid programme for the Soviets until its territorial claims regarding four islands in the North are settled. Recovery of the Northern Islands is now a primary object of Japanese foreign policy. But there is an internal debate on whether disintegration of the Soviet Union would help achieve the goal. There is a view that if Japan now takes a leading part in a programme to help Gorbachev's policy it might help its own territorial cause later. No definite has been formulated yet but a middle course is being followed: no large scale economic aid has been promised, but emergency assistance is being given in the form of high-interest loans.

Emperor Akihito's enthronement in November 1990 was a brilliant piece of Japanese diplomacy. Some high-ranking delegates from 160 governments including the chief executives of the United Nations and the World Bank attended the ceremony which lasted only 30 minutes. But the occasion was fully used by the Japanese Prime Minister and his foreign minister over three days to receive more than fifty Prime Ministers and Presidents from the Third World countries who were effectively encouraged to ask for Japanese aid. They all went back homes issuing statements of gratitudes for Japan's worldwide economic role. They were all also turned over to various Japanese business houses. Japan's Uruguay Round diplomacy consisted many in two approaches: go with the US on issues both Tokyo and Washington are mutually agreeable, but resist all pressure on Japan's agriculture market on grounds of national security, an idea it is trying to sell, so far without much success.

It is universally agreed that the world community saw Japan emerging in 1990 as a great power backed by its own money and sometimes support of the United States but the Japanese suspect that is impresses none except those who are vying for its aid. Japan has now honed aid into a sharp and keen foreign policy tool. Never being innovative to the post-War years, Japanese diplomacy continues to be reactive.

Economic growth that has been Japan's lodestar from which it did not deviate during 1990. The Japanese further consolidated their recently gained position as the richest in the world. It does not matter if the quality of life is far below the average of the industrially advanced world. They are happy on their own terms and standards and defend their level of happiness without measuring it by the Western standards. The nation's wealth does not equitably reach them but the Japanese are traditionally capable of vicarious pleasure from what belongs to the nation though not to themselves, individually. Though the international oil prices increased due to the Gulf crisis, the effect on the Japanese economy remained less than that of the past two oil crises. The economy remains buoyant, with the GNP in 1990 estimated at $3.2 trillion. Politically, economically as well as socially, Japan remains the most stable of all nations throughout the post-War period. With unemployment rate at a low 2 per cent, inflation less than 3 per cent and growth rate around 5 per cent, exceptionally high for an economy like Japan, Japan has not cause for anguish and worry. What is required is a greater global responsibility commensurate with its economic status that the world expects from Japan.

JAPAN AT A TURNING POINT

Japan now stands at a turning point as the last decade of the 20th century begins. The shift to democracy under US Occupation policy was the foremost achievement. The other success has been the pacifism embodied in the constitution in which Japan renounced war and the threat or use of force as a means of settling international disputes. Japan also pledged not to maintain any war potential. This idealistic constitution contributed greatly to Japan's development. Yet this pacifism appeared selfish to some leading nations as Japan, already an economic power, moved towards becoming a political power but did not respond promptly enough to US requests, based on UN resolutions, for Japan's contributions to a solution to the Gulf crisis. Thus a friction emerged between pacifism and an international role demanded of Japan.

The Gulf crisis of 1990 and domestic politics of 1989 revealed the limits of Japan's potential contributions to international security. In an interview to *The Japan Times* in January 1991, the Foreign Minister Taro Nakayama reminded the Japanese people of their role in help keep world order. He stressed that the value of essential constancy in Japan's defence and foreign policies was demonstrated by the announced intention by the former Soviet foreign minister Eduard Shevardnadze to resign. Prime Minister Kaifu's firm resolve to play an active role in achieving real peace and stability in Asia, though achieved limited success, it also exposed his limitations to sea the controversial UN Peace Cooperation Corps Bill through the Diet.

Influential personalities such as Eiji Suzuki, chairman of the Japan Federation of Employer's Association (Nikheiren) have exhorted that Japan should voice its opinion on international affairs and become actively involved in the development of a changing world order in the post-Cold War era. It is argued that Japan's reluctance to share in the pain and responsibility of managing world affairs, especially the developments in the Persian Gulf, does not enhance Japan's prestige. While it is laudable that Japan is not involved in any armed conflict since World War II and has been enjoying the success of economic progress, it is regretted that Japan has remained a bystander in world affairs and shirking its responsibility in helping to maintain a new order in the post-Cold War period.

NARCISSISM

The role of the Japanese in world order has been analysed from the economic, political, strategic, diplomatic and cultural points of view. However, Japanese role can best be understood in psychological terms, especially in terms of national narcissism. The main elements of narcissism are an abnormal sense of self-importance, extreme sensitivity to any kind of criticism and an inability to appreciate other people's point of view. Narcissism, with its inflated sense of self-importance, is imbedded in Japan's culture. Japanese sensitivity to criticism is legendary, as is their inability to differentials criticism of what they do or say from who they are. In the post-World War II years, all Japan's critics have directed their attacks at Japanese deeds, none at who they are. Yet, at even a whiff of criticism of actions of statements, spokesmen of the Japanese establishment claim Japan-bashing or racism. This tactic has proved to be successful because Americans do not want to appear racist or to bash their most important ally. The end result is that the tactic achieve only a pyrrhic victory for Japan as crises of Japan-bashing stifle any intelligent dialogue with its allies and get Japan on a collision course with Americans and Europeans. The pity is that Japanese appear to have become professional victims—another aspect of narcissim—who truly believe that the world conspires against them when, in fact, the world only objects to some of their actions. What the world this time objected was the Japanese hesitation for an active role in the Gulf crisis.

The other major narcissistic trait exhibited by the Japanese was their inability to accept on appreciate the point of view of the non-Japanese. Therefore, because the Japanese public is against military role for Japan, the Kaifu government could not send the SDF in a combat role in the Gulf, nor could it pass the controversial UN Peace Cooperation Corps Bill in the Diet. The constitutional limitation was only a convenient cover. What in fact Japan wanted on the Gulf crisis was a policy of non-involvement but had to yield to some extent to the US pressure by making a financial contribution just not to attract international ostracism and world criticism. But it did in fact reveal its real Japanese policy. The same is true when it comes to business. No wonder, Japan rejects the American argument that Japan should open up its markets for the American goods. But what Japan wants is that the US should spend less time in opening up Japanese markets and more time straightening out its own economy. Because of their lack of appreciation of others' points of view, the Japanese are continuously surprised at others' negative reactions to Japan's actions. In their relationships with the rest of the world, most Japanese view life and the world as a zero-sum game, one in which there are only winners and losers. The notion that life can be, and most of the times is, a positive-sum game, in which both or all parties that meets with great scepticism from members of the Japanese establishment. If one accepts the zero-sum-game view of the world, one naturally wants to be a winner, at all times, in all circumstances. If a country can not "share" winning, that country is generally not appreciated. This reaction is not Japan-bashing or racism; it is a reaction to what the winner-take-all attitude has characterised Japan's world view. Thus Japanese narcissistic behaviour prevents Japan from gaining the genuine and ungrudging admistration its accomplishments have earned it. In other words, Japan's world view is not projected to a long term perspective.

Thus there are signs that Japan is distancing itself from the ideology of paramount national interests, as seen in the market integration of the European Community. True, international politics is still in the main conflicts of national egoism as demonstrated by the Iraqi invasion of Kuwait. It was in this vortex of complex of international change and international conflict that Japan was increasingly found wanting, for not dealing with the situation effectively and properly. It is thus necessary that if Japan wants to have a competitive edge in the arena of international politics, it will have to improve certain characteristics of its society and its disposition. It is in the areas of freedom of speech, the economy, literacy rate etc., that Japan can justifiably feel proud. It has refrained from making nuclear weapons notwithstanding its capability to do so, desisted from extending a helping hand to a military government through military aid, and provided the largest amount of foreign aid in the world. What Japan fails to realise that these gestures fail to earn her goodwill and trust from other countries. These are few diseases that Japan suffer from.

It used to be said that Japan is like a raft without an engine, with a concomitant implication that it was unable to travel on its own and simply allows itself to drift. It is said now that Japan has an engine but no rudder and there is no knowing in what direction it is proceeding. It is unable to show a clear philosophy on its pacifist diplomacy and, at the mercy of external pressure, goes in a direction it has never intended. Instead of using its no-war constitution as pretext, it floats it as its ideal and loses no time in building up philosophical Japan.

Kenneth E. Boulding, an American economist, once said his impressions of Japanese history was that the Japanese was the most continuous, non-dialectical and non-revolutionary people in the history of mankind. Japanese seem to have a visceral aversion to change. Even when conditions around change, Japan is hesitant to adapt to the changing situation. While the hawks insist that the Cold War had not come to an end even after the Malta summit, the left claim that what fell apart was Stalinism and not Marxism. It was on August 2, 1990 that Iraq invaded Kuwait and it was only on October 12 the Diet came into session to discuss measures to contribute to resolving the Persian Gulf crisis. Such laggardness it nothing less than morbid. What Japan needs is a more nimble system that acts more promptly in a turbulent world. Consequently, as Japan dithered and missed good timing, neither its financial contribution to the Gulf crisis nor aid to the Soviet Union and to disaster areas got the gratitude they deserved.

The Japanese people are hypersensitive to anything that appear alien to their mind. It was therefore viewed as a deliberate attempt by some to undermine the basic tenets of its non-war constitution, perhaps out of eagerness to go along with the US when the Peace Cooperation Bill was sought to be passed in the Diet. Moreover, the government and the ruling LDP are so preoccupied with 'harmony' within the party and its factions that they place too much emphasis on partisan and factional interests. Partly due to lack of tradition of change of government among different parties, it is rare in Japan that constructive compromise comes out of conflicts of partisan interests. No wonder therefore, the Peace Cooperation Corps Bill which envisaged the dispatch of the SDF personnel to beef up the multinational forces in the Gulf was defeated.

There is an unwillingness in Japan, especially among the people of the establishment, to admit its mistakes before and during World War II. Unless, Japan and its people face history more squarely, people outside Japan will inevitably look on the Japanese with more vary eyes. Given its 'economic powerhouse' status in the world, attitudes and behaviour that befit a small and inward-looking country cannot fail to attract attention as 'extraordinary'. Many in Japan opt for a greater political responsibility in the world while abiding by the non-war constitution. In order to gain understanding and support from the international community, it is necessary that Japan defines a more outward-looking, if not a high-voltage, foreign policy that would be acceptable to the international community. What Japan has specialised now is the dynamics of an inward-looking policy, totally disregarding international politics. Unless Japan transforms itself, Japan which benefited from the Cold War would be come an orphan in the days of rapprochement.

THE UN PEACE COOPERATION CORPS BILL

The Japanese government, torn between pressures from outside and an allergy to anything to do with a war and the SDF insides hastily prepared a piece of legislation called the UN Peace Cooperation Corps Bill. This innocuous sounding bill seemed to be an attempt by the government to meet the conflicting requirements of satisfying both sides. The bill contained serious shortcoming which reflected the lack of global and historical perspective in Japan's thinking on secutiry issues.

The UN Peace Cooperation Corps was to have consisted of volunteers, including members of the SDF. They were supposed not to be involved in combat activities and to carry no weapons when they engaged in medical or logistic support activities. Members of this corps had to be prepared to go fairly dangerous places if they were to undertake the activities stipulated in the bill. It was difficult to envisage how a medical team could have operated effectively in such places without proper armed protection. What was more serious was the basic concept on which the bill was drafted.

The bill presupposed a situation under which the UN member countries would act unitedly and positively and left the judgement of the appropriateness of the dispatch of the 'corps' entirely to such UN activities. Such a thinking was not only ridiculously dangerous in the reality of international politics but meant nothing but a declaration that Japan placed secondary importance on the alliance with the US and decided to entrust its security to the UN. Whatever the real intention and motivation behind the attempt at this legislation, the concept literally expressed in the bill could not be read otherwise. Such an implication was especially striking because the bill was the first presentation of Japan's idea of international order after 45 years of silence on this important subject. If Japan, which had been so reluctant to participate in the activities of US and multinational forces, was willing to dispatch the SDF for the sake of the UN, it implied that Japan no longer had faith in the alliance with the US. If indeed the government was trying to suggest to the world its intentions to revise the alliance with the US, this was the single most fundamental foreign policy change in post-War Japan.

However, if Japan was merely using the UN as an expedient to bridge the wide gap between domestic public opinion and the international situation without such a perspective, it was playing a very dangerous game. There was obviously no benefit in Japan's declaring cooperative action with the UN. The UN's peacekeeping functions had rarely been effective in the past, as seen in various cases of UN involvement in regional conflicts. In the case of the Iraqi invasion of Kuwait, consensus resolutions were successfully adopted in the Security Council in the wake of changes in Eastern Europe and the Soviet Union but it is doubtful if such unanimity will be witnessed in the UN again if Japan faces a critical situation in the future. Therefore, it was argued that the UN Peace Cooperation Bill promised no single merit to Japan while the potentials for irreparable damage to the Japan-US relationship were great.

But could Japan afford to remain the only country with such poor security policies at such a critical moment when the future of the country deepened much on the decisions taken at the time? What appeared more reasonable for Japan at the time was to adopt policies which were within the framework of the constitution. The Gulf crisis thus inaugurated a debate on national security policy, including the relevance of the country's constitution. The debate was to define the role and responsibility of Japan in international society in the future. If Japan took no meaningful measures in response to the Gulf crisis, it would find itself in the most awkward position when the US and multinational forces take military action against Iraq and soldiers of many nationalities jointly fight a war. The extent of international opprobrium that Japan will earn in such eventuality is just unimaginable. The SDF has the capacity to contribute to the operations in the Gulf but Japan cannot and will not use it. When would then the SDF be used and for what? The answer is, only when Japan is attacked. But the point is, the post-War defence posture of Japan has been constructed upon the basis of Japan-US security arrangements, and the SDF is not organised or equipped to defend Japan by itself. Therefore, the security of Japan depends on whether the US will act quickly for the defence of Japan at a time of emergency. If, however, scepticism becomes dominant in the US about the worth of the alliance with Japan, the basic promise of the country's security policy collapses. That, however, is unlikely since Japan continues to serve America's global and strategic interests in the Far East. Nevertheless, it is Japan's responsibility to arrest such scepticism in the US for gaining an upper hand which otherwise might compel a reassessment in the US of its global strategy. In turn, the argument in Japan for building up an independent defence capability; leading to a heavy armed and militarised Japan would be strong and a policy change towards that direction would become inescapable. Japan once plummeted down the slope towards international isolation after its break up of its alliance with the United Kingdom when it tried to secure its security by itself and finally ended up in a devastating war. If, therefore, Japan behaves like a deserter from it duties, it may risk the same course of self-destruction again.

Japan did contribute funds totalling $ 4 billion but the point is Japan did not offer it voluntarily; it was provided only after strong request and exhortation from the US. Again, public opinion rejected the dispatch of SDF personnel overseas and the Peace Cooperation Bill was killed in the Diet. The origin of Japan's peace diplomacy is based on self-reflection over the mistakes made in the past. But if such diplomacy lacks the spirit of self-sacrifice for the sake of peace, it is no different from a military non-intervention policy adopted solely in the interests of one's nation. That is selfish pacifism. That is how the world would look at to Japan's foreign policy and diplomacy. One reason why Japan's peace diplomacy tends to be regarded abroad as egoistic is that it involves no sacrificial contribution. From pre-War days and throughout the War, Japanese society was mobilised by the military under the rallying cry of 'self-sacrifice to serve the nation'. Unbelievably, great sacrifices were demanded and were made. The spirit of sacrifice did continue after the War. The amazingly hard work performed by employees devoted to their companies led to the miraculous recovery and growth of the Japanese economy. But the spirit of sacrifice has remained in the narrow confines of the island nation and has failed to embrace more important and emerging problems such as global warming and other environmental problems that demand global response. Unfortunately Japan's response to address to these emerging global problems continue to remain inadequate. It is necessary therefore that Japan comes out of its narrow cocoon of inward-looking policy and embraces larger global issues as of primary concern and does its bid to tackle such global problems that demand urgent global response.

30

Japan: The Land of Rising Sun

VERINDER GROVER*

On a map of the world, Japan is a chain of islands laying off the eastern coast of the Asian mainland. In history books, it is an ancient country whose traditions reach back into the mists of mythology. Yet a few countries belong so actively to here and now of the modern world. Though indeed old, Japan has the energy of youth and the vitality of spirit that constantly is seeking to improve the old and discover the new. Once isolated from the rest of the world for two-and-half centuries, Japan is today contributing its share to the peace and prosperity of the world as a member of the comity of nations.

Japan is one of the four countries in the world whose history as a sovereign nation goes back to the pre-Christian era. Japan is unique in that it has undergone two major revolutions within the space of a century. As back as 3rd January, 1868 constitutional government was introduced in Japan after the overthrow of the Tokugawa Shogunate. This resulted in the restoration of Imperial rule. On 14 April, 1875 the Emperor by an Imperial Rescript established a bicameral legislature consisting of *Genroin* (the Upper House) and the *Chihokandaigi* (the Lower House). The law-making power of these houses was very much limited since the

* Former Reader, Department of Political Science and Managing Editor, *Indian Political Science Review*, University of Delhi, Delhi.

Dajokan (the Executive Council) had the power to indicate to the legislature whether it should give a decision or only study and discuss the Bill put before it. The Rescript also provided for the introduction of constitutional government in gradual stages.

The next step in the direction of constitutional government was the Imperial Rescript of 1881 which promised the establishment of a Parliament (Imperial Diet) in 1890. Accordingly on 11th February, 1889 a written constitution, known as the Meiji Constitution, was promulgated which came into force in 1890.

Under the Meiji Constitution, the supreme political power rested with the Emperor. He was not only the head of the executive department but also exercised legislative powers with the consent of the Imperial Diet. The Diet was bicameral, consisting of House of Peers and House of Representatives. The House of Peers consisted of members of the Imperial family, the nobles and other nominated by the Emperor. The House of Representatives, on the other hand, consisted of elected representatives of the people. The adult male suffrage was introduced in 1925 but women had no right to vote.

The Diet had limited legislative powers. The Emperor alone had the power to give sanction to laws and to order them to be promulgated and executed. The emperor's power to make laws by ordinance was also very extensive. The Cabinet was responsible to the Emperor and not to the Diet. The budget was passed by the Diet but the expenditure of the Imperial House was non-votable. The Meiji Constitution also provided for a Privy Council to deliberate upon matters of State. The Emperor, the Cabinet and the Privy Council shared most of the powers of government between them. The final power was with the Emperor.

The Meiji Constitution of 1889 was replaced by a new Constitution which came into force on 3rd November 1946. In the new Constitution the Emperor is the symbol of the State and of the unity of the people. Sovereignty resides with the people. The preamble of the Constitution clearly lays down that the Government is a sacred trust of the people, authority for which is derived from the people.

The present Constitution further guarantees fundamental rights to its people. All people are equal before law irrespective of race, creed, sex, social status, or family origin. Peerage has been abolished and no religion enjoys special privilege. The executive power is vested in the Cabinet consisting of a Prime Minister and other Ministers of state who are responsible to the Diet. They remain in office as long as they collectively enjoy the confidence of the Lower House of the Diet. The Prime Minister is elected by the Diet and the other Ministers are selected by the Prime Minister.

The legislative power vests solely in the Diet, a bicameral body consisting of a House of Representatives and a House of Councillors, both of which are composed of elected representatives of the people. The members of the House of Representatives are elected for a term of 4 years and those of the House of Councillors for 6 years. Though Bills normally require passage by both the Houses to become law, a Bill passed by the House of Representatives but rejected by the House of Councillors may still become law if voted for again by the House of Representatives by a two-thirds majority. In other matters such as deciding upon the budget, approving a treaty of designating the Prime Minister, if the two Houses disagree of if the House of Councillors fails to take a decision, the decision of the House of Representatives prevails. The House of Representatives may be dissolved by a Cabinet against whom it has passed a no-confidence motion.

The Judicial power is vested in the courts, of which the highest and the Court of last resort is the Supreme Court. The Executive has no disciplinary power over the Judges, who are subject to removal only by public impeachment before a court especially constituted for the purpose by the Diet, or if judicially declared to be incompetent to perform their duties. The Supreme Court has the power to determine the constitutionality of all laws, orders, official acts, etc.

APPENDIX I

THE CONSTITUTION OF THE EMPIRE OF JAPAN*

Preamble

Having by virtue of the glories of Our Ancestors, ascended the Throne of a lineal succession unbroken for ages eternal; desiring to promote the welfare of, and to give development to the moral and intellectual faculties of Our beloved subjects, the very same that have been favoured with the benevolent care and affectionate vigilance of Our Ancestors; and hoping to maintain the prosperity of the State, in concert with Our people and with their support. We hereby promulgate, in pursuance of Our Imperial Rescript of the 12th day of the 10th month of the 14th year of Meiji, a fundamental law of State, to exhibit the principles by which We are to be guided in Our conduct, and to point out to what Our descendants and Our subjects and their descendants are forever to conform.

The rights of sovereignty of the State, We have inherited from Our Ancestors, and We shall bequeath them to Our descendants. Neither we not they shall in future fail to wield them, in accordance with the provisions of the Constitution hereby granted.

We now declare to respect and protect the security of the right and of the property of Our people, and to secure to them the complete enjoyment of the same, within the extent of the provisions of the present Constitution and of the law.

The Teikoku Gikai shall first be convoked for the 23rd year of Meiji, and the time of its opening shall be the date when the present Constitution comes into force.

---

* The Constitution was promulgated on the 11th February, 1889 (22nd year of Meiji).

When in the future it may become necessary to amend any of the provisions of the present Constitution, We or Our successors shall assume the initiative right, and submit a project for the same to the Teikoku Gikai. The Teikoku Gikai shall pass its vote upon it, according to the conditions imposed by the present Constitution, and in no otherwise shall Our descendants or Our subjects be permitted to attempt any alteration thereof.

Our Ministers of State, on Our behalf, shall be held responsible for the carrying out of the present Constitution, and Our present and future subjects shall forever assume the duty of allegiance to the present Constitution.

(His Imperial Majesty's Sign-Manual)

(Privy Seal)

The 11th day of the 2nd month of the 22nd year of Meiji.

(Countersigned) Count Kuroda Kiyotaka,
Minister President of State.
Count Ito Hirobumi,
President of the Privy Council.
Count Okuma Shigenobu,
Minister of State for Foreign Affairs.
Count Saigo Tsukumichi,
Minister of State for the Navy.
Count Inouye Kaoru,
Minister of State for Agriculture and Commerce.
Count Yamada Akiyoshi,
Minister of State for Justice.
Count Matsugata Masayoshi,
Minister of State for Finance and Minister of State for Home Affairs.
Appendices
Count Oyama Iwao,
Minister of State for War.
Viscount Mori Arinori,
Minister of State for Education.
Viscount Enomoto Takeaki,
Minister of State for Communications.

THE CONSTITUTIONAL LAW OF THE EMPIRE OF JAPAN

CHAPTER I
THE TENNO

ARTICLE I

The Empire of Japan shall be reigned over and government by a line of Tenno unbroken for ages eternal.

ARTICLE II

The Imperial Throne shall be succeeded to by Imperial male descendants, according to the provisions of the Imperial House Law.

ARTICLE III

The Tenno is sacred and inviolable.

ARTICLE IV

The Tenno stands at the head of the Empire, combining in Himself the right of sovereignty, and exercises them, according to the provisions of the present Constitution.

ARTICLE V

The Tenno exercises the legislative power with the consent of the Teikoku Gikai.

ARTICLE VI

The Tenno gives sanction to laws, and orders them to be promulgated and executed.

ARTICLE VII

The Tenno convokes the Teikoku Gikai, opens, closes and prorogues it, and dissolves the House of Representatives.

ARTICLE VIII

The Tenno, in consequence of an urgent necessity to maintain public safety or to avert public calamities, issues, when the Teikoku Gikai is not sitting, Imperial Ordinances in the place of law.

Such Imperial ordinances are to be laid before the Teikoku Gikai at its next session, and when the Gikai does not approve the said Ordinances, the Government shall declare them to be invalid for the future.

ARTICLE IX

The Tenno issues or causes to be issued, the Ordinances necessary for the carrying out of the laws or for the maintenance of the public peace and order, and for the promotion of the welfare of the subjects. But no Ordinance shall in any way alter any of the existing laws.

ARTICLE X

The Tenno determines the organization of the different branches of the administration and the salaries of all civil and military officers, and appoints and dismisses the same. Exceptions specially provided for in the present Constitution or in other laws, shall be in accordance with the respective provisions (bearing thereon).

ARTICLE XI

The Tenno has the supreme command of the Army and Navy.

ARTICLE XII

The Tenno determines the organization and peace standing of the Army and Navy.

ARTICLE XIII

The Tenno declares war, makes peace, and concludes treaties.

ARTICLE XIV

The Tenno declares a state of siege.

The conditions and effects of the state of siege shall be determined by law.

ARTICLE XV

The Tenno confers titles of nobility, rank, orders and other marks of honor.

ARTICLE XVI

The Tenno orders amnesty, pardon, commutation of punishments and rehabilitation.

ARTICLE XVII

A Regency shall be instituted in conformity with the provisions of the Imperial House Law.

The Regent shall exercise the powers appertaining to the Tenno in His name.

CHAPTER II

RIGHTS AND DUTIES OF SUBJECTS

ARTICLE XVIII

The conditions necessary for being a Japanese subject shall be determined by law.

ARTICLE XIX

Japanese subjects may, according to qualifications determined in laws or ordinances, be appointed to civil or military or any other public offices equally.

ARTICLE XX

Japanese subjects are amenable to service in the Army or Navy, according to the provisions of law.

ARTICLE XXI

Japanese subjects are amenable to the duty of paying taxes, according to the provisions of law.

ARTICLE XXII

Japanese subjects shall have the liberty of abode and of changing the same within the limits of law.

ARTICLE XXIII

No Japanese subject shall be arrested, detained, tried or punished, unless according to law.

ARTICLE XXIV

No Japanese subject shall be deprived of his right of being tried by the judges determined by law.

ARTICLE XXV

Except in the cases provided for in the law, the house of no Japanese subject shall be entered or searched without his consent.

ARTICLE XXVI

Except in the cases mentioned in the law, the secrecy of the letters of every Japanese subject shall remain inviolate.

ARTICLE XXVII

The right of property of every Japanese subject shall remain inviolate.

Measures necessary to be taken for the public benefit shall be provided for by law.

ARTICLE XXVIII

Japanese subjects shall, within limits not prejudicial to peace and order, and not antagonistic to their duties as subjects, enjoy freedom of religious belief.

ARTICLE XXIX

Japanese subjects shall, within the limits of law, enjoy the liberty of speech, writing, publication, public meetings and associations.

ARTICLE XXX

Japanese subjects may present petitions, by observing the proper forms of respect, and by complying with the rules specially provided for the same.

ARTICLE XXXI

The provisions contained in the present Chapter shall not affect the exercise of the powers appertaining to the Tenno, in times of war or in cases of national emergency.

ARTICLE XXXII

Each and every one of the provisions contained in the preceding Articles of the present Chapter, that are not in conflict with the laws or the rules and discipline of the Army and Navy, shall apply to the officers and men of the Army and of the Navy.

CHAPTER III

THE TEIKOKU GIKAI

ARTICLE XXXIII

The Teikoku Gikai shall consist of two Houses, a House of Peers and a House of Representatives.

ARTICLE XXXIV

The House of Peers shall, in accordance with the Ordinance concerning the House of Peers, be composed of the members of the

Imperial Family, of the orders of nobility, and of those persons who have been nominated thereto by the Tenno.

ARTICLE XXXV

The House of Representatives shall be composed of Members elected by the people, according to the provisions of the Law of Election.

ARTICLE XXXVI

No one can at one and the same time be a Member of both Houses.

ARTICLE XXXVII

Every law requires the consent of the Teikoku Gikai.

ARTICLE XXXVIII

Both Houses shall vote upon projects of law submitted to it by the Government, and may respectively initiate projects of law.

ARTICLE XXXIX

A bill, which has been rejected by either the one or the other of the two Houses, shall not be again brought in during the same session.

ARTICLE XL

Both House can make representations to the Government, as to laws or upon any other subject. When, however, such representations are not accepted, they cannot be made a second time during the same session.

ARTICLE XLI

The Teikoku Gikai shall be convoked every year.

ARTICLE XLII

A session of the Teikoku Gikai shall last for three months. In case of necessity, the duration of a session may be prolonged by Imperial Order.

ARTICLE XLIII

When urgent necessity arises, an extraordinary session may be convoked, in addition to the ordinary one.

The duration of an extraordinary session shall be determined by Imperial Order.

ARTICLE XLIV

The opening, closing, prolongation of a session and the prorogation of the Teikoku Gikai, shall be effected simultaneously for both Houses.

In case the House of Representatives has been ordered to dissolve, the House of Peers shall; at the same time be prorogued.

ARTICLE XLV

When the House of Representatives has been ordered to dissolve, Members shall be caused by Imperial Order to be newly elected, and the new House shall be convoked within five months from the day of dissolution.

ARTICLE XLVI

No debate can be opened and no vote can be taken in either House of the Teikoku Gikai, unless not less than one-third of the whole number of Members thereof are present.

ARTICLE XLVII

Votes shall be taken in both Houses by absolute majority. In the case of a tie vote, the President shall have the casting vote.

ARTICLE XLVIII

The deliberations of both Houses shall be held in public. The deliberations may, however, upon demand of the Government or by resolution of the House, be held in secret sitting.

ARTICLE XLIX

Both Houses of the Teikoku Gikai may respectively present addresses to the Tenno.

ARTICLE L

Both Houses may receive petitions presented by subjects.

ARTICLE LI

Both Houses may enact, besides what is provided for in the present Constitution and in the Law of the Houses, rules necessary for the management of their internal affairs.

ARTICLE LII

No member of either House shall be held responsible outside the respective Houses, for any opinion uttered or for any vote given in the House. When, however, a Member himself has given publicity to his opinions by public speech, by documents in print or in writing, or by any other similar means, he shall, in the matter, be amenable to the general law.

ARTICLE LIII

The Members of both Houses shall, during the session, be free from arrest, unless with the consent of the House, except in cases of flagrant delicts, or of offences connected with a state of internal commotion or with a foreign trouble.

ARTICLE LIV

The Ministers of State and the Delegates of the Government may, at any time, take seats and speak in either House.

CHAPTER IV

THE MINISTERS OF STATE AND THE PRIVY COUNCIL

ARTICLE LV

The respective Ministers of State shall give their advice of the Tenno, and be responsible for it.

All Laws, Imperial Ordinances and Imperial Rescripts of whatever kind, that relate to affairs of State, require the countersignature of a Minister of State.

ARTICLE LVI

The Privy Councillors shall, in accordance with the provisions for the organization of the Privy Council, deliberate upon important matters of State, when they have been consulted by the Tenno.

CHAPTER V

THE JUDICATURE

ARTICLE LVII

The Judicature shall be exercised by the Courts of Law according to law, in the name of the Tenno.

The organization of the Courts of Law shall be determined by law.

ARTICLE LVIII

The judges shall be appointed from among those who possess proper qualifications according to law.

No judge shall be deprived of his position, unless by way of criminal sentence or disciplinary punishment.

Rules for disciplinary punishment shall be determined by law.

ARTICLE LIX

Trials and judgements of a Court shall be conducted publicly. When, however, there exists any fear, that such publicity may be prejudicial to peace and order, or to the maintenance of public morality, the public trial may be suspended by provision of law or by the decision of the Court of Law.

ARTICLE LX

All matters, that fall within the competency of a special Court, shall be specially provided for by law.

ARTICLE LXI

No suit at law, which relates to rights alleged to have been infringed by the illegal measures of the administrative authorities, and which shall come within the competency of the Court of Administrative Litigation specially established by law, shall be taken cognizance of by a Court of Law.

CHAPTER VI

FINANCE

ARTICLE LXII

The imposition of a new tax or the modification of rates (of an existing one) shall be determined by law.

However, all such administrative fees or other revenue having the nature of compensation shall not fall within the category of the above clause.

The raising of national loans and the contracting of other liabilities to the charge of the National Treasury, except those that are provided for in the Budget, shall require the consent of the Teikoku Gikai.

ARTICLE LXIII

The taxes levied at present shall, in so far as they are not remodelled by a new law, be collected according to the old system.

ARTICLE LXIV

The expenditure and revenue of the State require the consent of the Teikoku Gikai by means of an annual Budget.

Any and all expenditures overpassing the appropriations set forth in the Titles and Paragraphs of the Budget, or that are not provided for in the Budget, shall subsequently require the approbation of the Teikoku Gikai.

ARTICLE LXV

The Budget shall be first laid before the House of Representatives.

ARTICLE LXVI

The expenses of the Imperial House shall be defrayed every year out of the National Treasury, according to the present fixed amount for the same, and shall not require the consent thereto of the Teikoku Gikai, except in case an increase thereof is found necessary.

ARTICLE LXVII

Those already fixed expenditures based by the Constitution upon the powers appertaining to the Tenno, and such expenditures as may have arisen by the effect of law, or that appertain to the legal obligations of the Government, shall be neither rejected nor reduced by the Teikoku Gikai, without the concurrence of the Government.

ARTICLE LXVIII

In order to meet special requirements, the Government may ask the consent of the Teikoku Gikai to a certain amount as a Continuing Expenditure Fund, for a previously fixed number of years.

ARTICLE LXIX

In order to supply deficiencies, which are unavoidable, in the Budget, and to meet requirements unprovided for in the same, a Reserve Fund shall be provided for in the Budget.

ARTICLE LXX

When the Teikoku Gikai cannot be convoked, owing to the external or internal condition of the country, in case of urgent need for the maintenance of public safety, the Government may take all necessary financial measures, by means of an Imperial Ordinance.

In the case mentioned in the preceding clause, the matter shall be submitted to the Teikoku Gikai at its next session, and its approbation shall be obtained thereto.

ARTICLE LXXI

When the Teikoku Gikai has not voted on the Budget, or when the Budget has not been brought into actual existence, the Government shall carry out the Budget of the preceding year.

ARTICLE LXXII

The final account of the expenditures and revenue of the State shall be verified and confirmed by the Board of Audit, and it shall be submitted by the Government to the Teikoku Gikai, together with the report of verification of the said Board.

The organization and competency of the Board of Audit shall be determined by law separately.

CHAPTER VII

SUPPLEMENTARY RULES

ARTICLE LXXIII

When it has become necessary in future to amend the provisions of the present Constitution, a project to that effect shall be submitted to the Teikoku Gikai by Imperial Order.

In the above case, neither House can open the debate, unless not less than two-thirds of the whole number of Members are present, and no amendment can be passed, unless a majority of not less than two-thirds of the Members present is obtained.

No modification of the Imperial House Law shall be required to be submitted to the deliberation of the Teikoku Gikai.

No provision of the present Constitution can be modified by the Imperial House Law.

ARTICLE LXXV

No modification can be introduced into the Constitution, or into the Imperial House Law, during the time of a Regency.

ARTICLE LXXVI

Existing legal enactments, such as laws, regulations, Ordinances, or by whatever names they may be called, shall, so far as they do not conflict with the present Constitution, continue in force.

All existing contracts or orders, that entail obligations upon the Government, and that are connected with expenditure, shall come within the scope of Art. LXVII.

THE IMPERIAL OATH AT THE SANCTUARY OF THE IMPERIAL PALACE

We, the Successor to the prosperous Throne of Our Predecessors, do dumbly and solemnly swear to the Imperial Founder of Our House and to Our other Imperial Ancestors that, in pursuance of a great policy co-extensive with the Heavens and with the Earth, We shall maintain and secure from decline the ancient form of government.

In consideration of the progressive tendency of the course of human affairs and in parallel with the advance of civilization, We deem it expedient, in order to give clearness and distinctness to the instructions bequeathed by the Imperial Founder of Our House and by Our other Imperial Ancestors, to establish fundamental laws formulated into express provisions of law, so that on the one hand, Our Imperial posterity may possess an express guide for the course they are to follow, and that, on the other, Our subjects shall thereby be enabled to enjoy a wider range of action in giving Us their support and that the observance of Our laws shall continue to the remotest ages of time. We will thereby give greater firmness to the stability of Our country and to promote the welfare of all the people within the boundaries of Our dominious; and We now establish the Imperial House Law and the Constitution. These laws come to only an exposition of grand precepts for the conduct of the government, bequeathed by the Imperial Founder of Our House and by Our other Imperial Ancestors. That we have been so fortunate in Our reign, in keeping with the tendency of the times, as to accomplish this work, We owe to the glorious Spirits of the Imperial Founder of Our House and of Our other Imperial Ancestors.

We now reverently make our prayer to Them and to Our illustrious Father, and implore the help of Their Spirits, and make to Them a solemn oath never at this time nor in the future to fail to be an example to Our subjects in the observance of the Laws hereby established.

May the Heavenly Spirits witness this Our solemn Oath.

THE IMPERIAL SPEECH ON THE PROMULGATION OF THE CONSTITUTION

Whereas We make it the joy and glory of Our heart to behold the prosperity of Our country and the welfare of Our subjects, We do hereby, in virtue of the supreme power We inherit from Our Imperial Ancestors, promulgate the present immutable fundamental law, for the sake of Our present subjects and their descendents.

The Imperial Founder of Our House and Our other Imperial Ancestors, by the help and support of the forefathers of Our subjects, laid the foundation of Our Empire upon a basis which is to last forever. That this brilliant achievement embellishes the annals of Our country, is due to the glorious virtues of Our Sacred Imperial Ancestors, and to the loyalty and bravery of Our subjects, their love of their country and their public spirit. Considering that Our subjects are the descendants of the loyal and good subjects of Our Imperial Ancestors, We doubt not but that Our subjects will be guided by Our views, and will sympathize with all Our endeavours, and that, harmoniously cooperating together, they will share with Us Our hope of making manifest the glory of Our country, both at home and a broad, and of securing forever the stability of the work bequeathed to Us by our Imperial Ancestors.

THE IMPERIAL SPEECH SANCTIONING THE IMPERIAL HOUSE LAW

The Imperial Throne of Japan, enjoying the Grace of Heaven and everlasting from ages eternal in an unbroken line of succession, has been transmitted to Us through the successive reigns. The fundamental rules of Our Family were established once for all, at the time that Our Ancestors laid the foundations of the Empire, and are even at this day as bright as the celestial luminaries. We now desire to make the instructions of Our Ancestors more exact and express and to establish for Our posterity a House Law, by which Our House shall be founded in everlasting strength, and its dignity be forever maintained. We hereby, with the advice of Our Privy Council, give Our Sanction to the present Imperial House Law, to serve as a standard by which Our descendants shall be guided.

(His Imperial Majesty's Sign-Manual.)

(Privy Seal.)

The 11th day of the 2nd month of the 22nd year of Meiji.

THE IMPERIAL HOUSE LAW

CHAPTER I

SUCCESSION TO THE IMPERIAL THRONE

ARTICLE I

The Imperial Throne of Japan shall be succeeded to by male descendants in the male line of Imperial Ancestors.

ARTICLE II

The Imperial Throne shall be succeeded to by the Imperial eldest son.

ARTICLE III

When there is no Imperial eldest son, the Imperial Throne shall be succeeded to by the Imperial eldest grandson. When there is neither Imperial eldest son nor any male descendant of his, it shall be succeeded to by the Imperial son next in age, and so on in every successive case.

ARTICLE IV

For succession to the Imperial Throne by an Imperial descendant, the one of full blood shall have precedence over descendants of half blood. The succession to the Imperial Throne by the latter shall be limited to those cases only when there is no Imperial descendant of full blood.

ARTICLE V

When there is no Imperial descendant, the Imperial Throne shall be succeeded to by an Imperial brother and by his descendants.

ARTICLE VI

When there or no such Imperial brother or descendant of his, the Imperial Throne shall be succeeded to by an Imperial uncle and by his descendants.

ARTICLE VII

When there is neither such Imperial uncle nor descendant of his, the Imperial Throne shall be succeeded to by the next nearest member among the rest of the Imperial Family.

ARTICLE VIII

Among the Imperial brothers and the remoter Imperial relations, precedence shall be given, in the same degree, to the descendants of full blood over those of half blood, and to the elder over the younger.

ARTICLE IX

When the Imperial heir is suffering from an incurable disease of mind or body, or when any other weighty cause exists, the order of succession may be changed in accordance with the foregoing provisions, with the advice of the Imperial Family Council and with that of the Privy Council.

CHAPTER II

ASCENSION AND CORONATION

ARTICLE X

Upon the demise of the Tenno, the Imperial heir shall ascend the Throne, and shall acquire the Divine Treasures of the Imperial Ancestors.

ARTICLE XI

The ceremonies of Coronation shall be performed and a Grand Coronation Banquet (Daijosai) shall be held at Kyoto.

ARTICLE XII

Upon an Ascension to the Throne, a new era shall be inaugurated, and the name of it shall remain unchanged during the whole reign, in agreement with the established rule of the 1st year of Meiji.

CHAPTER III

MAJORITY INSTITUTION OF EMPRESS AND OF HEIR-APPARENT

ARTICLE XIII

The Tenno, the Kotaishi and the Kotaison shall attain their majority at eighteen full years of age.

ARTICLE XIV

Members of the Imperial Family, other than those mentioned in the preceding Article, shall attain their majority at twenty full years of age.

ARTICLE XV

The son of the Tenno who is Heir-apparent, shall be called "Kotaishi." In case there is no Kotaishi, the Imperial grandson who is Heir-apparent, shall be called "Kotaison."

ARTICLE XVI

The institution of Empress and that of Kotaison shall be proclaimed by an Imperial Rescript.

CHAPTER IV

STYLES OF ADDRESS

ARTICLE XVII

The style of address for the Tenno, the Grand Empress Dowager, the Empress Dowager and the Empress, shall be His, or Her or Your Majesty.

ARTICLE XVIII

The Kotaishi and his consort, the Kotaison and his consort, the Imperial Princes and their consorts, and the Princesses shall be styled His, Her, Their or Your Highness or Hignesses.

CHAPTER V

REGENCY

ARTICLE XIX

When the Tenno is a minor, a Regency shall be instituted.

When He is prevented by some permanent cause from personally governing, a Regency shall be instituted, with the advice of the Imperial Family Council and with that of the Privy Council.

ARTICLE XX

The Regency shall be assumed by the Kotaishi or the Kotaison, being of full age of majority.

ARTICLE XXI

When there is neither Kotaishi nor Kotaison, or when the Kotaishi or Kotaison has not yet arrived at his majority, the Regency shall be assumed in the following order:-

1. An Imperial Prince or a Prince.
2. The Empress.
3. The Empress Dowager.
4. The Grand Empress Dowager.
5. An Imperial Princess or a Princess.

ARTICLE XXII

In case the Regency is to be assumed from among the male members of the Imperial Family, it shall be done in agreement with the order of succession to the Imperial Throne. The same shall apply to the case of female members of the Imperial Family.

ARTICLE XXIII

A female member of the Imperial Family to assume the Regency, shall be exclusively one who has no consort.

ARTICLE XXIV

When, on account of the minority of the nearest related member of the Imperial Family, or for some other cause, another member has to assume the Regency, the latter shall not, upon the arrival at majority of the about mentioned nearest related member, or upon the disappearance or the aforesaid cause, resign his or her post in favour of any person other than of the Kotaishi or of the Kotaison.

ARTICLE XXV

When a Regent or one who should become such, is suffering from an incurable disease of mind or body, or when any other weighty cause exists therefor, the order of the Regency may be changed, with the advice of the Imperial Family Council and with that of the Privy Council.

CHAPTER VI

THE IMPERIAL GOVERNOR

ARTICLE XXVI

When the Tenno is a minor, an Imperial Governor shall be appointed to take change of His bringing up and of His education.

ARTICLE XXVII

In case no Imperial Governor has been nominated in the will of the preceding Tenno, the Regent shall appoint one, with the advice of the Imperial Family Council and with that of the Privy Council.

ARTICLE XXVIII

Neither the Regent not any of his descendants can be appointed Imperial Governor.

ARTICLE XXIX

The Imperial Governor can not be removed from his post by the Regent, unless upon the advice of the Imperial Family Council and upon that of the Privy Council.

CHAPTER VII

THE IMEPRIAL FAMILY

ARTICLE XXX

The term ''Imperial Family'' shall include the Grand Empress Dowager, the Empress Dowager, the Empress, the Kotaishi and his consort, the Kotaison and his consort, the Imperial Princes and their consorts, the Imperial Princesses, the Princes and their consorts, and the Princesses.

ARTICLE XXXI

From Imperial sons to Imperial great-great-grandsons, Imperial male descendants shall be called Imperial Princes; and from Imperial daughters to Imperial great-great-grand-daughters, Imperial female descendants shall be called Imperial Princesses. From the fifth generation downwards, male descendants shall be called, Princes, and female ones Princesses.

ARTICLE XXXII

When the Imperial Throne is succeeded to by a member of a branch line, the title of Imperial Prince or Imperial Princess shall be specially granted to the Imperial brothers and sisters, being already Princes or Princesses.

ARTICLE XXXIII

The births, namings, marriages and deaths in the Imperial Family shall be announced by the Minister of the Imperial Household.

ARTICLE XXXIV

Genealogical and other records relating to the matters mentioned in the preceding Article shall be kept in the Imperial archives.

ARTICLE XXXV

The members of the Imperial Family shall be under the control of the Tenno.

ARTICLE XXXVI

When a Regency is instituted, the Regent shall exercise the power of control referred to in the preceding Article.

ARTICLE XXXVII

When a member, male or female, of the Imperial Family is a minor and has been bereft of his or her father, the officials of the Imperial Court shall be ordered to take charge of his or her bringing up and education. Under certain circumstances, the Tenno may either approve the guardian chosen by his or her parent, or may nominate one.

ARTICLE XXXVIII

The guardian of a member of the Imperial Family must be himself a member thereof and of age.

ARTICLE XXXIX

Marriages of members of the Imperial Family shall be restricted to the circle of the Family, or to certain noble families specially approved by Imperial Order.

ARTICLE XL

Marriages of the members of the Imperial Family shall be subject to the sanction of the Tenno.

ARTICLE XLI

The Imperial writs sanctioning the marriages of members of the Imperial Family, shall bear the countersignature of the Minister of the Imperial Household.

ARTICLE XLII

No member of the Imperial Family can adopt any one as his son.

ARTICLE XLIII

When a member of the Imperial Family wishes to travel beyond the boundaries of the Empire, he shall first obtain the sanction of the Tenno.

ARTICLE XLIV

A female member of the Imperial Family, who has married a subject, shall be excluded from the membership of the Imperial Family. However, she may be allowed, by the special grace of the Tenno, to retain her title of Imperial Princess or of Princess, as the case may be.

CHAPTER VIII

IMPERIAL HEREDITARY ESTATES

ARTICLE XLV

No landed or other property, that has been fixed as the Imperial Hereditary Estates, shall be divided up and alienated.

ARTICLE XLVI

The landed and other property to be included in the Imperial Hereditary Estates, shall be settled by an Imperial writ, with the advice of the Privy Council, and shall be announced by the Minister of the Imperial Household.

CHAPTER IX

EXPENDITURE OF THE IMPERIAL HOUSE

ARTICLE XLVII

The expenses of the Imperial House of all kinds shall be defrayed out of the National Treasury at a certain fixed amount.

ARTICLE XLVIII

The estimates and audit of accounts of the expenditures of the Imperial House and all other rules of the kind, shall be regulated by the Finance Regulations of the Imperial House.

CHAPTER X

LITIGATIONS AND DISCIPLINARY RULES FOR THE MEMBERS OF THE IMPERIAL FAMILY

ARTICLE XLIX

Litigation between members of the Imperial Family shall be decided by judicial functionaries specially designated by the Emperor to the Department of the Imperial Household, and execution issued, after Imperial Sanction thereto has been obtained.

ARTICLE L

Civil actions brought by private individuals against members of the Imperial Family, shall be decided in the Court of Appeal in Tokyo. Members of the Imperial Family shall, however, be represented by attorneys, and no personal attendance in the Court shall be required of them.

ARTICLE LI

No member of the Imperial Family can be arrested, or summoned before a Court of Law, unless the sanction of the Emperor has been first obtained thereto.

ARTICLE LII

When a member of the Imperial Family has committed an act derogatory to his (or her) dignity, or when he has exhibited disloyally to the Imperial House, he shall, by way of disciplinary punishment and by order of the Tenno, be deprived of the whole or of a part of the privileges belonging to him as a member of the Imperial Family, or shall be suspended therefrom.

ARTICLE LIII

When a member of the Imperial Family acts in a way tending to the squandering of his (or her) property, he shall be pronounced by the Tenno, prohibited from administering his property, and a manager shall be appointed therefor.

ARTICLE LIV

The two foregoing Articles shall be sanctioned, upon the advice of the Imperial Family Council.

CHAPTER XI

THE IMPERIAL FAMILY COUNCIL

ARTICLE LV

The Imperial Family Council shall be composed by the male members of the Imperial Family, who have reached the age of majority. The Lord Keeper of the Privy Seal, the President of the Privy Council, the Minister of the Imperial Household, the Minister of State for Justice and the President of the Court of Cassation shall be ordered to take part in the deliberations of the Council.

ARTICLE LVI

The Tenno personally presides over the meeting of the Imperial Family Council, or directs one of the members of the Imperial Family to do so.

CHAPTER XII

SUPPLEMENTARY RULES

ARTICLE LVII

Those of the present members of the Imperial Family of the fifth generation and downwards, who have already been invested with the title of Imperial Prince, shall retain the same as heretofore.

ARTICLE LVIII

The order of succession to the Imperial Throne shall in every case relate to the descendants of absolute lineage. There shall be no admission to this line of succession of any one, as a consequence of his now being an adopted Imperial son, Koyushi or heir to a princely house.

ARTICLE LIX

The grades of rank among the Imperial Princes, Imperial Princesses, Princes and Princesses shall be abolished.

ARTICLE LX

The family rank of Imperial Princes and all usages conflicting with the present Law, shall be abolished.

ARTICLE LXI

The property, annual expenses and all other rules concerning the members of the Imperial Family, shall be specially determined.

ARTICLE LXII

When in the future it shall become necessary either to amend or make additions to the present Law, the matter shall be decided by the Tenno, with the advice of the Imperial Family Council and with that of the Privy Council.

APPENDIX II

CONSTITUTION OF JAPAN (1946) & RULES THEREUNDER*

Imperial Edict

I rejoice that the foundation for the construction of a new Japan has been laid according to the will of the Japanese people, and hereby sanction and promulgate the amendments of the Imperial Japanese Constitution effected following the consultation with the Privy Council and the decision of the Imperial Diet made in accordance with Article 73 of the said Constitution.

Signed: HIROHITO, Seal of the Emperor.

This third day of the eleventh month of the twenty-first year of Showa (November 3, 1946)

Countersigned:

Prime Minister and concurrently Minister for Foreign Affairs	YOSHIDA Shigeru
Minister of State	Baron SHIDEHARA Kijuro
Minister of Justice	KIMURA Tokutaro
Minister for Home Affairs	OMURA Selichi
Minister of Education	TANAKA Kotaro
Minister of Agriculture and Forestry	WADA Hiroo
Minister of State	SAITO Takao
Minister of Communications	HITOTSUMATSU Sadayoshi

Courtesy: *The National Diet of Japan Publications*, 1946.

Minister of Commerce and Industry	HOSHIJIMA Niro
Minister of Welfare	KAWAI Yoshinari
Minister of State	UEHARA Etsujiro
Minister of Transportation	HIRATSUKA Tsunejiro
Minister of Finance	ISHIBASHI Tanzan
Minister of State	KANAMORI Tokujiro
Minister of State	ZEN Keinosuke

The Constitution of Japan

(Promulgated on November 3, 1946)

We, the Japanese people, acting through our duly elected representatives in the National Diet, determined that we shall secure for ourselves and our posterity the fruits of peaceful co-operation with all nations and the blessings of liberty throughout this land, and resolved that never again shall we be visited with the horrors of war through the action of government, do proclaim that sovereign power resides with the people and do firmly establish this Constitution. Government is a sacred trust of the people, the authority for which is derived from the people, the powers of which are exercised by the representatives of the people, and the benefits of which are enjoyed by the people. This is a universal principle of mankind upon which this Constitution is founded. We reject and revoke all constitutions, laws, ordinances, and rescripts in conflict herewith.

We, the Japanese people, desire peace for all time and are deeply conscious of the high ideals controlling human relationship, and we have determined to preserve our security and existence, trusting in the justice and faith of the peace-loving peoples of the world. We desire to occupy an honoured place in an international society striving for the preservation of peace, and the banishment of tyranny and slavery, oppression and intolerance for all time from the earth. We recognize that all peoples of the world have the right to live in peace, free from fear and want.

We believe that no nation is responsible to itself alone, but that laws of political morality are universal; and that obedience to such laws is incumbent upon all nations who would sustain their own sovereignty and justify their sovereign relationship with other nations.

We, the Japanese people, pledge our national honour to accomplish these high ideals and purposes with all our resources.

CHAPTER I
THE EMPEROR

Article 1. The Emperor shall be the symbol of the State and of the unity of the people, deriving his position from the will of the people with whom resides sovereign power.

Article 2. The Imperial Throne shall be dynastic and succeeded to in accordance with the Imperial House Law passed by the Diet.

Article 3. The advice and approval of the Cabinet shall be required for all acts of the Emperor in matters of state, and the Cabinet shall be responsible therefor.

Article 4. The Emperor shall perform only such acts in matters of state as are provided for in this Constitution and he shall not have powers related to government.

The Emperor may delegate the performance of his acts in matters of state as may be provided by law.

Article 5. When, in accordance with the Imperial House Law, a Regency is established, the Regent shall perform his acts in matters of state in the Emperor's name. In this case, paragraph one of the preceding article will be applicable.

Article 6. The Emperor shall appoint the Prime Minister as designated by the Diet.

The Emperor shall appoint the Chief Judge of the Supreme Court as designated by the Cabinet.

Article 7. The Emperor, with the advice and approval of the Cabinet, shall perform the following acts in matters of state on behalf of the people:

Promulgation of amendments of the constitution, laws, cabinet orders and treaties.

Convocation of Diet.

Dissolution of the House of Representatives.

Proclamation of general election of members of the Diet.

Attestation of the appointment and dismissal of Ministers of State and other officials as provided for by law, and of full powers and credentials of Ambassadors and Ministers,

Attestation of general and special amnesty, commutation of punishment, reprieve, and restoration of rights.

Awarding of honours.

Attestation of instruments of ratification and other diplomatic documents as provided for by law.

Receiving foreign ambassadors and ministers.

Performance of ceremonial functions.

Article 8. No property can be given to, or received by, the Imperial House, nor can any gifts be made therefrom, without the authorization of the Diet.

CHAPTER II

RENUNCIATION OF WAR

Article 9. Aspiring sincerely to an international peace based on justice and order, the Japanese people forever renounce war as a sovereign right of the nation and the threat or use of force as means of settling international disputes.

In order to accomplish the aim of the preceding paragraph, land, sea, and air forces, as well as other war potential, will never be maintained. The right of belligerency of the state will not be recognized.

CHAPTER III

RIGHTS AND DUTIES OF THE PEOPLE

Article 10. The conditions necessary for being a Japanese national shall be determined by law.

Article 11. The people shall not be prevented for enjoying any of the fundamental human rights. These fundamental human rights guaranteed to the people by this Constitution shall be conferred upon the people of this and future generations as eternal and inviolate rights.

Article 12. The freedoms and rights guaranteed to the people by this Constitution shall be maintained by the constant endeavour of the people, who shall refrain from any abuse of these freedoms and rights and shall always be responsible for utilizing them for the public welfare.

Article 13. All of the people shall be respected as individuals. Their right to life, liberty, and the pursuit of happiness shall, to the extent that it does not interfere with the public welfare, be the supreme consideration in legislation and in other governmental affairs.

Article 14. All of the people are equal under the law and there shall be no discrimination in political, economic or social relations because of race, creed, sex, social status or family origin.

Peers and peerage shall not be recognized.

No privilege shall accompany any award of honour, decoration or any distinction, nor shall any such award be valid beyond the lifetime of the individual who now holds or hereafter may receive it.

Article 15. The people have the inalienable right to choose their public officials and to dismiss them.

All public officials are servants of the whole community and not of any group thereof.

Universal adult suffrage is guaranteed with regard to the election of public officials.

In all elections, secrecy of the ballot shall not be violated. A voter shall not be answerable, publicly or privately, for the choice he has made.

Article 16. Every person shall have the right of peaceful petition for the redress of damage, for the removal of public officials, for the enactment, repeal or amendment of laws, ordinances or regulations and for other matters; nor shall any person be in any way discriminated against for sponsoring such a petition.

Article 17. Every person may sue for redress as provided by law from the State or a public entity, in case he has suffered damage through illegal act of any public official.

Article 18. No person shall be held in bondage of any kind. Involuntary servitude, except as punishment for crime, is prohibited.

Article 19. Freedom of thought and conscience shall not be violated.

Article 20. Freedom of religion is guaranteed to all. No religious organization shall receive any privileges from the State, nor exercise any political authority.

No person shall be compelled to take part in any religious act, celebration, rite or practice.

The State and its organs shall refrain from religious education or any other religious activity.

Article 21. Freedom of assembly and association as well as speech, press and all other forms of expression are guaranteed.

No censorship shall be maintained, nor shall the secrecy of any means of communication be violated.

Article 22. Every person shall have freedom to choose and change his residence and to choose his occupation to the extent that it does not interfere with the public welfare.

Freedom of all persons to move to a foreign country and to divest themselves of their nationality shall be inviolate.

Article 23. Academic freedom is guaranteed.

Article 24. Marriage shall be based only on the mutual consent of both sexes and it shall be maintained through mutual cooperation with the equal rights of husband and wife as a basis.

With regard to choice of spouse, property rights, inheritance, choice of domicile, divorce and other matters pertaining to marriage and the family, laws shall be enacted from the standpoint of individual dignity and the essential equality of the sexes.

Article 25. All people shall have the right to maintain the minimum standards of wholesome and cultured living.

In all spheres of life, the State shall use its endeavours for the promotion and extension of social welfare and security, and of public health.

Article 26. All people shall have the right to receive an equal education correspondent to their ability, as provided by law.

All people shall be obligated to have all boys and girls under their protection receive ordinary education as provided for by law. Such compulsory education shall be free.

Article 27. All people shall have the right and the obligation to work.

Standards for wages, hours, rest and other working conditions shall be fixed by law.

Children shall not be exploited.

Article 28. The right of workers to organize and to bargain and act collectively is guaranteed.

Article 29. The right to own or to hold property is inviolable. Property rights shall be defined by law, in conformity with the public welfare.

Private property may be taken for public use upon just compensation therefor.

Article 30. The people shall be liable to taxation as provided by law.

Article 31. No person shall be deprived of life or liberty, nor shall any other criminal penalty be imposed, except according to procedure established by law.

Article 32. No person shall be denied the right of access to the courts.

Article 33. No person shall be apprehended except upon warrant issued by a competent judicial officer which specifies the offense with which the person is charged, unless he is apprehended, the offense being committed.

Article 34. No person shall be arrested or detained without being at once informed of the charges against him or without the immediate privilege of counsel; nor shall he be detained without adequate cause;

and upon demand of any person such cause must be immediately shown in open court in his presence and the presence of his counsel.

Article 35. The right of all persons to be secure in their homes, papers and effects against entries, searches and seizures shall not be impaired except upon warrant issued for adequate cause and particularly describing the place to be searched and things to be sized, or except as provided by Article 33.

Each search or seizure shall be made upon separate warrant issued by a competent judicial officer.

Article 36. The infliction of torture by any public officer and cruel punishments are absolutely forbidden.

Article 37. In all criminal cases the accused shall enjoy the right to a speedy and public trial by an impartial tribunal.

He shall be permitted full opportunity to examine all witnesses, and he shall have the right of compulsory process for obtaining witnesses on his behalf at public expense.

At all times the accused shall have the assistance of competent counsel who shall, if the accused is unable to secure the same by his own efforts, be assigned to his use by the State.

Article 38. No person shall be compelled to testify against himself.

Confession made under compulsion, torture or threat, or after prolonged arrest or detention shall not be admitted in evidence.

No person shall be convicted or punished in cases where the only proof against him is his own confession.

Article 39. No person shall be held criminally liable for an act which was lawful at the time it was committed, or of which he has been acquitted, nor shall he be placed in double jeopardy.

Article 40. Any person, in case he is acquitted after he has been arrested or detained, may sue the State for redress as provided by law.

CHAPTER IV
THE DIET

Article 41. The Diet shall be the highest organ of state power, and shall be the sole law-making organ of the State.

Article 42. The Diet shall consist of two Houses, namely the House of Representatives and the House of Councillors.

Article 43. Both Houses shall consist of elected members, representative of all the people.

The number of the members of each House shall be fixed by law.

Article 44. The qualifications of members of both Houses and their electors shall be fixed by law. However, there shall be no discrimination because of race, creed, sex, social status, family origin, education, property or income.

Article 45. The term of office of members of the House of Representatives shall be four years. However, the term shall be terminated before the full term is up in case the House of Representatives is dissolved.

Article 46. The term of office of members of the House of Councillors shall be six years, and election for half the members shall take place every three years.

Article 47. Electoral districts, method of voting and other matters pertaining to the method of election of members of both Houses shall be fixed by law.

Article 48. No person shall be permitted to be a member of both Houses simultaneously.

Article 49. Members of both Houses shall receive appropriate annual payment from the national treasury in accordance with law.

Article 50. Except in cases provided by law, members of both Houses shall be exempt from apprehension while the Diet is in session, and any members apprehended before the opening of the session shall be freed during the term of the session upon demand of the House.

Article 51. Members of both Houses shall not be held liable outside the House for speeches, debates or votes cast inside the House.

Article 52. An ordinary session of the Diet shall be convoked once per year.

Article 53. The Cabinet may determine to convoke extra-ordinary sessions of the Diet. When a quarter or more of the total members of either House makes the demand, the Cabinet must determine on such convocation.

Article 54. When the House of Representatives is dissolved, there must be a general election of members of the House of Representatives within forty (40) days from the date of dissolution, and the Diet must be convoked within thirty (30) days from the date of the election.

When the House of Representatives is dissolved, the House of Councillors is closed at the same time. However, the Cabinet may in time of national emergency convoke the House of Councillors in emergency session.

Measures taken at such session as mentioned in the proviso of the preceding paragraph shall be provisional and shall become null and void unless agreed to by the House of Representatives within a period of ten (10) days after the opening of the next session of the Diet.

Article 55. Each House shall judge disputes related to qualifications of its members. However, in order to deny a seat to any member, it is necessary to pass a resolution by a majority of two-thirds or more of the members present.

Article 56. Business cannot be transacted in either House unless one-third or more of total membership is present.

All matters shall be decided, in each House, by a majority of those present, except as elsewhere provided in the Constitution, and in case of a tie, the presiding officer shall decide the issue.

Article 57. Deliberation in each House shall be public. However, a secret meeting may be held where a majority of two-thirds or more of those members present passes a resolution therefor.

Each House shall keep a record of proceedings. This record shall be published and given general circulation, excepting such parts of proceedings of secret session as may be deemed to require secrecy.

Upon demand of one-fifth or more of the members present, votes of the members on any matter shall be recorded in the minutes.

Article 58. Each House shall select its own president and other officials.

Each House shall establish its rules pertaining to meetings, proceedings, and internal discipline, and may punish members for disorderly conduct. However, in order to expel a member a majority of two-thirds or more of those members present must pass a resolution thereon.

Article 59. A bill becomes a law on passage by both Houses, except as otherwise provided by the Constitution.

A bill which is passed by the House of Representatives, and upon which the House of Councillors makes a decision different from that of the House of Representatives, becomes a law when passed a second time by the House of Representatives by a majority of two-thirds or more of the members present.

The provision of the preceding paragraph does not preclude the House of Representatives from calling for the meeting of a joint committee of both Houses, provided for by law.

Failure by the House of Councillors to take final action within sixty (60) days after receipt of a bill passed by the House of Representatives, time in recess excepted, may be determined by the House of Representatives to constitute a rejection of the said bill by the House of Councillors.

Article 60. The budget must first be submitted to the House of Representatives.

Upon consideration of the budget, when the House of Councillors makes a decision different from that of the House of Representatives, and when no agreement can be reached even through a joint committee of both Houses, provided for by law, or in the case of failure by the House of Councillors to take final action within thirty (30) days, the period of recess excluded, after the receipt of the budget passed by the House of Representatives, the decision of the House of Representatives shall be the decision of the Diet.

Article 61. The second paragraph of the preceding article applies also to the Diet approval required for the conclusion of treaties.

Article 62. Each House may conduct investigations in relation to government, and may demand the presence and testimony of witnesses, and the production of records.

Article 63. The Prime Minister and other Ministers of State may, at any time, appear in either House for the purpose of speaking on bills, regardless of whether they are members of the House or not. They must appear when their presence is required in order to give answers or explanations.

Article 64. The Diet shall set up an impeachment court from among the members of both Houses for the purpose of trying those judges against whom removal proceedings have been instituted.

Matters relating to impeachment shall be provided by law.

CHAPTER V
THE CABINET

Article 65. Executive power shall be vested in the Cabinet.

Article 66. The Cabinet shall consist of the Prime Minister, who shall be its head, and other Ministers of State, as provided for by law.

The Prime Minister and other Ministers of State must be civilians.

The Cabinet, in the exercise of executive power, shall be collectively responsible to the Diet.

Article 67. The Prime Minister shall be designated from among the members of the Diet by a resolution of the Diet. This designation shall precede all other business.

If the House of Representatives and the House of Councillors disagree and if no agreement can be reached even through a joint committee of both Houses, provided for by law, or the House of Councillors fails to make designation within ten (10) days, exclusive of the period of recess, after the House of Representatives has made designation, the decision of the House of Representatives shall be the decision of the Diet.

Article 68. The Prime Minister shall appoint the Ministers of State. However, a majority of their number must be chosen from among the members of the Diet.

The Prime Minister may remove the Minister of State as he choose.

Article 69. If the House of Representatives passes a no-confidence resolution, or rejects a confidence resolution, the Cabinet shall resign *en masse*, unless the House of Representatives is dissolved within ten (10) days.

Article 70. When there is a vacancy in the post of Prime Minister, or upon the first convocation of the Diet after a general election of members of the House of Representatives, the Cabinet shall resign *en masse.*

Article 71. In the cases mentioned in the two preceding articles, the Cabinet shall continue its functions until the time when a new Prime Minister is appointed.

Article 72. The Prime Minister, representing the Cabinet, submits bills, reports on general national affairs and foreign relations to the Diet and exercises control and supervision over various administrative branches.

Article 73. The Cabinet, in addition to other general administrative functions, shall perform the following functions:

Administer the law faithfully; conduct affairs of state. Manage foreign affairs.

Conclude treaties. However, it shall obtain prior or, depending on circumstances, subsequent approval of the Diet.

Administer the civil service, in accordance with standards established by law.

Prepare the budget, and present it to the Diet.

Enact cabinet orders in order to execute the provisions of this Constitution and of the law. However, it cannot include penal provisions in such cabinet orders unless authorized by such law.

Decide on general amnesty, special amnesty, commutation of punishment, reprieve, and restoration of rights.

Article 74. All laws and cabinet orders shall be signed by the competent Minister of State and countersigned by the Prime Minister.

Article 75. The Ministers of State, during their tenure of office, shall not be subject to legal action without the consent of the Prime Minister. However, the right to take that action is not impaired hereby.

CHAPTER VI
JUDICIARY

Article 76. The whole judicial power is vested in a Supreme Court and in such inferior courts as are established by law.

No extraordinary tribunal shall be established, nor shall any organ or agency of the Executive be given final judicial power.

All judges shall be independent in the exercise of their conscience and shall be bound only by this Constitution and the laws.

Article 77. This Supreme Court is vested with the rule-making power under which it determines the rules of procedure and of practice, and of matters relating to attorneys, the internal discipline of the courts and the administration of judicial affairs.

Public procurators shall be subject to the rule-making power of the Supreme Court.

The Supreme Court may delegate the power to make rules for inferior courts to such courts.

Article 78. Judges shall not be removed except by public impeachment unless judicially declared mentally or physically incompetent to perform official duties. No disciplinary action against judges shall be administered by any executive organ or agency.

Article 79. The Supreme Court shall consist of a Chief Judge and such number of judges as may be determined by law; all such judges excepting the Chief Judge shall be appointed by the Cabinet.

The appointment of the judges of the Supreme Court shall be reviewed by the people at the first general election of members of the House of Representatives following their appointment, and shall be reviewed again at the first general election of members of the House of Representatives after a lapse of ten (10) years, and in the same manner thereafter.

In cases mentioned in the foregoing paragraph, when the majority of the voters favours the dismissal of a judge, he shall be dismissed.

Matters pertaining to review shall be prescribed by law.

The judges of the Supreme Court shall be retired upon the attainment of the age as fixed by law.

All such judges shall receive, at regular stated intervals, adequate compensation which shall not be decreased during their terms of office.

Article 80. The Judges of the inferior courts shall be appointed by the Cabinet from a list of persons nominated by the Supreme Court. All such judges shall hold office for a term of ten (10) years with privilege of reappointment, provided that they shall be retired upon the attainment of the age as fixed by law.

The judges of the inferior courts shall receive, at regular stated intervals, adequate compensation which shall not be decreased during their terms of office.

Article 81. The Supreme Court is the Court of last resort with power to determine the constitutionality of any law, order, regulation or official act.

Article 82. Trials shall be conducted and judgement declared publicly.

Where a court unanimously determines publicity to be dangerous to public order or morals, a trial may be conducted privately, but trials of political offenses, offenses involving the press or cases wherein the rights of people as guaranteed in Chapter III of this Constitution are in question shall always be conducted publicly.

CHAPTER VII
FINANCE

Article 83. The power to administer national finances shall be exercised as the Diet shall determine.

Article 84. No new taxes shall be imposed or existing ones modified except by law or under such conditions as law may prescribe.

Article 85. No money shall be expended, nor shall be State obligate itself, except as authorized by the Diet.

Article 86. The Cabinet shall prepare and submit to the Diet for its consideration and decision a budget for each fiscal year.

Article 87. In order to provide for unforeseen deficiencies in the budget, A reserve fund may be authorized by the Diet to be expended upon the responsibility of the Cabinet.

The Cabinet must get subsequent approval of the Diet for all payments from the reserve fund.

Article 88. All property of the Imperial Household shall belong to the State. All expenses of the Imperial Household shall be appropriated by the Diet in the budget.

Article 89. No public money or other property shall be expended or appropriated for the use, benefit or maintenance of any religious institution or association, or for any charitable, educational or benevolent enterprises not under the control of public authority.

Article 90. Final accounts of the expenditures and revenues of the State shall be audited annually by a Board of Audit and submitted by the Cabinet to the Diet, together with the statement of audit, during the fiscal year immediately following the period covered.

The organization and competency of the Board of Audit shall be determined by law.

Article 91. At regular intervals and at least annually the Cabinet shall report to the Diet and the people on the state of national finances.

CHAPTER VIII
LOCAL SELF-GOVERNMENT

Article 92. Regulations concerning organization and operations of local public entities shall be fixed by law in accordance with the principle of local autonomy.

Article 93. The local public entities shall establish assemblies as their deliberative organs, in accordance with law.

The chief executive officers of all local public entities, the members of their assemblies, and such other local officials as may be determined by law shall be elected by direct popular vote within their several communities.

Article 94. Local public entities shall have the right to manage their property, affairs and administration and to enact their own regulations within law.

Article 95. A special law, applicable only to one local public entity, cannot be enacted by the Diet without the consent of the majority of the voters of the local public entity concerned, obtained in accordance with law.

CHAPTER IX
AMENDMENTS

Article 96. Amendments to this Constitution shall be initiated by the Diet, through a concurring vote of two-thirds or more of all the members of each House and shall thereupon be submitted to the people for ratification, which shall require the affirmative vote of a majority of all votes cast thereon, at a special referendum or at such election as the Diet shall specify.

Amendments when so ratified shall immediately be promulgated by the Emperor in the name of the people, as an integral part of this Constitution.

CHAPTER X
SUPREME LAW

Article 97. The fundamental human rights by this Constitution guaranteed to the people of Japan are fruits of the age-old struggle of man to be free; they have survived the many exacting tests for durability and are conferred upon this and future generations in trust, to be held for all time inviolate.

Article 98. This Constitution shall be the supreme law of the nation and no law, ordinance, imperial rescript or other act of government, or part thereof, contrary to the provisions hereof, shall have legal force or validity.

The treaties concluded by Japan and the established laws of nations shall be faithfully observed.

Article 99. The Emperor or the Regent as well as Ministers of State, members of the Diet, Judges, and all other public officials have the obligation to respect and uphold this Constitution.

CHAPTER XI
SUPPLEMENTARY PROVISIONS

Article 100. This Constitution shall be enforced as from the day when the period of six months will have elapsed counting from the day of its promulgation.

The enactment of laws necessary for the enforcement of this Constitution, the election of members of the House of Councillors and the procedure for the convocation of the Diet and other preparatory procedures necessary for the enforcement of this Constitution may be executed before the day prescribed in the preceding paragraph.

Article 101. If the House of Councillors is not constituted before the effective date of this Constitution, the House of Representatives shall function as the Diet until such time as the House of Councillors shall be constituted.

Article 102. The term of office for half the members of the House of Councillors serving in the first term under this Constitution shall be three years. Members falling under this category shall be determined in accordance with law.

Article 103. The Ministers of State, Members of the House of Representatives and judges in office on the effective date of this Constitution, and all other public officials who occupy positions corresponding to such positions as are recognized by this Constitution shall not forfeit their positions automatically on account of the enforcement of this Constitution unless otherwise specified by law. When, however, successors are elected or appointed under the provisions of this Constitution, they shall forfeit their positions as a matter of course.

CHAPTER I
CONVOCATION OF THE DIET AND OPENING CEREMONY

Article 1. The Imperial Rescript convoking the Diet shall be promulgated, setting the date for assembling.

The Imperial Rescript for convocation of an ordinary session shall be promulgated at least twenty days in advance.

The promulgation of the Imperial Rescript for convocation of an extraordinary session or of a special session (a session convoked under Article 54 of the Constitution of Japan) need not follow the provision of the preceding paragraph.

Article 2. An ordinary session shall be annually convoked in December as a rule.

Article 2-II. A special session may be convoked in combination with an ordinary session.

Article 2-III. When a general election is held because of the expiration of the term office of Members of the House of Representatives, an extraordinary session shall be convoked within thirty days from the date when the term of office of Members begins. This shall not apply, however, if an ordinary session is convoked within the period, or if the period overlaps a time during which a regular election for Members of the House of Councillors is to be held.

When a regular election for Members of the House of Councillors is held, an extraordinary session shall be convoked within thirty days from the date when the term of office of Members begins. This shall not apply, however, if an ordinary session or a special session is convoked within the period, or if the period overlaps a time during which a general election because of the expiration of the term of office of Members of the House of Representatives is to be held.

Article 3. To demand a decision to convoke an extraordinary session, a written request must be presented to the Cabinet through the President of either House under the joint names of at least one-fourth of the total membership of that House.

Article 4. Deleted.

Article 5. Members of the Diet shall assemble at their respective Houses on the date designated by the Imperial Rescript.

Article 6. On the day of convocation, each House shall elect its presiding officer or deputy presiding officer, or both, if their posts are vacant.

Article 7. Pending the election of the presiding officer and deputy presiding officer, the Secretary General shall perform the duties of the presiding officer.

Article 8. The opening ceremony shall be held at the beginning of a session.

Article 9. The opening ceremony shall be presided over by the Speaker of the House of Representatives.

In the absence of the Speaker of the House of Representatives, the President of the House of Councillors shall preside.

CHAPTER II

TERM OF SESSION AND RECESS

Article 10. The term of an ordinary session shall be one hundred and fifty days. If, however, the term of office of the Members expires during the session, the session shall end on the day of expiration.

Article 11. The term of an extraordinary session or of a special session shall be determined as agreed by both Houses in their respective resolutions.

Article 12. The term of a session may be extended when both Houses agree in their respective resolutions.

The term of a session shall not be extended more than once for an ordinary session and twice for a special session or an extraordinary session.

Article 13. If the two Houses do not pass the same resolution on the matter under the two preceding articles, or if the House of Councillors has not passed a resolution thereon, the decision of the House of Representatives shall prevail.

Article 14. The term of a session shall be counted as from the date of convocation.

Article 15. An agreement by both Houses in their respective resolutions is required for the Diet to go into recess.

Even during the recess, if the presiding officer of a House deems it urgent, or if one-fourth or more of the total membership of a House demands it, a plenary sitting of either House may be called after consultation with the presiding officer of the other House.

The days of the plenary sitting called under the preceding paragraph shall be considered as part of the recess period provided for by the Constitution of Japan and by law.

A House may resolve to go into recess for a period not exceeding ten days.

CHAPTER III
OFFICERS AND EXPENDITURE

Article 16. The Officers of each House shall be as follows:

(1) Presiding Officer
(2) Deputy Presiding Officer
(3) Temporary Presiding Officer
(4) Chairmen of Standing Committees
(5) Secretary General

Article 17. There shall be one presiding officer and one deputy presiding officer for each House.

Article 18. The term of office of the presiding officer and the deputy presiding officer of a House shall coincide with their term of office as Diet Members.

Article 19. The presiding officer of a House shall maintain order in the House, arrange its business, supervise its administration and represent the House.

Article 20. The presiding officer may attend and speak at Committee meetings.

Article 21. If the presiding officer of a House is unable to attend to his duties, or if the post is vacant, the deputy presiding officer shall act as presiding officer.

Article 22. If both the presiding officer and the deputy presiding officer are unable to attend to their duties, a temporary presiding officer shall be elected to perform the duties of presiding officer.

When an election under the preceding paragraph is held, the Secretary General shall act as presiding officer.

A House may entrust its presiding officer with the nomination of the temporary presiding officer.

Article 23. If the post of the presiding officer or of the deputy presiding officer has become vacant in either House, or if both the posts have become vacant, an election shall be held without delay to fill the vacancy or vacancies.

Article 24. In the case of the election mentioned in the former part of the preceding Article, when the deputy presiding officer or the presiding officer is unable to attend to his duties, or in the case of the election mentioned in the latter part, the Secretary General shall act as presiding officer.

Article 25. The Chairman of each Standing Committee shall be elected in each House from among the members of the Committee.

Article 26. A House shall have one Secretary General, secretaries and other necessary personnel.

Article 27. The Secretary General shall be elected in each House from among those other than Members of the Diet.

The secretaries and other personnel shall be appointed and dismissed by the Secretary General, with the consent of the presiding officer and the approval of the Committee on Rules and Administration.

Article 28. The Secretary General shall, under the supervision of the presiding officer, administer the secretarial work of the House, and sign official documents.

The secretaries shall work under the direction of the Secretary General.

Article 29. If the Secretary General is unable to attend to his duties or if the post is vacant, a secretary designated in advance by him shall perform the duties of Secretary General.

Article 30. An Officer may resign with the permission of the House. While the Diet is not in session, however, permission for resignation may be given by the presiding officer.

Article 30-II. In case of special necessity, a House may dismiss the Chairman of a Standing Committee from his post by a resolution of that House.

Article 31. No Officer may hold concurrently any official post of the Government or of a local public entity, or any post of executive or staff member of a public corporation, except as otherwise provided for by law.

If a Member holding a post referred to in the preceding paragraph has been elected an Officer, he shall be automatically relieved of the former post.

Article 32. The expenditures of the two Houses shall be appropriated independently in the national budget.

The appropriation in the preceding paragraph shall include a contingency fund.

CHAPTER IV
MEMBERS OF THE DIET

Article 33. During a session of the Diet, a Member of a House shall not be apprehended without the consent of his House, unless he is in the very act of committing a criminal offence outside the House.

Article 34. With regard to the consent of a House to the apprehension of one of its Members, the Cabinet must ask for it, producing a copy of the request, upon receiving a written request sent by the competent court or judge prior to the issue of a warrant of apprehension.

Article 34-II. If a Member has been apprehended prior to the opening of a session, the Cabinet must communicate the Member's name, together with a copy of the warrant of apprehension, to the presiding officer of his House at the beginning of the session.

If a judge decides, during a session, to extend the detention period of a Member who has been apprehended prior to the opening of the session, the Cabinet must inform the presiding officer of his House to the effect.

Article 34-III. To propose a request for the release of a Member apprehended prior to the opening of a session, a written request with an explanatory statement must be presented to the presiding officer of the House, under the joint names of twenty or more Members.

Article 35. Members of the Diet shall receive an annual payment not less in amount than the highest remuneration for public employees in the regular government service.

Article 36. Members may receive a retirement allowance, as provided for separately.

Article 37. Members may travel freely on the Japanese National Railways system during a session or on official business, under the regulations separately made.

Article 38. Members shall receive allowances, as provided for separately, for mailing official documents and for communications of official nature during a session.

Article 39. A Member cannot hold concurrently, during his term of office, any official post in the Government or in any local public entity, or any post of executive or staff member of a public corporation, except the post of Prime Minister, Minister of State, Deputy Chief Cabinet Secretary, Deputy Director General of the Prime Minister's Office, Parliamentary Vice-Minister, and any other posts provided for by law. A Member may, however, during his term of office, be appointed as a member of a commission, adviser, counsellor, or other functionary of similar nature in any body of the Cabinet and of the executive branch, when both Houses agree to it in their respective resolutions.

CHAPTER V
COMMITTEES AND THEIR MEMBERSHIP

Article 40. Each House may have two kinds of committees, namely, Standing Committees and Special Committees.

Article 41. Standing Committees of each House shall consider the measures (including resolutions), petitions and other matters which may come into their respective spheres of work.

The Standing Committees of the House of Representatives shall be as follows:

(1) Committee on Cabinet
(2) Committee on Local Administration
(3) Committee on Judicial Affairs
(4) Committee on Foreign Affairs
(5) Committee on Finance
(6) Committee on Education
(7) Committee on Social and Labour Affairs
(8) Committee on Agriculture, Forestry and Fisheries
(9) Committee on Commerce and Industry
(10) Committee on Transport
(11) Committee on Communications

(12) Committee on Construction
(13) Committee on Science and Technology
(14) Committee on Environment
(15) Committee on Budget
(16) Committee on Audit
(17) Committee on Rules and Administration
(18) Committee on Discipline

The Standing Committees of the House of Councillors shall be as follows:

(1) Committee on Cabinet
(2) Committee on Local Administration
(3) Committee on Judicial Affairs
(4) Committee on Foreign Affairs
(5) Committee on Finance
(6) Committee on Education
(7) Committee on Social and Labour Affairs
(8) Committee on Agriculture, Forestry and Fisheries
(9) Committee on Commerce and Industry
(10) Committee on Transport
(11) Committee on Communications
(12) Committee on Construction
(13) Committee on Budget
(14) Committee on Audit
(15) Committee on Rules and Administration
(16) Committee on Discipline

Article 42. Members of Standing Committees shall be appointed by each House at the beginning of a session, and shall hold their membership until their term of office as Members of the Diet expires.

Every Member shall serve on at least one Standing Committee. However, the presiding officer, deputy presiding officer, Prime Minister and other Ministers of State, the Deputy Chief Cabinet Secretary, Deputy Director General of the Prime Minister's Office, and Parliamentary Vice-Ministers, may resign the Standing Committee membership assigned to them.

If a Member resigns Standing Committee membership under the proviso of the preceding paragraph, another Member of the party or group to which the Member belongs may assume the membership.

Article 43. Each Standing Committee may have an official with professional knowledge (to be called "Semmon-in" or Professional Adviser), and researchers.

Article 44. A Standing Committee of one House may hold a joint meeting with a Standing Committee of the other House after consultation between the two Committees.

Article 45. A House may set up Special Committees in order to consider matters which are deemed necessary by the House or particular matters which do not come under the jurisdiction of any Standing Committee.

Members of a Special Committee shall be appointed by the House, and shall serve until the matter which was referred to the Committee is decided upon by the House.

The Chairman of a Special Committee shall be elected by its members from among themselves.

Article 46. Membership of Standing Committees and of Special Committee shall be allocated to political parties and groups in the House in proportion to their numerical strength, and then the Committee members shall be appointed according to this allocation.

If, after members have been appointed in accordance with the provision of the preceding paragraph, there arises a need for redistribution of the membership so allocated by reason of a change in the numerical strength of the political parties and groups, the presiding officer may alter the membership with the consent of the Committee on Rules and Administration, notwithstanding the provisions of paragraph 1 of Article 42 and paragraph 2 of the preceding Article.

Article 47. Standing Committees and Special Committees shall consider the matters referred to them, only while the Diet is in session.

Even while the Diet is not in session, however, Standing Committees and Special Committees may consider matters (including those of discipline) specifically referred to them by a resolution of the House.

When a disciplinary matter is put to consideration while the Diet is not in session, in accordance with the provision of the preceding paragraph, it must be a case which occurred during the preceding session.

When it has been decided to continue consideration even while the Diet is not in session, in accordance with the provision of the second paragraph, the presiding officer of the House concerned shall inform the other House and the Cabinet to that effect.

Article 48. The Chairman of a Committee shall arrange its business and maintain order in the Committee.

Article 49. No business may be transacted and no decision taken in a Committee unless at least one-half of its members are present.

Article 50. All matters shall be decided in a Committee by a majority of the members present. In the case of a tie, the Chairman shall have the casting vote.

Article 50-II. A Committee may propose a bill concerning matters under its jurisdiction.

The Chairman of the Committee shall be the proposer of such a bill.

Article 51. A Committee may hold open hearings on important measures and matters of popular concern and for general purposes, and may hear views from the interested parties or people of learning and experience.

Open hearings as mentioned in the preceding paragraph must be held on the overall budget and important bills concerning revenue. This provision does not apply, however, to matters which have the same content as those on which open hearings have already been held.

Article 52. No persons other than Diet Members are admitted to a Committee meeting as visitors. However, this provision does not apply to those engaged in news service or any others who have obtained the permission of the Chairman.

A Committee may hold closed meetings if it so decides.

For the maintenance of order, the Chairman may order any of the visitors to leave the meeting room.

Article 53. The Chairman shall report to the House the proceedings and results of his Committee's meetings.

Article 54. A minority opinion rejected by a Committee but supported by one-tenth or more of the members present may be reported to the House by a member of the minority opinion, following the Chairman's report. In this case, the member of the minority opinion must present to the presiding officer of the House a brief written report on the opinion under the joint names of its supporters.

The presiding officer may allocate the time for the report on the minority opinion.

The written report shall be recorded in the minutes of the House, together with the Committee's report.

CHAPTER VI
PLENARY SITTINGS

Article 55. The presiding officer of a House shall decide the Order of the Day and inform the House of it in advance.

If the presiding officer deems it urgent, he may call a plenary sitting by notifying Members of only the date and time of such a sitting.

Article 55-II. The presiding officer may consult with the Chairman of the Committee on Rules and Administration and members of the Proceedings Conference selected and appointed by the Committee, concerning the order of business and any other matters which he deems necessary. In this case, if they fail to come to an agreement, the presiding officer may give a decision.

The presiding officer may entrust the Chairman of the Committee on Rules and Administration with the chairmanship of the Proceedings Conference.

The presiding officer may hold the Proceedings Conference at any time, whether the Diet is in session or not.

Article 56. For a Member to present a measure, it is necessary to secure the support of twenty or more Members in the House of Representatives, and ten or more in the House of Councillors. In the case of a bill requiring budgetary action, however, it is necessary for a Member to secure the support of fifty or more Members in the House of Representatives, and twenty or more in the House of Councillors.

When a measure is introduced or presented, the presiding officer shall refer it to an appropriate Committee, and, after consideration by the Committee, shall put it to consideration in a plenary sitting. In case of urgency, however, and at the request of the introducer or the proposer, consideration by the Committee may be omitted by a resolution of the House.

A measure which the Committee has decided need not be brought before a plenary sitting, shall not be laid before the sitting. The measure must be brought to a plenary sitting, however, if this is demanded by twenty or more Members of the House within seven days, excluding the period of recess, from the day the Committee has made such a decision.

If no such demand is made in accordance with the proviso of the preceding paragraph, the measure shall be dropped.

The provisions of the preceding two paragraphs shall not apply to a measure sent from the other House.

Article 56-II. When the Committee on Rules and Administration deems it necessary, a House may hear in its plenary sitting the explanation of the purport of a measure introduced or proposed to the House.

Article 56-III. A House may, in case of necessity, call for an interim report by a Committee on a pending measure or matter.

With respect to a measure or matter on which such an interim report has been made, the House may, in case of urgent necessity, set a time limit for the Committee consideration or proceed to deliberate it in a plenary sitting.

If a House has allocated the time for the Committee consideration and the consideration has not been completed within that time, the House shall begin to consider the matter in a plenary sitting. The House may, however, extend the time for consideration, if the Committee requests an extension.

Article 56-IV. Neither House may consider a measure which is identical with a measure sent from the other House.

Article 57. A motion of measure amendment to be taken up in a plenary sitting must be supported by at least twenty Members in the House of Representatives, and at least ten in the House of Councillors. However, a motion of bill amendment which brings about an increase of the budget or which will require budgetary action must be supported by at least fifty Members in the House of Representatives, and at least twenty in the House of Councillors.

Article 57-II. A motion of budgetary amendment to be taken up in a plenary sitting must be supported by at least fifty Members in the House of Representatives or at least twenty in the House of Councillors.

Article 57-III. A House or a Committee must afford the Cabinet an opportunity to give its opinion on an amendment to increase the total amount of the budget, on a bill presented by a Committee or a Member which requires budgetary action, or a bill amendment which brings about an increase of the budget or which will require budgetary action.

Article 58. When the Cabinet has presented a measure to either house, the same shall be sent within five days to the other House for preliminary consideration.

Article 59. To amend or withdraw a measure presented by the Cabinet, which a House or a Committee has already begun to consider, the Cabinet is required to obtain the consent of that House. The Cabinet may neither amend nor withdraw a measure, however, after it has been decided upon by one of the Houses.

Article 60. With respect to a measure presented by either House, the Chairman (or his proxy) of the Committee concerned or the introducer of the measure may explain the reason for its introduction in the other House.

Article 61. The presiding officer of a House may allocate the time for questions, debate and any other speaking, unless otherwise resolved beforehand by the House.

When one-fifth or more of the Members present raise an objection to the time allocated by the presiding officer, he must put the case to a vote of the House without debate.

Any part of a Member's remarks which he fails to say because of the time allocation shall be recorded in the minutes of the House, to the extent approved by the presiding officer unless otherwise resolved by the House.

Article 62. A House may close its sitting to the public, by a decision of the House adopted by a majority of two-thirds of the Members present, on a motion made by the presiding officer or by ten or more Members.

Article 63. Concerning the record of proceedings in a closed sitting, a House may not make public any part of it which the House especially decided to keep secret.

Article 64. When the post of Prime Minister becomes vacant, or when the Prime Minister tenders his resignation, the Cabinet shall notify the fact to both Houses immediately.

Article 65. With respect to a measure requiring a resolution of the Diet, the presiding officer of the House which made the final resolution, or, in the case that the resolution of the House of Representatives has become the resolution of the Diet, the Speaker of the House of Representatives, shall present it to the Throne through the Cabinet if it is to be promulgated, or to the Cabinet in other cases.

The designation of the Prime Minister shall be reported to the Throne by the Speaker of the House of Representatives through the Cabinet.

Article 66. A law shall be promulgated within thirty days from the day of its presentation to the Throne.

Article 67. In the case of a special law that is applicable to only one local public entity, it shall be referred, after the final resolution in favour of it in the Diet, to a vote by the inhabitants of that local public entity in accordance with a separate law. If there is a majority in favour, that resolution of the Diet shall be fixed and shall become a law.

Article 68. A measure or matter on which no resolution has been made during a session shall not be carried over to the next session; except that when a measure or a disciplinary matter is being considered under the provision of paragraph 2 of Article 47 while the Diet is not in session, it shall be carried over to the next session.

CHAPTER VII

MINISTERS OF STATE AND GOVERNMENT DELEGATES

Article 69. The Cabinet may, with the approval of the presiding officers of both Houses, appoint government Delegates to assist Ministers of State in the Diet.

Article 70. When a Minister of State or a Government Delegate desires to speak at a plenary sitting or a Committee meeting, he shall give notice to the presiding officer of the House or the Chairman of the Committee.

Article 71. A Committee may, through the presiding officer of its House, request the presence of any Minister of State or Government Delegate at its meeting.

Article 72. A Committee may, through the presiding officer of its House, request the President and Commissioners of the Board of Audit to attend its meeting and give an explanation.

At his own request and with the consent of a Committee, the Chief Justice of the Supreme Court or a deputy designated by him may attend and give an explanation at the Committee meeting.

Article 73. Reports on a plenary sitting and committee meetings shall be delivered to Ministers of State and Government Delegates at the same time as they are distributed to Members of the Diet.

CHAPTER VIII
QUESTIONS

Article 74. When a Member of a House desires to put a question to the Cabinet, he is required to obtain the approval of the presiding officer of the House.

The question must be presented to the presiding officer as a concise statement in written form.

If a Member raises an objection regarding a question of his to which the presiding officer has not given approval, the presiding officer must put the case to a vote of the House without debate.

When it is demanded by a Member, the presiding officer shall record in the minutes of the House a statement of the question to which he or the House has not given approval.

Article 75. The presiding officer of a House shall transmit to the Cabinet statements of questions which he or the House has approved.

The Cabinet must answer a question within seven days from the day of receipt of the concise statement. If an answer cannot be made within the period, the Cabinet is required to state clearly the reason, and the time by which an answer can be given.

Article 76. A question of an urgent nature can be made orally by a resolution fo the House.

Article 77. Deleted.

Article 78. Deleted.

CHAPTER IX
PETITIONS

Article 79. A person who desires to make a petition to a House shall present it in writing through a Member of the House.

Article 80. Resolutions on petitions shall be passed by the House after they have been considered by the competent Committee.

Petitions which the Committee has decided need not be brought before a plenary sitting, shall not be laid before the sitting. They must, however, be brought to a plenary sitting, if this is demanded by twenty or more members of the House.

Article 81. Petitions which have been adopted by a House and are considered appropriate for Cabinet action shall be transmitted to the Cabinet.

The Cabinet shall annually report to the House concerned on how the petitions mentioned in the preceding paragraph have been dealt with.

Article 82. Both Houses shall separately receive petitions, and shall not interfere with each other.

CHAPTER X
RELATIONS BETWEEN THE TWO HOUSES

Article 83. When a measure requiring a resolution of the Diet is passed or amended by House A, it shall be sent to House B; when the measure is rejected by House A, the fact shall be notified to House B.

When House B adopts or rejects a measure sent from House A, the fact shall be notified to House A.

When House B amends a measure sent from House A, the amended measure shall be sent back to House A.

When House A agrees or disagrees to the amendment sent back from House B, the fact shall be notified to House B.

Article 83-II. When the House of Councillors rejects a bill sent from the House of Representatives, the bill shall be returned to the House of Representatives.

If the House of Councillors disagrees to a bill sent back by the House of Representatives, and if a meeting of the Conference Committee of both Houses demanded by the House of Councillors fails to be held through the refusal of the House of Representatives, or if the House of Councillors does not call for a meeting of the Conference Committee, the bill shall be returned to the House of Representatives.

When the House of Councillors rejects a budget or a treaty which was considered first by the House of Representatives, it shall be returned to the House of Representatives. When the House of Representatives, rejects a treaty which was considered first by the House of Councillors, it shall be returned to the House of Councillors.

Article 83-III. If the House of Representatives determines, according to the provision of paragraph 4 of Article 59 of the Constitution of Japan, that failure by the House of Councillors to take final action upon a bill has constituted a rejection, the House of Representatives shall notify the House of Councillors to that effect.

When the resolution of the House of Representatives on a budget or a treaty becomes the resolution of the Diet under the provision of paragraph 2 of Article 60 or Article 61 of the Constitution of Japan, the House of Representatives shall notify the House of Councillors to that effect.

When notified as provided for under the preceding two paragraphs, the House of Councillors shall immediately return to the House of Representatives the matters sent from or sent back by the House of Representatives.

Article 83-IV. When a measure sent from House A is considered continuously in House B while the Diet is out of session and is resolved upon in the subsequent session, Article 83 shall apply.

Article 84. When the House of Representatives disagrees to a bill sent back to it by the House of Councillors or when the House of Councillors rejects a bill sent to it from the House of Representatives or disagrees to a bill sent back to it by the House of Representatives, the House of

Representatives may call for the meeting of a Conference Committee of both Houses.

Notwithstanding the provision of the preceding paragraph, the House of Councillors may, only when it disagrees to a measure sent back from the House of Representatives, call for a meeting of the Conference Committee at the same time as it notifies its disagreement. The House of Representatives may, however, refuse this request for a meeting of the Conference Committee.

Article 85. When the House of Representatives disagrees to a measure sent back to it by the House of Councillors in respect of the budget or a treaty which was considered first by the House of Representatives, or when the House of Councillors rejects the budget or treaty which was sent to it from the House of Representatives, the House of Representatives must call for a meeting of the Conference Committee.

When the House of Councillors disagrees to a measure sent back to it by the House of Representatives in respect of a treaty which was considered first by the House of Councillors, or when the House of Representatives rejects a treaty sent to it from the House of Councillors, the House of Councillors must call for a meeting of the Conference Committee.

Article 86. When either House resolves upon the designation of a Prime Minister, the fact shall be notified to the other House.

When the two Houses do not come to the same resolution on the designation of the Prime Minister, the House of Councillors must call for a meeting of the Conference Committee.

Article 87. With respect to a measure or matter requiring a resolution of the Diet, other than a bill, the budget or a treaty, when the House which subsequently considered it disagrees to a resolution of the House which considered it first, the former House shall send back the measure or matter to the latter, together with notification to that effect.

In the case of the preceding paragraph, the House which considered first may call for a meeting of the Conference Committee.

Article 88. When either House calls for a meeting of the Conference Committee, the other House may not refuse it, except in the case mentioned in the proviso of paragraph 2 of Article 84.

Article 89. The Conference Committee shall be composed of twenty members, elected in each House in equal number.

Article 90. Meetings of the Conference Committee are presided over alternately by a Chairman from each House who is elected by the Committee members of that House from among themselves. The Chairman for the initial meeting shall be chosen by lot.

Article 91. No business may be transacted and no decision taken in a meeting of the Conference Committee, unless at least two-thirds of its members from each House are present.

Article 91-II. When a member of the Conference Committee is absent from meetings without good reason, or, in disregard of repeated requests for his presence by the Chairman, does not present himself, the presiding officer of the House to which the member belongs may regard him as having resigned from the Conference Committee.

In the case of the preceding paragraph, the House to which that member of the Conference Committee belongs shall immediately hold an election to fill the vacancy.

Article 92. In a meeting of the Conference Committee, a draft compromise becomes a final compromise when it has been decided upon by a majority of two-thirds or more of the members present.

All matters, except as provided for in the preceding paragraph, shall be decided by a majority of the members present. In the case of a tie, the chairman shall have the casting vote.

Article 93. A final compromise reached by the Conference Committee shall first be considered by the House which called for its meeting, and shall then be sent to the other House.

The final compromise shall not be subject to any further amendment.

Article 94. If the Conference Committee fails to reach a final compromise, the Conference Committee Chairman of each House shall report the fact to his House.

Article 95. The presiding officer of either House may attend a meeting of the Conference Committee to express his views.

Article 96. The Conference Committee may request the presence at its meeting of Ministers of State and Government Delegates.

Article 97. No outsider shall be admitted to a meeting of the Conference Committee.

Article 98. rules of the Conference Committee other than those provided for in this Law shall be made as agreed by both Houses in their respective resolutions.

CHAPTER XI
EMERGENCY SESSION OF THE HOUSE OF COUNCILLORS

Article 99. When the Cabinet seeks an emergency session of the House of Councillors, the Prime Minister must make the request to the President of the House of Councillors, fixing the date for assembly and indicating the measures or matters to be considered.

When the request is made under the provision of the preceding paragraph, the President of the House of Councillors shall notify each Member to that effect, and Members must meet at the House of Councillors on the designated date for assembly as mentioned in the preceding paragraph.

Article 100. During an emergency session of the House of Councillors, a Member of the House shall not be apprehended without the consent of the House, unless he is in the very act of committing a criminal offence outside the House.

If a Member of the House of Councillors is apprehended before the opening of an emergency session of the House, the Cabinet must communicate the Member's name, together with a copy of the warrant of apprehension, to the President of the House by the day before the date of assembly.

If a judge decides, during an emergency session of the House of Councillors, to extend the detention period of a Member of the House who has been apprehended before the opening of the emergency session, the Cabinet must notify the President of the House to that effect.

A Member of the House of Councillors who has been apprehended before the opening of an emergency session of the House of Councillors shall be released during the term of the emergency session upon the demand of the House.

To propose a request for the release of a Member apprehended before the opening of an emergency session of the House of Councillors, a written request with a statement giving the reason must be presented to the President of the House under the joint names of twenty or more Members.

Article 101. At an emergency session of the House of councillors, Members may present measures or matters only if they are related to any of those indicated under the provision of paragraph 1 of Article 99.

Article 102. At an emergency session of the House of Councillors, petitions may be presented only if they are related to the measures or matters indicated under the provision of paragraph 1 of Article 99.

Article 102-II. When all the emergency measures or matters have been decided on, the President shall declare the close of the emergency session.

Article 102-III. When the measures or matters have been passed at an emergency session of the House of Councillors, those which require promulgation shall be presented to the Throne by the President of the House of Councillors through the Cabinet while the others shall be sent to the Cabinet.

Article 102-IV. For the consent of the House of Representatives to the steps taken at an emergency meeting of the House of Councillors, the measure or matter shall presented by the Cabinet.

Article 102-V. In applying the provisions of Articles 6, 37, 38, 47 par. 1, 67 and 69, "convocation" (Arts. 6) shall read "assembly"; "session" (Arts. 37, 38 and 47 par. 1) shall read "an emergency session"; "after the final resolution in favour of it in the Diet" (Art. 67) shall read "after the resolution in favour of it in an emergency session of the House of Councillors"; and "the Diet" and "both Houses" (Art. 69) shall read respectively "an emergency session of the House of Councillors" and "the House of Councillors"; and in applying Provisions of Article 121-II, "the closing day of a session or on the day before" shall read "the closing day of an emergency session of the House of Councillors or on the day before"; "the House had not resolved that consideration of it should continue while the Diet was out of session" shall read "the Committee had not finished consideration" and "the previous session" shall read "the emergency session of the House of Councillors following the close of the previous session."

Chapter XII

RELATIONS OF THE HOUSES WITH THE GENERAL PUBLIC AND WITH GOVERNMENT AGENCIES

Article 103. A House may send out its Members for the purpose of considering measures and so forth, or investigating into state administration, or whenever the House deems it necessary.

Article 104. The Cabinet, government and public entities' offices and others must comply with requests of a House or its Committees for production of reports and documents necessary for their consideration or investigation.

Article 105. Deleted.

Article 106. When a House calls a witness or informant for its consideration or investigation, travelling expenses and per diem shall be paid to such a person according to the scale separately provided for.

CHAPTER XIII
RESIGNATION, RETIREMENT, FILLING OF VACANCIES AND CHALLENGE TO MEMBER'S QUALIFICATION

Article 107. A House may accept the resignation of its Members. While the Diet is out of session, however, the resignation may be accepted by the presiding officer of the House.

Article 108. When a Member of either House becomes a Member of the other House, he shall be automatically retired from the first House.

Article 109. A Member of a House shall be retired from his office when he has lost the legal eligibility for election.

Article 110. When a vacancy occurs in the membership of a House, the presiding officer of the House shall notify the Prime Minister of the fact.

Article 111. When a Member's qualification is challenged in a House, the House shall decide on it after consideration by the competent Committee.

Such a challenge must be presented to the presiding officer in writing under the name of a Member of the House.

Article 112. The Member whose qualification is challenged in a House may retain not more than two counsel to defend his case.

The expenses for one of the counsel mentioned in the preceding paragraph shall be borne by the State.

Article 113. A Member is not denied his seat and the rights attached to it until he has been proved disqualified. He may not, however, vote at the meeting in which the challenge to his qualification is considered, though he may defend himself.

CHAPTER XIV
MAINTENANCE OF ORDER AND POLICING

Article 114. In order to maintain order in a House during a session of the Diet, the presiding officer of the House shall exercise police power within the House in accordance with this Law and the Rules of the House. The same shall apply also while the Diet is out of session.

Article 115. Police personnel needed for a House shall be sent by the Cabinet upon the request of the presiding officer of the House and shall be placed under his direction.

Article 116. When, at a plenary sitting, a Member acts contrary to this Law or the rules of procedure, or conducts himself in a disorderly manner, or impairs the dignity of the House, the presiding officer shall wan or restrain him or cause him to retract his remarks. If the presiding officer's order is not obeyed, he may forbid the Member to speak until the day's sitting is over or, if the proceedings, are to be carried over to the following day, until the end of the proceedings; or he may cause the Member to leave the Chamber.

Article 117. The presiding officer may temporarily suspend or adjourn the sitting for the day, if the Chamber goes out of control.

Article 118. If a visitor in the gallery obstructs the proceedings in the Chamber, the presiding officer may cause him to leave or, if necessary, hand him over to the police authorities.

The presiding officer may order the gallery to be cleared if it becomes too clamorous.

Article 118-II. If a person other than a Member creates a disturbance in a House, the presiding officer may cause him to leave the House or, if necessary, hand him over to the police authorities.

Article 119. No insulting language shall be used or remarks made in a House on another person's private affairs.

Article 120. A Member who has been insulted at a plenary sitting or at a Committee meeting may appeal to the House for disciplinary action.

CHAPTER XV

DISCIPLINARY MEASURES

Article 121. When a disciplinary case occurs in a House, the presiding officer shall refer it first to the Committee on Discipline for consideration, and, after debate in a plenary sitting, he shall pronounce the verdict of the House.

When a disciplinary case occurs in a Committee, the Chairman must report it to the presiding officer for disciplinary action.

A Member may make a motion for disciplinary action with the support of forty or more Members in the House of Representatives and twenty or more in the House of Councillors. This motion must be made within three days from the date when the alleged case occurred.

Article 121-II. With respect to a disciplinary case occurring on the closing day of a session or on the day before the closing day, the presiding officer of the House may refer it to the Committee on Discipline within three days from the date of convocation of the next session, if the presiding officer had failed to refer it to the Committee on Discipline, or if it had been referred to the Committee but the House had not resolved that consideration of it should continue while the Diet was out of session, or if the Committee had finished considering it but the House had passed no resolution on it.

If a disciplinary case occurs on the closing day of a session or on the day before the closing day, and if no time is allowed for a motion for disciplinary action to be made, or if such a motion is presented but the House does not pass a resolution upon it, or if the case is referred to the Committee on Discipline but the House does not resolve that consideration of it shall be continued while the Diet is out of session, or if the Committee finishes considering the case but the House does not pass a resolution on it; then a Member may, with the support of the required number of Members provided for in paragraph 3 of the preceding article, present a motion for disciplinary action within three days from the date of convocation of the next session.

In the first session of the House of Representatives convoked following a general election of the Members of that House, and in the first session of the House of Councillors convoked following a regular election of the Members of that House, the provisions of the preceding two paragraphs shall not apply to a disciplinary case which occurred on the closing day of the previous session or on the day before the closing day.

Article 121-III. When a disciplinary case occurs in a Committee or any other place within the House while the Diet is out of session, the presiding officer may refer it to the Committee on Discipline within three days from the date of convocation of the next Diet session.

When a case occurs in a Committee or any other place within the House while the Diet is out of session, a Member may, with the support of the required number of Members provided for in paragraph 3 of Article 121, make a motion for disciplinary action within three days from the date of convocation of the next session.

Article 122. Disciplinary actions shall be as follows:

(1) Admonition in an open plenary sitting;

(2) Apology in an open plenary sitting;

(3) Suspension of attendance at the House for a certain period; and,

(4) Expulsion.

Article 123. Neither House can refuse an expelled Member if he is re-elected.

Article 124. The presiding officer shall specially issue a writ of summons to a Member who does not respond to convocation of the Diet without good reason within seven days from the date of the convocation, or does not present himself without good reason to a plenary sitting or a Committee meeting, or remains absent beyond a period of leave of absence; and, if, within seven days from his receipt of the summons, the Member still fails to present himself without excuse, the presiding officer shall refer the case to the Committee on Discipline.

CHAPTER XVI
IMPEACHMENT COURT

Article 125. Impeachment of a judge shall be heard by the Impeachment Court which is composed of members elected in equal number in each House from among its Members.

The President of the Impeachment Court shall be elected by the members of the Court from among themselves.

Article 126. Removal proceedings against a judge shall be instituted by the Indictment committee which is composed of members elected in equal number in each House from among its Members.

The Chairman of the Indictment Committee shall be elected by its members from among themselves.

Article 127. A member of the Impeachment Court may not become concurrently a member of the Indictment Committee.

Article 128. When the members of the Impeachment Court or of the Indictment Committee are elected in each House, their reserves shall also be elected.

Article 129. Matters relating to the Impeachment Court and the Indictment Committee other than those provided for in this Law shall be prescribed by a separate law.

CHAPTER XVII
NATIONAL DIET LIBRARY, LEGISLATIVE BUREAU AND MEMBERS' OFFICE BUILDINGS

Article 130. The National Diet Library shall be established in the Diet by a separate law, in order to assist Diet Members in their study and research.

Article 131. A Legislative Bureau shall be established in each House to assist Diet Members in drafting bills.

Each Legislative Bureau shall have one Director General, secretaries and other necessary personnel.

The Director General of the Legislative Bureau shall be appointed and dismissed by the presiding officer with the approval of the House, provided that, when the Diet is out of session, the presiding officer may accept the resignation of the Director General of the Bureau.

The Director General of the Legislative Bureau shall administer the business of the Legislative Bureau under the supervision of the presiding officer.

The secretaries and other personnel of the Legislative Bureau shall be appointed and dismissed by the Director General, with the consent of the presiding officer and the approval of the Committee on Rules and Administration.

The secretaries of the Legislative Bureau shall work under the direction of the Director General.

Article 132. In order to assist Members in carrying out their duties, two secretarial assistants shall be provided for each Member, and Members' Office Buildings shall be constructed to provide Members with office space.

CHAPTER XVIII
SUPPLEMENTARY PROVISIONS

Article 133. Any period of time under this Law and the Rules of each House shall be regarded as including the day of beginning.

(This Law shall become effective on the day of enforcement of the Constitution of Japan.)

The Rules of the House of Councillors

CHAPTER I

OPENING OF SESSION AND ELECTION OF OFFICERS

Article 1. Members shall assemble in the House of Councillors at 10 a.m. on the day designated in the Imperial Rescript for convocation.

Article 2. Members who attend the House for the first time since their election are required to present to the Secretariat their certificates of election and have them checked with the list of those elected.

Article 3. When members assembled have reached one-third of the total membership, the President shall take the Chair.

Article 4. When the posts of both the President and the Vice-President are vacant on the day of convocation, the House shall elect the President after members assembled have reached one-third of the total membership.

The election of the President shall be held by secret ballot with single entry.

Article 5. Each Member shall, when his name is called, take his ballot paper and wooden name-plate to the rostrum for voting.

Secretary A shall receive the name-plate, secretary B the ballot paper, and on behalf of the Member they shall put them respectively into the name-plate box and the ballot box.

Article 6. When all the Members present have voted, the Secretary General declare the closure of the ballot box. After this declaration no more voting shall be allowed.

Article 7. On completion of the voting, the Secretary General shall immediately have the secretaries count the name-plates and the ballot papers and examine the ballot papers.

When the number of the ballot papers exceeds that of the name-plates, a further vote shall be held, unless the result of the election is unaffected by this discrepancy.

Article 8. When all the ballot papers have been examined, the Secretary General shall announce to the House the result of the election.

Article 9. The member who has obtained more than half the votes is declared elected. If no Member has obtained a majority, a deciding vote shall be taken between the two who have obtained the largest number of votes; and the one who obtains the greater number of votes is declared elected.

In case of a tie on the occasion of selecting two Members between whom a deciding vote is to be taken, or of deciding the members to be declared elected, the selection or the decision shall be made by lot.

Article 10. If a question arises about an election in the House, the Secretary General shall put it to the House for decision.

Article 11. After the election of the President, the House shall elect the Vice-President.

The election of the Vice-President shall be held in the same manner as that of the President.

Article 12. When the President and the Vice-President have been elected, the Secretary General shall present them to the House and conduct the President to the Chair.

Article 13. If the post of either the President or the Vice-President is vacant on the day of convocation, the House shall hold an election in the same manner as provided for in Article 4 and under.

Article 14. The President shall assign a seat in the Chamber to each Member at the beginning of each session; although he may change it whenever necessary.

Each seat shall be numbered and shall have the Member's name-block attached to it.

Article 15. Deleted.

Article 16. If the post of the Chairman of any Standing Committee is vacant on the day of convocation, the House shall hold an election in the same manner as that of the President.

The House may, however, delegate the selection of a Chairman to the President.

Article 17. If the post of the Secretary General is vacant on the day of convocation, the House shall hold an election in the same manner as that of the President. The House may, however, delegate the selection of the Secretary General to the President.

Article 18. Deleted.

Article 19. The election of the President, the Vice-President, the Chairman of a Standing Committee, or the Secretary General, whose post has become vacant while the Diet is in session, and the election of a President pro-tempore shall be held in the same manner as provided for in Article 4 and under.

CHAPTER II

DESIGNATION OF PRIME MINISTER

Article 20. The Member who is to be designated Prime Minister shall be chosen by open ballot with single entry.

The Member who has obtained more than half the votes cast shall be the one to be designated.

If no one has obtained more than half the votes cast, a deciding vote shall be taken between the two who have obtained the largest number of votes; and the one who obtains the greater number of votes is declared designated.

In case of a tie on the occasion of selecting two Members between whom a deciding vote is to be taken, or of deciding the Member to the declared designated, the selection or the designation shall be made by lot.

The House may also choose the person to be designated, not by ballot, but by the motion or by other means.

CHAPTER III

OPENING CEREMONY

Article 21. The date, time, and place of the opening ceremony shall be fixed by the President in consultation with the Speaker of the House of Representatives.

CHAPTER IV

DETERMINATION AND EXTENSION OF THE TERM OF A SESSION AND RECESS OF THE DIET

Article 22. The term of an extraordinary and a special session shall be resolved by the House, after the President has conferred with the Speaker of the House of Representatives. In this case the President must previously consult with the Chairman of Standing Committees to obtain their opinions of the legislative program for the session.

The result of a decision as provided for in the preceding paragraph shall be notified to the House of Representatives and the Cabinet.

Article 23. The provision of the preceding Article shall apply *mutatis mutandis* to an extension of the term of a session of the Diet.

Article 23-II. The provision of Article 22 shall apply *mutatis mutandis* to recess of the Diet.

Recess of the House shall be decided by the House upon the proposition of the President. In this case, the President must previously consult with the Chairmen of Standing Committees to obtain their opinions.

Even while the House is in recess, a sitting may be held, if the President deems it of urgent necessity or if at least one-fourth of the total membership makes a request for it.

When the plenary meeting has been held under the provision of the preceding paragraph, recess of the House shall have ended.

CHAPTER V
INTRODUCTION AND WITHDRAWAL OF MEASURES

Article 24. When any Member desires to introduce a measure, he must submit it, signed jointly by the required number of supporters, to the President with the reasons in writing attached. If the measure is a bill which requires a budgetary action, a written statement of the expenses needed for the implementation of the law shall be attached.

The President shall have the introduced bill printed and distributed to each Member.

The provisions of the preceding two paragraphs shall apply *mutatis mutandis* to the bills presented by the Committee.

Article 25. When any measure mentioned in the preceding Article requires the decision of the Diet, the President shall, besides distributing it to each Member, send it to the House of Representatives for preliminary consideration.

Article 26. When the introducer or proposer of a bill intends to request the omission of a Committee's consideration on the introduced or proposed bill, he must inform the President to that effect in writing simultaneously with its introduction, proposition or sending.

When the request is made under the preceding paragraph, the President must put it to the House for decision.

Article 27. When measures are presented by the House of Representatives or the Cabinet, or when measures are sent from the House of Representatives, or when measures are sent from the House of Representatives or the Cabinet for preliminary consideration, the President shall have them printed and distributed to each Member, unless they are the same measures as have already been distributed for preliminary consideration.

Article 28. When a Member desires to withdraw a measure he has introduced, the request must be made by all the proposers.

To withdraw a measure after a Committee or the House has begun to consider it, the permission of the Committee or of the House is required respectively.

CHAPTER VI

REFERENCE OF MEASURES

Article 29. The President shall refer a measure and a measure sent for preliminary consideration to an appropriate Standing Committee.

As to a measure deemed specially necessary or a special measure not coming under the jurisdiction of any Standing Committee, the President shall put it to the House for decision and create a Special Committee, to which the measure shall be referred.

In case of reference of matters other than measures to Committees, the provisions of the preceding two paragraphs shall apply, unless provided for otherwise in these Rules.

Article 29-II. A bill submitted by a Committee shall not be referred to a Committee, but to a plenary sitting of the House. However, the one deemed specially necessary by the President may be referred to a Committee.

Article 29-III. The President may refer to a Special Committee any measure or matter related to one which has been referred to that Committee.

CHAPTER VII

COMMITTEES

SUB-CHAPTER 1

GENERAL PROVISIONS

Article 30. Members of Committees shall all be nominated by the President.

The permission of resignations of Committee members shall be given by the President.

Article 31. A Committee shall have one or more directors.

Directors shall be mutually elected from among the Committee members by secret ballot. However, the appointment may be made, not by ballot, but by motion or other means.

A director shall perform the duties of the Chairman when the Chairman is unable to attend to them or when the position becomes vacant.

The permission of resignation of directors shall be made by the Committee concerned.

Article 32. Deleted.

Article 33. A Committee may hold its meeting to consider or investigate the measure or matter referred to it.

Article 34. Deleted.

Article 35. A Committee may set up sub-committees to consider or investigate the measure or matter referred to it or the matter on which an approval has been given by the President.

Article 36. A Committee may hold a combined meeting with other Committees by arrangement, if it needs to do so for consideration or investigation.

Article 37. No Committee shall during a plenary sitting of the House without the permission of the President.

Article 38. The Chairman of a Committee shall fix the date and time for a Committee meeting.

When requested by at least one-third of the Committee members, the Chairman must hold a meeting.

The Chairman shall declare the operating, recess or closing of a Committee meeting.

Article 39. When a measure has been referred to a Committee, the Committee shall first hear its purport and then consider it.

Article 40. Deleted.

Article 41. With regard to a measure presented by the House of Representatives or an amendment made by the House of Representatives to a measure which was presented by the Cabinet, the Committee may request an explanation from the Committee Chairman and the proposer or the introducer of the amendment of the House of Representatives.

Article 42. Committee members may freely ask questions and express opinions on the subject under consideration.

When Committee members ask for permission to speak, the Chairman shall grant it according to the order of the requests.

Article 43. The Chairman of a Committee is authorized to attend meetings of other Committees and express his opinions on behalf of his Committee.

Article 44. A Committee may hear an opinion or permit a speech of any Member not on the Committee.

Article 45. When the Chairman desires to participate in a debate himself, he must take a seat of a Committee member.

If the Chairman participates in the debate, he shall not return to his seat as Chairman pending completion of decision by vote on the subject.

Article 46. Any member who desires to move an amendment to a measure must submit it in writing beforehand to the Chairman.

When the amendment under the preceding paragraph is one to a bill and is to bring about an increase of the budget or is to require budgetary action, a written statement shall be attached clarifying expenditure needed as a result of the amendment.

Article 47. The Chairman of a Committee may allocate the time for questions, debate, and so on, as the Committee may decide.

Article 48. A Committee member may make a motion to close questions and debate.

Article 49. When the debate on a matter is closed, the Chairman shall announce the question and put it to a vote.

Article 50. When a Committee desires to present a bill that will affect the budget, the Cabinet shall be given an opportunity to express its opinion in advance of the Committee's decision.

As to a bill introduced by a Member, affecting the budget and referred to the Committee, the Chairman must, before putting it to a vote, give the Cabinet an opportunity to express its opinion. The same shall also apply to an amendment to increase the total amount of the budget and an amendment to a bill, creating an increase of the budget or affecting the budget, submitted by a Committee member.

Article 51. When a Committee member acts contrary to the Diet Law or these Rules, or conducts himself in a disorderly manner, or impairs the dignity of the House, the Chairman shall restrain him or cause him to retract his remarks. If the member does not obey the Chairman's order, the Chairman may forbid him to speak for the rest of the day's meeting or cause him to leave the room.

Article 52. The Chairman may declare a recess or adjourn the meeting, if the business of the Committee goes out of control.

Article 53. When a Committee intends to continue its consideration or investigation of a special measure or matter after the Diet is no longer in session, a request must be made to the President with the reasons in writing attached.

When a request under the preceding paragraph is made, the President must put it to the House for decision.

Article 54. Deleted.

Article 55. Deleted.

Article 56. A Committee shall compile the minutes of meetings.

Article 57. The minutes of the Committee shall be signed by the Chairman or the director who has presided over the Committee meeting for the day and kept in the Secretariat.

Article 58. The minutes of the Committee shall be printed and distributed to each Member of the House, except those parts of minutes of closed meetings which the Committee has decided to keep secret, and those remarks which the Chairman has ordered to be retracted under the provisions of Article 51.

Article 59. Except as provided in the preceding three Articles, the provisions of Articles from 156 to 158 shall apply *mutatis mutandis* to the Committee minutes.

SUB-CHAPTER 2
OPEN HEARINGS

Article 60. A Committee may hold open hearings to consider measures.

Article 61. When a Member or anyone who is not a Member of the House desires to have an open hearing held on an important measure, he shall send in to the Committee Chairman in writing clearly his reasons.

Article 62. When a Committee desires to hold an open hearing, the President's approval must be obtained.

Article 63. An open hearing may be held also for preliminary consideration.

Article 64. The subject matter of an open hearing shall be decided by the Committee Chairman after putting it to the Committee for decision.

Article 65. The Chairman shall announce to the public the date and time and the subject of the hearing.

Article 66. Any person who desires to express his opinion at an open hearing shall beforehand send into the Committee in writing his reasons and his opinion for or against the subject.

Article 67. The persons interested, men of learning and experience and others whose opinions are to be heard at an open hearing (to be called 'speakers') shall be selected by the Committee from among those who have volunteered to speak and from other persons, and shall be notified of their selection.

Diet Members or other public service employees shall not be prevented from becoming speakers.

At open hearings, the number of speakers for and against the subject as well as the length of time allotted to them shall be impartial.

Article 68. A speaker at an open hearing shall confine himself to the matters.

When a speaker at an open hearing deviates from the subject or when his words or actions are considered improper, the Chairman may stop him or order him to leave the room.

Article 69. A Committee member may question a speaker at an open hearing.

Article 70. Neither debate shall take place nor vote be taken at an open hearing.

Article 71. A speaker may not state his views through a proxy or in writing. However, this shall not apply to the case when a special permission has been given by the Committee.

SUB-CHAPTER 3

COMMITTEE REPORTS

Article 72. When a Committee has completed the consideration or investigation of a measure or matter referred to it or approved, it shall prepare a report and submit it to the President through the Chairman.

The report of the preceding paragraph shall be attached a written summary containing a brief explanation of the reasons for its decision, expenses and other matters.

When a Committee has given the Cabinet an opportunity to express its opinion under the provision of Article 57-III of the Diet Law, the gist of this opinion shall be included in the written summary.

Article 72-II. A report on the minority opinion shall be submitted promptly to the President through the Chairman.

Article 72-III. When a Committee does not complete its consideration or investigation of a measure or matter before the beginning of the next session, the Chairman must prepare a written report to that effect and submit it to the President.

Article 72-IV. The President shall have the report under the Preceding three Articles printed and distributed to each Member.

Article 73. When a Standing Committee intends to make an interim report to the House on the matter under its investigation with the approval of the President, the Chairman shall make a written request to the president to that effect.

When a request as mentioned in the preceding paragraph has been made, the President shall put the case to a vote of the House.

SUB-CHAPTER 4

STANDING COMMITTEES

Article 74. The number of members and the jurisdiction of each Standing Committee are as follows:

1. Committee on Cabinet 20 members
   (1) Matters relating to the Imperial Household
   (2) Matters relating to national administration organization
   (3) Matters relating to national public officials
   (4) Matters relating to pensions
   (5) Matters relating to national defence
   (6) Matters relating to honours
   (7) Matters relating to general statistical investigation
2. Committee on Local Administration 20 members
   (1) Matters relating to local public entities
   (2) Matters relating to local administration
   (3) Matters relating to local finance
   (4) Matters relating to elections
   (5) Matters relating to police
   (6) Matters relating to fire defence
3. Committee on Judicial Affairs 20 members
   (1) Matters relating to laws and regulations of civil, criminals and other judicial affairs
   (2) Matters relating to judicial system and judicial administration.
   (3) Matters relating to public prosecution
   (4) Matters relating to judges and public prosecutors
   (5) Matters relating to lawyers
   (6) Matters relating to execution of penalty
   (7) Matters relating to amnesty, rehabilitation and protection
   (8) Matters relating to safeguard of human rights

(9) Matters relating to nationality, census registration, inhabitant registration, notarial act, registry and deposit

(10) Matters relating to control of entry and exit and registration of aliens

(11) Matters relating to litigation in relation with national interests

(12) Matters relating to regulation of destructive groups

4. Committee on Foreign Affairs 20 members

(1) Meteters relating to diplomacy

(2) Matters relating to treaties

(3) Matters relating to international conferences and international organizations

(4) Matters relating to overseas Japanese nationals and overseas commerce

(5) Matters relating to voyage abroad and migration

(6) Matters relating to other international relations

5. Committee on Finance 25 members

(1) Matters relating to national accounts

(2) Matters relating to national taxation

(3) Matters relating to national bonds

(4) Matters relating to national properties

(5) Matters relating to monopolies (excluding alcohol monopoly)

(6) Matters relating to currency

(7) Matters relating to foreign exchange

(8) Matters relating to banking, trust, insurance, mutual financing and other financing

(9) Matters relating to stock transaction

(10) Matters relating to enterprise accounts

6. Committee on Education 20 members

(1) Matters relating to education and educational system

(2) Matters relating to religion

(3) Matters relating to science

(4) Matters relating to art, cultural properties and other cultures

(5) Matters relating to national language and authorship and publication

(6) Matters relating to physical education

7. Committee on Social and Labour Affairs 21 members
   (1) Matters relating to social welfare
   (2) Matters relating to livelihood protection
   (3) Matters relating to public health and sanitation
   (4) Matters relating to social insurance
   (5) Matters relating to labour conditions and protection of labours
   (6) Matters relating to labour unions
   (7) Matters relating to coordination of labour relations
   (8) Matters relating to security of employment
   (9) Matters relating to population problem
   (10) Matters relating to repatriation and demobilization
8. Committee on Agriculture, Forestry and Fisheries 25 members
   (1) Matters relating to agriculture
   (2) Matters relating to livestock breeding
   (3) Matters relating to forestry
   (4) Matters relating to sericulture
   (5) Matters relating to fisheries
   (6) matters relating to food
   (7) Matters relating to agricultural land and reclamation
   (8) Matters relating to fishing ports and fishing boats
   (9) Matters relating to insurance of agriculture, forestry and fisheries
   (10) Matters relating to groups of agriculture, forestry and fisheries
9. Committee on Commerce and Industry 21 members
   (1) Matters relating to commerce
   (2) Matters relating to foreign trade
   (3) Matters relating to industry
   (4) Matters relating to mining
   (5) Matters relating to medium and small size enterprises
   (6) Matters relating to electricity, gas and atomic energy
   (7) matters relating to measures and weights
   (8) Matters relating to inventions, practical new designs, devices and trade marks

(9) Matters relating to alcohol monopoly
(10) Matters relating to fair trade
(11) Matters relating to comprehensive planning to economy
(12) Matters relating to insurance of commerce and industry.
(13) Matters relating to commercial and industrial groups

10. Committee on Transport 20 members
(1) Matters relating to land transport
(2) Matters relating to water transport
(3) Matters relating to aviation
(4) Matters relating to harbours
(5) Matters relating to ships and railroad rolling stock
(6) Matters relating to seamen
(7) Matters relating to maritime safety
(8) Matters relating to marine accidents inquiry
(9) Matters relating to tourism
(10) Matters relating to warehouses
(11) Matters relating to meteorological observation

11. Committee on Communications 20 members
(1) Matters relating to postal service
(2) Matters relating to postal savings, postal money order and postal book-transfer savings
(3) Matters relating to post office, life-insurance and post office, annuity
(4) Matters relating to telecommunications
(5) Matters relating to radio regulation
(6) Matters relating to broadcasting

12. Committee on Construction 20 members
(1) Matters relating to national land planning, local planning and city planning
(2) Matters relating to roads, rivers, seashores, public water surface, canals and erosion control
(3) Matters relations to flood defence
(4) Matters relating to public engineering, building and housing
(5) Matters relating to land expropriation

(6) Matters relating to survey and maps

13. Committee on Budget 45 members

(1) Budgets

14. Committee on Audit 30 members

(1) Auditing

(2) Matters relating to the approval of expenditure from the reserve fund

(3) Complete returns on commitments of the national treaty

(4) Complete returns on the increase and decrease and the current value of national property and property leased rent-free

(5) Matters relating to examination of accounts by the Board of Audit.

15. Committee on Rules and Administration 25 members

(1) Matters relating to the House administration

(2) Matter relating to the Diet Law, Rules and Regulations of the House

(3) Matters relating to administration of the National Diet Library.

(4) Matters relating to the Judges Impeachment Court and Judges Indictment Committee

16. Committee on Discipline 10 members

(1) Matters relating to disciplinary action against Members of the House

Article 74-II. A Member of the House shall not serve concurrently on more than two Standing Committees. In case he serves on two Standing Committees, one of the two shall be limited to the Committees on Budget, Audit, Rules and Administration or Discipline, except for the case of paragraph 3, Article 42 of the Diet Law.

Article 74-III. A Standing Committee is authorized to investigate matters approved by the President, besides the measures or matters referred to it.

To obtain the President's approval, the Standing Committee shall submit to him a written request specifying the name of the matter, purpose, method, period and other details of the intended investigation.

When the President has approved the Committee request, he shall inform the House of it.

Article 74-IV. As to the total budget under consideration, the Committee on Budget may request any other Committee with a time limit to consider parts of the total budget which come under the jurisdiction of said Committee.

The Chairman of the Committee which has been requested consideration as provided for in the preceding paragraph, shall be deemed to report, after the consideration, a summary of the consideration to the Committee on Budget.

The Committee on Budget, when it deems specially necessary, may consider the total budget even if it is within the period of consideration requested in accordance with the first paragraph of this Article.

Article 74-V. The Committee on Rules and Administration may hold its meeting at any time while the Diet is in session with respect to administration of the House and of the National Diet Library.

Article 75. The Budget Committee and the Audit Committee and may divided themselves into several working committees for convenience of the consideration.

Each working committee shall elect a chief and an assistant chief from among its members by secret ballot. However, a motion or other means may be employed for its selection instead of voting.

Pending the election of a chief and an assistant chief, the business pertaining to a work committee shall be conducted by the eldest person in the working committee.

The chief may add to the Chairman's report in the House.

When the chief is unable to attend to his duties or when the position becomes vacant, an assistant chief shall perform the duties of the chief.

The resignation of the chief or the assistant chief requires the approval of the working committee.

Article 76. When a Standing Committee desires to hold a joint meeting with a Standing Committee of the House of Representatives, it shall make a decision to that effect after its Chairman has consulted with the Committee Chairman of the House of Representatives.

Article 77. A Standing Committee may not take a vote on a measure or matter put to a joint meeting until the latter has completed its consideration.

SUB-CHAPTER 5

SPECIAL COMMITTEES

Article 78. The number of members of a Special Committee shall be decided by the House. The House may, however, increase the membership whenever necessary.

Article 79. Deleted.

Article 80. Members of a Special Committee shall elect a Chairman from among themselves by secret ballot, and the person who has obtained the greatest number of votes shall be declared elected. In case of a tie, the decision shall be made by lot. However, the Chairman of a Special Committee may also be elected not by ballot but by a motion or by other means.

Until the Chairman is elected, the eldest person in the Committee shall perform the duties of the Chairman.

The resignation of the Chairman of a Special Committee requires the approval of the Committee.

CHAPTER VIII

PLENARY SITTINGS

SUB-CHAPTER 1

OPENING, CLOSING AND ADJOURNMENT OF SITTING

Article 81. The sitting shall start at 10 a.m. This does not, however, apply if the President deems it necessary.

Article 82. When the business of the measures or matters put on the Order of the Day is brought to an end, the president may declare the sitting closed. Even if some business remains to be dealt with, the President may adjourn the sitting, putting it to the House for decision when he deems it necessary, or without putting it to the House for decision when it is past 4 o'clock in the afternoon.

Article 83. When the time for the sitting comes, the President shall take the Chair and, after reporting on various matters, shall declare the sitting open.

No one may speak on the business of the sitting until the President has declared the sitting open.

Article 84. When the Members present do not form a quorum, the President shall declare to adjourn the sitting. When the absence of the quorum is proved because of the Members leaving their seats during a sitting, the President may declare a recess or adjourn the sitting.

When the President deems that the number of the Members present will possibly fall short of a quorum during a sitting, he may prohibit the Members from leaving their seats or request the Members who are outside the Chamber to present themselves in the Chamber.

When the number of the Members present is deemed to lack a quorum, a Member may request the President to count the number of the Members present.

Article 85. After the President has declared the closing, adjournment or recess of the sitting, no one may speak on the business of the sitting.

SUB-CHAPTER 2
THE ORDER OF THE DAY

Article 86. The date and time for opening a sitting, the measures and matters to be laid before it and their order shall be placed on the Order of the Day.

The Order of the Day shall be notified in advance to each Member through the Official Bulletin of the House of Councillors and published in the Official Gazette.

Article 87. When the President has notified the Members of the date and time for a sitting only, he must fix the Order of the Day prior to the opening of the sitting.

Article 88. When the President deems it necessary, or a motion is made by a Member, the President may alter the order in the Order of the Day, or add other measure or matter to it after putting the case to a vote of the House without debate.

Article 89. If any business on the Order of the Day has not been taken up or the business has not been finished, the President must place it again on the Order for another day.

SUB-CHAPTER 3
MOTION

Article 90. Except for special stipulations made in the Diet Law or these Rules, all motions shall require one or more supporters to be brought up before a sitting.

Article 91. When a Member wishes to withdraw a motion, the request for withdrawal shall be made by all the members who have submitted the motion with him. In order to withdraw a motion after it has been brought to a sitting, the permission of the House is necessary.

SUB-CHAPTER 4
SPEAKING

Article 91. A Member who desires to speak in the sitting is required to give notice to a secretary of the House in advance, as far as circumstances permit.

Article 92. Deleted.

Article 93. A Member who gives notice to debate must make it clear at the time of notice whether he is going to speak for or against the subject.

Article 94. As to the notices of questions or debates, the secretary shall put them on the Speaking List in the order of the notices received, and report them to the President.

In allowing questions or debates, the president shall name each speaker in the order of their names on the Speaking List.

For those who do not comply with the naming mentioned in the preceding paragraph, the notices shall become invalid.

Article 95. Members who have not given notice may not speak until all the Members who gave notice have finished speaking.

Article 96. A Member who desires to speak without having given notice may do so after obtaining the President's permission by standing up, calling the President and giving his own name.

Article 97. When two or more Members stand up and ask for permission to speak, the President shall give permission to speak in the order in which he considers the Members stood up.

Article 98. All speaking must be done from the rostrum. However, when speaking is extremely short or when the President grants permission, a Member may speak from his assigned seat.

Article 99. The President may at any time order a Member speaking from his assigned seat to speak from the rostrum.

Article 100. Speakers may not derivate from the subject under consideration or go beyond its scope.

Article 101. No speech shall be interrupted halfway by another one.

Article 102. A member who has not finished speaking owing to an adjournment of the sitting or a recess, may continue when the business on the matter is resumed.

Article 103. No Member is permitted to read out any written statement in a sitting. This provision does not, however, apply to a brief note which has been prepared for the purpose of quotation or report.

Article 104. When a measure or matter which has been referred to a Committee is brought to a sitting, the Chairman of the Committee shall first explain the contents of the measure or matter, and then report on its proceedings and results before questions on the measure or matter begin.

As to the measure or matter with which the consideration or investigation of a Special Committee has been finished while the Diet is not in session, the ex-Chairman shall make the report mentioned in the preceding paragraph.

Article 105. In making the report, the Chairman must not add his own opinion to it.

Article 106. Following the report by the Chairman, a member of a minority opinion shall report that opinion. In case there are several minority opinions, the order of the reports shall be decided by the President.

Article 107. When a measure on which Committee consideration has been omitted is brought to a sitting, the introducer or the proposer shall first explain its purport and contents.

Article 107-II. As to a bill introduced by a Member, requiring budgetary action on which Committee consideration has been omitted, the President must, after the explanation by the introducer of the purport of the bill, afford the Cabinet an opportunity to give its opinion. The same shall apply to an amendment presented by a Member to increase the total amount of the budget or an amendment to a bill, which brings about an increase of the budget or which will require budgetary action.

Article 108. Members may question the Chairman, the reporter of the minority opinion, the introducer or the proposer.

Article 109. In questions, a member may not state his own opinion.

Article 110. Questions may not be made on the same subject more than three times.

Article 111. When there has been too long a succession of questions and there seems no likelihood of an end, a Member may make a motion to close the questions with the support of twenty or more Members.

When the motion in the preceding paragraph has been made, the President shall decide it after putting it to a vote of the House without debate.

Article 112. When questions have ended, the President shall declare the closure of questions.

Article 113. When questions have closed, a debate shall be opened.

Article 114. Deleted.

Article 115. Deleted.

Article 116. In a debate, the President must let the opposer take the floor first, and, as far as circumstances permit, must let the supporters and opposers speak alternately.

When all the members on one side who gave notice have finished speaking, Members on the same side who die not give notice may ask for permission to speak even before all the Members on the other side who gave notice have not finished speaking.

Article 117. A Member may not debate two times on the same subject under consideration.

Article 118. A Chairman or a reporter of the minority opinion may speak several times in order to explain the purport of the report.

An introducer or a proposer may speak several times in order to explain the purport of the measure.

Article 119. If the President desires to participate in a debate himself, he must give notice to that effect in advance and take his assigned seat.

When the President has participated in the debate, he may not return to the Chair until a vote has been taken on the matter.

Article 120. After two or more Members have spoken for and against, or when two or more Members have spoken on one side and there is no one to speak on the other side, a Member may make a motion to close the debate with the support of twenty or more Members.

When the motion under the preceding paragraph has been made, the president shall decide it after putting it to a vote of the House without debate.

Article 121. When, after a debate ended or a motion to close a debate was carried, the introducer or the proposer has made a speech on the subject under consideration, it shall be deemed that the further debate has been entered upon.

Article 122. When a debate has ended, the President shall declare its closure.

Article 123. A member who desires to speak on a point of order is required to give notice of its purport to a secretary of the House in advance.

The time to grant permission to speak on a point of order shall be in the discretion of the President.

SUB-CHAPTER 5

AMENDMENTS

Article 124. Deleted.

Article 125. A motion of amendment must be made in advance to the President with the proposed amendment, signed by the proposer and the prescribed number of supporters.

When the amendment under the preceding paragraph is one to a bill and is to bring about an increase of the budget or is to require a budgetary action, a written statement shall be attached clarifying expenditure needed as a result of the amendment.

The President shall have the amendment printed and distributed to each Member.

Article 126. A motion of amendment withdrawn by the proposer may be reopposed by another Member together with the prescribed number of supporters.

Article 127. Deleted.

Article 128. An amendment reported by a Committee shall be brought up before a sitting without need of any supporters.

Article 129. An amendment proposed by a Member must be voted upon before one reported by a Committee.

Article 130. When several amendments are proposed by Members on the same subject, precedence shall be given to the amendments according to how far they depart from the original bill or measure. The order of voting on them shall be decided by the President.

But in case twenty or more Members present object to the order, the President shall decide in after putting it to the House for decision without debate.

Article 131. If all the amendments have been rejected, the original bill or measure shall be voted upon.

Article 132. If both the amendments and the original bill or measure fail to secure majority support but the House resolves not to drop the matter yet, the House may order a Committee to draft a new bill or measure; when such a new bill or measure is reported, it may be brought to a sitting.

Article 133. The House may delegate to the President adjustment of the article and words or phrases which have been amended and resolved.

SUB-CHAPTER 6
VOTING

Article 134. A vote must be unconditional.

Article 135. No Member who is not present in the Chamber at the time of voting is entitled to vote.

Article 136. When the President desires to take a vote, he shall announce the question to be voted on.

After the President's announcement, no one may speak on the subject.

Article 137. In taking a vote, the President shall ask those members who are for the matter to stand up, and, ascertaining whether they are in the majority or in the minority, he shall declare the result of the vote.

When the President finds it difficult to ascertain whether the standing members are in the majority or not, or when one-fifth or more of the Members present have raised an objection to his declaration, he must put the matter to a vote by open ballot.

Article 138. When the President deems it necessary, the vote may be taken by open ballot. When one-fifth or more of the Members present demand it, the vote must be taken by open ballot.

Article 139. In an open ballot, those Members who are for the matter shall cast white ballots with their names on them, and those against, blue ballots with their names on them, into the respective ballot boxes.

Article 140. While a vote by open ballot is being taken, all entrances to the Chamber shall be closed.

Article 141. When the voting has finished, the President shall declare the result to the House.

Article 142. No Member is permitted to ask for alteration of his vote once cast.

Article 143. The President may ask the House whether any Member has any objection against a given matter, and if he finds no objection raised, he shall declare the matter passed. If an objection is raised, however, against the President's declaration by Members present, the President must take a vote in accordance with the other means provided in this sub-chapter.

SUB-CHAPTER 7
DELETED

Articles 144-152: Deleted.

CHAPTER IX
QUESTIONS

Article 153. The President shall have printed and distributed to each Member a written question approved by the House or by him, together with the Cabinet's written answer to it.

Article 154. The Cabinet may give oral answers to questions.

On such oral answers, the questioner may put another question orally to the Cabinet.

Article 155. When a written question is to be recorded in the minutes under the provision of paragraph 4 of Article 74 of the Diet Law, the President may have the written question put into a concise form if he considers it diffuse.

CHAPTER X
MINUTES

Article 156. All the proceedings of sittings must be recorded in the minutes by means of shorthand.

Article 157. Matters especially provided for in the Diet Law, matters especially decided by the House and matters deemed necessary by the President shall be recorded in the minutes.

Article 158. A Member who spoke may ask for correction of his remarks not later than 5 p.m. on the day after the distribution of the minutes.

The correction, however, shall be limited to words or phrases and the gist of his speech may not be changed. The same shall apply to Ministers of State, Government delegates, and others who spoke in a sitting.

When an objection is raised by a Member against matters entered in the minutes or against corrections of the minutes, the President shall decide the case after putting it to a vote of the House without debate.

Article 159. The minutes to be kept in the Secretariat shall be signed by the President, or by the Vice-President or the President pro-tempore who presided over the sitting of the day, and by the Secretary General or the secretary who is his proxy.

Article 160. The minutes shall be printed and distributed to each Member and be available to the general public.

Article 161. The minutes to be distributed and to be available shall not contain the parts which the House has decided to keep secret under the provision of Article 63 of the Diet Law, and any words which the President has ordered to be retracted under the provision of Article 116 of the same Law.

CHAPTER XI
PETITIONS

Article 162. All petitions must contain the names (in the case of juridical persons, their names) and addresses (if there is no residence, a dwelling place) of the petitioners.

Article 163. No petition in the name of a delegate shall be accepted, except in the case of juridical persons.

Article 164. A petition must be expressed in moderate terms and must be submitted in a peaceful manner.

Article 165. The President shall have a list of petitions prepared, printed and distributed weekly to each Member.

The list of petitions shall contain the purport of each petition, the name and address of the petitioner, the name of the introducing Member and the date of receipt.

Article 166. At the same time as the list of petitions is distributed, the President shall refer them to the appropriate committees.

Article 167. In the case of a petition asking for the removal of a judge, the President shall send to the Judges Indictment Committee without referring it to any other Committee.

Article 168. A Member who has introduced a petition must make an explanation on the purport of the petition when requested by the committee.

Article 169. Only such petitions as have been resolved by the House shall be printed and distributed.

Article 170. The Committee, according to the results of their consideration, shall classify the petitions as follows, and submit the reports to the President:

(1) Those needing to be laid before a sitting to the House.

(2) Those not needing to be laid before a sitting of the House.

The petitions needing to be laid before a sitting of the House shall be further classified as follows:

(1) Those needing to be sent to the Cabinet.

(2) Those not needing to be sent to the Cabinet.

Article 171. As to the petition which the Committee has decided on needing to be laid before a sitting of the House, the Committee may attach a written opinion to the report of the preceding Article.

Article 172. When the committee has decided that a petition does not need to be laid before a sitting of the House, the decision of the Committee shall be final, unless demand to lay it before a sitting of the House is may by twenty or more Members within seven days.

Article 173. Deleted.

CHAPTER XII

RELATIONS WITH THE HOUSE OF REPRESENTATIVES

Article 174. When a measure is to be sent to the House of Representatives, the President shall have the Secretary General deliver it to the Speaker of that House.

Article 175. When a measure is received from the House of Representatives, the President shall report it to the House.

Article 175-II. A Committee Chairman or an introducer or a proposer of an amendment may make an explanation in the House of Representatives on the measure presented by the House of Councillors or the part amended by the House of Councillors of the measure presented by the Cabinet upon the request of that House.

Article 176. The election of members of the Conference Committee shall be held by secret ballot with plural entry.

The members who have obtained the largest number of votes shall be declared elected. In the case of a tie, however, the decision shall be made by lot.

The House may delegate the appointment of members of the Conference Committee to the President.

The House is authorized to accept the resignation of a member of the Conference Committee.

Article 177. The election of the chairman of the Conference Committee shall be supervised by the eldest Committee member.

Article 178. A measure sent back by the House of Representatives or a final compromise arrived at by the Conference Committee of both Houses shall not be referred to any Committee.

Questions and debate on a measure sent back shall be confined within the scope of the amendments contained in it.

In respect of a final compromise of the Conference Committee, questions and debate shall be confined within the scope of that compromise.

Article 179. Regulations concerning the Conference Committee and the joint meetings of Standing Committees of both Houses shall be resolved by the House after the President has conferred with the Speaker of the House of Representatives.

CHAPTER XIII

RELATIONS WITH GENERAL PUBLIC AND GOVERNMENT AGENCIES

Article 180. Sending members out for consideration, investigation or for other purposes requires the resolution of the House. However, when it is urgently necessary or when the Diet is not in session, the President may decide to send Members out.

Article 180-II. A Committee may, with the approval of the President, send Committee members out for consideration or investigation.

When a Committee desires to send Committee members out, a written request must be submitted to the President, stating the purpose, names of members, destination, period and expenses.

Article 181. When a Committee calls for the production of records or documents from the Cabinet, offices of government and public entities and others for consideration or investigation, the request must be made through the President.

Article 182. When a motion is made to call a witness at a plenary sitting for consideration or investigation, the President shall decide it after putting it to the House for decision and request his presence.

When a Committee has resolved to call a witness at its meeting, the request of his attendance must be made through the President.

Article 183. The President or the Committee Chairman may request a witness to submit, in advance, a summary of his testimony.

Article 184. A witness must present himself to the House to give testimony. However, under unavoidable circumstances, a written statement may be presented instead of testimony.

Article 185. A witness shall confine his speaking to the matter on which he is asked to testify.

Article 186. A Committee may hear the views of informants for consideration or investigation.

A request by a Committee for the attendance of informants must be made through the President.

CHAPTER XIV

LEAVE OF ABSENCE AND RESIGNATION

SUB-CHAPTER 1
LEAVE OF ABSENCE

Article 187. When a Member expects that he will be prevented from attending the House for several days for some cause, he shall present to the President in advance an application in writing for leave of absence, stating the reason and the length of time.

The President may grant leave of absence for a period within seven days. As to leave of absence for a period more than seven days, the President shall decide it after putting it to the House for decision.

When a Member has been prevented from attending the House due to official duties, illness, or other circumstances of a temporary nature, he must give the President a written notice of non-attendance stating the reason.

Article 188. A Member who takes a journey with leave of absence must, at the time of his departure and return, notify the President to the effect.

Article 189. When a Member who has been granted leave of absence attends the House before it expires, the leaves shall lapse.

SUB-CHAPTER 2
RESIGNATION

Article 190. When a Member desires to resign, he must submit his resignation to the President.

Article 191. The President shall have the resignation read out and decide whether to accept or reject it after putting the case to a vote of the House without debate.

Article 192. If the President considers that the resignation contains some insulting remarks, he may report its substance to the House instead of reading it out. In this case, the President may refer the resignation to the Committee on Discipline for examination.

CHAPTER XV
CHALLENGE TO MEMBER'S QUALIFICATION

Article 193. A Member who desires to challenge another Member on his qualification must submit to the President a written charge in duplicate, duly signed, containing the substance, reasons and evidence for the allegation.

Article 193-II. When a written charge has been submitted, a Special Committee on Challenge to Member's Qualification is deemed to have been established.

The Special Committee of the preceding paragraph shall be composed of 10 members.

Article 194. The President must fix the term of examination after putting it to the House for decision and refer the written charge to the Committee, and at the same time send the duplicate to the Member whose qualification has been challenged (to be called 'the defendant Member'), notify him of the term of examination by the Committee and have him submit a written answer by a fixed date.

If the defendant Member proves that he is unable to submit his answer by the fixed date by reason of natural calamity, illness or other unavoidable cause, the President may fix another date for his answer.

Article 195. When a written answer is submitted by the defendant Member by the appointed date, the President shall immediately send it to the Committee.

Article 196. The Committee shall examine the matter on basis of the written charge and the written answer. When an answer has not been submitted by the appointed date, the examination may be conducted with the written charge alone.

Article 197. The defendant Member may engage counsel at any time after he has received the duplicate of the written charge. In this case, he must inform the President to that effect.

Article 198. Counsel may, at the request or with the permission of the Committee, speak before the Committee in defence of the defendant Member.

Article 199. The Member who has instituted the suit (to be called 'the prosecuting Member') and the defendant Member may attend the Committee and speak with its permission.

Article 200. When the Committee deems it necessary for the examination of the case, it may, through the President, call the prosecuting Member and the defendant Member and may question them.

Article 201. The Committee may request the President to extend the term of examination.

Article 202. When the Committee has submitted to the President its written report of examination, the President shall have it printed and distributed to each Member.

Article 203. The defendant Member may speak several times at a sitting of the House in defence of the case.

Article 204. The counsel may speak at a sitting of the House in vindication of the case.

Article 205. The verdict of the House on a Member's qualification shall be rendered in the form of a resolution of the House.

No reason shall be attached to the verdict of the House.

Article 206. When a verdict is rendered by the House, the President shall have copies of the verdict prepared and send the copy of it to the prosecuting Member and to the defendant Member.

CHAPTER XVI
DISCIPLINE AND POLICE

SUB-CHAPTER 1
DISCIPLINE

Article 207. Members must respect the dignity of the House.

Article 208. Members shall use terms of respect for each other in the Chamber and in Committee meeting rooms.

Article 209. No one shall enter the Chamber or Committee meeting rooms with a hat, overcoat, scarf, umbrella, cane and the like on or with him. However, a member who has obtained the permission of the President may carry his cane.

Article 210. No smoking is allowed in the Chamber.

Article 211. No one shall read newspapers, books, etc., during the sitting except for reference materials.

Article 212. No one shall make unauthorized utterances or behave in a disorderly manner during the sitting so as to create a disturbance while other Members are speaking.

Article 213. No one shall ascend the rostrum without the permission of the President.

Article 214. The House shall come to order when the President rings the bell.

Article 215. At the close or recess of a sitting, no Member shall leave the Chamber until the President has retired.

Article 216. All questions relating to discipline in the House shall be decided by the President. The President, however, may decide them after putting them to the House without debate.

SUB-CHAPTER 2
POLICE

Article 217. The President shall exercise police power within the House by directing the guards and the police.

Article 218. The guards shall be on police duty within the House.

The Police shall be on police duty outside the House building. When the President deems it necessary, however, he may cause the police to be on duty inside the building.

Article 219. When a person is found in the very act of committing a criminal offence in the House, the guards or the police shall arrest the offender, make the report to the President and ask for directions from the President. In the Chamber, however, no arrest shall be made without the order of the President.

CHAPTER XVII
VISITORS

Article 220. The visitors' gallery shall be divided into sections for the Imperial family, foreign diplomats, Members of the House of Representatives, public officials, the general public and the press.

Article 221. When public officials desire to visit the House through the offices of the Ministry or the Agency to which they belong, the Secretary General shall send a limited number of admission tickets to the Ministry or the Agency.

Article 222. Half of the seats for the general public shall be allotted to those who obtain admission tickets for the general public section issued by the Secretary General on each day of a plenary sitting. These tickets shall be given to the people on a first-come, first-served basis at the House before the sitting.

The other half of the seats for the general public shall be allotted to those who, at the invitation of a Member, carry admission tickets for the general public section with the date indicated, previously issued by the Secretary General to the Member.

Article 223. Visiting badges valid throughout a session shall issued to newspaper companies and news agencies.

The number of visiting badges shall be decided, under the direction of the President, by the Secretary General at the beginning of each session.

Article 224. The President may order the guards or the police to make a body search of visitors, when he deems it necessary.

Article 225. A person carrying firearms or any other dangerous object, a person under the influence of alcohol, or any person who is regarded by the President as affecting the maintenance of order, shall not be admitted to the gallery.

Article 226. The President may limit the number of visitors to be admitted when he deems it necessary to do so for the maintenance of order.

Article 227. Visitors must show their admission tickets or visiting badges to the guards and follow their directions.

Article 228. Visitors must observe the Visitors' Regulations made by the president.

Article 229. No visitors may enter the Chamber under any circumstances.

Article 230. When all visitors are to be excluded on account of the House resolution to hold a closed sitting or because of noise in the gallery, or when any visitor is ordered out of the gallery for obstructing the proceedings, the President shall instruct the guards to execute his order of expulsion.

Article 231. Provisions of Article 224 and succeeding Articles shall be applied *mutatis mutandis* to visitors to Committee meetings.

CHAPTER XVIII

DISCIPLINARY MEASURES

Article 232. When a disciplinary case occurs at a sitting, the President may declare a recess or adjourn the sitting or cause the offender to leave the Chamber.

Article 233. When a disciplinary case occurs at a Committee meeting, the Chairman of the Committee may declare a recess or closing of the meeting.

Article 234. When a disciplinary case occurs in a sitting or a committee meeting, or otherwise within the House, the President shall refer it to the Committee on Discipline.

Article 235. If any person does not yield to the President's restraint or disobeys his order to retract offensive remarks, the President, besides taking appropriate action under Article 116 of the Diet Law, may also refer it as a disciplinary case to the Committee on Discipline.

If any person does not yield to the Committee Chairman's restraint or disobeys his order to retract offensive remarks, the Chairman, besides taking appropriate action under Article 51, may also report to the President for action as a disciplinary case.

Article 236. If any person has disclosed to others the matters not to be publicized under Article 63 of the Diet Law, the President shall refer him to the Committee on Discipline as a disciplinary case.

Article 237. Any Member may make a motion for a disciplinary measure, even if the Chairman does not consider the case as needing discipline.

Article 238. When a motion for a disciplinary measure is made, the President must put it to the sitting of the House without delay.

In case of the preceding paragraph, the President shall put it to a vote for a resolution of the House without debate and refer it to the Committee on Discipline.

Article 239. The Committee on Discipline may, through the President, ask for the presence of the defendant Member and other members concerned and may question them.

Article 240. A Member may not join the sitting or Committee meeting at which his disciplinary case is examined. He may, however, speak in his own defence or have another Member to do so in his stead, with permission of the President or the Chairman.

Article 241. Of the disciplinary actions the text of the admonition or the apology in an open sitting shall be drafted by the Committee on Discipline and submitted to the President with a report on the case.

Article 242. Suspension of attendance at the House shall not exceed 30 days.

Even if several disciplinary offences have been concurrently committed by the same Member, the suspension shall not exceed the period mentioned in the preceding paragraph.

Article 243. A Member who has been suspended from attendance at the House shall lose his Committee membership of the Special Committee or the Conference Committee.

Article 244. If a Member who has been suspended comes to the House during the period of his suspension, the President shall immediately order him to leave the House. If the Member disobeys the order, the President may take necessary action and refer the matter again to the Committee on Discipline.

Article 245. The House is authorized to suspend from attendance at the House or expel any Member who commits a beach of order in the House or impairs the dignity of the House in a particularly reprehensible manner.

Article 246. When the recommendation for expulsion made by the Committee on Discipline is not adopted by a majority of two-thirds or more of Members present, the House may inflict other disciplinary actions on the offending Member.

Article 247. When the House has decided on a disciplinary action, the President must declare the verdict of the House in an open sitting, even if the decision is made in a closed sitting.

CHAPTER XIX

ELECTION OF MEMBERS OF JUDGES IMPEACHMENT COURT, MEMBERS OF JUDGES INDICTMENT COMMITTEE AND OTHERS

Article 248. The election of members and reserve members of the Judges Impeachment Court, and the members and reserve members of the Judges Indictment Committee shall be held by secret ballot with plural entry.

The Members who have obtained the largest number of votes shall be declared elected. In the case of a tie, the Member to be elected shall be decided by lot.

The House may delegate the designation of members to the President.

Article 249. Where an election of more than one member occurs among the Members of the House of Councillors for a Committee or other function under the law, other than those provided for in the preceding Article, the provisions of the preceding Article shall apply *mutatis mutandis* to their election.

Article 250. Where an election of any member occurs among Members of the House of Councillors for a Committee or other function under the law, the election shall be held in the same manner as that of the President.

The House may delegate the designation of the member to the President.

CHAPTER XX
EMERGENCY SESSION

Article 251. The Members must assemble in the House of Councillors at 10 a.m. on the day designated for an emergency session.

Article 252. In applying the provisions of Articles 4, 13, 14, 16, 17, 19, 74-V and 223, "convocation" shall read "assembly"; "each session" shall read "an emergency session"; "while in session" or "throughout a session" shall read "while in an emergency session."

CHAPTER XXI
SUPPLEMENTARY PROVISIONS

Article 253. All questions concerning any part of the Rules of the House shall be settled by the President. The President may, however, settle the questions after putting them to the House for decision.

THE RULES OF THE HOUSE OF REPRESENTATIVES

CHAPTER I
OPENING OF SESSION AND ELECTION OF OFFICERS

Article 1. Members shall assemble in the House of Representatives at 10 a.m. on the day designated in the Imperial Rescript for convocation.

Article 2. Members are required to present to the Secretariat their certificates of election and have them checked with the list of those elected.

Article 3. When the posts of both the Speaker and the Vice-Speaker are vacant on the day of convocation, the House shall elect the Speaker after Members assembled have reached one-third of the total membership.

The election of the Speaker shall be held by secret ballot.

Article 4. Each Member shall, when his name is called, take his ballot paper and wooden name-plate to the rostrum for voting.

Secretary A shall receive the name-plate, Secretary B the ballot paper, and on behalf of the Member they shall put them respectively into the name-plate box and the ballot box.

Article 5. When all the Members present have voted, the Secretary General shall declare the closure of the ballot box. After this declaration no more voting shall be allowed.

Article 6. On completion of the voting, the Secretary General shall immediately have the secretaries count the name-plates and the ballot papers and examine the ballot papers.

When the number of the ballot papers exceeds that of the name-plates, a further vote shall be held, unless the result of the election is unaffected by this discrepancy.

Article 7. When all the ballot papers have been examined, the Secretary General shall announce to the House the result of the election.

Article 8. The Member who has obtained more than half the votes is declared elected.

If no Member has obtained a majority, a deciding vote shall be taken between the two who have obtained the largest number of votes; and the one who obtains the greater number of votes is declared elected.

In case of a tie on the occasion of selecting two Members between whom a deciding vote is to be taken, or of deciding the Member to be declared elected, the selection or the decision shall be made by lot.

Article 9. After the election of the Speaker, the House shall elect the Vice-speaker.

The election of the Vice-Speaker shall be held in the same manner as that of the Speaker.

Article 10. If the Member elected declines to accept the office another election shall be held.

Article 11. All questions about an election in the House shall be settled by the House.

Article 12. When the Speaker and the Vice-Speaker have been elected, the Secretary General shall present them to the House and conduct the Speaker to the Chair.

Article 13. If the post of either the Speaker or the Vice-Speaker is vacant on the day of convocation, the House shall, after Members assembled have reached one-third of the total membership, hold an election.

The election shall be held in the same manner as provided for in Article 4 and under.

Article 14. The Speaker shall assign a seat in the Chamber to each Member at the beginning of each session; although he may change it whenever necessary.

Each seat shall be numbered and shall have the Member's name-block attached to it.

Article 15. The elections of the Chairmen of Standing Committees shall be held in the same manner as that of the Speaker.

The House may, however, delegate the selection of a Chairman to the Speaker.

Article 16. The election of the Secretary General shall be held in the same manner as that of the Speaker.

The House may, however, delegate the selection of the Secretary General to the Speaker.

Article 17. The election of a Speaker pro-tempore shall be held in the same manner as that of a Speaker.

CHAPTER II

DESIGNATION OF PRIME MINISTER

Article 18. The Member who is to be designated Prime Minister shall be chosen by open ballot.

The Member who has obtained more than half the votes cast shall be the one to be designated and the result of the ballot shall be deemed to be the resolution of the House for the designation.

If no one has obtained the majority vote, the Member to be designated shall be chosen by applying *mutatis mutandis* the provisions of paragraph 2 of Article 8, and the decision on the designation shall be deemed to have been made for that person.

The House may also choose the person to be designated, not by ballot, but by a motion or by other means.

CHAPTER III

OPENING CEREMONY

Article 19. The date, time, and place of the opening ceremony shall be fixed by the Speaker in consultation with the President of the House of Councillors.

CHAPTER IV

DETERMINATION AND EXTENSION OF THE TERM OF A SESSION, RECESS OF THE DIET, AND NOTIFICATION OF THESE

Article 20. The term of an extraordinary session shall be decided by the House, after the Speaker has taken the views of the Chairmen of Standing Committees and conferred with the President of the House of Councillors.

The term of special session shall be resolved by the House, after the Speaker has conferred with the President of the House of Councillors.

Article 21. The provision of paragraph 1 of the preceding Article shall apply *mutatis mutandis* to an extension of the term of a session.

Article 22. Recess of the Diet on account of national events, the year-end and New Year holidays, and for other reasons, such as circumstances in relation to measures, shall be decided by the House, after the Speaker has conferred with the President of the House of Councillors.

Article 22-II. Recess of the House on account of circumstances in relation to measures and for other reasons shall be decided by the House.

Even while the House is in recess, a sitting may be held, if the Speaker deems it of urgent necessity or if at least one-fourth of the total membership makes a request for it.

The days of a meeting as provided for in the preceding paragraph shall be counted into the recess period of the House.

Article 22-II. The Speaker shall immediately notify the House of Councillors and the Cabinet of the result of a decision as provided for in the preceding four Articles.

CHAPTER V

ELECTION OF MEMBERS OF JUDGES IMPEACHMENT COURT, MEMBERS OF JUDGES INDICTMENT COMMITTEE AND OTHERS

Article 23. The election of members and reserve members of the Judges Impeachment Court shall be held by single secret ballot.

Members shall be declared elected in descending order of the number of votes they receive, until the required number of members has been reached. In the case of a tie, the Member to be elected shall be decided by lot.

To be declared elected in accordance with the preceding paragraph, a Member must secure at least one-fourth of the total number of votes divided by the number of Members required to be elected.

If there are not enough successful Members to reach the required number, a further election shall be held in accordance with the preceding three paragraphs in order to make up the number.

The House may, however, dispense with the election and delegate the designation of members to the Speaker.

Article 24. The provisions of the preceding Article shall apply *mutatis mutandis* to the election of the members and reserve members of the Judges Indictment Committee.

Article 25. The reserve members mentioned in the preceding two Articles shall perform the duties as members according to the number of votes received. In the case of a tie, precedence shall be decided by lot.

Article 26. Where an election of more than one member occurs among the Members of the House of Representatives for a Committee or other function under the law, other than those provided for in Articles 23 and 24, the provisions of Article 23 shall apply *mutatis mutandis* to their election.

Article 27. Where an election of any member occurs among Members of the House of Representatives for a Committee or other function under the law, the election shall be held in the same manner as that of the Speaker.

The House may, however, dispense with the election and delegate the designation of the member to the Speaker.

CHAPTER VI
INTRODUCTION AND WITHDRAWAL OF MEASURES

Article 28. When any Member desires to introduce a bill or other measure, he must submit it, signed jointly by the required number of supporters, to the Speaker with the reasons in writing attached. If the measure is a bill which requires budgetary action, a written statement of the expenses needed for the implementation of the law shall be attached.

The Speaker shall have the bill printed and distributed to each Member.

Article 28-II. When any Member desires to make a motion or introduce a resolution of confidence or non-confidence in the Speaker or the Vice-Speaker, he must submit it in writing, with the reason attached and signed jointly by at least fifty supporters, to the Speaker.

With respect to a motion or a resolution of confidence or non-confidence in the Speaker pro-tempore, the same procedure shall be followed as in the proceeding paragraph.

With respect to a motion or a resolution for the release of the Chairman of a Standing Committee, the same procedure shall be followed as in paragraph 1.

Article 28-III. When any Member desires to make a motion or introduce a resolution of confidence or non-confidence in the Cabinet, he must submit it in Writing with the reason attached and signed jointly by at least fifty supporters, to the Speaker.

Article 29. When any measure mentioned in Article 28 requires the decision of the Diet, the Speaker shall, besides distributing it to each Member, send it to the House of Councillors for preliminary consideration.

Article 30. As to the measures presented by the House of councillors or the Cabinet and those sent from the House of Councillors, the Speaker shall immediately have them printed and distributed to each Member, unless they are the same measures as have already been distributed for preliminary consideration.

Article 31. When a measure is introduced or presented, the Speaker shall refer it to an appropriate Standing Committee besides distributing it.

Article 32. When no jurisdiction can be fixed easily for a measure or matter, the Speaker shall refer it to a Standing Committee as the House may decide.

Article 33. When a Special Committee has been set up for a measure or matter which the House deems specially necessary or for a measure or matter not coming under the jurisdiction of any Standing Committee, the Speaker shall refer to that Special Committee the measure of matter which comes under its jurisdiction.

Article 34. The Speaker may, as the House decides, refer to a Special Committee any measure or matter related to one which has been referred to that Committee.

Article 35. The preceding five Articles shall apply *mutatis mutandis* to the measures sent from the House of Councillors or the Cabinet for preliminary consideration.

Article 36. When a Member desires to withdraw a measure he has introduced or motion he has made, the request must be made by all the proposers. To withdraw a measure or motion after a Committee or the House has begun to consider it, the permission of the Committee or of the House is required respectively.

Article 36-II. If a measure introduced by a Member comes to lack the required number of supporters before the House makes a decision on the measure, the deficiency must be filled without delay.

If the deficiency stated in the preceding paragraph cannot be filled, the measure shall lapse.

CHAPTER VII
COMMITTEES

SUB-CHAPTER 1
General Provisions

Article 37. Members of Committees shall all be nominated by the Speaker.

Article 38. A Committee shall have one or more directors who are elected by members of the Committee from among themselves.

A director shall perform the duties of the Chairman when the Chairman is unable to attend to them.

Article 39. Those who have been nominated as Committee members may not resign their posts without good reason.

When a Committee member desires to resign his post, he must apply through the Chairman for the permission of the Speaker, stating the reason for his resignation.

Article 40. Vacancies in the membership of a Committee shall be filled by the Speaker.

Article 41. No Committee shall meet during a plenary sitting of the House without the permission of the Speaker.

Article 42. Deleted.

Article 43. A Committee may set up sub-committees.

Article 44. When any bill has been referred to a Committee, the Committee shall first hear its purport and then consider it.

Article 45. Committee members may freely asked questions and express opinions on the subject under consideration.

When Committee members ask for permission to speak, the Chairman shall grant it according to the order of the requests.

If any objection is raised to the order of speaking, the Chairman must put it to the Committee for decision.

Article 46. With respect to a measure or matter under consideration or investigation, the Committee may request the attendance of any Member not on the Committee to hear his opinion, when the Committee deems it necessary or when a Member not on the Committee asks to speak.

Article 47. Any member who desires to move an amendment to a measure must submit it in writing beforehand to the Chairman.

When the amendment under the preceding paragraph is one to a bill and is to bring about an increase of the budget or is to require budgetary action, a written statement shall be attached clarifying expenditure needed as a result of the amendment.

Article 47-II. To make a motion of confidence or non-confidence in a Committee Chairman, the support of at least one-fifth of the total membership of that Committee is required.

Article 48. The Committee may set up a sub-committee to consider the proposed amendment to a measure.

Article 48-II. When a Committee desires to present a bill that will affect the budget, the Cabinet shall be given an opportunity to express its opinion in advance of the Committee's decision.

Article 48-III. When a Committee presents a bill which affects the budget, a written statement of the expenditure needed for the implementation of the law shall be attached.

Article 49. When the Chairman desires to participate in a debate himself, he must ask a director or nominate a proxy from among the Committee members to take the chair in his place.

Article 50. When the debate on a matter is closed, the Chairman shall announce the question and put it to a vote.

Article 51. No Committee member who is not present at the time of voting is entitled to vote.

Article 52. No Committee member is permitted to ask for alteration of his vote once cast.

Article 53. A Committee is authorized to summon, through the Speaker, witnesses for consideration or investigation.

Article 54. A witness shall confine his speaking to the matter on which he is asked to testify.

When a witness strays from the subject, or his speech or action is considered to be improper, the Chairman may forbid him to speak or order him to leave.

Article 55. When a Committee desires to send Committee members for consideration or investigation, the approval of the Speaker must be obtained.

Article 56. A Committee is authorized to demand through the Speaker that the Cabinet, offices of government and public entities, and others, produce necessary reports or records for consideration or investigation.

Article 57. When a Member asks to inspect the minutes of a Committee or other reference materials, the Committee must permit this as long as it does not interfere with its consideration or investigation.

Article 58. No one is permitted to take out of the House of minutes of a Committee or other reference materials mentioned in the preceding paragraph.

Article 59. When a Committee which has completed the consideration of a measure or matter deems it urgent, that Committee may ask the Speaker to hold a plenary sitting of the House on it.

Article 60. A Committee may hold a combined meeting with other Committees by arrangement, if it needs to do so for consideration or investigation.

Article 60-II. With regard to an amendment made by the House of Representatives to a measure which was presented by the Cabinet, the Chairman of the competent Committee or the proposer of the amendment may explain its purport in the House of Councillors upon the request of that House.

Article 61. A Committee shall compile the minutes of meetings and record the following particulars:

(1) Date and time of opening, recess and closing
(2) Names of Committee members present
(3) Names of Members of the House other than Committee members present
(4) Names of Ministers of State and Government Delegates present
(5) Changes of Committee members
(6) Titles of the measures or matters referred to it
(7) Titles of the measures or matters taken up
(8) Proceedings
(9) Results of votes taken
(10) Summary of decisions
(11) Open Hearings
(12) Witnesses
(13) Informants
(14) Sending out of Committee members
(15) Requests for production of reports or records
(16) Reports
(17) Other important items

Article 62. The minutes of the Committee shall be signed by the Chairman and the directors and kept in the House.

Article 63. The minutes of the Committee shall be printed and distributed to each Member of the House, except those parts of minutes of closed meetings which the Committee has decided to keep secret, and those remarks which the Chairman has ordered to be retracted under the provisions of Article 71.

Article 64. The provisions of Articles 226-231 shall apply *mutatis mutandis* to the admission into Committee meetings of persons other than Members of the House as visitors.

Article 65. The provisions of this Chapter shall apply *mutatis mutandis* to Committee consideration to be conducted while the Diet is not in session.

SUB-CHAPTER 2
Powers Of Committee Chairmen

Article 66. The Chairman of a Committee shall arrange the business of the Committee, maintain order in it and represent it.

Article 67. The Chairman of a Committee shall fix the date for a Committee Meeting.

When requested by at least one-third of the Committee members, the Chairman must hold a meeting.

Article 67-II. The Chairman of the Committee on Rules and Administration may, in case of urgent necessity, hold a Committee meeting at any time during the session. While the House is sitting, however, the Chairman is required to obtain the permission of the Speaker.

Article 68. The Chairman of a Committee may allocate the time for questions, debate, and so on, as the Committee may decide.

When the Chairman allocates time beforehand, the time allocated must be the same for all members of the Committee.

Article 69. The Chairman of the Committee may explain to the House of Councillors, upon request of that House, the purport of a measure which has been presented by the House of Representatives and is under the jurisdiction of his Committee.

Article 70. The Chairman of a Committee is authorized to attend meetings of other Committees and express his opinions.

Article 71. When a Committee member acts contrary to the Diet Law or these Rules, or conducts himself in a disorderly manner, or impairs the dignity of the House, the Chairman shall restrain him or cause him to retract his remarks. If the member does not obey the Chairman's order, the Chairman may forbid him to speak for the rest of the day's meeting or cause him to leave the room.

Article 72. The Chairman may declare a recess or adjourn the meeting, if the business of the Committee goes out of control or a case for discipline occurs.

Article 73. The Chairman may admit into a Committee meeting those engaged in news service or any others who are not Members of the House.

Article 74. When it is necessary for maintaining order in a Committee meeting, the Chairman may order any of the visitors to leave the room.

Article 75. When the Chairman considers that there is a disciplinary case in the Committee meeting, he shall report it to the Speaker for action.

SUB-CHAPTER 3

Open Hearings

Article 76. A Committee may hold an open hearing to consider measures referred to it by the House or the Speaker.

Article 77. A Committee may hold an open hearing also for its preliminary consideration.

Article 78. When a Committee desires to hold an open hearing, the Speaker's approval must be obtained.

Article 79. When the Speaker's approval for holding an open hearing is obtained, the Chairman shall announce to the public the date and time of the hearing and the subject on which opinions are to be heard.

Article 80. Any person who desires to have an open hearing held on an important matter or who desires to express his opinion at an open hearing shall beforehand send in to the Committee in writing his reasons and his opinion for or against the subject.

Article 81. The persons interested, men of learning and experience and others whose opinions are to be heard at an open hearing (to be called 'speakers') shall be selected by the Committee from among those who have volunteered to speak and from other persons, and shall be notified of their selection.

If those who have volunteered to speak include both supporters and opposers, the Committee must select speakers for an open hearing impartially from both sides.

Article 82. When a speaker at an open hearing desires to speak, he shall obtain the permission of the Chairman.

Article 83. A speaker at an open hearing shall confine himself to the matters on which his opinion is sought.

When a speaker at an open hearing deviates from the subject as mentioned in the preceding paragraph, or when his words or actions are considered improper, the Chairman may stop him or order him to leave the room.

Article 84. A Committee member may question a speaker at an open hearing, but a speaker may not question a Committee member.

Article 85. A speaker at an open hearing may, with the consent of the Committee, state his views through a proxy or in writing.

Article 85-II. A Committee may, if necessary for consideration or investigation, request the attendance of an informant to hear his views.

To call an informant, the Chairman shall notify him to that effect.

With respect to an informant, the provisions of Articles 82-84 shall apply *mutatis mutandis*.

SUB-CHAPTER 4

Oral and Written Reports

Article 86. When a Committee has completed the consideration or investigation of a measure or matter referred to it, it shall prepare a report containing a brief explanation of the reasons for its decision, expenses and other matters, and submit it to the Speaker through the Chairman.

When a Committee has given the Cabinet an opportunity to express its opinion, under the provision of Article 57-III of the Diet Law, the gist of this opinion shall be included in the report.

Article 87. When a measure or matter referred to a Committee is taken up for consideration by the House, the Chairman shall report to the House on the Committee proceedings and the results.

The Chairman may delegate a Committee member to make the report mentioned in the preceding paragraph.

The Chairman of a sub-committee or the chief of a working committee may add to the Chairman's report.

Article 88. A member who desires to report to the House a minority opinion rejected by a Committee must prepare a report on the opinion, signed by the required number of supporters, and submit it to the Speaker through the Chairman of the Committee before the Committee's report is sent in.

Article 89. This Speaker shall have Committee reports and reports of minority opinions printed and distributed to each Member of the House, except any part of the minutes which is deemed secret by the Committee and any remarks which are retracted by the order of the Chairman under the provisions of Article 71.

Article 90. When a sub-committee has completed its consideration or investigation, its Chairman shall report its proceedings and results to the Committee.

Article 91. When a Committee does not complete its consideration of a measure or matter before the beginning of the next session, a written report to that effect must be submitted to the Speaker at the beginning of the next session.

SUB-CHAPTER 5

Standing Committees

Article 92. The number of members and the jurisdiction of each Standing Committee are as follows. The number of members and the jurisdiction of a committee may, however, be changed by a resolution of the House.

1. Committee on Cabinet 30 members
   (1) Matters under the jurisdiction of the Cabinet
   (2) Matters under the jurisdiction of the National Personnel Authority
   (3) Matters under the jurisdiction of the Imperial Household Agency
   (4) Matters under the jurisdiction of the Administrative Management Agency
   (5) Matters under the jurisdiction of the Hokkaido Development Agency
   (6) Matters under the jurisdiction of the Defence Agency
   (7) Matters under the jurisdiction of the Okinawa Development Agency
   (8) Matters under the jurisdiction of the Prime Minister's Office not coming under the jurisdiction of any other Standing Committee
2. Committee on Local Administration 30 members
   (1) Matters relating to local public entities
   (2) Matters under the jurisdiction of the Ministry of Home Affairs.
   (3) Matters under the jurisdiction of the Public Safety Commission
3. Committee on Judicial Affairs 30 members
   (1) Matters under the jurisdiction of the Ministry of Justice
   (2) Matters relating to the judicial administration of the Courts

4. Committee on Foreign Affairs 30 members
   (1) Matters under the jurisdiction of the Ministry of Foreign Affairs
5. Committee on Finance 40 members
   (1) Matters under the jurisdiction of the Ministry of Finance (excluding matters under the jurisdiction of the Committee on Budget and the Committee on Audit)
6. Committee on Education 30 members
   (1) Matters under the jurisdiction of the Ministry of Education
   (2) Matters under the jurisdiction of the Board of Education
   (3) Matters under the jurisdiction of the Science Council of Japan
7. Committee on Social and Labour Affairs 40 members
   (1) Matters under the jurisdiction of the Ministry of Health and Welfare
   (2) Matters under the jurisdiction of the Ministry of Labour
8. Committee on Agriculture, Forestry and Fisheries 40 members
   (1) Matters under the jurisdiction of the Ministry of Agriculture, Forestry and Fisheries
9. Committee on Commerce and Industry 40 members
   (1) Matters under the jurisdiction of the Ministry of International Trade and Industry
   (2) Matters under the jurisdiction of the Economic Planning Agency
   (3) Matters under the jurisdiction of the Fair Trade Commission
   (4) Matters under the jurisdiction of the Environmental Disputes Coordination Commission (only matters relating to the use of land for mining and other purposes)
10. Committee on Transport 30 members
    (1) Matters under the jurisdiction of the Ministry of Transport
11. Committee on Communications 30 members
    (1) Matters under the jurisdiction of the Ministry of Posts and Telecommunications
12. Committee on Construction 30 members
    (1) Matters under the jurisdiction of the Ministry of Construction
    (2) Matters under the jurisdiction of the National Land Agency

13. Committee on Science and Technology 25 members
    (1) Matters under the jurisdiction of the Science and Technology Agency
14. Committee on Environment 25 members
    (1) Matters under the jurisdiction of the Environment Agency
    (2) Matters under the jurisdiction of the Environmental Disputes Coordination Commission (excluding matters under the jurisdiction of the Committee on Commerce and Industry)
15. Committee on Budget 50 members
    (1) Budgets
16. Committee on Audit 25 members
    (1) Auditing
    (2) Matters relating to the approval of expenditure from the reserve fund
    (3) Matters relating to the approval of transfer to revenue of money from the account settlement adjustment fund
    (4) Complete returns on commitments of the national treasury
    (5) Complete returns on the increase and decrease and the current value of national property and property leased rent-free
    (6) Other matters under the jurisdiction of the Board of Audit
17. Committee on Rules and Administration 25 members
    (1) Matters relating to the House administration
    (2) Matters relating to the Diet Law, Rules and Regulations of the House
    (3) Matters about which advice is sought by the Speaker
    (4) Matters relating to the Judges Impeachment Court and Judges Indictment Committee
    (5) Matters relating to the National Diet Library
18. Committee on Discipline 20 members
    (1) Matters relating to disciplinary action against Members of the House
    (2) Matters relating to challenge to qualification of Members of the House.

Article 93. Deleted.

Article 94. A Standing Committee is authorized to investigate, with the Speaker's approval and only during a session of the House, matters relating to government which come under its jurisdiction.

To obtain the Speaker's approval, the Standing Committee shall submit to him a written request specifying the subject, purpose, method, period and other details of the intended investigation.

When the Speaker has approved the Committee's request, he shall inform the House.

Article 95. When a question on jurisdiction arises between two or more Standing Committees, the Speaker shall settle it after putting the case to a vote of the House.

Article 96. Deleted.

Article 97. The Budget Committee and the Audit Committee may divide themselves into several working committees as required for their consideration. Each working committee shall have a chief who is elected by its members from among themselves.

Article 98. When a Standing Committee desire to hold a joint meeting with a Standing Committee of the House of Councillors, it shall make a decision to that effect after its Chairman has consulted with the Committee Chairman of the House of Councillors.

Article 99. A Standing Committee may not take a vote on a measure or matter put to a joint meeting until the latter has completed its consideration.

SUB-CHAPTER 6
Special Committees

Article 100. The number of members of the Special Committee shall be decided by the House when it is being set up. The House may, however, increase the membership whenever necessary.

Article 101. Members of Special Committee shall elect a Chairman from among themselves on the day of their selection as Committee members or the next day.

The election of the Chairman of a Special Committee shall be held by secret ballot, and the person who has obtained the greatest number of votes shall be declared elected. In case of a tie, the decision shall be made by lot.

The Chairman of a Special Committee may also be elected not by ballot but by a motion or by other means.

Until the Chairman is elected, the eldest person in the Committee shall perform the duties of the Chairman.

Article 102. The resignation of the Chairman of a Special Committee requires the approval of the Committee.

CHAPTER VIII

PLENARY SITTINGS

SUB-CHAPTER 1

Opening, Closing and Adjournment of Sitting

Article 103. The sitting shall start at 1 p.m. This does not, however, apply, if the House resolves otherwise, or if the Speaker deems it necessary.

Article 104. When the time for the sitting comes, the Speaker shall take the Chair and, after reporting on various matters, shall declare the sitting open.

No one may speak on the business of the sitting until the Speaker has declared the sitting open.

Article 105. When the business of the measures or matters put on the Order of the Day is brought to an end, the Speaker shall declare the sitting closed.

After 6 p.m. the Speaker may adjourn the sitting without putting it to the House for decision, even if some business remains to be dealt with.

Article 106. When the number of Members present does not reach one-third of the total membership, the Speaker shall have them counted against after a reasonable interval of time. If the presence of the quorum is still not established at the second counting, the Speaker must adjourn the sitting.

When the absence of the quorum is provide during a sitting, the Speaker must declare a recess or adjourn the sitting.

Article 107. After the Speaker has declared the closing, adjournment or recess of the sitting, no one may speak on the business of the sitting.

SUB-CHAPTER 2

The Order of the Day

Article 108. When the Speaker desires to hold a sitting, he shall arrange the Order of the Day and inform the House of it in advance.

Article 109. The date and time for opening a sitting, the measures and matters to be laid before it and their order shall be placed on the Order of the Day.

Article 110. The Order of the Day shall be published in the Official Bulletin of the House of Representatives as well as in the Official Gazette and shall be distributed to each Member.

Article 111. When the introducer or proposer of a measure or matter desires to omit the Committee consideration of it, he shall make a written request to the Speaker to that effect at the time of introduction or presentation of such a measure or matter.

If the Cabinet did not request committee consideration to be dispensed with in the House of Councillors, it cannot make such a request in the House of Representatives in respect of the same measure.

When a request as mentioned in paragraph 1 has been made, the Speaker shall place it on the Order of the Day, for the House to make a decision as to whether the Committee consideration should be omitted or not.

Article 112. When the Speaker deems it necessary, or a motion is made by a Member, the Speaker may alter the order in the Order of the Day, or add other matters to it after putting the case to a vote of the House without debate.

Article 113. If any business on the Order of the Day has not been taken up or the business has not been finished, the Speaker must place it again on the Order for another day.

SUB-CHAPTER 3
Proceedings

Article 114. To bring up a measure or matter before a sitting, the Speaker shall announce it.

Article 115. When a measure or matter which has been considered by a Committee is brought to a sitting, the Chairman of the Committee shall first report on its proceedings and results, and then a member of a minority opinion shall report that opinion.

In making the report mentioned in the preceding paragraph, the Chairman or the member of a minority opinion must not add his own opinion to it.

Article 116. After the Chairman and the member of the minority opinion have finished their reports, the Speaker shall call from an explanation of the purport of amendments.

Article 117. When a measure on which Committee consideration will be omitted is brought to a sitting, the introducer or the proposer shall be asked to explain its purport.

Article 118. When Members' questions are finished, the measures or matter shall be put to debate, and upon completion of debate, to a vote.

Article 119. After the report of a Standing Committee, the House may refer the measure or matter back to the same Committee or refer it to a Special Committee. With regard to a measure or matter on which a report has been made by a Special Committee, the House may refer it back to the same Committee or to another Committee.

Article 120. After resolving on a measure, the House may, if necessary, delegate to the Speaker adjustment of conflicting items in it, articles, paragraphs, words, figures and the like.

Article 121. If a request to omit consideration of a measure in a Committee is refused, the Speaker shall refer the measure to an appropriate Committee.

Article 122. Deleted.

SUB-CHAPTER 4

Speaking

Article 123. All speaking must be done from rostrum. If the Speaker grants permission, however, this provision does not apply.

Article 124. The Speaker may order a Member who is speaking from his assigned seat to come up to the rostrum.

Article 125. A Member who desires to speak in the sitting is required to give notice to a secretary of the House in advance, as far as circumstances permit.

Article 126. Members who have not given notice may not speak until all the Members who gave notice have finished speaking.

Article 127. A Member who desires to speak without having given notice may do so after obtaining the Speaker's permission by standing up, calling the Speaker and giving his own name.

Article 128. When two or more Members stand up and ask for permission to speak, the Speaker_ shall give permission to speak in the order in which he considers the members stood up.

Article 129. The time to grant permission to speak on a point of order shall be in the discretion of the Speaker, except where it relates directly to the items under consideration, or, if it is deemed necessary to dispose of it immediately.

Article 130. A Member who has not finished speaking owing to an adjournment of the sitting or a recess, may continue when the business on the matter is resumed.

Article 131. A Chairman or a member of a minority opinion may speak in order to supplement his report.

Article 132. A Member whose qualification has been challenged or who is charged with committing misconduct deserving disciplinary action may speak in his own vindication.

Article 133. No Member is permitted to read out any written statement of his views or reasons in a sitting. This provision does not, however, apply to a brief note which has been prepared for the purpose of quotation or report.

Article 134. Speakers may not deviate from the subject under consideration or go beyond its scope.

Article 134-II. The same Member may not ask questions more than three times on the same subject under consideration.

Article 135. A Member who desires to debate on a measure or matter on the Order of the Day must give notice, stating whether he is going to speak for or against the subject.

Article 136. A Committee may appoint debaters from among its members and notify the fact to the Speaker. Those debaters recognized by the Speaker must be allowed to speak ahead to others who have given notice.

Article 137. In a debate, the Speaker must let the opposer take the floor first, and, as far as circumstances permit, must let the supporters and opposers speak alternately.

When all the Members on one side who gave notice have finished speaking, Members on the same side who did not give notice may ask for permission to speak even before all the Members on the other side who gave notice have not finished speaking.

Article 138. If the Speaker desires to participate in a debate himself, he must give notice to that effect in advance and take his assigned seat.

When the Speaker has participated in the debate, he may not return to the Chair until a vote has been taken on the matter.

Article 139. When a question or debate has ended, the Speaker shall declare its closure.

Article 140. When there has been too long a succession of questions and there seems no likelihood of an end, a motion to close the questions may be made with the support of twenty or more Members.

Article 141. After two or more Members have spoken for and against, or when two or more Members have spoken on one side and there is no one to speak on the other side, a motion to close the debate may be made with the support of twenty or more Members.

Article 142. When a motion to close questions or debate has been made in accordance with the preceding two Articles, the Speaker shall decide it after putting to a vote of the House without debate.

SUB-CHAPTER 5

Amendments

Article 143. A motion of amendment must be made in advance to the Speaker with the proposed amendment, signed by the proposer and the number of supporters required for it to be taken up at a sitting. An amendment proposed by a Committee, however, needs no supporters.

When the amendment under the preceding paragraph is one to a bill and is to bring about an increase of the budget or is to require budgetary action, a written statement shall be attached clarifying expenditure needed as a result of the amendment.

The Speaker shall have the amendment printed and distributed to each Member.

Article 144. An amendment proposed by a Member must be voted upon before one proposed by a Committee.

Article 145. When several amendments are proposed by Members on the same subject, the order of voting on them shall be decided by the Speaker. In making this decision, he shall give precedence to the amendments according to how far they depart from the original bill or measure.

Article 146. If all the amendments have been rejected, the original bill or measure must be voted upon.

Article 147. If both the amendments and the original bill or measure fail to secure majority support but the House resolves not to drop the matter yet, the House may order a Committee to draft a new bill or measure.

SUB-CHAPTER 6

Voting

Article 148. No Member who is not present in the Chamber at the time of voting is entitled to vote.

Article 149. A vote must be unconditional.

Article 150. When the Speaker desires to take a vote, he must announce the question to be voted on.

After the Speaker's announcement, no one may speak on the subject.

Article 151. In taking a vote, the Speaker shall ask those Members who are for the matter to stand up, and, ascertaining whether they are in the majority or in the minority, he shall declare the result of the vote.

When the Speaker finds it difficult to ascertain whether the standing Members are in the majority or not, or when one-fifth or more of the Members present have raised an objection to his declaration, he must put the matter to a vote by open ballot.

Article 152. When the Speaker deems it necessary, or when one-fifth or more of the Members present demand it, the vote shall be taken by open ballot.

Article 153. In an open ballot, those Members who are for the matter shall cast white ballots, and those against, blue ballots, into the respective ballot boxes.

Article 154. While a vote by open ballot is being taken, all entrances to the Chamber shall be closed.

Article 155. When the voting has finished, the Speaker shall declare the result to the House.

Article 155-II. When the Speaker has set a time limit for voting in an open ballot, he may regard those Members who did not vote within that time as having abstained from voting.

Article 156. No Member is permitted to ask for alternation of his vote once cast.

Article 157. The Speaker may ask the House whether any Member has any objection against a given matter, and if he finds no objection raised, he shall declare the matter passed. If an objection is raised, however, against the given matter or against the Speaker's declaration, by twenty or more of the Members present, the Speaker shall take a vote by asking Members to stand.

CHAPTER IX
QUESTIONS

Article 158. The Speaker shall have printed and distributed to each Member a written question approved by him or by the House, together with the Cabinet's written answer to it.

Article 159. When the Cabinet's written answer is too vague or evasive, the questioner may submit another question in writing.

Article 160. The Cabinet may given oral answer to questions.

On such oral answers, the questioner may put another question orally to the Cabinet.

Article 161. When a written question not approved by the Speaker or the House is to be recorded in the minutes, the Speaker may have the written question put into a concise form if he considers it diffuse.

CHAPTER X
DELETED

Articles 162-170: Deleted.

CHAPTER XI
PETITIONS

Article 171. All petitions shall contain the names and addresses of the petitioners (in the case of juridical persons, their names as well as the names of their representatives).

Article 172. A petition must be written in ordinary Japanese. When a petition is written in a foreign language owing to unavoidable circumstances, a Japanese version must accompany it.

Article 173. A Member who introduces a petition to the House must affix his signature or full name stamped with his seal on the cover of the petition.

Article 174. The Speaker shall have a list of petitions prepared, printed and distributed to each Member.

Article 175. The list of petitions must contain the names and addresses of the petitioners, with the purport of each petition, the name of the introducing Member and the date of receipt.

In a petition signed jointly by several petitioners, the description of the names of the petitioners shall be entered as "Petitioner A and —others".

When there are several petitions with the same purport and introduced by the same member, their number shall be entered in addition to the description ''Petitioner A and—others''.

Article 176. At the same time as the list of petitions is distributed, the Speaker shall refer them to the appropriate committees.

Article 177. In the case of a petition asking for the removal of a judge, the Speaker shall send it to the Judges Indictment Committee without referring it to any other Committee.

Article 178. The Committees, according to the results of their consideration, shall classify the petitions as follows, and report them to the House:

(1) Those needing to be laid before a sitting of the House

(2) Those not needing to be laid before a sitting of the House

The petitions needing to be laid before a sitting of the House shall be further classified as follows and reported to the House:

(1) Those to be adopted

(2) Those not to be adopted

When any petition among those to be adopted is considered proper to be sent to the Cabinet, a note to that effect shall be added.

Article 179. When the Committee has decided that a petition does not need to be laid before a sitting of the House, the decision of the Committee shall be final, unless demand to lay it before a sitting of the House is made by twenty or more Members within seven days, excluding days in recess, from the date of the Committee's report.

Article 180. The Speaker shall send to an appropriate Committee for reference any representations or other documents which he deems necessary.

CHAPTER XII

LEAVE OF ABSENCE AND NON-ATTENDANCE

Article 181. When a Member expects that he will be prevented from attending the House for several days for some cause, he shall present to the Speaker in advance an application in writing for leave of absence, stating the reasons and the length of time.

Article 182. The Speaker may grant leave of absence for not longer than seven days. The House may grant leave of absence for longer than seven days. No leave of absence for an indefinite period may be granted.

Article 183. If a Member is still prevented from attending the House for some cause after the leave of absence has expired, he must present another written request.

Article 184. When a Member who has been granted leave of absence attends the House before it expires, the leave shall lapse.

Article 185. When a Member is unable to attend the House, he shall give the Speaker notice of non-attendance stating the reason.

CHAPTER XIII
RESIGNATION

Article 186. When a Member desires to resign, he must submit his resignation in writing to the Speaker.

Article 187. The Speaker shall have the resignation read out and decide whether the accept or reject it after putting the case to a vote of the House without debate.

Article 188. If the Speaker considers that the resignation contains some remarks which are insulting or derogatory to the dignity of the House, he shall report its substance to the House instead of reading it out.

In the case of the preceding paragraph, the Speaker may refer the resignation to the Committee on Discipline for examination.

CHAPTER XIV
CHALLENGE TO MEMBER'S QUALIFICATION

Article 189. A Member who desires to challenge another Member on his qualification must submit to the Speaker a written charge in duplicate, duly signed, containing the substance, reasons and evidence for the allegation.

Article 190. The Speaker shall refer the written charge to the Committee concerned, and at the same time send the duplicate to the Member whose qualification has been challenged (to be called 'the defendant Member'), and have him submit a written answer by a fixed date.

If the defendant Member proves that he is unable to submit his answer by the fixed date by reason of natural calamity, illness or other unavoidable cause, the Speaker may fix another date for his answer.

Article 191. When a written answer is submitted by the defendant Member by the appointed date, the Speaker shall immediately send it to the Committee.

Article 192. The Committee shall examine the matter on the basis of the written charge and the written answer. When an answer has not been submitted by the appointed date, the examination may be conducted with the written charge alone.

Article 193. The defendant Member may engage counsel at any time after he has received the duplicate of the written charge. In this case, he must inform the Speaker to that effect.

With respect to a counsel who desires to have his remuneration defrayed by the State, the defendant Member must notify the Speaker of this, together with the above information.

Article 194. Counsel may, at the request or with the permission of the Committee, speak before the Committee in defence of the defendant Member.

Article 195. The Member who has instituted the suit (to be called 'the prosecuting Member') and the defendant Member may attend the Committee and speak with its permission.

Article 196. When the Committee deems it necessary for the examination of the case, it may, through the Speaker, call the prosecuting Member and the defendant Member and may question them.

Article 197. The defendant Member and his counsel may speak at a sitting of the House in vindication or defence of the case.

Article 198. The verdict of the House on a Member's qualification shall be rendered in the form of a resolution of the House.

The decision to disqualify a Member requires a majority of two-thirds of the Members present.

No reason shall be attached to the verdict of the House.

Article 199. When a verdict is rendered by the House, the Speaker shall send a copy of it to the prosecuting Member and to the defendant Member.

CHAPTER XV
MINUTES

Article 200. The following items shall be recorded in the Minutes:

1. Date and time of opening, recess, closing and adjournment of the sitting
2. Order of the Day
3. Names of the Members who responded to the call

4. Matters pertaining to the opening ceremony
5. Changes of Members
6. Assignment and changes of Members' seats
7. Receipt of written requests; dispatch and receipt of notices
8. Matters pertaining to the report to the Throne
9. Matters pertaining to introducing, proposing, referring, sending, sending back and withdrawing of measures
10. Names of the Ministers of State and Government Delegates who attended the sitting
11. Measures or matters taken up at the sitting and their substance
12. Reports of Committees and reports of minority opinions
13. Reports by the Speaker
14. Proceedings
15. Written questions and written answers
16. Names of the Members who voted in an election or open ballot
17. Extensions of remarks
18. Other matters which the House or the Speaker deems it necessary to record

Article 201. The proceedings of sittings shall be taken down in shorthand.

Article 202. When a Member desires to have a brief note entered in the minutes as a reference for his speech, he must obtain the permission of the Speaker.

Article 203. A Member who spoke may ask for correction of words or phrases in his speech not later than 5 p.m. on the day after the distribution of the minutes. He may not, however, change the gist of his speech.

Article 204. When an objection is raised against a correction of matters entered in the minutes or against the minutes themselves, the Speaker shall decide the case after putting it to a vote of the House without debate.

Article 205. The minutes shall be signed by the Speaker, or by the Vice-Speaker or the Speaker pro-tempore who presided over the sitting of the day, and by the Secretary General or his deputy, and shall be kept it in the House.

Article 206. The minutes shall be published in the Official Gazette. The parts which the House has decided to keep secret under the provision of Article 63 of the Diet Law, however, and any words which the Speaker has ordered to be retracted under the provision of Article 116 of the same Law, shall not be published.

Article 207. The minutes published in the Official Gazette shall be distributed to each Member and be available to the general public.

CHAPTER XVI
POLICING OF THE HOUSE AND ORDER

SUB-CHAPTER 1
Policing of the House

Article 208. The Speaker shall exercise police power within the House by directing the guards and the police.

Article 209. The guards shall be on police duty within the House.

The police shall be on police duty outside the House building. When the Speaker deems it necessary, however, he may cause the police to be on duty inside the building.

Article 210. When a person is found in the very act of committing a criminal offence in the House, the guards or the police shall arrest the offender and then ask for directions from the Speaker. In the Chamber, however, no arrest shall be made without the order of the Speaker.

SUB-CHAPTER 2
Order in the House

Article 211. Members must respect the dignity of the House.

Article 212. Members shall use terms of respect for each other.

Article 213. No one shall enter the Chamber with a hat, overcoat, scarf, umbrella, cane and the like on or with him, unless he has obtained the permission of the Speaker on account of sickness or for other reasons.

Article 214. No smoking is allowed in the Chamber.

Article 215. No one shall read newspapers, books, etc., during the sitting except for reference materials.

Article 216. No one shall make unauthorized utterances or behave in a disorderly manner during the sitting so as to create a disturbance while other Members are speaking.

Article 217. No one shall ascend the rostrum without the permission of the Speaker.

Article 218. The House shall come to order when the Speaker rings the bell.

Article 219. At the close of a sitting, no Member shall leave the Chamber until the Speaker has retired.

Article 220. All questions relating to order in the House shall be decided by the Speaker. The Speaker, however, may decide them after putting them to the House without debate.

CHAPTER XVII
VISITORS

Article 221. The visitors' gallery shall be divided into sections for distinguished guests, diplomats, Members of the House of Councillors, civil servants, the general public and the press.

Article 222. The section for the general public shall be divided into reserved and unreserved seats.

Those who take the reserved seats must carry admission tickets issued at the invitation of a Member.

Those who take unreserved seats must carry general admission tickets issued on a first-come, first-served basis.

Article 223. Visiting badges valid throughout a session shall be issued to newspaper companies and news agencies.

Article 224. Visitors to a sitting must write their names, addresses and ages on their admission tickets.

Article 225. Visitors must show their admission tickets to the guards and follow their directions.

Article 226. No visitors may enter the Chamber.

Article 227. Visitors must observe the Visitors' Regulations made by the Speaker.

Article 228. The Speaker may order to the guards or the police to make a body search of visitors, when he deems it necessary.

Article 229. A person carrying firearms or any other dangerous object, a person under the influence of alcohol, or any person who is regarded by the Speaker as affecting the maintenance of order, shall not be admitted to the gallery.

Article 230. The Speaker may limit the number of visitors to be admitted when he deems it necessary to do so for the maintenance of order.

Article 231. When all visitors are to be excluded on account of a House resolution to hold a closed sitting or because of noise in the gallery, or when any visitor is ordered out of the gallery for obstructing the proceedings, the Speaker shall instruct the guards to execute his order of expulsion.

Article 232. Admission tickets and visiting badges shall be issued, under the direction of the Speaker, by the Secretary General, who shall decide how many there shall be.

CHAPTER XVIII
DISCIPLINARY MEASURES

Article 233. When a disciplinary case occurs at a sitting, the Speaker may declare a recess or close of the sitting or cause the offender to leave the Chamber.

Article 234. When a disciplinary case occurs in a sitting or a committee meeting, or otherwise within the House, the Speaker shall refer it to the Committee on Discipline.

Article 235. Any Member may make a motion for a disciplinary measure under the provisions of paragraph 3 of Article 121 of the Diet Law, even if the Speaker or the Chairman does not consider the case as needing discipline.

Article 236. When a motion for a disciplinary measure is made, the Speaker must put it to the sitting of the House without delay.

If such a motion is made after the close of a sitting, the Speaker must bring it up at the next sitting.

Article 237. The Speaker shall put a motion for a disciplinary measure to a vote for a resolution of the House without debate and, according to the result of the vote, shall refer it to the Committee on Discipline.

Article 238. If any person does not yield to the Speaker's restraint or disobeys his order to retract offensive remarks, the Speaker, besides taking appropriate action under Article 116 of the Diet Law, may also refer it as a disciplinary case to the Committee on Discipline.

Article 239. A Member may not join the sitting or Committee meeting at which his disciplinary case is examined. He may, however, speak in his own defence or have another Member do so in his stead, with the permission of the Speaker or the Chairman.

Article 240. The Committee on Discipline may, through the Speaker, ask for the presence of the defendant Member and other Members concerned, to hear their explanations.

Article 241. If the Committee on Discipline regards it proper to make the offending Member apologize in an open sitting, it shall draw up the text of the apology and submit it to the Speaker with a report on the case.

Article 242. Suspension of attendance at the House shall not exceed 30 days. This shall not apply, however, where several disciplinary offences have been concurrently committed by the same Member, or where another disciplinary offence is committed by a suspended Member during the period of his suspension.

Article 243. A Member who has been suspended from attendance at the House shall lose his Committee membership, notwithstanding the provisions of paragraph 1 of Article 42 and paragraph 2 of Article 45 of the Diet Law.

The provision of the preceding paragraph shall also apply to the case of a member of the Conference Committee.

Article 244. If a Member who has been suspended comes to the House during the period of his suspension, the Speaker shall cause him to leave the House. If the Member disobeys the order, the Speaker may take necessary action and refer the matter again to the Committee Discipline.

Article 245. The House is authorized to expel any Member who commits a breach of order in the House or impairs the dignity of the House in a particularly reprehensible manner.

Article 246. When the recommendation for expulsion made by the Committee on Discipline is not adopted by a majority of two-thirds or more of the Members present, the House may inflict other disciplinary measures on the offending Member.

Article 247. When the House has decided on a disciplinary measure, the Speaker shall declare the verdict of the House. When the decision is made in a closed sitting, he shall pronounce it in an open sitting.

CHAPTER XIX

RELATIONS WITH THE HOUSE OF COUNCILLORS

Article 248. When a measure is to be sent to the House of Councillors, the Speaker shall have the Secretary General deliver it to the President of that House.

Article 249. When a measure is received from the House of Councillors, the Speaker shall report it to the House.

Article 250. The election of members of the Conference Committee shall be held by secret ballot with plural entry.

The Members who have obtained the largest number of votes shall be declared elected. In the case of a tie, however, the decision shall be made by lot.

The House may dispense with the election and delegate the appointment of the Committee members to the Speaker.

Article 251. The House is authorized to accept the resignation of a member of the Conference Committee.

Vacancies in the membership of the Conference Committee shall be filled in the same manner as in the original election.

Article 252. Members of the Conference Committee shall elect the chairman from among themselves on the day of the election of the Committee members or the next day.

The election of the chairman shall be supervised by the eldest committee member.

Article 253. A measure sent back by the House of Councillors or a final compromise arrived at by the Conference Committee of both Houses shall not be referred to any Committee.

Questions and debate on a measure sent back shall be confined within the scope of the amendments contained in it. In respect of a final compromise of the Conference Committee, questions and debate shall be confined within the scope of that compromise.

Article 254. Regulations concerning the Conference Committee and the joint meetings of Standing Committees of both Houses shall be resolved by the House after the Speaker has conferred with the President of the House of Councillors.

CHAPTER XX
RELATIONS WITH THE GENERAL PUBLIC AND GOVERNMENT AGENCIES

Article 255. Sending Members to ascertain or investigate some matter requires the resolution of the House. This does not apply, however, in the case of Article 55.

Even when the Diet is not in session, the Speaker may decide to send Members out.

Article 256. When the House has resolved to call for the production of records or documents from the Cabinet, offices of government and public entities, and others, for consideration or investigation, the request shall be made through the Speaker.

Article 257. When the House has resolved to call a witness or informa for consideration or investigation, the Speaker shall notify the witness or informant to that effect.

Mutatis mutandis, the provisions of Article 54 shall apply to the witness and those of Article 83 to the informant.

CHAPTER XXI
SUPPLEMENTARY PROVISIONS

Article 258. All questions concerning any part of these Rules shall be settled by the Speaker. The Speaker may, however, settle the questions after putting them to the House.

APPENDIX III

COMMUNICATION FROM THE GOVERNMENT OF INDIA TO THE GOVERNMENT OF THE UNITED STATES ON JAPANESE PEACE TREATY (23rd AUGUST, 1951)

The Government of India have the honour to acknowledge with thanks the receipt of the reply of the Government of the United States of America to the representations which they had made on the Japanese Peace Treaty in their communication dated the 30th of July 1951. They fully appreciate the consideration given to their views by the US Government and wish to assure them that the present reply is conceived in a spirit of frank and sincere friendship for the USA.

Throughout the negotiations that have taken place between the two Governments on the subject of the Treaty, the Government of India have laid emphasis upon two fundamental objectives:

(i) the terms of the Treaty should concede to Japan a position of honour, equality and contentment among the community of free nations;

(ii) they should be framed as to enable all countries specially interested in the maintenance of a stable peace in the Far East to subscribe to the Treaty, sooner or later.

The Government of India have, after most careful thought come to the conclusion that the Treaty does not, in material respects, satisfy either of these to criteria.

Condition (i): (a) It is only natural to expect that Japan should desire the restoration, in full, of her sovereignty, over territory of which the inhabitants have a historical affinity with her own people and which she has not acquired by aggression from any other country. The Ryukyu and the Bonin islands fully satisfy this description. Nevertheless, the Treaty proposes that until the US Government seek and obtain trusteeship over these islands, they should continue to be subject to the legislative and administrative control of the US. It is apparent to the Government of India that such an arrangement cannot but be a source of dissatisfaction to large sections of the Japanese people and must carry the seed of future dispute and, possibly, conflict in the Far East.

(b) The Government of India recognize that, as a sovereign nation, Japan should have the right to make arrangements for her defence as provided in Article 5 of the Treaty. If, in exercise of this right, Japan should decide to enter into defensive agreements with a friendly power, no one could reasonably object to this. But the right should be exercised by the Government of Japan when Japan has become truly sovereign. A provision in the Treaty which suggests that the present occupation forces may stay on in Japan as part of such a defensive agreement is bound to give rise to the impression that the agreement does not represent a decision taken by Japan in the final enjoyment of her freedom as a sovereign nation. The effect of this, not only on the people of Japan but upon large sessions of people in Asia, is bound to be most unfortunate.

Condition (ii). As already stated, the Government of India attach the greatest importance to the Treaty providing that the island of Formosa should be returned to China. The time and manner of such return might be the subject of separate negotiations but to leave the future of the island undetermined, in spite of past international agreement which attempts to regulate the relations of Japan with all Governments that were engaged in the last war against her, does not appear to the Government of India to be either just or expedient. *Mutatis Mutandis* the same argument applies to the Kurile island and to S. Sakhalin.

For the foregoing reasons, the Government of India have decided, with regret, that they cannot be parties to this Treaty. It is their sincere hope that lasting peace will prevail in the Far East and, to that end, they will continue to cooperate with the US and other Governments in such manner as may be open to them, consistently with the principle on which their foreign policy is based. As a first step, it is their intention, as soon as this may be practicable, to put an end to the state of war between them and Japan, and to establish full diplomatic relations with that country.

It has already been announced that the Conference convened at San Francisco to consider the draft peace treaty with Japan will not be open to negotiation, through attending Governments will be free to state their views on the Treaty. The Government of India feel that statement of their views on the Treaty contained in this reply, should be adequate to clarify their own position to the Conference. It is their intention, if the US Government have no objections to communicate this reply to their own Parliament, which is now in session, on the 27th of August. Once the document has been published, it will be available for the information of the Conference, and the Government of India will be glad if the Government of the United States, which will act as host to the Conference, will have this reply circulated to its members. As, for the reasons already stated, the Government of India will be unable to sign the Treaty, they think that it is not necessary for them to send representatives to it.

APPENDIX IV

SECOND COMMUNICATION FROM THE GOVERNMENT OF INDIA TO THE GOVERNMENT OF THE UNITED STATES OF AMERICA ON JAPANESE PEACE TREATY (28th AUGUST, 1951)

The Government of India have the honour to acknowledge the reply to their Note of the 23rd August, 1951 received on the 26th August by telegraph from their *Charge d' Affairs* in Washington to whom it was delivered.

The Government of India welcome the assurance that the over-riding desire of the Government of the United States is peace in Asia. The Government and people of India have striven to this end, to the best of their ability, because they consider peace of paramount importance to the world and more especially, to the countries of Asia, which have suffered for many generations under alien domination. Nothing could be more disastrous for Asia than war which would make impossible of early fulfilment the hopes of development that fill the minds of the people of this great continent. It is with this single aim of preserving peace that the Government of India have considered every problem with which they have been confronted. In the task of maintaining peace and developing and nations of Asia, they would always gladly cooperate with the United States and with other countries.

The Government of India also welcome the assurance of the Government of the United States that they do not want to be a party to colonialism or imperialism. Opposition to colonialism and imperialism has been the basis of India's struggle. Having experienced the burden and the injury that flow from both, the people of India are convinced that continuance of them in any form and in any part of the world cannot lead to peace or progress or to the happiness of the people concerned. World peace can only be assured when the domination of one country over another ceases.

Turning to certain specific points relating to the Treaty which arise out of the reply of the Government of the United States, the Government of India wish to make the following observations:

(i) The Government of the United States have expressed the belief that their view of the proposed treaty is shared by the Government and the people of Japan. The Government of India regret that their appreciation of the situation does not tally with that of the United States Government.

(ii) Commenting upon the Government of India's suggestion that the treaty should restore in full Japan's sovereignty "over territories of which the inhabitants have a historical affinity with her (Japan's) own people and which she has not acquired by aggression from any other country", the Government of the United States point out that the Government of India have never questioned the Potsdam terms of surrender during the five and a half years during which India served as a member of the Far East Commission, which was established to ensure the fulfilment of those terms. In suggesting the return of the Ryukyu and the Bonih groups of islands to Japanese sovereignty, the Government of India are not challenging the Potsdam terms of surrender. As the Government of the United States have themselves pointed out, those terms left room for the addition, by agreement, of some minor islands to the islands of Honshu, Hokkaido, Kyushu, and Shikoku, over which Japan was to be allowed to exercise sovereignty. Nor have the Government of India any intention whatsoever of applying dissimilar principles to different parts of territories which have a historical affinity with Japan and which Japan did not wrest from any of its neighbours. If they excepted the Kurile Islands from the scope of their suggestion, it was because the Yalta Agreement provided, without any reservation, that "the Kurile islands shall be handed over to the Soviet Union." The Government of India cannot be held responsible for an inconsistency which is the result of the Yalta Agreement.

(iii) In discussing the Government of India's views regarding defensive arrangements to be made by Japan, the Government of the United States describe them as tantamount to leaving Japan defenceless against proved aggressors. The Government of India fail to find any warrant for such a conclusion from anything they have said. The draft treaty recognizes that Japan as a sovereign nation possesses the inherent right of individual or collective self-defence and that Japan may voluntarily enter into collective security arrangements. Adequate provision is thus made for Japan independently to make whatever arrangements she considers necessary for her self-defence as soon as she has signed the peace treaty and it is not clear to the Government of India why there should be any "period of total defenselessness" of Japan.

(iv) In regard to Formosa, the Government of India have suggested that, in keeping with international obligations, it should be stated clearly in the treaty that it would be returned to China. That would determined the future of Formosa leaving the time and manner of such return to be settled at a future date. The Government of India have been and are of opinion that a declaration that Formosa shall be returned to China will help in creating conditions for a settlement in the Far East. But the Government of India has at no time insisted or even suggested that a Japanese peace treaty should be deferred until there is final agreement with respect to the future of Formosa.

(v) The Government of India have been anxious that a peace treaty with Japan should be signed and the military occupation of Japan terminated at the earliest possible moment. All that they have urged is that what they consider to be imperfections of a major character in the draft treaty should be removed, so that the terms of the treaty may promote the prospects of a peaceful settlement of outstanding issues in the Far East. The Government of India do not wish to come in the way of any nation which is satisfied with the terms of the present treaty and is prepared to sign it. They only claim for themselves their inherent and unquestionable right not to sign a treaty with the terms of which they are not fully satisfied. Of their own resolve to establish the friendliest possible relations with Japan, they have already given proof for, as they have informed the Government of the United States they intend to terminate the state of war with Japan and to establish normal diplomatic relations with her as soon as possible.

The Government of India have no intention of proposing to Japan a treaty of peace, which would in any way be controversial or which would run counter to the provisions of the Draft Treaty of Peace. Their action is not being represented at San Franscisco Conference and in making a separate treaty of peace with Japan, should not, therefore, adversely affect either the friendly relations that exist between the Government of India and the Government of the United States or the cooperation of the two Governments in everything "which is practical and fruitful for peace".

The Government of India hope that the observations made in the foregoing paragraphs reveal a unity of outlook between them and the Government of the United States in many vital matters that affect the future of the people of Asia and of humanity in general. The differences that exist between them are differences of method and approach. Such divergences of opinion are bound to occur even amongst the friendliest nations and should not be allowed to cause resentment that might come in the way of mutual understanding and community of effort.

APPENDIX V

OPEN LETTER ADDRESSED TO THE PRIME MINISTER OF INDIA ON THE QUESTION OF JAPANESE PEACE TREATY (15th SEPTEMBER 1951)

Although the Government of India has refused to attend the San Francisco Peace Conference, India's Prime Minister, Pandit Nehru, stated some time ago in a speech before the Indian Congress that the Indian Government had decided to conclude a simple and straight forward pact with Japan after she regains her independence and a formal declaration of the ending of the state of war has been issued by India.

Insofar as India has always been inclined towards warm friendship for and trust in Japan, it appears not at all unlikely that normal and full diplomatic relations between the two countries will be restored in the very near future. Consequently, the non-participation of India in the San Franscisco Conference need not cause us too much worry.

There are, however, several good reasons why the Japanese public should heed the explanations offered by India for her non-attendance. And we also feel that it would not be out of place to address an open letter to Prime Minister Nehru.

According to memorandum sent by the Indian Government to the United States of America, the Japanese peace treaty fails to satisfy two requirements which India believes to be absolutely essential. One of them is that Japan be accorded an equal, honourable and satisfactory positive in the society of free nations; and the other is that opportunity be given, sooner or later, to all nations particularly concerned with the maintenance of stability and peace in the Far East to become a signatory to the Treaty.

The memorandum points out that in the fulfilment of the first requirement the Treaty fails because of the provisions for UN trusteeship over the Ryukyu and Bonin Islands and the stationing of occupation forces in these areas. In regard to the second requirement it is urged that Taiwan be restored to Communist China and the Kuriles and South Sakhalin be formally ceded to the USSR.

In so far as the Ryukyu and Bonins are concerned, the Indian note probably speaks for the majority of the Japanese who, consequently, should be extremely grateful. But with the disposition of the Kuriles and South Sakhalin, the Japanese find it impossible to agree. For, in the case of the Ryukyus and the Bonins, the territories in question were not acquired by aggression or by force but have long been an integral part of Japan. It may be that India, lying almost within the sphere of Soviet influence, has felt it necessary to humour the Kremlin. If this be the case, we cannot but voice our feeling of regret.

As for the stationing of foreign troops on Japanese soil, we do not believe that Nehru is entirely against it. For, with Japan stripped of arms, there is no power in the Far East capable of maintaining peace and security. Not only for Japan's security alone but for the maintenance of peace throughout East Asia it is absolutely essential to have adequate forces stationed in the Japanese islands.

It appears, therefore, that the only matter left open to question is whether or not Japan will be able to uphold fully the sovereignty she has regained. That India should be particularly interested in regard to this question is understandable, knowing that she herself was under British domination for more than a century. And we, as Japanese, feel that nothing should be neglected to ensure full enjoyment of the privileges of independence.

In these pages, we have contended that the leasing of military bases and the stationing of United States armed forces should be discussed and agreed upon after the ratification of the peace treaty, with Japan participating in the talks as a sovereign nation enjoying equal rights as the other power. We made this recommendation because we felt that otherwise the impression of compliance under duress would be created, and this could detract from the effectiveness of any working arrangement.

It seems that the Indian memorandum correctly brings out this point; and we believe that in this respect gratitude must be shown for Prime Minister Nehru's deep concern.

APPENDIX VI

GOVERNMENT OF INDIA NOTIFICATION TERMINATING THE STATE OF WAR WITH JAPAN (28th APRIL, 1952)

It is hereby notified for general information that the Government of India, bearing in mind that active hostilities with Japan were ended by Japan's signature of the instrument of surrender nearly six years ago and that a Treaty of Peace with Japan has been concluded and signed at San Francisco on the 8th September, 1951, by a large number of the Allied Powers, have determined that the state of war between India and Japan shall cease to exist as soon as the said Treaty of Peace comes into force for any State in accordance with the provisions contained in Article 23 thereof.

The Government of India propose to conclude at the earliest practicable date a separate bilateral Treaty of Peace with Japan whereby the relations between themselves and the Government of Japan would be brought into conformity with the amity which existed between them before the declaration of war with Japan.

In that Treaty the Government of India intend to stipulate provisions which will secure to themselves and the nationals of India all rights, privileges, indemnities and advantages, together with the right to enforce the same which under the Treaty of San Francisco have been stipulated in favour of the Allied Powers and their nationals.

APPENDIX VII

TREATY OF PEACE BETWEEN INDIA AND JAPAN

(9th JUNE, 1952)

Whereas the Government of India have by public notification issued on the ninth day of June, 1952, terminated the state of war between India and Japan.

And Whereas the Government of India and the Government of Japan are desirous of cooperating in friendly association for the promotion of the common welfare of their peoples and the maintenance of international peace and security in conformity with the principles of the Charter of the United Nations.

The Government of India and the Government of Japan have therefore determined to conclude this Treaty of Peace, and to this end have appointed as their Plenipotentiaries:

The Government of India

and

The Government of Japan

Who, having indicated to each other their respective Full Powers, and found them good and in due form, have agreed on the following Articles:

Article I

There shall be firm and perpetual peace and amity between India and Japan and their respective peoples.

Article II

(a) The Contracting Parties agree to enter into negotiations for the conclusion of treaties or agreements to place their trading, maritime, aviation and other commercial relations on a stable and friendly basis.

(b) Pending the conclusion of the relevant treaty of agreement, during a period of four years from the date of the issue of the notification by the Government of India terminating the state of war between India and Japan—

(1) the Contracting Parties shall accord to each other most-favoured-nation treatment also with respect to air traffic rights and privileges;

(2) the Contracting Parties shall accord to each other most-favoured-nation treatment also with respect to customs duties and charges of any kind and restrictions and other regulations in connection with the importation and exportation of goods or imposed on international transfer of payments for imports or exports and with respect to the methods of levying such duties and charges and with respect to all rules and formalities in connection with importation and exportation and charges to which customs clearing operations may be subject; and any advantage, favour, privilege, or immunity granted by either of the parties to any product originating in or destined for any other country shall be accorded immediately and unconditionally to the like products originating in or destined for the territory of the other Party;

(3) Japan will accord to India national treatment, to the extent that India accords Japan the same, with respect to shipping, navigation and imported goods, and with respect to natural and juridical persons and their interests —such treatment to include all matters pertaining to the levying and collection of taxes, access to the courts, the making and performance of contracts, rights to property (tangible and intangible), participation in juridical entities constituted under Japanese law, and generally the conduct of all kinds of business and professional activities:

Provided that in the application of this Article, a discriminatory measure shall not be considered to derogate from the grant of national or most-favoured-nation treatment, if such measure is based on an exception customarily provided for in the commercial treaties of the party applying it, or on the necessity of safeguarding that party's external financial position or balance of payments, or on the need to maintain its essential security interests, and provided such measure is proportionate to the circumstances and is not applied in an arbitrary or unreasonable manner:

Provided further that nothing contained in sub-paragraph (2) above shall apply to the preferences or advantages which have existed since before the 15th August, 1947, or which are accorded by India to contiguous countries.

(c) No provision of this Article shall be deemed to limit the undertakings assumed by Japan under Article V of this Treaty.

Article III

Japan agrees to enter into negotiations with India, when India so desires for the conclusion of an agreement providing for the regulation of finishing and the conservation and development of fisheries on the high seas.

Article IV

India will return or restore in their present form all property, tangible and intangible, and rights or interests of Japan or its nationals which were within India at the time of the commencement of the war and are under the control of the Government of India at the time of the coming into force of this Treaty; provided that the expenses which may have been incurred for the preservation and administration of such property shall be paid by Japan or its nationals concerned. If any such property has been liquidated, the proceeds thereof shall be returned, deducting the above mentioned expense.

Article V

Upon application made within 9 months of the coming into force of this Treaty Japan will, within 6 months of the date of such application, return the property, tangible and intangible, and all rights and interests of any kind in Japan to India and her nationals which was within Japan at any time between the 7th December, 1941 and the 2nd September, 1945 unless the owner has freely disposed thereof without duress or fraud.

Such property will be returned free of all encumbrances and charges to which it may have become subject because of the war, and without any charges for its return.

Property the return of which is not applied for by or on behalf of its owner or by the Government of India within the prescribed period may be disposed of by the Japanese Government in its discretion.

If any such property was with Japan on the 7th December, 1941 and cannot be returned or has suffered injury or damage as a result of the war, compensation will be made on terms not less favourable than the terms provided in the Allied Powers Property Compensation Law of Japan (Law Number 164, 1951).

Article VI

(a) India waives all reparation claims against Japan.

(b) Except as otherwise provided in this Treaty, India waives all claims of India and Indian nationals arising out of action taken by Japan and its nationals in the course of the prosecution of the war as also claims of India arising from the fact that it participated in the occupation of Japan.

Article VII

Japan agrees to take the necessary measures to enable nationals of India to apply within one year of the coming into force of this Treaty to the appropriate Japanese authorities for review of any judgement given by a Japanese Court between December 7, 1941, and such coming into force, if in the proceedings in which the judgement was given any Indian national was not able to present his case adequately either as plaintiff or as defendant, Japan further agrees that when an Indian national has suffered injury by reason of any such judgement, he shall be restored to the position in which he was before the judgement was given or shall be afforded such relief as may be just and equitable in the circumstances of the case.

Article VIII

(a) The Contracting Parties recognise that the intervention of the state of war has not affected the obligation to pay pecuniary debts arising out of obligations and contracts (including those in respect of bonds) which existed and rights which were acquired before the existence of the state of war, and which are due by the Government or nationals of Japan to the Government or nationals of India, or are due by the Government or nationals of India to the Government or nationals of Japan; nor has the intervention of the state of war affected the obligation to consider on their merits claims for loss or damage to property or for personal injury or death which arose between the existence of a state of war, and which may be presented or represented by the Government of India to the Government of Japan or by the Government of Japan to the Government of India.

(b) Japan affirms its liability for the pre-war external debt of the Japanese State and for debts of corporate bodies subsequently declared to be liabilities of the Japanese State, and expresses its intention to enter into negotiations at an early date with its creditors with respect to the resumption of payment on these debts.

(c) The Contracting Parties will encourage negotiations in respect to other pre-war claims and obligations and facilitate the transfer of sums accordingly.

Article IX

(a) Japan waives all claims of Japan and her nationals against India and her nationals arising out of the war or out of actions taken because of the existence of a state of war, and waives all claims arising from the presence, operations or actions of forces or authorities of India in Japanese territory prior to the coming into force of this Treaty.

(b) The foregoing waiver includes any claims arising out of actions taken by India with respect to Japanese ships between September 1, 1939, and the coming into force of this Treaty, as well as any claims and debts arising in respect to Japanese prisoners of war and civilian internees in the hands of India; but does not include Japanese claims specifically recognised in the laws of India enacted since September 2, 1945.

(c) Japan recognises the validity of all acts and omissions done during the period of occupation under or in consequence of directives of the occupation authorities or authorised by Japanese law at that time, and will take no action subjecting Indian nationals to civil or criminal liability arising out of such acts or omissions.

Article X

Any dispute arising out of the interpretation or application of this Treaty or one or more of its Articles shall be settled in the first instance by negotiations, and, if no settlement is reached within a period of six months from the commencement of negotiations by arbitration in such manner as may hereafter be determined by a general or special agreement between the Contracting Parties.

Article XI

This Treaty shall be ratified and shall come into force on the date of exchange of ratifications which shall take place as soon as possible at New Delhi (or Tokyo).

IN WITNESS WHEREOF, the undersigned Plenipotentiaries have signed this Treaty;

DONE in duplicate at Tokyo this Ninth day of June 1952 in the English language. Hindi and Japanese texts of this Treaty will be exchanged by the two Governments within a month of this date.

For Japan,
Sd./- Katsuo Okazaki

For India,
Sd./- K.K. Chettur

Select Bibliography

Akidzuku Satsuao, *La Constitution japonaise: son espritson but* (Bouloghesure Seine: 1919)

Allen, Charles (ed.), *Tales from the South China Seas: Images of the British in Southeast Asia in the Twentieth Century,* Futura, London, 1983.

Allen, Louis, *The End of the War in Asia*, Beekman/Esanu, New York, 1979.

Amaya Naohiro, 'Nation must back up values, Constitution', *Japan Economic Journal*, 31 January 1987.

Aoki Takeshi, *Taiheiyo Seicho no Torainanguru* ('The Growth Triangle in the Pacific: Structural Adjustment between Japan, the United States and Asian NICs'), Nihon Hyoron-sha, Tokyo, 1987.

Asai, K., *An Introduction to the Constitutional Larvs.*

Barnds, William (ed.). *Japan and the United States: Challenges and Opportunities,* Macmillan, London, 1980.

Barnett, R.W., *Beyond War: Japan's Concept of Comprehensive National Security,* Pergamon-Brassey, Washington, 1984.

Baylis, John. *Anglo-American Defence Relations, 1939-1984,* Macmillan, London, 1984; in Japanese translation, *Domei no Rikigaku,* Toyo Keizai Shinpo-sha, Tokyo, 1988.

Beckmann, George, *The Making of the Meiji Constitution* (Lowrence, 1957).

Beedham, Brian, 'A Special Strength: Survey of Japan', *Economist*, 31 March 1973.

Braddon, Russel, *The Other 100 Years War: Japan's Bid for Supremacy, 1941-2041*, Collins, London, 1983.

Bridges, Brian, *Korea and the West*, Chatham House Papers 33, Routledge & Kegan Paul, for the Royal Institute of International Affairs, London, 1986.

Broinowski, Alison (ed.), *Understanding ASEAN*, Macmillan, London. 1982.

Buckley, Roger, *Occupation Diplomacy: Britain, the United States and Japan, 1945-1952*, Cambridge University Press, Cambridge, 1982.

Chapman, J.W.M., Drifte, R., and Gow, I.T.M. *Japan's Quest for Comprehensive Security*, Pinter, London, 1983.

Chen Qimao, *Taiheiyo Kyodotai to Higashi-Ajia* ('The Pacific Community and East Asia'), Presented to a symposium of Waseda University, Tokyo, October 1985.

Chia Lin Sien and MacAndrews, Colin, *Southeast Asia Seas: Frontiers for Development,* Institute of Southeast Asian Studies, Singapore, 1981.

Chin Kin Wah, *The Defence of Malaysia and Singapore: The Transformation of a Security System, 1957-1971*, Cambridge University Press, Cambridge, 1983.

Colegrove, K., *The Constitutional Development of Japan* (Evanston, III. 1951).

Cortazzi, Hugh, *Higashi no Shimaguni Nishi no Shimaguni* ('The Island Countries in East and West'), Chuo Koronsha, Tokyo, 1984.

Curtis, Gerald, *The Japanese Way of Politics*; in Japanese Translation, *Nihongata Seiji no Honshitsu*, TBS Buritanica, Tokyo, 1987.

Darby, Phillip, *Three Faces of Imperialism: British and American Approaches to Asia and Africa, 1870-1970,* Yale University Press, New Haven, 1987.

Dore, Ronald, *Taking Japan Seriously: A Confucian Perspective on Leading Economic Issues,* Athlone, London, 1987.

________, 'Neo-mercantilism clouds trade issue', *Japan Economic Journal,* 11 April 1987.

Dower, J.W., *Empire and Aftermath: Yoshida Shigeru and the Japanese Experience, 1878-1954*, Harvard University Press, Cambridge, Mass, 1979.

Downen, R.L., and Dickson, B.J., *The Emerging Pacific Community: A Regional Perspective,* Westview Press, London, 1984.

Drifte, Reinhard, 'The European Community and Japan: Beyond the Economic Dimension', *Journal of International Affairs,* Vol. 37, No. 1, 1983.

Drucker, Peter F., 'Japan's Choices', Foreign Affairs, Summer 1987.

Eguchi Yujiro and Usui Tsutomu. *Kan Taiheiyoken no Jidai* ('An Age of Pacific Basin'), Aki Shobo, Tokyo, 1988.

Eto Shinkichi, 'Evolving Sino-Japanese Relations', in Joshua Katz and Tilly Friedman-Lichtschein (eds.), *Japan's New World Role,* Westview Press, London, 1985.

Freedman, Lawrence (ed.), *The Troubled Alliance: Atlantic Relations in the 1980s,* Heinemann, for the Royal Institute of International Affairs, London, 1983.

Fujii, Shinichi, *Teikoko kempo to keneko haku* (The Imperial Constitution and Count Keneko). (Tokyo: 1942).

________, *The Essentials of Japanese Constitutional Law.* (Tokyo: Yuhikaku, 1940).

Fujisawa, C., *Political Philosophy of the Yamato Race.*

Funabashi, Yoichi, *Managing the Dollar: From the Plaza to the Louvre,* Institute of International Economics, Washington, 1988.

________, *Sumitto no Shiso* ('A Thought of the Summits'), Asahi Shimbun-sha, Tokyo, 1980.

Furnivall, J.S., *Netherlands India: A Study of Plural Economy,* Cambridge University Press, Cambridge, 1944.

Giraud, Pierre-Noel, and Godet, Michel, *Radioscope du Japon, Economica,* Paris, 1987.

Goh Keng Swee, *The Economics of Development,* Asia Pacific Press, Singapore, 1972.

Grover, V., *The Constitution of Japan,* New Delhi, 1964.

Gubbins, J.H., *The Making of Modern Japan,* London: 1922.

Hanabusa Masamichi, *Trade Problems between Japan and Western Europe,* Saxon House, for the Royal Institute of International Affairs, Westmead, 1979.

Harris, Stuart, and Bridges, Brian, *European Interests in ASEAN,* Chatham House Papers 19, Routledge & Kegan Paul, for the Royal Institute of International Affairs, London 1983.

Higgott, Richard, and Robison, Richard (eds.), *Southeast Asia: Essays in the Political Economy of Structural Change*, Routledge & Kegan Paul, Melbourne, 1985.

Hooper, Paul F., *Building a Pacific Community*, East-West Center, Honolulu, 1982.

Hosoya Chihiro (ed.), *Nichi-ei Kankei-shi 1917-1949* ('A History of Anglo Japanese Relations'), Tokyo University Press, Tokyo, 1982.

Howe, Geoffrey, *East-West Relations: Realism, Vigilance and Open Mind,* Prepared for the Foreign and Commonwealth Office by the Central Office of Information, 1987.

Hozumi, Yatsukata, "Kempo seitei no yurai" (The origin of the establishment of the constitution), *Meiji bunka zenshu*, V. 419-28.

Ike, Nobutaka, *The Beginnings of Political Democracy in Japan,* (Baltimore: 1950).

Ito, Hirobumi, *Commentaries on the Constitution of the Empire of Japan*, Second edn. (Tokyo; 1906). Translated from the Japanese by Ito Myoji.

________, *Kempo Shivyo* (Materials on the Constitution), 3 Vols. (Tokyo: 1931).

Ito, H. Prince, *Commentaries on the Constitution of Japan* (Tokyo: 1931).

Jansen, Marius B., *Japan and its World: Two Centuries of Change*, Princeton University Press, Princeton, 1980.

Japan Center for International Exchange and Japan Society. *Report of the Seventh Shimoda Conference,* Oiso, 1987.

Japan International Development Co-operation Study Group. *Toward a New Perspective for International Co-operation*, Tokyo, July 1987.

Japan National Committee for Pacific Economic Co-operation Conference. *Nijyuisseiki no Taiheiyo Kyoryoku* ('Pacific Co-operation towards the 21st Century'), Jiji Press, Tokyo, 1988.

Kakehi, K. *Fundamental Principles on the Japanese Constitution.*

Kissinger, Henry A. *American Foreign Policy: Three Essays*, Norton, New York, 1969.

Kosaka Masataka, *Kokusai Masatsu: Taikoku Nihon no Yowatari Gaku* ('International Friction: Japan's Worldly Wisdom'), Toyo Keizai Shinposha, Tokyo, 1987.

________, *Saisho Yoshida Shigeru* ('Premier Yoshida Shigeru'), Chuo Koron-sha, Tokyo, 1968.

Kuroda, K., *A Treatise of the Japanese Constitution (Vols. I, II).*

Lqu Teik Soon, 'Defence Expenditure of ASEAN States: The regional strategic context', in *Defence Spending in Southeast Asia*, Institute of Southeast Asian Studies, Singapore, 1987.

Lehmann, Jean-Pierre, 'Agenda for action on issues in Euro-Japanese relations', *World Economy*, Vol. 7, No 3, September 1984, pp. 257-76.

Leifer, Michael. Indonesia's Foreign Policy, Allen & Unwin for the Royal Institute of International Affairs, London, 1983.

________, *Conflict and Regional Order in Southeast Asia*, Adelphi Paper No. 162, International Institute for Strategic Studies, London, 1980.

Lim Chong-Yah (ed.), *Learning form the Japanese Experience*, Maruzen Asia, Singapore, 1982.

Maekawa Report. *Economic Structural Adjustment for International Harmony*, Submitted to Prime Minister Nakasone, April 1986.

Matsumoto Hiroshi and Noordin Sopiee (eds.), *Into the Pacific Era: Southeast Asia and its Place in the Pacific,* Institute of Strategic and International Studies, Malaysia, Kuala Lumpur, 1984.

Matsunami, N., *The Constitution of Japan.*

Mendl, Wolf, *Western Europe and Japan between the Superpowers,* Croom Helm, London, 1984.

Merlini, Cesare (ed.), *Economic Summits and Western Decision-making*, Croom Helm, with European Institute of Public Administration, London, 1984.

Mori Kazuko, 'Ajia-Taiheiyo ni Mukau Chugoky no Me' ('China Looks Asian-Pacific'), *Kokusai Mondai*, February 1986.

Morris, James, *Pax Britannica: the Climax of an Empire*, Penguin Books, London, 1979.

Morrison, Charles E. and Suhrke, Astri *Strategies of Survival: The Foreign Policy Dilemma of Smaller Asian States,* University of Queensland Press, Queensland, 1978.

Morse, Ronald A., 'Japan's drive to pre-eminence', *Foreign Policy*, Winter 1987-88.

Motono Moriyuki, 'World trade issues require more than a piecemeal approach', *World Economy*, Vol. 7, No. 3, September 1984.

Murata Ryohei, 'Political relations between the United States and Western Europe: their implication for Japan'; *International Affairs*, Winter 1987-88.

Nagai Yonosuke, *Reisen no Kigen: Sengo Ajia no Kokusai Kankyo* 'Origins of the Cold War: the International Environment of Post-war Asia', Chuo Koron-sha, Tokyo, 1978.

________, *Gendai to Senryaku* ('Our Times and Strategy'), Bungei Shunjyu, 1985.

Nakatani Iwao, *Bodaresu Economi: Sakoku Kokka Nihon eno Keisho* ('The Borderless Economy: Alarm for Japan's National Isolation'), Nihon Keizai Shimbun-sha, Tokyo, 1987.

Nakamura, Y., *Studies on Japanese Constitutional Laws.*

Nakano, T., *The Power of Military Command of the Tenno.*

Naya Seiji, 'The Private Sector as a new Engine of Growth: Implications for the Asia Pacific', unpublished paper presented to the Japan Institute of International Affairs Conference, Tokyo, March 1988.

Nish, Ian (ed.), *Anglo-Japanese Alienation, 1919-1952: Papers of the Anglo-Japanese Conference on the History of the Second World War*, Cambridge University Press, Cambridge, 1982.

Nishihara Masashi, *East Asian Security and Trilateral Countries,* Report to the Trilateral, Commission: 30, New York University Press, New York, 1985.

Nixon, Richard, *Real Peace,* Sidgwick & Jackson, London, 1983.

Nomura, J., *A Manual of the Japanese Constitution.*

Nomura, S., *A General Survey of the Japanese Constitution* (Revised).

Ohmae Kenichi, *Toriado Pawa: Nijyuisseiki no Kokusai Kigyo Senryaku* ('Triad Power: International Business Strategy towards the 21st Century'), Kodansha, Tokyo, 1985.

Oishi, H., *Fundamental Problems of Politics.*

Okawara Yoshio, *Koritsuka wo Sakerutameni* ('To Keep Clear of Isolation'), Sekai no Ugoki-sha, Tokyo, 1985.

Okazaki Hisahiko, *Kokka to Joho: Nihon no Gaiko Senryaku wo Motomete* ('The State and Information: in Search of Japan's Strategy'), Bungei Shunju, Tokyo, 1980.

________, 'Magarikado no Nichibei Domei' ('A Turning Point of the Japan-US Alliance'), *Chuo Koron*, July 1988.

Okita Saburo, *Japan's Challenging Years: Reflections on my Lifetime*, Australia-Japan Research Centre, Australia National University, Canberra, 1983.

_______, *Economisuto Gaisho no 252 Nichi* ('252 days of the "Economist" Foreign Minister'), Toyo Keizai Shinpo-sha, Tokyo, 1980.

Owen, Davis, Brzezinski, Zbigniew, and Okita Saburo, *Democracy must Work*, A Task Force Report to the Trilateral Commission, New York University Press, New York, 1984.

Ozaki, Robert S., and Arnold, Walter (eds.), *Japan's Foreign Relations: A Global Search for Economic Security*, Westview Press, London, 1985.

Pacific Economic Co-operation Conference. *Pacific Economic Outlook: Dynamism and Adjustment,* Summary Statement of the Standing Committee of the Sixth Pacific Economic Co-opeation Conference, Osaka, May 1988.

Patrick, Hugh, and Rosovsky, Henry (eds.). *Asia's New Giant: How the Japanese Economy Works,* Brookings Institution, Washington, DC, 1976.

Peterson, Peter G., 'A New Pacific Compact', paper prepared for the joint meeting of Keidanren and Atlantic Institute, Tokyo, April 1987.

Prasert Chittiwatanapong, 'Japan's Role in the Asia-Pacific Region: The Political Dimension', unpublished paper presented to the Japan Institute of International Affairs Conference, Tokyo, March 1988.

Putnam, Robert D., and Bayne, Nicholas. *Hanging Together: The Seven-power Summits,* Heinemann, for the Royal Institute of International Affairs, London, 1984.

Randolph, R. Sean, 'Pacific Overtures', *Foreign Policy,* Winter 1984-85.

Rosovsky, Henry (ed.). *Discord in the Pacific: Challenges to the Japanese-American Alliance*, Columbia Books, Washington, 1972.

Saeki Kiichi, 'Outlook for a Pacific Era', unpublished paper delivered at the Pacific Energy Co-operation Conference, Tokyo, March 1987.

Saito Shiro, *Tenkanki no Sekai-zo* ('The World Image in Transition'), Asahi Shobo, Tokyo, 1972.

Sakamoto Masahiro, *Pakkusu Americana no Kokusai shisutemu* ('The International System of Pax Americana'), Yuhikaku, Tokyo, 1986.

Sato Seizaburo, 'Japan's Politico-military Role in the Asian Pacific Region', unpublished paper presented to Japan Institute of International Affairs Conference, Tokyo, March 1988.

Sasaki, S., *The Essentials of the Japanese Constitution.*

Satomi, K., *A Study of Laws with Special Reference to the National Policy.*

Sato, U., *Lectures on the Japanese Constitution.*

Satoh Yukio. 'Western Security: A Japanese Point of View', *Naval War College Review*, September-October 1983.

Scalapino, Robert A., *Asia and the Road Ahead: Issues for the Major Powers*, University of California Press, Berkeley, 1975.

________, *Parties and Politics in Contemporary Japan*, Calfornia, 1962.

Sasaki, S., *The Essentials of the Japanese Constitution.*

Sato, U., *Lectures on the Japanese Constitution.*

Shimizu, S., *Article-by-Article Lectures on the Japanese Constitution.*

Shibusawa Masahide, *Japan and the Asian Pacific Region: Profile of Change*, Croom Helm, for the Royal Institute of International Affairs, London, 1984; in Japanese translation, *Nihon wa Ajia Ka*, Simul Press, Tokyo, 1985.

Sinha, Radha, *Japan's Opinions for the 1980s*, Croom Helm, London, 1982.

Sonoda Sunao, *Sekai Nihon Ai* ('The World, Japan and Affection'), Shincho-sha, Tokyo, 1986.

Sopiee, Noordin, 'Kampuchea: The Way Forward', unpublished paper presented to the Third Malaysia-Japan Colloquium, Kuala Lumpur, June 1988.

Soviet National Committee for Asia-Pacific Economic Co-operation. *SOVNAPEC Newsletter*, Vol. 1, No. 1, May 1988.

Spero, Joan E., *The Politics of International Economic Relations*, St. Martin's Press, New York, 1985; in Japanese translation, *Kokusai Keizai Kankeiron*, Toyo Keizai Shinpo-sha, Tokyo, 1988.

Steel, Ronald, *The End of Alliance: America and the Future of Europe*, Viking Press, New York, 1964.

Stockwin, J.A.A., *Japan: Divided Politics in a Growth Economy*, Weidenfeld & Nicolson, London, 1982.

Suzuki, Y., *The Birth and Development of the Science of the Japanese Constitution.*

Tabata, N., *Lectures on the Japanese Constitution.*

Tanaka Toshiro, 'Oshu Giteisho to Ekinai Shijo' ('The Single European Act and the internal market'), *Kokusai Mondai*, July 1988.

Tanino Sakutaro, 'Japan and the United States: Partnership in East Asia', in *Annual Review, 1983-84*, Center for International Relations, Harvard University.

Thorne, Christopher, *The Issue of War, States, Societies, and the Far Eastern Conflict of 1941-1945,* Hamish Hamilton, London, 1985.

Tokuyama Jiro, *Taiheiyo no Seiki* ('The Pacific Century'), Diamond, Tokyo, 1978.

Turner, Louis, *Industrial Collaboration with Japan*, Chatham House Papers: 34, Routledge & Kegan Paul, for the Royal Institute of International Affairs, London, 1987.

Uesugi, S., *An Interpretation of the Japanese Constitution, A New Study.*

United States-Japan Advisory Commission. *Challenges and Opportunities in United States-Japan Relations,* report submitted to the President of the United States and the Prime Minister of Japan, September 1984.

Urata Masutaro, 'Japan's Market Structure and Industrial Policy in International Trade', in *Annual Review, 1983-84,* Center for International Relations, Harvard University.

Vasil, Raj K., *Governing Singapore*, Eastern Universities Press, Singapore, 1984.

Vogel, Ezra F., 'Pax Nipponica?', *Foreign Affairs*, Spring 1986.

Wallace, William, 'What Price Independence? Sovereignty and interdependence in British Politics', *International Affairs*, Summer 1986.

Watanabe Akio, 'From the Old Triangle to a New Great Crescent?

Southeast Asia in US-Japanese Relations in the Early Post-war Years', unpublished paper prepared for the US-Japanese Relations from 1950 to 1980 Conference, Hawaii, January 1984.

———, (ed.). *Sengo Nihon no Taigai Seisaki* ('Post-war Japan's External Policy'), Yuhikaku, Tokyo, 1985.

Watanabe, Ikujiro, *Meiji tenno to rikken seiji.* (The Emperor, Meiji and Constitutional Government) (Tokyo: 1937).

_______, *Nihon kempo seitei shi ko* (Lectures on the history of the establishment of the Japanese Constitution). (Tokyo: 1939).

Watanabe Toshio (ed.)., *The Policy Recommendations on the Structural Adjustment of Economies of Japan, US, and Asian NICs,* Japan Forum on International Relations, Tokyo, March 1988.

Wilkinson, Endymion, *Japan versus Europe: A History of Misunderstanding,* Penguin Books, London, 1983.

Williams, Phil., 'The limits of American Power: from Nixon to Reagan', *International Affairs*, Autumn 1987.

Wilson, Dick, *The Sun at Noon: An Anatomy of Modern Japan,* Hamish Hamilton, London, 1986.

Wolferen, Karel G. van., 'The Japan Problem', *Foreign Affairs*, Winter 1986-87.

Wong, John, *ASEAN Economy in Perspective: A Comparative Study of Indonesia, Malaysia, the Philippines, Singapore and Thailand,* Macmillan, London, 1979.

_______, *The Political Economy of China's Changing Relations with Southeast Asia,* Macmillan, London, 1984.

Yamasaki, K., *Constitutional Laws.*

Yoshida, K., *The Characteristics of the Japanese Constitution.*

Yano Toru, *Nihon no Nanshin to Tonan-Ajia* ('Japan's Southern Advance and South-east Asia'), Nihon Keizai Shimbun-sha, Tokyo, 1975.

_______, *Reisen to Tonan-Ajia* (''The Cold War and South-east Asia'), Chuo Koron-shà, Tokyo, 1986.

Yamasaki, K., *Constitutional Laws.*

Yoshida, K., *The Characteristics of the Japanese Constitution.*

Yoshida Shigeru, *Kaiso Jyunen* ('Reflections on the Ten Years'), Shinchosha, Tokyo, 1957.

_______, *Japan's Decisive Century 1867-1967,* Frederick A. Praeger, for Encyclopaedia Britannica, New York, 1967.

Sakaria, Haji Ahmad, 'Obstacles to Greater Pan-Pacific Cooperation: a View from ASEAN', in *Into the Pacific Era*, ISIS Malaysia, Kuala Lumpur, 1986.

Index